M

ALSO EDITED BY HARRIET BROWN

Mr. Wrong: Real-Life Stories About the Men We Used to Love

FEEDME!

BALLANTINE BOOKS   NEW YORK

FEED ME!

Writers

Dish

About

Food,

Eating,

Weight,

and

Body Image

EDITED BY HARRIET BROWN

A Ballantine Books Trade Paperback Original

Published in the United States by Ballantine Books,
an imprint of The Random House Publishing Group,
a division of Random House, Inc., New York.

BALLANTINE and colophon are registered
trademarks of Random House, Inc.

ISBN 978-0-345-50088-5

Printed in the United States of America

www.ballantinebooks.com

9 8 7 6 5 4 3 2 1

Book design by Debbie Glasserman

ACKNOWLEDGMENTS

For a few of the extraordinary women I've been privileged to know:

Ellyn Satter, who taught me not to be afraid
Pam Reilly, whose Dutch oven I use every day
Carrie Arnold, who made the necklace
Laura Collins, who reached out
Jane Cawley, who sent the Ancel Keys dinnerware
Joan Laurion, who listened and shared and walked
Mimi Orner, who walked the talk
Kasey Brown, who shares the genotype
and my daughters, who keep me honest.

And with love and thanks to Miriam Altshuler, the best agent in the world; Lea Beresford, editor par excellence; Nancy Miller, who first believed in this book; and all the women (and men) who sent me their stories.

CONTENTS

INTRODUCTION
Harriet Brown

The one piece of jewelry I never take off is a necklace, a gold chain with a single gold charm in the shape of a fork. I wear it the way other people wear a cross or a Star of David—to hold close something as necessary as life itself. I wear it to remind myself to celebrate food and not fear it, to enjoy it and not abuse it.

I wear it to remember (as if I could forget) how my daughter fell down the rabbit hole of anorexia, and how food was the medicine that cured her. Six times a day our family sat down to-gether and ate, bite after agonizing bite. Food nourished her body and brain, mind and heart and soul, back from the terrible borderlands of anorexia.

I wear the necklace in honor of the power of food. We eat the way we breathe—instinctively, without being taught, as a matter of survival. You can live without booze or drugs, but you can't live without food, not for long, any more than you can not breathe, not drink, not sleep.

And maybe that's why the act of eating is so fraught in this culture: because it's not optional. Because we have to do it, three or four times a day, every day. It calls to mind our creaturely origins and holds the potential to affect our physical selves. In an appearance-driven culture, we believe—we seem to *want* to believe—that food can make us large or small, powerful or weak, attractive or ugly. We are, increasingly, judged by both what we eat and how we look.

And man, are we judged! I doubt there's been another time in American history when what you put in your mouth has come with such a heaping side of *should*s and *don't*s. It's the rare woman today who doesn't know the dark side of the fork, the way food can be a curse rather than a cure, a source of anxiety rather than sustenance. No wonder so many of us have "issues" around food and eating. I've seen grown women cringe at the sight of a plate of pasta. I know women who swear they'd be happy if they just Never. Had. To. Eat. Again. I've felt that way myself. As much as I love food (and I do), I have on occasion wished I could just give it up forever.

The essays in this collection explore many aspects of the relationship between food and looks, eating and body image, appetite and desire. They are poignant, thought-provoking, wise, and hilarious. And they reflect not only the experiences of this talented group of writers—they reflect the experiences of so many of us in the twenty-first century. Whether they're describing the indignities of shopping for clothes in a size zero world, the paradigm shift of another culture's perspective on weight, or the dawning understanding of a mother's experience with food and love, these writers speak to all of us who have ever worried about how we look or what to eat.

The pressure to be thin is now felt by both women and men. It starts earlier than ever, a fact that may explain why children as young as six are now suffering from eating disorders. Wendy McClure's poignant essay, "Day One," describes the first day of the first diet of her life, at age ten. Alas, it was only the first of many diets McClure embarked on out of her longing to fit into the cultural mainstream—a longing most of us can relate to all too well, whether we're just ordinary folks or elite models like Magalei Amadei. Amadei's essay, "Top Model," describes her ironic struggle with body hatred and bulimia even as her face was gracing the covers of *Vogue, Elle, Glamour,* and other fashion magazines.

The conflation of eating and appearance affects every corner of our lives, as Joan Fischer points out in her mordantly funny essay, "Take This Cake and Shove It." Fischer's only slightly tongue-in-cheek piece offers a Swiftian solution to the interior conflicts of food and appearance, food and sex, food and love.

The average American woman eats about eighty thousand meals as an adult, and each and every one of them involves choices about fat and sugar, carbs and calories, organic and processed, how much and what. Every choice can and often does trigger a tidal wave of feelings, from self-loathing to celebration. In modern-day America, feeding yourself is an act of bravery.

It doesn't start out that way. We're born knowing hunger and satisfaction. Babies practice sucking in the womb. But if you've ever tried to get a baby to eat when she's not hungry, you know how powerful the internal self-regulation mechanism can be. Women especially are taught early on to ignore our appetites and to deny ourselves what we're longing for. There are consequences to such self-denial, as Dana Kinstler notes in her bittersweet essay, "Sugar Plum Fairy," a chilling description of anorexia from the inside out.

In fact, I think that's the true definition of disordered eating: eating that's divorced from real hunger. *Our* real hunger, not what our parents or our doctors or the media tell us we should be hungry for.* By the time we're adults, many of us have only the faintest sense of our own appetite. We don't know when we're hungry and when we're full. No wonder we obsess over the numbers on the scale, the curve of our hips, the fat content of our yogurt. No wonder we struggle with so many food-related fears: The fear of not getting enough. The fear of not being able to stop. The fear of taking up too much room.

No wonder, really, that we've become so afraid of food. I've been reading studies and books and following news stories and blogs about fat for the last two years. In that time we've been warned that fat can cause diabetes, heart disease, cancer, and even global warming. Fat is contagious—if you've got a fat friend, even if she lives hundreds of miles away, you are (supposedly) more likely to get fat yourself. Fat has become a moral issue, and what and how you eat is now a religion. A piece of chocolate cake isn't just flour, butter, cocoa, sugar, eggs, baking powder, and milk; it's now a dangerous object, something that can kill you and then send you straight to hell.

On the other hand, a Baggie full of celery sticks might as well come with a halo. It's one more way to abnegate the self, something we women are trained from an early age to aspire to do.

* There's another reason to want to stay connected to our appetites: A 1970s study showed that when you enjoy what you're eating, you get more nutrition from it. See Harriet Brown, "Go with Your Gut," *New York Times,* Feb. 20, 2006, op-ed page.

Like the joke about the miser who feeds his horse less and less each day until finally the horse dies of starvation, and the miser complains to his friend, "Why did he have to go and die just when I had him trained to live on nothing?"

Why indeed?

And so I wear the necklace to remind myself (to paraphrase the song) that a fork is just a fork, whether it holds lettuce and tomato or fettuccini Alfredo. A fork is a means to an end, and on good days, that's how I think of food, too. It's a way to care for myself, and for those I love, through the steady, courageous, often fraught act of eating, one spoonful at a time.

The words *fat* and *thin* exist only in relation to each other. Think about it. I might look fat standing next to one person, thin next to someone else. What's pleasingly plump to one is unacceptably obese to another. What looks normal to me seems emaciated to you. The words we use to describe these physical conditions run the gamut from positive to negative—and sometimes encompass both ends of the spectrum:

Plump, zaftig, voluptuous, thick, big, curvy, chubby, stocky, husky, overweight, fat, obese, morbidly obese.

Skinny, slim, wiry, athletic, lithe, slender, skeletal.

On the whole, though, anti-fat hysteria has come to dominate the public dialogue about food and body image. *Obesity* is the ace of spades in the blame game, a word that's become code for much more than weight. People who are obese aren't just fat; they're gluttonous, lazy, smelly, stupid. Fat prejudice, either overt or subtle, is not just socially acceptable; it's become pretty much de rigueur. I'm thinking, for instance, about a children's book that was published a couple of years ago, a collaboration between two of my former favorite children's writer/illustrators. The book depicts a sloppy, slovenly family (including children) who sit on the couch all day drinking soda and eating junk food, and whose collective hefts break a waterslide in an amusement park and various other presumably solid structures. The heavy-handed moral of the story is that all these characters have to do is stop stuffing their faces, eat salad, and take a little exercise, and they, too, can join the "normal" majority.

More recently, a schoolteacher felt compelled not only to make her students sing a song about how fat Santa is but to videotape them doing it and put the video on YouTube. The lyrics include lines like "Oh! Santa Claus, Santa Claus, how much do you weigh? I'm glad I'm not a reindeer that has to pull your sleigh!" Imagine how an overweight child would feel, reading this book, singing this song, hearing this message in the voices of adults she trusts.

In this oh-so-politically-correct society, people who would never dream of saying *nigger* or *kike* have no trouble whatsoever taunting those who are fat. I learned this the hard way, on a summer afternoon when a group of neighbors had gathered spontaneously in someone's backyard to eat cake. We had a feel-good schmoozefest, at least until one woman mentioned a plump (but hardly morbidly obese) movie and TV actress and added, "She's so fat, I can't stand watching anything she's in. I'm afraid she's going to have a heart attack any minute."

Aside from the magical thinking involved (um, the movie or TV show has *already been filmed*), the sheer thoughtlessness of this comment blew me away. I thought, *She doesn't mean to be cruel.* But actually she did, as evidenced by the fact that she kept talking about this fat actress, pontificating along the way about how unhealthy fat people are, why don't they simply eat less, she'd gained a couple of pounds after each pregnancy and had just cut back on her eating until the pounds came off, and so on and on and on—all while she sat right beside me, seemingly unaware of the irony of the fact that she was forking up a piece of cake *that I'd baked*. Eventually I gathered my courage and said that it offended me to have her characterize and criticize overweight people that way, that there's plenty of evidence to suggest not only that fat is *not* unhealthy but that overweight people may live longer.* Over the next few weeks, I raised this with her a couple of times. She insisted that she couldn't understand why I was offended, that "everyone knew" being fat was bad for you, that she *liked* this actress and was only expressing concern about her health.

This neighbor, by the way (do I have to say that she's naturally thin?), is the kind of person who goes light-years out of her way to champion diversity on every level, to speak and write in defense of the poor, the differently colored and abled, the underclass.

Everyone, in fact, except the weight-challenged.

Okay, the *fat*. For years I avoided that word. I used euphemisms to talk about myself and others. I—or they—were overweight or pleasingly plump or stocky. *Fat* was giving up, letting your stomach out, wearing muumuus and mules. *Fat* was for other people. *Fat* was for losers.

When I began writing about food and eating, I realized I had to desensitize myself to the word. I had to learn to use it without inflection, as a simple descriptor, as in "I have more fat on my body than you do" or "She's got some fat around her middle." This kind of desensitization is a cornerstone of the fat

* Katharine Flegal et al., "Excess Deaths Associated with Underweight, Overweight, and Obesity," *Journal of the American Medical Association,* April 20, 2005, pp. 1861–67.

acceptance movement, which promotes the (shocking! subversive!) notions that fat is a noun or adjective, not a statement of morality; that health is *what you do,* not *what you look like;* and that you can, in fact, be healthy even if you're fat.

Not only that: You can be fat and not conform to our cultural stereotypes of fat people, which are so often reinforced by those photos of headless and morbidly obese people that accompany each news article and press release about obesity. For years, whenever I'd fret about being fat, my husband's automatic rejoinder was "But you're not fat." What he meant was "You're not ugly, you're not stupid, you're not a loser." And it's true; I'm none of those things. But it took me a long time to separate them from the physical realities of my body.

The other side of the association of fat with moral turpitude is our national conviction that to be thin is to be healthy, morally superior, and attractive—even if you're emaciated to the point of death. Three years ago, when my daughter was ill with anorexia, she was regularly complimented by salespeople, technicians at the pediatrician's office, and even strangers on the street for her "fabulous figure," for her "natural slimness," and for "getting the thin genes, lucky you!"—all at a time when she looked severely unwell and was literally on the verge of hospitalization. But here's the most disturbing thing: Now that she's at a healthy weight, slim but muscular, smiling, her skin glowing with health, far more beautiful than she was at seventy pounds—the compliments have stopped.

No wonder we're so fucked up about food and eating.

Through my blog, also called Feed Me!, I've connected with many women who read, write, and think about issues relating to body image, weight, and food. My blog is part of "the fatosphere," a loose collection of bloggers who write about body image and eating and size acceptance, meaning an attitude toward fat that's nonjudgmental—the notion that bodies come in different shapes and sizes, and you can be healthy (or unhealthy) no matter what size you are. Writer Kate Harding is also part of this fat-acceptance movement, one of a growing number of young women who are challenging the conventional wisdom around fat and thin. Harding's wonderful essay, "You're Not Fat," deconstructs some of this fat-related baggage, and explains why she goes out of her way to wear the label like a badge of honor.

The fat-acceptance movement is gaining momentum, but it's not without its own complications. What's the role of ideology and politics when it comes to your own body, your own feelings, your own size and shape and eating habits? Politics and ideology are abstract concepts—they're "shoulds." We *should* feel proud and happy no matter our size or shape. We *should* feel comfortable with our own appetites. We *should* be okay with taking up room in the world. But human beings have a funny way of not reacting well to the notion of *should,* as Ophira Edut notes in her essay, "Battle of the Bulge." Edut's tale of the conflict between her work as a "body activist" and her own relationship with her body is bound to cause controversy, but it's truly a universal conflict. How many of us grapple with the contradictions of weight and body image and food? I'd guess Edut is in the vast majority of American women.

Like so many other women, I've wrestled with issues of weight and body image and food for a long time. I came late to the notion that not every woman can or should have a body like Audrey Hepburn or Keira Knightley, and that each of us is hardwired to have a certain physical size and shape. That weight and BMI and other numbers don't tell the story. That you can be fit and active and have, as Ellyn Satter says, a "joyful, competent relationship with food" at any size.

About ten years ago, I got to know a woman named

Mimi Orner, who taught women's studies at the University of Wisconsin–Madison. We had daughters in the same family child-care home, and we chatted now and then during drop-off and pickup. Mimi had been diagnosed with ovarian cancer when her daughter, Sophie, was two, and she went through one horrific treatment after another, trying to stay alive as long as possible.

Mimi was a woman of size in every way—generous, big-hearted, and fat. Her capacity for joy was compelling. "Let's go play!" she would say, and off we'd go to the park for ice cream cones and to watch our daughters climb around the playground. The fact that she openly enjoyed food astonished me at first. Here was a fat woman who ate with pleasure, who wasn't obsessed with the scale or the mirror, who didn't even pay lip service to the gods of thinness. I asked her once, "You mean it's okay to eat ice cream if you're fat?" I'd spent so much time feeling I should apologize for weighing more than 110 pounds that Mimi's behaviors seemed radical to me.

As the cancer progressed, Mimi fought pain and weakness, but she held on to her appetite and her enjoyment of food. We met occasionally at a Chinese restaurant for lunch, and she tucked into the Hunan chicken—her favorite—with the same gusto she always had, despite the morphine pump she now wore in a fanny pack. It wasn't until a month or so before she died that her appetite deserted her—the beginning of the end, she called it, and she was right.

At Mimi's memorial service, friends and students, colleagues and neighbors got up one by one to remember and grieve and tell stories about her. Every one of those speeches was moving, but the one I remember best—the one I can't get out of my mind—was by a young woman who stood, tears streaming down her face, to explain why she and Mimi had parted ways.

"Mimi was my inspiration," she said. "She loved her body and accepted it. But I just can't do it. I can't come to terms with myself. And Mimi couldn't understand that. She thought everyone was as brave and smart as she was." She raised her head and looked around the crowded room. "And I'm just not."

Mimi died in 2000, but that young woman's words still echo in my head each time I look in the mirror and wince, or see myself in a photograph and feel my heart sink, or choke on the words of self-loathing that lie on my tongue like stones. Words have so much power—the ones we say to ourselves and the ones we share with other people. A therapist once suggested that if a friend followed me around saying half the things I say to myself all the time, I'd ditch her in a heartbeat. Point taken. I began trying instead to channel my inner Mimi, to imagine what my friend would say or do in a given situation.

I wrote a pledge about loving your body and posted it online, inviting people to print it out, sign it, and put it somewhere they could see it every day—preferably beside a mirror. And they did. Several colleges have used it as part of body image awareness seminars and events. It's been passed around LiveJournal and blogs and other people's websites.

The response has made me, for the first time, feel more hopeful. Hopeful that if we talk openly about fat and food, bodies and weight and longing, that we can begin to heal the wounds inflicted on every woman in this society. That we can learn to eat when we're hungry, know what we're hungry for, and stop eating when we're full. That we know, really know, the meaning of enough. That we can feed ourselves with pleasure and competence and joy, and use the power of the fork for good.

THE I-LOVE-MY-BODY PLEDGE

I pledge to speak kindly about my body.

I promise not to talk about the size of my thighs or stomach or butt, or about how I have to lose 5 or 15 or 50 pounds. I promise not to call myself a fat pig, gross, or any other self-loathing, trash-talking phrase.

I vow to be kind to myself and my body. I will learn to be grateful for its strength and attractiveness, and be compassionate toward its failings.

I will remind myself that bodies come in all shapes and sizes, and that no matter what shape and size my body is, it's worthy of kindness, compassion, and love.

FEED ME!

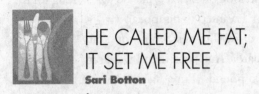

HE CALLED ME FAT;
IT SET ME FREE
Sari Botton

We were snuggling cozily after one of our first nights together when Brian, the man who would later become my husband, basically called me fat.

"This is interesting—I think I've grown emotionally," he decided out loud. "You're the most voluptuous, full-figured woman I've ever been with, and before now, I would have had a hard time being attracted to that."

My jaw dropped. My heart sank. My cellulite seemed to expand.

Most of the women he'd been with before, he went on, had been skinny. "I've been fighting with myself for a long time, trying to get past what the media programs you to be attracted to, and let me tell you, it's hard for guys," he insisted. "But this shows me that I'm able to see a whole person and be attracted to someone more deeply, on many levels."

He had this proud look on his face, like he was waiting for me to congratulate him. I wanted to disappear.

Mind you, even at my heaviest I am not a large woman by most people's standards. And back then I was at my dating skinniest, just about 105 pounds. I'm a hair under five feet, so 105 pounds on me is lean but by no means skeletal. I've got some diet-proof curves, and I'm a double-D cup. But I was pretty darn trim at the time.

I can't remember how I responded exactly in that stunning moment, but I recall having a hard time finding words. I wasn't sure what I was supposed to have heard, either. On the one hand, this so-far great new guy in my life was saying he was into me. On the other, I was pretty sure I had been insulted.

After no small amount of tears, a long discussion about body image issues, and great effort on Brian's part to extract his foot from his mouth—including assurances that what he had been trying to express, rather clumsily, was that I was attractive to him—we tried to put it behind us.

In time, this painful encounter would turn into an incredible gift. It would set me free from a lifetime of dieting and overexercising. I'd allow myself to gain some weight, essentially make peace with my softer shape, and even come to like it. And I'd come to understand that it's not just women but men, too, who are in their own way oppressed by the media standards for women's bodies. But not until I was done silently suffering.

I replayed Brian's monologue in my head more than a few times, dissecting it, weighing it for meaning and intentions, and trying to reconcile it with the way I felt about my body before that incident. I was thin! I was sure of it! How could he have seen me as anything else?

I'd been so proud of how thin I'd gotten, too. The year before, when a relationship with a younger guy ended, I'd turned to the Zone as part of a breakup makeover that included shearing my waist-length hair to right below my increasingly prominent jawline.

A few weeks into Zone-ing, though, fewer and better carbs somehow turned into nearly zero carbs. Sushi turned into sashimi, sandwiches on sprouted whole-grain bread turned into chef's salads, PB&J on rice cakes turned into peanut butter on a spoon, and I found myself swept up in the Atkins craze of 2002. I burned almost everything I ate and more, running four to five miles six mornings a week and walking over two miles to and from work each day. I sort of knew my attention to diet and exercise was bordering on an obsession, but so many people around me were doing the same thing, making it seem almost normal. Plus, in my mind, it was paying off because I felt great and I looked great. Or so I thought.

It wasn't the first time in my life that I'd taken to an extreme what began as an effort to trim down a little. In my teens, like so many girls who first encounter the mushy reality of the influx of female hormones and a slowing metabolism, I wrestled with an eating disorder, starving and aerobicising my slightly puffy adolescent form down to as little as eighty-seven pounds.

Eventually, the severe deprivation stopped, but never a certain secret desire to be super-thin, nor the sense that everything in life would be perfect if only I could reach and maintain that perfectly flabless model weight. Through my twenties and thirties, I kept rigorous track of everything that went into my mouth and felt ashamed if I ate anything extra or fattening. I exercised religiously, punitively, and was hard on myself when I took days off. My weight fluctuated by a few pounds now and then, but I was always able to fit into the same sizes, two and four, depending on the brand. I wasn't skinny-skinny, but I was pretty slim—and always a little stressed out about trying to stay that way.

I realize that's not very original. The idea that society's standards of weight and beauty have a negative, neurotic impact on girls and women—well, we all know that sad story. What is news, to me at least, is how tortured some men are by those body standards and how conflicted they feel about them.

It's not just Brian: In the past year, I've heard about three similar encounters. We're talking about *three* different men, nice men, basically telling *three* different, perfectly lovely women, "Wow—look at my progress! I'm able to see past your fat to your soul!"

One friend of mine wanted a medal from his girlfriend because he was finally open to dating a woman who wore a size six after a lifetime of going out exclusively with zeroes and twos. Another begged his new love to give him time to become attracted to her physically because, he explained, he was very drawn to her emotionally but had a hard time being turned on by someone who wasn't rail-thin. In the third case, a guy I know who for years gave his hearty wife a hard time about not being model-like finally got it. Having met a not-so-friendly model when he was out with a friend, he discovered that what was on the outside wasn't necessarily an indication of what was on the inside.

These stories don't exactly inspire sympathy for those men. But I can see how, for them, becoming attracted to women who look different than what they've been trained to expect feels like a noble victory over shallowness and vanity. I can relate; it's the same proud feeling a woman has when she matures to the place where she's able to be attracted to a nerd or an ugly guy for the first time. I have no illusions that women are immune to a degree of looks-ism, but we are a lot more forgiving. And no woman I know would ever say to a man, "Look how far I've come! I'm able to be attracted to you even though you're *so not cute*!" Clearly, these guys still have insensitivity to conquer.

Maybe I was naive, but before that difficult body-type conversation with Brian, it hadn't fully occurred to me that the images in magazines and on television and movie screens affected nice, sensitive, emotionally intelligent guys, the kind who do yoga and go to therapy of their own volition, who wear Tibetan meditation beads and talk about their feelings. *These* guys feel like they've failed if they haven't attracted a woman who lives up to those ridiculous body standards?

I was also unaware of how ridiculous those standards are, that if you aren't super-skinny, you are essentially fat. Recently, I was flipping through *Details* at my physical therapist's office when I came across a short piece entitled "Why Fat Is Back in Hollywood," about how suddenly bones are out and curves are in. The softer-edged Scarlett Johanssons and Rachel Weiszes of the world, writer Holly Millea suggested, are gaining popularity over their harder-bodied, emaciated sisters. Great. But why is the word *fat* in the headline? Who'd call those women *fat*?

In any case, this "fat" trend sounds great to me, although I don't trust it. I feel like I've read that story a hundred times in the past twenty years, and still nothing has really changed. The preference for "real bodies" in movies and on television never seems to stick, nor to completely sink in with men—or women. At least not in the United States.

Maybe a change will come about in Europe, now that

Madrid's fashion-week executives are banning underweight models from the catwalks. Men from Mediterranean cultures are already known to prefer their women with some meat on their bones, regardless of trends. And God bless them. Keith, the flirtatious Jamaican super in the East Village tenement where I lived for eleven years, used to practically coo when I'd bloat up during PMS. "Oh, you're putting on some *size*, baby!" he exclaimed once when I came back from a run. I nearly burst into tears on the spot.

"Do you not know that you never tell a woman she's gained weight?" I demanded, my voice cracking.

Keith seemed stunned. "No—no!" he pleaded. "I told you that because I think you look good! I like women like that!" Part of me didn't believe him, but he wore an almost lecherous smile that didn't lie.

Fortunately, Brian seems to have joined the ranks of these men who appreciate a softer belly, an ample derriere, a rounder shape overall—not to mention a happier wife who doesn't deprive herself of the pleasures of good food and wine. One afternoon this summer when I was wearing a bathing suit, he embraced me from behind, nuzzled my neck, and held me tight. He asked, "Do you remember that conversation we had early on about how you were more voluptuous than I was used to?" Um, *vaguely.* "Well, I'm a total convert now. You are so incredibly sexy to me, and I want you to know that I just love your curves and your softness."

It's a good thing, because I've only gotten curvier and softer since we met. After we had that awful conversation early on, I sort of threw my hands up. I figured if I'm depriving myself and overexercising and he still thinks I'm padded, I surrender. Hello, rice and potatoes. Hello, wine. Hello, dessert now and then. I stopped running as often, then altogether, because of injuries. I substituted walking, yoga, and other gentle exercise. I started enjoying myself more. My face filled out a little; everything filled out a little.

I can't tell you exactly how much weight I've gained. I am guessing it's about fifteen pounds—a lot on my frame, although I still don't fall into the overweight category. I feel like I've got an extra little layer of woman on me, and it feels good, like this is the weight my body is meant to be. The reason I can't tell you exactly how much weight I've gained is because I don't know. I never weigh myself—except, of course, when I'm in the vicinity of about 105 pounds. When I go to the doctor, I face away from the scale and ask the nurse not to tell me the numbers, even though no nurse or doctor has ever told me I need to lose weight. Alas, I have some leftover body image baggage. It may never go away completely.

But I've made tremendous progress—with the help of an adoring and now more evolved husband who, by the way, seems even sexier to me now that he appreciates my body the way he does. Last month I tried on a skirt that had been one of my favorites the fall that Brian and I met. And I could barely squeeze into it. It was the first time in my adult life that my clothes didn't fit, and I started to freak out. I immediately shifted back to my default settings and started scheming about how I would get myself back down to that size (two, to be exact). I vowed to fit into it in three months—no, two; no, one! Then I took a deep breath. I looked at myself through kinder, wiser eyes, the eyes of a real woman who is loved by a real man, the eyes of a woman who likes her rice and potatoes and dessert sometimes. And I threw the skirt away.

THE GRIEF DIET
Caroline Leavitt

We're all at dinner. The restaurant is one of Manhattan's fanciest, with white tablecloths and a hushed quiet and waiters in black suits, and the menu is so long that I joke it might as well be a novel. My boyfriend, Rick, whom I've been living with for six months, has invited his parents to eat with us. His mother, all frosted yellow hair and overstuffed dress, talks about her latest diet. His father, tall and lean and handsome, jokes, "In my next life, I'm marrying someone skinny."

Everyone except me laughs. I push my bread plate away, the slice of semolina uneaten even though it looks delicious and I'm so starving I could eat my shoes. Rick watches and takes my hand and squeezes it encouragingly.

I'm five feet four. Size two. One hundred and three pounds. My ribs and hip bones show. The last time I was this thin, I was seventeen.

I nibble at my dinner, and when the waiter brings the dessert tray around, Rick's mother urges me to have some. "Go on, live a little," she says, "a skinny Minnie like you." But when I point to the chocolate cake, Rick frowns. I know what's coming. "We'll split it," he says sharply, and when it comes, he quickly cuts it into halves, his half being seven eighths, mine a sliver. It doesn't matter, because by now my appetite is gone. Rick has moved his hand off my thigh, his body edging away from mine at the table. I fake a smile, I eat, the sugar melting on my tongue. It's so delicious.

Outside, we say goodbye to his parents, people he has urged me to call Mom and Dad, and we have a fight about it because although they're nice enough people, they're hardly my parents, and I feel stiff and uncomfortable calling them anything but Mr. and Mrs. Usually, I don't call them anything at all. "Goodbye!" Rick calls to them, and then he draws me closer in a hug, and his parents beam, seeing the affection. I relax right up until his grip tightens. "Did you have to eat that chocolate cake?" he hisses, and when I push away from him, he grabs my hand and kisses it. "Darling," he says, "I'm just thinking about you."

That night we come inside our apartment, a huge prewar on the Upper West Side. "Come here," Rick says, and he kisses me passionately, and I forget that I couldn't eat dessert. The way he trails his hands along my spine makes me forget that he thinks I'm fat. I peel off his shirt and kiss his chest, which is golden from the sun, and he smells of soap and cinnamon and I'm starving for him, greedy for his kisses. He burrows into the thicket of my hair, and then we're rolling on the floor and kicking off his pants and I'm sliding out of my thin little dress and every cell in my body is switched on like New Year's Eve, that's how much I want him. He sits up and looks at me, amused.

"What?" I say.

He points to my belly. "You've got a little pot." He sees me wince, and he kisses my shoulder. "Oh, sweetie," he says. "It's okay. Now I know what you'll look like pregnant with our child." All the passion drains from me. I am fat and I have a pot. I'm frozen with shock, but he's pulling me down, kissing me, urging me into sex; now I'm dry and it hurts, and I push away from him at the end. He looks at me with deep concern, smoothing back my hair. "Do you want to talk to someone?" he asks quietly.

"About what?"

He rolls me against him and holds me tight. "Many women get frigid," he says, "but it's a problem we can work on together." I break free of his grip and go into the bathroom, running the shower as hot as I can stand it. Oh, and I lock the door.

I know what you're thinking. What's wrong with me that I stay with someone who is clearly torturing me? Why don't I have any self-respect? Why am I with him?

I moved in with Rick three weeks after we met, and I have to endure this because the alternative is simply too terrible. If I leave Rick, I'll have to grieve for another man, one I really loved, who loved me back, who didn't care if I ate sixty desserts, let alone one.

Backpedal six months. I had been living with a man I adored. We traveled everywhere, we ate out, we gorged on movies, books, films, and of course, each other. I was 120 pounds and a size six and radiant. Two weeks before we were supposed to be married, he woke up in the middle of the night. "I don't think I feel so good," he said, and before I could grab my keys, he was prone on the floor, dying in my arms.

Of course I grieved. I spent a thousand dollars going cross-country, talking to psychics, mediums, priests, and rabbis. I got a grief counselor and went to group meetings of young widows. My friend Beth moved me into her apartment and took care of me, shuffling me to meals, to movies, to go shopping with her, and I admit I spent most of my time sobbing. I cried so hard in my apartment that the neighbors knocked on the door, terrified something new had happened. I burst into tears in the middle of the subway, in the supermarket, in the shower, everywhere. Everything looked black and white and faded. I began to think that it wouldn't be the worst thing in the world if a truck ran me over. "I can't do this anymore," I told my therapist. "Yes, you can," she said.

I read a lot about grief, and when I read that widows often found love again, and because it had been so good the first time it was even better the second, I thought that might be my salvation. If I were in love again, I'd have another person to think about. I wouldn't feel so empty and hollow.

I wanted to be in charge. But mostly I wanted not to grieve, not to think, and when I saw Rick's ad in the *New York* magazine personals, I answered it. On our first date, he took me on a picnic. He brought cheese and apples and a bottle of wine and sweetly presented me with my own novel to sign. I felt something new: happiness. Of course it was sweet in the beginning. He called me twice a day, he was interested in what I was interested in. He held my hand and held me at night, and when he talked, his conversation was filled with the future. We'd go places, we'd be together, we'd have a child, we'd marry. There was no place for grief.

"Isn't this a little early?" my mother asked me, shocked. "Are you sure this is what you should be doing?" my friends said. And when I told my therapist and she said, "You're running away," I stood up. "I don't want to come back to therapy," I told her and gave her her last check.

As long as I am with Rick, I know I won't grieve. Rick is the reason I can go to sleep at night. His body warmth keeps me from having to think about my fiancé. Rick's filling our schedule with endless trips to visit his family, to restaurants, to concerts means I don't have to think about how alone I am for a second. His whole family converges on their summer cottage every weekend, cousins and relatives, and I don't mind going. There's a lot of distraction.

Rick first comments on my eating habits four months into our relationship. "Seconds?" he says when I grab another handful of grapes. "That's an awfully big potato for one girl," he says. At first I laugh, but then I see Rick isn't laughing. Dinner is often broccoli and a baked potato (no butter, of course), and if I am a bit hungry, I tell myself, well, it's certainly better than crying, isn't it?

After one of our dinners, I go to see my friend Jane. "Caroline!" she says, shocked. "You look like a twig!"

"I guess I lost some weight," I tell her.

She has made lunch, but I'm so used to not eating that I pick at the food. I lose weight. I go from size six to four and down to two, and when I'm there, Rick asks me to marry him. I know I don't love him, that my heart is a hollow little fist of grief, but I nod and whisper yes, because this means I will never have to grieve, not ever again.

We tell his parents, who are delighted, and then my mother, who is upset. She takes my arm. "First of all, you look like hell," she says. "And second of all, you're still grieving, honey."

I smile at her. "No, I'm not."

"Oh yes, you are," she says. She starts to tell me that she doesn't like Rick, there's something about the way he treats me that she doesn't like, some hardness, and when I begin to cry, at first I think that it's about her disliking my boyfriend, but then the tears get harder and I'm starting to cry for my dead fiancé, great gulping sobs.

She wraps her arms around me and I burst into tears. "You have to leave him," she warns. "You're doing a disservice to both of you. Do you love him?"

I shake my head no.

"Do you want to stay with him?"

"I have to stay with him," I tell her. "If I leave, I'll remember what I lost, and I won't be able to stop crying."

My mother grabs both my hands. "You're my daughter and you're a skeleton," she tells me. "That's not love, what he's doing. Grief you go through and then you're done. But this—" She holds up my wrist. "This breaks my heart and makes me grieve for you."

When my mother leaves, I feel a seismic shift. I keep hearing her words in my head; I keep thinking that she's grieving for me. Plus, to tell someone the truth of what I'm doing somehow unlocks something.

At work I no longer want to rush to get home, because then I'll be monitored. Instead I work overtime so I'm given a raise, and when I call Rick to say I'm going to be late, I'm eating a bagel! Imagine, a bagel! I wake up early and get out of the house, leaving the one piece of toast I'm allowed for breakfast without comment. I work at Macy's. Marlise, my friend, sets something down in front of me. A gooey warm cinnamon bun from downstairs. She touches my arm. "Share it with me," she orders. I take a bite.

I go and buy half a dozen candy bars. I wolf down three and save the others, and when I come back, Rick is staring sullenly at the computer. He gets up and puts an arm around me and says in that tender voice, "You know, honey, you were so beautiful when I met you. I just hate to see you fat."

I jerk my arm away. I can still taste the candy. "My friends tell me I look terrible. My mother says I look like a skeleton."

"Well, they aren't sleeping with you," he says and kisses me on the cheek, and anger flares up in me like a lit match. I think, *Well, neither are you.*

Rick keeps asking me, "When are we getting married?" I put him off. I tell him I need six months to decide if I can marry him, and when the six months are up, I tell him I need more time. "Why?" he asks. He wants to have a baby. He wants a life. When I reach for a T-shirt of his that night because I'm cold, he takes it from me. "I'm saving that for my son," he tells me.

Please don't get me wrong. There is sweetness here. He is not a totally bad person. He holds me when we sleep. He tells me I am beautiful. He's smart and funny and politically aware. He's like the idea of Santa Claus that you hope and hope will be true. Also, I'm lying to him about myself all the time, so maybe I don't deserve Santa Claus. Maybe I deserve the coal.

In the end, it isn't food that does us in. It isn't when he goes onto my computer and adds jokes to the novel I am writing because, he says, "it's too serious."

There's something else. I come home one day and he's reading mail on the couch, frowning. "What's up?" I ask, and he shakes his head and then looks at me. "You told your friend Jo about our fights?" he says. His face is crumpled in hurt, and everything in me freezes.

I grab the paper from him. "You read my mail?"

"We're a couple," he says. "We're one. What's mine is yours, isn't it? Why, do you have something to hide?"

I don't know what to do. I call Jo and ask her not to write anything personal to me anymore. "What?" she says, astonished.

"Rick's reading my mail," I say.

Something snaps on the wire. "I will not stop telling you what I want to tell you," she says, and her voice rises in anger. She tells me we are friends, that I can't let another person destroy that friendship and control it. She tells me this has to stop. "Our friendship is based on the truth!" she says.

The truth. When was the last time I faced the truth about myself? I get off the phone with Jo and then go find Rick. "You can't read my mail anymore," I tell him. We argue, and suddenly he says, "You dress like a religious fanatic! Can't you be more feminine? Would it kill you to wear a ruffle?"

That night we break up, and three weeks later, I have a new apartment, a big studio in Chelsea where the previous tenant died of AIDS. I stand in the middle of the apartment, alone, and I feel all the grief coming back, and I sob and sob and sob.

I grieve. Of course I grieve. Four months, six months. A year of hard grieving and four more years of lesser grief. What I most feared is happening, and somehow the grief, having been dormant, has gained power and I can't shut it off. My friends take care of me, inviting me over, and each time, they place food in front of me. Eat, they say. We're here. It's okay. You can eat. Jane puts soup in front of me. "If you don't take a sip, I'll be so hurt I won't know what to do with myself," she says, and so I do. My stomach clenches. I take another bite. And then another.

I know people who ballooned up when they broke up, who

would buy a whole tub of ice cream and polish it off. Alone, I eat cereal for breakfast, bread sticks and cheese at lunch, and for dinner, I try to make pasta and eat a few bites. I go to a grief counselor who doesn't condemn me for my time with Rick; she nods. "Do you know what a brave thing it is you did?" she tells me. "You just have to get through it," she says, "one bite at a time."

It's a whole year and a half later when I meet this smart, funny journalist named Jeff. I'm a little wary, but I tell him right off the bat about my fiancé. I don't mention Rick. Jeff nods and takes my hand, and then we go out to eat, and of course I'm self-conscious and order the lightest thing on the menu and eat only half of it, taking tiny little nibbles. Mouse bites. "Aren't you hungry?" Jeff asks, concerned, and I smile and eat a little more. When the waiter clears the table, I start to get ready to leave. "Wait a minute, wait a minute," Jeff says, pulling me down. "We have to have dessert."

Stunned, I sit down. The waiter gives us a menu. "What's the most decadent thing on here?" Jeff asks him. I stare at the descriptions as if they were classic literature. White apricot mousse. Lemon chiffon pie. Chocolate turnovers. My mouth waters, and I swear my hands shake. "You decide," Jeff says to me.

"We could share the mousse," I say hesitantly. I've picked the richest thing on the menu, and I feel fabulously guilty.

Jeff nods. "We should get the death-by-chocolate cake, too," he says and beams happily, reaching across the table for my hand.

That's when I fall in love. That's the beginning of what turns into a marriage as rich and sweet as any dessert.

WITH HANDS
Diana Abu-Jaber

I was raised with my hands in the food. My father's Bedouin family ate standing up at a communal tray under a tent thundering with wind. First the men ate, with great delicacy, making sure to leave plenty behind for the women, each group attending to its specialized forms of gossip.

The first time we moved to Jordan, I was seven years old and inexperienced. My mouth and fingers stung for weeks because one is meant to eat *mensaf* quickly, as soon as it's poured from the pot to the tray, while the food is tender and steaming hot.

There's an art to the way you scoop the lamb and rice and bread into your hand, palm it to your fingertips, and push the morsel into your mouth. You eat from your own section—

whatever destiny has put in front of you, no roaming or second-guessing—and when you're done, you say, "Thanks be to God," so grace comes after the meal instead of before: the gratitude of a full stomach.

Auntie Mina spent years combating what she called "savagery." Bedouin by birth, she was educated at the French Catholic school, where she came to the understanding that silverware (not art, say, or philosophy) was the benchmark of civilization. She moved her life indoors and anchored her table with ornate place settings. Her resolutely Bedouin husband, my uncle Saeed, refused all cutlery and was subsequently banished to the back porch. So Auntie Mina served two separate trays of food: one for the "civilized eaters" in the dining room and one for the Bedouins on the back porch.

When I was eight, my parents, sisters, and I returned to silverware. Back in the States, I discovered that knives and forks had become cumbersome. What was more, they ensured a small but permanent distance from what was eaten. I was hesitant, wondering whether it was possible to truly enjoy food if you couldn't touch it. But this was what Americans did, my mother told me. It was part of the deal, like speaking English and walking quickly and rigidly on the sidewalk. And I had decided that was what I would do—I would go American.

So it was a pleasure, almost a relief, when, a couple of years after we returned to the States, my forkless uncle Saeed reappeared. Seemingly on a whim, he up and moved his entire family—wife, kids, grandkids—to the States. They lived in a big, noisy, crazy house on the other side of Syracuse, and our families were constantly visiting each other.

Saeed was actually a distant relation—the uncle of some-body's cousin—but we all called him Uncle Saeed to show respect. Respect was a big, important concept in our house: If you didn't show it, everything might fall apart, and in America, meta-physically speaking, everything was always on the verge of falling apart. Uncle Saeed was a "real old-time Bedouin," Dad said. He wore slacks when he drove his Crown Victoria around town, but as soon as he got home, he'd shed the confining Western clothes and slip a soft white djellaba over his head, its long skirt swishing around his feet.

Uncle Saeed and Aunt Mina always prepared *mensaf* for our gatherings—the grand feast of meat and rich, slippery, oniony yogurt sauce and bread. This was Uncle Saeed's favorite, so it was everyone's favorite. It reminded Dad and his immigrant family of their long-lost home; it was the closest any of them could come not only to that place but to that time when the family squeezed together at one table—Dad, his seven brothers and one sister, and their startled, exhausted parents. All of them eating hot food from one big round tray: What greater intimacy could there be?

I've generally found Arabs to be very warm, intense, affection-ate, and tender, even the Jordanian Bedouins, who are reputed to be formal, traditional, and reserved. Bedouin men and women alike dote on their children—on all children. In my own experience, some of the most well-adjusted young people I've ever met were those who grew up in the warm bath of their Arab family's adoration—knowing beyond a doubt that they were treasured for the simple fact of their existence. These same young people were offered almost no material goods: no allowances, new clothes, cars, computer games, or cell phones. They were offered kisses, home-cooked meals, warm embraces, and were told over and over, in no uncertain terms, that they were brilliant, beautiful, adorable, and beloved.

Children were also considered community property; our hair was fretted with and finger-combed, our arms manipulated, our teeth and tongues examined, our foreheads felt, cheeks pinched, knees and feet and reflexes tested. One of the truest, surest communications of affection between elder and child—a natural extension of this physical ownership—was to feed your nearest and dearest *min eedi,* meaning "from my hand." To my father, that meant picking up the crispy bits of chicken from the bottom of the pan and feeding us these shreds with the tips of his fingers. To my uncle—on the other end of the spectrum—it meant scooping up the biggest handfuls of *mensaf* he could and stuffing them into our mouths.

It was actually a little frightening to be fed by Uncle Saeed. He was a big guy, well over six feet, with a huge, muscular frame and a laugh that could just about shake the glass in the windows. He fed us the same-size mouthfuls he was accustomed to. And he didn't brook any of our childish fussing over which bits looked appealing and which, ineffably, did not. To him, the equation was simple—the more food you can stuff into your children, the more you love them, the bigger and stronger they'll grow.

My sisters and I lived in dread of these weekly family meals: Would Uncle Saeed's fearsome gaze fall on us or pass benignly by? I hated being called to his side, when—one arm scooped around my narrow shoulders—he'd hold up the dumpling-like palmful of meat and rice intended especially for me. The sheer amount of it always seemed impossible, unchewable, unswallowable: Breathing became difficult, tears filled my eyes, my head swam. Only with the greatest of effort could I undertake the massive gulp to get it all down. And I'd be free of the awful *min eedi* for another meal.

It never occurred to me that there might be anything optional about Uncle Saeed and his terrible feedings. He was a fact of family life. To refuse something that had come *min eedi* was like refusing love, the nutrients of life itself. It would be disrespectful. And without respect, well, there was no telling what would come after that.

I must have been eleven or twelve years old the day I overheard my mother talking to one of her sisters-in-law on the phone. Like Dad, several of my uncles had moved to the States and married Americans; the rest had stayed home and married Jordanians. I could tell from the tenor of Mom's voice that she was speaking to one of her American sisters-in-law.

They were discussing, among other things, Uncle Saeed and *min eedi*. My American mom struggled valiantly with Jordanian customs, at times wholeheartedly embracing the culture—learning Arabic, mastering the art of baklava baking, and preparing shish kebab and hummus that would stand up to the best. But sometimes I thought I detected a certain weariness in her. She was a soft-spoken only child who'd married into a sprawling, boisterous Arab clan, and I suspected the sheer effort of it all was exhausting.

"I am really getting sick of it—yeah—yeah—you, too? I know. I don't want all that food in my mouth at once. I can hardly breathe. It's gross. Yeah. I know." We used to hear from the relatives that Dad had become "Americanized." Which referred to the fact that he combed his curly black hair out straight and flat (until it sprang up in stiff curls an hour or so later); that he'd shaved his grand mustache (and grown it back and shaved it again); and that he had become entranced with square dancing, of all things. Every Friday and Saturday night (to my mortification), he'd don a big silver belt buckle, a bolo tie, and an embroidered shirt and take Mom to a hoedown.

Apparently, an American flatness of syllables had also crept into his pronunciation of Arabic, and—according to certain of the relatives—he had an "American-liberal attitude" that included helping my mother with the housework and taking an interest in his daughters' education.

Uncle Saeed, however, had concocted his own blend of American and Arab attributes: He spoiled his fourteen-year-old daughter, Loula, sending her off on shopping sprees at JCPenney but not requiring her to attend school. ("What for? She doesn't like it so much. For a girl, it's just extra.") He treated his wife—and all women—like favored servants and children, speaking to Mina in the same way he spoke to his granddaughter: "Mina, come here. Let me kiss your head. Please take this coffee away now and bring me more cake. What a good wife."

Mealtimes aside, I loved Uncle Saeed's sweetness and felt jealous of Loula—*no school! unlimited clothes!* At the time, I didn't have the emotional vocabulary to progress much beyond this. When Uncle Saeed beckoned Mom to his side and tried to feed her in his joshing, affectionate way, I didn't see a thing wrong with it. Perhaps there wasn't. Is it just my chilly Western imagination that leads me to imagine that it might not have been appropriate?

Not long after that, Mom took me aside. "Listen," she said, her eyes hard and intent. "Do you like it when Uncle Saeed offers you food?"

I really had to consider this. For me, the family had never been a matter of like or dislike. It wasn't something I could choose; it was a fact of existence, like the color of the sky. I knew that I dreaded the moment Saeed held up his great heaping palmfuls, though I couldn't have said exactly why. I couldn't have talked about issues like control or boundaries or intrusion.

All I knew of family was that it was in charge—a plural identity—and it was my job, as a child, to obey and fatten up, and to do it all respectfully. As an adult, I'd be expected to marry and serve my husband and to continue to nurture the family. Uncle Saeed told a story about when a Bedouin married: He'd place a golden bracelet around his wife's ankle, and the goal was for her to gain so much weight, as a happy, cooking, childbearing bride, that the anklet would not come off.

So when Mom asked me her impossible question, I could only answer, "I don't know."

But something shifted after that. The next time we all got together for dinner, Mom sat moodily through the long meal, eating little, talking less, her eyes set on some internal middle distance.

The dreaded *min eedi* moment arrived about midway through dinner. Uncle Saeed fed whichever of his children happened to be sitting closest to him at the table. Then his eyes lit on me: "Diana, *yella, imshee!*" He gestured for me to get over there, and he held up a great bolus of food.

My mother put a restraining hand on my arm. She shook her head and looked Uncle Saeed in the eye. "No," she said.

It's possible that, up until that day in his seventy-third year, my uncle Saeed had never before heard the word *no* from a woman. I remember a certain astonished frisson passing through his neck and shoulders. His eyes refocused, as if he were having trouble figuring out who'd spoken. His mouth opened in the shape of a great laugh, and he said, "How else can I fatten her up?"

My mother, her voice cool and smooth as stone, said, "I don't want my daughters *fattened up*."

I think the secret to happiness may be a simple matter of proportion. Too little of certain things obviously brings anguish, starvation, or a grinding, soul-consuming envy. Then there's the tricky problem of too much. I've seen children who were raised with too much—in particular, too much money and too much freedom. I wonder if it seems un-American to speak of too much money or freedom. Or perhaps it sounds like sour grapes, as I was raised with neither.

But there are always problems with extremes, and our subtle, sinuous minds try to remedy states of imbalance in indirect ways. Too much freedom, for example, can also feel like too little love or attention, and a person raised without limits might grow up to be a whiny, materialistic, self-medicating brat.

Make no mistake, I hated being raised with so many bonds, restrictions, and shackles—all in the name of Family and Respect and its corresponding codicil of obedience. But it also meant that I spent my childhood growing within myself, intensifying my sense of self, and plotting for my escape.

I was intensely relieved the day my mother said no to Uncle Saeed. But as I look back on it, I sense a deep underlying grief settling into that room as well. Yes, I think *grief* is the word for it: mourning an inevitable sort of loss. At that moment, after Mom said no, Uncle Saeed—who, from what I could tell, had never before really seen me as an individual, as anything apart from the mass of children—allowed his gaze to sharpen. He looked at me, then at my defiant mother. "Okay," he said mildly, surrendering.

Uncle Saeed and his family moved back to Jordan not so long after that. America was "too cold," they told Dad, as if Syracuse stood in for the entire nation. As if winter in Jordan weren't also sharp and biting. I understood then that I would never again stand under my uncle's arm and be fed too much food. Perhaps none of us would. I was very sorry to see them go.

SECONDS
Jenny Allen

I'm afraid there's no way to say this without sounding pitiful, so I'm just going to say it.

I used to eat cookies out of opened packages on supermarket shelves. I was a child, but still, it was an odd thing to do. I'd go to the supermarket with my mother, then ditch her to find the cookie aisle. In my adult life, I've rarely seen an opened package of cookies in a supermarket, so I can't explain why I seemed to see them all the time as a child, but I did. And when I found an opened box or torn cellophane wrapping, I would stand in the supermarket aisle and furtively shove the cookies in my mouth, *pop pop pop*.

The thrill of finding the packages was like one of those dreams when you find twenty-dollar bills blowing all over the sidewalk—only better, at least to a child, because it was Mallo- mars and Oreos and ginger snaps and Nilla wafers. Pecan sandies. Vienna Fingers. Whatever they called the spicy ones shaped like windmills, studded with slivers of almond. Oh, the joy of it.

I told a friend about this the other day. I thought she was going to tell me she'd done it, too; I'd always assumed it was one of those things that most children did, like biting your own toe- nails or playing with candle wax.

She looked like she was going to cry. "That is so sad," she said.

I had to wonder: Why had I spent my childhood trolling for food in the cookie aisle at Gristede's?

Oh, that's right. My mother didn't feed me.

That's not entirely true. She fed us—my brother, sister, and me; my parents were divorced—but that's about all you could say. My mother had other virtues, my mother had been handed some real lemons in life, my mother was doing the best she could. But boy. We had food, three or four different dinner en- trées—fried hamburgers and lima beans, corned beef hash with an egg on top, fried lamb chops, liver and bacon. That was it, that was the repertoire. And so little of it: I don't remember being offered seconds. I remember staring at the refrigerator shelves, empty except for, say, celery sticks sticking out of a glass of ice cubes and a jar of green olives, there to be made into cream-cheese-and-olive sandwiches for my school lunch, which I hated and which mortified me.

You never knew when you were getting fed. You weren't al- lowed to ask; you weren't even allowed in the kitchen half the time. She needed it to herself, the better to curse my absent father and burn things. This was as bad as the sameness and not-enoughness of the food—the tension around the food, the resentment with which it was served.

College food was like a dream. I couldn't believe it: every day, three times a day (the *same* three times a day!), cheerful ladies in hairnets produced food so delicious it made me want to weep with gratitude. London broil one day, Swedish meatballs the next, barbecued ribs, roast chicken, fish not in a stick. Food cooked with spices that weren't paprika.

And that was just lunch. Five hours later, incredibly, they did it again. I couldn't believe all the choices—it took weeks to repeat an item, and you even had a choice of dishes within a meal: filet of sole or Salisbury steak; shepherd's pie or chicken parmigiana. And sometimes there would be a theme—Chinese Banquet (water chestnuts! crunchy noodles!), South of the Border, Mangia Italia. The other kids made fun of theme nights, but I thought they were wonderful. I couldn't believe they were making such a fuss over us.

There was dessert every night—Jell-O with little ridged minarets of whipped cream, tapioca pudding and rice pudding and bread pudding and chocolate pudding. Chocolate cake. Chocolate cake! On any old Tuesday night! It was like a party every day, a party celebrating us for no reason other than that we existed.

And there were seconds. "Sure, honey, hand me your plate. You must really like broiled scallops." Yes, I surely do, and may I have a little bit more of that butter sauce on top, please?

The next morning there would be sausage and French toast, and a choice of scrambled or fried eggs, and bagels and muffins. I never ate the fresh fruit—why fill up space in my stomach that could be better served with six or seven slices of bacon?

It took me about two weeks to gain twenty pounds. I didn't care. I was in heaven.

I am in heaven just writing about it, just remembering it. It's not like I'd never experienced big, tasty meals before I went to college—my father and his new family loved to eat, and I had many delicious meals at their house. But college food, the orgy of it, was the antidote to the food at my mother's house. It kept coming at you, and there was nothing expected in return, nothing to remind you of the strings-attached quality of family food, expectations even in my father's happier household— reasonable expectations, like tribal loyalty, but which made me extremely nervous, stranger in their midst as I was. At college, the food was laid on you, given to you (I know, my father paid thousands of dollars a year for it, but it felt that way).

That excitement about eating has stayed with me every single day of my adult life. Three times a day—more if I feel like it— I can choose things I like to eat and eat them in peace. I never take this freedom for granted, I never get tired of it. I always anticipate eating with pleasure.

This is how much I love eating: The first time I ate soft-shelled crabs—if you have never tried one, you should do it today—I broke out in hives, head to toe. It is the only time I've ever had an allergic reaction to something I've eaten. The second time I ate soft-shelled crabs, I— You know, I think that's all I need to say: The fact that there *was* a second time, the fact that I tried them again, hoping against hope that the hives had been some kind of freak event, sort of says it all, doesn't it?

You are wondering how fat I am. Let me say this: If I lived in most places in America, where the all-you-can-eat restaurant is part of the landscape, I would probably weigh 350 pounds. But I live in Manhattan, where the ridiculous rents won't allow for family-style restaurants, so I'm usually about twenty pounds overweight. At the moment I weigh 155 pounds. I am tallish—five-eight—and "big-boned," so I carry it off, more or less. I try to lose five pounds sometimes, and sometimes I do, but then I sort of slip and forget I'm trying to do it.

I look all right. I wish I had thinner thighs, I wish I had a more pronounced waistline, but I don't wish these things so much that I have made them happen. I go to the gym four or five days a week, I put in a half hour on the elliptical and try to do two or three of the weight-lifting machines, but these efforts are mostly to get my heart pumping and to maintain some semblance of muscle tone.

I have been heavier than I am now, but I thought I looked okay then, too. For a few years, I generally weighed about ten pounds more than I do now, and it was not unusual for me to need a size sixteen. And I have been heavier even than that. When I was pregnant, I was hungry all the time, and I used to eat cheeseburgers and drink vanilla milk shakes for a little mid-morning snack. By the time I was eight months pregnant, I had gained fifty pounds. I weighed 185. I thought I was allowed; I thought I looked fine. "You think that after you have this baby, you're going to lose all the weight," my obstetrician said to me. "But the baby is going to weigh about seven pounds. So you'll weigh seven pounds less than you do now."

He was right. I didn't think I looked great after I had my baby, when I did indeed weigh 177 pounds, but I didn't worry about it that much. I just wore my maternity dresses for a few months until I could fit into my old clothes again. Shortly after my daughter was born, I went to a cocktail reception in the elegant Manhattan town house that belongs to the Cuban government. I sat down on the thick glass-topped coffee table in the beautifully appointed living room, the better to talk to someone on the sofa. The thick glass broke, and I fell through the table frame to the floor, where I had to be delicately (and, amazingly, unharmed) lifted out. I thought it was hilarious. It was only after telling this story for a year or two that I realized I'd gone through the coffee table *because I was fat*.

Except for my pregnancy binge, I seem to be able to check myself before I get truly tubby. I had to interview Martha Stewart not long ago. She doesn't weigh herself, she told me, doesn't "watch" her weight, but she does go on diets. "When?" I asked. "All the time," she said. "Why?" I asked. "So I can zip up my pants," she said. I have a lot of thoughts about Martha Stewart, some of them quite critical (this is how she diets: She doesn't eat), but I will say that I was with her on the pants thing. That's how I know I need to decline dessert and the restaurant dinner rolls and the urge to polish off the mushroom ravioli my husband has left on his plate.

Even though I always use that line about weighing 350 pounds if I lived outside Manhattan, the truth is that I have outgrown the stuff that's really bad for you. Even I prefer my open-faced hot turkey sandwich sans that thick caramel-colored gravy; even I usually turn down sausages with my eggs and french fries with my hamburgers.

But I have a lasting affection for institutional steam-table food—for the food itself, the scalloped potatoes and stuffed eggplant, and for the sheer heaping plenty of it. I have spent some of the happiest hours of my adult life in cafeterias: employee cafeterias, YMCA cafeterias, the cafeteria at my daughters' public school, where I ate on days I volunteered at the library. I like the little milk cartons. I don't mind plastic utensils. I don't even mind sporks. I am probably the only person you will ever hear say that she enjoyed her meal in the cafeteria at

Sing Sing (I went on a tour of the prison): sloppy joes, macaroni and cheese, red beans and rice, canned pears. I don't even hate most airplane food, and I am actually nostalgic for it when I am handed the seven peanuts in a foil bag they give you now in lieu of a meal.

I like the one-step-removed quality of institutional eating. I like the cheerful servers, but they don't have to be cheerful. There don't even have to be servers. One of the most memorable food moments I ever had was eating what was billed as a fresh ham sandwich about twenty-five years ago in the Horn & Hardart Automat on Forty-second Street and Third Avenue in New York: thick slices of tender, warm roast pork inside a big fresh roll. The idea that such a perfect, delectable thing came out of an anonymous window was exciting to me in a way that—now that I am trying to describe it—I realize sounds sort of kinky. The impersonal quality seems to have been the clincher.

As long as I am going down this road, let me say another thing about me and food: I like paying for it. I like the cleanness of that exchange. I love restaurants for that reason, but the kind of restaurant I like best is the casual, unfussy kind where the waitperson does not introduce himself or tell me he is going to be my server this evening or ask me whether I am finding my entrée satisfactory. I love coffee shops not only because I like the kind of food they serve but because my server is not that interested in me. There isn't a lot of pressure on our relationship; it's more of a one-meal stand (oh dear, there's that kinky thing again). I like the café car on Amtrak. I like snack bars and coffee wagons and souvlaki stands.

But I also like it free. I don't think I have ever passed up an opportunity for free food. I don't sneak food off store shelves anymore, you'll be relieved to know, but I never turn down food when it's there: platters of brownies during Curriculum Night at my children's schools, platters of doughnuts in college admissions offices, leftover birthday cake in the office kitchenette. One of the markets where I do my food shopping sets out samples of cheeses—sometimes so many different varieties that it's like running a gauntlet of cheese samples. I am as happy as I am at a cocktail party, where I also never let a tray of hors d'oeuvres pass by me without plucking off one or two or five.

The corollary of always anticipating eating is being fretful about not getting enough to eat. I don't like being separated from food for too long, and I always need to know where my next meal is coming from. This summer my friends John and Goldie gave me a ride home at the end of our mutual vacations, which their family and mine had spent on Martha's Vineyard (the rest of our families had gone home earlier). The drive from Woods Hole—the mainland town where the ferry from the Vineyard docks—to New York City is about five hours long. I brought with me four hard-boiled eggs, two yogurts, a package of baby carrots, and many Fig Newtons, all in a cooler.

Some of these items had been in my refrigerator, which I had cleaned out that morning. But that wasn't why I'd brought my food. I'd brought my food because I had never been on a car ride with John and Goldie, and even though I have known them for twenty years, I didn't know their position on food while traveling: Would they turn out to be the kind of people who didn't need to eat for hours? Would I have to request a bathroom break at one of the infrequent McDonald's on the interstate in order to get something to eat, something pallid and microwaved that I would hate?

Goldie and John didn't bring anything; it turned out that their position on food while traveling was to stop for a civilized lunch. We chose a restaurant off the highway that looked like a

New England inn on the outside but offered, it turned out, an all-you-could-eat buffet. John and Goldie were disappointed, I could tell. I felt like I'd won the lottery.

If I need to know where my next meal is coming from, I also need to know where my family's next meal is coming from. This can be anxious-making (my friend Angeline likes to say that she "forages" in her cupboards when it's suppertime at her house; when she told me this long ago, my first reaction was to be astonished that her family still liked her), but mostly it has been a pleasure.

An enduring pleasure. I am not a great cook, but I am a good cook. You would like my leg of lamb and roast pork. You would like my mushroom risotto and my penne with cauliflower. You would like my pineapple upside-down cake. I am killing many birds with one stone when I cook—mending that sad old sense of deprivation and taking care of people I love.

This is how much I love eating: Ever since writing the words *chocolate pudding* in this piece, I have not been able to get chocolate pudding out of my mind—how much I used to love it; how, for some reason, I haven't had any in years. If you get it with whipped cream on top, you can fold the whipped cream into the pudding, which turns it a café au lait color and makes it taste even more delicious.

Thinking about it makes me want some right now.

I'm on a train. If I didn't have someone meeting me at the end of my trip, and if the next stop on the train were at a town that had a diner within view of my train window, I'd get off the train, I'd walk to the diner, and I'd have a big helping of chocolate pudding and whipped cream, hopefully in a tall glass sundae dish. Then I'd wait for the next train, and I wouldn't mind waiting one bit.

MY WORST EXCESS
Amity Gaige

I was not born a liar. I became one in the early eighties when, in the household of my youth, candy was outlawed. My mother, already wary of anything smacking of excess, had read several popular books on health, and these books confirmed her suspicions about the unhallowed nature of saturated fats. She scoured our house of all butters and lards. With them went the thing I loved best—sugar.

These staples of my childhood diet were replaced with items of dubious edibility, sounding less like food than like the capitals of foreign cities: Quinoa. Carob. Couscous. If my sister and I begged for something sweet, my mother would say, *Have a honey ball. Have a sesame biscuit.* I felt as if we, as a family, had reverted to a primitive age—before flavor, before accent, before the birth of the recipe, when we ate whatever we could club to death. The catch was, I knew my mother had a wretched sweet tooth. I had seen her swoon over a spoonful of chocolate mousse, eyes rolling upward, the napkin touched lightly to her lip. Why, I wondered, should we fight it so? But fight it we did. Together. After the candy ban became law, while eating my desserts of raisins and whey, I used to close my eyes and dream there was a lollipop in my mouth. It's the *smoothness* of hard candy that makes it so necessary, the infinite suckability, how the hot little mouth-warmed orb of a cherry lollipop bumps against the teeth like a sweet, stupid fish in the dark.

To get my fix, I would sneak to the corner store, where the candy was arrayed in gorgeous, foiled rows. Standing before these choices, I felt the fullness of my previous intimacy with them all. The less plausible the design of the candy, the more I liked it. This one looked like chewing tobacco. That one exploded when you placed it in a can of Coke. I bought whichever caught my fancy. It became sickening to try to finish the candy before I got home, so after a while I began to smuggle it in and consume it in secret. On one occasion, I tried to eat an entire grocery bag full of candy, which I had been carefully stockpiling over a period of weeks, in one sitting. I was thwarted in this goal by a solid chocolate Santa Claus, which I'd bought at the drugstore for twenty-five cents at a post-Christmas discount. I remember Santa's density in my hand and the portentous noises of my stomach as I gazed at his gnawed-off head.

Memories of my prepubescent self circle sharklike around these themes—lying, eating, dreaming of eating, lying about eating. Did I ever do anything nice? Did I have a tendency to stand up for the underdog? Was I brave on skates? I was a big girl with a round belly and vitamin-rich hair. Once I got going, I could run pretty fast. Photographs show me cartwheeling. I remember dressing up in my mother's nightgowns and going door-to-door with some crude instrument, performing for money. Oh, who might I have been, what sort of noble being, if I had only been allowed a bit of candy in my youth? For after the candy ban, one thing led to another. My excess with candy became excess in other forums. In college, I drank, I ate, I smoked, I partied, I did whatever I wanted. I became who I thought I was—an immoderate person, a somewhat happy, immoderate American, that creature who never denies herself an outrageous emotion, a love affair, an opinion, or a candy bar.

One day in the midst of these excessive years, I went to lunch with my mother. I had convinced her to go to one of those highway chain restaurants I loved, the kind with a penny press and a popcorn machine in the foyer and a glass box full of stuffed toys eternally out of reach of the mechanical arm. It was no accident that such places tended to be the home of the outrageous portion size, so that I left them with a feeling I liked—being stuffed to the gills.

In those years I enjoyed being with my mother for many reasons, but my bid to become my own independent spirit often put an unnatural cast on the quality of our conversations. I was always quietly out to convince her that I was right about fights we'd had years ago. She, for her part, was a force of immovability. She is Latvian, and like all Latvians, she has a sober bearing and a quick wit, and is capable of mighty silences. When we went to restaurants together, it was as if we had returned to some distant dinner table at which we were still silently debating the merits of the candy ban. I would order the greasiest thrice-fried foods—the bacon nachos or beer fries with a side of blue cheese dipping sauce. And my mother would choose the most healthful item on the menu—say, a salad with nonfat vinaigrette and water with no ice. When the waitress would ask for our dessert order, I would request the most debauched offering on the menu—for example, a molten rainbow cake with whipped cream and action figures—while my mother would look away, as if to give me a kind of shabby privacy. But the worst was when she would ask for a second spoon. This meant that when my rainbow cake arrived and I began to eat, my mother would sample it with a tentative bite and then, setting down her spoon, she would say softly, "Yuck."

Yuck. That always did it for me. Thereafter, I would eat without tasting. I would eat to make a point. For I knew, in the end, she was right. My rainbow cake *was* disgusting. She had science on her side, not to mention age, grace, and dignity. All I had was an abstract devotion to pleasure, to the idea that it was healthy to throw off caution, to be unburdened by consequence. Cartwheeling, cartwheeling.

Anticipating all this at our lunch, I cleared my throat and asked my mother the big question: "What are you having?"

She had, to my surprise, already shut her menu and was staring into middle distance. She looked beautiful and incongruous under the green glass shaded lamps, a wall of baseball memorabilia behind her.

"Split pea soup," she said.

"Really?" I said, taken aback. "Didn't you see? It comes with a side of cheese logs. Those are pretty high in fat."

My mother didn't take the bait. She was looking out the window now. It was a rainy day. Cars sluiced by below billboards.

No one walked, except across parking lots, slowly, their heads down.

Then she gave me an answer I did not anticipate.

It was a story. A story about the war.

At five years old, my mother is a serious, obedient child. A good girl with slick, unraveling brown braids. Her world is a farmhouse in Latvia set amid a field of flax. Gooseberries grow there, fat and seedy, tangy currants, cherry trees. Her days are busy—there are farmhands to pester, field mice to portage in the skirt of her dress. There is a soft mongrel dog for a playmate, a favorite cow, and two sisters, one only a baby. And although the Soviets invade Latvia in 1940, under the pretext of protecting it from the Nazis, and in that one year orchestrate a wave of killings and deportations that breaks the back of any resistance, my mother, in her farmhouse, feels no fear. The sun rises and falls over the goldenrod, the rhubarb. In the kitchen, pots clash, and in some beautiful alchemy the currants find their way into tart jellies, the apples into turnovers, and the table, at noonday, is crowded with people. Then one June night in 1944, on the eve of the return of Stalin's army, a force that was to violently occupy the Baltics for the next fifty years, my mother is bundled into a horse cart to begin her five years as one of World War II's displaced persons.

The family passes through Riga at night, the city quiet as a seashell, its red clay roofs like a thousand leather books left open along the shores of the Daugava. They catch the last ship out of Liepāja, which takes them to Poland. A year of travel follows— by train, by foot, with thousands of others. And little to no food. Only the hand of her mother, tearing bread. When there isn't enough, she distributes four portions: one for each daughter, one for her husband, and none for herself. Years later, it is this gesture on her mother's part, the sacrificing of her own bread, that is to be my mother's weightiest memory.

Once they arrive at the DP camps, the monotonous provisions there seem like bounty. My mother tells me: *When we were in the camps, we used to get so tired of the food. Food would arrive in big trucks, always one item in huge quantities. Sometimes it was cabbage. Sometimes cornbread. You'd have cornbread for weeks and weeks. Hard, stale cornbread, until you swore you would never in your life eat cornbread again.* She spends the next five years of her childhood living in a barracks, and yet the barracks always seem like a high old time compared to the fate she might have had if her escape had failed, or if, along the refugee trail, she had succumbed to her semistarvation. *But you know the food I remember best? It was the pea soup. Endless pea soup. You'd stand in line for a long time, and then you'd get some disappointing pea soup in your bowl. Good enough, though, if you were a hungry little girl.*

In 1945, an aid worker at a DP camp in Germany asserted that out of all the terrors of the war—loss of property, loss of nation, the threat of death—"the strongest language" of complaint among the refugees of World War II was reserved for "the deadly monotony of the diet." Of the hundreds of camps spread throughout the western zones of Germany, Austria, and Italy, some were famous along the refugee trail for having particularly bad food. A U.S. Army director at a camp in Italy reported that more than half the complaints he received were about the food. As for pea soup, its ubiquity has been noted with a surprising amount of documentation. The Latvian refugees even invented a term for it: *zaļās briesmas*—the Green Horror.

The end of war is always ambiguous. When Stalin forcibly annexed the Baltic nations—Estonia, Latvia, and Lithuania—at the conclusion of the war, the Allies turned a blind eye. Those who had not fled were subjects of a new totalitarian regime, and many were harassed, killed, or swept off to Siberia. For the ones who had fled, the world was disorder. Nothing was solid or whole or familiar. Amid all this, I can see how palliative it might have been, how beautifully *real,* to settle down in a mess hall not to watery *zaļās briesmas* but to cake and tea. A slice of hazelnut torte, perhaps, with a strong, hot Darjeeling and a sleeve of sugar. This was, in fact, the sort of delicacy my grandmother, my *vecmamma,* would produce during family gatherings in this country long into her old age—layers of cake, cream, and currant-jelly cake sprinkled with the broken meat of toasted hazelnuts. This torte seems to me now an offering to ghosts. It was what she wished she could have offered her three daughters decades ago in the barracks instead of bread or, worse, no bread.

A hungry body never forgets hunger. And a body that has once been hungry always retains its hungry ghost. In November 1944, at the same time my mother was on the refugee trail, a man named Ancel Keys began to study her condition in his now-famous Minnesota Starvation Experiment. To help treat and refeed the wrecked civilian populations of World War II, Keys studied thirty-six healthy American men as they experienced six months of controlled semistarvation. As these previously healthy and stable men succumbed to a shockingly uniform series of physical and psychological pitfalls, one symptom in particular came to the fore: food obsessiveness. The preoccupation with food became absolute. Gone were the topics of sex, sports, politics. The subjects were incapable of *not* speaking about food. Their bodies' drive to regain weight drove them into a neurotic agitation. When several of the men broke down and consumed extra calories, they suffered deep shame and self-disgust. During the refeeding period, the men found themselves utterly out of control, eating so much they became sick. No matter how full they were, some subjects were unable to find a point of satiation. It was as if the peace of the *fed body* was lost to them.

Once, as a teenager, when coming into a room where my mother was unloading groceries, I accidentally kicked a loaf of bread on the floor. My mother stood, pointing, and an expression so fierce crossed her face that I caught my breath. It was not the first time I had wandered, haplessly, into my mother's childhood.

Growing up, I wanted to hear about it. I did. I wanted to know what had happened to my mother during the war years, but we never knew quite how to talk about it. I was restless, keen to hear the most dramatic moments. For her part, she seemed unrelieved by the act of telling. Her voice quieted, and she would be seized with uncertainty that anyone really wanted to hear her story. Some of it she did not remember. And so her memories often drifted into ellipses, and I was forced to chatter on about my known life, while hers was a secret, right there in plain view.

In 2004, my husband and I went to live in Latvia. The country was liberated by then, the U.S.S.R. having collapsed in 1991. For the entire five months of our stay, we lived like the Latvians and dressed like the Latvians, and yet not once were we ever mistaken for Latvians. "It's because you smile so much," said my friend Inta. "You smile all the time." But off the streets, in their small, body-warmed rooms, I discovered that the Latvians were themselves enamored of a curiously cheerful ritual: cake for lunch. *Come have lunch in the faculty room,* Inta would say, *we are having cake.* Cake for lunch! It shone through my American density like a sunbeam. A group of slender, hardworking men and women huddling over a cake. Sometimes there was an occasion, but sometimes there was not. Any kind of cake would do. Mocha cakes, marzipan cakes, cakes with cherries, with chocolate shavings, cakes moist with liqueurs.

My favorite was the most traditional: *medus kūka*—honey cake. The honey in Latvia was potent, a demanding sweetness spiked with lavender. It retained a sharp, outdoorsy bitterness, as if you'd cut your tongue when you tasted it. Whenever I ate honey cake, I remembered a life I'd never had. The life, I suppose, I might have lived as a Latvian. A woodstove crackled in the gaps between imagination and memory. My mother turned from this stove, wearing an apron made of sackcloth, and smiled at me. *Are you happier here?* I whispered. *Is it better now?*

Upon my arrival home, I was excited to tell my mother about Latvians and their guiltless preoccupation with sweets. I felt I had made some sort of crucial connection between myself and my ancestors. Also, I felt vindicated. There is nothing wrong with cake, I would announce to my mother. There is only something wrong with you. You can't enjoy yourself.

I had planned to say all this, but I didn't. Standing before her on U.S. soil—how I'd missed her!—I realized that, in the end, this was my most outrageous bid to win our argument about food. I wanted her unqualified approval of my habits. I wanted her to give me permission to eat cake. I wanted her to say, *Be joyous, be guilt free.* I went all the way across the world for this permission. But what new information did I have? What could I tell her that she didn't already know? I had never stood in a long line for food. I had never treasured a bowl of soup. She had been raised in a barracks. Did I expect this fact to be solved by a sweet? And why was I so keen to fix it, anyway? Is the rupture of exile something that can even be fixed? I thought about my own dissolute behavior, and for the first time I considered that I was attempting, well into my thirties, to eat my mother's candy. To drink my mother's wine. I was attempting to eat and drink *for her*. And that this sort of desperate discomfort with her experience was, in itself, my worst excess.

Two years ago, my parents separated after forty-four years of marriage. My mother moved into a condominium on the outskirts of our city. Here, so late in life, was another journey. One more transit, one more passage. When I visit her there, my head spins. I look for my father. I look for myself as a child, for my sister in braces. But instead, in scoots a little boy who looks a lot like me. My own son.

During a recent visit, I find myself scouring the kitchen cabinets for something that might interest this towheaded two-year-old. The condominium, sunny and new, is crowded: my family, my sister, her husband and their two children. My mother announces her plan to jump in the shower, and I take the opportunity of her absence to open the floor for discussion.

"What's here for breakfast?" I ask the room.

"There's a box of Sticks 'n Oats," says my husband. "You should try it. Good, if it doesn't coagulate in your throat."

"I liked the Tree Bark Chews," says my brother-in-law, smirking.

I roll my eyes. My mother's unflagging zeal for health food has become a joke, something charming yet intractable, something by which we identify her, like a birthmark.

"Come on," I say. "What about for the kids? Isn't there Cheerios or something?"

"There's some desiccated goat's milk," says my sister. "Just add water."

"Ha," I say. "I almost believe you guys."

Back behind a box of toasted soy nuts, I see a glint of something silver. I push aside the boxes and reach in. Can it be? My fingers close around the familiar shape, that dopey, wide-assed figure of a Hershey's Kiss. In fact, there is a whole cache of them, way back there in a Baggie. I pull one out and stare at it for some time, the conversation going on without me. Then I loosen the Kiss from its little foil jacket and slide it into my mouth. I close my eyes. Creamy, yielding, a kind of chocolate Eucharist for the devout.

There is a tap on my shoulder. I turn to face my mother.

"What are you doing?" she asks.

I stare at her. Finally, I open my hand, revealing the ball of foil and its tiny white flag of surrender.

"Rather," I say, "what are *you* doing?"

She looks at the evidence for a moment. I can see her reach down into the wells of reason and attempt to make this into a tactical interchange.

"They say it's good for you, cacao," she explains airily. "They're saying that now. There's evidence. A lot of studies." Then a look of indifference flits across her face. She selects her own Kiss, defoils it, and pops it into her mouth. We chew.

I look at her—her beautiful lined face—and I am possessed with a kind of radiant understanding of her mystery and a sense

that I am destined to love her without ever being able to completely understand her, heal her, or ask quite the right question,
and even if I could, she would never be able to give the answer
that satisfies all questions.

What if I had asked her, that day we had lunch together, Why
pea soup? Why pea soup now? Why eat the Green Horror now
that you're safe? Nothing against pea soup, but what if it's an
emblem of one's starvation? Maybe she would have answered,
I'm ordering it because I can. Because it's *my choice* now what I
eat. I am no longer *being fed;* I am eating. Maybe she would have
winked at me and said, Just as you used to sneak to the corner
store for candy because you wanted some control back. *(You
knew about that?)* Or maybe she would have told me that she has
fond memories of the Green Horror because it was what she ate
in her childhood, just as I ate Chuckles in mine, and childhood
is supposed to be happy, and if you can't remember yours with
any happiness, what hope have you later, when life starts handing you fresh grief?

Or maybe she would have spoken of the ghosts. The ghosts
of all the people she'd left along the road. The people who
never made it to the refugee camp, or who were exterminated
in camps of a different kind. The nonsurvivors, who sometimes scare themselves up in the lamplight of a summer
evening. Or maybe her answer would have been simpler, as
perhaps it was for the subjects of Ancel Keys's study: Listen,
you have to feel it to understand. Hunger is the space in which
truth is simultaneously gained and lost. For refugees the world
over, the basic properties of food are eclipsed by the getting,
the losing, the sharing, the hoarding, and the intimation that
one's human worth is somehow reflected in the small or watery
portions.

Thought of in this light, the asceticism of my mother's diet suddenly becomes sensible to me. Health food is whole; it requires little preparation; you can eat small amounts of it and still be fortified. It is eminently unwasteful. It is, in a way, my mother's comfort food. It makes the most sense with the world she has seen. I cannot eat her cake, you see, because the cake tastes different in my mouth.

And me and my candy? Did my slavering obsession with sweets really belie some deeper flaw, something essentially insatiable about myself or my American childhood? Or could it be that, for me, candy symbolizes a blessed life, a life I should just be grateful for? The sponsors of Keys's starvation study concluded the following: "Many of the so-called American characteristics—abounding energy, generosity, optimism—become intelligible as the expected behavior response of a well-fed people." Some Americans, well-fed Americans like myself, have lives of overabundance. But overabundance, in essence, is a good thing—feasts, harvests, rain—and does not, in itself, hurt the spirit. Excess hurts the spirit, but with a little wisdom, excess does not have to be the end result of overabundance.

I think of another ghost, my grandmother, passing small hunks of bread to her little girls on a train halfway across Poland, headed into the thick of an angry, lightless night, and I know, though she is gone, she would never want any debate between my mother and me on this score. *Eat,* she would say. *Eat what you want. And love.*

A shriek of pleasure interrupts my mother's chocolate moment. It is my son in the other room, amused by some outrageousness of his cousin's. I can almost see his small face widening in surprise. He shuffles into the kitchen, where we stand, full of a story he does not have all the words to tell. My mother and I stoop to listen. I would give him my bread, of course I would. If we were both hungry, I would give him mine. And that would not be an act of heroism, really. It would not be anything that would require his lifelong indebtedness. It would be love. Love, simple as wheat.

SISI, YOU'RE GETTING FAT
Courtney E. Martin

Sisi, you're getting fat," said my nine-year-old companion playfully as she poured thick milk over her granola. "I can see that your body is changing."

I felt like I'd had the wind knocked out of me. Pause. Pause. Pause. "Nodidi, that's not a nice thing to say to someone," I finally managed to spit back at her with all the righteousness of a Sunday-school teacher. But even as I was scolding her, I knew I was wrong.

Her comment wasn't nice. It also wasn't mean. It was just her observation. And in South Africa, in a still economically obliterated township, to a little girl who adored me—her study-abroad student from America—beyond measure, it happened to be what had popped into her head. Because she hadn't been sufficiently brainwashed by American advertising that told her fat was tantamount to leprosy, Nodidi saw the thickening of my middle as a sweet reminder that I had eaten well under her mother's roof, that I had enjoyed my chicken dinners and *samp* (a kind of cornmeal) with beans, that I had been happy.

So why, I wondered, couldn't I experience it that way?

I'd always known I wanted to study abroad. I'd had the privilege of traveling quite a bit as a kid—my dad's liberal Western law firm gave its partners three months off every five years. My parents reserved those three-month stints for massive international adventures. We'd forgo country-club memberships and the name-brand clothes of our neighbors in favor of daylong airplane flights to exotic locations. By the time I was seventeen, I'd fed stray cats in Athens, been shocked by topless women on the beaches in Nice, witnessed an "authentic" Masai Mara ceremony in Nairobi, snorkeled the Great Barrier Reef, and floated next to an Alaskan iceberg.

After a few years of political theory and sociology courses at Barnard College, I was convinced that my next destination should be South Africa—home of apartheid and those who dismantled it. I was obsessed with race. Growing up white in suburbia with hip-hop music, watching the L.A. riots unfold on the news right as I was becoming politically conscious, and, more recently, dating Nik, a Caribbean-American who was born and raised in Brooklyn, I found that racial politics were omnipresent in my life. In my romantic view, South Africa would be a place where race played out in stark and understandable ways—a dynamic I thought might be refreshing in comparison to the messy political correctness and complexity of racial politics in America.

When I boarded South African Airlines out of JFK on a cold winter day, I never could have guessed that what I would learn during my six months abroad would have to do not only with the color of people's skin but with the shape of my own body.

Right away I realized that I couldn't eat like I had at Barnard—careful meals, sometimes as painstakingly planned as my term papers. Few carbs (a word I hadn't even known until arriving at the Hewitt, renamed Spewitt, cafeteria). Salads okay. Desserts generally not. Avoid anything hot and steaming in metal trays—sure to contain lots of fat. Never eat rolls. No granola.

That last rule had been a real wake-up call for me. I am a Colorado native, and as clichéd as it sounds, granola had felt comforting to me in those scary early days of being a college student. While everything else was foreign—the skyscrapers, the intellectualism, the unfriendliness—granola reminded me of my kitchen table at home, scarred with years of family meals, wear, and tear. Within weeks, one of my new girlfriends explained to me that while it might be comforting, it was going to garner me the dreaded freshman fifteen in no time if I wasn't careful. Needless to say, I stopped eating granola.

In South Africa, granola was a staple breakfast food, and everything seemed to be hot, steaming, and full of fat. *Carb* wasn't even a part of the Xhosa language, the native tongue spoken by our host families in Langa township, but they sure loved 'em. An average dinner included a heaping spoonful of white rice and a small plate with a tall stack of sliced bread for each

diner. Indian food—delicious samosas and creamy saag pa-
neer—was everywhere, seemingly the only alternative to traditional South African cuisine, which was usually a variation on
chicken.

In fact, the first night I arrived, my host mom, Nokwezi,
made sure her ex-husband came over with a live chicken, which
he showed me and then promptly strangled in the backyard.
Nokwezi cooked it up, and that was my meal of honor and welcome. I can still remember her round, beaming face as she
dished out huge pieces of chicken and enough rice to serve a
small Japanese village. I was touched—a little horrified by how
much I had to consume in order to appear grateful, but totally
touched.

At first I tried to control my environment in little ways. I
would use half whole milk and half water with my granola in the
morning. I would tell Nokwezi that we'd eaten a *huge* lunch at
school in hopes that she'd make my serving a bit smaller than
usual. When other students would grab snacks during break
times, I would stick to juice. I wanted to try the Cadbury candy
bars, too, but I was petrified that I'd be on a slippery slope from
there.

Denying myself those little indulgences was especially hard
because I was craving some kind of comfort. Studying abroad
had proved far more difficult than my family vacations years before. I would lie in my tiny bed at night, watching a line of ants
crawl across the floor, listening to gunshots in the distance, and
wonder why the hell I'd thought this was such a good idea. I
missed my boyfriend, Nik, whom I was newly in love with. I
missed my family. But perhaps most of all, I missed control.

I also couldn't exercise like I had at Barnard. After being a serious high school athlete, I had struggled to figure out a healthy

way to exercise as a civilian. My entire first year of college, a time when other kids are sleeping in and partying late, I'd woken at eight A.M. sharp, run at least a few miles, grabbed a piece of fruit from the dining hall, and headed off to Italian class. I was utterly committed to this routine five days a week. It allowed me to eat during the rest of the day without worrying too much, a justification—I now realize—for basic nutrients and the enjoyment of food.

If I'd woken up at eight A.M. and thrown on some running gear in Langa, I would have been seen as certifiably crazy. No one exercised in a neighborhood where just having enough food was, for some, a new and welcome experience, and for others, not necessarily a foregone conclusion. The only spandex that entered the township gates was surely coming from foreign clothing donations.

The University of Cape Town, where I took classes, was another story. There, American anxiety about exercise and unattainable standards of thinness had been imported along with the McDonald's near campus. A short walk down from where we took our classes was a small track, maybe a quarter of a mile around, designed for campus athletes. I asked our supervisor, a clumsy Zimbabwean gent, if it was okay for me to run around the track on our afternoon break. He looked puzzled, scratching his shiny bald head, but granted me permission.

Soon a few other girls—equally neurotic and searching for control amid the uncontrollable—joined me. We would run round and round, trying not to sweat because there were no facilities to wash up, hoping that we could burn a few calories in our incessant circling.

I remember feeling a certain amount of relief from these short runs, but I simultaneously struggled with guilt over the new realization that I *needed* that relief. I was so rule-bound when it came to my body—what I ate, how I moved—that anything less made me feel anxious. Studying abroad brought that awareness home.

One of the girls who joined me admitted to also jumping and running in place in her bedroom in Langa at night. I couldn't imagine what her host family must have thought of this petite American girl running to nowhere. It seemed so embarrassing. So hopelessly American. But the more I reflected on her behavior—on all of our behavior—the more I realized that most of the young women on that study-abroad trip were *that* girl.

We were clinging desperately to an ideal weight, convinced it meant something more than a number on the scale—beauty, competence, control, sheer worthiness. Our quickly adding pounds were a constant source of collective consternation, a frequent conversation topic on the van rides to and from our houses, exasperated P.S.'s in our e-mails to friends. We didn't want it to ruin our time in South Africa, but we also couldn't stomach the idea of our expanding bellies. Looking back, I realize that so many of us were only half there—learning, experiencing, changing—and half inside ourselves, managing our own anxiety, trying not to lose our first-world bodies. In truth, our worst nightmare wasn't being caught up in the violence that surrounded us but returning home to our boyfriends and families fatter.

Nodidi and I sat cross-legged on her tiny concrete front porch and played a mean game of Egyptian Rat Killer, a card game of rowdy slapping and matching that I had learned a decade earlier at Camp Shady Brook. Neighborhood kids wandered past her front gate to see what all the commotion was about and stuck around, laughing along with us when we collapsed into giggles following a really raucous slap. Eventually, they wanted to join, but the game wasn't great for that many kids.

"What about Spoons?" I exclaimed, nine years old myself again. The motley crew of kids looked at me with quizzical looks. "What's she talkin' about?" one asked Nodidi, as if she could translate for the strange American girl. Nodidi shrugged.

"Everyone go back to your houses and get a spoon. Meet back here in five!" I said, relishing my new role as township captain. A dozen kids scattered in different directions, taking the mission very seriously.

When it was just Nodidi and me again, she knelt behind me and started playing with my long, curly hair, an activity she was becoming accustomed to. One day she had even invited friends over to see how my hair became dark and sleek when I got out of the shower. I was shocked when I walked out of the bathroom in a towel and was greeted by three curious faces, eyeing me as if I were an animal in the zoo.

"Courtney, I didn't mean to hurt your feelings when I said that this morning," Nodidi said quietly.

"Oh, honey," I said, spinning around so I could look into her huge, sweet eyes and grab her hands in mine. "I thought more about it, and I don't think you should feel bad at all."

"I shouldn't?"

"No, you weren't trying to be mean. You were noticing. There's nothing wrong with that. I just have this really American idea about gaining weight—that it's this terrible, horrible thing," I said, straining to explain something that I was realizing more and more was ridiculous.

"Why is it so bad?" she asked. "I mean, Destiny's Child all has big ol' butts!" She jumped up and sashayed around the porch in her best Beyoncé impression. She started belting out her favorite hit, "Bootylicious." Nodidi had a beautiful voice. She did not, however, have a big ol' butt. In fact, as I smiled and laughed, watching her, I realized that she had the same body that I did prepuberty—that stringy, all legs, no torso figure that prompts nicknames like "chicken legs" and "string bean." I remembered hating my skinny legs, even tearing up a basketball-team photograph after a friend pointed them out and lovingly teased me. Unlike me back then, Nodidi had no time for self-hate.

"It's not," I screamed above her singing. "It's not bad at all!"

All the kids started coming back with spoons clutched in their tiny hands, and we sat down in a lopsided circle to play. They loved Spoons—a game, like musical chairs, that involves lots of anticipation, laughter, and very little skill. We shuffled cards and smacked them down, grabbed for spoons, huffed and puffed in fake anger, giggled and teased one another as the sun set, turning the sky a striking shade of bright orange and pink.

Eventually, Nokwezi threatened to make us watch bad soap operas all night if we didn't come get dinner, so we said goodbye to our gaggle of card-playing friends, scooped up the scratched spoons, and headed in.

As I lay in bed that night, blissfully exhausted, I wasn't thinking about the size of my thighs or the occasional shout or car backfiring coming in from my barred window. I was thinking about Nodidi's long, skinny legs, the self-conscious girl I used to be, Nodidi's definitively unself-conscious dancing, and the lesson in all of this. What matters in life—not South African life but life everywhere—boiled down to very few things. The sun setting on a raucous card game, tiny hands tangled in your hair, and unadulterated joy all counted.

When I got off the plane at JFK, I *was* about ten pounds heavier. I was also exponentially smarter. I'd learned so much about social change—not the romanticized, *Free to Be You and Me,* melting pot, diversity schlock of my youth, but real, fundamental political paradigm shifts (still in process almost fifteen years after the fall of apartheid). I'd articulated a more nuanced idea about my own role in that social change; I finally understood that to be of service to others, I had to understand them first. And I had developed incredible, life-changing friendships with my host family and a half-dozen other locals (Spoons-addicted neighborhood kids among them).

I spotted Nik right away in the crowd of friends and families waiting excitedly for their loved ones to exit baggage claim. We walked toward each other slowly, almost shyly, and then I buried my face in his chest and he wrapped his long arms around me tightly. As in all moments that really matter, my weight was the furthest thing from my mind.

MY TEN PLAGUES
Harriet Brown

I grew up going to Passover seders, where my favorite moment was always the recitation of the ten plagues God visited on Pharaoh in order to spring the Jews from slavery and set them on the long road to freedom. Of all the rituals of the seder, my favorite was when we dipped our pinkies in our glasses, leaving drop after drop of wine (or grape juice) on the side of the plate as we solemnly chanted the Hebrew name of each plague: Frogs. Boils. Darkness. Somehow this is the image that comes to mind when I think of my history with food: a story of slavery and suffering with something of a happy ending, though not the one I spent years fantasizing about. That story starred a svelte, glamorous me who maintained her dream weight, unfazed by hunger, obsession, or guilt. The reality—let's just say it's a different neighborhood in the promised land.

Cookies. *My weight: 20 pounds.* Specifically, a tin of cookies on the bottom shelf of a kitchen cabinet. I'm not walking yet, but I know where the cookies are. And one day I crawl purposefully into the kitchen and head straight for the cookie cabinet. I get the door open and the lid off and I'm elbow-deep in the tin when a flash of light makes me look up. My mother takes another photograph to make sure she catches the expression on my face: a mixture of pleasure, confusion, and shame. *Gotcha!,* she said years later whenever she pulled out the black-and-white photos—too often—and showed them to friends and family. But which part, exactly, was wrong: the end or the means? Eating the cookies or sneaking into the kitchen to get them? And why were they on the bottom shelf, anyway, if I wasn't supposed to eat them?

Challah. *My weight: 50 pounds.* On Friday nights my family eats dinner with my grandparents. My elegant grandmother makes extra portions of my favorite dish, so for years I think chickens come with four wings. My grandfather, a stocky Russian Jew with atrocious table manners, urges me to eat. "Put a little butter on that," he says, jabbing a fork at a slice of challah on my plate. I don't like butter, but I love the pretty, braided loaf my grandmother buys at the Jewish bakery. In fact, I love everything about these Friday-night dinners except the inevitable comment from my grandfather as I get ready to take my first bite of challah. "You know, doll," he says, "you're putting on a little weight." A shred of herring adheres to his bottom lip. The challah might as well be cardboard. I chew and swallow anyway, hoping the bland mush in my mouth might taste as good as it looks. It never does.

Cake. *My weight: 90 pounds.* Specifically, my (other) grandmother's checkerboard cake, which is famously dry and tasteless, at least according to my mother. But I love the way the squares of vanilla cake alternate with the squares of chocolate, the way they're all mixed up and yet still separate. How does my grandmother do that? My mother, who's always on a diet, wraps the cakes in tinfoil and hides them at the back of a shelf in the upright freezer that stands in the hall between the laundry room and garage. All kinds of things disappear into that freezer: cases of Tastykakes, gallons of ice cream, a side of kosher beef, and my grandmother's cakes. The freezer door is always locked, and only my mother knows where the key is—at least until the afternoon my sister unearths it. From then on, whenever our parents are out, I dig out one of the solid silver-wrapped squares and wolf it down, standing in front of the open door. Freezer burn gives the illusion of moisture. I eat whole cakes this way, hiding the crumpled foil balls at the bottom of the kitchen garbage, waiting for my mother to catch me. She never says a thing.

Carrots. *My weight: 115 pounds.* Sophomore year in high school, my mother and I join Weight Watchers, each of us hoping to lose twenty pounds. We go to weekly meetings at a church in the next town so we don't have to see anyone we know. I like the routine of the meetings: waiting in line to be weighed, chatting with the other women (I'm the only teenager, which embarrasses me), all of us a little nervous. Then being called behind the screen, slipping off shoes and belt and even earrings, stepping on the scale for the moment we've waited for all week. The number that makes the scale balance is the number we will obsess over for the next seven days. If it's lower than last week's number, I spend the rest of the night in a haze of pleasure. If it's gone up even a little, I'm plunged into self-loathing. Between meetings, I record every bite in my preprinted food diary, checking off boxes: three servings of fat, three breads, five proteins, three milks, three fruits, and as many vegetables as I want. I'm a born-again when it comes to dieting, oh yeah, a true believer whose salvation lies in playing by the rules. No deviation, no rationalization; I never cheat, not even by a single jelly bean. Every Sunday my mother makes a week's worth of individual bread "puddings" from bread, egg whites, and artificial sweetener. I carry carrot sticks everywhere in plastic Ziploc bags, chewing until my jaw hurts and my painfully empty stomach protests. And it pays off: in fourteen weeks I've lost twenty pounds, and that summer, for the first time, I have a boyfriend. My mother becomes a Weight Watchers lecturer, toting her own collection of markers, posterboard, and inspirational sayings to a different church every week. I attend a few maintenance meetings and then stop. I have nothing in common with these people. I'm never going to be fat again. Never.

Frosting. *My weight: 140 pounds.* Specifically, chocolate frosting, the kind that comes sealed in a can with a reusable plastic lid. By my senior year of college I've gained back the twenty pounds I lost, plus five more. I make nightly two A.M. sorties to the off-campus Wawa, buying cake mix and cans of chocolate frosting. I throw out the cake mix, but I'm not fooling the Wawa clerk, and I'm sure as hell not fooling myself. I eat the frosting by the tablespoon when I can't sleep, which is pretty much every night. Some nights I eat a whole can, then lie awake until dawn, listening to the clamor in my head. *I'm a fat pig, I deserve to feel sick, I'm a terrible person.* My boyfriend says that when I pull on stockings, my legs look like sausages. Then he breaks up with me. I don't know what I'm going to do after graduation. These are the best years of my life, aren't they? Then why am I so miserable?

Salad. *My weight: 106 pounds.* I love everything about New York City—the people, the noise, the feeling of urgency that pervades every conversation. I love knowing where to stand on the subway platform so I'm in exactly the right spot when the doors open. And I love the food. I eat curry for the first time, and sushi. Homemade ravioli from the little Italian shop around the corner. Blackout cake from the Jewish bakery down the block. I walk miles and miles each day and eat pretty much whatever I want, and slowly, the pounds come back on. So eight years after moving to New York, I find myself back at Weight Watchers. This time I'm determined to lose twenty-eight pounds, enough to get married in my mother's wedding dress. Once more I'm compulsive about sticking to the diet, recording each tomato and pretzel stick. I'm just as obsessed with food as I was back in college, only now, instead of eating, I focus on weighing, measuring, and recording what I eat. I'm hungry all the time. I dream about three-layer chocolate cakes with raspberry filling, bowls heaped with cream-drenched pasta, buttered toast. The only way I can stay on the diet is to eat exactly the same meals every day. So breakfast is three strawberries and two slices of diet bread spread thinly with cottage cheese, sprinkled with cinnamon and artificial sweetener, and broiled. Lunch is a salad from the Korean greengrocer down the block—two kinds of lettuce, cucumbers, shredded carrots, and chickpeas, topped with a teaspoon of diet dressing and four pretzel sticks. Dinner is broiled chicken or fish, a cup of cooked pasta, steamed veggies, a fat-free yogurt, and an orange. I'm not tempted to cheat, even when confronted with ice cream, because I've fallen in love with the vision of myself in my mother's wedding dress, a confection of lace and seed pearls. After three months I can zip it up the back; after five, the waist has to be taken in. I wear a size two for the first time in my life. I wear my shirts tucked in under wide cinched belts. I wear sleeveless tank tops and don't flinch at the sight of my upper arms. Though my weight is in the normal range for my height, I'm weak with hunger most of the time. But when I walk down the aisle in that dress, I feel almost beautiful.

Milk. *My weight: 150 pounds.* When my grandmother (she of the extra chicken wings) dies, I'm shocked by an overpowering urge to have a child. Two weeks later, I'm pregnant. For the first time in my life, I'm *supposed* to eat. My old enemy, food, is suddenly my friend. I eat when I'm hungry, without trying to distract myself, without chewing on carrot sticks, without sneaking or binging or self-loathing. I drink big glasses of milk and eat cheese and ice cream. My body gets bigger, but for the first time in my life, I'm okay with that, at least until the midwife scolds me for gaining too much and gives me a copy of *What to Expect When You're Expecting,* pointing out the recipes for low-cal "treats." I throw the book away. I fall in love with my daughter the minute she's born, and count it a testament to biology that I continue to love her despite her severe colic. Dairy products make her scream—my dairy products, that is, since I'm breast-feeding— and so I give up milk, cheese, and ice cream. I lose weight and barely notice. Four years later, my younger daughter is born, and she, too, is colicky. Once more I give up dairy, but this time I don't lose weight. By the time the baby is walking, I still weigh more than I did when I delivered the first time.

Bread. *My weight: 205 pounds.* When a major depression smacks me in the brain, I drag my weeping, panicking, insomniac self to the doctor and get a prescription for antidepressants. Three weeks later, I feel better than I've felt in years. But the medication has an unexpected side effect: I can't stop eating. This is not the binging behavior of my teens and twenties; I don't feel shame, and I'm not lonely. In fact, I'm happier than I've ever been. It's just that I never *ever* feel full. I'm not exactly hungry all the time, but I'm always ready to eat. And I do. After I gain the first twenty pounds, I stick to plain bread without butter, vegetables and fruits, lean meats. I take up cycling and put a thousand miles on my bike in a single summer. Still, the pounds pile on. Catching sight of myself in the mirror is a shock, but otherwise I feel normal. My body is strong and capable. It gets me where I want to go. It's just, well, fat.

Crackers. *My weight: 185 pounds.* After five years, I go off the antidepressants. Gradually, about twenty pounds disappear, and my appetite subsides to pre-SSRI levels. But the unmedicated me has to grapple once more with food and eating. I don't want to spend the rest of my life obsessed with food; I don't know how not to. I make a few perfunctory visits to Weight Watchers, but I can't bring myself to weigh and measure and worry about every bite I put into my mouth. I can't diet anymore. There must be another way. I sign up for a ten-week eating program with a therapist who specializes in eating disorders. In our first session, she asks me to take a cracker from a box she offers. *Look at the cracker,* she says. *Really look at it.* I look at the cracker. I notice that its edges are not perfect, and its surface is bumpy, speckled with bits of black pepper. I spend fifteen minutes observing, touching, and smelling the cracker before the therapist tells me to put it into my mouth. *Don't chew,* she instructs. *Don't swallow.* The cracker sits on my tongue, all sharp corners and salt. It feels enormous in my mouth; it feels big enough to choke me. I want to snap my teeth around it once, twice, and swallow. I want, I realize, to get it the hell out of my mouth. This realization is so surprising that I forget to panic. I look up, meet the therapist's eyes. She is smiling. I come back to her office again and again and eat crackers and bread with her, noticing the taste and texture and smell of each bite. Then I move on to the scary foods—chocolate bars and cookies and cake. I learn to be tuned in to my hunger, to eat slowly and attentively, to recognize when my stomach is full. Along the way, I learn to recognize feelings, too: anger and sorrow, terror and joy. It takes much longer than ten weeks; in fact, our work together takes nearly ten years. The process changes much more than the way I eat and my relationship with food. It changes my life.

Pasta. *My weight: 168 pounds.* The rest of the world is on the Atkins diet, or some variation thereof, but I'll never diet that way again. I enjoy pasta in every form: Spaghetti in tomato sauce with tiny shrimp. Linguini in lemon-wine sauce. Rigatoni with olive oil, grated pepper, and Parmesan. Baked ziti covered in mozzarella. Soba noodles in miso broth. Most of the time I savor the crunch and flavor of whatever I'm eating. Most of the time I like the way I feel after a good meal: *satisfied.* And if there are moments when I still feel that urgent hunger, still want to chew for the sake of chewing, I've made my peace with it. I've also made my peace with a number on the scale that would have horrified me thirty years ago. As I tell my daughters, all bodies have flesh on them; some have more than others. My body has more than, say, their father's or their grandmother's. If I can name it and acknowledge it, this information becomes simply another part of who I am: I have green eyes and curly hair. I am smart and funny. And—oh yes, I am fat.

TOP MODEL
Magali Amadei

*Forty-two percent of first-to-third-grade girls want to be thinner.
Eighty-one percent of ten-year-olds are afraid of being fat.
Forty-six percent of nine-to-eleven-year-olds are "sometimes"
or "very often" on diets.*

—The National Eating Disorders Association

At six A.M. the TV studio lights burned into every ounce of me. I was no stranger to early call times, but this was the first time I had been up at the crack of dawn to talk about my eating disorder on a morning news show. I talked about my years as a top model—the covers of *Vogue, Glamour, Cosmopolitan,* and *Elle;* ad campaigns for L'Oreal, Dove, Banana Republic, and Pantene; runway shows for designers like Ralph Lauren and Versace. I revealed the not so glamorous truth behind all those picture-perfect images: I had suffered from bulimia for seven years, through the height of my modeling career.

At the commercial break, a production assistant rushed over

to remove my microphone. The anchor leaned in and said, "My three-year-old daughter just asked me if she looked fat! Isn't that incredible? I think she must have overheard me saying something about my weight. Anyway, it's great that you're telling your story." She shook my hand and thanked me for coming.

That was over seven years ago. I now have a daughter who was born in 2005. Today the anchor's story has a whole new meaning for me. And I understand my own story in a very different way.

As a teen, I never opened an issue of *Allure, Mademoiselle,* or *Glamour.* I didn't know who Steven Meisel, Peter Lindbergh, Steven Klein, or Albert Watson was. My idea of fashion was cutoff jean shorts and a tank top. My sense of "in" and "out" was nonexistent. I simply didn't care. I remember going to see Etienne Daho (the heartthrob of all French teenage girls) in concert wearing a black-and-white-checkered jacket that my mother had made me. I thought it was great, and I lived in it for months. I didn't care so much about what I was wearing, but I did care about other things. I tried to be the best at everything, from ballet to piano. I grew up in an Italian family in which feelings weren't often a topic of conversation; when my brother got into a life-threatening motorcycle accident, everyone shut down. I communicated by trying to be the perfect girl. My shock and fear over the accident got twisted into an intense drive for achievement.

The first time I linked that perfectionism to what I "should" look like was one day at school, when someone told me I looked fat. I was fourteen. My body was changing, and some curves were beginning to show, but I was far from fat. Reality didn't matter, though. Those three words sent me down a slippery slope. *You look fat.* It's what the experts call a trigger. For me it was the first shot fired in the battle.

My bulimia started as a game. I found someone at school (or rather, we found each other) who had discovered the same trick. She would come to my house for cheese and pasta, and I would go to hers for latkes, and then we would guard the bathroom door for each other while we vomited. After a while we both denied we were still doing "it." Of course we were both still purging, but we lied. We lied to each other because it was too shameful to admit that the bulimia was already controlling us, not the other way around. So we nodded, knowing our secret. We never spoke of it again.

Every night at the dinner table, my father would ask me the same questions in a valiant attempt to reconnect: *Are you okay? Do you need anything? Is anybody bothering you? How are your classes going? Do you need any money?* This became the dining-table mantra, much as I imagine the Catholics hold hands and say grace. My answers would be as monotonous as the rhythm of the questions—monosyllabic yeses and nos. At that point I had pretty much given up on verbal communication.

I came to Manhattan in the summer of 1991 on a two-week vacation that turned out to be the start of my modeling career. I never intended to become a model. Pauline Bernatchez, the owner of Pauline's NYC and Paris, spotted me in my hometown and was intent on signing me to her agency. After two years, she finally persuaded my parents and me that New York City would be a fun place to visit. After two months in New York, I became a model in demand. I was a star, but I hated the attention. The fashion industry was the worst place for a girl who didn't know how to speak up for herself. I felt like a fraud when I saw myself on the covers of magazines. I knew every millimeter of my face by heart because I had to stare at myself for hours every day while I was being made up. I could paint my lips to make both sides of my upper lips match, pluck the smallest undesirable eyebrow hair, and shade my nose to look straight all while sipping coffee, smoking a cigarette, and answering my agent's calls. I became my own worst critic. I saw myself as fat, stupid, and completely insignificant.

I was in a downward spiral of repressing my emotions to appear always happy, always worry- and problem-free. My inner voice was a harsh, reprimanding, unloving bitch. I'd forgotten what hunger was and was completely consumed by my weight obsession. I weighed myself from morning to night, using laxatives and purging by vomiting so often that I didn't have time to think of anything else.

I was naive to the consequences of having an eating disorder. I didn't even know that there was a name for what I was doing to myself. I had no idea I could damage my reproductive system, though I did begin to notice that my periods were getting further and further apart. I had permanent dark circles around my eyes, and brittle hair and nails. I was unaware that using laxatives could impair my bowel control, and I never could have imagined that I would end up with seven dental caps, eleven root canals, a bridge, and two implants.

While bulimia took its physical toll on me, my mental health was also deteriorating. I was very depressed. I was having panic attacks and couldn't get out of bed. That was when I had to face the reality that I had a problem. I wrote a letter to my then-boyfriend, confiding my dark and shameful secret. After he read it, he held me and told me everything would be okay. I felt relief for the first time. I'd reached out and the impossible had happened: I could be me, all of me, and still be loved and accepted. That was my starting point, the point where I relearned to feel, relearned to be myself, and rediscovered the power of having opinions and making choices.

Simple things have been my pillars of recovery. I haven't weighed myself in years. I don't restrict any food I eat, and I've adopted an anti-fat-free policy. Learning to recognize my hunger was a big challenge, and trusting that my body would self-regulate was at times trying. Early on in my recovery, I had no idea what it meant to feel full. My first instinct was to watch peers to find out more about this foreign concept of eating to the point of satisfaction. I've always been a good parrot—I have the ability to copy people's mannerisms, accents, and styles—so I put those skills to work. I started observing what a dinner looked like where people actually seemed to enjoy themselves from start to finish! I assessed my own satisfaction by being with other people instead of withdrawing from them.

I started consciously reviewing basic feelings such as happiness, sadness, joy, and anger. I hadn't expressed anger in over seven years. I knew there were plenty of moments in my life when I should have felt furious, but that anger never came out.

At the height of my career and of my eating disorder, I often would leave on two- to three-week work trips. I would visit one city in a different country every few days: Start in New York, go to Paris, then Morocco, on to Venice, then Spain, and so on. On one of those trips, I arrived in Venice, but my suitcase did not. Two days later, I was scheduled to be on a flight to Paris. I didn't have anything with me, not a toothbrush, not a change of clothes, nothing. I didn't say anything; I think I didn't even feel anything. I pretended it wasn't affecting me and brushed it off. I brushed it off for ten days—that's how long it took for us to be reunited, my suitcase always missing me by a day or two. I never uttered a cuss word or a complaint. I kept it all in and controlled that anger through constant binging and purging.

Being bulimic was like scuba diving to me. I was in a world but removed from it. My eating disorder was the air tank. It was my life. It replaced my friends, my lovers, anyone close. Recovering meant I had to find the surface, to come up and walk around for a while with the tank on my shoulders and gain trust that the air was breathable. I breathed regular air and tank air intermittently, until I had enough confidence to give up my tank altogether.

I also had to stop working as a model while I focused on getting well. I didn't know how to deal with criticism and constant judgment of my appearance. I learned to speak up for myself when I heard those flippant weight comments. Most important, I learned that if I wanted to continue modeling, I would need to work with people who respected me—and I would have to be open about what I had been through.

Being part of the fashion industry was always a challenge for me. Not only was I a seventeen-year-old bulimic who'd gotten thrown into the most critical and superficial business, I was also *part of the message that was hurting me.* Advertisers sell the idea that what you look like defines you, that physical beauty is the answer to all of life's problems. The fact that every picture is retouched only reinforces the illusion of perfection. Getting over my own eating disorder helped me understand my responsibility to the millions of people who read those magazines and compare themselves to those images.

I *know* what happens in the studios. I've been through countless hours of hair and makeup. I've waited and waited until the ideal lighting is set up. I've seen how pictures of me have been drastically altered with a few clicks of a mouse. Models and actresses on the glossy pages are reshaped, recolored, and reinvented. When we understand that simple fact, we can begin to recalibrate our ideas about what's real and what's fantasy. Fashion can actually be a lot of fun when we stop believing that our lives would be better if we could hop inside a *Vogue* magazine spread. Here's my personal beauty tip: *No one can.*

Not too long ago I was on a photo shoot for a magazine, and the stylist kept trying clothes on me. She'd envisioned a certain look and certain clothes, but they didn't fit. She snapped to the photographer while I was standing right there, "She's too fat for the clothes, she's too big!" In the past, I would have felt ashamed. I probably would have gone back to my hotel to binge and purge. But not that day. Instead I snapped right back, "Her clothes are too small for me! I'm not fat or big—she picked clothes that are too tiny." The stylist ignored me and walked away. But I felt great. Some people don't know that the things they say are hurtful, and others don't care. Before an image appears on the pages of a magazine, a real person has to stand in front of that camera. The images don't have a voice, but I do.

My eating disorder has shaped who I am. It has also brought me an awareness of what kind of mother I want to be. A few months after my daughter was born, I was struck by the comments my dear, well-intentioned friends were making about her: *She is so gorgeous! She is so cute!* I started wondering if they would be making the same comments if she were a boy. Each day I became more aware of how girls and women are given the message that appearance should be the focus of their lives. Other moms asked me questions about my "baby weight," and I took note of their puzzled expressions when I responded that I don't own a scale.

I think about that television anchor a lot these days. I look at my own daughter and I am filled with a fierce determination to do everything in my power to ensure that she never questions who she is or feels the need to ask, "Do I look fat?" Instead of telling her how beautiful she looks, I talk to her about how much I appreciate her talents and her unique personality. I encourage her to express her feelings and help her understand that what she looks like does not define who she is.

Motherhood is a powerful reflection of my past, present, and future. Now when I look in the mirror, I don't lean in closer to search for imperfections. I see who I am. Sometimes I'm fearful and sometimes I'm courageous. Sometimes I see tears and other times it's a big, happy grin. This is me. This is how I define beauty.

READER, I ATE HIM
Brenda Copeland

The first thing to say is that I was thirty. If I left that out, you might think I was younger when this story took place—twenty-five, sixteen, maybe even twelve. But I was thirty and old enough to know better.

I was living in Toronto at the time, taking classes at the university during the day and working as a legal secretary in the evening, the five-to-midnight shift at one of those big corporate law firms. I'd left college years before without getting my degree, which didn't seem to be a problem at the age of twenty-two. With a steady paycheck and a steady boyfriend, anything seemed possible. But things look different in the harsh light of thirty, so after several years and a string of unsatisfying jobs, I found myself in a classroom once again. Though it wasn't quite a fresh start, it was a time of industry and resolve when I was trying to right past wrongs and live up to what everyone told me was my potential. I guess that's why I was also on a diet.

There was nothing unusual about my being on a diet, I'm sorry to say. I had been dieting one way or another since I was nine: Scarsdale, Slim-Fast, Weight Watchers, Metracal, Ayds—you name it, I tried it. I never knew what would set me off. Sure, there were the usual motivators like a party or an interview, a new dress or a new year. For these I could count on magazines and friends to help me through. But there were other reasons for my diets: a harsh word, a nameless worry, loneliness. These incentives never appeared in the bold, bulleted lists of magazines, and they terrified me. I don't know which approach was more effective. (It was the old carrot-or-the-stick question, I guess, only in my case the stick was likely to be a chocolate-covered pretzel.) All I know is that for years I measured the success of my day by what and how much I ate. I would lose weight, keep it off for a time, then gradually gain it back . . . and more. That's the way with diets.

It was toward the end of the second week of this particular regime, and I was Being Good, which meant that I was being strict with myself, measuring portions, saying no to fats and sugars (anything with taste in it, really), being careful to drink my eight glasses of water and write down everything I ate in my little blue notebook. I'd bought the notebook for this purpose, resolved that this one wouldn't get tossed into the drawer alongside the red notebook with the flowers, the purple notebook with the stripe down the side, or the black vinyl one with FOOD DIARY stamped on the front. Recording my day in this way gave me purpose, a way to shape my intention and document my struggle. I was Anaïs Nin, Anne Frank, and Go Ask Alice all rolled into one—only I wasn't writing about lovers or Nazis or an addiction to drugs. I was writing about my battle with food, about Doritos, chocolate, Szechuan beef, and those little marshmallows shaped like peanuts. I was pitiful. I was tortured. And I wasn't even fat.

Two weeks of this and I'd lost five pounds. They were familiar, those five pounds, and even though they were my bad penny, losing them gave me a *maybe this time* sense of optimism. But I was hungry and could feel my determination waning. I'd spent the past couple of weeks avoiding coffee shops and vending machines, the leftover food in the conference room. I was pretending that a Lean Cuisine could make a satisfying meal and that I preferred my salad without dressing. Still, as much as the rules of the diet had kept me going, as much as I tried to fill myself up on Diet Coke and celery, it wasn't enough.

So I tried to distract myself. I took a bubble bath and lit a vanilla-scented candle. I reminded myself that nothing tastes as good as thin feels. I cut out pictures of skinny models and taped them to the fridge. I focused, smiled at myself in the mirror, and tried to visualize my thinner, better self, and as I did, I remembered a commercial from some twenty years before in which a pretty blond woman, sassy in that seventies way, walks along the street window-shopping. It isn't your typical Main Street with a dress shop and a sporting-goods store. This is Eden before the serpent, and every window frames an apple. Only it isn't an apple, it's a luscious ice cream sundae, a gooey chocolate cake, a fresh-from-the-oven apple pie. The pretty blonde, more troubled now than sassy, stops at each window. She furrows her brow and licks her lips or makes some other gesture to indicate her struggle.

"You're on a diet," the voiceover says. "Your willpower is getting weak." At that the woman stops and enters a store. Her hunger is palpable. The moment is tense. And then she comes out, a little yellow box in hand. Chiclets. She exhales, pops one into her mouth, and a look of satisfaction that is undeniably sexual comes across her face. Crisis averted. Appetite thwarted. Problem solved. A mere twelve calories.

At least that's the way I remembered it.

My appetite felt larger than that. It felt lusty and shameful, something to be hidden, even from me. That's how it was as I walked down my main street, my own dark serpent whispering in my ear. I didn't want the ice cream or the cake or the pie, and I certainly didn't want Chiclets. I wanted something else, some other kind of sweetness. I wanted sugary sour, maybe even friendly and bright, something hard that was slightly obnoxious with a teeth-rattling crunch. No doubt about it: I wanted candy.

That shouldn't have been such a big deal—a bag of sourballs or a roll of LifeSavers was hardly a binge. As far as dieting sins go, it didn't even rate. But what if I couldn't stop? Sure, I could have a couple of LifeSavers; they were practically breath mints, for God's sake. I could enjoy them (reds first), then write them down in my blue notebook and be done with it. But could I be done with it? Could I buy one little package of candy and stop there? I had always wanted to be the type of woman who comes across some half-eaten candy in her purse, who finds it down there along with an old to-do list and a receipt for the dry cleaning. But that was never me, would never be me. If I had it, I ate it.

That's what I was thinking that afternoon as I made my way home after class. It was warm with the suggestion of spring, one of those promising days that make you want to talk about the weather. Mid-March, and most people were still wearing their heavy coats, only they wore them unbuttoned today, unzipped.

That made me nervous. The idea of shedding the woolly layers and comforting camouflage of winter made me uneasy. I wasn't prepared to give them up. I wasn't ready. I kept my coat fastened and went into the nearest store.

It was a drugstore, one of the big bright chains with harsh fluorescent lights and large tempting displays, and everywhere giant-size posters (smiling babies, young-marrieds, active senior citizens) all meant to indicate good health and goodwill. I wandered the aisles feigning interest: toothpaste, tampons, milk, magazines, hair dye, diet aids, cigarettes, battery-operated fans, bathtub toys. And then I came upon the candy aisle. There was no "just one" about anything here. Everything came in value-size multipacks with low unit prices, great for Halloween or a family of four but hardly what I was looking for, or so I told myself. I really didn't know why I'd entered the drugstore in the first place, to buy time or buy candy, but I wasn't ready to give in. I still held on to the promise of the diet. So I turned away from the candy aisle with exaggerated nonchalance, like a felon fleeing the scene. That was when I saw the Flintstones vitamins.

Just how long can you keep yourself in check? How long can you deny your appetite and tell yourself that you really don't want what you know you desire? It's an interesting split. You tell yourself you're being good to yourself by being good. But it's a lie. Dieting—the sort of dieting I'm talking about, the sort of strict dieting that, ironically, has left me with a lifelong weight problem and a wardrobe that spans three sizes—denies not only the experience of food but the wonder of appetite and taste. And it *is* a wonder. To want, to need, to crave—how important that is, how human and real. What could be better than to anticipate, to eat, to enjoy, to savor the experience and then move on? What could be better than biting into the apple?

—

I waited until I got home. For some reason that was important. I locked the door. I unbuttoned my coat and draped it over the back of a chair. I may have whistled. I walked to the window and saw with relief that it was getting dark, that the burden of the day was lifting. I didn't close the curtains—I wasn't weird about it or anything—I merely sat down on the couch and tore open the bag.

Barney came first. It wasn't what I wanted—not quite—but it was close, and in the moment that was enough. Betty came next, hands on her hips, then Bamm-Bamm, his club propped on his shoulder like a Jurassic baseball bat. Then it was Fred. There was another Barney (mauve this time), a green Fred, a pink Pebbles, and a puzzling little creature I later remembered as Gazoo, the green spaceman visible only to Fred. I looked over each tablet before popping it in my mouth. All the shapes had the same vague sweet-tart taste, and there was no discernible difference between the colors, but I still looked. After I ate my fourth Wilma, it was game over. I'd known it all along. Despite telling myself that one would do, deep down I'd known I wouldn't—couldn't—stop. I'd known it in the store. I'd known it walking down the street. I'd known it the very moment I ripped open the blister pack and lined up the arrows on the child-proof cap. The dosage on the side of the bottle (one-half tablet for children two and three years of age, one tablet for adults and children four years of age or older) was as meaningless as the portion sizes printed so reliably on snack-food packages. The vitamins were supposed to be a compromise, but diets don't lend themselves to compromise. At least not mine.

In the end it was just me and the empty bottle of Flintstones.

It wasn't pretty. I knew I would joke about it in time, that I would make cracks about *Yabba-dabba-doo* and *Bam! Bam!,* not to mention Bedrock ("Bedrock? Ha! Don't get me started!"). But the truth was, I was in pain. Grinding gears of pain engaged my stomach and lurched forward like a taxi in a traffic jam. It was nasty and noisy. Worse still was the knowledge that I'd caused—*deserved*—every clench and rumble. I called in sick for work that night. I had no choice. It wasn't just the stomachache or the noxious farts. I was in that place again, with room for little else but shame and defeat. I looked around my apartment. I was disappointed now. Sad. The pretty yellow walls, so sunny and optimistic, must have been painted by someone else. I was a beast, and beasts don't live in cheery yellow apartments.

I'd like to say that this was a turning point for me, that I had reached rock bottom (the Bedrock joke again) and from that moment decided to look at food as something other than the enemy, my appetite as something to be enjoyed rather than conquered. But it wasn't. It was an episode, not a lesson, and as I'd predicted, it became a joke, a tale to tell, a story to trot out at parties along with the cocktails and the snacks. Some people find it hard to believe that an otherwise responsible woman would consume an entire bottle of children's vitamins. Other people tell me they understand the impulse before sharing their own version of the story.

It's funny how we can play with our shame, how much we can entertain ourselves with the discrepancy between who we are and who we want to be. Or maybe not. I'm still drawn to the gaudy promise and the happily-ever-after extravagance of diets, but I know that for me, at the end of each leap, there's usually a fall. Call it a setback, call it a splurge, call it a binge, but it's a fall into darkness, and it's in direct proportion to the austerity of the diet.

So why diet? Why, indeed. It's just that my dieter's belief in transformation is proving hard to give up. Years (and many humiliating experiences) later, I'm not ready yet. But I'm getting there. I'm getting closer. I'm finally getting my daily dose of the truth: If it's not what you want, it's never enough.

THE TWIN PARADOX
Susan O'Doherty

I steadied myself at the bathroom sink with my right hand, stabbing blush onto my cheeks with my left. I felt like a teenager prepping for her first terrifying dance, but now I looked like a geriatric barfly. I rubbed off the blush and started again.

My husband came up behind me. "Isn't all that going to wash off in the pool?"

"I just want to look normal when I get there."

Bill put his hand on my shoulder. "You look fine. Skinny but gorgeous."

He lied.

Seven months earlier, I had felt, if not gorgeous, healthy and vibrant. The eating disorder I'd flirted with in adolescence and early adulthood was long gone. For the past twenty-five years, except when I was pregnant, I had maintained a steady, healthy 130 pounds through sensible eating and recreational swimming. I even liked that my weight was a few pounds over the actuarial "ideal" for my five-five frame. When I dropped into the 120s, I stopped menstruating and became cranky. I took my refusal to dip into the danger zone as a sign that I was done with body-image nonsense.

At fifty-three, I felt at the top of my form. Then, on a Wednesday morning in May, I was jerked awake by intense chest pains and nausea. I staggered into the bathroom and vomited, and I couldn't stop. My eyes throbbed so I could barely see, and every inhalation was a knife wound.

"We're going to the emergency room," Bill said, but I refused. I couldn't go through that humiliation again. Four times over the past twenty years, I'd rushed to emergency rooms and doctors' offices with milder bouts of whatever this was, and they never found anything. My body would be prodded, measured and assessed, and finally decreed unworthy of serious consideration. The doctors who had taken Bedside Manner 101 in med school tended to explain the concepts of stress and anxiety in words of two syllables or less; the others used terms like *all in your head* or, once, *hysterical conversion disorder*. However they phrased it, I always ended up feeling like a naughty, pushy girl for taking up space in the important professionals' schedule with my imaginary ailments. The symptoms subsided in a few days and disappeared within a week, but the shame lingered. I would tough this one out.

The following week, when I wasn't better, I decided it was a particularly vicious case of the flu. After two weeks, I reluctantly called my doctor.

Four months later, I could barely walk without gasping for breath and was reduced to a diet of saltine crackers and ginger ale because anything more substantial made me throw up. My temperature would build all day, peaking at 103, then dropping rapidly to 96, leaving me shaken and exhausted. My clothes hung on me, when I was able to get dressed. Still no cause had been found—once again, hypochondria and anxiety emerged as the default diagnoses, and I was shamed for my complaints.

I knew this was all wrong, that my body was sending out frantic distress signals that needed to be attended to, yet I doubted myself. I was haunted by the idea that I was fabricating or exaggerating symptoms to get attention, once again wasting everyone's time with my nonsense. I got the clear message that the doctors I consulted wished I would disappear—and I almost did.

When I was at last delivered to the genius rheumatologist who diagnosed me on the spot with Still's disease—a lupus-like inflammatory disorder whose symptoms are manageable when episodes are caught early, but that can wreak havoc on the organs if left to run amok—I weighed 112 pounds. MRIs showed severe inflammation and fluid buildup in my left lung and the lining of my heart. I was alarmed by the diagnosis, which carries with it the likelihood of unpleasant long-term consequences, but at the same time relieved to learn that I hadn't been making it all up, that my body's cries for attention had a basis in physical reality—that I wasn't just asking everyone to drop their important work and look at me.

My doctor put me on prednisone to control the inflammation. After a few weeks I was able to keep food down, and my hunger returned tenfold, thanks to the drug's appetite-stimulating properties and the hours I was forced to spend lying on the couch, bored. The catch was that I wasn't allowed to eat much of anything. Corticosteroids, my doctor explained, can trigger a stroke or diabetes, so it's necessary to severely restrict fat and carbohydrates while taking them. She put me on a regime that basically allowed me to eat minuscule portions of low-fat cottage cheese, lettuce, string beans, and tofu (steamed, not fried). I was instructed to ignore my cravings and stick to the diet; any deviation could be disastrous.

During my three months of enforced deprivation, I dreamed of food the way a starstruck teenager dreams of her unattainable idol. I devoured *Martha Stewart Living* and *Gourmet* as though they were fanzines, longingly ripping out pictures of my crushes—chocolate-mousse tortes, wine-and-cheese pairings, pyramids of sugar-dusted grapes—filing them away against the day I was declared "over it."

During the height of my illness, my son, Ben, then eleven, had developed severe insomnia, fearing I would be dead when he woke up. A child who had never, even in toddlerhood, raised a hand against another living being, he began getting into fights at school. We found a therapist who suggested that he and I engage in a hopeful, forward-looking project together. We decided to plan the big party we'd give as soon as I had recovered, making lists of invitees and dishes we would serve. I pretended that my obsessive collecting of food porn was research for this party, to make it seem more normal. In the meantime, terrified that the disease could domino into lifelong invalidism, I followed my doctor's instructions religiously and continued to starve myself even as I thought of nothing but food.

Adolescence had been something like this. I started my period at fourteen, in 1966. That year I sprouted hips, pubic hair, and the conviction that everyone was looking at me, and not in a positive way. I had never been particularly self-confident, but before, my insecurity had expressed itself in the feeling that I was insignificant. Now I felt too large, too much. I was sure I smelled bad, that I was enormous and always in the way, that everything about me was glaringly wrong.

My closest dieting buddy, Christina—a peach-skinned blonde with an hourglass figure that Lillian Russell might have envied— and I developed the habit (more like a religious ritual) of meeting downtown on Saturdays for a "bakery tour." There were four first-rate bakeries, and we would visit each one, poring over the display cases of shiny black-and-white cookies, dark-chocolate petits fours topped by pink spun-sugar flowers, and elaborate charlottes russes. We inhaled the mingled aromas of fresh-baked bread, sugar, and chocolate until we had settled on our most desired delicacy—the one item that exemplified the reward we would give ourselves on that longed-for day when we had become thin enough. Then we would move on to the next bakery. After the tour, we would go to Stefan's, our favorite soda fountain, where we would sip Tabs and discuss the relative merits of our choices at each site, narrowing down our selections to one agreed-on perfect morsel.

This game was too dangerous to play alone—the temptation to jump the fence and actually order and devour a petit four or éclair was great. So on those Saturdays when Christina was unavailable, I would manufacture a term paper or upcoming exam and spend the day at the library. What I really did was park myself in the periodicals section with a stack of fashion magazines.

At home, I subscribed to the nice-girl gazette, *Seventeen,* which featured at least marginally healthy-looking models and sensible diet tips. At the library, I went for the hard-core: *Mademoiselle, Glamour,* and, most seductive of all, *Vogue.* I studied the models cavorting on the beach in skimpy bikinis, their perfectly toned and waxed bodies betraying not even a smidgen of swimmer's fat; or dancing gracefully in slinky, form-fitting sheaths, escorted by handsome, adoring men. Thinness seemed to be the key: confidence, poise, glamorous friends, fabulous boyfriends. It was impossible to imagine these elegant, balletic women tongue-tied at parties, fighting with their brothers, or knocking over their milk. I felt their grace would attach to me, too, if I could only manage to ignore the demands of my greedy body.

I would enter the pictures the way I ate the bakery treats, imaginatively but so intensely it felt real. I would insert myself into a beach-volleyball game or holiday fete, and because my spreading hips and chipmunk cheeks would have magically melted away, I also would have mastered the stunning repartee and thought-provoking political observations that would certify me as a legitimate member of the circle.

The same magazines featured lavishly illustrated recipes for rich hors d'oeuvres and desserts—dishes we would presumably serve to the handsome boyfriends and chic party guests who would be the rewards of our self-denial. I inhaled these as well. When I actually attended parties, I never ate. Usually, I would congregate with other girls and exchange recipes for "chocolate cake" made from pulverized Special K, Sweet'N Low, egg whites, and artificial chocolate flavor, or "malteds" consisting of powdered nonfat milk and diet cherry soda.

My grandmother, who was raised on a farm and appreciated a good meal, might have been counted on to intervene, reassuring me that I looked better with a little meat on my bones, but she and my grandfather had retired to Florida. My mother and my friends' mothers, all suburbanites, caught the diet fever themselves. Television commercials shamed middle-aged women for "unsightly midriff bulge," which could be disguised only with expensive and uncomfortable undergarments. Mother-daughter dieting became a popular bonding ritual. My own mother joined Weight Watchers and bought a postage scale to weigh and record every crumb she ingested. Other mothers took more extreme measures. My friend Ellie swiped her mom's Dexedrine and reported that it addressed all of her issues at once—it suppressed her appetite, loosened her social inhibitions, and allowed her to stay up late to study without resorting to M&M's and malted milk balls. I was tempted, but there was no way one prescription could support three of us without attracting notice. Ignoring my body's messages, as the magazines suggested, seemed to be the most reliable road to salvation.

After a few weeks of extreme deprivation, my natural hunger would always reassert itself so powerfully that I would end up binging on whatever I found in the kitchen—a loaf of bread, a bag of potato chips, a quart of ice cream. I didn't enjoy these "treats," certainly not the way I imagined savoring every slow, delicious bite of the bakery petits fours and mousse cakes. I hardly tasted them. I pulled them into myself the way I would later gasp for air in my illness. Afterward I would lie on my bed, overcome with self-loathing. Once again I had demonstrated my essential baseness, my shameful inability to control my body. I would never be worthy of the magazine-spread life I dared to aspire to. I deserved the drab, tacky life of a fat loser. I would flagellate myself mentally for a day or so, then resume my celery-and-Tab regime.

At the height of this frenzied cycle, I was introduced to the Twin Paradox. This is a problem physics teachers present to students for the purpose of short-circuiting their reasoning faculties. A pair of twins splits up. One takes off into outer space in a rocket approaching the speed of light. The other stays home.

The adventurous twin returns younger than the homebody. In the Disney cartoon on relativity that our class watched, the younger twin emerges from his spaceship virile and energetic, while his now older brother, bald and toothless, greets him from a wheelchair. I watched, transfixed, as I realized all at once that I was enacting this paradox in my own person—the Sue of my imagination was living out the glamorous adventures portrayed in the magazines that preoccupied me, sporting slinky, expensive dresses on her slender, graceful frame, charming the haut monde, and enjoying chocolate confections without negative consequences; the corporeal Sue haunted bakeries and hunkered in the library, denying herself actual experiences in favor of chasing after unattainable fantasies, getting older while going nowhere. It struck me with the force of a newly discovered but suddenly obvious physical law: It was time to stop.

I forced myself to override my self-consciousness and participate in my life. I made myself try out for school plays, and to my surprise, I was cast in comic character parts. I threw myself into them, and I participated in the social life of the drama club by pretending I was one of the outgoing characters I played. I started dating actual boys who, unlike the discriminating paragons of my fantasy life, thought I looked fine and laughed at my awkward jokes, though I still couldn't eat in front of them.

I looked better, but I wasn't over it. I remained a sucker for every loopy fad diet that came along. I was still disgusted by the fat on my hips, and I starved myself before dances and performances, binging after I'd come down from the excitement. In college, I discovered the appetite-suppressing powers of caffeine and nicotine, developing two tenacious addictions. When diminished lung power forced me to choose between smoking and swimming, I stuck with my two-pack-a-day habit, convinced that without chemical aids, my traitorous body would once again get the upper hand.

I finally broke the dieting cycle—for good, it seemed—in my mid-twenties. I suffered what was probably an early flare-up of Still's disease but was diagnosed as a panic attack by yet another condescending doctor. My rheumatologist believes that this event and my three subsequent episodes of "hysterical conversion" were early, self-resolving forerunners of the attack that felled me that May. After flaring up, Still's can remit and lie latent in the system, leaving its victim symptom-free in the years in between, adding credence to the assumption that the attack was fabricated to begin with. Taking my complaints seriously at any point could have staved off the damage I eventually sustained. Even so, I'm grateful to that doctor for his condescension, because I believed the panic diagnosis and sought therapy for it.

Marianna, the therapist I consulted, was brilliant, accomplished, dedicated—and very fat. My "panic disorder" evaporated fairly quickly, but I stayed on to examine every other facet of my history and current life. Weight and body image issues came to the forefront almost immediately. Marianna's pointed, relentless questions forced all of my half-conscious, never articulated assumptions up into the light, where they crumbled like stale sugar cookies.

Together, we explored the messages behind those magazine spreads I'd swallowed without chewing—the desirable life I was made to feel excluded from; the hope, always just out of reach, of achieving it through adherence to impossible standards and purchasing unnecessary stuff. Marianna made me articulate the loathing I felt for my healthy body and my conviction that starvation was the road not only to attractiveness but to virtue and accomplishment—an idea that, once I put it into words, was so ludicrous I couldn't continue holding it in my head. She disclosed details of her own life—the Fulbright scholarship that had allowed her to attend a prestigious doctoral program; her husband and four children; her spacious Upper West Side brownstone—to challenge my association of obesity with loserhood.

And one day I got it, as viscerally and suddenly as I'd recognized my enactment of the Twin Paradox back in high school. "They want to make me disappear," I blurted, not exactly sure who "they" were but certain, in my gut, that I was right. "I'm supposed to be little and weak, not big and scary. Fuck that!"

It was as though a fever had broken after a long illness and I could think once more. With Marianna's encouragement, I quit dieting and smoking and started swimming again. I learned to eat when I was hungry and stop when I was full. I found my right size and stayed there. (We worked on the coffee addiction, too, but she was a therapist, not a miracle worker.)

I thought I was cured, but it turned out to be a twenty-five-year remission. Like Still's disease, the eating disorder lay latent in my system, waiting for a stressor to lower my resistance.

The morning I prepared for my return to the pool, I was officially over the worst of the illness. Though still on medication, I was cleared to resume limited activity, starting with an experimental dip. I knew I looked like hell, and this was an appearance-oriented crowd. I felt everyone would be looking at me and judging me negatively.

My weight had dropped to a hundred pounds. The formerly firm flesh on my arms and legs sagged. New lines were etched around my eyes and the corners of my mouth, and for the first time I noticed jowls. Even my hair had lost its texture; it hung around my face, thin and flat. I imagined the pitying looks I'd get, the whispers. I considered putting off my entrance, but I knew I couldn't hide at home forever. So I painted myself up as well as I could and walked with my new, halting gait toward the door. "Seriously, you look great," Bill said. In thirty years of loving support, this may have been his most outrageously gallant moment.

The reactions I was preparing for would have been painful and embarrassing. The ones I got ricocheted my psyche back to adolescence, even as my body continued on its accelerated-aging trajectory.

On my way to the gym, a neighbor stopped to greet me. I'd known Bob casually for ten years; his wife, Sally, and I had been playground buddies when our kids were small. "You look great!" he said, echoing my husband's words. I figured he had heard about my illness and appreciated his tact.

"Thanks," I said.

"So what's your secret? I'll have to pass it on to Sally."

Was he flirting with me? I decided this was a misplaced but well-meant stab at neighborly support. I smiled and moved on.

At the gym, I was barraged with the same question—"What's your secret?"—over and over, in the locker room and the pool. This despite my geriatric appearance and bearing, my difficulty with the simplest strokes, and my need to leave after less than ten minutes because without my accustomed insulation, the water temperature was unbearably cold. When yet another pool buddy approached me as I shivered in my underwear in front of my locker and said, "Boy, have you lost weight! What's—," I snapped, "A life-threatening illness," assuming that would quiet her.

"Well, it paid off," she said.

Later that day I called my friend Jan and tried to quell my growing unease by joking about the "social X-rays" at my gym and their distorted idea of attractiveness. "They're probably wondering why the hell I don't get my eyes done," I said.

She laughed, but not entirely naturally. There was a pause, then she said, "I'm envious, too. I haven't worn a size two since I was a toddler."

I didn't want this—but what was she seeing now that had been absent or obscured before? And now that I had it, how could I give it up?

A few days later, a neighbor brought her son over to play, and they stayed for an impromptu dinner of takeout pizza. I explained that I would be dining on cottage cheese and salad because I was still on prednisone. Sara, chic and bony in her tight jeans, munched delicately on a quarter-slice. "Maybe this illness is a blessing in disguise," she said, "if it makes you cut out all that fat you used to eat."

I dropped the pizza knife. *What fat?* I love cheese. I make a mean lasagna with hand-rolled noodles, and asparagus-and-Gruyère omelets are a specialty. I have to mix double batches of holiday cookies because half the dough tends to disappear, and before my illness, I'd been perfecting a chocolate-truffle recipe. But those were occasional or seasonal treats interwoven with fresh fruits and vegetables, beans, and whole grains. Even the fact that I had to remind myself of this was nuts, wasn't it? I had been in good shape. Hadn't I? I had looked fine, right?

I picked up the knife and pushed down the mushrooming conviction that I had been fooling myself all these years—that in reality I had been so gross-looking that everyone saw my current emaciated state as an improvement. That my hips had indeed been as disgusting as my adolescent self had believed. "I didn't eat *that* badly," I protested, but it came out more like a question.

"Of course you didn't," Sara agreed.

When my doctor pronounced me well at last, Bill and Ben insisted we celebrate. They took me to my favorite local restaurant, a mildly pretentious "international" bistro whose main attraction was its lethal Mississippi mud pie, which I dutifully ordered. When it arrived, I stared at it, trying to summon my prednisone-fueled fantasies of rolling silky bittersweet chocolate on my tongue, but what came to mind was the troupe of tutu-clad hippos mincing through "Dance of the Hours" in Disney's *Fantasia*. I picked up my fork and put it back down. Ben said, "So now we can plan that party for real!"

"For real," I agreed. But how could I cook all those treats we'd planned—the recipes I'd collected so obsessively—without eating them? And if I ate them, I'd get fat again. I'd be a loser. Again. "I guess I'm too tired to eat right now," I said. I had the pie wrapped to take home, and the next day I threw it out.

I stuck with the cottage cheese and string beans for another week. Then I ran into my neighbor Bob again. "You are looking so good," he said. I smiled and edged away. He grabbed my arm. "*So* good," he repeated. "If you were my wife, I'd never let you out of the house."

In a flash, I was transported back to Marianna's office, struggling to articulate my newly discovered truth, saying, "I'm supposed to be little and weak, not big and scary. Fuck that!" *Fuck you,* I thought. I felt myself grow larger. I took a deep swimmer's breath as my soul reentered my body. I sent Marianna a telepathic message of thanks across the years and returned to the Brooklyn street corner, where I disengaged my arm from Bob's grasp.

"That's why I'd never marry someone like you," I told him. Then I went home to start dinner.

ATTACK OF
THE XL GIRL
Laurie Notaro

As soon as I opened the door to the boutique and took a quick look around, I shook my head, sighed, and went on in. It had been this way all day.

Every stop my friend Meg and I made was like another flash of bad skinny-girl déjà vu. I'd open the door, take two steps in, and there we were, confronted by racks filled with nothing but really cool funky designer clothes.

Initially, I was in heaven. I was visiting Meg in Seattle shortly after she had her baby, Carmen, and I was more than excited about my shopping opportunities. In my hometown, pickings are slim, and unless I wake up each day with the desire to dress "drone" and head to my local Gap, Banana Republic, or J. Crew like everyone else, I'm a little more than slightly out of luck. Since Meg, being a new mother with an infant, had been basically confined to the house for eight weeks, she was itching to get out. "I want to go shopping. I'm dying to buy something without an elastic panel that stretches from my crotch to my waistband," she said to me over the phone a couple of days before I arrived. "I don't even care that I'm completely fat right now, I am just dying for some real clothes!"

Secretly, I was a little delighted because Meg had always been my rail-thin friend who made me look like a Pittsburgh Steeler when I stood next to her. She could eat troughs of any given dairy product without consequence and once actually wrinkled her nose at a box of Godiva, explaining chirpily, "You know, I'm just not a chocolate kind of person."

Although Meg lacked the very qualities that I counted as some of my finest and I somewhat doubted that her DNA was indeed human, she had remained a wonderful friend for over a decade, and now, for once, I was going to see her fat!

After my plane landed, I met Meg at the curb, where she picked me up in her Bronco, which was now outfitted with a baby seat. As she jumped out of the front seat and ran to open the tailgate, I stood back and screeched.

"Liar! Liar!" I yelled as I pointed at Meg and her "I had a baby basically yesterday but am going to the Oscars tonight in a dress made from Cling Wrap" figure. "Who are you, Sarah Jessica Parker? Come on, you said you were FAT, and I gorged on pretzels and Pepsi the whole way down here thinking that for once our butts were going to be in the same BMI category! This is so not fair! If you don't show me a stretch mark right now, I'm grabbing a bag of Hershey's Kisses and a six-pack and I'm getting back on that plane!"

"I can do better than a stretch mark," Meg said as she laughed at me. "I had a nine-pound baby and got forty-four stitches as a reward!"

"Ewwww," I said with a gasp. "That's what you get for being Miss Healthy! See, this is where a slothlike lifestyle packed with sugar, processed foods, and caffeine would have really paid off for you and given you a baby with a small little softball head!"

"Oh my God, look at how fat I am!" Meg cried, outstretching her arms. "I now have two fat rolls!"

"Oh, Meg," I said, putting my arms around her. "Poor, sweet, skinny Meg. Those aren't fat rolls, my friend; those are your boobies."

So not only was Meg still Depression-era thin, she now had cleavage to boot, which up until then had been the one and only area between the two of us where I reigned supreme, even if I had it on my back, too.

As if the fact that Meg was now buxom wasn't enough to drive me mad, once we went shopping the next day, things began falling apart more quickly than a Twinkie dipped in hot chocolate. There, in front of me, were rows and rows of the kind of clothes I struggle to find, all laid out before me simply for the taking. Overwhelmed by excitement and the possible damage these incredible finds were going to have on my Visa bill next month, I made fashion sparks fly from my fingertips as I flipped through the items on the rack like they were a deck of cards. Again and again, I caught my breath and gasped, "Oh!" with desire to a brown velvet waistcoat with antique jet buttons—but it was a size six. Not gonna work with my 38C torpedoes unless the whole thing was made out of very forgiving spandex and a Seal-a-Meal machine. "Oh!" to a striped pair of corduroy bell-bottoms à la Janis Joplin in her heyday (which I guess translates to "alive"), but alas, that size four wasn't going to fit unless I was able to clone the original pair and sew the two of them together. "Oh!" to the most darling fifties-style aqua poplin day dress, but then the size-two tag squashed my hopes like a potato bug beneath the sole of a strappy, three-inch, skinny-heeled sandal. Not compatible with this user, unless the dress came with a hidden expansion panel the size of a movie screen.

This happened again and again and again. Size six. Size four. Two. Zero. And then, when I saw that a slovenly size-eight skirt on the clearance rack was the fat lady in this circus, I knew I was in the wrong freak show.

I was in a Skinny Store, where double-digit girls were not allowed, mainly because in this single-digit world, they plainly didn't exist.

I was dully reminded of an experience several months previous when I wandered through SoHo during a short trip to New York City. I had decided that during my trip, I would allow myself one extravagance, and I had decided I was going to buy a dress—maybe even a "not on sale" dress—in one of the funnest parts of the coolest city in the world. That was going to be my gift to myself. A great, wonderful, expensive dress. I was dying to throw my money away, I was dying to simply give someone my money, I tell you, but alas, no one would take it. Nanette Lepore didn't want it, and neither did Anna Sui or Cynthia Rowley. I might as well have been on a scavenger hunt with no clues, because that's the kind of luck I was having trying to find a size L dress in New York City. Fat money was apparently no good there. Salespeople looked at me as if I were a mythical beast, something only whispered about in the safety of a shadowy stockroom. Even size eights didn't belong in this world, because the only clothes displayed were the zeroes, twos, fours, and sixes. I felt like the biggest girl in the universe—as if I had been exposed to Chernobyl-like amounts of radiation and had just flattened entire Japanese villages simply with the crumbs that had fallen from my mouth.

After being submerged in the Land of Protruding Ribs for so long I had a craving for barbecue, I finally lost it when a salesgirl asked if she could help me.

"Honestly, it's useless, because you don't have my size, I need a fourteen, and I am a giant in your world," I said, throwing up my hands. "Apparently everyone who shops here is the size of a Keebler elf or a first-grader."

The salesgirl actually laughed, putting me a little at ease. "We do have other sizes," she said nicely. "Is that the dress you like? I can pull it from the back, where we keep our plus sizes."

Now, I didn't know whether to run or shove a Suzy Q in her face in protest. The plus sizes? An eight was a plus size? Okay, sure, my size dress requires more material than, say, a dress for an Olsen twin, but come on, it's not the size of a car! I suppose you can never be too careful, though; put a size-fourteen dress on a rack, and who would really be surprised if the whole fixture was just ripped right out of the wall and took an entire building down with it?

I left before the salesperson returned with the dress, even though I'm sure she had to hire several men right off the street and maybe a forklift to help her carry it. Even if that dress fit me perfectly, my Fat Money was not going to be burned there.

I learned a lesson that day, and that lesson was that if a store is too embarrassed to have me as a customer, if a store is too skinny to carry my size and display it out in public with the thinner, cuter sizes, then I'm too proud to give them my money. And I felt the same way in the store in Seattle.

Before I could say, "Meg! Let's get out of here, the only people who could fit into this stuff are junkies!" I turned around
just in time to see her pluck a familiar aqua poplin day dress off
the rack and head to the dressing room with it in one hand and
Carmen in the other.

"I'm going to try this on," Meg giggled.

I nodded and smiled, trying to hide my dismay and encourage
my friend to have fun at the same time. "I'll watch the baby
while you're in the dressing room," I said.

The next boutique was the same—dresses that could only fit
a pretzel stick (nonsalt) or Meg—so I watched the baby after
scouring the racks and finding many adorable things but none in
my size. Finally, in subsequent stores that we visited, I didn't
even bother with the clothes section of the store and headed
straight for the "non-size" items, like body lotion and candles,
and then just sat in front of the dressing room with Carmen
until Meg was done. I should have brought some change to jin-
gle in my pocket, I thought; I have officially slipped into the role
of The Guy on shopping expeditions, except for the part when
other customers in the store would assume the adorable infant
was mine. Then I'd have to explain, "No, she's my friend's baby,"
at which Meg would pop out of the dressing room and the other
customer would gasp, "Oh! Yours? But you look so great!"

"You're not having any fun," Meg said sadly as we added another bag to her growing mountain of great, cool clothes finds.
"You haven't bought one thing! We should just go home."

I realized then that Meg didn't know that we were visiting
skinny-only stores, because Meg had been only one of two
things in her life: skinny or pregnant. I mean, the girl thought
that she was FAT simply because she finally filled something
out, even if it was just her nursing bra.

"No, absolutely not," I replied. "We are not going home. You've been dying to go shopping for months! We're going to hit every store you want and you're going to buy fabulous things. I just haven't found . . . the perfect fit yet, that's all."

At the next store, I exploded with manufactured enthusiasm over a fig-scented candle, asked the salesgirl some pertinent and pointed questions about acne cream, and then held up a pair of underwear the size of a cocktail napkin and bellowed to Meg, "I have been driven MAD trying to find these!"

However, the angry little miss inside my head was having a field day all her own: You know, in California every restaurant has to post its health-inspection grade in the front window so the customers know exactly what they're getting into. If you'd like to go home with your intestines intact, you pick an A joint; if you have a decent co-pay and want some paid time off from work, choose option B; and if you're angling for long-term disability or an alternative to gastric bypass surgery, C is your way to go. The same should go for boutiques. I say, don't waste my time, just say what you are. Let me know right off if I have a better chance of fitting into something at Baby Gap than I do in your store. I want to see it posted in your front window—"Sizes Six and Under: For Paris Hilton, women with tapeworms, and young boys"; "Super Small Sizes: For Lara Flynn Boyle, political prisoners on hunger strikes, and everyone else 180 calories away from death"; and "Teeny-Weeny Sizes: For skeletons that hang in doctors' offices, mummies, and Prada models."

I have been a frequent visitor to sales racks in almost every major department and clothing store, and guess what's on them? XS's and S's. Sizes zeroes, twos, fours, and sixes. Rarely at Banana Republic will you spot a hallowed L on the sales rack, and ditto for J. Crew. The large sizes are always the first ones to get picked (for a change). Which tells me one thing: There's way more of us out there than there are of them, and they'd better watch it. Should we decide to declare war on them, well, my Fat Money is on the Fat Girls. We don't need bullets; all we need is to pass around a box of See's chocolates for some extra energy and then huff and then puff and then blow their bones down.

I mean, can it get any worse than this? Any worse than stores that house the larger-than-chic sizes away where no one can see them, and shops that simply don't carry them at all? Will they become like the airlines and start weighing people at the door before they're allowed access? "Oh—a size fourteen? Hmmmm. Well, you, with your waterbed-like ass, take up as much room as two Lilliputian size zeroes. You'll have to wait until those attractive thin girls over there leave before you can come in. But don't you dare handle any of our stock too much. We don't want you passing the fat gene to our clothes, you size LARGE!!"

"Jeans?" Meg cried delightedly, and I suddenly realized that the little angry voice inside my head hadn't been completely contained there after all. "Did you find jeans? Did you find something cool to get? I knew you would find something here! This is my favorite store, you know!"

"Not yet, but I'm on a mission!" I assured her. "I'm sure this is the place."

While Meg met her match in the dressing room, I strolled around the shop with Carmen, desperate to find anything so Meg wouldn't feel so bad about me not being able to fit into a tank top the size of a panty liner. I finally sighed with relief when I spotted a lightweight butt body shaper with some pretty lace around each leg in the lingerie section. I flipped to the tag and nearly gasped. What I saw there nearly took my breath away and almost made me drop the baby. L. I saw an L. What on earth a girdle was doing in this shop I didn't know and I didn't care—it had probably been misordered and had sat there for years, been used as a dust rag, to stuff a couple bras, kill some bugs, who knew—but finally I was going to buy something and walk out with a bag of my own.

I raced up to the counter with the girdle and pulled out my credit card. The owner of the shop—a pretty, young, skinny-Minnie girl with collarbones so prominent they could be used for rock climbing—picked it up, looked at it for a moment, and with a little laugh said, "Oh! This is NOT the right size for you!"

I smiled, excited, pleased, and humbled that she had mistaken me for a medium, since all she had really seen for such a long time were miniature-size people that she had absolutely forgotten what a real human looked like. "Oh," I said. "It's okay. That's a good size for me."

"No, really," the woman said, nodding vigorously. "You need an extra-large, and that's not a size we carry in the store regularly, but I can order it for you. I can have it here next week."

And then she tilted her skinny little head.

And then she smiled at me.

Even the girdle I wanted to buy was too small. The woman, that awful, awful woman, wouldn't even let me buy that stupid LARGE girdle. I WAS TOO FAT FOR THAT.

My face started burning around the edges and I didn't know what to say. I was stunned and embarrassed and mortified and I was FAT and I felt like I was in the seventh grade again and a cheerleader had just told me my pants were too tight and I had also just had my period in them.

"Should I order it?" the owner said.

"I don't think so," I finally said, looking right at her. "My fat ass doesn't live here."

Feeling as big as a Kodiak bear, I then sat down on the Skinny Store couch, mumbling something aloud about hoping that it could support my weight. I thought very, very hard about farting on it for a simple yet effective form of revenge, but then remembered I had an innocent baby in my presence and gracefully, though reluctantly, refrained (although I did not refrain from leaving a tiny wad of now flavor-depleted Bubble Yum underneath it).

But wait.

There are such things as happy endings, even for a size fourteen wandering the streets looking for a fabulous dress to take home. On my next trip to New York, I found Jill Anderson, a small boutique in the East Village that sells fantastic clothes in XS, S, and M, and then dares to put an L on a tag, too, and mean it. Not only was there a size fourteen dress right out there on the sales rack next to a six, a four, and a two, but there in that dress was room for my boobs, my butt, and my hips. I no longer felt like a Chernobyl monster. I felt like a girl and I felt pretty and I felt good. When Jill was named Best Women's Designer in New York by a prominent media outlet this year, my heart swelled with joy, not only for her, but for all of the L's out there who had finally found her at last.

Although there will never be world peace, I do find much comfort in the fact that there is a place out there where size doesn't matter, where all that matters is that you're a girl (and sometimes that doesn't even matter so much because on one occasion, I was trying on the same dress that a man was, and it may be up to debate, but I will still argue to this day that I looked better in it than he did). Despite the shame of the "plus sizes" hidden away in stockrooms or the XL's that are only available by special order in other places in the universe, there is one place in the East Village where a size two and a size fourteen accidentally touched butts in a dressing room and war didn't break out. No one screamed and no one called the Fat HazMat team. They both laughed, the size fourteen was lacerated by the jutting hip bone of the size two, but after a little hydrogen peroxide and a Band-Aid, all was dandy and then the fourteen and the two told each other just how great they looked in their dresses. The cut scabbed over, but I'll always have that dress.

In the East Village at Jill's, we'll just wait until the rest of the world catches on.

SUGAR PLUM FAIRY
Dana Kinstler

I was under the spell of *The Nutcracker*. How did that tree grow until it touched the ceiling, like Jack's beanstalk? It pierced the membrane that kept us from nearing heaven too soon, and like the opening scene—a drawing room whose exterior panel went from opaque to see-through in a thrilling sleight-of-hand that exposed me to *stage magic*—the exuberant gesture was heightened by the sighting and sounds of silver flutes, piccolos, violin bows, and a golden harp.

The music grew mice into boy-kings, toy soldiers to generals, and girls into graceful ballerinas, en pointe. One of my neighbors was in this scene. I'd crossed the street with her the other day in plaid school attire; now she was a candy-cane girl wearing white pajama pants and a small cap.

But it was the appearance of the Sugar Plum Fairy, in white tights and toe shoes, white ribbons laced around her bony ankles, that held me captive. The Sugar Plum Fairy was the embodiment of spirit, the essence of the Land of Sweets, promising to take me to a place where candy grew and kept growing, like that expansive Christmas tree. She moved in and around the other sweets—French marzipan shepherdesses, Spanish chocolate ladies, the sinewy Arabian coffee girl, human Chinese tea bags popping out of their boxes—blessing them, grazing them, all to the "heavenly sweet sound" played by the celesta, the instrument that inspired Tchaikovsky when he'd first heard it played in Paris, my mother read from the ballet notes. The Sugar Plum Fairy's legs inched her spindly body around, her arms reaching up and beyond into the otherworld, one I could not see, which spilled its innards out onto the stage in sticky, colorful display.

Afterward, my mother and I hopped in a Checker cab, riding downtown past the silver-lit trees in the avenue dividers, slivers of undeveloped real estate. Still in my eyes were the dancers in their poufy skirts, their long, slender legs like stilts beneath—legs just like mine. Bouncing in the fold-down seat, pointing my toes inside black patent-leather Mary Janes, I replayed the Sugar Plum Fairy's tune; it seemed as if the music had been plucked from the harp by those strongly pointed toes. Silk straps crisscrossed around the ballerina's ankles, her joints bony and protruding. Viewing the dancers through the binoculars had embarrassed me, as if spying on a skeleton in dress-ups. Up close, more bones—collarbones, knobby elbows, finger knuckles, arms stretched out to the length of a rope.

In another ten years, I'd aspire to dancing en pointe—several years too late. I'd try to work my body back to what it had been when I was a girl. The ballet master calls all company members "boys and girls," and I would figure out how to get there. I mean, at eighteen, to work my body back in time to eight years old.

White noise of sugar. A million grains pouring down a chute into bins, then bagged by the ten pounds, divided into neat piles, siphoned into plastic pouches, boxed, cubed, poured into paper restaurant packets. A photo of me at two; I sit in diapers, Indian-style, the sugar bowl between my legs, a cube on my lips.

Returning from their days off in Camden, Maine, where they'd spent our petty cash, our summer camp counselors handed each of us a bag from a seaside grocery store. These went directly under our cots; at night we sneaked out with flashlights, trading, dipping into bags of Butterfingers, Hershey's Kisses, Reese's Pieces, and gummy flowers, fish, worms, brains, stars, but I never shared my frosting. Alone in the cabin between activities, I'd take a lick here, a blob there, feeling the rush of excitement, the pleasure and anger from that synthetic high, and then a bellyache and guilt afterward. I was the most homesick kid in the camp.

A month later, I'd morphed from City Girl, my moniker (as if I were the only New Yorker in Maine), to Rising Sun camper, discovering kinship in the cozy cabins and divinity in the secret knolls of the light-dappled forest. The sweetness of summer— its arc and pending decay, the eventual bus ride back to New

York City, the end of shady forests and pine-needle campsites and swimming in the lake with girls I might never see until next July, which was as far away as never, bags of discarded wrappers, tins, spoons, the end of this private pleasure. Always a sorrow coming toward me as the nights cooled and the island loons cried, their babies hatching, soon to be heading south. I never wanted to go home again.

The gymnastics leotard was purple with short sleeves. I'd worn it all summer in camp, learning front and back walkovers, cartwheels, and splits on the balance beam. Back in New York City, the school gym teacher, a Russian fencing champion, had won the bronze medal in the 1972 Summer Olympics, frightening us with tales of gunmen taking hostages in Munich, sending eleven people to their death.

Then she nudged my belly, which was sticking out, with the back of her hand—swift. "Vat ees deese?"

During basketball, she tossed me the ball, fast. I ducked. I was used to that.

"You scared of zeh ball?"

I couldn't answer. I noted right away that during after-school gymnastics, I earned little recognition for my floor routine, learning to push myself even though no one was watching. I knew instinctively that despite my flexible body, the girls who looked like Gumby dolls with near-flat chests, long muscular legs, and sinewy arms would make the team. When I saw my chubby form in photos, I feared I was a disappointment to my parents, too.

My big sister took dance class at Alvin Ailey, attended tennis camp in the summer, had the natural abilities of an athlete and dancer. She had what I didn't: self-control. On a family trip, the boys from the other family told me they wouldn't play with me: "You're fat." They preferred my sister. My belly was a shield. With her sleek shape and unattached attitude, my sister was desirable; her thinness gave her confidence, gave her status among her peers. I quit the competition.

Into high school, I kept the weight, armor against the attention I'd always wanted but was simultaneously terrified to have; I watched my sister go out with the basketball players. One afternoon after school at our apartment, her best friend spied while I waited on a melted cheese sandwich glowing in the toaster oven. "You'll get fat if you keep eating those," she said. She meant: *You already are.*

Once I got to college, away from New York City, my family refrigerator, city bodegas, everything changed.

The dining hall—I'd never seen so much food, already paid for. Regional dishes: amandine scrod, twice-baked potatoes, Boston cream pie. The rising scent met me just outside the swinging door. The possibility of endless eating inspired both anxiety and repulsion. For the first time in my eighteen years, I questioned each bite. Was I really hungry? Or was this habit? I wanted to know exactly how little would fill me up: When was I full? I had never asked myself these questions. In the middle of harvest meal at the cafeteria, I threw away my plate of pork chops with applesauce and went off meat. Pretty soon I gave up dinner, too.

I started to dance once a week, then every day.

I moved off campus to a college-owned house, to a room with a dark wood interior, glass French doors, and a fireplace. My roommate broke her leg and disappeared; I was left alone.

I went off the school meal plan. At night I'd wait until the rest of the house left for the dining hall, then I'd put one sweet potato into the microwave oven; I'd divide it into seven parts to last the week. Rarely could I finish a sliver, preferring to wrap the remainder in tinfoil, place it back in the small refrigerator, go to bed with belly pangs, taking pride in my ability to ignore the ache, waking up repeatedly wishing I could eat, forbidding myself to eat.

Alone in the off-campus house, I finally had utter control.

At home, there had been a breakup, then another. On a weekend trip back, I discovered my mother's closet empty; she'd left the state. Then my first love, a close friend and summer boyfriend, broke up with me. These primal cuts I would not talk about. Instead, I danced and signed up for an accelerated Italian-language course, where I read a novel in Italian, penciling the English into the margins in Italo Calvino's *Marcovaldo,* a postmodern story of a man living in an imaginary city. Dizzy from lack of nourishment, I looked up words, then again, still unclear as to the meaning of a sentence, a paragraph.

I grew downy facial hair. My period did not come.

The snow was drifting up against the glass doors. The spindly branches of pine trees were covered with opera gloves of heavy, wet snow. I was perfecting my pirouettes, using my Salvation Army chair as a bar. I had years to make up for. In religious studies, I read Saint Augustine, who struggled with his bodily needs, renouncing them, always in a state of attempting to overcome satisfaction. In his *Confessions,* he called eating "a dangerous pleasure."

Chocolate milk shakes, the silky insides of the Milky Way bar, the shiver of whipped cream inside each cream-filled doughnut. What was caramel, creamy, chocolate, vanilla, white, crunchy, covered with nuts, I translated: *mou, cremoso, ciaccolato, vaniglia, bianco, croccante, di noce,* all made of *sugar: lo zucchero, zuccheroso, molto zuccheroso.* Reading in Italian, I spoke flavors I would not taste. I mastered the trick of creating a fantasy of words, rolling their voluptuous sounds in my mouth, just not touching a sweet to my lips.

My black velvet catsuit, found in an off-campus vintage clothing store, hung baggy; I'd gone from size ten to eight to four, then two. On campus, I went to donate blood and was turned away: "You're too thin." A hundred pounds on my five-feet-five-inch frame.

Still, I didn't think anything was awry. I'd finally reached the aesthetic I'd longed for, my femininity had been sanded down to a pointy, androgynous form, no signs of being able *to mother:* no identifying marks to the one who had created me. Something about leaving home included severing the bonds visually but not emotionally. I wanted to transcend family, but simultaneously, I wanted to hold on to *before,* that early time, of family closeness and girlhood freedoms; thinning down my disappearing act, lessening, becoming all angles, razor-edged, then vapor, my body the closest it could be to spirit in pure form.

Always there was someone behind me at the barre who looked thinner. The less I ate, the more I felt total ownership over my body. Over *everyone:* I was no longer at the disadvantage of being a plump roving target, the dough girl getting her belly poked, always picked last for the team. I couldn't stand to look down unless it was concave between my hip bones. I was un-afraid to wear tight clothes, and an edgy quality emerged to accompany my pointy self, just as a friendly, nonjudgmental vul-nerability had disappeared along with my extra girlhood weight. My thinness gave me autonomy; losing weight, I'd come unat-tached from the human race. I thought I didn't need approval.

But I didn't actually want to be alone all the time. I preferred my one sweet potato—peasant's earth food—to a Thanksgiving dinner I wouldn't share again with my family.

I could see there was still one problem. The thinking. The thinking was not, contrary to my intents, freed from longing for food. No, the thinking was all about food: *What are they serving over in the cafeteria or in the other cafeteria on that other part of campus, no, can't go there, what about the snack bar underneath the cafeteria, only open at night, where a cute guy makes falafels, I can put some cucumbers on a salad plate and no one I know will be there to see me while I am eating.*

I couldn't stand to be seen eating.

If you do two dance classes today, you can eat a half-banana later, or some soup. Just the broth, though. Maybe a package of saltines. Just one saltine.

And so on.

This thinking consumed me.

It was impossible to read a book without being interrupted by the thinking. I couldn't hold conversations because I couldn't hear anyone's words. Just as people who gave some but not enough of themselves became the most desirable to me, so being half starved kept me enveloped in *longing*. With beer and M&M's, I found a perfect meal, usually in the late afternoon. The emptiness of sugar, once the rush left, the loneliness and the waste. I could buy an entire box of sugar-coated doughnuts with coffee-cake topping, lick a little, maybe eat a few crumbles, then toss the rest. Knowing the garbage wouldn't go out until later threatened my control, so I'd leave the doughnuts in a can away from my house.

At home on Christmas break, I baked elaborate cookies from the glossy cooking magazine, filling up boxes with chocolate-glazed stars and raspberry-jam-filled hearts, green-frosted trees. My cousin devoured them, watching as I handed them out, instructing me to try one; when I shook my head, he took me aside: "I'm worried about you."

He was perhaps the only one I believed. Not my sister, who said I was too thin, nor her best friend, who commented that I used to be nicer *before,* and by *before,* I knew she meant *when you were fat.* I'd already slept with her ex-boyfriend, a long-overdue violation, since I'd introduced them back when I was fat.

But—the excitement and danger of deprivation.

I do not have a particular day in mind for when I stopped starving myself to death.

I dropped out of college, moved back home, and announced my plan to my father: "I'm going on toe shoes!" I took class three times a day with a small rising company; there, I witnessed New York City dancers, front-row girls, perpetually in the mirror, corrected by the company's director. Reality check—these girls had been dancing all their lives.

A friend from college dance class came to visit and said, "If you don't come back now, you'll never get out of here." I knew she was right. I scared myself, cleaving to home, as if I'd remain in my childhood bedroom forever, shrinking down to a size when I was happy, my family intact, my mother at home. Moving back to college, no longer in love with the ballet, I wondered who I was.

I started eating more at almost twenty years old. I ate with shame and self-disgust, unable to stop from satisfying my hunger. Fullness: I thought I'd overcome that—a return to a childhood state of mind. Suddenly I wanted to gobble up everything I'd denied myself, like a female Pac-Man gone wild in the banquet hall.

I gained weight. I got too heavy again. Then I got help. I quit dance. No more anatomy studies in the dance studio mirrors, skeleton-to-skeleton, no more leotards and leggings and soft leather slippers all day long. Men cared less about my body fat than I did. Eventually, I found a good boyfriend who stuck. I had two babies, gaining then losing exactly sixty pounds each time. Pregnant, I ate as I once had, post-anorexia, making up for years of deprivation, eating for two for all I was worth.

Now the starvation point unsettles me. When people tell me they think I'm too thin, I listen. If I can see my clavicle or sternum, or start to feel frail, I've gone too far. Pendulum swings back; I assume that's a lifetime job.

Sometimes I drive past a jogger wearing sweatpants in the middle of a hot July day, her body an apparition in the swirl of gas exhaust, her head overpowering a bony chest, dark hair on her cheeks, wiry arms boxing at her waist, her whole being like an insect with glowing eyes, breakable legs. In my rearview mirror, she looks eighty years old, she looks eight. If I pulled over, would she listen?

I would like to write about food without writing about hunger—my own personal hunger, a craving that occasionally quiets down. I'd also like to write about food without writing about my body. I'd like to list the meals I've eaten, as my grandmother could, claiming she could track every restaurant meal she'd ever had and in which city: clams on the half-shell followed by steak au poivre and haricots verts in Tours in 1968. I'd like to list every meal as if it were only glamorous pleasure.

When my eight-year-old daughter draws girls, they are rail-thin, concave, carved out of nothing; she fits twelve girls on one page.

I hide fashion magazines, not wanting her to see who wears the pretty clothes, this year's models more waif than woman.

When I take her to see *The Nutcracker,* she leans in to me, whispering, "She's the leader! Look, they're all watching *her.*" She points at the Sugar Plum Fairy. I've put my daughter in ballet class, and I'm dismayed when she wilts to the floor, tutu all around, crying that she's bored. Also, I'm relieved.

Now, in the middle of the Dance of the Snowflakes, I'm spellbound. Flurries come down, the corps de ballet step over the new-fallen snow. Night is approaching, and the Nutcracker Prince has emerged from his wooden utensil form. Clara is set free into the unknown forest, leaving family to be with her prince, the love object come to life. As the girls move through the night forest and snowflakes cover their hair, their pointe shoes mark the floor with a satisfying scrape. The eerie dreamscape is fully formed, neither woods nor stage, figures in geese formation, children masquerading as grown lovers; they dwell in an outward manifestation of inner space, one where I once found the stillness of my unseen forest, where I knew Tchaikovsky had guessed my secret, beckoning me to believe that a grown-up understood the child's heart, where I once attempted to capture the timelessness of a chord, a *pas de chat,* a pirouette, in tutu, *sur la pointe,* a sweet candy become stick figure in toe shoes.

SKY GIRL
Ann Hood

During winter break in my senior year of college, my parents asked me what my plans were for the future. Graduation was six months away, and, with my degree in English, they were not hopeful about my options. Years earlier, I had sat in my seventh-grade guidance counselor's office and he had asked me the same question. For reasons that remain mysterious to me, I'd looked Mr. Stone in the eye and said, "I want to be an airline stewardess."

This was in 1969. National Airlines had a TV commercial in which a pretty blonde looked into the camera and said, "I'm Cheryl. Fly me." Braniff had the air strip—stewardesses disrobed piece by piece during the course of the flight. Southwest called their stewardesses Love Birds. And my future employer, TWA, offered foreign-accent flights with theme-costumed stewardesses: Olde English dressed like wenches, French wore gold minis, and Italian featured togas. Just two years earlier, *Coffee, Tea, or Me?: The Uninhibited Memoirs of Two Airline Stewardesses* had been a best seller. The book promised that this "hilarious jet-age journal offers a gold mine of anecdotes from the aerial and amorous lives of those busty, lusty adventurous young 'stews' of the swinging '60s."

Perhaps all these things were on Mr. Stone's mind when he burst out laughing at my response. "Ann," he said, "smart girls do not become airline stewardesses."

"Why not?" I asked him. All I wanted was to get out of the depressed old mill town where I lived and see the world.

Mr. Stone stroked his muttonchop sideburns and told me, "Smart girls become teachers or nurses. Or," he added brightly, "they get married."

It was 1969, but in West Warwick, Rhode Island, smart girls did not have a lot of options. Teacher, nurse, or wife did not offer me a chance to see the world and have adventures. I left Mr. Stone's office and went directly to the library, where I took out a book called *How to Become an Airline Stewardess*. The book promised me lunch in Paris and dinner in Manhattan. It promised me boyfriends around the world. It promised me sophistication and elegance. All I had to do was be tall (check); under the age of twenty-five (check); single (check); a high school graduate (likely check); and weigh under 115 pounds (my adolescent body weighed in at 112, so; check). I was on my way to a career as an airline stewardess, my brains and Mr. Stone be damned.

By the time my parents questioned me eight years later, many things had changed since 1930, when Ellen Church, the first sky girl, worked on a twenty-hour, thirteen-stop flight from San Francisco to Chicago. Back then sky girls had to be trained nurses, and Steve Stimson, the manager of Boeing Air Transport who hired them, decreed that he wanted "no funny little ones nor great big ones"; they were required to greet the captain and his copilot with rigid military salutes. Six years later, they were serving hot meals. By 1942 the nursing requirement had been dropped. And in the 1950s, wearing girdles, hats, and gloves, sky girls became airline stewardesses, giving men on certain all-male flights cigars that they lit for them, and mixing cruets of cocktails. It wasn't until 1968, a year before my meeting with Mr. Stone, that the marriage ban got lifted.

My college roommates majored in business and bought gray suits with floppy ties for job interviews. They went to résumé workshops and flooded banks and corporations with their polished results. My parents drove me to Logan Airport, where I walked from terminal to terminal collecting one-page job applications. Stewardesses were now flight attendants, but not much else about the job seemed to have changed since I'd read *How to Become an Airline Stewardess*. I was advised to wear a skirt to my interviews to show off my legs, to avoid turtlenecks so the interviewer wouldn't suspect I was hiding something, and to answer most questions with the reply "I love people and I love to travel."

Looming large in every brochure from every airline was a chart that had the acceptable heights down one side and the corresponding acceptable weights. At five-seven, I had a maximum accepted weight of 135 pounds. But my *preferred* weight was 125 pounds. I stepped on my parents' scale and held my breath. For four years of college, it had never occurred to me to weigh myself. My standard uniform was a pair of boy's khakis, 28 × 30, and a closet full of sherbet-colored Izod shirts. Too busy as student body treasurer and sorority sister, not to mention a double major, I decided to forgo the meal plan and subsist instead on Hostess cupcakes and coffee for breakfast and a variety of cheap meals at campus pubs for dinner. No lunch. Lots of beer at night, perhaps offset by frantic dancing at parties. All of this, I saw with a sigh of relief, had left me at 122 pounds, three pounds below the preferred weight.

I mailed off a dozen applications, already dreaming of training with Pan Am in Honolulu, or wearing TWA's Ralph Lauren uniform while I jetted around Europe, or moving to Houston for Braniff and spending all my time in South America. I breezed through all of these preliminary interviews and more—United, Eastern, Northwest—and got ready to move on to the final ones. These were three-day visits to the training centers, and soon tickets to Miami, Kansas City, and New York began arriving. I bought a black suit with a short skirt, pale pink lipstick, and a pretty pink silk scarf that I tied jauntily like the flight attendants tied theirs.

In this final stage, we would be given math tests, psychological tests, physicals, drug tests, several more interviews, and our first official weigh-in. My overachieving self began to worry. Unable to control how well I did in any of these—except the drug test—I decided to lose a few pounds. Sure, I was already below the preferred weight for my height. But what if I was way below it? Then I wouldn't have to worry if I gained a couple extra pounds at some point. By the time I reached Kansas City, I weighed in at 118 pounds.

I did not have to starve myself to get there. I just didn't eat very much for a couple of weeks. Some days I ate only Hostess cupcakes. Some days I ate only dinner. Some days I didn't eat at all. When TWA hired me, I turned down the other airlines and left for chilly Kansas City and six weeks of training. That was when I learned that the weight we weighed in at during that last visit was considered our hiring weight. For the next six months, while we were on probation, we had to maintain that weight. Go above it, and we could get fired.

Even though my hiring weight was almost twenty pounds below the maximum weight allowed for my height, I couldn't go above 118 pounds. I wasn't alone. Most of the women had done the same thing, arriving at their final interview well below the preferred weight in an effort to win the job. Now we all had to stay thin. Really thin. Every week of our six-week training period, we had scheduled weigh-ins, squeezed right between TROUBLESHOOTING THE COFFEEMAKER and EVACUATING THE 727. That meant we could eat normally until a few days before the weigh-in, and then we would basically stop eating. For me, that meant lots of coffee, the occasional cookie, and sometimes a piece of roast beef. At night, women worked out for hours in our common suite. They shared weight-loss secrets: Drink a lot of water, drink a lot of coffee, and don't eat after three in the afternoon.

By the time I left flight attendant training, I weighed 115 pounds. My Ralph Lauren uniform was a size two. And I loved the way I looked. I loved to run my hands over my sharp hip bones as they pressed against the navy blue fabric. I loved how concave my stomach became when I lay down, a deep canyon between those jutting hip bones. I loved how each rib stood out in the bathroom mirror after a shower. I loved how the waistband of those old khakis of mine, 28 × 30, was loose enough for me to put my entire hand inside.

My graduating class was based in Boston. Six of us rented a

large three-bedroom apartment near the aquarium, with pano-
ramic views of the bay and the airport beyond it: two secretaries,
a sales rep, a Playboy Bunny, a telephone operator, and me—
twenty-one years old and just out of college. One day my roommate Linda came in from a flight pale and upset. Our supervisor
had been waiting for her at the gate when she deplaned. The supervisor measured the dangle of her earrings, the heel of her
shoes, and then took her downstairs and weighed her. Linda,
also five-seven, had a hiring weight of 120 pounds. At her surprise weigh-in, she was 122. "Three strikes and you're out," the
supervisor told her.

We had been warned about these surprise checks, how we
could get off a flight anywhere, anytime, and find a supervisor
waiting. We would get demerits for not wearing lipstick, for not
wearing our uniform jackets (required during boarding, deplan-
ing, and in the airport), for heels too high or too low, for earrings over the required length, for using nonregulation luggage
(we were issued one crew kit and could not take anything extra,
no matter how many days we were away from home), and a
dozen other infractions. Then we would be weighed.

"I have to lose two pounds," Linda said. "Fast."

If Linda had to lose two pounds, didn't we all? At any time,
we could be weighed and come in over our hiring weight. Flying
all the hours that we did caused bloating. Then there were our
erratic schedules, flying redeyes one week, the dreaded six A.M.
six-stop Ohio Valley trips the next. We changed time zones as
often as our underwear. We never slept. We ate pilfered chateau-
briand left over from first class, or crew meals that resembled
Swanson TV dinners. On layovers, we drank margaritas and ate
greasy Mexican food, or, if the layovers were too short or too
late to go out to eat, we relied on airport food: popcorn, hot
dogs, and coffee, coffee, coffee. Sometimes my schedule was

such that I didn't remember the last time I'd eaten. Then I would come home and join my roommates at T.G.I. Friday's, where we drank sugary cocktails and ate cheap appetizers like loaded potato skins and steak on a stick.

We hatched a plan to help Linda and ourselves. Someone's boyfriend could get us diuretics—"water pills"—that would keep off the extra water weight that came from all that flying. Eagerly, we accepted our share and took them during each flight. Someone else learned that the Y on Tremont Street had a sauna where we could go and sweat off extra pounds for free. Every day that we were home instead of away on a trip, we would walk to the Y, put on our bathing suits, and sit in that sauna, our bones protruding, our cheeks sallow. Someone heard you lost more weight if you drank water while you were in the sauna. So we brought in liters of water and drank while we sweated. More than once I nearly fainted in there and had to crawl across the cold, dirty floor to the cool air of the locker room, where I sat guzzling water on the old cracked tiles.

Still, when Roslyn had a surprise weigh-in, she, too, had gained two pounds. No matter how much we starved and sweated and peed, our lifestyles made it impossible to maintain our weight. When Linda was met again after a flight, her weight had moved up to 125 pounds—still ten pounds below the maximum for her height, but five pounds over her hiring weight. And strike two.

Despite everything, I loved the job. I loved walking across the broad expanse of an airport in my uniform, shiny silver wings pinned to my jacket, my lipstick the same cranberry as the stripes on my sleeves. I loved standing in front of an airplane full of people and pointing out the emergency exits. I loved working the redeyes to San Francisco, stumbling exhausted and bleary-eyed off the airplane and dropping immediately to sleep in the luxurious beds of the Mark Hopkins Hotel. The six-month probation period was almost over, and then I would have unlimited free tickets everywhere that TWA flew. Our timetable was the thickest and most exotic of any airline, and sometimes, as the L-1011 flew west and the passengers slept, I sat on my jump seat and planned trips to London and Cairo and Athens.

I loved the job and did not want to get fired for two pounds or five pounds. It became easier and easier to consume only crab Louis and a few Ramos gin fizzes one day, then nothing the next. Or a Cobb salad and water for two days, then coffee for two days. Or to eat an entire first-class meal, then only chips and salsa and a margarita the next night. The hollowness I felt became normal. I was never full. But I was also never met at a flight for a surprise check.

With a month to go before probation ended—and with it our weigh-ins—I came home from a trip and found Linda packing her things. She'd had another surprise check and weighed in at 128 pounds. Strike three. She was fired on the spot. Through her tears and her anger, she threatened lawsuits and discrimination. "I mean," she said "it's 1979, and women can still be fired for their weight?"

I don't know whatever happened to Linda. Out of embarrassment or rage, she went home to Long Island and disappeared. Later, I heard that she went to work for Northwest Airlines, that she did sue TWA and won her job back, that she sued and won a fat settlement.

I do know, of course, what happened to me. For years I continued this relationship with food. Although I stopped taking diuretics and sweating in saunas, I kept eating only once a day, or having just coffee if I felt like I was gaining weight. My size-two uniform skirt could completely spin around my waist. I started wearing a size zero. When I look at pictures of myself in my twenties, all of the eight years that I was a flight attendant, I look gaunt. I see that now. I see, too, that Linda was right: Getting fired for your weight was outrageous. But so were most of the requirements forced upon us. We were called flight attendants, but in many ways, we were still just sky girls.

In 1986, after I stopped flying and began to live on a more regular schedule, my weight landed at 125 pounds and pretty much stayed there until I had children and added a stubborn three more pounds. I remember that day in 1978 when I stepped on a scale for the first time and held my breath. Sadly, that is still what I do every time I step on a scale. Even today, if I see that needle inching toward 130, I don't panic. I just drop my meals down to one a day, increase my coffee intake, and in no time I'm back. Not only back to my desired weight but back to that time when weight and what I ate were obsessions. Until that needle lands at 128 again, I think too much about how to get it there. I know that a lunch of rotisserie chicken breast and fresh mozzarella cheese and tomatoes eaten for three days with nothing else but coffee and wine will get me there fast. I know that I can go two full days without eating before I get light-headed and queasy. I know that if I eat only grilled salmon and salad for three days, my waistbands will loosen, my cheeks will hollow, and I will relax. I should be able to accept that middle-age weight, a dress size higher than a six, a softening not just on my body but in the way I see myself. I should be able to, but I can't. When I am thin, I feel light as a balloon, and like a balloon, I fly.

PLUS WHAT?
Lisa Romeo

I am a fat girl. At many times in my life I have been thin, but right now I am fat. So it may surprise you that last week I reported to a photographer's studio in trendy downtown Manhattan, got made up, styled, coiffed, and posed for about 250 photos, one of which, if all goes as planned, will appear in a national magazine with a one-letter name I cannot reveal.

Now, let me be clear. I am not a plus-size model, which as we well know is a normal-size woman who wears a ten or twelve or, very occasionally, a fourteen (in a Lane Bryant ad). I am not one of those girls, although if I lost forty pounds, I could be—that is, if I were attractive and not just fat. I am just fat; I wear a size eighteen and sometimes a twenty. And it shows, especially in photos.

Every two or three years I manage to banish the thin person who appears in my mirror. I was at the photo shoot because the magazine editor suspected that many other women over forty (her demographic) ping-pong back and forth their entire lives, gaining weight, losing weight, and gaining it all back again (usually more), just like me.

What happened was this: A few years ago I lost sixty-five pounds through a combination of an obsession with Tae Bo videotapes and a food journal (*Altoid at 10:12 A.M.—alert the media!*). I chimed in on a question posted on the website that is home to this nameless magazine and its nameless namesake's talk show, submitting my "tips that helped me lose weight." Weeks later, a fact-checker called to ask if they could use my information in the magazine. Apparently, putting a treadmill in the laundry room, buying exercise videos on eBay, and getting a notebook and marking it FOOD DIARY are brilliant breakthroughs in dieting. Okay, I said.

When the issue hit the stands in 2003, passing acquaintances, forgotten coworkers, relatives I'd assumed were dead or living in foreign lands called or e-mailed to say, "Hey, I saw your name and quotes in that one-letter magazine." Thus the trouble began. Nothing kills a fresh weight loss faster than the pressure to keep it up (or rather, down) for others, so that I would not be humiliated by the town librarian who was once a stranger but smiled conspiratorially when I returned my kid's Goosebumps book, or the local funeral home director who was previously a nodding acquaintance but now called out "Hey, skinny" when he passed me in Foodtown, or Father Greg, who confessed his weight-loss woes on the church steps after Mass.

So I did what I always do after a dramatic weight loss—charged a new wardrobe in a smaller size, colored my hair, signed up for a gym membership (Tae Bo classes live!), started wearing thong underwear, and bought expensive knee-high real leather boots without a zipper.

I got two seasons out of the boots before I needed to spritz PAM on my stockinged calves and put the boots on lying down; I did wear the underwear (which my husband enjoyed more than I did); and I absolutely used the gym membership (although six trips in eight months worked out to $118.75 per class, which wasn't authentic Tae Bo anyway).

Then I did the next thing I always do: I gained it all back. Plus more.

The wait was over, the other shoe had dropped, the knife had turned. Truth is, when I gain weight, I am home, I am comfortable again; I arrive, I can rest. People I do not know that well (and never liked) can stop telling me how "fabulous" I look. Back up in the attic go the skinny clothes (if you can call twelves and fourteens skinny; I do), and down come the loose, long sweaters, the elastic-waist velour sweatsuits, and the maternity nightgowns from 1993 (hey, I am a *frugal* fat person!).

How it works is like this: I overeat compulsively, I binge, I get lazy, I stop exercising, I make peanut-butter-and-marshmallow-fluff sandwiches on pasty white sliced bread at one A.M. I eat all the refreshments at the fund-raising meeting when the other moms leave, I stop at Foodtown on the way home from an Overeaters Anonymous meeting for a box of Yodels, I finish the leftover birthday cake and say I brought it to the office.

Enterprising person that I am, however, I made fat work for me this time. I kept going back to page through that magazine and think: Magazines love follow-up stories: *Let's revisit Brenda,*

*who lost forty-five pounds on the Eat Only Your Own Sweaters diet . . .
and here she is, still slim two years later, with an exciting higher-paying job,
a hunky fiancé, and three marathons behind her.* Only this time I had a
different follow-up in mind: *Here's Lisa, the "successful dieter" . . .
three years later, she's fat again, does not exercise, and recently had to buy
size-eighteen stretch jeans.*

Why not a follow-up? Why not give the 90 percent of dieters
who studies say regain all the weight, plus more, someone to relate to on those glossy pages? Why not?

I will tell you why not. Because I know how editors usually
think—with their eyes and their "happy brain." They wonder: *Is
he/she wildly photogenic?* or *How hard will the cosmetologist/hair-
dresser/stylist/photographer have to work? Is this a happy ending?* or *How
can we spin/shade/gloss it over?* So I knew that suggesting a "Here's
the fat girl" story had as much a chance as a piece about the
downside of positive thinking. Still. I envisioned not a before-
and-after story but a during piece—here's one of our former diet
successes, now a diet failure gal. Let's try to figure out why she
and so many others keep doing this to themselves.

I know that I am not alone, that millions of other women
who would see such a story might think, *Finally, someone like me,*
and that the story might be a hit. On the other hand, readers
might recoil, drop the magazine on the coffee table, and head
for the secret Halloween-candy stash they told their kids they'd
donated to the school's Treats for Homeless Tots.

What did I have to lose? Certainly not any weight! And what
American girl wouldn't want to appear in a popular magazine
looking as if she weighs 220 pounds (because she does)?

So I wrote a letter. The pitch: Revisit someone you held up as
a success and is now a failure, and tell us what a yo-yo dieter (a
fattie, a binger, an overeater, a slug) can do to break the cycle

(and I do *not* mean go on another diet). I was stunned when the magazine said, Yes, let's talk about weight gain *after* weight loss, about chronic re-gaining, and about why some women get stuck in the cycle amid depression, frayed nerves, negative thought patterns, and self-loathing, not to mention the bitch of trying to find boots that fit a seventeen-and-a-half-inch calf.

The editors would assign their famous, expensive-but-pragmatic life-coach columnist to spend ninety days getting inside my head and hopefully helping me get out of my pantry.

I spent an hour every few days talking to this incredibly smart woman who seemed to have a direct line into my thoughts. I wrote her copious e-mails daily, did my assigned homework, and *did not* go on a diet. Result: I lost eighteen pounds, which was nice, *and* I stopped binging (much nicer and more important). Now she was going to write all about the psychology of it, and I was going to write all about the day-to-day "mood-food-brood" swings. They wanted a photo of me to go along with the articles. Which brings me to the modeling part and why it sucks to be America's Next Top Fat Model.

When I arrive at Studio 3, I get my fifteen minutes, and let me tell you this: It is everything you have imagined. And so much less.

Rolling racks bulge with clothing I cannot afford, in gorgeous colors, some bejeweled, tags affixed, all in size extra large! On the floor, the stylist's assistant has lined up fifty-seven pairs (yes, I counted) of stilettos, boots, and sling-backs in luscious suede, patent leather, reptile skin; designer names I have seen only on Carrie Bradshaw's feet or read of in *Vogue*. I inspect, and yes, they're all in my size, nine and a half! How will I ever choose?

The stylist is friendly and sweet and kind and funny, and he makes me laugh—right up to the moment he leads me to a makeshift curtained changing area where he has assembled the outfits and shoes *I* will be wearing: black stretchy pants (implied message: active girl!), plain white tees in short- and long-sleeve and a variety of necklines, and black jackets. No Jimmy Choos for me, just nice but not naughty black-and-white walking sneakers.

And for this I gained seventy pounds?

The makeup artist erases my genetically stubborn under-eye circles, smothers my too-young-to-have-'em-but-I-do age spots, and gives me the long, curled, deep dark eyelashes normally reserved for eight-year-old boys. She skips over a blemish that seems horribly obvious to me. "Oh, sweetie, they'll airbrush that out." Of course. Will they also airbrush out my bulging thighs, dimply upper arms, saggy double chin, pudgy fingers, rounded droopy shoulders, and poochy gut? No, then there would be no *story*!

I peel off my jeans and plain black T-shirt (worn because that's how models arrive backstage, no?) while the gay stylist and gay prop master hover and chatter about how great and fabulous and cute everything is. I pull on pair after pair of black stretchy pants—cropped, capri, ankle-length, and tapered—followed by white tees with long and short sleeves or no sleeves at all, covered up by black jackets, zipped or unzipped. The men smooth buckled fabric, run lint rollers over my breasts, buttocks, and elbows, and when I am feeling completely morose, they tell me to remove my necklace, bracelet, and earrings, and that no, I won't be layered in borrowed bling.

The better to *see* the fat, I suppose.

Except for me and the magazine photo supervisor, who is lovely but lingers in the background to allow the photo pros their artistic leeway, no one actually on the set where we are shooting—not the photographer or assistants, not the excitable stylist or the prop master, not the makeup artist or hairstylist—has a clue what this article is about. I explain that it's about gaining and losing weight, but it's not a diet piece, not a before-and-after article, not a makeover. That's when the prop manager tells me about friends who have lost twenty-five pounds on a diet of lemonade, honey, and cayenne pepper. "Try it," he advises. I nod politely and learn that my shoot will not entail my swanning about striking poses or swishing hair. I will be standing quite still, one leg bent just so, leaning slightly back against the white backdrop but not too far back because the paint is still wet.

"What?" I tease the stylist. "No sparkly jewels, no fancy duds, not even a quirky hat or funky scarf?" In my best diva voice, I declare that if I do not get to wear at least one gorgeous thing, I may act like a real model and sneak a pair of Christian Louboutins out in my backpack.

He hugs me. "Sorry," he says, "they want you to look very simple, serene."

"Right, because weight gain is so simple and makes one so serene," I deadpan.

"I know what you mean," he says. "As a gay man in New York City, I know everything about staying slim; have you tried doing cardio twice a day and biking fifteen or twenty miles each weekend?"

Only the makeup gal, who gives me what she calls a natural, earthy look (translation: not a speck of shimmering eye shadow, bronzer, or dollop of drama), seems to notice my hidden inner model. "You know, I like working on real people better anyway," she says. I suppose this is a compliment, or at least a kindness, but I don't feel any better.

As the fattest person in the room (except for a workman who delivers a ladder), I do not indulge in the catered breakfast now that I am wearing the final steamed and lint-rolled outfit, with my lips caked in color. So I wait, slightly bored and, to tell the truth, feeling rather ignored and, how can I put this, *in the way*. Talk whirs, little of it directed at me.

How is it possible to be the largest person in the room and yet be invisible? What are they all thinking? Is the photographer, used to super-slim twentysomethings, wondering how to make me look even the ten pounds lighter that his camera will add? I'm reminded of the movie *Tootsie,* when Dustin Hoffman, in female persona and full makeup, steps on the set and the director asks the cameraman how much farther he can pull back to make Hoffman appear more attractive: "How about Cleveland?"

On the set, I glance around to find . . . nothing but a white backdrop, a white drop cloth on the floor, white everything; but with my fat encapsulated in slightly tight, stretchy black pants and jacket, I'm good to go. So I go, or try to go, with the flow, smiling, tilting, bending (but not too much), looking up, looking down, looking out, looking pensive. When I begin to relax the tiniest amount, the photographer asks, "How would you like to see how great you're doing?" He grabs my elbow and moves me next to his assistant, whose laptop computer screen erupts into a virtual moving picture of me in 171 poses. Here is what I see: black-white-FAT-black-white-FAT. Which is when I need to vomit.

I don't, of course. I want to, but there doesn't seem to be anyplace appropriate to do so on this white set or in the cramped staging area filled with clothes and shoes (which I learn are meant for the magazine's columnist, who happens to wear my size but somehow never looks it in her photographs, and who is arriving momentarily). I dab my watery eyes, ask for more concealer where I have smudged my lower-lid mascara, and get back to "work."

Two hours later, back in my jeans, I collect my umbrella, snitch a chocolate-chip-peanut-butter cookie from the catered lunch, and wave bye as everyone tells me I "did great" and that I won't believe how good I am going to look in the magazine. I try to make a weak joke, but they are all distracted by one of the numerous slim twentysomething assistants demonstrating how to eat quiche without consuming a crumb of fat-laden crust by scraping out the eggy filling with her teeth.

The prop manager presents me with the red silk journal and handsome pen I admired, and the stylist winks and says I can keep a pair of black stretchy pants. Cramming these treasures into my tote, I realize my fifteen minutes are over. I am free to move about my life and possibly, on the way to the subway station, grab a croissant at the bread shop next door. When I get there, I select a ham-and-cheese-filled croissant, a black-olive baguette, a mini provolone-and-red-pepper semolina loaf, two everything bagels, and a pesto focaccia.

Whether I ate them all on the subway and train rides back to my little suburban life, or whether I daintily ate one and saved the rest, I will not reveal, at least not here. For that, you must buy the magazine (on newsstands soon), or preorder the forthcoming memoir (due out in time to coincide with my appearance on the book-club segment of the talk show hosted by the eponymous magazine's perennial cover girl). It will be a stunning work of high literary art, a breathtakingly honest look at this tumultuous and life-altering experience.

I am going to call it *A Million Little Reese's Pieces.*

ESS, ESS
Rochelle Jewel Shapiro

When my father was a boy, he escaped from the burning village where most of his siblings were murdered and hid in the woods from the Cossacks and their dogs. He survived by eating berries, roots, and tree bark. In a way, he never left those woods. When I was growing up and the dinner table was heaped with food, he ate so fast that his hand, holding the fork, was a blur. As he chewed, the veins stood out on his forehead and his eyes never left his plate. There was no dinner conversation, only anxious chewing. "*Ess, ess*" (eat, eat), he'd always tell me, but if he thought there was a potato left on my plate, he'd spear it and wolf it down though I might not have finished.

I didn't have memories of starvation, like he did, but I did fear not having enough to eat when he was around. I had to eat as fast as he did, or his big hand would descend on my plate. He worked so many hours in his grocery store that sitting down at the table with me, no matter how ferociously he ate, seemed like a time of grace, a blessing. Even when I was little, I understood that the abundance on the table was his triumph and reward for what he had gone through, and I was strangely happy for him. I was average weight; I didn't have a belly like his. But I found myself eyeing food wistfully, knowing that it wasn't going to be there for long. I joined him in his speed-eating even though it made me choke. The crazy thing was, he would yell at me for choking.

"Stop *vorfing* yourself with food," he'd holler. He didn't seem to realize that I was trying to keep up with him.

Oblivious, my mother stayed on her feet, serving him as if he were an eating machine that had to be stoked. "Your father is a good provider," she'd always say as she ladled more gravy onto his plate.

Sometimes, when he took half a day off on Sundays, we'd have lunch at Central Delicatessen. One day when I was five, while eating my frankfurter too quickly, I began to choke and couldn't breathe.

"I told you not to eat so fast," my father yelled, and he sprang up out of his chair and pounded me on the back with his prize-fighter fist. (He had earned the money for his grocery store from boxing.) When the pounding didn't work, he said, "God, don't let her die," and grabbed me by my ankles and turned me upside down, my felt poodle skirt hanging down to my chin, my pink Lollipop panties on display for the whole corned-beef-and-pastrami set to see.

There was never anything left over in our house. Every crumb would be eaten immediately. When I went to a friend's house and saw part of a cake under a glass dome, I was amazed that it was possible for food to sit out for someone to eat later. One Passover as I lay in bed, I couldn't stop thinking about the can of coconut macaroons my mother had bought and put in the closet. I was afraid my father would get to them before me and I wouldn't get a chance to taste one. I got out of bed and tiptoed into the kitchen. In the dark, I climbed on a chair and got down the can. It was impenetrable, like a locked vault, but there was a key on top, like on a can of sardines. As soon as I'd opened the can enough to stick my hand in, I reached inside for a macaroon and my wrist caught on the sharp metal cover. I was bleeding into the macaroons, but I still ate them. I kept eating even though blood dripped onto the linoleum, even though my wrist burned like fire. When the blood kept flowing, I was frightened and ran to my parents' bedroom. "Mommy!" I cried through the closed door.

When she came out and saw the blood, she turned white and swayed as if she'd faint. "What happened?" she sputtered.

"I wanted a macaroon," I admitted.

She wrapped my hand in a towel, threw on a dress, and drove me to the hospital. On the way, she said, "Didn't you know those macaroons were for your father?"

As a grown woman, I still have that jagged scar on my right wrist. When people see it, their eyes widen and the question pops out of their mouths—"Is that from a suicide attempt?"

My father died from a heart attack when I was twenty-five. Twelve years later, I was married with two children, and I still found myself eating as quickly as if he were at the table with me. I scalded my lips, my tongue, and the roof of my mouth on food and drinks that were too hot. I swallowed fish and chicken bones. I couldn't keep cake or cookies or a box of chocolates in the house for unexpected company because I'd eat it all in one sitting, or standing. I was so worried about setting the same example for my children that I avoided eating with them. My husband worked late at night, so most nights he wasn't home for dinner. Like my mother, I didn't sit down to eat with my children. Like her, I stood on my feet, serving them, then washing the dishes as they ate.

My friends called me Spot—I was always spilling things on myself. Once I brought a cup of cocoa to my lips so quickly that it sloshed up into my face. My seven-year-old son looked at me with knitted brows. "Mommy, did you do that on purpose?" he asked.

My ten-year-old daughter rolled her eyes. "Mom, what you need is a full-body bib," she said.

I was most embarrassed when I had to face my dry cleaner. "What's this stain from?" he'd ask. "And this one?" He'd been a journalist in China before Tiananmen Square and went about dry cleaning with the same investigative intensity he'd had as a reporter, putting small bright stickers on each of my stains while the other customers tapped their feet or smirked.

When he found out I was a writer, we developed a rapport. One day he asked what I thought of his logo—ADEQUATE CLEANERS. "I found *adequate* in the thesaurus," he said proudly.

"No!" I cried in alarm. "*Adequate* means barely good enough. Your cleaning is perfection." After that, every time I walked into the store, he smiled and gestured toward his new sign—PERFECTION DRY CLEANING.

Then one day I was in a pizza shop, wolfing down a slice as if the Cossacks were after the pepperoni, the cheese and tomato sauce sliding down the front of my white silk blouse, when the dry cleaner walked in. This was worse than bringing in the soiled garment. It was being caught in the act.

I knew I'd miss the friendly exchanges but I begged my husband to bring in my clothes on his way to work at the pharmacy.

"What do I say if he asks me what the stains are from?" my husband complained.

Thinking of what my husband told his customers about their medications, I said, "Tell him they're generic."

I swore to myself that I'd slow down, that this was it. But working at home as a phone psychic and writer, I was always dangerously close to the refrigerator.

The next day, while I stood at the open refrigerator, gobbling down skinless, boneless tuna, I got a clump of it stuck in my throat. I gagged and gagged, but I couldn't cough it up, and I was having trouble breathing. I drank water and choked more. I tried to push it down with bread. The bread got stuck along with the tuna. Thinking I was going to die, I ran out into my apartment hallway. No one was around to help. I banged on the door across the hall.

"Who . . . is . . . it?" called my neighbor in his rusty old voice.

I couldn't even say my name. I banged on his door with both fists. The peephole opened.

"Just a minute," he sang out. "I gotta get my pants on."

Panicked, I remembered a poster I'd seen of how to do the Heimlich on oneself. I pressed my fist hard below my bra line, and by the time the neighbor opened the door, the tuna was hidden in my hand.

"Never mind," I said to my neighbor and went inside, where

I put my back against the door. My heart was pounding. My speed-eating had to stop, or one day my children would come home and find me dead. I decided to go to an eating-disorders therapist recommended by one of my clients who binged.

"Why are you here?" the therapist asked me the following week. "You're not overweight."

I told her about my father and how I couldn't stop eating like him.

"It took me years to get my own eating disorder under control," she said earnestly. "But I've been symptom-free for seven years, and it's been such a pleasure." She handed me a framed photo of a heavy, unsmiling woman. "That was me," she said. "Don't worry," she added, "I've helped hundreds of people with your symptoms."

She had a Ph.D. Her voice was so soothing, her manner so confident, that I thought I'd get well just as she had. She went on to ask me questions about what thoughts and feelings I was having before I choked on the tuna, but I was distracted by a sickly-sweet odor. I knew what it was—mouthwash. My mother drank, and she used to try to mask it by rinsing her mouth with Lavoris. Was the therapist an alcoholic? And then I noticed something shiny in her dark hair. I leaned forward in my chair as if I were hanging on her every word and looked more closely. Vomit—a piece of vomit was in her hair! She was managing her weight by throwing up. She was bulimic. There was nothing I could learn from her. She was more fragile than I was. I knew I wouldn't be coming back.

In my apartment lobby, a stack of New Age newspapers sat on the table, along with menus from a Chinese restaurant. For no reason, I leafed through one. There was an ad for a meditation class that promised stress relief, anti-aging, and physical, emotional, and spiritual healing. I read on. *Slow down your eating,* it said. I did a double take and realized it read, *Slow down your breathing.* But I felt that my mistake wasn't really an accident, that this meditation class could help me, that somehow the universe was providing me with a solution. I felt saved.

The group met in a house that was perfectly round, like a miniature stadium. A dozen people sat in a circle, legs folded in the half-lotus position, backs against the couches or the walls, depending on how early they'd arrived. The teacher asked us to become aware of the breath entering our nostrils, lungs, diaphragms, then coming out of our mouths and traveling up into our noses. She told us to say to ourselves *in* as we inhaled, *out* as we exhaled. After about five minutes, I was overcome with fidgets. *Zitsflaish,* my father would have called it. It was like torture. Every muscle in my body rebelled. I couldn't wait for it to be over.

When I got home, I flung myself onto my bed and cried. I felt even more hopeless. Nothing could help me. I got up and scarfed down a stale bagel. (My father had taught me never to waste food.) I ended up swallowing the temporary cap my dentist had put on my right molar.

A couple of days later, to my surprise, I got into the lotus position and began to do the *in* and *out* mantra as I breathed. I could stay like that for only a few minutes, but the next morning I tried it again. I did find it relaxing and began to do it a few times a day for short periods by myself. Within three months, I was able to meditate for fifteen minutes at a stretch.

One afternoon, as I meditated, I felt linear time dissolve; I was rocked in the hammock of my own breath. Then I heard, in my own voice, "The Cossacks aren't after you. There's plenty of food in America. You're safe." I'd told myself things like that before, but in meditation, the words came from such a deep place inside me, as if wrung from my solar plexus, that they broke the terrible spell.

After that, I was able to sit calmly at the table, chew slowly and thoroughly, and swallow without incident. Our cleaning bills were halved. There were no more blisters on my tongue or the roof of my mouth. No emergency doctor probed my throat for fish or chicken bones.

Now my children are grown and living in their own homes. My husband still works late at the pharmacy, so I often eat before him. Recently, on the thirtieth anniversary of my father's death, I lit a *yahrzeit* candle in his memory. I could have gone out to dinner with a friend, but it didn't seem right. Instead, I stayed home and made my father's favorite meal, *flanken,* a stew made from the short ribs of beef. (He liked it covered with horseradish.) The table was set for two. When I began to eat, I imagined my father's spirit sitting down beside me. I imagined him so vividly that I could see his auburn curls, his blue eyes. I could see what he was wearing—a yellow nylon shirt with a plastic pocket protector for his pens. I was so happy to see him. "*Ess, ess,*" I said; I wanted to give him the gift of his favorite food the way he'd given me the gift of his presence. He stared into his plate and began to eat like in the old days, his hands blurring with haste, his eyes never leaving the plate.

"Daddy," I said, "there's plenty of food in America. There's enough for both of us."

His pale blue eyes looked into mine, and he smiled at me, but then he went back to eating at top speed.

After decades of eating slowly and carefully, I felt compelled to go back to gobbling my food before he speared my portion like he used to, thinking I had finished when I hadn't. Shaking, I put my fork down, concentrated on my breathing as I did in meditation.

To my great relief, I was able to take a small bite slowly, chewing over and over. Taste flooded my mouth, garlic and bay leaf and black pepper. The warmth and slightly grainy texture of the meat dissolved on my tongue, and I looked at the food, amazed, as if I had never seen it before in my life.

IN THE HOUSE OF JEAN NIDETCH
Whitney Otto

Wednesday night in our house was Liver Night, in accordance with the Weight Watchers directive to dine on liver once a week. This would be the Weight Watchers of founder (and owner until 1978) Jean Nidetch, which was nothing like the current Fergie-shilled, points-system version. The entire place reeked of calf's liver sautéed in water with dehydrated onion flakes. At fourteen years old, I would sooner be force-fed a used athletic sock than to be in our house on Liver Night. It wasn't just the liver; old-school Weight Watchers was a culinary contradiction made of equal parts portion control, sensible dietary recommendations, and astronaut food. My mother, a modernista and Nidetch devotee, loved Weight Watchers since it dovetailed nicely with three of her primary preoccupations: her obsession with the ongoing twenty-pound problem, her adoration of anything new, and her informal career as Everybody's Friend.

1. The Twenty-Pound Problem

My mother's twenty-pound problem was the gateway issue that led to Weight Watchers. Her weight history, told and retold in my youth in the tribal oral tradition favored by my mother, was roughly as follows: Slim as a child until her first job at age fifteen, manning the pastry cart at B. Altman in New York City. Job over, weight gone. Young lithe woman, always stylishly dressed, until after the birth of her second child (my introduction into the litany), when she couldn't shake the extra twenty pounds. Then my brother, the Handful, was born, causing the weight to come off from sheer frustration and exhaustion. Then my sister came along; weight on. Harried with four kids; weight off.

My mother falls in love with the man soon to be my stepfather. She's happy! Weight on! Twenty pounds! She's unhappy about the weight, of course, and in the past, unhappiness meant the weight would come off, but in defiance of her own personal biological logic, this time the weight doesn't budge. She thinks about joining my stepfather, who diligently dieted the second he gained five pounds by embarking on the Drinking Man's Diet. Here is an excerpt from the book *The Drinking Man's Diet* (1964):

> Did you ever hear of a diet which was fun to follow? A diet which would let you have two martinis before lunch, and a

thick steak generously spread with Sauce Béarnaise, so that you could make your sale in a relaxed atmosphere and go back to the office without worrying about having gained so much as an ounce? A diet which allows you to take out your favorite girl for a dinner of squab and broccoli with hollandaise sauce and Chateau Lafitte, to be followed by an evening of rapture and champagne?

As you can see, the advantage of the Drinking Man's Diet is being able to drink, and, frankly, if one is that involved with liquor, how important is food to you? Are you really going to fret about your reduced M&M's intake, or the fact that bread is off the menu? Doesn't bread soak up the alcohol, anyway? It's kind of a win-win situation where you can't eat everything you want but you're too buzzed to care. Unfortunately, my mother didn't drink.

2. Anything New

My mother is what as known in the marketing game as "an early adopter," which is sort of a consumer's version of being first in line. First boom box I ever saw? Years before anyone of any age? My mother. Car phone? My mother. Surveillance equipment—like recording devices for no reason beyond the fact of their being gadgets? My mother. Anything that can be plugged in or battery-fed, my mother bought when it was bigger, less efficient, more expensive, and not yet mainstreamed. Other facts about my mother? She will live only in a house no one has lived in before. She loves her bedroom because it resembles an anonymous hotel room. Things you should never give her? Flowers, plants, or pets. Nothing that ever had a will to live.

Now, old-school Weight Watchers was a kind of nirvana for those who preferred their food from, say, a lab as opposed to a farm. Dehydrated onion flakes were the spice staple in our house, even though onions aren't exactly a spice. When I asked my mother years later if she liked the dehydrated onion flakes, she replied, "Could you imagine me chopping onions?" as if chopping an onion was on a par with any other improbable, intricate task, like repairing a disabled spacecraft while tethered to the mother ship. Or like cooking. I can't remember my mother ever really cooking. Mostly, it seemed she sort of assembled stuff, then carelessly broiled or boiled. As if cooking was less about *preparing* the food and more about changing its location ("Look—it was on the stove, now it's on the table!").

In addition to the liver, we had to have fish four times a week: frozen milky blocks of what I think might have been halibut (sometimes sole), served with frozen textured blocks of green that usually turned out to be chopped broccoli. Or peas. Or Brussels sprouts. Asparagus came from a can and was so soft it was practically pureed. Chicken was always skinless and buried in an avalanche of dried oregano, then broiled.

Breakfast was synthetic cottage cheese (no curds) mixed with cinnamon and artificial sweetener, slathered on a slice of bread, then broiled. Lunch was cabbage soup—cabbage, salt, and water—its boiled smell rivaling the liver aroma. Dessert? Usually frozen strawberries, sometimes blended with some sort of powdered-milk product, ice, and sweetener. And everything was washed down with Tab or Fresca.

In an unspoken acknowledgment that Weight Watchers was the hair shirt that the entire family wore as a response to the wages of adult food sin, my mother began to indulge us with a variety of processed snacks to break the monotony of processed fish and vegetables. Space Food Sticks, Scooter Pies, frozen spareribs, imitation instant mousse mix, grape soda, Pop-Tarts, Instant Breakfast drink, any cereal with chocolate or dried marsh-mallows. There was even this thing on the market—briefly—a concentrated "ice cream" that, when stirred into a regular glass of milk, turned the milk into a shake. We kids skipped the milk and ate the outrageously thick dairy product directly from its container.

Our house was very popular among the neighborhood kids. Even in the 1960s, most people didn't go to the supermarket and come home with packages of fake food—it was so twentieth-century. Most people in my parents' world had some grasp on the connection between health and the dinner table. And at the time my mother discovered Weight Watchers, we lived in south-ern California, where perpetual summer yields year-round fresh food. While we ate frozen strawberries, our neighborhood liter-ally sat in the middle of strawberry fields.

By the time I was an adult, I had no idea how to cook—I could only emulate my mother and shove things under the broiler until they were jerky. More to the point, I had no idea how to eat. I was always very thin because I was the family's picky eater, something I now recognize as some primal variety of defense mechanism. The freshman ten bypassed me com-pletely; I hardly ate when I was in the dining hall because I couldn't recognize anything. Once I plucked a piece of fresh spinach out of my salad and asked my tablemates what it was.

From then on my life was like the scene at the end of *The Mir-acle Worker,* when Helen Keller is frantically touching everything as Annie Sullivan signs into her hand and exclaims, "It has a name!"

3. Weight Watchers Is Very Social, or Everybody's Friend

My mother, who grew up in an extended Italian-Sicilian-American family in a crowded Bronx apartment, never adjusted to Los Angeles life. "They're always in their houses! Or in their cars! And no one drops in on anyone!" This rant usually concluded with one of two words: *WASPs,* or, for variation, *Germans,* since (according to my mother) these were the two coldest, most emotionally barren groups in existence. That they had nothing directly to do with Los Angeles didn't matter.

On the other hand, she loved the sun, and locating a previously unlived-in house in L.A. was fairly effortless.

My mother, who already had a burgeoning relationship with the Avon Lady, was ready to expand her consumer/friend base. The Avon Lady was unhappily married to a man on whom she regularly cheated. This astonished my mother—not the sleeping-around part, since my mother is more curious about people's lives than judgmental—but because the Avon Lady was, well, how to say it? A little like a giant Pekingese, with wide-set, slightly bulging eyes and straight blond hair that she wore brushed back from her forehead in the style of Kim Hunter in *Planet of the Apes.* My mother was less fascinated by the details of each encounter than by there being more than one such encounter.

Weight Watchers began as a group effort, with Jean Nidetch and friends meeting first in her kitchen, then in rented conference rooms. The forum was designed for someone like my mother: a place where she was encouraged to talk about what she ate and what she weighed in a relaxed, social atmosphere. The other aspect of the organization in those years was the encouragement to become friendly with your group leader.

Enter the group leader. She and my mother became so

friendly that she confessed over dinner one night that she was "married to a homosexual," which was kind of a big deal in that time (late 1960s) and place (suburbia). It seems she had been longing to tell someone, anyone, about her secret life. Soon she was calling my mother for support instead of my mother calling her.

I enjoy reading food memoirs, with their lavish, usually ethnic meals and fabulous family anecdotes. Everything is crazy and colorful and everyone always loves everyone, even when they don't. A close relation is the often cinematic narrative depicting a group of diverse people who become a makeshift family, with the final scene taking place around a crowded table, heavily laden with what looks like the sort of meal that's going to keep you in your chair for a few hours. That is, until you move to the sofa. The movies and the memoirs are as potent an idealization of the American family as *Father Knows Best*. And just as seductive.

My mother's upbringing was an endless series of such multi-course Italian dinners where the relatives ate, talked, argued, ate, laughed, ate, indulged the kids, ate, watched baseball on TV, bragged about who made the best sauce, played with the kids, argued, laughed, then did it all again the next week. A kind of *50 First Dates,* Italian-style.

When I was twenty-four, I moved to San Francisco, where I began a sentimental education that included all kinds of food. Despite sampling and learning to love a vast variety of ethnic cooking (and becoming quite an enthusiastic eater in the process), I remained thin. Partly because I walked everywhere, partly because I had a pretty impressive metabolism, and partly because I was young.

My first kid came along when I was in my mid-thirties, along with my first twenty-pound problem. Around this time my mother, who had taken an extended hiatus from her rigid weekly Weight Watcher menus, returned to the kinder, gentler point-system Weight Watchers and said farewell to her twenty-pound problem for good. And thus, the child (me) became the parent.

These days my mother encourages me to join her in the new Weight Watchers, reassuring me that it's nothing like the old program—something I believe is her unspoken apology for enveloping our home in a weekly noxious liver cloud. She never talks about calories, only "points," which makes me feel as if Weight Watchers has replaced bad cuisine with low-level math. Mostly, my mother wishes me to return to the fold so we can continue our lifelong discussion about her weight obsession. She wants to talk about my twenty-pound problem, about what we eat each day, what we're allowed to eat, what we shouldn't eat. We can talk about "substitutions" and "cheating" and pounds and clothing sizes. She can comment on who's gained or who's lost weight; she can model an endless series of belts. It's like quantum physics for fat, taking the overweight world down to its molecular level.

I grew up listening to the wistfulness in my mother's voice as she described her youth of extended family sharing marvelous meals, as our own little nuclear family tucked into what we called dinner, with me moving food around on my plate as if I were trying to arrange the furniture in a living room. This had the effect of my wanting the life she described, not the one we lived. I used to wonder how she ever could have left New York for Los Angeles. She would say she wanted adventure, to see what the world held, and by the time she understood that what she most wanted was what she had left, there was no turning back.

She met and married my father, had us, married my much adored stepfather, who felt it was important to sit down together at dinner each night, even if we were eating weird space-age diet dinners, in a house where no one had lived before, with me patiently waiting for my own life to begin. Then my stepfather got sick, and after he died we rarely shared a dinner at the table. I once thought the only dinners a person could pine for would be like the dinners of my mother's youth. But I'm older now and understand much more about food and family and what there is to miss.

YOU'RE NOT FAT
Kate Harding

few weeks ago, I went out for dinner in Manhattan with a friend I've known since high school. We went to a typical restaurant in the West Village, which is to say a place with seating for thirty in the approximate square footage of a refrigerator box. Along one wall was a banquette with tables lined up in front of it, close enough to one another that if you ordered anything requiring the use of a knife, elbowing a stranger in the chin would become a real concern. So when the hostess led us to one (which is to say, she took two steps and pointed at a table) smack in the middle, I immediately turned to my tall, thin friend and said, "The squishy seat is all yours. No way my fat ass is getting back there."

I watched her eyes flash and her mouth open slightly before she caught herself and chose *not* to say the words she's said about nine gazillion times to me over the last two decades: *You're not fat!*

We've talked about this. She knows that I blog every day about body acceptance, that I believe *fat* is a useful adjective that should be no more emotionally loaded than *blue-eyed* or *curly-haired,* and that I am indeed significantly wider than she is (she has functioning eyes, after all). And she knows that for all those reasons and many others, the words *You're not fat* drive me up a goddamn wall. But old habits die hard. Since we were teenagers, she's been conditioned to respond to any mention of my weight with "You're not fat!"—as automatically and mindlessly as I would murmur "And also with you" to a priest. She makes a real effort not to say it anymore, bless her heart, but it's going to take either a couple more decades of practice or a course of electroshock therapy to get her to also stop making the *I want to say it* face.

The thing is, at various points during the time we've known each other, it was true: I wasn't fat. During high school, when I'd reached my full adult height of five-two and weighed around 135 pounds, I really wasn't fat by any rational standard—unfortunately, adolescent girls aren't known for their rational standards regarding weight, so I fully believed I was the Fattest Girl in Recorded History. When I was dieting in my twenties, there were times when I clearly wasn't anything approaching fat, yet I still wasn't satisfied with the amount of weight I'd lost; when I'd gotten myself down to size four jeans and extra-small T-shirts, all I could focus on was getting a pair of *size-two* jeans past my thighs. People telling me I wasn't fat didn't make a damn bit of difference to my profoundly warped self-image in those days, but at least they weren't lying.

At other times, though, they were. For much of my adult life, I've worn plus sizes, struggled to fit into airplane seats, and been clinically obese according to the body mass index (BMI) charts that determine everything from the price of my insurance premiums to whether doctors will hand me a Weight Watchers brochure when I see them about an ear infection. I once asked a doctor for help with excruciating knee pain following a spill down some stairs, and the only prescription she offered was "Lose weight." (OH, OKAY. But since I'm probably not going to lose enough to reduce pressure on my joints in the next ten minutes, and my knee hurts RIGHT NOW, do you think maybe you could MAKE WITH THE PAINKILLERS, BITCH?) I was once standing on the street talking to a business contact I hoped to impress, when a homeless man came up and asked us for change. The man I hoped to impress said he didn't have any, and the homeless guy spat, "Oh, fine, you just keep talking to the *fat girl,* then!" Which meant the business contact spent the next five minutes sputtering about how that guy was crazy and I shouldn't think anything of it, while my face flamed and I stammered, "It's . . . okay, really, it's . . . please . . . it's *fine.*" So much for the awesome professional image I was hoping to project.

I may not be as big as some of my friends and family members, and I may not be the size most people mentally associate with the word *obese,* but I am bloody well fat, and I have been most of the time since college. The homeless man might have been crazy, but he wasn't wrong. The friends who kept insisting "You're not fat!" were the ones out of touch with the truth.

But then the truth was never really the point. Thin women don't tell their fat friends "You're not fat" because they're confused about the dictionary definition of the word, or their eyes are broken, or they were raised on planets where size twenty-four is the average for women. They don't say it because it's the *truth*. They say it because *fat* does not mean just *fat* in this culture. It can also mean any or all of the following:

- Ugly
- Unhealthy
- Smelly
- Lazy
- Ignorant
- Undisciplined
- Unlovable
- Burdensome
- Embarrassing
- Unfashionable
- Mean
- Angry
- Socially inept
- Just plain icky

So when they say "You're not fat," what they really mean is "You're not a dozen nasty things I associate with the word *fat*." The size of your body is not what's in question; a tape measure or a mirror could solve that dispute. What's in question is your goodness, your lovability, your intelligence, your kindness, your attractiveness. And your friends, not surprisingly, are inclined to believe you get high marks in all those categories. Ergo, you couldn't possibly be *fat*.

But I am. I am cute and healthy and pleasant-smelling (usually) and ambitious and smart and lovable and fun and stylish and friendly and outgoing and categorically *not* icky. And I am fat—just like I'm also short, also American, also blond (with a little chemical assistance). It is just one fucking word that describes me, out of hundreds that could. Those three little letters do not actually cancel out all of my good qualities.

That's what I told my old friend about a year ago, when I finally mustered the nerve to ask her to quit telling me I'm not fat, on the grounds that we both know it's a crock. And like I said, she's stopped. But thin friends aren't the only ones who insist that I *really do* magically appear skinny everywhere except in doctors' offices, on the street with strangers, on airplanes, in dressing rooms, and in my own mirror. Since my blog about body image and fat politics has developed a strong readership and I've become more visible in the fat-acceptance community, I'm getting it from the other side now, too: According to some people bigger than me, I'm not fat enough.

What do you know about size-based discrimination? You're not fat!

What do you know about how hard it is to find clothes that fit? You're not fat!

What do you know about trying to find a partner in a culture where fat is almost universally considered unattractive? You're not fat!

One more time for those who missed it: Yeah, actually, **I am fat.** Granted, I am not fat enough to have suffered truly vicious discrimination from medical professionals, employers, or landlords. I'm not fat enough to have been asked to buy two seats on a plane; I've never had fast-food containers chucked at my head while I was out for a walk; and I don't have any trouble getting around or taking care of myself. I am incredibly grateful for all of that and conscious of my relative privilege, but it still doesn't make me *not fat.* It only makes me less fat than some, just as I'm fatter than others. It makes me kinda small for a fat person. If I were thinner than the average American woman, I might call myself kinda big for a thin person instead. But I'm not. I am, as it turns out, **fat.**

It's okay to say it out loud. It's also okay to point out that I'm not *that* fat, so I've never personally been the victim of the worst fat hatred our culture has to offer—that's the plain truth. But telling me I'm *not fat* is a goddamned lie.

In response to a similar ornery outburst on my part, I once had a commenter on my blog say, "I've never seen anyone work so hard to convince people that she *is* fat." I'm honestly not sure if that was meant as an insult or an amused observation; either way, it cracked me up. But in all seriousness, let me tell you why I'm so bulldoggy about hanging on to that word and refusing to let go.

Because I *have* taken shit for my size—the kind of shit my thin friends rarely observe and can't quite imagine—and that's an ineradicable part of my history. Telling me I'm not fat doesn't make those wounds disappear.

Because *fat* should mean only *having more adipose tissue than the average person,* but it doesn't. And every time you ignore what's in front of your face to tell me I'm not fat because you can't bring yourself to put me in that nasty, ugly category, you're buying in to the idea that *real* fat people are all sorts of nasty, ugly things I'm not. Horseshit. I *am* a real fat person, and very few real fat people live up to the worst stereotypes wielded against us.

Because whenever you read an article about THE OBESITY EPIDEMIC BOOGA BOOGA BOOGA, you should know that they're talking mostly about people who look like me—and like your mom, your neighbor, your coworker, your kid's teacher, not like the headless, poorly dressed, extremely fat people inevitably used to illustrate those articles (who are no less deserving of human rights and dignity than any of the rest of us, I hasten to add). Only about 6 percent of the adult population is categorized as severely obese. The vast majority of people classified as obese are about as fat as I am, in the BMI thirty-to-thirty-five range. I *am* the face of the obesity crisis everyone's so worried about, and yet I constantly have people telling me I'm *not fat.* There's some, uh, food for thought.

But mostly, I want to be called fat because it's the simple truth. I am not overweight, which suggests there's some objectively ideal weight for me that's less than I weigh now, when I exercise regularly and eat as much food as my body needs. That makes no sense at all. I'm definitely not thin, which is what everyone seems to be implying when they tell me I'm not fat; I take up space, I'm curvy as a mountain road, and I've spent more money at Lane Bryant in the last six months than the people who sew their clothes probably make in a year. And although I know some people prefer euphemisms like *big beautiful woman* or *person of size* or *voluptuous* or *plump* or *fluffy,* I am really, really not one of those people. (I mean, seriously, *fluffy*? Are you fucking kidding me?)

I'm fat. You wouldn't think that simple fact would be so confusing. And yet.

My favorite comment ever, among the thousands I've gotten since I started blogging, is from a woman who wrote:

> Back when I first saw pictures of you, in your personal history entry, I felt so cheated and disappointed. "So that's her? The poster child of fat bloggers? Just another thin girl with body dysmorphia? Big deal for HER to accept her body." I could just barely restrain myself from writing a righteously enraged comment about that. [Recently], I finally found the courage to step on a scale after several years. I was so scared, sweating and shivering like it was a bloody bungee jump. **And I found that I'm almost exactly your size.** That makes my initial feelings wrong on so many levels, I don't even want to start on it.

Emphasis mine.

That right there might be the number one reason why I stubbornly claim the word *fat* for myself. Because too many women
look at me and think, *She can't be fat—she looks fine,* then look at
themselves and think, *I'm so fat—I can't possibly look (or be) fine.*
Even ones who are built *exactly like me.* As long as the horseshit
stereotypes persist—that fat women can never be healthy,
smart, driven, disciplined, fashionable, attractive, and eminently
lovable—women who are all those things *and* fat will keep seeing themselves as fundamentally disgusting and unworthy. So
every time someone tries to tell me I'm not fat simply because I
don't fit those stereotypes, I'm gonna keep telling them I *am, too,*
fat, dammit! *Le fat, c'est moi.* This is what fat looks like.

I am a kindhearted, intelligent, attractive, person, *and I am fat.*
There is no paradox there.

MY BINGE YEAR
Jane E. Brody

My distorted relationship with food began early, probably earlier than I can remember. My earliest memories date back to age three, when I was a wisp of a girl weighing a mere twenty-five pounds. (Point of reference: My youngest grandson weighed thirty-four pounds at age two.)

I remember my parents coaxing me to eat with games like Open Sesame and threats (at least that's how I perceived them) like "Eat! The children in Poland are starving." It didn't take me long to think of an appropriate reply: "So send them my food!"

Through such wheedling and cajoling I learned to associate food and eating with love and acceptance. If I ate, my parents rejoiced, and to make sure I would eat they catered to my every culinary whim. While the rest of the family supped on shoulder lamb chops or beef liver (cheap), I got baby lamb chops or calf liver (expensive). The peas had to be Libby's—if they were Del Monte I could tell and wouldn't eat them.

I stayed thin enough for breezes to pass through me until puberty, when hormones kicked in that seemed to stimulate my appetite and interest in all kinds of food, including pizza. By the time I graduated from high school, I was what one might kindly call zaftig—not fat, but not slender, either.

College dining rooms in my time were a far cry from the eating plans students have now. We were served our meals, and dinner was presented family-style—big bowls of all kinds of food sitting on the table for everyone present to share. That's when those starving children in Poland reared their ugly heads. I couldn't stand to see the food wasted, so when everyone else at the table had had their fill, I ate what was left in the serving bowls.

I also kept a stash of Oreos and other goodies to nosh on in my dorm room while I studied. Needless to say, this soon added up to the freshman ten, which I determinedly shed the summer between my freshman and sophomore years by eating lots of fresh fruits and vegetables—I worked that summer at an agricultural experiment station where a quart of luscious strawberries cost a dollar and corn could be cooked and eaten sans butter within a few hours of being picked.

All was normal for the next three years. I stayed at a comfortable 102 pounds, just right for my five-foot frame.

Then I moved from my beloved New York State to the Midwest for graduate school. My boyfriend moved to the West Coast for his graduate work, and our romance took a turn for the worse. I never felt like I belonged in Wisconsin, and my feelings of displacement, combined with my dissipating love life, took its toll. Little by little, I turned to food for solace. After all, to me it meant love and acceptance. When I began to gain weight, I went on a diet and lost it, only to regain what I lost when I went off the diet. Still, I wasn't what anyone would call fat when I took a job at the *Minneapolis Tribune,* then one of the nation's top newspapers.

Although Minneapolis provided me with more of a sense of belonging and a number of friends who remain dear to me to this day, it wasn't long before several problems turned my head to food. My job soon became tedious and not at all what I'd been promised when hired. My boss was a misogynist who did everything possible to thwart my success. My love life was in complete disarray.

Food was about the only thing I could count on for pleasure. And not just any food. Candy bars, ice cream, cookies, crackers, chips, cereal. Note the carbohydrate content and overall lack of nutrients. I also learned how to drink, in those days almost a necessity if you wanted to be part of the newspaper crowd. (Fortunately, I never got hooked on their smoking habits. Alcohol was bad enough.) I began to gain weight despite daily physical activity. Naturally, I tried nearly every diet that had been invented, including the Drinking Man's Diet (which at least allowed me to continue to socialize with my newspaper colleagues). And naturally, I would soon abandon each diet and regain what I'd lost and then some.

Eventually I discovered that once I started eating, I couldn't stop. So I decided not to eat during the day. I waited until I got off work (usually ten P.M. or later), and then the gorging began. I soon learned where all the all-night mom-and-pop shops were located and raided them on my way home for that night's consumption.

The pattern of my nightly binges went from sweet to salt and then back to sweet—a half-gallon of ice cream was only the beginning—until sleep overcame me. I often awoke in the morning with partially chewed food still in my mouth. And since I'd never heard of purging (not that I was likely to go that route, since I'd long considered throwing up one of life's most unpleasant events), my binges simply added pounds to my little frame until I weighed a third more than I did in college. When I reached size fourteen, I stopped buying clothes off the rack and began making my own so I wouldn't have to face the size.

As you might expect, I became more and more unhappy with my life. One night, after a particularly destructive binge, I became desperate. I was no longer in control of my food, it was controlling me, and I felt I could not go on living that way. I contemplated ending my life as the only way out of my entrapment by food. But I was still rational enough to reach out for help. At my lowest point in the middle of the night, I called a psychologist I knew at his home, and his offer to see me first thing in the morning got me through the rest of the night.

He reassured me that I was not the only one in the world with a binge-eating problem, and that was enough to keep me alive, barely. But he couldn't help me control my binges. That remained for me to do on my own, since no one at the time had treated such an eating disorder or even had a name for it.

I made a decision: If I was going to be fat, at least I could be healthy. At least I could eat foods that were good for my body. I stripped my apartment of the junk I consumed during binges and filled the refrigerator with fruit, vegetables, meat, poultry, eggs, cheese, bacon, and began eating three hearty meals a day, with a midafternoon snack of a small treat—two cookies, a sliver of cake or pie, two tablespoons of ice cream—so I wouldn't develop uncontrollable cravings for such no-nos.

Much to my amazement, in a month's time, I had lost seven pounds. I continued eating this way and continued losing weight gradually—two pounds a month. As I lost weight, my stomach shrank, and little by little, I ate less and less at meals. Little by little, I lost weight, until after two years, I was back to what I had weighed in college. And I have stayed that way, give or take a few pounds here and there, ever since—by eating! And by exercising, every day, no excuses.

As it turns out, the route I chose to cure myself is how the experts now treat people with binge-eating disorder. They call it cognitive-behavioral therapy, and it starts with insisting that patients eat three meals a day, with snacks, so that they go no longer than four hours without eating. This reduces the famished state, followed by uncontrolled eating, that commonly occurs when meals are skipped. Therapists also work to correct twisted or downright mistaken ideas patients have about food and eating.

About half of the patients are able to stop binging with this therapeutic approach. But—and this is an important *but*—they don't always lose weight as a result. So Dr. Thomas Wadden of the University of Pennsylvania has added another dimension to the therapy. He calculates how many calories patients need to maintain their current weight and devises an eating plan that contains about five hundred fewer calories per day and includes foods the patients enjoy, so cravings that can result in uncontrolled eating are less likely to occur.

In essence, this is what I did on my own to get my life and eating patterns back on a more normal track. And it's how I eat to this day, some forty years later. There are no fewer than eight half-gallons of ice cream in my freezer. They're all creamy, slow-churned, light ice cream, and none provides more than 150 calories per serving. A serving of ice cream—in case you don't know—is half a cup. That's how much I eat on any given day. I know because I dish it up in a half-cup container. I also have lots of chocolate and chocolate-covered nuts and pretzels around. Again, I allow myself one or two pieces, and that seems to satisfy my sweet tooth enough to keep me from gorging on the whole package.

My negative experiences with food and eating taught me some important lessons, which I applied when I raised my sons and am applying now when I take care of my grandsons. I did not, and do not, insist that the children eat any particular food or any particular amount. When they say they're full, the meal is over. And if they're full, we wait a while before offering a dessert—perhaps two cookies or a small dish of ice cream, often with fruit.

Children have to learn to eat in response to their own hunger signals and to stop eating in response to their own satiety signals. No parent or caretaker can know when those signals kick in. There should be no wheedling and cajoling, no bribing with dessert or anything else. If good food is available and children are hungry, they will eat it. When they are full, they will stop eating. End of story.

DAY ONE
Wendy McClure

Not too long ago I had a dream about myself. It was about my job, actually—I edit children's books for a living, and in the dream, I was flipping through the freshly printed pages of a book I had worked on. It was a project I'd recently completed in real life: a rhyming picture book called *Girl, You're Amazing!*, a spirited ode to all the wonderful things young girls can do—run fast, paint pictures, do quadratic equations. Encouraging stuff like that. And in my dream, while I thumbed through the pages, I came across the word *diet* in one of the verses. What the hell is that doing there? I thought. That word wasn't in the manuscript for *Girl, You're Amazing!*; it wasn't supposed to be there at all. I'd missed typos before (and dreamed about it), but this was much, much worse.

I hoped nobody would complain. Maybe readers would over-look it. But a few pages later, I saw the word *diet* again, in an-other verse: *You eat your diet food, oh yeah!* I had the worst sinking feeling. I knew people were going to hate the book: parents and teachers and librarians and critics and my bosses. There would be furious letters. Everyone would be outraged; how could I have overlooked the appalling fact that the word *diet* was in a *book for little girls*? The author of *Girl, You're Amazing!* wasn't re-sponsible—no, it was all my fault; in the dream, I knew that much for sure. Somehow the word *diet* had crept into the book on its own, and I'd failed to see it because I am a twisted, dread-ful person. I mean, I might as well have put the word in, since I was just as guilty for not deleting it. *I am so dead,* I thought. *I'm screwed.*

Then I woke up and remembered that in real life, the book does not have the word *diet* in it anywhere. Little girls will read it and nothing bad will happen. They'll be *fine.*

But I have to wonder about myself sometimes, about the way that word is apparently so profoundly stuck in my head that it surfaces and curdles my dreams. Then again, I went on my first diet in fifth grade. No shit. It lasted almost the whole day.

I was home sick from school by myself, though I don't remem-ber if I was actually sick to begin with. The symptoms, real or imagined, were minimal and vague. It could have been a slight fever, or it could have been boredom. But I also know that I woke up with the thought that I should *do* something, some kind of diet thing. At any rate, my mom called the school that morning and told them I wouldn't be in. Then I listened for her to leave for work (my dad had already gone to his office) so I could be alone.

Whether or not I was actually fat at the time almost doesn't matter. The one thing I knew for sure, and I knew it intimately, was that my mother was fat. At first I understood this the way any kid understands motherness: from picture books about animal babies and visits to the children's zoo, I'd managed to grasp that *mama* was, in a sense, *the big me*. It was simple enough—I was the calf, and she was the cow. For example, I mean, because I never thought of her as a cow in any other sense of the word, though in time I would worry that other people did. Certainly, on that day in fifth grade, I would have been old enough to worry.

My mother did plenty of worrying on her own, and plenty of work. I knew, because the books were in our house, that she did Weight Watchers and Atkins and Sugar Busters. Or that she was planning on doing them or had done them at one time. It was hard to tell. Once, for several months, there'd been a typed copy of the Scarsdale daily menu displayed on our refrigerator door, but otherwise I was never quite sure when she was dieting: she always was and she always wasn't. Was, because the kitchen cabinets had boxes of Figurines and packets of D-Zerta pudding and Alba shakes. Wasn't, because she was never not fat. Though these two things were at odds with each other, they seemed equally true. I began that first day with two competing truths as well: I wasn't really fat. And yet somehow that wasn't good enough, and I'd better diet anyway.

I know that Day One was a day in late January, when the second half of the school year had started but things were still formless and distracted and strange. It got dark early. The walk to school was a series of narrow paths where the sidewalk had been barely shoveled (there were bad blizzards that winter), and I trundled along in my puffy coat. It was the time of year when I felt like I had to move faster, try to overtake the shuffling slowness, the mess of noise and clothes and impulses that crowded me. I wanted, I think, a clear space to fill slowly and methodically with my good intentions. The empty house on a weekday morning seemed a good place to start.

I'd heard my mom leave for work—I'd listened for the sound of the heavy foyer door closing and then, more faintly, the slam of the porch door leading outside. I padded down the hall in my nightgown and slippers to watch her car pull out of the driveway, and I went to my room and put on pink sweatpants and a T-shirt. And then I decided to begin.

As far as I could tell, I had everything I needed. I had my mother's diet books—the supermarket paperbacks with warped covers, a few of them bookmarked with index cards on which my mom had jotted numbers (calories? carbohydrate grams?) or notes: ½ grapefruit. 1 slice toast w/lite bread. The books had lots of good ideas. I also had a collection of magazines: Between my mom's Woman's Day and my Young Miss subscriptions, there were plenty of recipes and exercises and tips, particularly in the January issues. Even my mom's Avon book—a big glossy-covered thing called Looking Good, Feeling Beautiful—had a section on calisthenics, where a model in a striped leotard solemnly demonstrated poses.

There was iceberg lettuce in the refrigerator and an exercise bicycle upstairs in the spare room. There was the entire day ahead of me. And there was still time—it was under a month into the second half of the school year. The magazines were full of New Year's resolution chatter, which buoyed me; it helped to know that everyone wanted to do this diet thing. All the women in the magazines and my mom and all the girls in my class—maybe they were like me, hoping for our ideal lives to stick.

But first things first: I needed a plan. I had to figure out what to do and what to eat. One of the principles of dieting, as I understood it at the time, was that food was sort of a mistake. Like once you got past the part where you needed it to stay alive and stuff, everything beyond that had the potential to screw you up. I saw it on television sitcoms all the time: People on diets ate cakes and then acted like it was a horrible accident. I mean, it *was* an accident; I wanted to believe it even as I knew, deep down, that if *I* ate the cake, it would be all my fault. Which was all the more reason to be careful and eat only the right food.

What *was* the right food, anyway? I had only the vaguest sense of nutrition. Most of what I knew came from well-meaning Saturday-morning cartoons that ran between the commercials and the real cartoons; from those I learned only that fruits and vegetables were "good," in much the same way that geometry was good, or the Constitution, whatever the fuck that was. I didn't think much of this kind of goodness—*goody*-goodness, really, with smiley-faced apples and dancing broccoli and things full of vitamins. No, I wanted the real stuff, the diet food, which, as far as I could tell, was specially fortified with dietetic intent. Things like my mother's Figurine bars and carrot sticks, and the scoop of cottage cheese I'd seen my grandmother order in a restaurant once when she said she was "reducing." Diet food included any food item legitimized in a diet book or a "low-cal" magazine recipe. Canned pears, sugar-free jam, melba toast—it's not like I thought these things were magic, but I was sure it would help if I ate them. I didn't yet understand that the rest of the time, I'd be hungry. If I was really doing it right, that is.

That first day, for lunch, I made a "simple, healthy pasta

salad," attempting to follow a recipe suggestion in *Woman's Day*. I tossed some vinaigrette salad dressing with a cup of chilled pasta, a bit of diced bell pepper, and olives. There was a Tupperware container of uncooked spaghetti in the cupboard, but how could I measure a cup? I opened a box of Kraft macaroni and cheese instead and poured out a cup of the dry macaroni. I cooked it dutifully—suddenly a cup was a lot—and stuck the steaming colander of it in the freezer while I searched the fridge and cupboards for the other ingredients. I made do with some Wish-Bone Italian dressing and a jar of green olive slices.

I tried the exercises in the Avon book. I made a point of skipping the sit-ups and any other move that I recognized from gym class. (I hated gym, and moreover, gym class wasn't dieting.) Instead, I did leg lifts, side bends, anything that looked sort of graceful.

I checked the clock. More than once.

I ate some of the pasta salad in front of the TV and picked out all the olives. Did it matter that I didn't eat them? After all, I didn't even *like* olives.

I rode the exercise bicycle in the spare room. I'd ridden it before—ever since my parents had bought it, my older brother and I had delighted in riding it as hard as we could until the whole thing rattled, and then letting the pedals spin free. But now I rode it conscientiously and watched the needle on the speedometer dance in wobbly arcs. I pedaled until the odometer nudged a crooked new digit into place, then another and another. I rode five miles, or five imaginary miles, really. I tried to feel the distance as if it existed somewhere within me.

I looked through the books and magazine articles again to see what more could be done. I would have to try *a daily brisk walk* another day; same thing with *order an appetizer instead of an entrée*. Everything else seemed to require something—ankle weights, or skim yogurt, or three mornings a week, or grape-fruit, or positive thinking. My improved life and the clear space I imagined for it began to feel different; there were cold spots, like in a haunted room.

I thought about dinner. I wondered what my mom would make and whether it would have anything that could be con-strued as diet food, anything that could "count." There was still half a plateful of oily macaroni in the fridge, but I didn't want it anymore. (I was mildly proud of this.)

I waited for my parents to come home. I turned on the TV in the family room and lost myself in plots about other people. On one show, there was a scene set in a hospital cafeteria where two women talked over trays crowded with plates of different sizes, holding bowls and sandwiches and small blocks of cake. I knew their conversation was the most important part of the scene, but I stared at their hands; I watched the women chew, amazed that they could carry on with their acting and practically ignore the food.

When my mother came home, she asked me how I was feel-ing.

I told her I was better, since in more ways than one, it was true. And I was relieved she was home.

She walked through the kitchen in her office clothes and her stockinged feet. She looked around; no doubt she could tell I'd been up to more than usual. She saw the colander. "Did you cook something for lunch?" she asked. "Macaroni and cheese?"

"I made a salad," I told her. "Pasta salad." I realized how strange it sounded. I'd never shown any interest in salads, not even the pasta kind. I might as well have said I'd whipped up a soufflé.

She raised her eyebrows; she seemed a little impressed. "What made you decide to do that?" she asked.

"Oh, I don't know," I said.

But she knew. "What else did you do today?" she asked.

Watched TV, I told her. Also did some homework and rode the exercise bicycle a little. "It was fun," I added after a moment.

"That's good," she said. "Just, you know, don't overdo it."

I told her I wouldn't.

All the same, it was confusing, that word *overdo,* because from what I could tell, dieting *was* overdoing—that was the nature of the thing. Everything you did, you did differently; every move was laden with deliberateness. You put one leg in front of the other to stretch; you put the fork to the food to the mouth. I hadn't thought ahead enough to consider what would happen after that, after the first day, and the second, and so on. Either you'd wear yourself back down into the ordinary, I thought, or else every purposeful move would be laid end to end to create a distance, and then you'd get away from yourself.

It's likely that my mom also meant *don't go too far.*

There were plenty of Day Ones after that over the years. Every now and then I'd make my way through the first week, and the second, and the third; at some point I'd feel the diet thing take hold.

I don't know what else to call it besides, well, *diet thing.* That sounds like a bad translation; in a way, I guess it is. The diet thing had its own secret frequency, and sometimes, after days and weeks of trial and error and vigilance and fine-tuning, I'd come across it at last; I'd tune in, find the clear in the static.

I found it the following summer when I'd allow myself only

half a container of cherry yogurt at a time. I rode my bike in circles around the block every morning as soon as school let out. I
did it all through June; the sun came up earlier every week, and
I felt I was making progress.

I found it again in my twenties when I first joined Weight
Watchers. The meetings I attended were in a converted office
suite, and I'd go to weigh in at lunchtime. Some days when I'd
walk back out to my car I could feel it—not a bad feeling, or
even really a feeling at all. It was more like a ticking—it was measured and purposeful, and I'd started to sense it in the background of all my Weight Watching thoughts. I associated it with
being On the Program, though occasionally, the feeling rubbed
off on other things, so that I felt it while driving or in the warm
and complicated dimness of the bars I went to on the weekends.
The *on and on and on* was supposed to be a good thing, and I
could keep it going for several weeks at a time.

Inevitably, though, I'd lose it. It might happen with a wrong
meal, or some other instance when I'd forget to be good—
though usually I didn't forget so much as I let myself be someone else, someone besides the girl I'd been trying to be. But
anything could disrupt the diet thing. There were also times
when it would flicker out all by itself, leaving me estranged and
feeling a disconcerting kind of hunger, where I knew I'd have to
eat too much in order to feel like myself.

As for my weight, it usually lurched back and forth a few
pounds either way. Once, I managed to sustain the diet thing
long enough to lose forty pounds in a year, but it seemed like a
clumsy kind of magic that I knew I'd never master.

The diet details, though, are a different story; they stick with
me. Breakfast for one diet was melba toast and a scrambled egg
made with one teaspoon of margarine. For another it was can-

taloupe (for once I didn't have to count how many slices).
Breakfast: half a container of yogurt. Breakfast: a Figurines bar
I swiped from a box my mom bought. Breakfast was always the
most superstitious meal of the day, especially when it was nothing.

I think I've stopped trying now; I've stopped listening for the
diet thing. I couldn't change my body, and yet it felt like my life
had become much smaller inside it, tiny and adrift and floating
too far away. I decided to come back.

When I remember the Day Ones and all the subsequent days,
it's hard not to think of them as only half formed, as if somehow
they didn't end with nights and sleep. But I know on that first
day I had dinner (it must have been an ordinary dinner, since I
have no memory of it); I must have gotten ready to go back to
school the next day; my life had started to return to its usual
shape, whatever it was. More than anything, I wish I could go
back and see how I was, and witness all the indifferent and
amazing things I did with my other days.

QUACKS
Kathi Kamen Goldmark

The Health Nook was the only health food store in our town, and it smelled funny. No gleaming aisles of fresh organic produce or free-range poultry for us—no sir. There wasn't any such thing as Whole Foods or Trader Joe's. It was the suburbs in mid-twentieth-century America, and the concept of health food had not yet caught on in popular culture—was in fact seen as vaguely subversive, perhaps even Communist. Back then "Better Living Through Chemistry," defined by a growing array of convenience foods, was the national model.

The primary aroma inside the Health Nook was pungent and yeasty, from the brewer's yeast powder sold in both bulk and tablet form, with light undertones of blackstrap molasses and sour milk. I called the owner Nurse Lady because she always wore a lumpy white uniform to dole out scoops of brown rice and millet from large wooden barrels. The walls were lined with shelves containing jars of powders, potions, and pills, as well as a few dusty books by people with names like Gypsy Boots and Adele Davis, writers my mother revered even though I once heard our trusted family physician dismiss them as "quacks." I pictured little ducks with tiny stethoscopes, quacking away.

My mother was stylish and energetic, with color-coordinated outfits and curly dark hair molded into a sensible do during weekly visits to the beauty parlor. She didn't *look* any different from the other mothers, but somewhere along the line, she'd developed a passionate interest in healthy eating. So while everyone else's mommy was shopping at the Grand Union supermarket, mine became (it always seemed) the Health Nook's one and only customer. Evidence supported this impression: There was never anyone else in the place, and we shopped there a lot. Every so often, if I'd been quiet and patient while the grown-ups held forth on the relative benefits of various vitamin brands, Nurse Lady would give me a "treat," a carob-based concoction that tasted pretty much like chalk with a hint of dirty gym sock. I learned to wait until we were leaving to pop the confection in my mouth, so I could tactfully spit it out on the curb.

At home we had unpasteurized, nonhomogenized whole milk, cream floating at the top, delivered to our door. Our meat came from an organic farm in Amish country, the few canned goods we consumed from Walnut Acres, a health food mail-order service. No processed flour or white bread, no sugared cereal or chocolate was allowed inside our house. And I had no idea how bizarre this all was until I hit first grade and saw how everyone else lived.

It turned out that my friends and their families lounged in their dens watching *The Honeymooners* and *I Love Lucy* and eating TV dinners in little compartmentalized trays, while we sat around the dining room table reading from *A Child's Garden of Verses* and consuming fresh whole food. My classmates' pantries were stocked with six-packs of soda, bags of candy and potato chips. Ours contained nuts in the shell, sunflower seeds, and those horrid carob things. Breakfast for others might include sugary cereals; we were allowed nothing more hedonistic than Cheerios, washed down by a blended drink that included mysterious powders, fresh-squeezed juice, and (I always suspected) a raw egg. Worst of all, robust health was an absolute household requirement, preventing everyone in my family from the sweet luxury of ever getting to stay home with a sore throat or a cold.

So despite glowing complexions and thick glossy hair, perfect school attendance, strong teeth, and boundless energy, my brothers and I felt weird and different. Other kids enjoyed school lunches consisting of peanut butter and jelly on Wonder Bread and a bag of chips; we had carrot sticks and sesame-tofu surprise on dark, coarse rye. When other kids took their slices of Wonder Bread and magically compressed them into lethal little balls to throw across the room, we were defenseless. We were food geeks.

It was those bread balls that made me feel the most left out, when I saw Alan Altman take a large, soft piece of baked white dough and squish it into a pellet no larger than his thumb, then sling it across the cafeteria at Alexander Katz—who reciprocated in kind. Wonder Balls existed in a magic land to which I was denied access, an alternate universe where you could eat endless sweets, like in my favorite song, "Big Rock Candy Mountain." I felt painfully deprived, stuck on Carob Island with the health-nut weirdos.

—

The day a huge moving truck pulled up across the street, everyone expected another typical suburban family: two regular-looking parents and a couple of kids. Instead, we got the Jamesons. There was a blue-eyed, redheaded girl my age named Janie who was a full head taller than I was, even though our birthdays were merely weeks apart. There was Sparky the poodle, clipped and poufed within an inch of her life. There was Aunt Eleanor, a petite woman with auburn hair worn in a fancy upsweep, who came out by train on the weekends. But there was no dad in evidence. Janie's mom, a tall, leggy blonde, was the first divorced working mother in our neighborhood and had once been a Radio City Music Hall Rockette. No one could imagine anything more glamorous, and as a result, Mrs. Jameson had a tough row to hoe in terms of being accepted by the other moms. Because Janie's mother went to work every day and her father didn't live at home, Janie felt even more different than I did. It didn't take long for us to become friends.

Janie often came over after school to play until her mother got home from work. If Mrs. Jameson was running late, Janie would stay for dinner, and I noticed that she pushed our strange food around on her plate and never ate much. She was a polite girl and always remembered to thank my parents afterward, but I knew she wished more than anything that her mother would get home in time to eat with her. After Mrs. Jameson finally arrived in her usual fashionable flurry, always "dressed to the nines" (as my mother liked to say) to whisk Janie away, I'd try to draw her outfit from memory with my crayons. She was exotic and fascinating and had a way of talking to us kids as though we were her girlfriends, instead of using that condescending tone most adults thought appropriate when speaking to children.

When Mrs. Jameson asked my parents if she could reciprocate our family's hospitality by taking me and my brothers on an excursion to a nearby park to feed the ducks, I couldn't wait for the special day to arrive. The next Saturday morning, my brothers and I joined a small group of other kids in the Jamesons' front yard, where Janie's mom made a big deal out of counting our noses. There were eight or nine of us, ranging in age from toddler to six or seven. It seemed every kid on the block who could walk had been invited. We lined up two by two and followed the divine Mrs. Jameson and Aunt Eleanor down our street, across the main road, and over a winding path through the park to the duck pond.

As we drew nearer to the pond, I heard splashing and quacking. Then we turned a corner and there they were—dozens of ducks swimming around, waddling up on the shore, mama ducks leading lines of little baby ducklings in and out of the water, daddy ducks preening, stretching their long green necks and pointing their beaks toward the sun. Janie's mom opened her large straw pocketbook and handed each child a paper bag with a cheerful "Here's your duck food, kids, come get your duck food!" Children started running toward the water's edge, shouting and throwing crumbs at the ducks, who seemed a little confused about whether they were being attacked or fed, but eventually decided to hang around and gobble the offered crumbs.

I stayed back, slowly opening my bag to see what was inside. When I saw what Mrs. Jameson was passing off as duck food, a wave of yearning came over me, a mixture of feelings and physical longing I would later know as lust. There was *no way* I was feeding this bounty to any old duck. Inside my paper bag was a treasure more precious than gold, the coin of the realm—white bread!

As discreetly as possible, I motioned to my brothers to follow me. They were younger, one in kindergarten and one in pre-school, and as a big first-grader, I still had bossing-around priv-ileges. I led them behind one of the bushes growing near the pond, out of sight of the group. "Look!" I squealed. "Look in-side your bags. She gave us white bread."

"I think we're supposed to give it to the ducks," five-year-old Paul said earnestly. He was always one to take the rules literally.

"What's dat?" Three-year-old Michael held up his bread, pointing to the kind of green stain that I would—much later in life—learn to identify as mold.

"I think it's jelly or something," I said with authority. "Come on, let's see what it tastes like."

"It smells funny," Paul offered.

"I think it's just what white bread smells like," I answered. "What are you, a scaredy-cat?"

Not wanting to be thought of as a scaredy-cat, even by his an-noying sister, he took a big bite. "Hmm, not bad," he allowed.

The three of us sat behind our bush, solemnly munching our bits of moldy bread. I would like to be able to say it tasted hor-rible, but compared to the Nurse Lady's carob treats, it wasn't all that bad. Add the excitement of subterfuge and the sweetness of forbidden fruit, and those hard old slices even tasted a little bit delicious, though not as puffy and soft as I'd expected.

Sitting in our circle behind the bushes, chomping away, we were startled by a piercing shriek.

"Oh my God! You poor children!" It was Mrs. Jameson, who had apparently discovered that her nose count was off by three and come looking for us. "I don't believe this," she shouted. "Oh, Eleanor, and in our neighborhood . . . who would think?"

Had we done something horrible? Did anyone really care if a
few crumbs of bread were diverted from their intended ducks?
I trembled, thinking I was in really bad trouble. After all, I'd
stolen bread meant to feed others. Not only that, I had coerced
my brothers into joining me—I was a ringleader! There was no
doubt about it. I had to protect them and take the fall. I stood
tall on shaky legs.

"It's all my fault, ma'am," I stammered. "Really, I made them
do it."

"Oh, sweetheart," she said softly. "It's not about being anyone's fault." Turning to Aunt Eleanor, she continued, "They
seem like such nice people. I had no idea this was happening in
front of our very noses. I should have seen the signs—Janie is
always ravenous when she gets home from their house. Come
on, kids, we're going back to my place. I'm going to fix you a real
meal."

The Jamesons' kitchen was a wonderland of all the newest,
trendiest convenience foods. I had never seen anything quite
like it, but then this was the first time I'd been in the kitchen of
a single working mother.

Mrs. Jameson settled us on the sofa in front of the TV, and as
we watched Tom and Jerry pound each other with mallets, she
whipped up a feast of macaroni and cheese, instant mashed
potatoes, frozen peas and carrots, and lime Jell-O topped with
Reddi-wip for dessert. My brothers and I ate ourselves silly. The
whole time, Mrs. Jameson talked quietly with Aunt Eleanor. I
heard only bits and pieces, but the gist was that something had
to be done to help starving children in our own backyard without hurting anyone's pride. An hour later, the three of us rolled
ourselves across the street and home, my brothers nodding
solemnly when I said that it was probably best if none of this
was ever mentioned to our parents.

I'll never know if the night of vomiting that followed was caused by gorging on moldy bread or feasting on my first meal of processed convenience food, impure chemicals coursing through my perfectly antioxidized cells for the very first time. My mother held my head in her hands as I threw up over and over again, clucking with sympathy while vowing to redouble her efforts at providing her family with perfect nutrition. She was sorry, but those carob treats were just going to have to go. In the weeks that followed, Janie's mother redoubled *her* efforts, too, and began picking Janie up in time for dinner. Janie was thrilled, and so was I, as I was often invited to join them, then urged to take the leftovers home.

My parents were mystified when sacks of food—mostly canned goods and powdered milk—began appearing at our back door. These peculiar gifts had no notes attached, and the intriguing items disappeared almost immediately after being discovered, never making it as far as our dinner table. I had a pretty good idea where the stuff was coming from, but I didn't see the point of tattling on a former Rockette, especially if I wasn't allowed access to the creamed corn and franks 'n' beans pictured on the cans' festive labels.

As it happened, Janie's mom got a new job and moved her little family away from our neighborhood before her charitable gestures had a chance to be discovered, so my parents never learned that their children were pathetic and starving. As the years went by, our neighborhood changed in other ways, too. The Health Nook and Nurse Lady got makeovers at about the same time: The store got a new floor and a paint job; hers was a nose job and a face-lift. That lumpy white uniform bit the dust, too, replaced by colorful dashikis and big dangling earrings. The bins of wheat germ and millet were replaced by an organic produce section and a deep freeze containing locally made fruit pies and strawberry sorbet. The store got busier as more people in town started looking for fresh, healthy food. My mother's reputation morphed over a decade or so from "Health-Nut Quack Weirdo" to "Woman Ahead of Her Time." She got her own radio show and wrote twenty-seven books with titillating titles like *Kamut: An Ancient Food for a Healthy Future* and *Everything I Know About Nutrition I Learned from Barley.* And as the world caught up to her, she began to relax a little—occasionally even springing for one of those pies.

We stayed in touch with the Jamesons for a while, and every Christmas they sent a parcel containing all sorts of treats: tins of sugared almonds, white-flour cookies with icing, fruitcake and plum sauce. My mother would open up the package, exclaiming over how thoughtful it was that Janie and her mom still remembered our hospitality and generosity, though they'd moved away so long ago. My brothers and I would be allowed to choose one treat each from the package; then our mother would wrinkle her nose.

"Really, this is all such garbage," she'd say. "Why don't you kids take this junkaroo down to the park and feed it to the ducks?"

"Sure," we'd reply, even though by then we were busy teenagers with way cooler activities in mind. We put on our hats and gloves and walked down our street in the direction of the duck pond. We knew exactly what to do.

BATTLE OF THE BULGE:
Notes from a Decade of Body Activism
Ophira Edut

The auditorium lights beam into my eyes as I step onstage. I try not to squint. The spots cast a halo over the crowd, dimming their figures like shadow puppets.

As my vision adjusts, I notice the seats are mostly full, and I'm relieved. My book, *Body Outlaws,* has been on the shelves for eight years, and to my surprise, it's still relevant to the college crowd. Body image is a charged topic for women who leave home for the first time, questioning everything. The collection of multicultural women's body-acceptance stories has become required curriculum at many colleges, and I visit campuses as a guest speaker.

I secure a stray blond lock behind my ear with a bobby pin

while the moderator introduces me. I've pulled my hair into a ponytail so nobody can tell how long and girlie it is. My jacket is carnation pink, so I've toughened it up with black boots. I know the audience is full of women's studies students who will analyze my lecture—and me—for their critical-thought papers. They will debate, in twelve-point Times Roman, whether a white Jewish woman can represent multicultural women, and if, at my current 145-pound weight, I really understand size discrimination.

I walk up to the podium and smile. "Hi, I'm Ophira." My tone is warm, familiar, intentionally disarming. "It's great to be here. And tonight I'm going to talk about what it *really* means to love your body."

Do I know? I still wonder silently.

I'm here to speak about women overturning the beauty standard and loving their bodies. Yet my clothes, my makeup, and my own body are under scrutiny, by the guests and by me. My outfit is as carefully chosen as my words, and my credibility, to an extent, rides on my looks. *Has she bought in to the status quo? Is she a hypocrite?* My former chin-length choppy bob suggested no, marked me as a riot grrrl, even though I've never been cool enough to claim the title. Tonight my long salon-highlighted hair could suggest that I've sided with the Anistons and Lohans of the world. (It will, however, endear me to the sorority members who cosponsored my visit.)

With nonthreatening hair/edgy black boots, soft eye makeup/risqué berry lips, underwired boobs/Beyoncé hips unleashed, sunless skin/my dad's Israeli nose, I pray I've achieved that fleeting balance—the third-wave feminist body image activist who's hip enough to be pop-culture stylish, yet conscious enough to be a credible face of body acceptance.

Now, I almost forgot—I have a speech to give. As I talk, I

grow animated. I wave my hands, drop slang, stride across the stage, leave my notes on the lectern and freestyle. I want to embody a woman unleashed, the union of confidence and curves. According to statistics, 90 percent of what women say is communicated through body language. My audience will listen to what I *don't* say as much as to what I do.

Later, they'll raise their hands with questions designed to find my weak spots. I love this part. With each challenging question, I thank them for having the courage to ask.

"How can you really understand this stuff? You're pretty— you're not even really fat," I've been asked.

"Positive body image is a state of mind," I tell them. "It goes so much deeper than that."

I didn't always feel this way. In 1992 you could find me most days in an XXL striped sweatshirt and leggings, paired with (horrors!) mauve Birkenstocks. I usually slapped on my ritual of liquid eyeliner, bronze shadow, and mascara, but it took all of two minutes to apply. For jewelry, I wore a Star of David necklace to display my newfound Jewish pride. I was five-one and 160 pounds, which classified me as "obese" at the University of Michigan health services clinic. Like I cared.

It was a radical shift from the year before, when I weighed 120 pounds. I was dedicated to thinness at all costs, and although I didn't have an "official" eating disorder, I kept my weight under tight control with exercise and diet. Occasionally, I'd binge on a large pizza, then walk for hours, even on dark, snowy winter nights, to work it off. For the most part, I thought I was a healthy eater, sticking to a thousand to twelve hundred calories per day and resisting temptation like a saint.

My body and food obsession had begun during my freshman year of high school. It hit me while I was making paper flowers for the homecoming parade float, where the student council members who enlisted me ignored me at the flower party. I realized that a klutzy, zaftig Jewess with braces and an after-school-snack belly was basically invisible to the popular crowd. Sure, I could toil as a schoolmate-serf to decorate their float, but I would never ride on it, at least not looking like this.

Not that I wanted to be popular, per se. I'd been in the gifted-and-talented program since fifth grade, and I took honors classes all day. I knew better. I didn't want to dumb down, I just wanted to pretty up—to stage my own "revenge of the nerds" on the popular girls. I envied and resented their Benetton sweaters that cost as much as my fall wardrobe, and their perfectly "poufed" bangs that my Conair curling iron could never imitate.

One morning my mom held up a newspaper section at breakfast. THE DEE-TROIT DIET, screamed the headline. *The Detroit News,* she explained, was sponsoring a Pritikin-style eating plan designed to cut weight over the course of several months. New menus and tips would be published every week. The diet required cutting out red meat and saturated fat and eating ten times the calories of my desired weight. It promised energy, delicious food, and a hot body. For the last item alone, I was in.

At my last checkup, the doctor had chided me for weighing 124 pounds and having high cholesterol. Maybe it was time to do something about it. I also wanted Eric, the cute varsity swimmer who smiled at me during biology, to fall in love with me. His smile suggested interest, but it was probably sympathetic, I reasoned. I could barely meet his blue eyes when he said hi to me in the hall.

But the Dee-Troit Diet was gonna change everything. For

the first few nights, I went to bed with hunger pains, my stomach filled with air and agony. To curb my appetite, I signed up for a community-center aerobics class. My twin sister and I faithfully did the one-hour cardio and tone-up routine seven days a week, wearing five-pound ankle weights filled with silicone. Unbelievably, I had the willpower of a marine. That's how disciplined a teenage girl can be when she wants to be thin and noticed.

Within a few months, I had dropped down to 113 pounds. My mother cheered, and I amazed myself by squeezing into a pair of size-zero jeans at the mall. By then my whole life was about numbers: fat grams, calories, pants sizes.

With obesity now the CNN topic du jour, I suppose my lifestyle was comparatively healthy and "heart-smart"—or it could have been, done in moderation. I certainly got more exercise and made better food choices than today's teens. But I was also an adolescent girl with body issues.

My self-esteem, assumed to be increasing as my weight decreased, was probably at an all-time low. Gone was the self-determined preteen Girl Scout who won art and writing contests, played first viola in the orchestra, and gorged on sundaes with my paper-route earnings. I was all about free weights, biker shorts, and the still-to-be-fulfilled hope of a popular boyfriend.

By then, Eric was dating Patti, a cheerleader from the wrong side of the tracks. Looking back, I think he probably could have liked the pre-Pritikin me if I had actually liked myself.

I met Darrell at the student union cafeteria early in my sophomore year. He claimed to be a premed student living in a dorm across campus. He talked loudly, with brash confidence, and his eyes glittered during our intense conversation. "We click," he kept saying, and I felt a surge of joy each time he declared that. For the first time, I felt *seen* by a "popular" guy.

We walked through the woods back to my dorm room, making animated conversation the whole way. Darrell wanted to see my artwork and writing, to get to know "everything" about me. Once we closed the door, the light in his eyes went cold. He pushed me down and forced himself on me. I cried, and eventually he stopped, but the damage was done. "You're crying. I'd better go home," he said flatly. I never saw him again.

The next day I didn't feel much like exercising. I was angry and confused about what had happened—in shock, really. Mostly, I felt numb. A week later, my ankle weights still lay untouched under my loft bed.

A Snickers bar in the lobby vending machine caught my attention. I hadn't eaten one in five years. The whole calorie-counting game seemed pointless at that moment. I barely had the energy to leave my room, much less power-walk across campus or check the wrapper for partially hydrogenated palm kernel oil. *Who was that girl?* I thought as I dropped two quarters into the coin slot and devoured my candy bar. I didn't enjoy it that much, but I ate another two of them.

Fortunately, a friend of mine who volunteered at the campus sexual assault prevention center directed me to counseling services and a bunch of educational resources about date rape. I joined her at a Speak Out (an open-forum rally where rape survivors can share their stories) and a Take Back the Night march. Hearing other women share their stories was shocking. I had never imagined my experience was part of a larger phenomenon.

My numbness gave way to a fierce anger—not just at Darrell but at the whole society. Suddenly I saw how much I'd bought in to this ridiculous body standard, how my poor self-worth had led me to bring a stranger to my room because I was starving— for food, for love, and for so much more. More than anything, I was starving to be seen, not as numbers on an SAT score sheet, a scale, or a dress label. I just wanted to be me, beautiful at any size, unconditionally loved as a goddess in the real.

I started with a juicy porterhouse steak and an Entenmann's cake that I ate in one sitting. As the pounds packed on, I laughed and said, "Screw you!" to the culture. I walked down the street eating candy bars, fancying myself a revolutionary. Where I'd once been desperate for men's attention, I now didn't want guys to look at me. Even in my armor of forty new pounds and bulky sweatsuits, I still got the occasional catcall.

A few months later, I started *HUES* (*Hear Us Emerging Sisters*) magazine with my twin sister and our friend Dyann Logwood. It was a magazine for women of all cultures and sizes to speak their truths. Our mission was to create the magazine we always wished for, one that would talk about women's lives as they really were, not spin some Madison Avenue fantasy. I used my nascent PageMaker skills and the school's resources to design and edit the first issue. Classmates modeled and wrote articles. We printed a thousand copies and passed them out around campus. The response was overwhelming. People mailed us articles, and letters poured in, thanking us for creating realistic, positive images of women.

The *HUES* Collective, our ever-expanding multiculti crew who wrote, edited, designed, and planned each issue, was an amazing group of fierce, powerful, and beautiful women. We were all trying to figure out femininity, navigating between mainstream media beauty standards and those of our own ethnic groups, which added an extra layer of demands. Black women discussed skin color and hair and debated whether black men were starting to prefer thinner women, now that hip-hop videos were becoming big-budget productions. Indian women traded arranged-marriage stories and shared their inner conflict between pleasing their parents and following their semi-Americanized dreams. They talked about sex, body hair, and other cultural secrets. I got quite an education. I learned that body image was about so much more than the pressure to be thin. It was woven into ethnic background, money, social class, sexuality, experiences with violence and trauma. And food.

I also unveiled my own cultural shame as I thought back to high school. Even as I triumphantly cinched the zipper on my size-zero Guess jeans, I was struck by the realization that I might be thin, but I couldn't diet my way out of being Jewish or Israeli. I was still an outsider on the inside, and there was no "cure" for that. I knew I was defeated, and I'd known it all along. I wanted to be a white American, stripped of so-called minority influences, down to my DNA. When people asked my national-ity, I didn't want to answer "Israeli" only to be asked, "What's that?"

It was a shame that my wake-up call came in the form of col-lege date rape, but I turned it into a triumph, as many women do. I wanted girls to read *HUES* so they would love themselves more than I had loved myself, know that they weren't crazy, and see the world through conscious eyes. I wasn't content to stop there, though. I wanted *HUES* to look as good as *Glamour* or *Cosmo,* to stand proudly beside these titles on the newsstand, like a zaftig Jewess reigning among thin Anglo homecoming queens.

——

By the time I was twenty-five, I'd developed *HUES* into a glossy national magazine and sold it to a publisher in Minnesota. Someone suggested I write a book, and after many false starts, I gathered a collection of essays by women of all cultures writing about body image. It was called *Adios, Barbie: Young Women Write About Body Image and Identity,* and it was published by Seal Press, an independent women's house in Seattle.

I'd healed tremendously from my experience, and I weighed around 150 pounds. For the most part, I was fine with it. I was dating men who liked "thick chicks," as I called myself, and I figured that this was my body's natural weight. I focused on loving my love handles and being happy at my larger size. I even defiantly wore a bikini at size fourteen, hoping to play a small role in expanding the world's range of acceptable sizes.

More than anything, the thought of dieting filled me with so much rage and disgust, I couldn't go near the subject. I could only associate it with feeling oppressed, and with the pain of starving myself in hopes of being liked. I never wanted to be that sad, pathetic girl again, desperate to be loved, unable to love herself. *Fuck you, diet industry!*

A year after the book's publication, the plastic powers that be at Mattel filed a lawsuit against my publisher. Apparently, the Seal Press jacket designer had used an actual Barbie doll's leg and shoe on the cover. Every Barbie limb, hair follicle, and accessory is under Mattel's ironclad trademark—the doll is more protected than the crown jewels—and we had violated it.

We changed the cover and renamed the book *Body Outlaws.* The philosophy: It's become so unusual for women today to actually like their bodies that those who do are considered freaks, out of touch, from another planet. A woman who eschews a lifestyle of dieting, clothes-whoring, and obsessing over her appearance lives on the fringes in an uncharted world.

A body outlaw, I declared, was a courageous soul who dared to resist and lived on her own terms. She might face harassment and rejection, but her rewards were freedom and self-determination. Every time I wore my bikini, I imagined myself as an outlaw, helping to reshape the culture one cellulite dimple at a time.

Colleges around the country adopted the book as a required text, and they flew me in as a keynote speaker. At the time, there was very little material on body image written from multicultural viewpoints, with a mix of straight and queer writers to boot. Professors were also hungry to include the honest next-generation voices that their students were demanding, and the students loved the stories.

At twenty-seven years old, I was tickled to be regarded as some kind of intellectual expert, booked in the same university auditoriums as Hillary Clinton and Spike Lee. All I'd done was ask all my friends (and their friends) to write from the heart about their struggles to accept their bodies. But it touched a nerve.

At the time I was a size twelve or fourteen, and there was a subversive element to my primping. In spite of the plus-size fashion movement's efforts, the general message I got was this: *You're not worthy of glamour, style, and a great wardrobe unless you get rid of that tummy bulge and trim those thighs.* To adorn my curves, to attend to style, gave the students an outlaw message that thick chicks could be sexy and self-confident, too. In fact, students often said that they were more impressed with how I carried myself—proudly—than they were with my words. "If she can do it, I can do it," one told me.

That was a true victory. At the same time, it was a contradiction. I knew that to be taken seriously by the eighteen-to-twenty-four set, I had to have style. My body language and my outfit were essential factors in how well the "love your body" message would stick. I had to *be* my message: a woman who didn't fit the cultural beauty standard and still dared to look good.

I was fine with being a size fourteen, for the most part. After all, 60 percent of women in America are a size fourteen or above. Sure, I was annoyed by the limited clothing choices, but my anger was properly directed toward the fashion industry instead of at myself. I was a consumer, but a conscious one, which, by my reasoning, allowed me to indulge in fashion's playground.

My message was never to ignore one's body—or its adornments, like clothes, makeup, hair, and style. I wanted women to reclaim beauty and style on their own terms.

In 2004 my microwave changed everything. I was thirty-one years old and still about 150 pounds. My mornings consisted of chugging coffee and writing until I was famished. (I didn't want to break my caffeine-fueled creative streak.) Then I'd grab cold handfuls of whatever was in the refrigerator; or, if it was empty (as it often was), I'd order a huge lunch from the Texas BBQ delivery menu. At my computer, I'd alternate between typing e-mails and shoveling down the fried-chicken lunch plate. I never exercised. I might have been a proud size twelve, but I didn't really take care of myself. My life was out of balance.

One morning my little sister, Leora, bounced into my apartment and asked to use my microwave. "What are you eating?" I asked as she tore open a cardboard package.

"Oh, it's my Jenny Craig French toast meal," she sang, peeling back cellophane from a black container. "It's really good."

"You joined Jenny Craig?" I gasped, horrified.

Leora is a licensed manicurist and makeup artist whose profession revolves around beauty. I was surer than ever that my mom had slept with the milkman, because there was no way I could be related to this . . . sellout.

"It's actually really good," she said, looking me straight in the eye. "You should consider it. They give you a lot of food, and I eat all day—it's almost too much food. The counselor is really supportive. And it's keeping me on a routine."

Leora poured a small cup of warm blueberry compote (included in the package, from what I could tell) over her steaming French toast. It looked appetizing. Then she threw down the gauntlet: "Tali's joining, you know."

My identical twin sister? My own genetic soul mate was not only fueling the diet industry but was going to lose a bunch of weight, leaving me to be called the fat twin?

I calmed down enough to face one simple truth: I was starving. Sure, my refrigerator wasn't full of the diet food I looked down on. But it wasn't full of anything else, either—and it hadn't been in a long, long time.

Had I won the battle but lost the war? I had to admit: It would be nice to eat three square meals a day. From a financial standpoint, I could get a week of meals for about $120—far less than I spent at New York City restaurants on my American Express card. And yes, if it meant my twin sister and I wouldn't look like Laurel and Hardy when we stood next to each other, I was willing to try. I could always quit.

Paranoid and shot with adrenaline, I slunk into Jenny Craig's midtown Manhattan center later that week. It was street level, with a huge plate-glass front window. I prayed nobody I knew was walking by.

I met with Denise, a sweet counselor who was an easy size fourteen herself. *Cool,* I thought. *At least the women here aren't anorexic.* She weighed me in at 149, snapped a Polaroid, and stapled it to my file. After explaining the Jenny Craig program, Denise helped me select a week's worth of packaged meals, and I left with an armload of white plastic shopping bags.

As soon as I brought the bags into my kitchen and opened the empty fridge, I burst into tears. It had been so long since I'd kept food at home, I didn't know what to do. Full refrigerators reminded me of my parents and grandparents. It was a grown-up's responsibility to keep food in the house, and now I *was* the grown-up.

Not feeding myself was a way of remaining a child, I suppose, of keeping my youth alive. It was an emotional challenge to see myself as capable enough to nourish myself. Yet the more I did it, the more womanly and free I felt—and I loved it. Following a weekly structure turned out to have its benefits, too. I got used to going to the Jenny Craig center, weighing in, and refilling my stash of frozen and packaged food. It was a challenge to make eating regular meals a priority, but I did it. Gradually, I lost fifteen pounds and stayed in a range of 132 to 137 while eating all my meals plus extra fruits and veggies. If I felt hungry, I honored my appetite and body rather than fall into the "cheating on a diet" mentality. Because I knew better, I approached it as a lifestyle rather than a diet.

Then I was invited to give a speech in Cleveland. A feminist theater group had adapted *Body Outlaws* into a staged monologue series, and they were performing it for two hundred area high school students. They asked me to kick off the performances by talking to the teens about body image and why I created the book.

My first thought was *Uh-oh. What if they knew?*

For the first time in my public speaking history, I wasn't the thick, curvy girl—the likely picture of a body image activist. I wore a six or eight instead of a twelve or fourteen now. I still had curves and ethnic features, but I didn't exactly look like a beauty-standard outcast living on society's margins.

Was I a hypocrite? I lectured about the multibillion-dollar diet industry, and now I was participating in it. What if my audience knew I was sleeping with the enemy? My credibility would be shot.

One thing I've always believed essential to progress is honesty. In editing my book, I coached writers toward full disclosure, open dialogue, the courage to tell the truth. Now I couldn't find that courage myself.

I'm still searching for it several years later. From my plus-size perch (which I've returned to several times since), it's easy to talk about creating a size-friendly world. Nobody raises a hand and asks, "What do you know about it? You're not fat. Why should I listen to you?"

What I yearn to reveal is this: Losing weight by taking better care of myself was one of the kindest things I've done for my body. I had to fight against my workaholic tendencies and fears to do it, to overcome an internal voice saying, *You're not worth three square meals a day. Ignore your appetite and your body's signals. Drive yourself harder, live an unbalanced life.*

I'd be lying if I said I didn't want to lose weight when I signed up for Jenny Craig. I knew I was carrying around some emotional poundage from the past, and I was ready to let it go. I didn't feel at home in my body. How could I, after spending punishing hours in my desk chair, never exercising, and scarfing fried food?

I began to realize that in some ways, body image has very little to do with one's body. It's our perception of our bodies, not the bodies themselves. After all, it's the brain that forms our images, that interprets messages from glossy magazines and TV shows and high school hierarchies.

I've also learned that the intentions behind my choices are the most important. I think we must ask ourselves: *What's the context, the spirit, in which I'm doing this?* At one point, my intention to eat chocolate cake with abandon was to overturn my teenage near-anorexic behavior—to release my rage and say "fuck you" to the machine. That was healthy in many ways. For the next phase of my body-loving revolution to happen at Jenny Craig seemed like an obvious contradiction, but it was the unlikely source of empowerment at that point in my life.

Eventually, I let my Jenny Craig membership expire, and I found my way into organic foods and actual cooking. Thick lentil soups, salmon fresh from the gourmet market—the pleasure of fresh food was downright titillating. I loved buying a swordfish steak, bringing it home wrapped in butcher paper, then pan-searing it with garlic and olive oil. My meals became events, daily indulgences, and bonding occasions.

I also started taking a gym class called intenSati. The creator, Patricia Moreno, combines kickboxing, martial arts, yoga, and dance moves with empowering affirmations. She believes that our muscles have memory, so students recite positive statements like "I am strong!" while training their bodies to move in new ways. My body image improved as I traded toxic thoughts and eating habits for affirming ones.

Tuning in to my body, through my appetite, exercise, or being in the moment, was so healing. Often I would discover a layer of emotions to work through. *You're fat! You're ugly! You're never gonna be loved or successful!* some inner voice would berate. Before, I would stuff down food to suppress that voice and the horrible feelings that resulted. Now I was able to let the feeling pass, to recognize that it was coming from an old place, and that it wasn't real.

A year later, I met my husband. As I developed a deeper intimacy with my body and myself, I was able to let others in, too. Jeffrey and his eight-year-old daughter, Clementine, loved me unconditionally, in a way that was initially a challenge to allow. Like food, their love was so nourishing that it overwhelmed me at first. It makes sense: A girl who grows up feeling unworthy of food and fearing fat will also believe there's such a thing as too much love. If I honored my wild appetite, would there be consequences? I had a lot to unlearn.

I'm still figuring out how to work this message into a speech. How do I communicate the journey to college women struggling with stress, academic pressure, the freshman ten, possible date rapes, and their first taste of independence? To some, the concept that they can actually like their bodies—cellulite and all—is revolutionary.

At thirty-five, with ever blonder highlights, a weight in the low 140s, and a husband, I'm not exactly the angry twenty-something who put that book together. I'm dealing with a new set of body baggage—aging and the wrinkles that grow a touch deeper around my eyes with each birthday. The party doesn't stop. I secretly hope that in the next five years, someone will develop an over-the-counter version of Botox that's as harmless as lip gloss. I wonder about having a baby and what will happen to my body during and after a pregnancy. I keep a close watch as

Clementine plays fashion-design games on Barbie.com, but I don't censor her fun, either.

Along the way, being a body outlaw has evolved for me. It's become about feeding myself in every way. For my college-age audiences, there's awareness to raise first. They must understand that they're not crazy; they must get angry at society and rebel their way into self-determination. There will be plenty to reclaim. Let's start with their appetites.

TAKE THIS CAKE AND SHOVE IT
Joan Fischer

So here's my latest food fantasy: I go to a plastic surgeon and ask him to remove my taste buds. Scrape them off my tongue, carve them out, do whatever needs to be done.

Because what, after all, are they good for? They allow me to enjoy something I am not allowed to enjoy. I love food, I love to eat, but I want to be slim, and therein lies the problem. Maintaining a low body weight may not amount to starvation, but it is a state of constant deprivation with very few indulgences—so few that I'd rather just lop off my taste buds and be done with it. Who needs a desire that cannot be satiated? Our culture has ruined food for me.

It's come damn close to ruining sex, too, or at least making it into a spectator sport in which I am a deeply flawed player. This goes back to food. I eat, therefore I'm pudgy, therefore I am a sexual untouchable with a stomach that is, well, not as flat as a board. There's so much sex on TV that we regularly see many of our favorite actresses positioned on all fours or bouncing on top of their partners, their stomachs completely flat, their breasts pointing upward, their skin free of cellulite, even in the danger zones. They are like moving Barbie dolls, sex action figures. They are everything I am not.

Small wonder that if my husband puts a hand on my stomach—maybe wanting a fistful for a sensually pleasurable squeeze—I respond as though electrocuted. The hand has learned its lesson: My stomach is surrounded by barbed wire, officially off-limits. Do not touch the tummy.

Second only to the bedroom is the battle of the beach. I have pretty much renounced wearing swimsuits, which to me—and to so many women—feels like being subjected to a humiliating inspection (while the guys, who don't even have cellulite, are allowed to wear baggy shorts). Here's another fantasy: a line called Dignity Swimwear. The most popular model would be the Burkini, a head-to-toe flowing garment that allows the wearer to revel in the ocean with pretty much only her sunglasses showing.

While it may be a good thing that women in their forties and beyond are now viewed as desirable, it is tragic that the model for beauty—to be a stick figure with big boobs—in no way concedes to age. "Desperate housewife" Teri Hatcher basically looks like a twenty-year-old with a few wrinkles. I didn't look like her at twenty, and I for sure don't in my forties. Celebrities who give birth at every age are regularly applauded in popular magazines for shaking off that baby weight before they even get home from the hospital. A competition is on to see who can get back in her skinny jeans the fastest. Unfortunately, I have seen the trend even among non-famous women I know.

Is this really progress?

Desire. In many ways, that word stands at the heart of it all. It's as simple as that old Cheap Trick song "I Want You to Want Me." Women famously confuse being desired with being loved, and let's face it: Sexual attraction usually is, for both sexes, a prerequisite for further acquaintance. So much of what we women put ourselves through—our punishing sessions in fitting rooms, our battles with swimsuits and jeans, our cruel diets, the billions we spend on cosmetics and surgery—is fundamentally a desire to be desired, a desire to be loved.

All humans feel that. But many cultures have designated the woman as the object of desire, the one who has to wait to be desired rather than simply going to get what she wants. Women are forever channeling their own wishes through the lens of desirability, which means judging themselves by the male gaze.

Naomi Wolf astutely described this "outside-in perspective," as she calls it, over fifteen years ago in her book *The Beauty Myth*. "What little girls learn is not the desire for the other, but the desire to be desired," she writes, noting that the books, magazines, and movies that girls see about sexual awakening are almost always told from the male perspective. "Women come to confuse sexual looking with being looked at sexually; many confuse desiring with being desirable." Given our unrealistic standards for beauty, the outside-in perspective quickly leads to what Wolf describes as "the ultimate anaphrodisiac: the self-critical sexual gaze."

When we survey our cultural landscape, we see that women have been willing accomplices, in some ways even leaders, in our own objectification. Even such new and apparently assertive forms of sexual expression as "do-me feminism"—the notion that women take their objectification into their own hands—still look and feel like self-degradation (like pornography, you know it when you see it). They also fully embrace the rigid beauty standards originally imposed upon women by men.

I am nearly Madonna's age, but to me, she has never represented women's sexual empowerment. Rather, she and her emulators (Britney Spears, the Pussycat Dolls) simply enact male fantasy, no matter how they try to frame it. Along the way, they've done indelible damage to the ways in which their young admirers, male and female, view women.

I noticed how hard it was to buy clothes for my daughter starting when she was ten or eleven; we could find few things designed to actually cover her body. It's hard to interpret those skimpy outfits as empowering. Nor are girls empowered when they wear thong underwear to school dances where mass dry-humping is common practice, or when they are pressured to give boys oral sex to avoid having intercourse. (More than half of teens say they have had oral sex between ages fifteen and nineteen—and 35 percent of boys and 26 percent of girls by age fifteen—according to the Centers for Disease Control and Prevention.) While little concrete data on younger age groups and who's giving oral sex exists, anecdotal evidence suggests that in the under-fifteen set, too, it is growing more common, and that it's more often the girls who drop to their knees.

No doubt they worry whether their tummies are sticking out while they do it. Thinness remains an essential mark of beauty. In the celebrity world, we see one actress after another growing so thin that her head looks oversize, her back ribs protrude, and her spindly legs can barely support her—all in the name of desirability.

We, the mothers, are not setting much of an example as we starve and nip-and-tuck ourselves to fit the unchanging beauty standards of our youth, often emulating the clothing and "hookup" lifestyles of much younger women (since so many of us are single and feel the pressure of being on the market). Married women in the suburbs are learning to strip and pole-dance for the viewing pleasure of their husbands. Now more than ever, we're embracing our own objectification as our correct role in sexual experience—indeed, it's the only role we know. We remain "entertainment for men," as *Playboy*'s enduring tagline puts it.

I'm not the only one who carries all this into the bedroom: the rigid standards of beauty, the emphasis on being desired, the feeling that I cannot measure up—and, on a deeper level, resentment that I should even have to. The impact of women's negative body image on our sexuality is strong enough for a group called Female Sexual Dysfunction Alert—which includes faculty members from such esteemed universities as New York University and the University of California at San Francisco—to have issued a manifesto calling for a new classification for female sexual dysfunction to replace the one developed by the American Psychiatric Association in its *Diagnostic and Statistical Manual of Disorders* (DSM). According to this group, the DSM, the bible of psychiatric counseling, takes male sexual dysfunction as a model for female sexual dysfunction, not recognizing that they often have vastly different causes. By not zeroing in on causes of sexual dysfunction in women, the DSM fails to give diagnosticians the tools to adequately treat them.

Under the very first category, "Sexual Problems Due to Socio-Cultural, Political, or Economic Factors," the group cites "Sexual avoidance or distress due to perceived inability to meet cultural norms regarding correct or ideal sexuality, including . . . anxiety or shame about one's body, sexual attractiveness, or sexual responses."

A growing number of studies document that much of that anxiety or shame revolves around body size. Thinness and desirability are closely linked. "I conceptualized body image self-consciousness during physical intimacy with a partner to be based on concerns over appearing fat," writes researcher Michael W. Wiederman in "Women's Body Image Self-Consciousness During Physical Intimacy with a Partner" (published in *The Journal of Sex Research* in February 2000). Wiederman based his premise on a number of studies: "Although there exists a small minority of men who prefer large women, males in the United States generally find thin women most sexually desirable. Larger women are stigmatized, especially with regard to sexuality and courtship. Indeed, women's general body dissatisfaction is typically measured according to perceptions of being too heavy or having particular body parts that are 'too large.' "

In his study of some two hundred college women, 35 percent of them said that focusing on their appearance and attractiveness during sex was a problem at least some of the time, Wiederman reports. A Body Image Self-Consciousness Scale had these women responding positively to such fat-specific statements as "If a partner were to put a hand on my buttocks I would think, 'My partner can feel my fat' "; "If a partner were to put an arm around my waist, I would think, 'My partner can tell how fat I am' "; and "During sex, I (would) prefer to be on the bottom so that my stomach appears flat."

And these are college-age women—women who, according to our youth-bound standards of beauty, will never again in their lives look so good. Small wonder that women over fifty would prefer to make love in a burka.

Reports sex researcher and author Leah Kliger, "Over the past six years I have traveled throughout the U.S. conducting research and seminars about older women's sexuality and sexual desire. I discovered that the single biggest factor that affects older women's sexual desire is negative body image. Over 50 percent of women in my research cited this. Many women told us they are so dismayed by changes in their bodies that they have taken to undressing in the closet and wearing long flannel nightgowns to bed. Their desire is negatively affected even if their partners/spouses tell them differently."

In the early 1970s, collectively bucking the beauty myth meant, or seemed to mean, things like not wearing a bra or shaving your legs and wearing baggy unisex clothes. I remember feeling conflicted about this as a fourteen-year-old when an anthology of feminist writings called *Sisterhood Is Powerful* swept through my summer camp. I felt traitorous for wanting to wear mascara, for wanting the boy I liked to like me back, to choose me at the dance.

"I want you to want me." We may be women, but men have us by the balls. There is no part of ourselves that is so tender or yearning or vulnerable as the part that seeks sexual acceptance. It will not be denied, it will not be excised, and it sure as hell won't go to the dance in an army jacket. The answer is not to hold hands and agree to go ugly but to insist collectively upon an expanded definition of beauty. This must include the participation—at least some of the time—of the industries and institutions that plague us.

God bless actors like Patricia Arquette, the Emmy-winning star of *Medium,* for insisting on playing her soccer-mom character rounded and real despite alleged demands from her producers to lose weight. Those same kudos go to Jamie Lee Curtis for publishing a photo of how she really looks in her underwear—back fat and all—before the interventions of trick lighting, airbrushing, and Photoshop. And to Sara Ramirez, Camryn Manheim, and a scant few others who are refusing to downsize. May their numbers grow.

I'm heartened by Dove's "Campaign for Real Beauty," the company's conscious effort to redefine our notion of beauty by featuring women of many sizes and ages in its ads. Yes, the campaign is a savvy attempt to sell product—so-called firming lotions are being marketed to those "real women with curves," and pro-age potions are being pushed to aging boomers. I'll take it anyway. That's how encouraging it is to see regular women onscreen and on the printed page. Ads showing these women—nearly naked but dignified and quietly proud—highlight by contrast the violation done to women in most other ads. These are our mothers, our grandmothers, our sisters, our girlfriends, ourselves. Don't men recognize them, too, as women they love and have loved in their lives?

We need reminders that a woman is more than a slender body; that sex is a private act of expression and response, not a spectator performance; and that food, our very sustenance, is not the enemy but a source of nourishment and pleasure. In the presence of a culture that sends us the opposite messages, and alongside a growing but still marginal collective will to work against them, these are things we need to tell ourselves.

It's a struggle, and much of the time I feel like an angry work in progress. I am as trapped by vanity, by a desire to be desired, as most women. I want to enjoy food and still be considered attractive in a culture that pretty much forces women into choosing between food and sex. Literally, I want to have my cake and eat it, too. And most days I feel conflicted and frustrated enough to say: *Take this cake and shove it.*

PIE
Joyce Maynard

The diagnosis reached me on Mother's Day 1989: My sixty-six-year-old mother was suffering from an inoperable brain tumor. They told us she had only weeks to live. Within twenty-four hours, I'd left my husband and our three young children to be at her side and take care of her at her home in Toronto. I didn't say it out loud, but secretly, I believed I might cure her. With my own strange, grief-crazed brand of magical thinking, I knew how I'd do it. I'd cook for her.

Cooking and Mother. Mother and food. Food and love. They were all tied up together, like multiple definitions in the thesaurus, under the umbrella heading SUSTENANCE. Or simply: LIFE. Little wonder, maybe, that when life itself was threatened, I would see food as the miracle cure.

My mother was many things in life: a teacher and a writer, a brilliant lecturer, a storyteller, an entertainer. Even, on occasion, a television talk-show host. But when I picture my mother, it's never her big accomplishments I think about.

I see her cooking. The image that comes to me always features her offering up some good thing to eat—setting a steaming casserole on the table, sliding a tray of cookies into the oven, running her finger around the rim of a bowl to test the sauce, ladling the soup, chopping the vegetables, munching on an apple. (She ate in the same manner she tackled life: with a big, zestful appetite, and nothing wasted. Give my mother a Cortland or a Mac, and she'd devour it, right down to and including the core.) Never a fancy cook so much as a hearty, instinctual one, she seldom followed recipes and tended to rich, spicy, hearty foods served up in abundance. She was a messy cook (as opposed to that other type, who cleans up as she goes along) and a joyful one—a woman who never quite believed that good food could come out of an immaculate kitchen. She was a woman who could take whatever lay in the bottom of her refrigerator crisper drawer and turn it into soup. I never tasted more wonderful roast chicken than hers.

Of all the foods my mother whipped up in her kitchen, though, one item remained her trademark. Give her a little flour, a little salt, sugar, water, cinnamon, fruit, and her trade-secret box of Minute tapioca, and fifteen minutes later, she'd be pinching the crust on one of her incomparable pies and brushing on the milk. For her, baking was an expression of love. Eating, an expression of acceptance. And something else: In a home filled with hidden sorrows, disappointment, anxiety, and pain, mealtime represented safety, security, comfort.

Ours was a household divided down the middle—one Jewish parent, one gentile; one sober, one drunk; one in the master bedroom, one down the hall. In a single place, we came together as a family: around the dining room table. For us, meals were a kind of communion, my mother's pie the sacrament.

This was not an easy family to grow up in, filled as it was with a mix of big love and big pressure—to please our parents, to lay at their feet the successes that had eluded them in their own lives. My role in our household was to make my parents happy, and I tried my darnedest to do it. If my sister was salt, I was sugar.

I was a baker from a young age. I loved to hang out in the kitchen with my mother, eating cookie dough straight out of the bowl and talking with her. She never actually instructed me in her method for making pie crust, but I took it in the way a baby learns speech, from life. I knew all my mother's mantras: *Crisco for flakiness, butter for flavor. Use as little water as possible. Don't cut up the apples so small you'll end up with applesauce. Never overhandle the dough.*

In our house, the words *packaged pie crust* or *Pillsbury mix* were as unthinkable to utter as obscenities.

In a household where food and meals played such a significant role, it's no big surprise that my mother struggled with her weight—always dieting, endlessly depriving herself of some treat or other. She counted calories obsessively, then snacked on cookies. She never went out without putting on her girdle, and she longed, I think, to be released from it. The winter I was seven, she got pneumonia and almost died—a terrifying period

for my sister and me, but one our mother remembered afterward with a certain nostalgia as the one time in her adult life
when she was really slim.

It didn't last. Maintaining skinniness was my job. Very early I
became the designated thin person in the family (along with our
father, who favored liquor over food), and as much as my
mother lamented the way I turned away from the wonderful
meals she prepared, there was a part of her that delighted in my
thinness. For my part, I recognized it as a source of power.
Whole mealtimes were dedicated to the project of getting me to
try some food or clean my plate of vegetables.

I picked at the foods my mother offered up, my goal to consume as little as possible. She cooked me special meals—swept
me away from school for a half hour at lunchtime (as late as ju-
nior high) so she could serve me one of the two foods I would
agree to eat: a soufflé of nothing but milk, flour, and eggs, put in
the oven to rise for the six minutes of the drive to school to get
me. Twenty minutes later—soufflé consumed—she'd whisk me
back to class.

We had a dance around food, eating, weight: my mother the
supplicant, begging me to eat, I the withholding one, fork resting on the place mat, meal untouched. I never articulated the
thought, but now, when I consider that behavior, I wonder if I
wasn't taking onto myself all the attention that might otherwise
have been focused on my father, as he brooded at the end of the
table with a couple of shots of vodka in him, headed for more.

Sometimes I ate, sometimes I didn't, always knowing how
much power I wielded with my choices. *You feed. I eat. Accept or reject. Binge or starve. Take a piece of pie or leave it.* There was a message
in every decision. Herself the daughter of a baking, cooking,
soup-making mother, my mother was carrying on an old family

pattern, learned in her own mother's kitchen, no doubt. *Feed me, own me. Deny food, reject love.* Eat as you want, feel guilty, and squeeze yourself into that girdle. Or deprive yourself, feel virtuous, and be slim. Though in my mother's case, neither alternative held true. She deprived herself endlessly and still did battle with the bathroom scale, basking in her daughter's thinness as she mournfully surveyed her own ripe curves.

At seventeen, I gained ten pounds and watched how my mother suffered the weight gain. At eighteen, I dieted away thirty pounds and noted her relief. Letters she wrote to my sister and grandmother over the next few years featured regular assessments of my weight, with ups and downs. Extra pounds, a signal of trouble.

At twenty-three, I married and started baking for my own little family. I took a photograph of the contents of my freezer during the winter I was pregnant—compelled to document the rows of baked goods I'd stockpiled, to guard against the wolf that seemed to hover just outside our door. That winter I barely let my husband taste the brownies before wrapping up every new batch for the freezer. Food was security. Food was protection. The one thing I could control in a life of uncertainty. I gained fifty pounds with that pregnancy, basking in the knowledge that for once in my life, I didn't need—couldn't have, in fact—a flat, hollowed-out stomach.

Two days after the birth of that baby, the first of our three, my mother came to visit. She was easy to spot as she made her way down the ramp from the plane, carrying Tupperware containers with four different kinds of homemade cookies and a whole roast chicken. I was thrilled to see her, knowing she'd take care of me—a talent my husband never mastered. But he—raised in a very different kind of household, where the parents kept a polite distance and stayed in hotels when they visited and took you out to dinner at their country club instead of whipping up casseroles—felt crowded, overwhelmed, and stressed. Within hours of my mother's arrival, he had a migraine. "She's staying for two weeks?" he asked, holding his throbbing head.

I fixed a pot of tea and sat there in our kitchen, new baby in my arms, trying to explain to each of these two people I loved how it was for the other. I thought I did a good job, but when the heart-to-heart was over, my mother made the baffling announcement that something unexpected had come up back home in Toronto, and she'd have to leave. Two days later—with all traces of my mother gone but the last of the cookies—I called her (collect, as always). Only this time she didn't accept the charges.

"I think it's best if Joyce and I discontinue our relationship," she told my husband when he called (while I lay on the couch, gasping for breath). "It's clear she doesn't want me around."

Eventually, she let me back in her life, though I never again felt the old safety and comfort of her kitchen, or what had once seemed to me like her inexhaustible acceptance and love. Now my daughter became my little emissary—traveling solo to her grandmother's house in Canada, where her favorite activity was baking with my mother. Cookies and pie. Audrey adored those visits, always coming home with baked goods and stories of adventures.

At thirty, unhappy in my marriage, I got very thin again. My mother—still beautiful at sixty-six, but dieting, as always—continued her endless struggle, love of good food on one side, longing to be slim on the other. *I'll tell you one thing,* she had written in a letter to a friend more than twenty years earlier. *If I ever get a brain tumor, I'm going to stop counting calories.* Nothing but death would release her from this struggle. And ultimately, it was death that would.

I was thirty-five when her cancer diagnosis came. Until that day, I believed I'd have decades left to work things out with my mother. Now it turned out I had only weeks.

With my mother facing death, the idea came to me that despite the terminal prognosis given by the doctors, I might once again provide, for my mother, what was needed to make everything okay—just as she had once believed she could do for me. With food, of course.

Years before, my mother had been the woman who'd defied the nurses on the maternity ward of the hospital where I was born to breast-feed her youngest child, me. When I was growing up, she buttered my toast on both sides to make it extra delicious, arranged my apple slices in the design of flowers, roasted chicken wings nightly (regardless of what the rest of the family might be eating) because for one whole year that was all I ate.

Now I'd be the one providing sustenance. From the day of my arrival at her house in Toronto, a crucial part of my role there was the maker of wonderful meals. I shopped that summer with the obsessiveness of an addict—traveling to three different produce markets to locate the best raspberries for my mother's breakfast tray, riding the bus to the Jewish bakery on the other side of the city where they baked the best challah.

My mother had always been not simply a great cook but a great hostess, with legions of devoted friends; with the news of her illness spreading, they came to see her. I tried to make the visits into something resembling the parties of before, only now I was the cook. I made carrot-ginger soup and salad with goat cheese and roasted pine nuts, pasta with fresh tomato sauce, and, for my mother's birthday in July, salmon encrusted in brioche dough with creamy lemon sauce and fresh dill on the side, the brioche sculpted into the shape of a smiling baby.

Nearly every day that summer, I baked a pie for my mother and her friends to eat during their farewell visits in her garden. One day it might be strawberry rhubarb. Next day, blueberry or apple. Sometimes late at night when she was sleeping, I made my way downstairs to the kitchen and took out the rolling pin, the pastry blender, the red Minute tapioca box. In the quiet of midnight, tears streaming down my cheeks, the kitchen in shambles, I rolled out the dough. Part of me still believed she couldn't die so long as I kept feeding her.

Still, my mother was going steadily downhill—no longer walking one week, her speech terribly garbled the next. By August came the most ominous sign: My mother had mostly lost interest in food. Maybe that was when I understood that she was really dying. Now when her friends came, she didn't touch the pie. They waylaid me in the kitchen to say, "We'll miss the food she cooked." And then the question: Could I give them the recipe for her pie crust?

Here's the thing about pie crust, I told them. It's not about the recipe. (Nearly every recipe for pie crust is identical.) It's about how you handle the dough. And the only way to learn is to stand as I did once, at the elbow of a baker who knows what she's doing. Once that was my mother. Now it was me.

A half-dozen times at least, that summer, I stood in my mother's kitchen with one or another of her old friends, teaching the lessons of pie, reciting her advice. I had thought the exercise was for them, but I found, as I baked, an unexpected comfort. For all the uneasiness and trouble of my history with my marvelous, difficult mother, on this subject at least no trace of ambivalence existed, only love.

My mother died that October, having hung on longer than any of the doctors expected. The week she died, my marriage—so long troubled—finally ended, and I found myself moving out of the home I'd shared with my husband for more than a dozen years, to a town a half hour's drive away. I slept in an unfamiliar bedroom. Cooked in a strange kitchen—though for a while there, I hardly cooked at all. No baking for me. No smell of soup on the stove. Of all the seasons of my life, this was the darkest and the hungriest.

My children were spending Thanksgiving that year with their father and his parents, making this the first year of my life I'd mark the fourth Thursday in November away from family, and the first year in more than a decade when I wouldn't be preparing a holiday meal.

As I thought about all those afternoons teaching my mother's friends how to make pie, an idea came to me to do the thing my mother always did so brilliantly—throw a party. I invited everyone I knew (many of them women heading off to family celebrations of their own a few days later) to come over for a pie lesson. More than a dozen showed up that first time, though later the guest list would double. They brought their own pie tins and rolling pins and pastry blenders, but the rest I provided. We spread our materials out over every available surface—not only the kitchen but the dining room table—and got to work. When the afternoon was over, everyone went home with a pie. We'd left them unbaked, not simply because I didn't have space in my oven but so each person's house could be filled with the smell of the apples as they baked, and so every baker would know the pleasure of reaching into her own oven and lifting out her own golden pie.

That was eighteen years ago. Many seasons later—living on the opposite side of the country now—the number of men and women to whom I have given my pie lesson probably numbers high in the hundreds. For years, when my children and I were living in New Hampshire, perilously close to being broke, I had delivered this line to them: "Even the richest man in America isn't eating a better pie than we are tonight." Then a man who was, briefly, the richest paid several thousand dollars to a charity I liked so I would teach his wife to bake a pie. But some things in life, I knew, cannot truly be bought, and a good pie is one of them.

I've baked pies to raise money for deaf children, for the homeless, for the scholarship program at my children's school, for a presidential candidate (who lost). I like to think of how, in states all over America, in kitchens like mine, pie bakers reach for the Minute tapioca box on my mother's say-so, reminding themselves "Crisco for flakiness, butter for flavor." Almost two decades since my mother uttered her last words, her mantra endures.

So does the old family pattern. The good part, anyway—the belief in the value of food made with one's own hands, a sit-down home-cooked meal you share with those you love.

All three of my children are grown and gone from home, a fact that still stabs at my heart sometimes, I miss them so achingly. But it is a source of pleasure that though I never set out to instruct them, any more than my mother did with me, each of them knows how to make a great pie. I reside in their kitchens in some small way, the same as my mother does in mine.

Now and then one of them calls me midcrust with a question: "What do you think about peaches, cranberries, and raspberries as a combination for filling?" my older son asks. (I think it's a terrific idea. "Just remember," I say, "to throw in extra tapioca to keep the filling from getting runny.") "I ran out of Crisco," my younger son tells me. "Do you think it's okay to throw in a little extra butter to substitute?" ("No problem" is the answer. One great thing about pie crust is how forgiving it is. More than one road leads to great pie.)

These days, apart from when I teach pie, I bake one only if friends are coming over. But sometimes, at night, alone in my kitchen, I still take out my rolling pin and pastry blender and my tins of sugar, flour, and salt and get to work. It is a kind of meditation for me—cutting the butter into the flour, rolling out the dough, and that risky moment when you flip the top crust over the fruit and, for one brief second, the circle of dough is neither on the counter nor on the pie but in midair. It's a moment when I still hear my mother's voice in my ear. Performing the act correctly is about confidence and faith, two qualities I have somehow acquired and retained over the years.

In the end, of course, I did not save my mother's life with pie. And though it would be overstating things a little to tell you that pie saved mine, this much is true: It is with the small act of making a pie—a handful of ingredients, twelve minutes of preparation, max—that I most consistently locate peace of mind. Something happens when I make a pie, and something else happens when I take out my pie server and cut a piece and set it on a plate for a person I care about, with French-vanilla ice cream on the side. It is a small act but, in its way, one of the more satisfying parts of life.

My mother was a complicated and frequently difficult woman,

and it was a complicated, difficult thing to be her daughter—the same words my own daughter might use, come to think of it, about being mine. But about the pie part, I feel no ambivalence. Pie is simple. *Easy as pie.* Pie is something a person can count on when so much else in life may seem to be in question. Pie is the place I go where I know I will feel nothing but love.

ABOUT THE CONTRIBUTORS

Diana Abu-Jaber's newest novel, *Origin,* is a literary psychological thriller. She has also written a memoir with recipes, *The Language of Baklava.* Her novel *Crescent* won the PEN Center Award for literary fiction. She teaches at Portland State University and divides her time between Portland, Oregon, and Miami, Florida.

Jenny Allen writes articles and essays for many magazines and is the author of *The Long Chalkboard,* a collection of fables for grown-ups. She has performed her one-woman show, *I Got Sick Then I Got Better,* in New York. She lives in New York and is married to cartoonist and writer Jules Feiffer; they have two daughters, Julie, thirteen, and Halley, twenty-three.

Magali Amadei is a former top model. In 1999 she created an outreach program with Claire Mysko, director of the American Anorexia Bulimia Association. The pair have traveled to schools across the country to share the message that physical beauty is not the key to happiness. Visit them at www.insidebeauty.org.

Sari Botton is a writer and New York City expat now based in upstate New York. Her articles and essays have appeared in *The New York Times, New York* magazine, *The Village Voice, Marie Claire, Self, Harper's Bazaar, Glamour,* and many other publications. She ghostwrites other people's memoirs for a living and hopes to soon publish her own.

Jane E. Brody has been the Personal Health columnist for *The New York Times* since 1976 and a science and health writer for the *Times* since 1964. She lectures frequently to lay and professional audiences on topics related to health and fitness. She is the mother of twin sons and the grandmother of four boys, including a pair of twins. She lives with her husband in Brooklyn.

Harriet Brown edited the anthology *Mr. Wrong: Real-Life Stories About the Men We Used to Love* and is the author of *The Good-bye Window: A Year in the Life of a Day-Care Center* and other nonfiction books, as well as a chapbook of poems, *The Promised Land.* Her essays and features appear in *The New York Times, Elle, Vogue,* and other national magazines and newspapers, as well as in her blog, Feed Me! (harrietbrown.blogspot.com). She often speaks to groups of parents, doctors, nurses, and students about eating disorders. She lives in Syracuse, New York, where she's an assistant professor in magazine journalism at the Newhouse School of Journalism.

Brenda Copeland is an executive editor at Hyperion Books. She has conducted writing workshops across the country and now teaches editing at New York University. She lives in Manhattan.

Ophira Edut is the editor of *Body Outlaws: Rewriting the Rules of Beauty and Body Image* (Seal Press), one of a few books to examine body image from multicultural perspectives. She owns Mediarology, an agency that creates empowering media projects for girls and women, and she lives in New York City. Visit her online at www.ophira.com and www.loveyourbody.org.

Joan Fischer lives in Madison, Wisconsin, where she works in communications for the University of Wisconsin.

Amity Gaige is the winner of a Truman Capote fellowship, a Fulbright fellowship, and a MacDowell Colony fellowship. In 2006 she was named one of "5 Under 35" outstanding emerging writers by the National Book Foundation. Her debut novel, *O My Darling,* was published in 2005. Her second novel, *The Folded World,* was named one of the best books of 2007 by the *Chicago Tribune.* She lives in Amherst, Massachusetts, and teaches creative writing and literature at Mount Holyoke College.

Kathi Kamen Goldmark is the author of *And My Shoes Keep Walking Back to You,* a novel, and coauthor of *The Great Rock 'n' Roll Joke Book, Mid-Life Confidential: The Rock Bottom Remainders Tour America with Three Chords and an Attitude,* and a monthly column in *BookPage,* and has contributed essays to several anthologies. A 2007 San Francisco Library Laureate, Kathi is the founder and a member of the all-author rock band the Rock Bottom Remainders, president and janitor of Don't Quit Your Day Job Records, author liaison for many high-profile literary events, and producer of the radio show *West Coast Live.* She likes to think she is ready for anything.

In 2007 **Kate Harding** founded Shapely Prose (kateharding .net), which swiftly became the most widely read fat-acceptance blog on the web. She's currently at work on a book about body image with fellow blogger Marianne Kirby. In the meantime, her writing can be found in the anthology *Yes Means Yes* and at the award-winning group blog Shakesville, as well as at Shapely Prose. She lives in Chicago.

Ann Hood is the author, most recently, of the novel *The Knitting Circle* and a memoir, *Comfort: My Journey Through Grief*.

Dana Kinstler won the *Southern Indiana Review*'s fiction prize in 2007 and the *Missouri Review* editor's prize in 2000. Her essays have appeared in the London *Sunday Telegraph*'s *Stella* magazine and in the anthologies *Mr. Wrong, About Face,* and *My Father Married Your Mother*. She lives in the Hudson River Valley with her husband and daughters.

Caroline Leavitt is the author of eight novels; the most recent is *Girls in Trouble*. A recipient of a New York Foundation of the Arts Grant and a Goldenberg Fiction Prize winner, she was also a finalist in the Nickelodeon screenwriting competition, a quarterfinalist in the Fade In Screenwriting Awards, and a National Magazine Award nominee in personal essay. She teaches novel writing at UCLA and is a book critic for *The Boston Globe, Dame* magazine, and *People*. Her work has appeared in *Salon, New York* magazine, *Redbook, Psychology Today, Parenting, More, Cookie,* and others. She lives with her husband, the writer Jeff Tamarkin, and their son, Max, in Hoboken, New Jersey.

Courtney E. Martin is the author of *Perfect Girls, Starving Daughters: The Frightening New Normalcy of Hating Your Body*. She's a freelance journalist and blogger whose work has appeared in *The New York Times, Newsweek, The Christian Science Monitor,* AlterNet, the Huffington Post, *Utne Reader, Women's eNews, Publishers Weekly, off our backs, BUST,* and *Bitch* magazine, among others. She blogs regularly for Feministing, Crucial Minutiae, and Women in Media and News. She was awarded the Elie Wiesel Prize in Ethics, a Clark Foundation Fellowship, and ChoiceUSA's Setting the Message Straight Award. She's currently an adjunct professor of gender studies at Hunter College. Read more about her at www.courtneyemartin.com.

Joyce Maynard is the author of nine books, including the memoir *At Home in the World,* which has been translated into fourteen languages. A frequent contributor to national magazines, she teaches memoir at her home in Mill Valley, California, and runs the Lake Atitlan (Guatemala) Writers' Workshop. Her website is www.joycemaynard.com.

Wendy McClure is a columnist for *BUST* magazine, a children's book editor, and the author of the memoir *I'm Not the New Me.* Her essays have appeared in *The New York Times Magazine,* the *Chicago Sun-Times,* and several anthologies, including *Does This Book Make Me Look Fat?* She has an MFA in poetry from the Iowa Writers' Workshop. She lives in Chicago and maintains a blog at www.poundy.com.

Laurie Notaro is the author of seven books, including *The Idiot Girls' Action Adventure Club* and *There's a Slight Chance I Might Be Going to Hell.* When her book contracts no longer get renewed, she plans on working at the Costco hot dog stand and intimidating senior citizens in the sample booths at lunchtime until they step aside and she can get full on free bite-size egg rolls and cups of granola.

Susan O'Doherty is the author of *Getting Unstuck Without Coming Unglued: A Woman's Guide to Unblocking Creativity*. Her work has appeared in numerous publications, including *Eureka Literary Magazine, Northwest Review,* and *Literary Mama,* as well as the anthologies *Sex for America: Politically Inspired Erotica, About What Was Lost: Twenty Writers on Miscarriage, Healing, and Hope,* and *It's a Boy!* Her story "Passing" was chosen as the New York story for *Ballyhoo*'s ongoing "Fifty States Project" and is distributed in chapbook form in bookstores and coffeehouses around New York State. Her popular advice column for writers, "The Doctor Is In," appears each Friday on M. J. Rose's book-promotion blog, Buzz, Balls, & Hype.

Whitney Otto is the author of *How to Make an American Quilt, The Passion Dream Book,* and other novels. Her mother is still on Weight Watchers.

Lisa Romeo's nonfiction has appeared in newspapers, magazines, literary journals, and anthologies, including *The New York Times, O, SportLiterate, Quay,* and *L'Année Hippique International.* She recently earned an MFA in creative nonfiction from the Stonecoast Program at the University of Southern Maine. A former public relations specialist and equestrian journalist, she's an editor for a magazine industry newsletter and is at work on a memoir of linked essays. She lives in Cedar Grove, New Jersey, with her husband and two sons. Visit her at LisaRomeo .blogspot.com.

Rochelle Jewel Shapiro's novel, *Miriam the Medium,* was nominated for the Harold U. Ribelow Award. She's published essays in *The New York Times, Newsweek,* and many anthologies, including *What Was Lost* and *"Have I Got a Guy for You."* Her poetry and short stories have appeared in *The Iowa Review, Negative Capability, Coe Review,* and other magazines. Like the heroine of her novel, Shapiro is also a phone psychic from Great Neck.

INVASION!

"They're coming!"

"Who is coming? What do you sense? Are you an empath?" How, he thought, could this off-worlder know of a danger to Nuala when he, an Atare, sensed nothing?

"Lunas. They turned my planet to ash, we had no shields, no military.... They melted the skin from my people. They will sear the life from this world...."

He shook his head. "This time it will be different. We have a shield." Yet even as he spoke, the impact of a bomb rocked the ground beneath their feet, and horrified, they heard the first chain reaction of explosions...

FIRE SANCTUARY

FIRE SANCTUARY

A NOVEL BY
KATHARINE ELISKA KIMBRIEL

POPULAR LIBRARY

An Imprint of Warner Books, Inc.

A Warner Communications Company

This story is a work of fiction. All characters are ficti-tious and any resemblance to actual persons, living or dead, is purely coincidental.

POPULAR LIBRARY EDITION

Copyright © 1986 by Katharine Eliska Kimbriel
All rights reserved.

Popular Library® and Questar® are registered trademarks of Warner Books, In

Popular Library books are published by
Warner Books, Inc.
666 Fifth Avenue
New York, N.Y. 10103

 A Warner Communications Company

Printed in the United States of America

First Printing: October, 1986

10 9 8 7 6 5 4 3 2 1

For my godson Justin,
who received a manuscript instead of a baptismal quilt

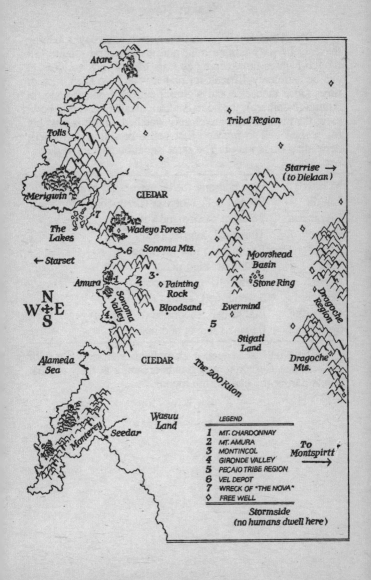

Atare

Tolls

Meriguin

The Lakes

← Starset

CIEDAR

7

Wadeyo Forest

Sonoma Mts.

6

Amura

1

2

3

Painting Rock

Bloodsand

Sonoma Valley

4

W N E S

Alameda Sea

CIEDAR

Wasuu Land

Monterey

Seedar

Tribal Region

Starrise →
(to Dielaan)

Moorshead Basin

Stone Ring

Evermind

5

Stigati Land

Dragoche Region

Dragoche Mts.

The 200 Kilon

LEGEND
1 MT. CHARDONNAY
2 MT. AMURA
3 MONTINCOL
4 GIRONDE VALLEY
5 PECAIO TRIBE REGION
6 VEL DEPOT
7 WRECK OF "THE NOVA"
◇ FREE WELL

To Montspirti →

Stormside
(no humans dwell here)

Nualan Time

The planet Nuala has a twenty-five-hour day, retaining the ancient sixty-minute hour and sixty-second minute, although Nualan timekeeping appears hazy to off-worlders. It can be extremely difficult for planet visitors to keep track of time, since moonrise and moonset can vary enormously. In Amura (Nuamura), the hours are canonical. Elsewhere, however, the moon cycles are closely watched, and it is possible for second bell to precede first bell—or follow third bell, depending on moonset. The same situation applies to moonrise.

Matins	First bell and the deepest point of night
Lauds	Second bell, moonset (firstmoon)
Canonical	Between matins and starrise
Prime	Third bell, starrise (Kee)
Tierce	Fourth bell, mid-morning
Sext	Fifth bell, high noon
None	Sixth bell, mid-afternoon
Vespers	Seventh bell, starset (Kee)
Compline	Eighth bell, moonrise (firstmoon)
Canonical	Between starset and matins

The Nualans' sequence also changes fractionally with the seasons. Compline and Lauds are rung at their median points during the dark of the moons.

Nualan Calendar

The Nualan year is an ecliptic orbit of 432 Nualan days, based on a twenty-five-hour day. Ancient Terran hours are used as the base measurement. Nualans divide the calendar into four seasons of 108 days each. These divisions are based on the rainy seasons; it rains almost thirty-six days straight at the beginning of spring and autumn. A Nualan month is thirty-six days. Nualans do not use any smaller fraction of the calendar between "month" and day. They refer to the passage of time according to festivals and religious feast days.

New Year	Firstday (first day of fall)
Festival of Masks	Thirtyfiveday
Feast of Souls	Thirtysixday
Yule	Onehundred Twentysevenday (midwinter)
Feast of Atonement and Anointing	Onehundred Eightyoneday (first day of spring)
Ascension Day	Twohundred Fortysixday
Midsummer's	Threehundred Fortythreeday
Feast of Adel	Fourhundred Twentyfiveday
High Festival	Fourhundred Twentysixday through Thirtytwoday

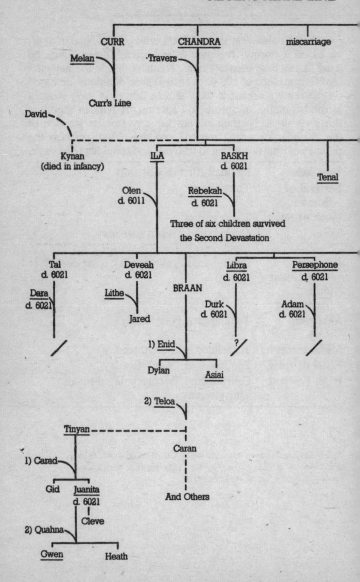

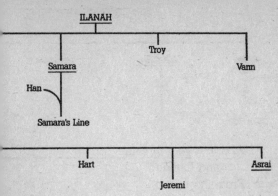

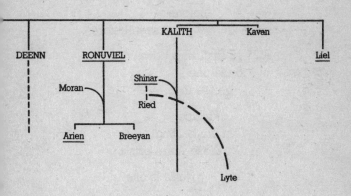

Ruling Atare and Ragaree are indicated by CAPITALS; although Kalith and Deenn did not rule for their lifetimes, they were anointed Atares. Deaths, when premature, are indicated—

And in a year of flame
and thunder,
From the womb
of a healer
life shall be born,
bearing sight
no one
has seen before.

And ye shall bow down
to the one
before them—

Rejoice!
In the healing
these Atare bring.

Nuala is one.

—Naitun

This is but a glimpse, a glimmer of end and beginning, exordium and terminus. For to understand *Nuala,* the word and all the nuance surrounding it, is a lifetime in itself. Nuala is many things—a solar system; a planet; a religion; a language; a people; a way of life familiar, and yet unfamiliar, to the senses of the human species. If you understand nothing else after you have heard this tale, understand this: *Nuala* means "survival." Survival against all odds, all enemies, all fortune. Survival.

—From the words of the Mythmaker,
in the reign of the 167th Atare.

CHAPTER ONE

The Gerrymander

"**A**ssassin takes king of spades. King of hearts to edifice, queen of hearts to crown, king of clubs to ascendant," the computer droned as it made its move. The duty officer winced visibly as his king was toppled from the peak of the pyramid.

Lyte did not allow his smile to reach his face. The computer's programming for edifice was elementary, and it played scarcely at an intermediate level. Knocking off the edifice card in the second round merely to introduce a pretender in the last tier was poor strategy—but then, computers had trouble with edifice strategy. It was too erratic a game for a machine, a fact that kept living, breathing dealers all over the republic in constant demand. Although this move put the computer's high card into the heir's position, it placed Lyte at edifice *and* ascendant—strong positions so early in the game. The duty officer, whose name Lyte did not remember, was in trouble.

Of course, the idiot had probably figured out his error two days ago, after the first three-hour session of cards. His anticipated "easy" opponent had turned out to be a professional gambler. Fortunately for Lyte, the man was too proud to admit he was overmatched, and the equivalent of a fourteenday's pay glittered on the divider between them. Lyte's sympathy had dimmed long ago—the officer was arrogant, almost contemptuous of his two passengers. *I would cheat to*

beat you, fool. If the Nualans hired you to prove they don't
discriminate against non-Nualans, they went too far. . . .

The 3AV hologram to his right winked at him, drawing
his attention. It was frozen in its hold mode, waiting for
instructions. Allowing himself a languid stretch, Lyte punched
the promotion tape back to its beginning. Noticing his distraction, the duty officer visibly searched for a good move,
his nostrils twitching in agitation. Lyte wasn't worried; he
probably didn't *have* a good move. Time to finish this hand
and start another; he was getting bored, and that shouldn't
happen in edifice.

"Pass," the man finally said, his nostrils now fluttering
frantically. The contrast of his nervous tic with his excessively
thin face was laughable, but Lyte controlled himself as he
requested another card. Jack of pretenders—not worth much.
He slid it under his other card.

All hail the biggest pretender of all, he thought wryly
as the computer bumped his pawn pretender and slid the king
of diamonds into the bottom tier. Four cards now computer-
controlled—time for an assassin card to turn up. *I am the*
pretender, the biggest pretender. Gods, Moran, hasn't it oc-
curred to you once that I've previously avoided Nuala like a
plague? That I'd stay on base and hustle dice before I'd take
my leave there, even with you? Gods, you'd be lousy in the
tratores—they'd read you like a signpost and take everything
you had.

The tape began once again. Lyte watched it with one
eye, his professional card sense taking over the game. He'd
memorized this tape, of course, as he had all the others, but
they had not told him enough. Even Moran couldn't really
tell him enough. After all, the man was smitten by that Nualan
princess, incapable of remembering the terror the word *Nuala*
conjured. "If you ever were afraid . . ." Lyte muttered aloud.

"What?" The duty officer jerked, as if startled.

"Nothing," Lyte said, wondering if the little man was
trying to figure out a way to cheat. Damn, why did the Axis
tapes have so little information about Nuala? As if it tried to
forget the colony existed. And this was basically an assignment; he couldn't afford gaps in his knowledge. Moran had
been forthcoming but simply hadn't understood his friend's

concern. Lyte glanced away from the 3AV toward his dozing partner. Moran always looked very peaceful when he slept, his smooth, classic features more appropriate for an artist or an entertainer than for a warrior of the Axis Forces. But his temper never showed through when he slept. Years ago, before Moran had taken classes in control, Lyte had seen his friend almost kill a man with nothing but his hands. Moran had learned the reason for his outbursts, and his temper rarely showed through; but unlike others, Lyte never made the mistake of thinking that this tranquil, soft-spoken individual was an easy mark. *Not since you pounded me into the ground for that prank I arranged on your twelfth birthday.*

"'My other half, dark to my light, but I am the darker brother,'" Lyte quoted, running his fingers through his own silver hair to straighten it.

"Are you playing or not?" the duty officer snapped.

"Are you passing?" Lyte responded mildly, fixing the man with a frost-tipped eye.

"I passed." It was muttered—they were playing strict edifice, which meant no discard, only three cards maximum. He was probably holding pawns and jacks.

Lyte drew a card. Another jack; gods, was the deck rigged? Maybe after two days of losses the guy was getting desperate.

The computer chose to draw and apparently didn't like its card. "Pretender queen removes jack of diamonds, pawn of hearts enters," it droned. The duty officer could not control a strangled gasp. The jack had been his last card in the pyramid.

"Can you do anything?" Lyte asked, ready to toss in his cards.

The man tossed his onto the small pile in disgust, punching the machine for another game. Lyte raked the cubiz to his side of the seat separator. Nearly five hundred cubiz— yes, this was close to a duty officer's salary.

"Double or nothing?" the man suggested quickly.

"Where's your stake?" Lyte countered. The man reached for the computer keys, and Lyte added, "Cubiz only. No credits."

"A regular game, then." The other sighed, sneaking a

glance at Moran as he pulled out a handful of cubes. Lyte could not help but smile—the fool had actually nudged Moran awake once to cut off a game he was losing. Not this time. He was too far away....

Lyte watched without comment as the computer once more dealt the cards, sliding them across the smooth seat separator with precision. The duty officer's face lit with pleasure, and he placed his first card, the queen of diamonds, at the edifice spot. Grimly amused, Lyte placed his king of clubs directly below and to the right, in the heir-apparent position. The computer took ascendant with the king of hearts, and then Lyte lost interest.

Nuala. He was going to Nuala, the enigma of the stellar system, the only populated radioactive wasteland, the— *Stop it, fool.* His unease surprised him; he had visited many dangerous planets in his time. Perhaps it was knowing that Moran intended to marry one of the natives. *Or maybe it's because an assassin stalks us ... and I fear to find out who did the hiring....*

"Where do I get the radiation pills I have to take?" Lyte casually asked the duty officer. Startled, the man looked up from the board. Lyte gave the cards a glance; he'd probably assassinate the computer's king of hearts, moving his king to the ascendant position.

"Pills? You're staying?" The tone was incredulous.

"Of course not. I always take my vacations on transport ships."

It took the duty officer several moments to realize Lyte was being sarcastic. The man slowly flushed. "We rarely carry non-Nualans.... They change you—the pills, I mean. So the food won't make you sick. I've never taken them, I eat ship food. But whoever meets your party will probably bring them. Your hotel guide or embassy rep." The man dropped the ace of diamonds on the computer's king and slid still another king into the tier.

"Assassin takes king of hearts. King of spades ascendant, king of diamonds enters," the computer announced.

So someone from the palace would bring the pills to him. He decided not to mention their connections—apparently this ship had never carried Moran to Nuala. He studied the board. The duty officer had four of the seven slots. Time to shake him a bit. Lyte pulled out his ace.

"Assassin takes king of spades, queen of clubs to ascendant, Jack of pretenders enters." This time Lyte allowed himself a slight smile. The guy would go crazy trying to figure out why he didn't take the edifice. The hand was young. . . .

"They say if you take the pills five days, you're safe. Unless you get injured while on the planet or something. But I guess they have good doctors there—they should. People don't die from rav anymore," the duty officer murmured, still studying the board.

"Rav is radiation poisoning by ingestion?" Lyte asked, his fingers toying with his final card. He had heard all this, of course, but he was interested in the officer's perspective. He worked with Nualans; his prejudices might be enlightening.

"It's when you eat their food without building up to it first. Don't eat the meat," he added. The nostrils started twitching again. That jack of pretenders had him worried— an assassin in disguise?

"Ingestion. Are the pills controlled doses of radiation?" Lyte went on, probing.

"No, I think it changes your immune system somehow, so it likes the radiation instead of fighting it. Only Dielaan radiation, though—not ultraviolet or plutonium or anything. I guess it changes you permanently. People only take the series once." Sighing, he drew a card. "Pass."

Lyte also drew. Another ace—good. "Pass. Are they good for the radiation in the air . . . and the people?"

The man's sudden laugh was slightly derisive. "You'll be two days by boat from any bad area *and* from the irradiated colonists. Don't lose sweat over it."

"Boat?" Lyte had not found any references to boats. In fact, the hot city, Tolis, had scarcely been mentioned at all.

"The hot city is so hot, normal metals don't survive there, and even Nualan stone gets gritty and pebbly on the surface. Why hook them into the rail system? Who'd go to visit? And water travel is cheap—they don't want to bother with a transport system. The land is fragile, I've heard." He drew. "Pass."

Lyte pounced, both hands moving with precision.

"Jack of pretenders turns assassin, king of diamonds falls," the computer droned. "Queen of pretenders enters."

The man's jaw dropped. Lyte heard Moran chuckle—how long had he been awake?

Afraid that the man would stop talking, Lyte smoothly asked, "Why haven't you taken the series?"

Composing himself, the duty officer leaned back in his seat. "If I took the series, I might get assigned to the terminal there. Since I don't want to take the pills, they won't force me, so I don't get ground assignment." He seemed smug about the situation. "They aren't pushy, the Nualans, I'll say that for them." He studied the remaining vacant spot in the pyramid, planning a strategy.

"People always say metals don't survive on Nuala. *Any* kind of metal? Am I going to lose my timespot?" Lyte said suddenly, annoyance creeping into his voice. He hadn't thought of that before—the ship was Nualan, of course, it was made of vandrun, which was impervious to Dielaan radiation. But what about his shaving tackle, his timespot?

"I'll put anything you have on you into a vandrun case. You can carry that to your room. Just don't ever wear it near the launchpads," the man muttered, glancing at the computer to see why it hadn't made its move.

"But it *could* eat my timespot if I wore it?" Lyte persisted. It was the last thing his mother had given him before his father kicked him out, which was why he hung on to it.

The duty officer shrugged. "I suppose. I've never been in the city. I don't know how it works."

"Moran, stop shamming and talk to me," Lyte said without turning his head. He was momentarily distracted as the computer moved, filling the open space with the queen of hearts. The duty officer looked disappointed.

"About what?" Moran asked companionably.

"My timespot, joker. How potent is the radiation? Will it eat my timespot?"

"Only if you strap it to the nose of the ship before reentry." The man straightened in his seat, stretching broadly before continuing. "The microbe's harmless unless Dielaan radiation speeds up its metabolism." Moran glanced over at the edifice board. "Didn't you read about the *sinisus* microorganism?"

Lyte felt his irritation rising. "I read every damn thing in the library, and it didn't say a damn thing about any damn microbe."

Moran smiled; the expression was, as always, disarming. "There are microbes native to the Nualan solar system that leach minerals out of rocks. Normally they work about as fast as, say, a glacier melting. However, when one variety, *Arachnobacillus sinisus*, is exposed to Dielaan radiation, its metabolism goes crazy. A Dielaan radiation belt encircles this planet, so a ship's hull is exposed as it enters the atmosphere. The *sinisus* microbes hop on board, mutate, and start eating at an incredible rate. They can devour a non-Nualan ship in about a thirtysixday. This ship is Nualan—its vandrun hull has been 'doped' so the microbes won't like it. They'll jump off the ship to find something to eat, but since all Nualan metals are doped, the microbes starve to death."

"What if they find my timespot?" Lyte was still annoyed. This was the kind of information he had wanted and had been unable to find.

"The duty officer will seal it in a small case made of vandrun. You'll carry it off in that. The microbes from the ships die quickly, Lyte—if we stay out of this area, it's unlikely anything will happen to it. You can have the stuff plated if you're worried."

"Why isn't it mentioned in the tapes?"

"It is—they say that all metal valuables will be sealed for visitor protection. Most people don't care what causes things—only that they and their possessions are safe. Few tapes refer to the microbe, Lyte. And what you just heard is all that is recorded off-planet. The Nualans are very jealous of their secrets." Moran's gaze was steady, in control. "Are you finished with your game?"

Game. He had completely forgotten the stupid game. The duty officer was *still* staring at the board. He had only one move; if he had an ace, he could assassinate the pawn in front of his jack and move one space. But it gained him no money, nor an extra card. Surely he'd wait to see....

The man dropped an ace on the ten of hearts. "Assassin

takes pawn of hearts," came the computer's voice. As the cards slid to the right to fill the void, the duty officer moved another card into the tier. "Jack of spades enters."

Lyte was tired of the game. He whipped out his ace.

"Assassin takes queen of diamonds. King of clubs to edifice, queen of clubs to crown, jack of clubs to ascendant." The pronouncement was sweet; so was the look on the duty officer's face. Obviously he was hoping Lyte was too addled to think clearly. The warrior placed his last card. "King of pretenders enters."

Lyte heard Moran chuckle, and felt his body's tension continue to unwind. He had won. There was only one assassin card out; even if the fool had it, he couldn't remove both edifice and crown. And Lyte had a pretender threatening both the man's board cards.

The computer drew a card. "Pass."

His nostrils almost vibrating in his agitation, the duty officer drew. "Pass." There was no emotion in that tone. Lyte almost felt sorry for him again.

The warrior drew and set the card facedown without looking at it. Only two cards left mattered—pawn of pretenders and the last assassin. Did he want to bother? A bright core of irritation said yes. He looked at the card. Assassin. But one cannot draw and assassinate in the same turn. "Pass."

"Pass." Startled, Lyte glanced at the computer. It had missed its move! Or had the duty officer changed its game programming? Some variations did not allow pretender displacement. But they had played that version for three days. . . .

"Stupid machine," the nameless idiot muttered, drawing the last card. No, no change in the game, just a flaw in the program. Perhaps it realized it could not win and did not wish to inadvertently aid either side. But missing a play *did* often aid a side. "Pass."

Hell freeze it. Lyte dropped the ace on the duty officer's jack of clubs.

"Assassin takes jack of clubs, queen of pretenders to ascendant," the computer announced. It then filled the last tier spot with its own queen of spades. "Pass."

The duty officer sat very still for a long moment. "I concede." He carefully folded his three cards and set them facedown on the divider, hiding either three pawns or two pawns and a jack, Lyte knew. With only twenty-five cards in the deck, edifice strategy depended on the first three rounds. "Actually, it's not that many hours until we land. I think I'll get that valuables box right now." Nodding tightly, the man stood and moved off down the aisle.

Picking up the deck of cards, Lyte touched the keypanel. The computer's edifice board pulled away from the seat divider and slid into the wall. Finally Lyte looked over at Moran.

"All right?" the man asked. Lyte nodded. "We're arriving in about twelve Nualan hours. Tomorrow night is one of the biggest parties of the Nualan year, the Feast of Adel. You'll have a great time. Trust me, the Nualans really know how to throw a party."

Still reassuring; did he really look that bad? "I know," Lyte said casually, gesturing at the promotional 3AV hologram. "I can't believe this tape. Parties to celebrate a kid being fertile, for gods' sake! I'm sorry we're going to miss the Festival of Masks, though. It's about forty days from now. Sounds like fun—everyone dressing up in ornate masks, acting crazy all night, keeping their identity a secret . . . they visit the extended family during the day, I guess. . . ." He toyed with the tape controls, stopping the tape. "And *two* wedding ceremonies—"

"Only one wedding ceremony. It's public, held in the temple, and usually not until a child is on the way. If the couple is sterile, then it's . . . an excuse to throw a party." Moran chuckled at how neatly he had fallen into Lyte's trap. "But the first 'ceremony,' if there is one, is private, called Bonding. It has deep religious meaning, which probably wouldn't interest you. But any birth, any healthy child, is reason to celebrate, so when an adolescent reaches puberty and tests positive, the family goes on a blitz of partying." Moran glanced at his tiny timespot. "We're almost there. Are you having fun with the propaganda tape? Is there more to Nuala than trine gold?"

Lyte allowed a dramatic sigh to pass his lips as his fingers started to riffle the cards. "All right. I've seen the landscape information, and it's not nearly as bad as I thought it'd be.

You have to admit I need *some* information about this radio-active wasteland."

"Wasteland!" Moran shook his head, not bothering to hide his smile. "I've heard tales of the desert people creating paradise out of sterile sand. And the sinis, the irradiated humans, farm the hot lands. Things do flourish on Nuala, Lyte."

There was silence for a time, the only sound the ruffling of the edifice cards. "Did you learn all this at one time?" Lyte asked abruptly. "When you came here three terrayear ago, with the ambassador's party?"

"A great deal of it. Roe has taught me quite a bit." He smiled faintly. "I've known her three Nualan years tomorrow night—we met at the palace party the night of the Feast of Adel." Moran's smile grew broader. "Relax! You're going to the most lavish party of the year. The Feast of Adel, ushering in High Festival and the new year—party before penitence, and then party again! And the women, Lyte! The women—"

"Can steal a man's soul. No thanks." Lyte smiled as he said it. "I just wish we could stay longer so I could find out why you like the place so much. You talk as if you've come home. . . . You have a home, Moran—I'm the one who was thrown out."

He had spoken easily, but Moran politely skirted the subject of his family. "A fifteenday furlough isn't bad—"

"Elevenday, Moran," Lyte reminded him casually, starting to set out the cards faceup in an intricate pattern. He carefully controlled his sudden tension. Moran was as skilled at "reading" emotional currents as any commando—perhaps more skilled than most. If he realized Lyte was blocking . . .

He knew—and that knowledge pained Lyte. Lyte could see the puzzlement in his eyes. Commandos usually did not "read" their friends, nor did they block each other. Moran *had* to wonder why Lyte was blocking. But he chose not to ask. *And that's why they sent me. You're too trusting.*

"I forgot. Why didn't Officer Matias tell me about the meeting? I would have scheduled my furlough earlier." Moran actually sounded annoyed. Interesting; he did not criticize his superiors very often. . . .

Lyte shrugged. "It came up quickly, I guess. They must have a special assignment for us or something." He grinned. "If we'd known in advance, I could have found a discount trip to Mercury 7—and you'd be traveling alone." Moran smiled at that. He had issued many invitations to Nuala over the past few years, but this was the first time Lyte had accepted. Usually the sumptuary worlds were too much of a lure.

Are you so in love with this woman that you can't see? Lyte wanted to shout. *It is friendship that brings me here, but not coincidence.* His fingers hesitated on a card. *They told me someone wants to kill you for even contemplating marrying a Nualan. And they told me to get you off the planet four days early. Did you think your furloughs to visit her on Nuala or at the university went unnoticed*? Lyte shivered at the implications of such an assassination. Moran might be the perfect warrior; he was a decorated war hero, even a scholar. He was also an aristocrat of the bluest blood, the eldest son of a wealth-poor, title-rich Secundus CSSI family. *I, too, am from the planet Secundus....* Lyte knew the bigotry of the CSSI system, knew its conscious and unconscious prejudices. It had a social system that married off strangers—his parents among them—and forced them to remain together, to produce heirs to great wealth. Lyte shook his head to clear it. He thought he had escaped Secundus. And now the values of CSSI had the power to reach across a stellar alliance and touch them once again....

He could believe such a tale; could believe it of the fanatical aristocrats of CSSI, the first system colonized by humans. *The Axis Tribunal ordered me to protect you, to entrap the assassin, if possible. So I'll stop him ... if he exists.* Lyte sighed inaudibly and set down the card in his hand.

There was more to it ... what, Lyte did not yet know. But the tribunal had withheld information—Lyte had "read" that fact as clearly as printed words. They told him to tell Moran there was a meeting. *Was* there a meeting? Had the war effort *really* calmed down enough for them to take a furlough? Nuala was only one system away from the front. Lyte had a feeling they were being used, but how? Why?

The only way to solve the mystery was to follow his orders and shadow Moran. A commando followed orders, he did not question them. On a planet where no one carried blasters, a commando should be safe . . . unless, like Moran, he was so smitten by the place that he had lost all caution. Lyte would provide the buffer.

"Just be careful, for my sake, all right?" Moran asked. "Don't offend anyone. You can bargain, and flirt, but . . . remember the old proverb: 'The Nuala do not lie and therefore are not easily deceived.' They are a highly civilized and moral race within their own laws, and they don't trust *off-worlders.*"

"Do they really never lie?" Lyte said, suddenly interested.

Moran made a wry face. "Nualans are instinctively, or culturally, like commandos—they are highly skilled at 'reading' emotional currents. So they are difficult to deceive face-to-face. But they have the same problems commandos have—the more people present, the harder to sift out the emotions of an individual. So Nualans don't try to lie to *individuals*; they may keep secrets or leave out information or avoid a topic . . . but they usually don't lie to each other— why risk it? Yet they're human. Their politics are as convoluted and scheming as any I've seen, and they have their share of criminals—not many, but some. Violent crimes are very rare there. More often it's theft, illegal trading. . . ." He returned to the question. "In other words, *I* wouldn't risk trying to cheat a trader in the bazaar, but if you can attract a crowd with your bargaining, *you'll* probably get away with it."

"Because I bargain better than anyone else you know?" Lyte inquired innocently.

Moran fixed him with a stern eye. "Just use whatever sense you have, all right? Remember, the Nualans are an interesting dichotomy where off-worlders are concerned— both hospitable *and* paranoid."

"If I had been abandoned after a colony mission backfired, I'd be paranoid too. It took the Axis hundreds of years to find the courage to start colonizing again after the Nualan disaster. How many people are born sterile today?"

"About seventy percent now, although they are still called

80s. Apparently fertility has nothing to do with 'hotness'; many sinis, irradiated humans, are fertile. However, an exceptionally large number of cool young people have been testing out fertile lately. For the Nualans, it's a reason to rejoice. Everything here is centered around gene recombination; the child rearing, the multiple spouses, the royal succession through the woman's line—all to keep the genes moving."

"Can you survive the intrigues of Baskh Atare's court, Moran?" Lyte suddenly asked bluntly. "Can you grasp the possibility of fathering a king and having no power yourself?"

"A king?" Moran shook his head in denial. "Ronuviel has two healthy older sisters, one of them pregnant. We will have our place. With Ronuviel as a hot healer and as the Mythmaker, we will have just enough connection to the capital to keep everyone happy. I've been a scientist, a historian, a musician, and a cartographer, and I was pretty good at all of them. I have only one more year of this tour to serve; then I'm going back to Nuala for the rest of my life." Moran looked thoughtful. "To live on a planet where they abhor killing—to never have to kill again. . . ."

Lyte was silent. He had suspected that Moran would not renew his service. But had he really thought out the current political situation? Lyte knew that the heir was a scientist, not interested in ruling Nuala—and that the second son was of fragile mind, possibly already insane. The third would probably make a fine ruler, if the various enemies of the ruling Atare House did not kill him first. One man had been trying to supplant the Atares for fifty years.

"A deceptive paradise," Lyte murmured, hoping Moran would think he meant the contrast of the harsh beauty of Nuala and the dangers of its radiation. "If more people are being born fertile, will they keep the polyandry and the polygyny? I'm not sure I'd like to be one of three husbands—that I could deal with it, I mean. How about you?"

"Anyone who marries an off-worlder can have only one spouse—they don't think we handle their ways very well, either. Roe and I will be considered a family unit, with whatever children we may have. They like to know who the parents

are to keep track of genetic disease, but other than that, they
don't care. There is no such word as *illegitimate* in Nualan,
by the way."

"Isn't polygamy the norm?" Lyte persisted. "The tape
mentioned—"

"No. It is totally free choice. Those who are fertile—
the 20s—are raised believing that they are responsible for
gene recombination and should try and find more than one
spouse, but it is up to the individual. Most prefer monogamy.
Only the off-worlders and Atares are bound to one spouse at
a time. Sometimes 20s will marry 80s, but they keep looking
for a 20."

"I'm getting confused again."

"I don't think you ever pay attention. Here's a real
example—Arrez, the high priest, has four wives. The first,
Elana, is a love match. The second was required because
he is high priest and she high priestess—it's part of the
religion. But he and the priestess decided to make a *real*
marriage out of it, not merely a symbolic one. Now, the
high priestess already had a husband when she married
Arrez. But there is nothing between her husband and Elana.
They are friends—maybe only casually, I don't know—
and show respect to a member of their extended family.
But for the two of them to get involved with one another
. . . well, it would be a little too much togetherness and
usually doesn't happen. It could, but the Nualans are very
conscious of possible tensions in families. That's why god-
parents help raise children for periods of time. It also makes
the kids more secure, knowing that more than one person
loves them. Am I making sense?"

"I think so. You're saying the morality is very strict
within Nualan religion and custom. I take it that it works?"

"So far," Moran answered, "five thousand years' worth.
They are a rather unique people. There's always enough
love for the Nualans . . . it never has a limit."

Lyte's eyes settled on the card in his hand—a king.
He kept his thoughts to himself. People go there by choice?
What draws you, Moran? What makes you choose Nuala?

MT. AMURA,   FOURHUNDRED   VESPERS
NUALA   TWENTYFOURDAY

SONOMA   NUALAN
MOUNTAIN   YEAR 4952
RANGE

Dusk fell slowly, subtly on Amura, shadows giving way to night. The street illuminaries blazed on in the distant city, and Roe searched for major buildings and forums. It was no use; the temple and the palace were simple enough to find, as well as the medical complex and fine arts center. All else vanished in the increasing glow of the capital. The synod's current yearly session would end tonight, if they could ever pass those last two bills, she thought wryly. Most likely the elders had personal worries. In less than one Nualan year elections for the 708th Synod would be held, and with the current heated debate on tariffs, immigration, and the ever-present 20s-versus-80s problem, quite a few men and women were finding their benches in jeopardy. One nice thing about the session ending—only the garden and honor lights would be on, and the inner-city residents could sleep with their blinds up and windows open.

The night deepened, and still she and her brother did not speak. Roe let her hearing sharpen, waiting for the symphony to begin. She could hear the furtive rustlings of ground-stalkers, the wild akemmi and the lante; the shifting of tiny baby silva birds in their nests deep in the caves behind them. It was late for silvas to be nesting. Soon the adults would begin to migrate. She wondered if the little ones would be able to keep up.

Roe glanced out of the corner of her eye. Braan had not moved in hours. A few cheeps and trills came from the treetops below. The night symphony was beginning. The soft insect harmony grew louder. More and more Faxmur birds began to sing as the last streaks of light vanished from the horizon. Roe sat up, looking for the Brethren. The Seven Systems were so called because of the extremely close proximity of seven stars, Nuala's young pale yellow sun the farthest out. The others soon appeared as the brightest constellation in the sky, shaped like the keystone of the Atare's office.

Roe moved again to pull her long dark hair free and abruptly noticed the waterfall, its flow momentarily interrupted. She waited, smiling—a splash followed. Some small animal was going for a swim. They loved the high pool as much as her family did. Braan rolled over and sat up, looking out over the wide valley below. Only the multitude of lights was visible, and even farther off, beyond the center of the city, the huge river Amura, the glowing orbs of the Brethren reflected in it. The sea was darkness—there were no moons yet this night. Zair moved, smelling the akemmi, his ears flicked forward. Roe put a gentle hand on his back to restrain him. The monstrous dog dropped his head.

"Shall we build a fire?" she asked. They were staying the night. For most it was a full day's climb simply to the bottom of the mountain and the way station; they planned to cut through the caverns. They would have to leave well before dawn to meet Moran's transport.

"If you are cold," Braan replied. Roe did not move. The dry season was ending and the rains beginning, but there was no frost yet. She had only wanted a bit of cheer, anything to snap him out of his mood. She studied the black shape of his square jaw in the backdrop of the capital lights. Enid had had a relapse, and the truth was on the lips of every citizen; she was dying. Finally, after more years than Roe cared to count. And no one could blame Braan for taking a few days away from her side. Indeed, many wondered that he had the strength to bear it, that he had not taken a lover long ago, Atares being barred by law from more than one mate. Six long years since the birth of their daughter; six years since Enid contracted the virus that had slowly destroyed her health, her mind, and now, soon, her life. Long ago she had ceased to recognize any of them. As a healer, Roe had never entertained such thoughts, but perhaps the burden that hung over their entire family would lift if only the poor woman would die in peace, take the Last Path, her soul free.

Braan, she was sure, did not desire fire or even conversation. He wanted only to sit in this glade, oblivious to

the world, his life, his responsibilities, his future. When
had things been simpler—six, seven terrayear ago? He had
been twenty-three terra then. . . . Ten years ago, serving a
short tenure as a trader, in reality searching the galaxy for
an intelligent, healthy woman brave enough to leave behind
everything for her man and an unknown future. It was the
same when their older brothers and sisters went searching,
in many ways harder for the women. A man strong enough
in himself to forsake all for the big planet was a rare man
indeed. No one came halfway to Nuala. . . .

"Moran will arrive for the feast?"

It was more statement than question, calling Roe back
to the moment. Strange that they had discussed Moran so
little, Roe thought. Usually they told each other everything,
these two, best-loved of their generation. Praise Mendulay
that their oldest brother, Tal, took no offense at Braan's
popularity, believing it could only help the royal family.
Deveah, however, who was second in line—that was a
different matter. His resentment of Braan was well-known
by all. Braan was careful, very careful, around Deveah.
But Tal was the heir. He loved Braan and respected Ronuviel's opinion of him. Stay healthy, Tal, very healthy.
. . . Never had there been a bloodletting over the throne, a
prodigious achievement. She prayed there never would be.

"Of course," Roe answered, "providing the transport
is on time. Sometimes I wonder if we are wrong, placing
such restrictions on freight and passenger ships, even those
crewed by our own people."

"We are right."

Ronuviel's lips tightened at the hardness in his voice.
Like Baskh Atare, Braan did not trust the Axis Republic,
the confederation governing their interstellar alliance. Someday they might turn their backs once again on Nuala . . . he
did not want his descendants to blame him for failing the
vigil.

"Will you announce the marriage then?" Braan continued.

"He has not formally asked for marriage," she answered, a chuckle in her voice. Braan snorted, stifling his

laughter. Roe wondered if he suspected that the first, private ceremony had already taken place.

"Does Moran know that you are pregnant?"

"Braan! I have run no tests, had no signs—I have not even spoken to Elana!" She could feel Braan's smile in the soft darkness, his pleasure at cracking her beautifully mannered facade. If the foremost healer on the planet had not questioned her health, why did he? He always knew everything. . . .

"Elana knows everything," Braan said gently, insistently, interrupting her thoughts.

"Not this time," Roe replied. "With so much illness in her family, and of course—"

"I know. She is often with Enid, and when she is not, Shinar stays with her. The child will make a good doctor someday." The image of Elana's lovely daughter brightened their thoughts momentarily.

"That 'child' is a year older than Liel, and there is already talk of sending our sister out traveling early," Roe murmured.

"No." Braan's voice was hard again. Of course, the decision was up to their mother, Ila the Ragaree, and their mother's twin brother, Baskh Atare. As Mother of the Heir and as Atare, their word was final. Only their father could have challenged the verdict, and he had been dead ten years. But no Atare, no Nualan, had left the planet before their sixteenth birthday, unless to emigrate. And Roe knew Braan saw no reason to change now. Only those values instilled before adulthood seemed capable of withstanding the wreckage the Axis had become. And Liel was very innocent; too innocent for Axis games.

"Do you like Moran? You have never really told me," Roe suddenly asked.

"You never told me if you liked Enid," Braan responded. "Strange, how no one questions the choice of an Atare, and yet few of us have chosen badly."

And yet I have always wanted your approval, and you have always wanted mine. . . . Ronuviel did not play at "who asked first."

"I grew to care for her. Enid's warmth was reserved for you and the children." Roe's voice was noncommittal, care-

ful, and Braan relaxed. It was true. Roe knew he was thankful
for the friendship she had offered Enid. The woman had
been—she was—a secretive woman, not cold but cool, a
bit overwhelmed by the joyous warmth of the Atares, of
Nuala. It was not what the average off-worlder expected.

"I shall be proud to call him brother," Braan answered.

Roe waited, her thoughts chaotic. His reply was as ambiguous as his turnabout question. A brilliant war hero, high
in the Axis eyes for one so young; yes, of course he is good
for the family. But Roe did not want it to be as Enid and her
were, always a barrier—

Braan turned toward her. "And, if he will let me, friend."

Now it was Roe's turn to relax. "You think too much,"
she began abruptly.

"So do you."

"But I do not brood." The tone was slightly accusing,
and Roe cursed it even as it passed her lips.

"You do not have anything to brood about," Braan replied, apparently not offended.

"You . . ."

Braan glanced up. "Touché" came the archaic answer.
He rolled over on his side, facing her. "Do not worry, I will
take a quick hike around the capital when we get back. Use
up all my excess energy." Roe flashed him an irritated look.
"Take a hike around the capital" was one of Baskh's favorite
brush-off sayings to his children, his sister's children, and
his advisers alike, used whenever they stepped out of line.
Braan heard it often, before he left the planet, and after,
before Enid's illness. For over five years he had kept silent,
openly volunteering no suggestions, no criticism of the regime. His friends worried about him and his detractors fretted,
expecting an eruption of the fiery Braan of old.

"What do you wait for, belaiss?" she asked gently, dropping down on one elbow. He stirred at the old endearment,
not looking up. A night breeze touched them, sending a shiver
through Roe and blowing Braan's dark hair away from his
face.

"For Enid to die . . . so I can try to live again" came the
steady answer.

"You know—"

"That is not what you mean? What can I do, Ronuviel?" Now he met her gaze, eyes very dark in the starlight. "I am well beyond the schooling of the young ones, and I have no specific interests other than sculpture. The art pays and I gain a name—but I need more. I do not have the heart to seek another woman. I am not sure I could bear the pain, should something happen again...." His voice was very soft, perfectly controlled, as he spoke of things she had no doubt he had told no one else. "Yet I do not think the synod would consider two children my full contribution to the gene pool and would bar me from the military. I know, such is the burden of a 20—what I would not give to be a nameless 80!"

"And the synod is also barred."

"I could give up my land holdings, even my claim to the throne. It would not be enough. If Tal sat the throne, 'they' would talk collusion. If Deveah, between us we would destroy the people. Shall I forsake home and family, never to return? Is freedom its own reward?"

"If Arrez—" Roe began very carefully. The high priest, so unlike what the off-worlders seemed to think a man of God should be, was Roe's dearest of friends. Even he walked as softly as akemmi on this subject.

"No!" Braan sat up abruptly, staring out over the distant, twinkling lights of Amura, the swift disintegration of a shooting star.

"I am sorry ... but, Braan, never have I felt the spirit so strongly in any man—as much as Arrez in deep prayer— and you wear it like another skin."

"Ah, yes, St. Braan." His attempt at self-mockery always failed; the spirit was too much with him.

"There is reason that the best to rule is third son, not first." Barely a whisper, though the *guaard* hidden on the ledge below would repeat nothing, ever. Braan turned to silence her, but she sat up, freezing his lips with a touch of her finger. "Tal is a scientist at heart, Deveah a fanatic. You know that. I do—Baskh does. As much as I wish you were as devoted to art as I am to medicine, I know that there is purpose in this. I fear it, but I know you will not be given a burden greater than you can bear. I love you, crazy brother, and I am not alone in that. Your time is coming. I only wish I could lighten your heart, to ignite the cunning, witty, brash young cad you used to be."

"I grew up."

"No . . . you aged. I do not think you will ever grow up." She smiled then, her perfect teeth reflecting starlight, her strange eyes, the only set like his in this generation, a kaleidoscope before him. He managed a faint smile, the burden of silence slipping from his shoulders. He held her a moment, sharing the invisible strength from her molten fire within.

"I wish to stop at the shrine on the way down. How about your fire?" He released her and dug around in the pack he had used as a pillow. Zair leapt up to help, the huge descendant of Terra's kingly dogs forgetting that he was no longer a puppy.

"Down, fool, you will crush the heat disks!" Braan tried helplessly to fend him off, the beast retaliating by pushing him over with a large paw and cleaning his face for him. Roe's low, golden laughter rang back from the waterfall.

CHAPTER TWO

AMURA,   FOURHUNDRED   SEXT
NUALA   TWENTYFIVEDAY,
                          4952

Braan leapt out of the solar car, still tying the waist sash of his long-sleeved mandraia shirt. *Idiot, slow down, you have beaten the transport, it has not even touched down yet!* His feet slowed to a walk as his mind continued to race. Moran and Lyte, Lyte and Moran—it had to be Lyte. Who else would be coming to Nuala at High Festival? He touched the packet of radiation pills in his pocket. Tourists remained in their hotels through the religious services, a sevenday of confinement—*We know what is in his file; we are prepared for him. Calm down.* Braan's kaleidoscopic eyes recorded the presence of his younger twin brothers, Kalith and Kavan. They lounged before the gates. One was sunning himself in the blazing rays of Kee, now at her zenith, while the other meditated in the shade of a towering neudeya evergreen.

"Tracking says the ship is here. Can we pull this spectacle together?" Both youths leapt at the sound of his voice.

"Braan! How did you get back so fast?" It burst from one of them, the energy and worshipful tone revealing him as Kavan long before Braan was close enough to see that his left iris was topaz-brown; his right, emerald-green. Kal's eyes were reversed; left green, right brown.

"Sprouted wings and flew. The duty officer sent word that he has two for us. Perhaps Moran finally talked Lyte into coming." Without a backward glance Braan sauntered toward the launching bay.

"We finally get to meet the mysterious Lyte?" Kal asked, his voice soft in the afternoon heat.

"He undoubtedly thinks just the opposite—that he is arriving on the mysterious Nuala," Braan replied. "Come, let us go." They started inside the huge landing bay. "Are you two ready to return to the Axis?"

Kavan's expression immediately turned to one of disgust. Kalith remained impassive, as Braan had expected. Only seventeen, the twins were already working at cover trades. Kal posed as a merchant's son, polishing his already considerable diplomatic skill, while Kavan worked as a navigator's apprentice, submerging his fierce Atare temper in endless detail. The High Festival marked the coming of autumn, the new year, and heralded their return to the Axis Guilds. Neither of them wanted to leave, but for different reasons. Kavan was having "feelings" about the Atare and did not want to leave the old man. And Kal did not want to leave Shinar. Ah, the problems that could bring, Kal and Shinar. . . .

But Lyte, now—why did he choose a serious religious festival as the time to visit, why *this* particular furlough? Moran had asked him many times, but the gambling worlds had always held a brighter lure. Now Lyte came to them . . . who was he, really? He had his own law and own sense of honor—this was well-known—and Braan doubted that they coincided with anyone else's. Moran alone had any control over him at all, and then only a strange, entwined mutual respect and friendship. The disowned son of aristocrats, the silvery, ice-eyed Lyte went his own way, always.

They stepped to the loading platform, and Braan's musings faded. The three stood elbow-to-elbow in the landing bay gateway, watching the drifting *Gerrymander* silently drop into the launch hole. Amazing how gently the self-propelled junk heap could set down when she— Braan's thoughts broke off at the tremendous squeal of the hatch hinges, grating as they opened. Two Nualan security guards appeared, as if from nowhere, and were behind them, just in front of the white pillars.

The legendary white pillars. Not the originals; they were in the museum. These were stone copies and filled with intricate devices capable of detecting anything from a gamma cannon down to the tiniest powdered poison. When the Nualans stated that theirs was a sanctuary planet, they did not jest, and the white pillars marked the beginning of Nualan domain. Following interstellar law, anyone passing through them was given a place of safety until they could, or wished to, continue their journey. Many never left. As it was difficult to lie to a Nualan, criminals did not bother trying to come to Nuala. Only those desperate—the misjudged, the oppressed, those without power or friends—came to Nuala.

Moran and Lyte hurried off the craft, their personal tackle in hand. Moran deflated visibly at the sight of the three men—Lyte noticed and smiled grandly, giving his friend a sly nudge. "My, we have the love sickness badly, don't we? You'd better check into clinic when we get back, take a pill or something."

Moran gave him an unsettling glance as Braan gestured to them.

"You finally talked him into it?" Kavan asked as they walked over. Kal poked him; the young man retreated for the moment.

"Atares, this is Lyte. Braan, Kalith, and Ka-van," Moran said clearly, raising an amused eyebrow at Kavan.

"Bra-an?" Lyte asked, trying not to stare at the trio's eyes. The man smiled faintly.

"Close—softer on the second *a*. Most humans miss that—the Setteos are better with our vowels for some reason."

"There is a lot of inflection in Nualan. In human terms it's a very old language," Moran said. "What did you do with my woman?"

"She is at the palace cleaning up. We were in the mountains last night. Shall we go? The solar car is right outside." As he spoke, Braan started walking toward the gate. Moran and Lyte followed, passing the pillars and stepping on the

platform before the actual exit. Lyte looked around curiously
as they stepped out into daylight, apparently glad to leave
the strange launch bay with its huge automatic ceiling hatch.
Braan received the impression that the man felt he had been
coerced into coming here. How to reassure him? Moran had
mentioned he liked mountains. . . .

---

*Running, running, stop—listen . . . run again. How long
had she been running? Running. Who would have believed
a military wheel had so many corridors? Running. Had security been alerted? A general alarm? Running. Running.
Damn! Why did you leave Mercury 7? Never, never on the
spur of the moment, you know better— She rounded the
corner to find herself in the midst of bodyguards, facing the
bottomless eyes of her patron—*

She awoke with a soft cry, quickly stifled by her own
fist. Fighting back tears, the woman tried to make herself
comfortable, rearranging her shapeless, cowled dress to make
the most of its heavy fabric. Why couldn't this dilapidated
heap of a transport ship—what was its name, *Gerrymander*?—be tempra-controlled? Too much of a luxury for the
cargo, she supposed. But she had traveled this way once
before, fleeing the bombed-out wreckage of Capricorn V.

Suddenly she noticed the change; the numbing vibration
of the floor and walls had ceased. They had landed. She was
on Nuala. *Nuala.* Her heart froze at the very thought. *Nuala.
Close to the war zone. A sanctuary planet. They aren't even
human here, not even—*

Stop it! She had seen only two Nualans in her entire
life. One was a handsome older man, an officer spending his
furlough on Mercury 7. The other was an example of the
genetic disasters caused by the Nualan System's natural radiation, a horrifying memory from a holographic history tape.
Ancient, ancient history, they're not like that anymore. . . .
Every myth and legend she had heard in the past tenyear rose
up to choke her. Forcing them down, she reminded herself
that it was merely sanctuary. She did not have to stay.

How would she live? It had been three long years since
she had worked as a planter—the restricted agriguilds had

seen to that. And what had Tyr said? "There are no hustlers on Nuala. They don't need them." Then her dissipated brother had laughed, abandoning her in the docking bay. What had he meant? How would she earn money to leave? How—

Calming herself, she reached into memory, dredging up her name, the name she had not spoken aloud in three years. And still could not—not yet. *Teloa. I was Teloa. I have survived the destruction of Capricorn V, the halfway camps, the tratore worlds. Nothing can be worse than Mercury 7.*

Quietly she clicked open the hatch to the passenger corridor. She was unable to control a smile. Fortunate that stowaways were so rare; it would have been harder to slip out the cargo doors. She allowed herself simply to listen for a while; what she could see and hear through the opening disturbed her.

Only two passengers for this sanctuary world. The pillars—she had to pass the pillars. They marked the beginning of Nualan domain. Gods, the outer hatch was going to close. It was now or never. She slipped out from behind the packing cube, through the inner hatch, and into the corridor. Teloa touched the outer railing, barely two steps down the ramp.

"Hey! You! Hold it right there!" It was the duty officer; it had to be. He knew every cube and passenger by sight, and she was certainly not on his list. Horror at returning to the military wheel lent wings to her feet. She charged down the porta-ramp and sprinted for the gateway. The duty officer hesitated a moment too long, not believing anyone could move that fast in such high-heeled shoes. Then he ran after her, still yelling.

It was impossible not to hear the commotion. As the group on the platform turned, Teloa pushed by one of the burly guards and through the wide pillars. The pale blond man moved first, grabbing her around the waist as she passed and pinning her in a commando grip. She struggled but could not break the hold. The two guards stepped forward and seized the young duty officer; much to his dismay, for the men were unbelievably tall and magnificently proportioned, as big as ober players. The duty officer's face was changing colors, his fury at the breaking point.

"She's a stowaway!! I claim Axis—" he began to screech.

"I seek sanctuary!" Teloa blurted out.

The officer stopped in mid-gasp. Teloa was startled at the immediate and almost imperceptible shift in the reactions of the Nualans. Before, they were observers. Now it was as if they were lined up behind her, supporting her. The two dressed as commandos also noticed; only the one restraining her seemed surprised. So it was true. On Nuala the ancient law still applied—the accused was innocent until proven guilty. It was one of the few places in the Axis Republic that this still held true.

"Why do you seek sanctuary?"

Teloa turned, recognizing the voice as the man who called himself Braan. He gestured at her silvery captor, who released her. Composing herself, she took in the Nualan's appearance at a glance. About her height—then she remembered the heels—graceful, compact, dark-haired, with intense green eyes that— She was startled. That were marbled with a soft topaz brown! She felt the assurance and knew this man was someone of importance. Amazement crept over her, and the woman quickly perceived why. Rarely did she encounter a man who was not covetous of her statuesque beauty or embarrassed, even angered, by her height. This man gave her a steady, all-encompassing gaze. He knew exactly what— even who—she was and did not care in the least.

"Why do you seek sanctuary?" he repeated gently. Teloa started to speak and hesitated. "The Nuala do not lie and therefore are not easily deceived. If you wish to stay, you must state your reason, even if you have lied all your life. When you pass through the gate, your past disintegrates. We do not care what you were or claim to be . . . only what you become."

"I was working on Mercury 7 and was invited by a wealthy man to tour the tratores of the Seven Systems at his expense. He arranged for my transport to the military wheel Annular 14 and then refused to pay my passage through. I— retaliated. . . ." Teloa began.

"In the traditional manner?" Braan asked.

"Yes." She gave him a direct glance with her clear gray eyes. "He turned out to be a powerful Axis councilmember, and he was not amused. He sought my arrest, or death, so—"

"But that's against the code!" the blond commando burst in, "I know it's not law, but if you cheat a hustler, you deserve what you—"

"My word against his?" Teloa interrupted, knowing him as Lyte by his voice. He paused, and looked as if he might speak again. Then he shook his head, turning to inspect the visible city. "I asked for transportation to the nearest sanctuary. I don't even—I didn't know where I was headed," she finished, aware she had a professional habit to leave behind, and quickly. There was a long pause.

"Kal, send for a temple minister." One of the youths quickly ducked into a narrow alley and disappeared. Braan turned back to Teloa. "You must stay at the temple until the ship leaves port, in case some of the off-world crew 'objects' to your sanctuary."

"Who let you on board?" the duty officer demanded. Teloa was silent.

"That would not be fair to expose such an . . . honorable, selfless deed." Teloa forced herself not to react to Braan's voice; to the dry, almost hollow sound. It was as if he knew her brother Tyr had abandoned her. The duty officer became offensive again. "Punch up a one-way ticket, man," Braan said abruptly. "You know you will be paid." The off-worlder departed toward the ticket point. Kalith returned and nodded to Braan, who indicated that the other men should wait for him outside. Then he walked over to the high rock wall, a soft mustard moss covering its rugged black side. There was a bench carved out of the same stone, and he indicated that Teloa could sit if she wished. The guards remained by the pillars, watching the duty officer prepare the ticket.

"The temple ministers will have some other clothes for you, and a hot tub. Have you ever had any . . . other skills? It is not necessary, but you could become bored here quickly," Braan continued, adjusting a small votive candle in a wall sconce.

"I was a planter on Capricorn V, before the bombs fell," she answered steadily.

"We always have need of planters. Stay as long as you wish." Stay as long as you wish? That was not what her brother had implied. Suddenly the duty officer reappeared and thrust a small support slab in front of Braan. Braan eyed the man a moment—the off-worlder looked away. The Nualan picked up the sconce candle and dripped some wax on the slab. As he read the recording he removed the ring on his finger and rolled it in the wax. "I believe you know where to be reimbursed?" The officer, a bit sour, nodded and returned to his ramp, carefully avoiding the guards. Braan glanced down the alley against the wall and turned to Teloa.

"Your name is . . . ?"

"Tele—Teloa. I was Teloa—Tay to family," she managed to get out.

"I am Braan of Atare. Welcome." He flashed her a gentle smile so charming that she returned it despite her fear. He turned and seemed momentarily surprised to see the woman who stepped forward. She wore an ankle-length white dress of some obscure natural fiber, corseted in a rich, dark sienna brown of the same material, only heavier. The brown lined her dress, peeping out of the long, slit sleeves, hood, and side slit. Looking closer, Tay saw that the rosy-cheeked, blue-eyed, crimson blonde was almost as tall as she, bearing a beauty mature, yet fresh. Perhaps thirty, thirty-two terrayears?

"I am Dr. Elana. You are . . . Teloa? Can you walk?" the woman asked, offering support.

Teloa tentatively reached for her hand, calming her inner shaking. "I can walk." Remembering her manners, she turned to Braan and, wrapping herself in the shreds of her dignity, said, "Thank you." Braan nodded, and the Nualan woman led her away.

———

Braan walked briskly to the solar car and hopped in. The *guaard* in the driver's seat punched up the numbers of the palace, and the car began to move.

"How do you know she wasn't lying?" Lyte asked.

"We know," Kavan offered. They drove on in silence.

AMURA   SEXT

In a daze, Teloa was led down into the center of the city. Pedestrians thronged around her, and she found herself still tall but not excessively so—most Nualan men were at least her height. Genetically altered to be so? she wondered, and all her fears crept back. She kept her eyes on the buildings—strange buildings—or on the flagstone road, avoiding the interested and admiring looks of the men. She felt dirty, ugly, and exhausted, and, at the least, a man was responsible for her current problems. A man had also remedied them, at least temporarily. Perhaps she could call that a fair trade. It was too much to think about. She understood that this was an older section of the city—what city was this?—and that no building seemed to be over four stories. Everything was stone, and she was aware of towers. She felt so tired, so confused.

They left the narrow walkway and stepped out into a wide-open space, grass-covered and thick with late-blooming flowers, bushes, and trees whose leaves were just beginning to darken to a greenish indigo. Off to the right, among dark trees, a small lake sparkled. Above the tall, strange foliage was an incredible brilliance, as if the afternoon star had settled onto the hill in the center of the city's park. Tay gasped as she realized the source.

There were other buildings within the Axis alliance with more gold-and-silver inlay, more jewels; taller, more extensive, even more ancient. None had the starkly simple and majestic tones of the Mendularion, the temple of Mendulay. It was unlike any existing building—totally unlike secular Nualan architecture.

"It is impressive, is it not?" the woman agreed. "I forget how it affects visitors to our world. The Mendularion is white marble, the roof gold. It is empty except for a few tiny candles, lit to signify a birth, marriage, or death, or occasionally a milestone in someone's life. The priests and priestesses are often seen there, busy with personal prayers or special requests. And there are no locks on the doors; citizens can spend the night if they feel the invisible pull of Mendulay."

Elana led Teloa to an area directly below and to one side

of the temple where they found a moving, snakelike metal runner. It seemed to have no track or containment, yet moved smoothly along at a moderate pace.

"Stand in the center," the woman told her. "Do not catch your heels underneath!" Teloa leapt and landed in the center. It felt good to stop walking; tiring to stand. Elana noticed. "The catwalk will take us beneath the temple to the living quarters. There are some guest rooms there, and you can sleep as long as you wish."

The catwalk was totally silent, hence its name. Teloa looked down to see that she was now standing on a step, and the walkway was moving swiftly uphill, approaching a small tunnel. Had she stepped from flat to stairs, or had the runner created its own stairway? She was almost positive she had not moved, so the runner must have done it for her. Good gods, she hadn't even noticed. . . .

"You keep your poise well. Most people are a bit un-nerved by the catwalk the first time they ride it," the Nualan said suddenly as they entered the tunnel.

"I—noticed a change," Teloa answered, not sure her statement made sense. Elana either did not notice or pretended not to—she indicated that Teloa should step off on an up-coming platform. Tay jumped again, to avoid catching her decorative heels, and watched the sheen of the walk as it passed, like a river of silver amphibians.

"Do not look too closely! You could become dizzy," Elana counseled, leading Teloa into the depths of the hill. They entered a wide, natural-stone corridor lit by shafts lead-ing to the surface. The area was cool but not cold. Teloa's guide stopped at a panel and pressed its corner. It was im-mediately lit, revealing a color-coded set of block catacombs, most of the cubes having a yellow dot in the centers. "One of the suites for visiting dignitaries is vacant, you are in luck! Sheer luxury. Come." She led off down the corridor.

Had Tay been alone, she would have become lost in the bewildering maze of rough white stairs and walkways, al-though she noticed several blank panels and assumed that they were also maps of some kind. Finally the woman reached tall double doors and opened them.

"Welcome." Elana walked straight ahead to the opposite

wall, and the distance was not short. She opened another set
of tall double doors and stepped into brilliant starlight, which
was just beginning to angle past the doorsill. As Tay walked
into the room she discovered that the living quarters were
built right into the side of the hill. Looking out the doorway,
she saw the mountains, their foothills covered with homes.
For a moment she said nothing; she had never seen mountains.
She could think of no words grand enough. Teloa tore her
eyes away at the sound of running water. A small, enclosed
garden was off to one side, lit, as was the room, by more
shafts. A fountain set in the wall bubbled merrily. She breathed
deeply of the scent—lush, exotic plants whose names she
did not know.

"Do you like it?" the woman asked with a smile. Tay
smiled in return, her eyes taking in the high, deep ceiling
arches, her fingers lingering on the rough-hewn walls of stone.
"The fireroses are in bloom, and they bring a heady scent to
the arboretum. Come and look." The woman led Teloa into
the garden, stopping under the sky shaft. Tay stood in the
warm starlight, closing her eyes and enjoying the sensation.
So long since she had felt natural heat . . . Between the star
and the murmur of the water . . . even the odor of the plants
conspired to put her to sleep. Many of the indoor trees were
taller than she, and the variety of colors ranged from soft
yellow-greens through blues and purples. One plant had brilliant yellow-and-orange blossoms. Elana reached out to touch
a vine, and Teloa followed her example. So long since she
had worked with living things . . .

"You do that as if you know plants," Elana said gently,
walking back into the main room and heading for a sunken
tub.

"I was a planter once—in the Caprican system," Tay
answered vaguely, following the Nualan to the sanitation.
She touched the wooden hot tub, studying the marble facilities.

"Look, Teloa, this is hot and this cold, and you may
blend them by—where are the sands?" Tay was startled until
she realized the woman's question was of general puzzlement
and not directed toward her guest. "As I was saying, the
water will circulate on its own and automatically shuts off

when your weight is removed from the bottom. Do not worry about all the water; it goes straight to irrigation. I shall get you some towels and some bath sands. I must apologize for the lack of sands and oil—all four grades of sand are supposed to be kept here at all times. I shall have to report it to Drau. What with the festival and feast, she is much too busy to monitor the younger priests and priestesses who keep these rooms stocked. But is important to her, all the same." At the question in Teloa's eyes Elana continued: "Drau is the high priestess, and her days are very full, but she has greeted the newcomers to our world since she was an initiate, and she is still very concerned about the comfort of our guests. I shall tell my godson, her eldest, and he will carry the message."

"Is . . . her husband a priest? I had forgotten that the clergy of Nuala marry," Tay said, sitting on the edge of the double bed.

"Her firsthusband is a scientist; her second, High Priest Arrez, as is our law. She is the second wife of Arrez."

"Second?"

"Yes. He has four."

Tay digested this information. "A . . . healthy man indeed," she managed. She was startled by Elana's silver laughter.

"Not exactly, although he is a 20. He married me because he loved me, Drau because he was appointed High Priest, and, as I said, it is our law. Mariah because her prophecies are disturbing and often violent, and only he and I can deal with her. And Chaka, out of sheer . . . cussedness, as our ancestors once said. I shall get the towels and sand and be right back. Play with the tub as you wish!" She quickly and silently slipped out of the room. Tay turned slightly and looked out the thermapane windows at the dazzling soft yellow light. She ached all over and wondered if lying in the star's rays would help. It was a young world, she decided. Capricorn V had been young. Her thoughts swirled back to the hot agra planet, its fertile fields stretching to the horizon, the glittering irrigation canals opening their wash gates. Her parents' pride when she was appointed Assistant Planter, her younger brother Telen's enthusiasm. Older sister Meer had desired only to leave the planet, and brother Tyr was always confused. Then the luna bombs came, the whistling luna bombs — and it was ambitious Meer who stayed, forever, and naive Teloa who became the wanderer. She had not seen Telen since the halfway camp, when she had given him her last hundred cubiz to aid his attempts to enter a trade. Being guildless, he had a small chance to build a new life. She wondered if he still lived. He'd be almost twenty terrayear now, and if he thought her dead . . .

The exhaustion, the release of tension, hit her like a tremendous weight, and she was crying, a torrent of tears, almost hysterically, something she had not allowed herself since the luna bombs devastated Capricorn V. Teloa did not hear the door open and did not protest the firm and gentle embrace she was drawn into; she was merely aware of years of pain and frustration, and memories that could never be anything else. Finally her shaking began to subside.

"It will get better, child. By Mendulay's grace you are alive, and the dawn will come. Let your heart be lightened." Through her tears Teloa saw long, slender hands pushing her hair out of her face. Elana was smiling. "I think you will be better able to see the brightness of the day after a hot tub and some rest. Are you hungry?"

"Maybe — a little. I am so tired. And I ache terribly."

Elana lifted several bottles. "Found! And we shall get you into a tub right away." She studied the Caprican's face intently and then asked, "You have not tasted the water, have you? You look pale."

"No," Teloa said quickly. She knew enough about Nuala to refrain from that, no matter how thirsty she was. "But I need some water." Her voice faded as she looked closely at the sand bottles. "Oh, I couldn't. I mean—" She looked up at Elana in amazement. "These are worth a week's salary each! I—"

"Not here. We make it here, and it is as cheap as gill soap. You are free of import taxes for the duration of your stay! Now get in and soak, and I shall bring you some saffra and your first pill. You must not drink or eat anything without first taking a pill, and your first fiveday here, eat only what I bring you! The radiation content of some of our foods could make you very sick. I am a doctor, and I shall bring my bag — I have a simple monitor that can determine your general health almost immediately. The water is safe for you to bathe in, please enjoy it. I shall be awhile this time." Elana dumped several capfuls of oil into the tub and then vanished again. Tay sat a moment, watching volumes of bubbles appear, letting her mind go blank. Then she slipped off what was left of her shoes. Carefully lining up the sand bottles, she removed the dark, cowled dress and lowered herself into the tub.

She discovered a wide ledge around the perimeter of the wooden bath. Sitting down, she reveled in the hot water, letting it soak to the chill of her bones. She had to shake herself awake, and then reached for the sand. How good to scrub away the dirt, the feel of everything before. A sharp stomach cramp sliced through her, and she seized the edge of the tub to steady herself. Gods, what was wrong? She had not touched the water, nor any food—no food in days. Hunger? It hurt too much to be hunger. Hustlers did not get sick. They died from alcohol or drugs or knives, but they did not become sick. An awful thought began to form in Teloa's mind. Narcotic dependency . . . palus, opiates, coca, ltima—any or all of them had probably been slipped into her drinks at one time or another. How much? Enough so that she'd show her dependency in two or three days? Suddenly she was frightened.

Forcing herself to continue, Teloa slowly washed her hair as well, living an old fantasy to wash all over in extra-fine Silva Sand. Then she crawled out of the tub, wrapping herself in the thick towels. The shaking would not stop.

There was a light rap of knuckles on the door. "Tay? I am coming in."

"Please—" Elana stepped over the threshold, a tray in her arms and a shapeless bag tossed over her shoulder. She took one look at the off-worlder and set the tray down on the dresser.

"What is wrong? Where is the pain?" Elana asked as she came to her side.

"My stomach—all over. I—am cold—" Tay gasped, shaking violently. Elana touched her forehead a moment.

"No, not cold. A fever. And you have not drunk any water, it is not rav—"

"I haven't! I swear it—" Tay said frantically, her voice cut off by another spasm.

"Rav is radiation poison by ingestion," Elana told her. "I can see you have not. Teloa, have you ever used...euphorics? I know they sometimes get into things...." The doctor was polite but firm in her need for information.

"Not by choice—but you never—" She doubled over. "You never know what a patron might have put into a drink."

"Try to reach the bed. You need to lie down until the fever burns itself out. I can ease the pain, and it will pass. Our people are passionate and often foolish but never that stupid—you cannot find drugs here, they will not tempt you." Elana helped her to her feet and to the bed. "I can stop the shaking, but you will be in bed several days. That is all right!" Tay sensed that Elana was trying to ease any worry her new patient had. "There is little to do during festival. As a new immigrant, you would have to stay inside most of the time. Now you can relax and read tapes and listen to music. I can find a few visitors for you and explain things when our people confuse you—" Tay gasped again, this time from the air hypo Elana shot into her arm. Then the woman quickly scanned her with a small metal object. "I have seen worse, but that is no comfort. Drink this, the rav pill is already in it. We can take no chances." Tay downed the fluid, conscious of its acid edge, herbs and pulp floating in its opaque, red body. Elana pushed her down onto soft pillows and pulled a light blanket up around her. "Rest. I shall stay with you awhile, and then one of my healers shall come. Do not think you will die—I never lose patients! If we must, I shall seek Ronuviel, and she will draw the fever out. Just rest—soon the pain will pass and you can seek a home and work." Her cool fingertips rested on the young woman's forehead a moment. "Rest ...Nualans have great skill with green things; even our deserts grow lush under Cied hands. But our ecology is very fragile. We always have need of planters."

Tay clung to that thought as delirium crept upon her.

AMURA, THE PALACE   SEXT

It was not far to the palace. Kal quietly played tour
guide, pointing out the capital, temple, park, medical complex, and fine-arts center. Lyte feigned disinterest, his eyes
absorbing and cataloguing everything. The buildings were
strange, occasionally even macabre—dreamlike configura-
tions that reminded him of something he could not name.
Colors were numerous, and Lyte thought of the stone called
marble, which he had seen on the planet Terra. The buildings
all had the same swirling, translucent effect, although not all
were highly polished. There were many, many towers, their
outsides textured as if they were dribble castles made of sand.
And the city was clean, as if scoured.

"You certainly know how to avoid pollution. Nova Terra
would give a lot to know your secret," Lyte began conversationally.

"Nova Terra? Have you been there?" Kavan could not
repress his excitement. Kal eyed him warningly—it was not
polite to pressure visitors into conversation after a long trip.
Lyte did not notice the discourtesy. He was more interested
in the people. He had never seen so many Nualans together
at one time. And he had made a discovery. They were not
all beautiful. Healthy, certainly, at least to the eye, but some
were far from beautiful. In fact, he saw no greater number
of attractive people than he would see on any CSSI system
street. Most were average—a few could be defined as dregs,
dogs, or *entiss*, depending on your native tongue. One woman
in particular fascinated him. He found her lanky, flat-chested,
almost buck-toothed appearance quite unappealing. But the
handsome young man on whose arm she hung was plainly
oblivious to it.

"Ah, yeah. I've been to Earth."

"Would we be so blasé if we could boast?" Moran added,
amused.

Braan was following Lyte's gaze, and smiled slyly. "She
is brilliant, and witty, and a 20," Braan said softly. "And,
from what her friends say, a compassionate woman. No higher
tribute can be made." He looked distant then, as if not noticing
Lyte's blank reply. What was Braan, a mind reader? Very

observant, Lyte decided. A man to be watched. He absorbed the little speech, aware of the sincerity behind it.

"I thought you people dealt in genetics," Lyte answered. He was rewarded for his error in interpretation by Kal's startled look and Kavan's obvious anger. Braan quickly spoke, smoothing the path.

"To correct the disabling, the mutilating, the dangerous genes. There is no beauty requirement. We have learned all too well, the hard way, the true meaning of beauty. And appreciate it all the more when it appears of its own accord." Lyte did not pursue it. There was no lack of looks among the Atares, that was certain. Braan, with his dark hair, tanned skin, and mysterious, brooding magnetism, was extremely attractive to most females. Lyte still heard his name mentioned with affection in the tratores. The twins were young yet, but with their narrower faces, high cheekbones, and oddly paired green-brown eyes, they were just as alluring. He had seen a hologram of Ronuviel's father, however—a very average-looking man. Despite Braan's words, Lyte suspected genetic tampering, but he said nothing.

Moran was merely breathing deeply; of the flowers, the air, the babble of voices from the market they passed through. Something occurred to him—he turned to Braan. "Should we have taken that woman somewhere? It seemed as if she had been through a lot."

Braan shook his head negatively. "She needed . . . privacy . . . more than transportation. Elana will take care of her. She was very uncomfortable with us." Satisfied with Braan's analysis, Moran turned back to watch the turquoise grass shimmer in the starlight.

"I hope she is happy here," Moran said finally. "As happy as I have been." They did not speak again until they reached the palace.

Lyte had not been paying attention and was mildly surprised when the solar car stopped. He was not sure what he had expected, but not such . . . massiveness. There were huge spiraling steps wide enough for ten men to walk abreast, the trees overshadowing them older than memory. The center door of the tri-portal was three times Lyte's height, the hourglass pillars before it even larger. Green, yellow, and turquoise patterns in the stone danced before his eyes, shadows playing tricks on him. Lyte extended a hand—the pillars were heavily textured with smooth, teardrop lumps.

"Don't worry, they've held for thousands of years, and strong ground tremors are common here," Moran whispered.

"Our years or their years?" Lyte retorted, still lost as to what the city reminded him of.

"Practically the same thing" was the rejoinder. The two turned in time to see the door wardens open the center portal to admit them. They were both copper-skinned, a blond man and a dark woman, and they were dressed, Lyte realized, in ancient space colonization suits—reflective silver and internally controlled. They did not react to the royal family or the warriors as the group walked in.

"The Atares' personal *guaard*, as is the gentleman in black skins following us. They will defend all the royal family if the need should ever arise and are silent companions in times of danger. Those suits are replicas of the original colonists' suits. The men and women trained for that duty are prepared much like your unit is." Commandos, sensitive-trained? A whole troop? Lyte filed the information away for future reference.

As they entered the palace Lyte immediately noticed the echo and stopped, looking up into darkness. He now understood what the Nualan structures reminded him of—caverns. Massive, entwining caverns. It was the underground city of Becoten, only on the planet's surface. He studied the white walls, their irregularly shaped depressions glowing fitfully from an unknown power source. The overall impression was of age, warmth, and closeness. He took in its great width; several men were setting up long tables at one end of the hall.

"Welcome to the Great Hall," Kal said. Kavan hurried ahead and threw his weight on two huge bronze doors at the opposite side of the barren hall. Lyte tapped his fingers on them as he passed and was shocked—they swayed slightly under his touch. They were of solid bronze and perfectly balanced to open at the thrust of a hand.

They had entered an octagonal corridor intersection, the hallways receding into infinity in three directions. Lyte was about to ask if this was fact or illusion when he noticed the mirrors. More than mirrors—they were the walls. In all three corridors the only supports visible were windows and mirrors. They looked hand-polished, their irregular shapes biomorphic, the huge fired clay frames almost oozing around their reflecting substance. He could see the glint of cast bronze at all three exits, figures in black standing next to them.

"This is the Hall of Mirrors. To the left is the Footpath to the Stars. The view out that door is the Mendularion and starset. To the right are the living quarters, and straight ahead is the throne room. We are expected for saffra and kriska in the family room."

Having finished his speech, Kal led on. Lyte glanced around as they walked down the passage and noted that Braan was using the mirrors to observe him. For nervousness? Disdain? Perhaps for something the man himself could not have named. They reached the doors sooner than Lyte expected— so the distance was illusion. Moran appeared relaxed, as if everything was routine. His initial excitement had mellowed into a delighted realization that Ronuviel was near.

Kal activated a palm-impression lock and opened the door. Moran grabbed Lyte's arm, stopping him. "We have to alert the computer to your presence."

"Computer?" His voice was expressionless.

Braan answered, "The interiors of the palace and sensitive medical and military areas have palm-impression locks on their portals. If you have clearance, you can walk right in. There was an assassination attempt made on my older brother's life when we were children . . . during a party. It was considered a prudent move to inhibit easy access to the living quarters."

"Them?" Lyte gestured at the warriors.

"They cannot memorize every stranger on the planet. The times are not dangerous; we do not use individual *guaard*."

"Place your hand on the panel and say your name. Just Lyte; no one uses titles here except the Atare," Moran instructed, setting his own hand on the panel. "After that, the computer will know your prints."

"What happens if you go in without clearance?"

"A silent alarm activates, and the *guaard* would find you so fast, it would make your life spin—what was left of it," Kavan answered, touching the panel. Flashing Lyte a smile, he disappeared inside. There was a silence.

"If you would prefer not, I can ask Liel to bring the saffra to the garden," Braan offered.

"No." Lyte set his hand on the panel and said, "Lyte." It was strange to hear his own voice say the word. The panel blinked and was again dark. Braan set his hand on it. The screen flared and was still. Moran opened the door and followed the twins' path.

The room was darker than Lyte had imagined, and cool, blocking out the mid-afternoon heat. Its construction was similar to the Great Hall, and it was filled with low, inviting chairs, and fibers decorating the walls and floor. A beautiful table of a dark, polished wood was piled high with trays of unknown edibles and glasses made of trine gold. Lyte's mouth dropped open. He could buy a whole army with one of those cups. Trine gold, rarest of metals; Nuala's wealth and its curse. . . .

A stronger light source from beyond caused Lyte to move to one side—he could see a window in an adjoining room. He wondered if the windows were rigged.

"The windows are also monitored," Braan said as he strolled into the room. Abruptly a young woman burst through the door frame.

She might have been called a girl but not without adolescent offense. Although Lyte had the impression of shiny, dark hair that fell to her elbows, the eyes were the arresting quality. One was blue and one green, and they sparkled with a liveliness, an awareness that hinted, inexplicably, of Braan. And with her heart-shaped face and turned-up nose, a beauty.

With a delighted laugh the girl threw her arms around Braan. Moran took advantage of the momentary diversion. "Careful, friend, she's brigbait," Moran whispered mischievously.

Lyte looked dour. "Not exotic enough for me."

"Those eyes should be exotic enough for anyone," Moran returned, lighting up as Liel walked over to him.

"Moran! When will you come and stay for a while?" She shyly slipped her arms around him and hugged him like a favorite toy.

"I've got elevenday off, what more could you ask?"

"Huh!" The woman tossed her head impatiently, for a moment still the child. "I could say a few things about what I think of your superiors, but I shall refrain."

"Youngest of the Ragaree, this is Lyte, my closest friend. The Serae Liel. Liel is fine." Lyte straightened and inclined his head slightly in the manner of a professional star-rover, used to meeting all forms of life. Liel gracefully swept her right hand arching away from her heart in the ancient Nualan greeting.

"Welcome, star warrior. You bring honor on our heads." She avoided looking straight at him. Braan broke her oration by tickling her.

"Be bold, little one! Your spirit cannot remain hidden forever!" She could not help but crack a smile, the hint of a dimple showing; she met Lyte's eyes, the gold in her green eye flashing. Liel gestured for the warrior to follow her to the table.

"One of the interesting properties of saffra is that it is often more refreshing heated and poured over ice than constantly chilled! We also have Tours day wine, or if there is anything special you would like . . . ?" Liel began.

"Got your pill?" Moran asked Lyte. Braan had handed him the packet while they were in the solar car.

"Right here. Did someone watch you as closely as you're watching me?" Lyte held up his hand as if to swallow the pill.

"Wait! They are very bitter. It is better dissolved in saffra and does not change the drink's taste." Liel grabbed his hand and pushed a glass of saffra toward him. Kal had poured it over ice, and the steam was thick. Lyte did not visibly hesitate, but he steeled himself for the unaccustomed taste. He was pleasantly surprised and had to force himself not to swallow the drink in one gulp. In the meantime Braan poured a glass for Liel while she greeted her other brothers.

"I wish Deenn was here, he would have enjoyed meeting you; but he is over on Niamh and will not be back until almost the end of the festival. He is the closest thing we have among the 20s to a professional warrior," Braan said conversationally. He handed a glass to Moran, smiling slyly as he did so. "She will be down soon; she should be almost ready."

"Did I hear 'almost'?" Lyte started involuntarily at the voice, low and slightly musical. He turned toward the sound. Moran managed a soft half smile.

Ronuviel was no challenger to the universal beauty; not in the popular sense of the statuesque tratore queens. Average height, numerically proportioned, flawless skin and teeth— all superficial traits of health. Her straight, turned-up nose and strange, haunting eyes, so much like Braan's, were disturbing, not attractive, as far as Lyte was concerned ... although the mahogany-brown hair that tumbled halfway to her knees was a definite asset. Lyte now understood her initial lure, however. How it worked, no. How it affected men, yes. She was at once sensual and earth mother, magnificent as a star and as humble as a madonna—totally at ease with, and unaware of, her "air" and her completeness as a woman.

Roe came straight to him, her face blazing in her pleasure, touching his arm in an intimate yet nonthreatening way. "Lyte! We are greatly honored! I was beginning to think there would be no one to give away the groom, should the need arise!"

"I'll be up to it, don't worry," Lyte answered. With a look for Braan, Ronuviel walked over to Moran and gently touched his face, her thoughts for him alone.

Lyte glanced away. He could deal with the physical couples, the clinging, adoring here-for-the-moment situations he saw in the tratores, though he did not like clinging men or women, himself. What was between Roe and Moran was something different. One thing he knew: Moran was crazy about this woman and her people and could no longer be objective about them. Lyte would have to stand a double vigil during their stay. If only they weren't so friendly ...

"Lyte, would you allow me to take charge of your personal case?" Kal asked, gesturing toward the tiny box they had carried from the transport. "We can have the items sealed against destruction or plated with trine gold, whichever you prefer."

Lyte stared at him a moment. No average citizen could afford trine plating, so he assumed it was a free offer of service, because of his connection to Moran. But did he really want to be wearing something he might get hit over the head for every time he wore it?

"Sealing doesn't change the color or—"

"You will scarcely be able to tell. It adds a slight sheen to matte finishes, that is all," Kal went on.

The warrior offered him the box. "Sealing sounds fine. Put it on my tab."

"There is no charge to you, our guest. I will also replace whatever currency you have with Nualan issue—it *is* in the box, is it not?"

So that's why Moran made me put it in there. "Thank you, I'd appreciate that."

"I do not wish to throw a damper on your party, Liel, but I must find Jaac. She has requested my presence," Braan suddenly said, setting down his glass of saffra. The twins glanced at each other but said nothing.

"I also intend to go," Roe told him, seizing Moran's hand and pulling him along. She paused a moment, remembering Lyte, and looked to Braan. They studied each other a second, and then Moran, perceiving that this was not a casual visit, spoke.

"Don't worry, I'll vouch for him."

Lyte remained impassive. In their simple glances he was reminded that the Axis Republic was still fighting a thousand-year war against the Fewha and the Malvevenian Empires— and that the Nualans were only one system away from the front.

The foursome walked back into the palace complex and outside, the trees of the garden shielding them from the blazing afternoon light. Roe, Moran, and Braan talked lightly of the trip over, the goings-on in the city—names and places totally unfamiliar to Lyte. He busied himself with trying to keep the direction of the temple in mind as a point of reference and started studying the greenery.

Nothing was familiar. In the thousand years the Nualans had been isolated and the following three thousand during which they had had no visitors, any desire for their previous

flora and fauna had vanished. Some names had come down
to them, and the many years had not changed the essential
natures of trees and grass, but the similarity ended there.
Even the predominant ground cover was not really grass but
instead was more clover-shaped and lichenlike, springy un-
derfoot. The dry, oppressive heat was offset by towering
succulents, some writhing like snakes, some with long, slender trunks and stiff, flat fronds. There were several barrel-
shaped bushes with thick, juicy leaves—Lyte bumped into
one and nearly fell from the slippery undergrowth.

"Everything is so green here! I thought, since the area
around Amura is primarily desert..." Lyte began.

"It is the time of the cold rains, though they are inter-
mittent and light, compared to spring. Thirtyday ago it would
have been dust here. We are closer to the equator—if you
want green wait until you go north, into the mountains!"
Ronuviel replied.

Suddenly a yawning entranceway appeared before them
and plunged downward. They went down a flight of stairs to
a corridor carved from solid rock. Walking to the end of the
hall, Braan activated the door lock and walked in. Moran and
Roe followed and, more slowly, Lyte. He did not like those
locks. Lyte almost bumped into Moran as he entered the
room.

"We're supposed to wait here. The connecting room is
the pillar-set computer. This is the *watch* room for the Nualan
civil defense. Jaacav is the first officer in charge," Moran
whispered. "Interplanetary Communications is over there—
and Interstellar Communications, Scope, and Navigation.
They're one of the most efficient in the Axis."

"One of? The best, First Officer." The tiny dark-haired
woman had broken off with the Atares and turned to them.
Lyte was stunned and dropped his usual mask.

"You!! Mercury 7!"

"Yes," Jaac answered, a faint smile curling at the corner
of her full lips. "We are familiar with the edifice tables, are
we not?" She turned back to Braan and Roe and continued
speaking softly in Nualan. "There has been no replacement
for the *Io*, and no explanation for the move. The Atare, Tal,
and the prime minister have the facts and the nuances, and

the twins and Liel have an inkling of what has happened. I
am not concerned enough to attempt to reach Deenn or your
sisters. The synod has not yet been informed. That is all."

"I cannot believe they would allow anything to happen
before the feast. If there were any 'accidents' involving guests
of their rank, the Axis Forces, not Nuala, would be blamed,"
Braan replied. "But afterward? Who knows?"

"We are safe until the festival. I have a—a premonition?" Roe shook her head, disturbed. Then she smiled at
Jaac. "You never told me you knew Lyte."

A secret smile behind those almond-shaped eyes... "You
never asked. If you will excuse me, I need to get back to
work." Nodding to the Atares, Jaac turned back toward the
communications board. Lyte unintentionally caught her eye—
her gaze settled on the object of his scrutiny, the scope. For
a moment their eyes met, and Lyte sensed worry. Was it
shared concern of what they both suspected, or was she anxious that he had seen the scope at all? She was too perceptive
a warrior not to realize the *wrongness*. And Lyte feared he
now knew what the whispered Nualan words had been about.

Gesturing to Moran and Lyte, Roe swept out the door,
Braan following. As they slowly made their way to the surface
and back toward the palace, Lyte found a moment to speak
to Moran alone.

"That's an extremely sophisticated setup. Why do they
need it? The surrounding protection ships take care of almost
all of that. They don't need to watchdog the Axis Republic."

"Quite simply, the Nualans trust everyone else about as
far as they can throw them. And it will take more than good
standing in the Axis Council to change their minds." Moran
had a look on his face that was at once knowing and distant.
Lyte did not voice his other thought—that from the scope
he could see, it appeared the two major guard ships were too
far out. One ship always moved in at the same speed as the
departing ship. Something did not fit, and Jaacav and the
Atares were aware of the missing pieces, but it was not yet
time to ask questions of their hosts. They had hours before
the feast was to start, and everyone had individual plans.
Later... He followed Moran back into the palace, unaware
that Moran was thinking the same thing.

The right wing of the palace had been the Atares' home for generations uncounted. Not only the family of the current Atare but of his sister as well, for her son would be the next to reign. The progeny of both families were raised with a strong sense of duty, although other outside relatives kept that force from becoming the overriding influence of their lives. When the children reached an age of majority, they left the palace, even if they did not leave the planet, and remained away for five Nualan years. After that time, if not yet married, they could return and live under the family roof.

The older Atare siblings all had homes of their own nearby. Ronuviel and one brother, Deenn, had both returned from their various cover trades single and had elected to remain under the sprawling dynasty roof. Although the atmosphere was occasionally stifling, Ronuviel had never seriously regretted the move. Otherwise she would never have known her younger sister and brothers so well, or known her mother as woman and not merely as Mother. After all, the thought lazily occurred to her, where else could she get such a spacious room, so close to the capital, so cheaply? Roe managed to chuckle, and she cast a quick glance at Moran, fearful that she had awakened him. Unlikely—she could feel his sleep pattern synchronizing with her healing waves, a deep and total relaxation. He almost always slept on his back, the light native blanket and sheet drawn up to his ribs and held with one arm, radiating a tousled contentment. Roe lay on her side, drawing the sheet up to her shoulders to shield herself from the overactive air-cooling system. Her eyes traveled from the glow pits buried in the walls to the numerous thermapane windows and finally rested on the slow, deep rise and fall of Moran's chest, light reflecting off the soft brown hairs and drawing gold from them. They became a golden blur and then merely light, fading as drowsiness stole over her.

He needed sleep. She knew he had been on short night shifts for almost a twentyday, and she did not like it. They would be lucky if he awoke for the feast. He did have some energy left, she reminded herself, smiling gently at the mem-

ory of the last hour. And it was partly the hour that had lulled
her fears. Lyte's presence and his obvious unease . . . it was
too simple to dismiss it as what it appeared to be. But there
was no change, no restraint in Moran. His loving was in
complete accord with his entire being: intricate, passionate,
unusually gentle, unusually honest. Though she rarely let him
know, let alone others, she could read this vulnerable man
like a monitor. True, he could do the same with her, but he
did not rely on his sensitive training. Nor did she. And they
used no blocks with each other. No—if there was something
wrong, Moran did not know about it. A momentary chill ran
through Roe as she imagined his reaction to being used. Dear
God, this man could love—and hate—with passion. An un-
dying friend or lover, he would be a dangerous enemy.

    Without thought she ran her hand down her stomach,
testing its contours. There did not seem to be much change,
no more than a lack of exercise or a few sweets might cause.
Roe frowned slightly. Her menses had cycled four times in
the past year, the average for a fertile Nualan woman. But it
had been onehundred twentyday since her last pass. Her mother
had been pregnant with her first onehundred sixtyday before
a routine physical revealed her condition. Nothing obvious,
no discomfort, yet Roe felt . . . different. That could mean
conception anywhere from an hour ago through—she
counted—one hundred days ago. The thought of being a third
of the way through pregnancy momentarily stunned her.

    Moran stirred slightly but did not awaken. He shifted
his body angle and reached out instinctively to the side Roe
always slept on, his left. She managed to pull herself back
to full consciousness long enough to creep into his embrace,
and to wonder, half guiltily if she should mention her suspicions about a child or confirm it with Elana first. No matter—
there was plenty of time.

CHAPTER THREE

Lyte awoke to the sound of furtive rustlings in the room. As his eyes focused, a figure cut off the light in his vision. But the light was pale, as if—as if the star was setting. *Damn, I fell asleep*. . . . Lyte gained full consciousness and realized Moran was looking at him. The man looked more rested than Lyte had seen him for a long time. Managing his famous winning smile, Lyte sat up.

"You're looking good. Have an enjoyable afternoon?" Lyte said.

"Very. How went your exploring?" he replied, turning back to his dressing. His voice was light, amused, and Lyte was certain Moran knew he had never left the room.

"How long until the feast?" Lyte asked instead, getting up and walking over to the shower basin. He recognized the tub and bypassed it, suspecting he'd fall asleep again. The water falling out of the wall was much cooler but effervescent and exhilarating to the touch. His skin tingled as he quickly worked up a lather.

"We can go the the Great Hall at any time. You won't recognize it." Moran moved to the mirror and carefully adjusted the starbursts that symbolized the rank of first officer.

"Ronuviel will meet us there. I think Braan brought some clothes to the palace, so he'll also show up quickly."

"I thought Braan lived in his own house," Lyte murmured, smearing a depilatory over his cheeks and chin.

"He does, but—I thought I told you about his wife." The face that Lyte turned toward him was puzzled. "Enid is dying," Moran went on quietly, "and she's been here at the palace for several years. It was thought too depressing for the children to have it all going on under the same roof. Braan divides his time among the children, his art and his wife's bedside, although she hasn't recognized any of them in over five years."

"There's a sadness about him. That explains a lot," Lyte answered. Rinsing off, he stepped out of the shower and dried himself as he walked over to his tackle. The black-and-silver dress uniform unfolded wrinkle-free, as always. There wasn't much Lyte hated more than a dress uniform, but protocol demanded it. The sheer number, much less the status of the dignitaries attending, made a simple dodge impossible. He carefully adjusted on his collar the even-armed crosses that were the insignia of his rank and reached for a hair rake. His hand brushed against his timespot. Intrigued, he picked it up and examined it. A sheen to the finish . . . They're quick here.

"Where do you know Jaacav from?" Moran suddenly asked.

Lyte, masking his surprise, did not look at him. "I don't, really. A couple of furloughs ago I played against her in a high-stakes edifice game on Mercury 7. There were maybe a half dozen of us. Never did catch her name," Lyte replied, attaching the timespot to his cuff.

"Don't sound so casual about it. You obviously recognized her."

Lyte glanced at him. Was Moran fishing or teasing? He decided he was getting paranoid. "And she recognized me. There aren't many people capable of holding their own in a game like that—especially in the military. A good-looking woman, a great gambler; of course I remember!" Lyte hoped he didn't sound defensive.

"Yet you didn't follow up on her while you were there."

"I couldn't—she left mid-game and had left the tratore

by the time I had finished." That was the truth. He hoped
Moran would leave it at that. The warrior seemed unper-
turbed.

"Well, now you have a chance to follow up on it. She'll
be here tonight."

"I have a lot of things I plan to follow up on," Lyte
finished, flashing Moran what he hoped looked like a confident smile. "It's time to explore a bit. See you there." He
started for the chamber door.

"Don't get lost!" Moran called by way of parting.

Lyte ducked out the door of their chamber and into the
spacious hallway. He had no desire to pursue the subject of
Jaac—now, or at any other time. He found her disturbing,
just as he had on Mercury 7, and that was a rare response
on his part to any woman. He had no time to think of this,
however, for he realized he had forgotten a turn. He saw a
figure up ahead enter the corridor and hurried to catch up.

"Hey, can you tell me— Oh, hi." For a moment he had
not recognized Braan. The man had changed into more formal
clothes; deep brown, loose-fitting mandraia pants and a pale
yellow gauze shirt that was embroidered in a rich brown on
the cuffs and pointed collar. "I'm lost. How do I get out?"

"Follow me." Braan glanced at Lyte's dress uniform.
"Do they never let you out of that thing?"

"Depends on what you mean. My swimming string is
blue, and I sleep in the raw. Does that count?" It was all he
could think of to say. The truth was, he owned three regulation
uniforms and a dress suit—nothing else.

"I suppose it is some sort of freedom. I have to make a
stop. Come." Braan turned and started back down the corridor. Lyte did not mind retracing his steps; he was thankful
Braan did not ask why he had left without Moran, or at least
remark on his being lost. Lyte decided to increase his observations. Moran had a lot of respect for this man. Again,
as earlier, he felt something different about Braan. Something
elusive. His feet made no sound on the stone floor, though
he wore boots.

Interesting...

They suddenly stopped before a door.

"You may wait here." He opened the door and walked

in. Braan had used the word *may*—a choice. Lyte looked in.
He was not prepared for what he found. It was apparently a
study that had been converted into a bedroom. A dark man
he did not recognize was present, passing a small, flat instrument about a meter above the bed. Lying on the bed was
a woman. At least he thought it was a woman; she appeared
no bigger than a ten-year-old. She was tiny, so incredibly
tiny, and very pale, with a mass of dark curls. Lyte noticed
a young woman sitting in a nearby chair. She had been reading
a tape console but now raised her head, startled by Braan's
presence. She glanced quickly at the window, and Lyte saw
a sundial.

"Go get dressed. You will not be late. Thank you for
staying, but you should be out more—your vacation is almost
over." She managed a lovely smile, then slipped out past Lyte
and into the corridor. She was small and slender but properly
endowed, with long, thick hair the color of raw bee's honey.
Lyte never missed the essential elements of a pretty woman,
no matter how young. Looking back, he saw that Braan had
moved next to the bed.

"No change," the healer offered. "I am staying the next
shift." His voice did not indicate that he had ever expected
any change. Lyte studied the tableau; Braan was expressionless. He slowly reached out toward her face, just barely touching a curl. Then he turned abruptly and moved to the door.
Lyte quickly backed up.

They swiftly left the room and continued on down the
corridor. Braan was still impassive, and Lyte refrained from
comment. The woman had to be Enid, and it was clear that
her condition was deteriorating. Such a contrast; what Braan
appeared to be and what old stories, now almost legends, had
to say about him. Years of watching his woman die; yes,
Lyte supposed it could wither a man.

"Her name is Shinar," Braan said quietly. Startled, Lyte
glanced at the man. The Atare smiled slightly. "The little
blonde you were admiring. Her name is Shinar reb Elana —
the daughter of Elana."

Lyte watched as the tension in the man slowly dissipated.
Fascinating the control this Nualan had over his body. Almost
like a commando. Amazing that he'd noticed anything beyond

his wife. Shinar . . . smooth on the tongue. Where had he heard the name Elana?

"I . . . prefer blondes," Lyte offered vaguely.

"So did I, but I married a brunette."

The conversation faded as they reached a set of bronze doors. They were now in the Hall of Mirrors. Darkness was falling fast, and the mysterious light source flared brighter, as if in response to the coming night. Instead of being in isolated wall pockets, each firegem was over a window, reflecting eerily in the mirrors on either side.

The two men quickly reached the dome and, as of yet, had met no one. The sound of music and voices could be heard coming from the Great Hall. Braan took hold of the chamber door and swung it inward.

It had been transformed. Lyte found it hard to believe that this room had been the dark, empty chamber of a few scant hours ago. The normal light sources were supplemented by blazing torches. They revealed a ceiling almost as tall as the dome, its face resembling interlocking tetrahedrons. The huge tables he had seen earlier were now covered with soft beige cloths and heaped with food both native and imported. All of the visible food containers or supports were blown out of glass or trine gold. Music was provided by one of Amura's excellent chamber ensembles. Lyte took it all in and quickly dug in his pocket and pulled out his next pill. As he popped it in his mouth Braan noticed the movement.

"You will regret that," he warned. Lyte could not cover his grimace. Even polished, the pill had quite an aftertaste. "You would think a technology like ours could do something about that. I suggest you get—" Braan broke off as a waiter passed and grabbed one of the tall glasses of saffra. "Here." Lyte did not protest, gratefully gulping the drink.

Someone chuckled behind him, and Lyte turned his head. A dark, handsome young man about his own age silently waited, amusement sparkling in his eyes.

"Be honest, Braan. Did you purposely wait to warn him about the pills?" the man asked. Braan's face took on an air of total innocence. The off-worlder's interest sharpened; this Nualan addressed an Atare by name.

"Lyte, I would like you to meet my Moran—Gid

reb Tinyan. This is Second Officer Lyte, Moran's alter ego,"
Braan said, dismissing the Nualan's questions with a gesture.
Still unable to speak, Lyte nodded a greeting. "I thought you
decided not to attend this night?"

"I wished to meet Lyte before I left for Tolis," Gid
answered. "And I have accomplished my task. I also need
to speak with Arrez. Have you seen him yet? I saw Shinar
in the hall a few moments ago, but she had yet to dress for
the feast."

"Does this feast have any special significance?" Lyte
asked when he had regained his voice.

"The harvest is in full swing. During the festival we
reap by day and give thanks by night. This is a fruitful planet
but not without great effort on the part of the planters. The
year will be good—already the deep grain vaults are full,
the vegetables and fruits sealed." Pride seemed to radiate
from Gid as he spoke. "We have great hopes for the grape
and berry crops of both the coast and the desert."

"Perhaps you would like to sample a few things," Braan
said casually. "Go light on the food, but if you normally hold
your liquor, the wines will be no problem. Do not eat any of
that." He pointed to a tray heaped with a type of meat or
meat substitute rolled in red leaves. "Even the pill cannot
counteract a few of those yet."

Lyte nodded his understanding and then gestured for a
cantinamaster to pour golden fire into a green-stemmed glass.
Braan's head suddenly shot up, and he strained to see past
the crowd. "Arrez and Elana just came in. Come, we shall
introduce you, and then feel free to mingle."

The high priest was easy to find in the crowd; he was
the only man wearing white. The robe was festive, made not
of the mandraia plant but of syluan, one of Nuala's two
priceless exports. Trine gold was merely the rarest of the
three types of gold, but syluan flowers were found nowhere
else in the known stellar systems. The faint glimmer always
associated with syluan gave him a slightly immaterial appearance, as if he were a dream. Arrez was tall, slender, and
patrician, his high cheekbones, sculptured features, and dark
coloring marking him of Latin ancestry. His flashing, dark
eyes gave an observer the impression that Arrez missed noth-

ing. Lyte immediately sensed a kinship between the priest and Braan, though they looked nothing alike.

Arrez's dark tan and long, dark, swept-back hair contrasted vividly with the woman beside him. Elana had chosen a swirling syluan dress the exact color of her deep blue eyes. Lyte had only a moment to wonder if she chose the illusionary outfit accidentally or by design, and then Braan's grip on his elbow propelled him before the pair.

"Arrez, I would like you to meet Moran's friend, Second Officer Lyte. This is the High Priest Arrez."

"My pleasure, warrior. Gid," Arrez added, nodding to the man. "Lyte, may I present Dr. Elana, my firstwife?" Arrez turned an open, interested, and amused face to Lyte, who was unabashedly staring at Elana. So familiar, so beautiful, and yet . . . not just at the transport ship . . . "Ah, and our daughter Shinar and Elana's son, Kire."

Lyte turned, and beside him was the lovely young woman of Enid's room, dressed in a riot of aqua syluan and silver netting. Her escort was a tall, handsome young man with dark auburn hair. Lyte stared a moment, and then said, "Your *daughter*?" He fought to control his embarrassment as he realized how it sounded, but both women were amused by his expression.

"You flatter me, warrior," Elana began in her warm, rich voice. "Come—tonight you may continue for an indefinite length of time." She took his arm and gently drew him off. With a quick greeting to Braan and Gid, Kire and Shinar vanished into the crowd, Kal suddenly appearing at Shinar's side.

Relieved of his obligation, Braan turned his full attention on Arrez and Gid.

"How are Mariah and Chaka?" he asked, inclining his head graciously to High Priestess Drau and her firsthusband as they entered the hall. Arrez's third and fourth wives were both in poor health.

"Chaka is ill again, and Mariah had a prophecy this afternoon and is sleeping things off."

"It was that bad?" Gid said, concerned. His family had been close to Arrez's for many years.

Arrez frowned and, gently taking hold of Braan's and Gid's elbows, steered them out of the mainstream.

"I really do not know. It is the second time she has had the same dream." The priest's voice was quiet, as if his words were not for the casual listener. "It begins more as an emotional thing—an overwhelming feeling of terror. I think much of her own fright comes from this weak, helpless feeling. Then she sees the temple, and Drau is at the altar, trying to protect the chalice. Stone is falling. I am a blur and then gone. Baskh is there and tries to drag Drau away from the altar." Arrez paused a moment. "And then there is fire—a veil of fire that rises and screens the scene, like syluan, she said—and it grows, consuming everyone, everything. Her last image is of the planet in flames. But they looked . . . artificial? I do not think it is a literal dream."

Braan glanced at Gid and was disturbed by the expression on his face; he was pale, his skin dusky. This was no jest on the priest's part—they had all ceased to play games with each other's minds a long time ago. They knew each other too well.

"Mariah dreams truly—" Gid whispered.

"Not always," Arrez broke in sharply. "She has a high accuracy rate, true, but no one can see all futures at all times. We have many paths before us."

"I wonder," Braan mused, letting his mind wander down an unpleasant path.

The crowd burst into excited whispering, and a turn of the head told Braan that Roe and Moran had arrived. He heard the murmurs—the perfect couple . . . Perhaps. Moran the dashing warrior, Roe heart-stopping in a flowing emerald dress. Braan amused himself wondering if anyone else had noticed that Roe had put on weight. He did not doubt the existence of a child.

"What do you think of him?" Arrez asked suddenly.

"I like him. We have not had time to talk at length, but what I have seen, I like."

The priest nodded, his eyes following the couple with obvious pleasure. Roe was his favorite of all the Atare children. "She will be happy with him. That is most important. He will be a good husband—I think a good father. One of us should talk to him, you know—more than idle chatter. Before he leaves the planet again."

"I shall work on it. Right now Lyte concerns me more." Braan had been studying the silvery warrior for several minutes. He was as usual surrounded by women, both Nualan and off-worlder, and was enjoying the attention.

"Lyte? You have been hoping he would come. Granted, he is infatuated with my wife and will undoubtedly seduce— or be seduced by—my eldest daughter before he leaves, but what has he done to concern you?"

Braan laughed. "You are not disturbed at the prospect?"

Arrez smiled in return. "Elana no longer strikes me as eager to continue having children, and a foreign source always increases the chances. But if it was her wish, I would want the best for her. Kire was off-world-sired, though I have never known who his father was. Accordingly, if Shinar finds a joy in Lyte, why not? To add to our family such a healthy child, as I know it would be—it would be marvelous. And a plus for her marriage status."

"Then you consider him the best?" Gid asked, his face sharp once more.

Arrez inclined his head slightly. "Mariah has dreamt of him and described him quite well, incidentally. She called him a wildman, a heathen king of tremendous loves and hates. She saw him two-faced, and the other was Moran's. I prefer to interpret it as meaning that there is much of Moran in Lyte and vice versa. Yes—I have a good feeling about him."

"So do I," Braan replied softly. "That is what worries me. He is sensitive-trained. He knows the empathy of our people, yet he is being very careful. Why? What is he hiding? I sense a fear in him, more than a warrior's nervousness at being among so many strangers. Lyte does not strike me as a man who frightens easily. If I could just get them away from Amura for a while . . ."

"That can be arranged," Gid said abruptly. "I have spoken to Baskh Atare. There are some rumblings up in Tolis, a disquieting air dealing with the current synod session. It is all explained in this capsule." Gid held up the tiny, glittering tome, the seal of Baskh visible on its side. "You cannot deny that my parents and the other sinis prefer to deal with you. They trust you as they have not trusted in centuries. It is an official trip and he would send Tal, but this needs your delicate touch. Why not take Roe, Moran, and Lyte and head north with me?"

Braan hesitated. "Enid is worse. . . ."

"I know, my friend. He hesitates to ask but for the seriousness of this business." Gid's voice dropped again. "It concerns the current star-shuffle and some land grabbing, among other things. My parents have not spoken openly of it, even to me. There is nothing you can do for Enid; there is much you can do for continued good relations between Amura and Tolis."

"Look cheerful, we have company," Arrez said in warning. He put on his warm, embracing smile as Roe and Moran came up to them.

"Gid! I thought you had left!" She embraced the dark man, who suddenly looked almost shy. "I have come to deposit my man safely in your arms, dear brother, and to borrow your man. We must go pick just the right wine for Moran. Arrez, I need your keen nose." Ronuviel gracefully took the high priest's arm and drew him toward the cantinamaster. Arrez's handsome maturity fell from him, his face lighting up boyishly as he escorted her into the crowd.

"Perhaps an herbidian chablis?" they heard him say as the two disappeared in the press.

"He'd do anything for her, wouldn't he?" Moran asked rhetorically, nodding a friendly greeting to Gid.

"As long as it was moral and honest, I would say yes," Braan replied.

"And legal?" the warrior added for him. Braan's sly smile crept out, and he shrugged.

Gid began laughing. "Come. Food and wine await. You have had the pill series?" Moran nodded in answer to Gid's question. "Then by all means try the cide."

Moran reached for a delicate pastry as Braan signaled the cantinamaster. "Dramiera, please." The warrior glanced back to see this favorite Atare drink, noting Gid's polite refusal. Then he looked in one of the hall's upper mirrors—and his expression froze. Seeing Moran's face, Braan looked up as well. Someone was using the mirrors for observation. An older man, tall, broad-shouldered, with snow-white hair and dark eyes—like pits, those eyes . . . The look was malevolent. Moran shuddered. The eyes seemed to recognize them and grew more intent. Braan evenly met the gaze.

"Meant for you?"

"I do not think so . . . not this time. We often use the mirrors like this, he and I. To my face he is quite cordial. That is Corymb Dielaan, the head of the Dielaan clan. He hates Atares. Especially Braan of Atare." Braan turned away and reached for a drink; Moran followed suit. "I do not envy whomever he is seeking." A tiny gasp of protest reached his ears. Braan's head snapped back, but only the cantinamaster was present, his face a mask.

"You spoke?"

"No, Seri. I made his drink weaker, and he has yours."

Moran sipped his liquor. "This is fine, not too strong."

"In the future please inquire first before you make such a judgment," Braan said tranquilly, watching the cantinamaster. The man returned no expression. Turning, the Nualan prince moved away from the table, Moran and Gid following.

"I wanted to ask you to come with me into the coastal mountains," Braan started. "I have been planning a vacation. However, something has come up, and Gid and I must go north to Tolis. I want to take Roe, though I have not yet asked her. You could bring Lyte, if you think he could handle the trip. You have never been, have you?"

"No, I haven't. The mountains would have fascinated him. Too bad . . ."

"Think about it. I know it is sudden. Here comes Roe."

The woman appeared before them, balancing three glasses of wine. "We decided on Sonoma River Chardonnay. Arrez was raving about it, but I think you should judge for yourself." Thanking her, the men took the glasses and tasted the wine. Always appreciative of fine wine, especially white, Moran quickly agreed with Arrez's taste. Gid and Roe laughed at them as they stood holding a glass in each hand, and then

Roe leaned over to whisper to her man. "Moran, I have to talk to you about something before Arrez announces that we are getting married."

"Announces? *Tonight*?"

Roe looked puzzled. "We decided on the Feast of Adel. That is tonight."

"That feast is *this* feast?"

She laughed at his bewilderment and took his arm. "Too late, Arrez is signaling." She took one of his glasses and started dragging him toward the speakers' platform. "Here comes Baskh Atare." Looking around wildly, Moran saw the aging ruler and his consort make their entrance to a grand ovation. Braan and Gid slipped away.

———

"Guests of the domain!" Arrez's authoritative voice boomed out over an unseen amplifier. "Now that our Atare is present, we wish to bring to your knowledge glad tidings for the people of Nuala." The conversation on the huge floor ceased; Arrez had everyone's attention as Roe struggled to reach the platform. "Tonight we wish to announce that another of the house of Atare, of the direct throne line of this generation, has decided to marry in the full sight of Most Holy Mendulay and of proper witnesses. I wish to announce the banns of Ronuviel reb Ila Atare and First Officer Moran of the Axis Forces." The uproar that followed drowned out anything else that Arrez intended to say, and finally, with a smile and a helpless shrug, he stepped from the platform and embraced Roe.

The next half hour was joyous, unnerving confusion. They were mobbed by family, diplomats, and citizens alike, and emotions ranged from radiant pleasure to tight-lipped formality. Roe was reminded that potential problems were not confined to house enemies and then pushed the thought out of her mind. Her sisters and brothers were full of congratulations and suggestions; even paranoid Deveah relaxed enough to join the small, encouraging group. As the conversation flowed, Roe was suddenly aware of a dark presence and turned to her husband-to-be. Moran was facing Corymb. The elder noticed her movement and smiled graciously, nod-

ding his head respectfully, but Roe could not rid herself of
discomfort. Corymb's smiles always meant something else.
She had never doubted that the attempt on the heir's life,
many years ago, had indirectly come from Corymb. Remove
Tal, and Deveah would be next in line . . . and Corymb controlled Deveah. Moran's features were carefully neutral, refusing to recoil from the death in Corymb's face and the lies
in Deveah's eyes. Deveah's eyes were the most disturbing—
one green eye glittered, and the other, the rare Sheel Split of
half green, half brown, was dull and lifeless.

Corymb would not allow a silence to settle. "The future
ragaree's husband is an agroengineer of some renown. I hope
your skills shall be as useful to the people." The elder's tone
was polite, interested—the consummate speaker.

"Ronuviel must think so," Moran replied. Roe knew that
voice—he was controlling anger. Moran was dangerous when
he was angry.

"Thank you for coming, Dielaan," Roe murmured swiftly,
using the title of respect for the man. "My man and I have
much to speak of. You will excuse us? It seems a good time
to leave."

"Of course." The colorful, pulsing crowd swirled, and
both Corymb and Deveah were gone. She felt Moran relax.

He turned to her. "Thank you. You wanted to tell me
something?"

"Yes." She drew him out of the mob and toward the
wall. "I have been trying to tell you that I think I am pregnant,
but there has not been time to take the tests. Braan suspects,
but no one else."

Moran looked a bit dazed by the news and stared at her.
Then he gently reached out to touch her cheek in a simple
caress. Her expression bloomed, and she hugged him.

"Come, get your drink. I want to see Jaac before she
takes Braan's children to bed. She is their godmother, you
know." Reaching to the cantina table, Moran grabbed his
Dramiera, swallowed the remainder, and then followed her.

———

Lyte floated among the guests, his face the blasé mask
of the tratores, his ears absorbing every word and nuance. A

familiar name caught his attention, and he paused near two consuls.

"Are you suggesting there are people who could profit from her removal?"

"When one is at the top of one's profession, life itself becomes a cat-and-mouse game. It's common knowledge what Elana has been working on for ten years. And I have seen the optics—the rumors of her findings are true!"

"You believe the Nualans are human, as we are human, and no longer need genetic tampering? Even if it is true, do you think her colleagues will stand by and watch their pet projects lose funding?"

So intelligence had been correct: Elana was currently in disfavor over her research. Something about cutting the Nu-alans loose from their medical intravenous tube and encouraging reproduction with no medical interference...

"You look much too preoccupied for a party. Can I point you to some diversion?"

Lyte turned and met Shinar's clear blue eyes. Thick blond hair tumbling at several levels, held by clasps—what was she, sixteen terra? Gods... "I think I just found it," he answered.

"Oh? For the moment, perhaps. You can save the charm because, yes, I am susceptible, and yes, I am on guard. You will have to make other plans for the rest of the evening."

"Don't worry, I'm probably twice your age, and that tends to put a kink in my style. Also, I don't trust Nualan women. They steal men's souls."

She laughed, the sound of it ringing in the crystal goblets. "Do not let it bother you. I have had lovers much older than you." And she was gone. Gods...

"I'm just as interesting as she is." Lyte glanced to his side. The woman was one he had talked with earlier, a person of importance; she was the under secretary of the Military Council and a second officer. She was also a lovely blonde. Lyte had a weakness for blondes.

"Who am I to disagree?" he returned, handing her a drink from the nearby cantinatable. She smiled demurely, turning on the charm. He smiled in answer, with no need to attempt to be charming. It was innate with him.

"Just be sure she's willing—there's no penalty for mutual seduction, but the penalty for rape is castration."

Lyte somehow hung on to his composure. "What about a—false accusation? Somehow an apology wouldn't, well—"

"Make up for things? The punishment for a false accusation is death." She laughed then, a perverse humor taking over in her. "Needless to say, they've had something like two rapes and one false witness in about four thousand years. I guess it works. The law *and* their social system."

Lyte nodded absently, intending to be very sure of Shinar's true feelings if he chose to pursue that course. "I don't know much about Nuala. Suppose we try a few local delicacies, and you can instruct me in some of the upcoming customs. I've heard about the grape harvest celebration. . . ."

"This way," she answered, taking his arm and leading him to a banquet table.

Something was very wrong. Moran tried to remember if he had taken an antirav pill and could not. Of course not, he took the series long ago. For a moment he couldn't remember where he was, and that frightened him. Suddenly someone was standing next to him, gripping his arm. He turned and tired to focus. Vertigo overwhelmed him. It was Ronuviel.

"Moran? What is it? You did not eat any chéraka, did you?"

He was having trouble focusing on her. "No, I know better than— Lords, I'm dizzy."

She flinched at the polytheistic off-world oath. "We must get you to a chair. You have a delicate stomach; maybe you need more pills. If that cantinamaster is watering the liquor, I shall have his license." She began to haul him toward a table.

"No! No, I just want to lie down awhile. Maybe I haven't eaten enough. Some of these liquors are strong . . . and I had wine. Shouldn't—shouldn't have mixed . . ." He stumbled, Roe barely able to steady him.

"Come on, then, let us go back to your room. I want to run some tests on you."

"I thought you . . . don't treat . . . family."

"I shall get Elana, then!" She pulled his arm across her shoulders. "Come on, this way. We do not want the guests to think you have been celebrating all day, do we?" Roe added, attempting to force humor.

———

Fortunately they were close to the bronze doors and quickly rounded the corner into the Hall of Mirrors. Moran looked up, and the lights reflecting in the mirrors threw him into such a spin, he collapsed to his knees. At that moment Jaac entered the hallway.

"Roe? What is wrong?" She hurried over to the couple.

"I do not know. I think it may be the water. Help us!"

"Is—not!"

Jaac went to Moran's other side, and the two hauled him to his feet.

"You must try, Moran," Roe said, wishing the *guaard* was not stationed inside the bronze doors tonight instead of outside them. "You must carry some of your own weight!" They were scarcely halfway down the hallway when it became apparent that he was not able to carry any weight. Finally the women let him sit down on the floor, Roe supporting his back and head.

"I shall go bring a stretcher," Jaac began, "and see if I can find Elana." She ran back down the hallway to the bronze doors, only to meet Lyte and the under secretary.

The man stopped her. "What's wrong? You—"

"It is Moran. He is ill, extremely ill. We need Elana."

"*What!*" Lyte dashed down the corridor to the huddled pair. "Never should have left him, never!" he muttered savagely under his breath. "Can you stand?"

"Yes. Room. Please." Lyte grabbed Moran in a body lock and slowly hauled him to his feet.

"Roe, balance him. Jaacav, get a doctor or somebody! He may have been poisoned!" The woman was already gone. He suddenly realized what he had said. "Oh—you're a doctor. I'm—"

"Forget it, I do not have my instruments. Let us hurry. If it is rav poisoning, he should be lying on his back." The two dragged him down the hall. The off-worlder woman, momentarily forgotten, followed them.

They left the blonde at the bronze doors, Lyte promising to return to her. It was not far to the guest room, and the *guaard* helped; only the turns and curves made it seem long. The group had barely set Moran on the bed when Elana, Jaac, and Braan entered the room. The doctor went straight to the man and whipped out a meter, passing it above his body while Roe made him comfortable. Using a tiny probe, she withdrew a single drop of blood from his arm and absorbed the fluid into her meter. Ronuviel felt her eyes widen as she read the flashing sequence of lights. Elana took an air-injection hypo out of her small bag and gave Moran a shot. The tossing man immediately relaxed, unconscious.

"What—" Lyte began.

"A common poison," Elana answered abruptly. She turned to Braan. "How could this have happened?" she asked in Nualan. "Who could have followed him and done this—and why?" Braan did not speak. A *guaard* signaled for Jaac's attention, and she left the room.

"We must leave the city," Roe whispered tightly. "Until Jaac can discover what is happening."

"That is not a problem. Baskh has requested we go to Tolis. I thought Lyte and Moran could travel with us."

"The radioactive city?" Lyte asked carefully, visibly grateful that they were speaking Axis once again.

"It will be one of the more memorable times of your life, Lyte—the trine mines are there. And it is the most secure city on the planet—the best place for Moran right now." Lyte nodded absently, the wheels visibly turning in his mind. Before he could frame a reply, Jaac returned.

"Curiouser—we have a body." The others stiffened in reaction to her words. "A cantinamaster—his neck is broken, and it could not have happened from a fall, the healer says."

"Cantinamaster?" Braan repeated sharply. "From what station?" Jaac told him, briefly describing the man. Braan nodded slowly and then spoke softly. "Lyte, there is nothing we can do for Moran now, except let the antidote run its course. We shall depart on *the Nova* with the tide, if you have no objections. Try to relax the rest of this evening— Roe is better qualified than any of us to care for Moran. She has the vested interest in his future." Elana nodded, her eyes on Braan. Then, with a nod to Roe, she swept out of the room, Jaacav following.

Lyte looked at Braan. The Nualan was pale; this had clearly frightened him. The warrior looked almost reassured at Braan's reaction as he slowly walked out of the room. Only after Lyte exited did the two *guaard* leave, the woman setting the door slightly ajar and stationing herself in front of it.

"There is one great problem, Roe....." Braan whispered.

"What?" she asked, not looking up as she loosened Moran's collar and cuffs.

"The drink of Dramiera—the cantinamaster meant it for me." Roe's head shot up, and they stared at each other a long moment. Braan turned to leave. "At tide."

CHAPTER FOUR

The council room was a dome of leaded glass, the floors polished to a brilliant ebony. By night the universe would settle on their heads, and by day, on a clear day, they could see almost to Amura's mountains, the council room being the highest point in Tolis. No benches—the synod of this city had stood during their meetings for as long as memory stretched; it made for shorter and more concise gatherings.

Today the room was almost deserted, echoing from Tinyan's footsteps. She had waited the afternoon there, her mind on one thing: Who had Baskh Atare sent? The prime minister was off-planet. Perhaps Tal, the heir? She prayed it would be Braan or Ronuviel. Only they understood. . . .

It was cool. Even this short distance north, the year had begun to turn. She drew the sides of her woolen poncho close as she stepped up to the side of the dome, trying to absorb the last rays of light. Carad found her there, as always, a flaming woman dressed in black against a flaming sky. He entered the dome, his traditional skin boots making no sound, the tread of an elkita master.

"Nowhere on Nuala does Holy Mendulay paint the sky as it is seen above Tolis," she remarked, not turning

"The brilliance of fire for a burning city," Carad replied, stepping to her side.

"They come," Tinyan went on, her voice still conversational. "Whom do you think he sent? The *guaard* on the transmission would not say."

"As long as it is not one of Dielaan's jackals, I do not care."

She did not miss the edge to his tone. "When Corymb comes, he comes on his own. Baskh Atare is many things, good and bad. A fool he is not." They stood awhile in silence, watching the sail top the horizon and swiftly approach the harbor.

"The winds of autumn begin. Rare for the southerners to come so late," Carad began.

"There is need," Tinyan answered, almost cutting him off. "Perhaps more than we suspect." She turned from the dying starlight. "Quahna must be informed."

"Not necessary" came Quahna's voice from the chamber doorway. They looked up to see the archpriest, his white robe blood-colored in the last rays from Kee. Tinyan managed a lovely smile despite her mood. She had not seen her second-husband in two days. They stood silent, the eternal triangle, as it had been since they were children plotting to have Tolis acknowledged as the power it could become. So Tolis had ... and why not? Did they not mine the trine gold? The radiation of the deeper veins held no terror for sinis. Had a sini not created the Nualan metal, vandrun, which was immune to Dielaan radiation? The keys to Nuala's return to the Axis had been found scant kilometers from Tolis.

There was a price to pay for such power; family, privacy, personal needs and desires had been swept aside. Many times over they had paid it. Only Tinyan had desired it, to become a co-minister; she had paid the highest price of all. Quahna, to his amazement, had been chosen archpriest scarcely a year ago. Carad preferred his old ambassadorial post, but the city needed him as a minister. There were no laws against a married couple holding the joint office; reluctantly he had accepted the position and had proved a fine minister.

"I wonder if the children might come." Tinyan's voice was almost musing.

"They would have called first, Tinyan," Quahna gently replied.

"Of course." She bit off the words, stiffening as she straightened the folds of her poncho. "Let us prepare the feast. They may bring off-worlders, so we must have appropriate food." She brushed past them into the corridor, disappearing into darkness. Quahna reached out for a piece of hair that had caught in the doorsill, absently wrapping the long, crimson strand around his finger.

"Over a thousand years to this end. Amazing we never thought past the moment of triumph," Quahna said aloud. The big black man nodded his agreement. Quahna glanced up, his own short, trim physique dwarfed by the mighty Carad. Age had not dimmed the co-minister, though his hair was now prematurely white.

"Gid could be on board, you know," Carad replied. "He loves to surprise us."

"I hope he is. She could use such a boost. I miss his dry humor and his relentless logic." Quahna paused. "It is hard to be the head of a city whose stated purpose is to remove the need for its existence, is it not?"

"She does not see the end in our lifetime and does not dwell on it," Carad said heavily. "She is proud our children were sent beyond the walls at birth. But it is hard, very hard. Let us prepare for our guests. The tone of the evening shall be set by the first off the moonraker. I wonder how they will phrase their report when they discover that we base our findings on 'feelings.'"

THE NOVA   VESPERS

Ronuviel was alone as she watched the mother star, Kee, set. The flaming ball dropped like a stone to the water's rim. Sea sounds overwhelmed her—the creaking wood, the crying birds, the fine mist whipping against her face. An arm slipped around her waist, and she turned sideways to see Moran. He looked much better than he had at dawn; a day of sweats and trembling had left him weak and drawn, suspicion clouding his features. Roe's stomach knotted again as she thought of the consequences—Braan's drink, Moran's life. *What is happening to us?* The pale shadow that was Lyte stood behind her lover—he was never far from Moran's side. He was worried, too, though he never mentioned it.

"Time to get into suits?" Moran asked, referring to the protective gear they would wear during their stay.

"Soon."

"How do you know when to get into suits?" Lyte asked.

"Every shipmaster has his own system," she explained. "This one waits until he can see the engravings on the dome. A small ship would have different ways. The marine life, the flora, tells you if you know what to look for. . . ."

"Someone said not to drag our hands in the cargohold water. I didn't realize that even the land is more radioactive here, much less the ocean. Some of the sailors have already changed," Lyte observed.

"A moonraker is too large a ship to be left unattended while people suit up. The new shift will not have to becalm the boat, as a smaller ship might. We should go below. Already I think we are too close." She gestured for them to follow.

"Do we wear them all the time?" Lyte asked.

"Except when we are in our own rooms, which are especially treated and sealed. Everywhere else we accommodate them. That is why Braan left Zair behind—we do not make suits for animals."

"Does Gid have to wear one?" Moran asked.

"Of course. Why do you ask?"

"I thought his parents were sini."

"The leaders of the city or something?" Lyte added.

"They are," Ronuviel replied, ducking a low sill. "But Gid is not. He is as vulnerable as we are. Tinyan, his mother, is a mild sini, a *mock* sini. We can be in her presence without suits for hours. Carad, Gid's father, is very hot—it is unusual that both his children are cool."

"How long has Braan known Gid?" Lyte asked suddenly. Roe glanced up—she sensed more behind the question.

"Since they were children. They were best friends and shared everything together. Gid feels a responsibility to the city of his birth, however, so now they see each other rarely.

It is true that there are fanatics in Tolis, as anywhere, Lyte, but Gid reb Tinyan is above suspicion. He would die for Braan, and he has no reason to hurt Moran." Desiring no more questions, Roe directed them to put on their climate-controlled suits. Always the garment had repelled her; she did not care that it was comfortable, impossible to rip, and took care of every bodily need. She felt alien within it. Only Braan wore it as if he was born in one—and only she knew he also dreaded wearing the suits. But it was wear a suit or remain isolated in a room. She demonstrated how to put one on and activate the functions and then led them back to the deck. Braan and Gid awaited them, the two men already encased in suits.

The city now loomed on the horizon. Its similarity to Amura was apparent, even from a distance. Tolis was lighter, however, as if made of white marble. It was pieced stone from the surrounding region—the radiation would destroy imported marble. She studied the beautiful inlaid mosaics and the ancient rock fortifications. Tolis was a city of contradictions, one of the most beautiful and deadly places on the planet. It occurred to her that it was not unlike the planet Nuala as a whole.

"They are not wearing suits," Lyte said suddenly. She squinted to see the wharf. A large crowd had gathered, the color of their robes muted in the twilight.

"Of course not. We are the aliens here. You will find the desert clothing comfortable, Lyte. We shall wear it within our own sector." The man turned and walked toward the stern, apparently watching the night creep in. Ronuviel felt a stirring of compassion—Lyte was more disturbed by this visit than he would ever admit. She reached for Moran's hand, and his responding grip was firm. "You will like Tinyan, Carad, and Quahna. They have fought many battles to reach what they want. They are individuals of great strength and courage." She could not tell whether or not he was reassured.

———

Their hosts were prepared for the huge crowd and quickly whisked them away to the minister's beautiful, austere home up in the cliffs. Normally the arrival of the Atares would have required a feast, but it was the secondday of High Festival, and that precluded formal entertainment. Quahna was needed at services and would join them later. In the meantime Carad and Tinyan offered their gracious hospitality in the form of a light meal and good conversation.

The dinner was a skillful blend of off-world and Nualan delicacies. Lyte sat at the bar in fascination while Carad tossed the main course together with the seeming abandon of a master. It contained the first meat they had seen, except for the feast, but it was a tiny portion of the whole. Tinyan sought Gid's help in preparing a steaming alcoholic beverage, and when it was ready, the newcomers went into the next room and removed their outer suits. Carad opened the drapes and, to Gid's amusement, waved through the nonreflective glass. An excellent intercom was activated, and with the tables as extensions of the wall, Roe occasionally felt as if they were all sitting in one room and talking. Certainly conversation and good humor were not lacking. Tinyan, glowing over the surprise of her eldest's visit, was in unquenchable spirits.

Roe studied the woman and her dark son, who were sitting so close together that only the thickness of the glass separated them. Gid was the image of his father, as close to Afrikanis as any man in the Axis Republic—that was the fault of Carad's family, fanatics who married only the blackest, the hottest. Carad gave up his past to marry the pale, red-haired firebrand Tinyan, and this little gathering was all the family he had: these friends, Quahna, and the three other children. How strange, to be cut off from roots . . . it was not the normal Nualan procedure. And how beautiful Tinyan was, as if she had not aged a day since Gid's birth over twenty years before. . . .

The thirdmeal dishes were being dropped in the autoton, and dessert and hot saffra were being served when there was a knock at the main door. Tinyan answered and ushered in Quahna. Carad pulled out another mug and plate.

"You are in time for saffra, my friend! Will you join us?"

"Thank you, yes, Carad. Now that the old man has arrived, it is time to get down to serious matters." Quahna's voice was gentle but unyielding, and Ronuviel felt a chill.

Now was the time for what they had come for—the true meaning of all the preceding pleasantries. The priest sat down next to his wife and took a sip of saffra. He stared through the glass at the visiting group and finally began to speak, choosing Axis over Nualan as a courtesy to their guests.

"Braan, there is no way to express our gratitude for your arrival. We are aware of Enid's failing health and give you our sympathy for your pain." Braan appeared untouched by the words, but Tinyan's fingertips against the glass in a futile outreach shook him visibly.

Carad continued the speech. "All the more because what you have come to hear is brief and cryptic, and what you will see are but pieces in a great puzzle. We are but pawns, whatever my pride may shout in argument." Carad paused, uncertain of how to proceed.

Tinyan had no doubts. "Forget the 80-20 problems, our civil rights, the border skirmishes with the Stigati Ciedärlien, all of it. Something potentially much more lethal is taking place right under our noses. We are losing land, Atares. Losing crucial land—and I suspect to one man."

"Specifically which land?" Roe asked.

"Mostly the Luna tracts," Tinyan replied.

Braan stopped twirling his eating utensil and looked up. "How much?"

"We do not know. That is why we are frightened and why we need you to discover what you can." Tinyan looked visibly worried, a rare occurrence.

"What are the Luna tracts?" Moran finally asked. Lyte also looked interested.

"The lands surrounding the gold mines," Roe answered. "There are literally thousands of square kilometers in the area. The nominal owners are the Atare clan, as the discoverers of trine gold, but all the people have a stake in the trade. Who do you think is buying up so much of the stock?"

"Corymb Dielaan." Tinyan's face registered no expression. Roe saw Moran and Lyte react to her voice—not to the tone but to the lack of tone, of any emotion at all.

"Our rabid, 80- and sini-hating friend. Interesting. No one can own more than ten percent of the released stock. How is he doing it?" Braan asked easily.

"We think he is buying the rights to off-world trade names, companies that have folded. He would never have to announce his holdings, you know. He could simply draw the profits and keep silent," Tinyan answered.

"No." Carad's voice was granite. "I know Dielaan; he is insatiable. That jackal will not be happy until he has all the trine mines. And he wants people to know he has these things."

"He wants love and respect most of all," Quahna said gently. "Which he cannot buy. He is doomed to fail."

"Perhaps ... perhaps not. With the stranglehold the synod has had our family in these last few years, Corymb's chances to unseat Baskh are better than ever. Not through election or war—through Deveah." Roe's words fell on silence, the thought sobering them all. "My question is why the synod turns a blind eye to him. Even the tribe of Dielaan grows ashamed of his deeds."

"They all have their little power games. They think he keeps Baskh on his toes," Tinyan replied sourly. "I would also be cautious if I feared a knife in my back. And our *watch* station has been put on alert by Jaacav—something about our Axis guard ships pulling back. There has been a change in the war. We are no longer right behind the front?" The first was not really a question; the second was.

"It is believed an offensive is coming, possibly an attack from two sides by both the Fewhas and the Malvevenians. But they would not have released Lyte and me for furlough if it was expected soon," Moran offered. Roe let her eyes rest on him, seeing his sadness as he realized that the Toli were not about to believe him. He had not lived with the fear, the paranoia, the hate—the knowledge that Nualans were expendable. He could not know. . . .

"Enough," Carad said with a wave of his hand. "You may check the records tomorrow and see for yourself. You traded the galaxy lines, Braan, you know what to look for. I think you will find what we fear." Toasting his guests, he drained his mug and, with a touch of his wife's hand, left the room.

Roe did not stand to move as the others did. She watched Tinyan, as always amazed that two strong-willed men like

Carad and Quahna could both be married to such a woman. Her magnificent, fiery beauty and intelligence possessed a heat far beyond radiation. Years before, Braan had nearly caused an uproar in the royal court over his unrequited love for his best friend's mother. Age was not the problem— Tinyan knew the old stories and knew better than to fall in love with a man who was barred from marrying even a Nualan 20. She was the one with two men and, by custom, would have had to make the first move—she had wisely kept silent. But Roe knew the truth of the attraction, and if Braan had been a nameless, faceless 80, Tinyan would have three husbands instead of two.

Oh, my brother, she thought with pain as Braan said his good nights and walked to the rooms prepared for them. *There is something cold within you, trying to protect what is left of your scarred heart. Even the children cannot reach you. Will you let no one try?* Tinyan had entered their side of the family room and was off by the window, joking with Gid.

Then her son looked serious and drew her to the couch, insisting that she listen. Roe wondered what Gid was up to; he could not have missed Braan's uncharacteristic aloofness of late. But once the families had been very close—she hoped some of that was left. Coming out of her thoughts, she looked up to find Moran patiently waiting for her to accompany him to their quarters.

"Thank you," she said simply, offering him her hand. They walked slowly back to the apartments.

———

Braan sat down on the edge of his double bed, clutching his caftan. He had stripped down to the long, loose, string-waisted pants, joqurs, the southerners preferred. Something in the night drew him, and he stared out of the tiny window at the silver of the firstmoon, Eros. *Holy One, things are getting worse. Do I have enemies on every front? Do they abandon us to the Fewhas, thinking we are as unarmed as Axis planets are supposed to be? And why bother to poison me, why is the third brother a threat? Malice . . . sheer hate . . .*

There was a knock at the hatch.

"Enter." Braan turned his head, saw Tinyan's etched

features by the light of the water candle, and let a smile slip across his face. "I was hoping to see you. Have you come for idle chatter, the latest gossip, or the truth about the Nualan Synod?"

Tinyan managed a deep-throated chuckle. "Actually, Gid sent me to entice you."

A quick rush of air followed this remark as Braan rolled his eyes and turned away, touching his forehead in a gesture of mock despair. "Not you two as well! I thought I was safe here!"

"Can you escape truth?" she asked, pulling the hatch closed behind her.

"Truth?" He was tired, unable to block. The all too familiar depression settled like a cloud.

Tinyan stepped over and sat on the low stool by the end of the bed. "There is a loving man behind that practiced smile. But it has been a long time since I have seen him."

Braan looked out the window again. "If you are getting into therapy as a sideline, Tinyan, then—"

"Can you believe that? Just because we both choose to be blind, do not call me insensitive as well. My son and friend, Gid, made a point I should have seen for myself." She reached up and clasped his neck with her cool, slim hand, turning him to face her. "When she dies, Braan, what will you do?"

"She is already dead, actually. We merely wait to bury her."

Tinyan could see no flicker of feeling, yet the emotions in the room were chaotic, collapsing. For once the ability of all Nualans to sense emotional currents was a help and not a hindrance. To other humans, nothing would be evident. He did not even sweat. "You can do better than that, Braan. Or shall you tell me I am being too familiar with royalty?" He started to turn away; only a slap would have been more insulting. "Braan, I have to tell you. I never told anyone— Gid, Carad, Quahna, none know—but now is the time. I spoke to Enid alone once, just before Asiai was born. Do you know what she told me? That she knew the child would be her death. She had not believed it until right then, but finally she did. And she did not care! In that grim, cool manner of hers she told me that for four years she had been a queen—not in name, but between your worship of her and the people's worship of you, close enough. And that too much of it was dangerous. She loved it and feared it. Did you know that when she was born, the doctors said she would never survive her childhood? But somehow, with her will to live, she hung on. She never told you, did she? You knew she looked fragile; you never knew she *was* fragile."

"Yes," he whispered, more to stop her than to answer her.

"She forbade her family, her friends, to say anything, wanting to go with you and knowing you loved her too much to take her if you knew. She always lived on borrowed time! No one here knew—everyone thought the air, the food was too much for her. No . . . Enid would have died on Orion, probably before this! They are very good at bringing weak fetuses to term, poor at adult medical care."

"Do not dare—"

"But that is fortunate for us! She gave you Dylan and Asiai and her love: the things she wanted you to have most of all. And she made me promise that if anything happened, I would remember and find a time to tell you. For I was the mother of your best friend, and Nualan—I would not dare lie. And I waited for the time to speak, thinking you would snap out if it, not truly realizing how . . . dangerous . . . your position was, how you had to seem to vanish to survive. How it finally affected you."

"Tinyan, please—" He kept waiting for her to cease, yet he had no strength to stop her.

"You gave her everything she ever wanted for as long as it was humanly possible. And now—will you withdraw into a shell as a testimony of love? It seems to me that choice would say, 'I made a mistake. The potential pain is not worth it.'" There was a long pause.

Braan studied the sinking moon. He turned back to her. "You always leap for the jugular, do you not?"

"Was it worth it?" she asked, ignoring his question. And Braan knew he had lost the argument.

"Yes." He slowly pulled away from her, propping his elbows up on his knees and dropping his head in his hands.

She waited, setting her other hand, still cool, like the night, on his shoulder.

Braan's thoughts were spinning. Could he have been that blind? Why not? It was possible. So many things he had always felt were unsaid. A mirthless smile crossed his face. If only the rumors were true and Nualans really did investigate the genes of their chosen ones. But then, they would never have been so happy. . . .

The man felt tears coming on and rose, facing the window. Tinyan stood to leave and looked to him again. He seemed so fractured, so unlike the man she knew and had always been a little in love with. Tinyan walked over and slipped her arms around him, hugging him briefly. As she began to pull away, his fingers seized her clasped arms, stopping her.

"What right do you have to come here, smelling of starset and singeing me with the fire of truth?"

"You like pain and self-pity?" Tinyan responded.

"No. What else do you offer?"

"The love and admiration of millions."

Braan softly snorted. "If I reject it and leave Nuala forever, will you come?"

Tinyan hesitated, wondering what he was really asking. "No glass partition would stop you?"

"Or bother me," Braan whispered.

"Yes. If you can look me in the eye and tell me to leave the fools to their doom, for doom is what I fear."

Braan slowly turned to face her and lightly rested his fingertips on her arms. "No," he answered. "As much as a part of me would like to do just that, I could not. As you know. I am too well trained."

Tinyan smiled. "You love them too much . . . as I love you. I tried to forget you a long time ago, with every foolish, antique, and unscientific excuse I could think of. Please do not think I was wholly untempted."

His strange eyes, dark in the light of the water candle, pierced her. "Ten years ago I risked friendship, dignity, and my Atare's wrath to chase you with adoration and roses the color of your hair. And then you enter with the words I have dreamt about!" He released his gentle touch and turned away, smiling faintly, sardonically, as he often did. "You are *bad*."

"I did not lie."

Braan slowly faced her again. "Why?"

Tinyan looked closely and saw the teasing humor in his eyes.

"Because . . . you must return to the living sometime. Are you not a bit afraid of the legend? That you cannot live up to it?" She smiled faintly. "If I am nothing else, my friend, I am a true lover—one who loves. I am not beguiled by the off-world pleasures. I ask nothing, expect nothing, and give everything; something no other child of Nuala could promise." Her grin was so wicked, Braan threw back his head and laughed.

"I have been told that what I thought was simple, honest mutual pleasure spoiled a lot of women," Braan replied.

"Most of them have forgotten what it was like to be the center of attention, if they ever knew. I have been told it was your manner, not your technique. But enough—I would like some firsthand knowledge."

Braan laughed again, softly, and shook his head, beginning to look away. The simple facts made her words incredible; Tinyan was still young, though she had borne four children. A foreign source always increased the odds, and Braan had once witnessed the parting of a mock sini and her child. He could not bear the thought of causing that, even if she did not fear it. Yet the mark of Nuala was free choice. . . . Then she touched the crook of his arm.

"Why not?" She stepped closer until she was right in front of him, her eyes almost meeting his. He took a half step back and studied her, the situation dawning on him. Braan felt his body temperature rise, his pulse increase slightly.

All his life this woman had floated through his mind like a cloud at starset: colorful, ethereal, lucid, remote. And he had always wondered if things had been different, if she had been cool, or he sini and tribeless, could she have cared for him, if only for a day, a night.

Things were not different; but she cared for him, and there was a night, and at least two and a half hours before he might get dizzy from radiation. He was so tired. Then he

smelled the wind in her hair, the scent of starset, and without
hesitation extended his arms and sought her mouth, as if it
were the most natural thing in their lives. She was fierce,
unaware until now of her own reaction to this slender man,
and traced the curve of his throat with her lips. Braan felt
that familiar heady feeling, as if he had touched a living
nerve, and for the first time in years did not fight it, did not
recycle and dismiss it. It had been so long, and he had almost
forgotten how wonderful it was. Almost.

He softly, quickly, almost carelessly kissed the length
and breadth of her throat and shoulders, carefully tracing the
uplift of her magnificent breasts. She shivered, and remembering an old boldness, he touched the clasp at her left shoulder. The caftan fell partially open, and it was all he could do
to keep his head. She chuckled at the soundless appreciation
of his look, pleased with their mutual pleasure. Tinyan slipped
off the sleeve and ruffled the light brown hairs on his chest
with her fingertips.

"If you did not know that a good woman improves like
fine wine, know it," she whispered in his ear. Braan paused,
almost in homage, to Tinyan's amusement, and then bent and
placed a kiss between her breasts that brought forth from her
an unanticipated moan. He suddenly scooped her up in his
arms, meeting her kiss and popping the other clasp as he did
so. He slipped her onto the bed, sweeping away the caftan
as he dropped down on his side next to her. With one hand
she delicately massaged the muscles of his chest while the
other hand pulled the string from his joqurs.

Braan tried to remember and savor each moment that
came afterward, as he had so often done before, but he could
not. He remembered tracing the delicate line of hairs down
her stomach, and then half-buried instinct took over. The fire
in that room was more potent than any radiation, the body
locked to his coaxing him on to endurance and insanity he
had forgotten was possible. His mind was in such a spin, he
thought radiation poisoning had taken over, but a few long
gasps later he could see again.

She was smiling at him, and he shyly managed to answer,
bending forward to kiss her raised shoulder. She stopped him
with a gentle touch, much as he had stopped her moments

ago when an errant move would have escalated things too swiftly. Then she slipped her arm around him and found a backbone muscle, gently kneading it while she followed the bones of his face with her left hand. Braan relaxed in her arms, torn between sleep and the half-restful, half-arousing touch of her hands. He quietly traced the curves and swells of her body, knowing that there was time for many things before she had to leave. . . .

When he awoke in the faint shiver of dawn, he was alone, and on the headrest next to his was a single reddish-gold rose.

CHAPTER FIVE

The morning dawned crisp and clear. Braan was up early, eating alone, trying to sort out the previous night. He could not analyze Tinyan—he accepted the situation and let it be. No doubt Enid *had* spoken privately with the Nualan woman. He had not been so addled last night that he could not read the truth. His eyes strayed to the sculpture standing before the plated window. Massive, rising with incredible strength, as if to break free of gravity ... *I was another man when I carved that....* Too long since he had touched laser to stone, releasing the soul within. He had tried to carve his impressions of Enid, but ...

Ronuviel was suddenly beside him, punching up a cup of cocoa. She slipped an arm around him and hugged him before sitting at the table. "You look as if you slept well! I never heard of Tolis being therapeutic for anyone except Gid!"

"You never know," he answered dryly. "Ready to play intelligence officer?"

"I think so. I suggest we copy everything," she continued. "There may be names we do not know that others might."

"Agreed. If we finish early, let us take them to the trine mine. I would like to see Lyte lose his composure over all that gold ore."

"You are *bad*," Roe replied, pleased with the resurgence of his mischievous streak.

"Who is bad?" It was Moran, already checking out his suit.

"Oh, nothing. Braan has some not-so-subtle torture planned for Lyte." Ronuviel could not control her smile.

"Such as?" Moran paused, looking over at her.

"The most valuable mine in the galaxy and he cannot touch any of it?" she offered.

Moran laughed. "Fiend!"

"Of course," Braan agreed. "Firstmeal?"

"Any egg strollen?" came a voice from the corridor. Gid appeared, followed by a disheveled Lyte. The men sat down and quickly demolished the food as fast as Braan could whip it up. Roe blended several fruit juices and left the balance for their hosts, who as a rule ate no solids in the morning.

Gid was reaching for his suit when a flashing light told them their hosts had arrived. Carad sauntered in, his feet making no sound on the tile floor. Quahna followed and headed straight for the fruit juice. "Ronuviel, you read my mind! Thank you for your thoughtfulness." He downed half a glass in one breath.

Carad, in no hurry this morning, slowly poured glasses for himself and Tinyan. "Are you ready to spend time in our archives?" he asked.

Braan sighed. "It is much too beautiful a day. Yes, as soon as you are finished, we shall leave." He looked over through the glass to see that Tinyan had slipped in unannounced, clothed in a brown caftan girdled in white. She had not yet put on her makeup or piled up her hair, and she looked no older than Roe.

She reached for a cup of juice and toasted the inner window. "Good morning all. I hope you slept with as much comfort as those vented rooms could provide. Are you going to the archives already, Gid?"

Braan finally looked away from her to the three men, who were checking each other's safety locks.

"We are off," Moran answered for Gid, opening the door. Lyte waited a moment, shrugged, and then followed. Rolling his eyes expressively, Gid pulled the door shut.

"Can he be trusted?" Tinyan asked after a suitable pause.

Roe glanced up. "Moran? Completely. Lyte—I think so. I hope so."

"We will find out soon, will we not?" Braan added easily. "I suppose he thinks we are crazy, looking for traitors. Let us pray he is right." He stood and reached for his suit.

———

The research room was unbearably hot. Ronuviel slowly sat up from her console, wishing for the hundredth time that there was some way to wipe the sweat from her brow. She glanced at Braan—he appeared cool and comfortable in his suit, going through the rote processing as if unencumbered by gloves. Tinyan and Carad had brought them the major programs and then turned the consoles on manual, giving their guests access to everything in the library.

She stared down at the bewildering mass of names and corporations. Most she knew as off-world conglomerates. For the first time this trip Roe was afraid. There were so many names, and most were meaningless. A few, strangely enough, were Ciedärlien, and that could not be coincidence. Roe stirred uneasily at the thought of Corymb dealing with the fierce desert dwellers. When she looked up again, she found Braan staring off into space, focusing on nothing. He might as well live in that suit, it is his second skin, she thought angrily. Then he looked at her.

"We are in trouble. A great deal of trouble. The synod ran out of time and did not start debate on the question of increased off-world ownership, but it passed committee with no problems," he said softly. "I think we have discovered this just in time."

"What?"

"Most of these names are meaningless, but a few I recognize as bogus off-world companies I ran into while trading in the Axis. They never have attempted to buy here, so there is no record preventing them from entering local trade and ownership."

"Is not the Land and Securities Exchange supposed to keep an eye out for those types?"

"Yes." They stared at one another. "Corymb is the chairman of that exchange," Braan added.

Roe suddenly felt very cold. A fool, power-hungry; Corymb was both, but this could be interpreted as treason.

In another part of the library Lyte punched up gold deed information and muttered his frustration. So simple to write them all off as paranoid. But what if—just suppose—he had not seen that scope in the watch room; he'd think they were all crazy. Ships had been out of position, however, and remembering his talk shipboard with Moran, he knew Moran was thinking of scopes too. His friend had also mentioned the bitter looks Braan had received from Corymb. For the first time it occurred to Lyte that the poison might not have been meant for Moran. *Great—now I have two people to protect. . . .* He punched the keys faster.

VESPERS

They finished the day by crossing the river and touring a trine gold mine. Gid laughed for five minutes at the look on Lyte's face when Braan dumped into his hands enough pellets of trine gold to buy the entire Seven Systems. Lyte was good-natured about his bad habits; he sighed, smiling, and said, "Now I can die happy." As usual, all found the ore extraction fascinating. When asked why no one was searched at the entrance, Roe chuckled and told Lyte that an intricate scan system determined how much gold each person wore when they entered. Any deviation when they left alerted security. She was surprised and gratified by the look of approval on his face.

The Atares had been hopeful that they could return the warriors to Tinyan's home without incident. As they passed a small parish near Tinyan's home, however, they met in the departing crowds several sinishur, the most horribly deformed of all Toli. The crowd, of course, was oblivious to their condition, and Gid knew one of them and exchanged swift pleasantries; but Moran was politely silent, and Lyte had on

his tratore face, using every ounce of self-control to keep
from bolting screaming into the street. To see an ugly alien
was one thing; for all he knew he might be appallingly ugly
to it. But to acknowledge the Nualans as human and then see
this Toli. . . . To be uncertain of its sex; its bones and its skin
subtly, painfully malformed beyond comfortable movement.
It was the stuff of which nightmares were made. After saying
good-bye Gid quickly steered them back down a side street.
No one said anything during the entire walk to the house.

Then, at the bottom of the long staircase, Gid spoke.
"Fortunately those who survive natural miscarriages and have
wits are without exception sterile. We actually have none so
badly deformed under forty terrayear."

"Were they male or female?" Lyte finally asked, his
voice thick.

"The sinishur I spoke to was a man. The other I do not
know. I am not sure it has a sex." In silence they ascended
the stairs to finish their last night in Tolis.

AMURA, THE   FOURHUNDRED   PRIME
MENDULARION   TWENTYNINEDAY

This time the music woke her. Teloa stirred, hovering
on the edge of sleep, resisting the call of the bells. But no,
the great bass bell was also tolling—once, twice, thrice.
Opening her eyes, she watched the mountain peak beyond
her outer doors slowly come to life, a healthy flush of pink
caressing its face. Welcome, Kee, star of Nuala, she thought
as the haunting melody drew to a close.

As she expected, a faint rap at the inner door echoed
through the chamber.

"Come in." Stretching carefully, she rolled over and
reached for the light temple robe she had worn for several
days.

"Good morning! Are you starting to adapt to our schedule?" Elana asked, bringing in a tray of food.

Teloa smiled. She had been so tired, she had scarcely
noticed that she had reversed her schedule. "What do the bells

mean?" she asked suddenly. "I know they ring at starrise and starset, but they ring during the day and night as well."

"Indeed they do—eight times during a normal day and night, and when deaths of important people occur," Elana began, setting the tray down on a small table. "I ordered some pants and a long-sleeved shirt for you from stores—you cannot walk around in the robe of a priestess! And also a poncho; the days are getting colder."

Slipping the robe in question over her head, Teloa slowly moved over behind the elegantly carved divider to the sanitation area. "The bells?"

"I have not forgotten." Elana seated herself at the table and started removing the food from the tray. "What have you been reading about us so far?"

"Mostly recent material,'" Teloa answered, pausing longingly by the hot tub. She could not admit to the woman that she feared to read the older writings—feared to find out the origins of the colony. Reading current information on their culture and politics was more reassuring.

"If you want to bathe first, please go ahead. But I will eat if you do not mind. I have lab work today."

"You are so kind to bring me my meals and keep me company, how can I let you eat alone?" Teloa asked, moving to sit opposite the healer. Elana chuckled and offered her the round pill she had to take before every meal.

"I must keep an eye on all my patients, and I must eat firstmeal. Why not together? Plus, I admit, I am always curious about those who take up a planet of mutants on their offer of sanctuary." Teloa blushed and lowered her eyes. Elana pretended not to notice. "Oh, I have lived off-planet for a time—I know what they say about us." She began to cut up the bread loaf.

"The bells?" Teloa prompted, quickly downing the pill with some saffra.

"The bells are how we keep time, as I am sure you have guessed. Here in Amura we ring the ancient canonical hours. Matins is midnight, lauds between matins and starrise. Starrise is prime, mid-morning tierce and sext high noon. The largest bass bell rings the hour, and matins is our first hour." Elana paused to smear a sweet spread on her still warm bread slice. "So what you just heard rung was third bell. The sixth bell is rung at mid-afternoon, and is none. Vespers, or starset, is seventh bell, and compline is between vespers and matins—my bedtime!" They both smiled. "Now, in smaller towns, lauds is rung at moonset—the firstmoon, Agape— and compline at moonrise. Which confuses off-worlders."

"Uh-oh," Teloa said aloud, remembering the patterns of Capricorn V's two moons. "Then that means—"

"I see you know your moon phases," Elana started, anticipating her comment. "It means sometimes lauds is rung *before* matins or even in the middle of the day!" She chuckled at the thought. "Most of our people are very aware of the moon cycles, especially in agricultural areas. So *we* have no trouble. But Amura changed a thousand years ago, to minimize the confusion of our visitors. This is the capital of the system, and we have many embassies here, although most of them are empty during festival. The nights are too quiet for the personnel!"

"Was this a religious settlement?" Teloa asked, pleased to get so many answers without digging through the library system.

"No. It was never truly a settlement." Elana looked thoughtful and a bit distant. "There were six thousand scientists and support personnel. . . . They were to set up self-supporting stations that would be the basis of the new colony. This is a large planet of great variety—a lifetime is not long enough to study it. Many of the finest scientific minds of the fledgling Axis joined the expedition. What the Axis neglected to mention before the three ships launched was the anomaly in the atmosphere. . . ." Elana's voice grew softer. "Because the nitrogen-oxygen mix was acceptable, the Axis colonization headquarters decided to let the scientific expedition define and name the unknown readings. It was not until after the ships left that they realized that the metal of the probe was deteriorating rapidly."

"You don't have to tell me this," Teloa said gently.

The healer looked surprised. "It is ancient history, Teloa— almost five thousandyear ago. It is always difficult for me to realize how careless they were, how foolish." She sighed. "But there was great political pressure then for colonization.

The media had no patience with scientists who said, 'Yes, it *looks* like a paradise, but we need to run more tests.' So the ships went, *the Atare, the Dielaan,* and *the Seedar*. And they landed . . . and they could not leave."

Teloa studied the woman as she spoke, listening to the formal cadence of her Axis speech; much more formal than Capricorn V's Axis speech. Gods, what if the Axis did not require everyone to learn a common tongue?

Elana finally focused on her again. "To shorten the story, there were several New Order Catholic priests and priestesses among the scientists and support group. They had a bell to announce their religious services, and they kept the monastic hours. Before it was over, we all were believers." She smiled faintly at Teloa. "Forgive me, that was too long a storytelling for one not a mythmaker."

"I am interested, and I should learn something about Nuala. I may be here a long time until I can earn passage elsewhere." She paused, nibbling on some cheese. "Elana, I didn't mean to be rude . . . about why I came here—"

Elana reached across the table and touched her hand. "No, Teloa—"

"Tay is fine for variety," the woman interrupted, offering the intimate form as an apology.

Elana smiled at that. "Tay, then. My comment was really a statement of fact. I am interested in people; that is why I am a healer as well as a geneticist. And you need not worry about your past here—if you wish it to remain private, no Nualan will question you about it. But sanctuary is part of our creed. We are mavericks, in a sense. Most planets in the Axis Republic belong to smaller confederacies, with various forms of government—most more centralized than ours. Our local synods, and the high families as judges, run just about everything here. The Atare is chief judge, and the temple a balance between synod and royalty."

"I noticed you have both elected and hereditary representatives," Teloa offered. "Something called a parliamentary system?" She began to spread soft fruit on her bread slice.

"Related but not quite; our Atare—king—and his sister, the Ragäree, are the supreme judges and have actual power. There is also a certain amount of power invested with the high priest and priestess, although not nearly as much as the Dragoche of the desert has; the Dragoche has absolute spiritual and temporal power over his people, the Ciedärlien."

"Who began the offer of sanctuary?" Tay asked softly, staring out the glass doors. Politics had never really interested her; it always meant struggle, and she had struggled enough in her life.

"The scientific expedition," Elana answered. "We have had it from the first. People forget how suppressed the Axis was then; the fighting, the expansionist propaganda, the censorship. Colonies were allowed to set up their own governments, as long as they held no standing armies and did not practice slavery. I personally believe the legend that says Habbukk, the captain of the ship *Atare*, knew the expedition was being abandoned and demanded the sanctuary clause. As a way of . . . justifying who and what they were? I do not know; no one is sure. Things have not changed a great deal. Expansion and trade wars continue, censorship rises once again in the greater Axis—"

"But we were attacked first," Teloa said tightly. "By the Malvevenians."

Elana was silent. "The Caprican System fell to the Malvevenians, did it not? That makes the truth all the more difficult."

"What truth?" Teloa turned away from the windows.

"The truth conveniently glossed over in most history 3AVs. The Malvevenians are merely continuing an import-export embargo that blew out of proportion. They are a refined and finished civilization, Teloa, with high technology, heavy industry, and shrinking markets. They desperately needed new trade outlets. At this very moment they trade peacefully with neutral planets, who either are merely cleaning up an excellent product source or are aware of the reasons the war began and oppose them. No, the Malvevenians tried to establish trade agreements with the Axis Republic. Tremendous industry lobbies, trying to avoid competition, squeezed the council to the point that they refused trade talks. The Malvevenians responded by going to individual planets to conduct separate treaties with major population centers, which is legal under planet rights. Several industry tankers, afraid for their jobs and trade routes, fired on the Malvevenian sample ships. At that time the Malvevenians had had more experience with pirates and smugglers—they were better armed. They blew the industry haulers into little pieces. Business went screaming to the Axis, and war began."

Teloa was silent a long time. She methodically ripped apart the rest of the bread as she stared out the glass doors. Why not? After what she had seen in the past three years, it was all too easy to believe. "The Fewhas?" she finally asked.

"Even more tragic. The Fewha Empire, like the Malvevenian, was crumbling—not for economic reasons but because it had become big and unwieldly, and under its totalitarian regime the people suffered and starved. The government needed to unite them behind a cause. It chose paranoia. Its propaganda convinced its people that the Axis Republic had no love for humanoids, especially outside ones, and planned to expand its boundaries and crush the Fewha's own search for good seed planets. Fearing eventual extinction, they attacked us first."

"Where did you find all this?"

"Most of it is in old press tapes and commentaries written when the wars started."

Another silence. Tay stood and walked slowly to the tub. She adjusted the hot water to a comfortable temperature and then slipped off her robe. "Why did you tell me this?" she asked finally.

"I had not intended to . . . the conversation simply turned that way." Elana gestured vaguely. "I am never sure which is easier, to learn of it in hints and whispers, finally seeking out the library archives, or being told in one massive tale. I am sorry if I have distressed you."

"And it is said that Nualans cannot lie," Tay murmured, slipping into the tub.

"Oh, they *can*. I can think of one man who is a very good liar. But he lived off-world for a long time. I think his ambition has warped him. Most of us find the truth safer. If you can always tell the truth, you do not need to remember what you tell people. The story never changes." She sighed. "I must return to work. You seem much better since Ronuviel healed you—I must find you some added entertainment."

Tay smiled faintly, her thoughts with the lovely young woman whose hands sped warmth to trembling limbs. Did it matter anymore how the war—a thousand-year war—had begun? "Come back," Tay said abruptly to Elana's retreating form. "When you can."

The scientist brightened. "Of course."

THE NOVA   FOURHUNDRED   PRIME
                      TWENTYNINEDAY

Kee had not yet risen in the sky when the *Nova* sped softly out of the harbor, bearing in her hull the ransom of empires. Braan sat alone on deck, except for the crew. Soon they could remove their suits; just in time for the dawn breeze. He was staring at Tolis, salmon-pink and violet in the first light of day. Shipmaster Oh'nel always liked to get an early start. Braan's eyes narrowed. Was another ship bound south? He studied the black speck at the harbor's mouth. Perhaps he had missed a buoy. The speck neither increased nor decreased in size. A stardancer, the only thing smaller than a moonraker that could maintain the same pace. Pirates?

"You have noticed, then?" Braan turned slightly and saw the suited outline of the big shipmaster. His tone was one of mild respect. "Most land people do not. It followed us to Tolis harbor, and now it trails us home. A shadow we do not need, not this late in the year. Storm coming." A frown furled his face, and the man turned and walked back to the wheel. He had a heavy cargo, Braan thought—two Atares, two high-ranking off-worlders, and enough trine gold to buy the Fewha confederation, no questions asked. The pirate trade was under control, but they still existed. And now a storm followed them from the north.

His mind rolled back to the previous night. Gid, the Atares, and the warriors had pooled their wealth of knowledge, and the answer had surprised no one—Corymb easily controlled twenty-three percent of the floating mine stock, a clear majority among owners unrelated to the Atare clan. When the subject was trine gold, it was no longer merely clan business—it was Nualan business, for the trine was the heritage of all Nualans. Everyone owned at least one piece of trine gold: the family crest, worn as a ring or earring. And everyone owned at least one piece of stock. Few Nualans felt the need to own more. The question was: What to do about Corymb? He owned vast corporations off-world, most of them legal. The synod could be tied up in courts for years in a futile attempt to prove that Corymb knew of the purchases in his name. The man was too clever to be snared that way. The evidence of treason had brought forth one other interesting result. Lyte had confessed that he had originally thought the Nualan paranoia about off-worlder threats to be ridiculous. Now, with the evidence of off-world money backing Corymb's wealth, he could no longer deny their problems.

Later Tinyan had spoken of many things. Under her leadership Tolis had prospered, but it still fell short of what it should have been: an equal voice in the politics of Nuala. And although she never said it openly, the meaning was clear; it was time for Braan to retake what was his, a voice in the court, and to push for changes he knew were necessary and had ignored for six long years.

The warmth of the previous night dissolved into the waters of the archipelago, the ocean becoming sky before his eyes. For six years he had mourned his wife's passing. If it was to be, then he swore to rejoice in the freedom of her soul after long suffering. The children would be relieved . . . also possibly resentful, torn between wanting their father happy again and mistrusting other women. No more would the throne influence his decisions. He would leave Nuala if he had to, and force the hand of the Atare as an independent council member of the Axis Republican Council. A jumbling of thoughts . . . He had a sculpture to finish.

"Mighty words," he murmured aloud.

"Silent ones" came Roe's voice. She sat down next to him, her suit gone, and unfastened his helmet. "Smell the air of autumn on the sea and be grateful for the chance to feel it." Her smile was warm and knowing. How much she guessed about the last two nights Braan did not know. He imagined she suspected everything. He smiled slightly and let her assist him in removing his suit.

The storm hit that night not long after they were in bed.
It was typical of the sea's winter storms, but early and violent
for the time of High Festival. Halfway through the night the
rudder snapped, and a lesser crew might not have made it.
But *Nova* was a watertight ship, and with her gold proving
to be the correct ballast, she made it to shore.

Lyte awoke at the silence. It was still dark. Nuala had
long days and nights, too long for him; he could not get used
to them. The ship was tilted crazily to one side and Lyte
realized that they were no longer in water. The silence was
appalling; he had to hear something! Not for the first time
he missed Gid's soft half snore. The Nualan would return to
Amura after the festival ended. Lyte stood and, dressing
quickly, carefully made his way up the ladder to the deck.

It was deserted. He heard the sounds of voices in the
distance and saw a fire. Wishing for a blaster, a knife, anything, he started to climb off the ship.

At the fire he recognized Ronuviel, laughing and talking
with several crew members and attempting to steal a biscuit
from the cook's tins. Lyte relaxed and came forward.

"So you finally noticed the storm! Only after it was over.
Have a seat and try a biscuit; this man is a chef." Lyte slipped
thumb and finger into his shirt pocket and pulled out his pill.
It was habit, especially after Tolis. Swallowing it, he quickly
bit into a biscuit to kill the taste.

"Now try one without an antirav," the cook advised, and
laughed.

"Where is Moran?" Lyte asked after a plate of soufflé
was passed his way.

"Off with Braan, getting a predawn tour. The crew and
shipmaster are assessing the storm damage, and then we will
start packing supplies. We should be gone before Kee reaches
the top of that valley," Roe answered, pointing to a distant
crevice that was slowly growing lighter.

Lyte tried to see beyond it, but right now the Nualan
star filled the lands eastward. "Gone? How bad was the storm
damage?" He felt a bit guilty; apparently he had slept through
a lot of excitement.

"We do not know yet. Bad—right now they are trying to decide if she will sail again." Lyte digested the unspoken meaning while she continued. "If she will sail again, it will not be in time for us to return to our temple obligations, and you would probably miss your ship back. We are going over-land, through the tip of the desert and the wadeyo forest. It will take, oh, a day and a half."

"Walking?"

"I hope not. Or we shall never get back. I am not sure what kind of settlements are in the area—an aircar is unlikely this far from a major center . . . and this close to the Ciedär. If we can borrow hazelles, we will. When you are done, throw together your things." She stood and walked to greet the dawn. Lyte watched her go and bent to his firstmeal.

In the meantime Moran and Braan had followed the shipmaster and were listening to the damage reports. The crew was solemn as the shipmaster's chief engineer was pulled back over the stern onboard. At her signal the rudder was hoisted up and onto the deck.

She pointed to the broken blades. "Cut." Her voice was flat. "Almost completely in half. The stern protected it until the first big swell—cross currents snapped it like a twig."

The shipmaster turned and gazed out over the water. "I wonder if they made it in. . . ."

"Of course," the engineer said dryly. "Their rudder was not cut." She cursed softly under her breath in Nualan and stalked off down the deck.

Braan stepped up to the shipmaster. "Shipmaster Oh'nel, will you and your crew be all right?"

The man turned and met his eyes. "We will be fine. It is you I am concerned about, Seri. We could have gone down in that—no pirate wants to lose his prey. It is not my cargo he wants, it is my passengers. Do you want to take *guaard*? It is owed."

"No," Braan replied quickly. "You will need every hand if you are to be afloat within fourteenday. We do not want to attract attention. I have confidence in my companions and myself. I would like hazelles, though."

"I will send my chief to the core settlement. Perhaps they sighted that stardancer. We shall spread the word; no

skipper would aid any who threatened the crown, not knowingly; they are loyal around these parts." Sobered by that
thought, the small group walked back to the fire.

Lyte was waiting for them. He had changed into the
loose robes of the northern desert dwellers and looked uneasy.

"What is it?" Moran asked.

"I heard the ship was tampered with. . . ."

"Yes, the steering mechanism was cut almost in half."
Lyte turned away, looking quite disturbed.

"Would you care to confide in us, Second Officer?"
Braan asked.

Moran glanced at the Nualan's expressionless face.
"Come on, Lyte, what is it? You've been on edge ever since
we left the military wheel," he said abruptly.

"Nothing. Nothing concrete, at least. I'd like to let it
go for now. I need to think." And plan, he continued silently.
Braan stared at him a moment longer and then walked away
from the fire, a sailor following. Lyte suddenly saw that Braan
was as suspicious of him as he was of the Nualan. The thought
was perversely comforting. Moran flicked a finger at him,
his irritation evident, and then started back to the ship. Feeling
helpless in the face of their condemnation, Lyte sought
Ronuviel.

She was standing by a small pile of bundles, helping a
sailor fill water gourds. Dressing in a flowing white mandraia
caftan, Roe looked like a sand spirit; not quite mortal, ready
to vanish at any time. She handed him an empty gourd.

"We have to carry all your water. The only oasis on our
trip has a pool with high rav content. Too high for you to
drink from, at least at this stage of your acclimation. Another
sevenday and you would be all right." Lyte bent to the well,
submerging the carrier. There was silence. The star rose from
the mountaintops.

"Such a wild, frightening land," Lyte said suddenly. He
did not know why he said it—the prairie that bordered the
desert looked innocent enough. But it was a deceptive tran-
quility, as if something were waiting for them. Plants brought
to life by the monsoons were blooming but had not yet seeded.
He saw many of the fleshy bushes and tall, narrow trees he

had seen near the palace. Faint, moving dots that Lyte suspected were wildlife intrigued him.

He was snapped from his thoughts by Roe's question: "What do you fear?"

He glanced at the sailor, who seemed oblivious. Roe shook her head. *Guaard?* Lyte instantly chose. "I thought it was for Moran's life. Now I'm not so sure." She looked steadily at him, making no move to interrupt. He let the words flow out. "I was practically ordered here, to guard against an attempt on Moran's life. My superiors feared reprisals by xenophobic groups who objected to your relationship. But I cannot believe ... " He gestured helplessly. "Your security is too good for your people not to suspect trouble. How could this attack happen blind? And to Braan as well? Atares have always married off-worlders, and many were warriors. But this appears—"

"Internal."

Lyte sat down on the well and looked at her. "Yes. But even so, it doesn't make sense *that* way, either! You and Braan are only third in line for Ragäree and Atare—to kill you is a wasted gesture. I'm supposed to be preventing a major incident between the Nualan system and Moran's home system, yet they told me not to contact Jaac—not to contact the superior officer of the planet! If they suspected you were on the hit list—our intelligence is better than this! Why didn't they cancel his furlough?" Lyte muttered the last, as he had so many times since he had received his orders.

Roe sat down next to him, slowly stoppering his gourd. "It is the gaps that disturb you," she said finally. "What do you read in them, warrior?

"It's what I feel in them," he answered, watching as a yellow-robed figure he recognized as Moran left the ship. "It's felt wrong from the beginning. Now I see little pieces coming together. I smell treachery. I don't think there ever was an assassin. It would have been a professional, a suicider who would not have bothered with a whole ship. Then why send us both, and why tell me to get Moran off Nuala fourday early?"

Roe raised her head at this, her gaze sharp. "No explanation? And you accepted that?"

"I am a warrior. I exist to receive and follow orders. And I don't always do that, so my status is at best shaky. I could be imprisoned for telling you all this."

Roe reached over and gripped his arm. "The words stop here. But what do you suspect, if no assassin?"

"Something I can't bear to believe." He was staring up now, away from the star of morning to where the battleship *Io* should be. "We are pawns. Screens to hide something. To keep someone from looking deeper..." He turned and faced her again. "All my life I have dismissed this planet as the home of a bunch of paranoid mutants. Tell me, paranoid mutant, if your paranoia is correct, can you defend yourself if the Axis turns on you? Or abandons you to the Fewhas?"

She did not answer. Lyte's last words had been delivered in a whisper. When Roe finally spoke, her words were no less soft. "We can defend. We cannot win. The planet will win, in the end. Only Nualan ships can pass through the barrier. The crews may be off-world, but the shipmasters, the captains are Nualan, and they would turn pirate or destroy their crafts before they would let them be confiscated. It would be a hollow victory for any conqueror, Lyte ... only we make rav pills. Only we can cure rav radiation. It is not an oversight that the information never left this planet. For any other creatures Nuala is slow poison of the deadliest kind. Very slow..."

Lyte did not answer, a chill passing through him. He stared out over the desert again, and the ghostly tendrils of a mirage came to his eyes. For a moment he saw a Durite death's-head, symbol of the dreaded death cult of Dur, the skull rotting in the early rays of Kee. A smile spread over the teeth. Lyte shook off the spell with difficulty and went to get his small tackle bag.

CHAPTER SIX

Lyte reached up and wiped the sweat from his forehead. If winter was coming, this place did not know it. "I can see why Nualans live on the coast," he said aloud. "You could roast here during the summer."

"Many Nualans live in the desert," Ronuviel answered.

Lyte looked over his shoulder. "Many?"

"The Ciedärlien, the sand dwellers. Hundreds of tribes are scattered throughout the Ciedär. It is a hard life, but they prosper. Their farming secrets make the desert fruitful."

Nodding absently, Lyte riveted his eyes to the horns of the beast he straddled. Had to keep his seat . . . A hazelle had a crazy, staggering gait that was torturous to the amateur and blissful to the expert. Roe and Braan were clearly experts; he and Moran reeked of inexperience. The beast lurched, and a soft exclamation of pain slipped past his lips. Moran glanced over his shoulder at him.

"We shall rest the hazelles at the top," Roe called forward. Lyte knew she knew and was trying to help them save face. He silently blessed her for that thoughtfulness.

The top of the gorge rose up before them—Moran's hazelle slipped, scrambling, and the man threw his arms around its neck. Lyte had a flash of impending disaster and was suddenly flying sideways through the air. He landed in a barrelbush, the thick, oozing leaves cushioning his fall, and lay without moving. Anything was better than that poor excuse for transportation. . . .

Roe leapt off her hazelle as she topped the rise. "Lyte! Are you all right? Do not move!" Her practiced hands quickly went over him, checking for broken bones. She looked relieved. "A few bruises—you will live." Lyte groaned.

"I suggest we squeeze some bara and treat the blisters before they are infected," Braan said, dismounting and dropping his reins. The beast moved to feed. Moran stiffly climbed down and let his hazelle follow suit.

While the others gathered broken pieces of the barrelbush and squeezed the juice into a cup, Lyte tried to sort through his daze. Starstroke? The hazelle floated above him, and the man studied it intently. The creature was a cross between a horse and a native Nualan animal, the tazelle. It still retained a horse's sleek coat, round hooves, and broad back and neck, but the head was more delicate, like a tazelle's, and the two spiraling horns that grew up and out from the head looked like nothing Lyte had ever seen before. They were all the same color, dark brown, with a white blaze on their faces and long white tails; this one had white to its knees. Reaching out to touch the beast's coat, he discovered that the skin underneath was black. The hazelle lowered its head and regarded him with soft eyes. It was not as intelligent as a horse could be but was more stoic, less skittish, and less likely to run in fear of its own shadow.

Roe's hand intruded into his vision, handing him the pure numbing agent. Lyte slowly sat up, nodding his thanks, and as the woman discreetly drew away, he removed his joqurs and laved the blisters with sap. Immediately his legs began to cool. Lyte glanced up, looking for Moran; he was waiting for the bara salve. Roe was standing next to Braan, who was staring toward the now distant sea.

"Maybe we should stop for secondmeal?" Roe called. "That will give you time for the salve to take effect."

"Fine. Let's make it a cold meal, please," Moran answered. She nodded and left Braan's side, reaching for her hazelle's pack. Braan continued to gaze back over the desert toward the sea, adjusting his viewing scope, watching the numerical distance finder.

"We are losing him," he muttered.

"How far back to the oasis?" Lyte called, handing the cup of sap to Moran.

"Two, three hours," Roe replied. She inspected the sky. Huge, dark clouds had crept inland and were slowly overtaking them. "Do you think we can make the grotto before the monsoon?" she asked Braan. Her brother nodded.

Dressed once again, Lyte moved carefully to Ronuviel's side. The smell of the cheese she was unpacking made his mouth water. He reached to unfasten the pocket containing his pills . . . and found it empty.

Lyte looked up to find Roe watching him, a smile teasing her lips. "Welcome to Nuala. You have finished the series; you are one of us."

Had he—? Of course. Ronuviel was a physician; she had kept a close eye on him. Still, it felt strange to take the sliver of native cheese from her hand, to bite into its smooth surface. He gently sat upon the ground and reached for a water gourd.

Braan folded up his viewing scope and approached them. "We must go faster. Eat and drink your fill; we shall not stop until starset." He arranged his robes and sat down on a rock. "We are being followed." Lyte winced, suddenly remorseful. Perhaps Braan should not have been so confident about commando abilities. The *guaard* had wanted to come . . .

Roe passed around a loaf of bread. "Is he gaining?" she asked quietly.

"No—falling back. If we are lucky, we can lose him in the forest. He is off-world; maybe he has a bad map." Braan ripped off the end of the loaf.

"How can you tell he's off-world?" Lyte said, his spirits improving as his pain decreased.

"To find a Nualan assassin you would have to go into the Ciedär, the desert, to the Ciedärlien tribesmen or even the mutants. They are excellent at killing, without hesitation or mercy. All Nualans worth their salt are legendary trackers;

if we do not intend to be seen while on the trail, we are not. That is why we make good spies."

"If a Nualan tribal was following us," Roe finished for him, "we would not see him until he was on top of us. This assassin is off-world." They ate in silence for a time, Lyte and Moran studying the desert. Its sands were pure white, dazzling and blinding, the scrub and trees blue-green against it. They could still see the ocean twinkling fitfully in the distance. Lyte slowly stood and gazed ahead. The giant evergreens could be seen several hours southeast, through shimmering waves of heat. The horizon was almost twice as far away as he expected it to be, lost in mist. Lyte shook his head at the strangeness and then groaned inwardly at the sight of the Atares picking up litter and stowing it away. Roe had already mentioned the fragility of the Ciedär ecosystem. He moved for his hazelle.

Braan was now standing by his beast, staring back toward the sea . . . toward the path of their unwelcome companion. The other three mounted and waited for him.

"Those who come to an alien planet have two choices," he suddenly said conversationally. "Adapt or die. I suspect this interloper will be little trouble." Braan quickly pulled himself up on the hazelle and gestured for Ronuviel to lead off. Moran and Lyte repressed shudders and followed. The truth of Nuala was ever below the surface—death to the unwary.

———————

They wandered on for several hours, the sky darkening above them. Lyte glanced over at Ronuviel and envied the easy way she kept her seat. She looked relaxed and happy, not at all concerned by the thought of someone following them. She never seemed to show her fears, he thought, no matter how open she appeared. Curiosity overcame his usual restraint; now seemed like a good time to get some answers to disturbing questions.

"Ronuviel?"

She raised her head and masked her surprise. He had never initiated conversation before. "Yes?"

"There's something I've always wondered about. I

understand if you don't want to answer. You live and grow on Nuala until you're of an age of majority, seeing few off-worlders except in court. It seems to me that—well, you might gather up good friends among your people, and even a lover. What do Atares do who fall in love with Nualans?"

She did not answer. Then her gaze skimmed over her shoulder—Braan was unaware of the conversation. Roe moved her hazelle closer to Lyte's. "Forget." She looked at him. "I was fortunate; I never had the problem. For a woman it is hard. If your lover is an 80, there are no difficulties, as long as you are discreet. If he is a 20, well..."

"Are there any past Atares who gained the throne who had Nualan fathers?"

"All the first thousand terrayear, of course. Otherwise, maybe two, or three. Many other brothers and sisters, I think, but most Ragärees are extremely careful until their heirs are born. If that heir dies, the second son or daughter may have a different parent."

"So the men can keep another woman because their children have no succession, but the women have to think of the throne. Perhaps... birth control?" Seeing her face, he rushed on, "I'm too frank, forgive me."

"It is not that. We do not have the concept of illegitimacy, Lyte. A woman who is a 20 may care enough for several men to spend time with them. Even I could have. My dead older uncle had a different father than my mother and her twin, Baskh. He was conceived before grandmother even met grandfather. The people trust their Ragäree. They may never know the father, the ragarr, but they trust that he is suitable to father their ruler. They trust her judgment. Why I look appalled is this; our fertility is too fragile to risk birth control. So when we choose a man, or a woman, we make a choice. If a child is conceived, we rejoice in it, and accept the commitment."

"Commitment?"

"Not *bonding*. That is even deeper, concerning a soul trust. Children are a lesser bond. For example," she continued, not missing a beat, "you are interested in Shinar. She in you. If you finally do sleep with her, Lyte, be aware that she is prepared for the possibility of a child and will commit herself to it if it becomes a reality. *And she expects the same of you.* Not money, not marriage, not even bonding"—Lyte was again aware, half consciously, of the Nualan differentiation between marriage and bonding—"but an emotional commitment to the healthy raising of that child. We take our pleasure gladly, aware of the consequences."

"Great. I'm being enticed by a pair of blue eyes into playing stud."

"Oh, no!"

"She only wants my genes, that's what you're saying." Lyte felt more heated over the idea than he'd like to admit.

"Perhaps a few might do that, out of desperation, but not Shinar. She is too willful and yet giving. She really would have to care for you. Not that she would be selfless . . . no, I can think of one healthy motive."

"What?" He was defensive and cursed it.

"To prove that she can bear a healthy child within the normal ratings. The health of your genes should be . . . comparable to an Atare's. If she could have with you a normal, healthy child, then she could do the same with—"

"Your brother." Lyte stared at her, ignoring the pain beginning again in his legs. "Kalith."

She looked over at him, cool admiration in her glance. "You noticed; I am surprised. They are very careful."

"I just remembered Kal being very attentive at the feast."

"They worry me . . . yet they may hail a new era."

"How?" It was Moran. Lyte wondered how long he had been listening.

"Because most Atares push their Nualan loves out of their minds and follow their duty. They marry in the temple and are happy with their mates and do not wonder what if? But Kal is not indulging in adolescent fantasy. He is a man in love with a woman. Atares have bonded, have married Nualans, but they have given up their place in the throne line. Kal wants Shinar and his inheritance. He will not renounce either. She loves him. Subconsciously she may think a healthy child will force the synod and temple to seriously consider their request."

"Why can't he just marry her, too, and not count their children as royal Atares or whatever?" Lyte asked.

"Kal wants it all." Braan's voice was unnervingly soft, startling the warriors. "He is braver than any of us were at his age. Under his cool facade he makes his own rules. He wants Shinar as bond, marriage mate, and serae, mother of his royal children. He will fight to blood for it."

"And he is frustrated." She smiled at this. "They abstain because he has it in his head that he cannot mock her with less than all that, and because he feels he cannot insult an off-world wife with less than bonding."

"Don't all Atares bond their mates?" Lyte asked, looking back at Moran.

Braan appeared puzzled. "No," he answered. Now Moran looked strange. "Roe is the first in generations."

She turned in her cloth saddle. "Not even—"

"I know Tal and Persephone did not, and Deveah's woman feared us and refused. I never asked Enid. I guess I always thought my soul belonged to you." There was simple dignity in Braan's words, and Lyte was moved, though he did not know why.

"Is Arrez bonded to all his wives?" Moran asked carefully.

"I do not know. It is possible," Braan replied.

"Then love is not the only criteria," Lyte continued.

"The love you speak of has nothing to do with it," Moran said. Lyte looked over at him and considered abandoning the conversation. It was obviously getting into religion, and he had enough difficulty accepting the ancient terran god. He had no interest in discussing foreign theology.

He ventured one more question. "Do you understand what you have gotten yourself into?"

"Not completely," Moran answered easily. "But enough."

"Moran, for all his short acquaintance with us, is deeply steeped in our lore. He is becoming more Nualan than many Nualans." Conversation ceased for a time, Braan's final comment moving thought into areas Lyte did not care to follow. He began to watch the clouds and changing scenery and saw that Moran was doing the same.

The sparse vegetation of the outer desert was giving way to grass, long, flexible, waving tubes that would have snapped with slower or heavier passage. The quick footfalls of the hazelles carried them swiftly toward the ever larger trees. Lyte suddenly noticed that the trees already looked huge, and they were an hour or more away.

"How tall are those trees?" he called to Roe.

"They average over a hundred meters," she replied.

"How can they survive that tall?"

"There are trees on Terra that tall," Moran threw in. "Remember?"

"These are taller. They are wadeyo, 'Long arm.' Cone-bearing evergreens, several of them with diameters wide enough to set the capitol building on their stump with room to spare. Black as night, that is why it looks so dark there, although the forest is two hours farther from the starset than we are. The branches are weird, almost ropy, and hang in graceful sweeps; they have branches hanging off them perpendicularly. But do not try to climb one—the branches start fifty meters up."

"What else grows there?"

"Nothing," Braan said, pulling up closer to them.

Lyte looked over his shoulder at the Nualan, grabbing his hazelle's neck for support. "Nothing?"

"They are invincible monarchs," the man went on. "Only a nuclear holocaust could destroy them, and a direct hit at that. No disease; no pests or parasitic vines; fire cannot harm their tough coats; and their dead needles change the soil so that only their own offspring can grow. If a seed lands in a lit spot. I think you will be impressed."

"How old are they?" Lyte persisted.

Roe smiled. "We shall show you."

WADEYO FOREST   VESPERS

Kee was low in the sky when they reached the edge of the wadeyo forest. Moran and Lyte were thankful for the rest stop and a chance to walk around the area. "Can we lead them and walk a little while?" Lyte asked, staring into the vast forest.

"Tomorrow, early; now we must reach the grotto," Braan told him. "If we are still being followed, I would rather face an enemy there. We shall be protected from the rain; he will be wet." The Nualan had been reviewing their tracks again. He handed the glass to Roe, whose eyes were keener.

"Nothing," she announced. "Do you think we lost him?"

"I do not know what to think," Braan murmured. "If he has followed us this long, he is a professional. I just hope he is not a Durite." The others reacted visibly to this. A humanoid race, the Durites were the most efficient assassins in the known universe. Given an assignment, a Durite would follow its prey until death—the victim's or its own.

"Durites resent briefing," Lyte ventured. "Maybe this one didn't want to know about the dangers here and poisoned himself."

"We can hope. Let us go." Roe recaptured her hazelle and hopped on it. She looked up at the towering giants before them, the diameter of the first one larger than her bedroom.

"Are they all this big?" Moran said.

Roe leaned over as she rode up to it and touched its smooth bark, still warm from the fading star. "This is but a child standing at the feet of its mother. Wait until you see the grandparents." She led off into the forest, followed by Moran, then Lyte and Braan. Almost instantly the darkness swallowed them.

As his eyes adjusted to the dim light Lyte found he could see better than he had expected. A feeling first of awe, and then dread, slowly crept over him. It was fine as long as he watched the dark, soft ground or listened to the sounds of the hazelle's hooves muffled by the deep pile of needles. But as soon as he let his peripheral vision take over, the columns began to affect him.

Like ancient columns. Smooth as glass, hard as diamond, glittering in the last fleeting rays that shot through the trees and warmed their backs. He tilted his head back, trying to see branches. All was fading into an early night. As they rode deeper into the forest the trees were larger, some taking several minutes to ride past. The feeling was not claustrophobic—far from it. They could easily ride four abreast on this path. But the overwhelming size of the trees bore down on Lyte. He felt as tiny and insignificant as a common microbe.

They rode on for over an hour, the twilight deepening around them even as the star began to set on their last resting place. Finally Roe slowed and pointed to a massive tree, visible down a side path.

"Watch that one." She broke into a fast trot. It was not until almost ten minutes later that Lyte understood that the elusive tree she had pointed out was still beside them, a solid wall behind its now fragile-looking relatives. They reached a tiny glade, wide enough for them all to dismount at Roe's bidding. At her side, about ten meters from the mammoth wadeyo, was a plaque set in stone. It was obviously cared for by someone; no dirt filmed the plaque, no moss crumbled the stone. Lyte and Moran moved closer and could see that it was written in a mode of ancient Third English, but they could not read the script.

"Do you read Third English?" Moran said in surprise.

"No. But every Nualan child knows these words from the day they are old enough to understand them." Ronuviel lovingly read the entire message aloud, and Lyte's thoughts paused at one passage: "This planet, 22XL37-C, or Nuala, shall be known as a sanctuary planet; and all of the universe's falsely accused, all who flee unjust laws and sentences, are welcome here. We ask only that you bring no harm to anything of Nuala, human or otherwise, and that you find your place in our collective existence."

From the very beginning . . . There was silence. The words might have been written by humans ignorant of the law, the attempt to sound grand merely stilted and vague. But Lyte could feel the haste, the urgency of the words; the need to establish, indelibly, the ground rules for the new venture those humans had begun. He knew this was written scarcely days after the crash. Lyte's eyes traveled down the list of men and women who led the first colonists. "This was composed before they realized what the radiation was doing to them?" he asked. Roe nodded as she touched the engraved signatures. "Funny that they used planet dating instead of stardates."

"Stardates are mainly used on ships. No doubt the scientists were eager to usurp the authority of the three captains," Moran said. His gaze stopped at Habbukk, Captain of the *Atare*. "They included the officers?"

"Anyone who was healthy was included," Braan answered, his gaze taking in the trees. "The captain of the *Seedar* was dead—Habbukk was a strong figure, although he did not take charge until almost a year later when the expedition had dissolved into chaos."

"It is remembered that they argued, you know," Roe suddenly said, as if coming back from a dream. "Whether it should be stardate or planet-date. The pillars stood over there." She gestured behind their hazelles. "The synod decided four thousand terrayear ago that the area was too special to be a spaceport, so it was set up in the new city of Amura."

"A spaceport?" Lyte began to see the significance of bringing them here. "You mean the ships crashed here? In this forest?"

"It was a huge field then, with only a few hundred trees moving slowly down the mountains. The plaque was once on that tree." She pointed to the huge wadeyo. "It grew so large, the plaque popped off, so we put it on stone."

"The night comes; we cannot linger," Braan told them. "Enough history lessons. Their naive beginning led to a great heritage. Let us not fail them by washing away in the monsoon." Jumping up on his hazelle, he indicated that they should follow him quickly. Slowly remounting, the three hurried off.

It was not far to the grotto. Lyte knew that Moran had been privately concerned; he did not like caves and had probably pictured a dark, tiny crevice with various unknown creatures crawling out of it. This cave was just the opposite. Its entrance soared up several meters and was nearly as wide, although blocked in several places by tumbled boulders. The hazelles went immediately to one side of the grotto, staking out their area; they had been there before. Roe and Braan pulled off the cloth bags they had sat on and proceeded to demonstrate how to wipe down a hazelle with hill grass. Then, taking the reins of two of the beasts, Braan led them and the men off to the stream. When they returned, Roe had a bright fire burning in an ancient fire pit.

"How long has this grotto been a rest stop?" Lyte asked, pulling up a piece of tree stump and carefully sitting down. He looked for the pot of barrelbush juice.

"Centuries," Roe replied, peeling the bark off a wadeyo branch and throwing it on the flames. "Start peeling; it will not burn with bark on it. We do not need much because it burns a long time."

"All peoples sojourn here in peace," Braan added. "Even Ciedärlien tribes that are normally enemies will allow each other to rest under this arch unmolested." As Moran set down the last of their water bags Braan began to fix dinner. It was simple and eaten in silence, the warriors more comfortable with another application of barrelbush juice. The combination of the huge trees and the massive stars peeking through their branches was a sobering sight. After she finished eating, Roe moved over next to Lyte and sat down.

"Did you understand our conversation this afternoon?" she ventured.

"I think so."

"Explain it to me, as you would to an off-worlder."

Lyte paused, thoroughly chewing the hard traveler's bread. "Bonding, although I do not fully understand the religious significance, is much like an off-worlder's marriage is *supposed* to be—a sharing of souls and lives, of turning only to one another for all the needs of mortal existence. Nualans, and the royal family in particular, are often in a strange and cruel paradox—"

"Until you have lived as we do, do not judge, only seek to understand," Roe interrupted. "Go on."

"As I was saying, they are often denied this important part of living. Marriage is a necessary thing for the survival of the species," he went on quickly, "not that you don't care for, even love, your mate. It's just a different love, a—"

"A separation of the three great loves—agape, philios, eros. All present but separate. The most any off-worlder seeks or expects," Roe clarified.

Startled to hear the ancient Greek words, although he knew they were the names of Nuala's moons, Lyte continued speaking. "It's as if you don't expect outsiders to understand, and so you don't attempt to explain it. Do outsiders, off-worlders, ever understand?"

"Sometimes—after years of living among us and watching how we live. To tell someone fresh off a ship that there is always enough love and that loving more than one person does not diminish the love for either . . . it is not believed. Oh, many of your people *pretend* they believe and go from mate to mate; but they do not believe. They are not raised with literally hundreds of doting friends and relatives, all telling and showing them how loved they are, even if they are not always liked. You are not raised to believe that if you lose one love, Mendulay will give you something else to love; and that if you love Mendulay first, all else follows." She turned to him. "You keep your loves shallow, wrap yourself in a cocoon, and let no one touch your core. You share good times but shrink from hard ones. No, you do not understand love."

"And Nualans are never neurotic or insecure?"

"Of course they are. We are human and affected by other humans. It is when we absorb the values of your society that we are in trouble—"

"Which is why you have no concept of illegitimacy," Lyte broke in, beginning to recognize something. "If you feel strongly enough about someone to share a separate love with them, then you—"

"Accept the consequences. Of eros, it may be a child, or temporary feelings of rejection if one lover turns elsewhere. In philios, it may be sacrifice. I know Braan's skin crawls every time he puts on a protectorate suit. But Gid is his friend, and Gid's parents live in Tolis. Friendship, true friendship, comes high."

"Agape? Is that not the hardest to reach? I mean, as a separate thing, not even mentioning bonding?" Moran asked. "To be required to do something for the good of the majority no matter what the cost to yourself?"

"Something like that," Braan answered softly. "And to bond is to say, 'I believe we can work daily toward it all.' It is the highest compliment we can give to an off-worlder, to bond from the beginning. Most may marry more than one; establish home and family. But they usually bond once. I personally think Arrez is only bonded to Elana, but only Arrez and Holy Mendulay know for sure—mates do not discuss that among themselves. It defeats the attempts to reach such a state. Some reach that state without ever saying the words of bonding, or—"

Braan never finished his sentence. The hazelles suddenly screamed, that weird half neigh, half whistle of fear they give when badly frightened. Dropping his cup, Moran leapt to his feet, oblivious to the pain in his legs. He saw as if in a dream a robed figure sprint crazily through the animals, staggering like a drunken man. Braan sat up and turned around, tensing in preparation for the assault.

"Moran, look out!" Lyte yelled the words before he realized it. Even as he stood and leapt for his friend, he was dimly aware that the unknown assailant was diving straight at Braan.

With a skill long unused, Braan twisted away from the fire and rolled out of the attacker's reach. Without hesitation Moran jumped the fire and was on top of the unknown, gripping the wrist holding the knife and attempting to subdue him with a commando hold. But the assassin was apparently wise to commando training and tore himself away. Moran still hung on to his wrist, trying to keep the knife from himself. Had he been alone, things might have been fatal for him, even though it was plain that their attacker was exhausted and using his last strength. As Lyte snatched the other flailing arm Braan reached in behind the man and grabbed his head and neck in a two-handed grip. Gagging, paralyzed, the robed figure went limp.

"Disarm him." Braan's voice carried such a note of command, Lyte was searching for other weapons before he thought of it himself. Roe reached over and carefully peeled away a needle hidden in one hand, and the men quickly relieved the intruder of several hidden knives, all of a variety used by Nualans to hunt wild tazelles. The young woman turned the man's left palm to the light. The tiny tattoo of the Durite death's-head could be seen at the base of his second finger. Braan forced the man to lie down; he did not argue.

Roe loosened the Durite's collar as they looked him over. His condition was pitiful. Roe recognized it as a combination of rav poisoning and external Dielaan radiation, already well advanced. Where he had been merely touched in the struggle, massive bruises were appearing, and he had been bleeding from the nose, eyes, mouth, and ears for some time.

"Release his wrists, you cause him terrible pain," Roe directed, reaching toward him to begin the healing energy, something few off-worlders had ever witnessed. The warriors looked unbelievingly at her and then to Braan. Ignoring them, shaking his head at Roe, Braan spoke directly to the assassin.

"We know what you are and that you are on a trail of blood. Be aware that I am holding you in an elkita grip. If you move suddenly, I will break your neck. Do you understand?" The Durite blinked twice, trying to clear his throat of blood. Braan went on, his voice controlled, merciless. "I want to know whom you are pursuing and why. Who hired you? How did you get on this planet?"

"The Durite dyes used in their tattoos show up on our monitors," Roe murmured to the two off-worlders. "Someone was bribed, a machine was tampered with, or he was landed away from the spaceport." The Durite, meanwhile, made no reply.

"You followed us into Tolis, did you not?" Braan said conversationally. "Unaware that the city was hot, too far behind our arrival to see our suits. You mingled with the robes of Tolis, ignorant of your peril. And now you will pay for your traditional refusal to be briefed about a planet. Know, Durite, that your boasts to blend in with any people have come true—you are now dying because you became one of us too quickly."

"I know my death," the Durite replied, a rattling noise in his voice. "Your threats cannot frighten me. Save them."

"I do not threaten. My people do not use torture to reach their ends. If you wish to die this way, your secret dies with you. But I warn you; the death from rav is slow and painful. Pain such as you have never dreamed. My sister is a healer and a doctor. She can ease your pain, but you are too far gone to live. We do not have the means with us, and we are too far from help."

"You cannot fool me, mutant. I know your spineless attitudes. You will not kill me, nor leave me to pain."

"You have been misinformed." Moran glanced up at the lifeless note in his voice. "Lift him." The warriors added their strength and carried the Durite over to the other end of the grotto entrance. "You may lie here and consider whether the pain is worth your silence." Without a backward glance Braan moved back to the fire.

The monsoon came late. The Durite broke later. Moran and Lyte exchanged subtle expressions, fascinated by the situation. Roe would not comment, saying only, "I have not the stomach for the darker side of kingship." She sat to one side, an air hypo in her hand, a faint luminescence about her, waiting for her brother to signal her to end the assassin's agony.

Braan was relentless in his questions, repeating them over and over until Lyte was tempted to throttle someone, anyone, for an answer. The Durite stammered and stuttered, choking on his own swollen, bloody throat, and slowly, like the tightening of a hand crank, the information came.

The first shock, at least for the warriors, was who he was stalking—Braan, not Moran. Lyte felt obligated to explain everything that had gone before, and so he and Moran retired to the fire to talk. Moran said nothing; he did not react even when Lyte said Roe had known all this since dawn. When Lyte had finished, the first officer stirred and stretched, as if waking from deep sleep.

"I wish you could have believed," Moran said. "I'm glad you found Roe to be a good confidante." He jerked suddenly as Braan sat down next to him. A glance showed Ronuviel giving the Durite a painkiller, her warm hands speeding the narcotic to its destination.

"Well?"

"I do not know whether to be enraged or flattered," Braan said dryly. "He was smuggled onto Nuala by an outside controller whose name he does not know. His contact was Corymb, who paid him an ounce of trine gold, in advance"—Braan held up a small marker on a leather thong—"to murder me far from home. It was preferable if it looked like an accident, but the main thing was to keep me from returning to Amura. He was to receive another ounce upon proof of my death."

"How?"

"He was going to take back one of my eyes," Braan

replied easily. "Since Roe was not marked for death, it could belong to no one except me. He does not know why I am to be killed—only that I am." Braan held up the marker again, watching the reflection, the shadows thrown. Moran looked over at the Durite, who was no longer writhing in pain.

"Is there anything we can do for him?"

"No. Only the complex could help, and the rav is so advanced, he would be a physical and mental cripple if he survived. He would kill himself as soon as he had a chance." Braan turned to Roe. "Is he unconscious?"

"He feels nothing."

Braan moved over to the Durite's head, probing gently to see if the 'man' was aware of them. Carefully getting a firm grip on the Durite's throat, Braan snapped his spine like brittle grass. The only reaction was the cessation of the sound of labored breathing. There was silence.

"I thought your people never killed, that it was a sin or something," Lyte said, his voice characteristically impassive.

Braan looked up, surprised. "We abhor violence. And it is a sin. But if it is necessary, we kill—quickly, efficiently. His life was my responsibility. Now, on the Last Path, I shall have to answer for its premature end. I hope the explanation satisfies the Holy One." Braan pulled the Durite's robe over his face and moved to stand.

The sound of rolling gravel brought all four of them to their feet. Lyte spun around, a knife in his hand. Standing in the dying light of the fire was a boy of about fifteen, fear and amazement plain on his face.

Braan moved toward him, exuding confidence. "What do you seek?"

"You, Seri," the boy finally answered. "Word has come from Amura. I have ridden this whole day from Vel depot, since a message came from the sailors telling of the wreck. It is your lady—she is dying." The boy looked over at the Durite, took in the scene of the struggle. "I shall take care of the burial and the rites. You must leave now, for she ebbed as I reached the mountain. If you do not race, you will be too late."

CHAPTER SEVEN

They were too late.

And as the exhausted group climbed the palace stairs Elana stood waiting for them at the open doors of the Great Hall. Ronuviel and Braan led the way, Lyte and Moran hobbling up behind them as best they could. Enid had died nearly an hour before, and except for informing the Atare, they had attempted to keep it a secret until Braan arrived. This had proved impossible, so the bells had been rung and preparations made for the cremation, which by temple law had to occur before the next dawn. Word spread like a whirling santana, and a strange, unnatural silence feel over the city. Those who looked for omens murmured uneasily— deaths at High Festival had always been few, and tradition said it foretold a bad winter. The faithful flocked to the temple early, to light candles for Enid's journey to the next life.

Braan stood impassively while Elana related the story. It had been peaceful—she had simply stopped breathing. With a stiff nod Braan led the group into the hall. The palace was full of attendants going about the business of preparing a quiet state funeral. Braan was aware of Elana leaving to be with the children. He felt wobbly, as if he might fall, and

was glad he had somehow found the stone bench near the
hall doors. Moran and Lyte had disappeared, and Ronuviel
sat with him, millimeters away, her fingertips touching his
wrist. The room was so very cold...

"Seri? Braan?" He glanced up at his name. A young
servant stood before him, her face red from weeping. "Do
you wish to—view her—your wife's body?"

Braan studied her a moment. "My wife died five years
ago," he answered softly, clearly. "And the period of mourning has gone on too long." He realized he was standing and
then walking through the bronze doors into the Hall of Mirrors. Without a backward glance he walked down the hall
and out into the courtyard and beyond. He was scarcely aware
of Kee setting, of the silence. Somehow he had expected
grief, and the absence of it frightened him, horrified him.
Had he grown so callous that he felt nothing at the death of
his wife?

He found himself at the side entrance of the Mendularion. Every side was nothing but stairs, and Braan started up
them.

———

The huge chamber was ablaze with light. Every altar,
shelf, and crevice was filled with a candle, forcing the shadows into retreat. It was between services, the huge sixthday
ceremony postponed for the wake before it. The altar was
already set up, one tall, unlit candle at its head, the eternal
flame burning in a standing socket at its side. Braan walked
to the dark wax column, not sure if anyone was in the temple
and not really caring. Then he reached for a slender wooden
taper. Moving to the huge fire basin now burning below the
Nualan cross, he lit the taper.

The Nualan light ceremony was lost in their past, its
beginnings shrouded by folklore and legend. But all knew its
purpose—to light the paths of the dead on their last journey.
Whether they went to paradise or tortured silence, all took
the Last Path, all received a light ceremony. Braan reached
over and lit the large beeswax candle and then stepped back
to watch its glow illuminate the apse.

I have faced them five years and more, Braan thought.

This is the last. I cannot face that ceremony. For me, you have been on the Path too long. Aloud he whispered, "You are free . . . we are free." He dumped the taper into the purifying fire basin and walked out the same door he had entered.

He stood a moment in the dying light of starset. Absently touching a tear on his cheek, he rushed down the stairs and onto the temple grounds.

He finally stopped running at the edge of the lake. The temple was hidden, and the tall trees of the meditation gardens blocked out all awareness of the city. Only the mountains were still visible, their heights lost in mist. There was a presence . . . he found Zair next to him. The dog must have tracked him from the palace. He sat down at the edge of the clear, sand-bottomed reservoir, his thoughts drifting, his hand reaching out to touch the fleshy leaves of the weeping, succulent tree.

I cannot weep . . . not really. It is release, my lady— from your prison, from my pain . . . No longer will your spectral image float before Dylan and Asiai. May they remember you as our holograms record your loveliness. . . . Her face rose up before him, delicate, coolly remote, fair beyond health. It brought on a passing tenderness, of the life they had shared and of the passion he had carefully steered away from her memory. His eyes traveled to the first star of evening . . .

Braan leaned back against the tree, the dog's head in his arms, trying to clear his mind, to think of his sculpture, of anything except the anger and bitterness and despair that threatened to burst from him. He heard a tiny splash, a ripple, and glanced up. Perhaps fifteen meters away from him he saw a woman. He was blank, and then recognized her as the voyager who had arrived on the *Gerrymander*. Since she was staying at the temple, of course she could, and would, come here to swim.

Braan studied her slow movements and suspected that she had been ill. That was not uncommon among first-time visitors. She must have tasted the water. Or—she was from the tratores. Perhaps an old addiction . . . Her face was unlined, relaxed, as if she had cast away the problems that had driven her to Nuala. At least no deeper shadows were visible on her features. Suddenly Braan's gaze widened, and he realized she had almost finished undressing. He hesitated. To speak now would not only startle but also probably embarrass her, off-worlders being notoriously self-conscious about their bodies. Better for her not to know. The artist in him took over, and he detached himself from his problems, from the scene. He was aware of beauty—scarcely aware of woman. Completely a warm honey bronze, the light from the rising moons flattering. A lamp treatment? No, he remembered that her palms were a mere shade lighter. Mostly natural; and with the flawless teeth and blonde hair, from the Caprican system . . .

Amazing how the light of the evening played tricks on the mind. Her legs seemed so long. She hesitated, poised on the edge, and then dived into the deep end of the small lake. Braan watched the ripples extend across the surface of the water, idly thinking that it was dangerous to swim alone. Glancing at Zair, he saw that the contented beast was already asleep. He stretched out on his back, watching the stars peep out and become brighter, as if they were exploding, diffusing . . .

———

Braan woke with a start, pain shooting through his leg. He gasped and threw up an arm for protection, aware of another's cry of surprise. Zair leapt to his feet, growling menacingly in his throat. Braan rolled over and up and recognized in a flash the reflection of golden hair, shimmering from the water still trapped within it.

"Are you all right?" he asked, grabbing Zair's choker chain.

She stifled a groan and quickly sat up. "Oh, I'm sorry! I didn't see you there. Did I hurt you?"

He realized her distress was genuine. "Nothing that will not mend on its own. You merely startled me out of a sound sleep. So the lake agrees with you?" he went on, his voice quiet.

"Oh, yes! I've never seen so much water before! It was so dry on our world—we had one public pool on the whole planet! We took sponge baths. I never dreamed of so much water just to look at!" She hesitated a second and then spoke again. "Thank you for letting me stay. It's almost impossible to be unhappy—" She cut herself off; so someone had told her about Enid.

"It is all right," Braan answered gently, pained for her embarrassment.

She looked away, steadying herself. Then she turned back to him, her direct gray eyes meeting his. "I am sorry."

Suddenly another person was beside them. It was Ronuviel. "I could not come any sooner. I took the children from Elana and left them with Moran and Lyte. Moran has been through this before with his father...."

"I have been sleeping," Braan said quickly. "Please assure this woman that my shins are sturdy and will not suffer from being soundly kicked. Teloa, my sister Ronuviel."

Roe smiled. "We have met. Ignore him. He will try to make you feel guilty just to tease you." Seeing that Braan had dealt with the situation, if only temporarily, she went on. "I hate to interrupt your meditation, but Baskh Atare needs you. We are summoned."

Braan arched an eyebrow. "Does he know of our findings?"

"No."

Braan stood, drawing both women to their feet. "Will you please excuse us?"

"Of course." And Tay remained standing by the water while the pair dissolved into dusk, Zair a dark shadow at their heels.

PALACE   COMPLINE

Baskh Atare sat carelessly, as he always did, the symbol of his birthright twinkling fitfully in the soft light. He did not touch it; unlike his predecessor, he never toyed with his chain of office. His full attention was on Roe, his deep green eyes boring into her, the square jaw jutting forward, the big vein in his forehead throbbing visibly. "Well?"

It was Braan who answered first. "The *Nova* was followed north, and on its return voyage as well. We were wrecked not by the storm but by sabotage, and our group was pursued across the Ciedär and into wadeyo country. Only the presence of the off-worlders saved both Roe and me. I do not think two could have stopped a crazed Durite, weak and dying though he was." Having gained the man's undivided attention, Braan tonelessly narrated the findings of the trip. Baskh closed his eyes through the recitation, unnaturally quiet as Roe outlined the records and spoke of Tinyan's, Carad's, and Quahna's fears.

"I think I see a part of this," Baskh said softly as the two trailed off. "Deveah's paranoia has crossed from sadness into danger. After the festival we shall have him hospitalized and observed. That puts a large dent in Corymb's plans. It was long before your births, my friends, but Corymb once attempted to unseat our house by popular vote. Now he tries other ways." He straightened in his chair. "Something I have always worried about . . . do you not think that having our yearly air-raid drill during festival is a good idea?" Braan began to smile.

"When people are away from home, unfamiliar with area shelters?" Ronuviel paused. "Yes, I think it is an excellent idea."

"We may have a tenday yet—or no days. I want no alarm, but that precaution I demand. Tomorrow morning, Amura time, planet-wide. Now . . ." He gestured with fingers of dismissal. "I must think and plan. It will be in my private memory bank in case . . . something happens to me. You and your siblings shall all receive it in your homes, tonight or by prime." He turned to Braan, who had stepped near the throne, and gripped his arm. "My sympathies, friend. At the least you are both free. Tonight is the ceremony of family. Let us go and sing praise for what joys we have received." He stood stiffly and indicated that they should follow him.

The bonfire behind the temple flared suddenly as they stepped out into the night. Ronuviel came up and slipped an arm around Braan as they stood motionless, watching the funeral pyre of Enid. They slowly moved toward the Mendularion, where the balance of their family awaited them. Moran met them on the walkway, Asiai and Dylan clinging to him and trying to appear in control, as befitted royal children. The man was a little pale. Roe embraced him, knowing that memories of his father's death haunted him. Then Braan lifted Asiai and, taking Dylan's hand, followed Baskh Atare up the path and into the Mendularion, the great hound Zair waiting patiently outside the door.

AMURA STREETS	FOURHUNDRED THIRTYTWODAY, 4952	TIERCE

Teloa was up early the last day of the festival, though Kee was already well into the sky when she finally left the temple complex. Elana had been harried as she brought the woman firstmeal, but she had promised to meet Tay in the market at the flower stand corner—at four bells? Teloa considered the meeting and decided that she had said four bells—tierce. The doctor had not volunteered any information about her uneasy state of mind. A direct question, however, revealed that all of her children had a childhood sickness, and a houseful of cranky little ones was not what Elana needed on the day of elder ceremonies. She added that Arrez's fourth-wife, Chaka, was worse, but Shinar was with her. That assistance, as well as knowing that her son Kire would represent her family at the evening services, seemed to relieve Elana immensely. Tay's offer to help was politely turned down, and Elana sent her off into the city with a gentle reminder not to eat or drink anything from the bazaar stalls.

Kee was bright in the autumnal morning and looked deceptively warm. Teloa pulled the woolen poncho close and was glad for the protection. Was it only sevenday ago that she had arrived on a sweltering summer day? Now winter was before them. Her idle walk into the center of town put her in the bazaar before she knew it. Color swirled before her eyes. Cloth, clothing, jewelry, leather goods, luxuries, foods, and plants were heaped on every stall. Tay soon forgot what planet she was on in her delight at examining everything. Several dealers tried to interest her in foodstuffs, and one charming gentleman offered her a free glass of newly pressed native grapes. She regretfully turned down the offer, thankful that her illness had passed and desiring no reoccurrence. Elana had warned her to move slowly with Nualan foods. As if perceiving the situation, the man gaily told her to return "in a few days, when no touch of Nuala deters you!" He whirled to face his friends at the press, and Tay chuckled when she realized they were trying to empty last year's wine bottles to make room for the first harvest.

She made her way to the flower corner, grateful that the bazaar was one area that did not close en masse for the festival. There were stone benches near the roads' intersection, and Teloa claimed one for her own. She was again aware of the admiring stares of several men and was surprised by it. The only women she had really seen were Elana and Ronuviel, and both had a unique beauty. She decided to watch other women to see if she was truly unusual or if it was only because of her blonde hair. True blondes, undyed and free of genetic tampering, were very rare.

The feeling of being observed was so intense, she turned around and found a tall, attractive blond behind her. He was dressed in an Axis Forces uniform and held an exotic flower in his hand. "You look much happier than the last time we met."

She stared at him, her eyes cool, trying to place him. The launching bay, of course, but his tone hinted at another place.

He offered the flower to her. "Second Officer Lyte. We met at a private party on Pacra II."

"I am Teloa."

The warrior nodded, flashing an unexpectedly charming grin. "A new name, a new destiny—I'm glad for you. I always thought you deserved a lot more."

Tay bristled inwardly, but the man appeared quite sincere. Her mind flashed back to Pacra II . . . party? It was an experience, the celebration to end all celebrations. She had accompanied the crown prince, a stupid man but a pleasant host. Lyte was . . . "You were one of the crown prince's bodyguards," she said aloud.

Lyte laughed. "Like I said, you deserve much better. I

can't remember his name, either. May I?" He gestured to the bench and, at her noncommittal reply, carefully sat down. "This is native to the planet. A firerose. Pretty, isn't it?" He held it out to her again. "It's all right—this is a no-strings-attached flower."

Tay smiled. "I don't mean to be rude, but I'm still very tired and—"

"You've had enough of men telling you how beautiful you are and meaning something more."

"Something like that."

"Not even a simple, early dinner?"

"Not even dinner," she replied, amused. "I can't really eat the native food yet, anyway."

"What's wrong?" Tay stared at him blankly. "The tension is winding in you like a spring." His bluntness disconcerted her, and she turned away. "It's all right. Seriously, that's not my standard line. I don't mean to offend you, but I'm a trained sensitive, and I can't just turn it off when I'm off duty. I meant what I said. I've been riding hard through the desert for two days, these crazy Nualan timetables have me pacing nights and falling asleep in my soup, and you're the prettiest thing I've seen in a long time—you and this flower. I wanted to see them together."

She wordlessly took the firerose from him. "Thank you," she finally managed.

Lyte slowly stood. "I'll be here for a while, and probably back in thirty- or sixtyday. If you feel like a night on the town, find me. I may even find you. I'll be able to take in the native restaurants when they open tomorrow, and I intend to . . . Have a good festival." He left, moving a bit stiffly, and Tay did not doubt his story about the desert. A confident man, one not threatened by rejection.

"You allow even that only on your own terms," Tay whispered aloud.

"Allow what?" Tay glanced to one side to find Elana sitting down next to her. She was watching Lyte's disappearing form. The off-worlder heard the sound of the great bell in the temple, tolling through the music of the carillon. "So you have met Lyte," Elana went on. "A character, is he not?"

"A charming one."

Elana smiled. "It is second—no, first nature with him! Shall we go see Lars, the head planter?" The exuberant look on Tay's face said all Elana needed to hear. She gestured for the woman to follow her.

———

The fields were a soft russet, floating with the almost indiscernible haze of morning. The reflection from the parallel irrigation ditches was like a row of gemstones. Tay drank it all in, feeling the slower life-style of the planters revolving around her. She was oblivious to the conversation between Elana and Lars. Huge mechanized implements were digging the furrows for the winter grain planting. It was a collective of sorts; why waste planters on things machines could do? Lars had greeted her with enthusiasm. His warmth had not disguised the probing nature of his conversation—it had been in the form of a test. Teloa was not concerned; she had not forgotten the feel of a seedling between her fingers, and it showed in her speech. She would be valuable here. The joy of that thought bit through her. She knew that finally she could work in experimentation, exploration, on the things she had briefly touched upon as an apprentice and despaired of ever doing again.

When Teloa looked to Elana, the doctor was smiling. "I must return to the city. It is lastday, and the Feast of the Elders. Since my family is ill, I am allowed to miss services, but I should be with them!"

"Feast of the Elders?"

"Lastday is the time when the two oldest children of each sex in each family unit must go to a service of purification and thanksgiving. The first son and daughter are always dedicated to Mendulay, and the second son and daughter to the people. Arrez is first son, I second daughter. Only Arrez and Kire shall represent us. Next year! I took the liberty of asking the Atares to bring you back—there, Liel! Will you come here, please?" Elana called. Turning to Teloa, she quickly whispered, "Kalith, Kavan, and Liel are here for the Elder Day Feast, which is the official beginning of the harvest of grapes and berries and the time of blessing the new plantings.

I think you will like them. They are still wild enough to have a good time—even during a solemn festival! And they see Enid's death as a time to rejoice in the freedom of her soul, so do not worry about that." At that moment the young Nualan woman came up to them. "Liel, this is Teloa, a newcomer to our world. The Serae Liel," Elana said informally. Teloa was dismayed and looked it.

The youngest Atare laughed. "Liel is fine. You are a planter, I hear? I am also interested in the plants. We will make an afternoon of it!"

Even as she finished her speech, a strange-high-pitched noise began. It pulsated, like a foghorn, but was swifter and more penetrating.

Alarmed, Lars grabbed Teloa and Liel by an arm and started running down the irrigation ramp, Elana in close pursuit. "Quickly, to the raid shelters! This way!" he shouted over the noise, dragging the half-paralyzed Teloa down a short flight of steps. With Elana's help he pulled her through a set of double doors and down another staircase. At the bottom they all halted to catch their breath, Tay folding to the floor. Although the doors were still open, more workers pouring in, the alert was now muffled, as if from a great distance.

Elana stooped to Tay, reaching as if to reassure her. "It is all right now, we are safe here, as safe as—" She stopped when she realized that the woman was calmly surveying her.

"I thought it was luna bombs. I couldn't bear that again. But I can't hear them. Anything else I can take, but not luna bombs..." Teloa stared off then, her beautiful face blank. "The horror of those things... When the whistling is so high-pitched that it hurts, then our doom is upon us." Elana raised her head and turned; the sound had changed to one constant tone. Then silence.

"That was the all-clear," Liel whispered. "It was a drill. I wondered if we might have it during festival, while everyone was in strange territory. We are safe."

"Are we?" The planters looked at Tay, puzzled. "How do you know when it's the real thing?"

"I suppose..." Lars began, "the alarm will keep sounding... until it is knocked out, or there is no one left to hear it." He extended his hand to pull her to her feet. "We live with it. We do not dwell upon it." Tay stood and started past the planters up the steps.

TEMPLE HEIGHTS   VESPERS

The star was low in the sky when Arrez finally started for the temple. Throwing up his hood, he hurried down the flagstone streets and into Oldtown, where the wealthier Nualans lived. The procession started at the foot of temple hill, and the catwalk was not working. The long way was necessary for appearances; the sight of the high priest charging down the grass knoll was not ceremonial. As he rushed down a hill, he saw at the bottom three figures. Two were in robes, and one wore the usual attire of a wealthy southerner. Arrez glanced up and thought for a split second that one was a priest—his robes were reflecting as Arrez's did. Then, shocked, he stopped in his tracks.

Apparently the trio did not see him. Arrez instinctively moved closer to the building, trying to catch its narrow shadow. He recognized the towner who faced him—Corymb. The other two were wrapped completely in their robes, bands tying a long strip to their heads. Arrez knew that if he was closer, only the eyes would be visible. A white Ciedär robe, and a beige one... only one man or woman of the Ciedär wore white robes. The Dragoche... Baakche, the Dragoche of the Ciedärlien clans. To think that he would enter Amura! With his shadow, undoubtedly the current chief of security—his best assassin. The tall, white-robed figure turned and slowly continued down the hill, the slighter individual following. Corymb returned to his home, and soon the pathway was deserted except for Arrez. The priest stood frozen and then went on down the street. He had seen Corymb's wife earlier, and she had told him that Corymb felt unwell and would not be at services. Arrez could wait. And find Braan after services.

CHAPTER EIGHT

Teloa was not really paying attention to the twins' bantering. They had drunk just enough wine to be lightheaded and were ribbing each other mercilessly, Kalith bringing up Kavan's appreciation of lovely women and his brother retaliating with a list of the new wines—all of which Kal had sampled. The Caprican was more interested in their younger sister, Liel. The girl was remarkably unspoiled for being the youngest of ten children, treating Teloa as a sister. Tay could see that Liel had been protected; there was a naive sweetness about her, an awe of the outside world that stopped just short of being provincial. Walking back to the city, they had been shy of one another, the presence of a *guaard* inhibiting conversation. But Braan's dog, Zair, had proved to be a bridge between them. Both loved animals, and now that he knew the off-worlder, the beast responded to Teloa's affection wholeheartedly.

   Their speech shot from one topic to another. Teloa was convinced that Liel had never conversed with an off-worlder before, other than ambassadors and her in-laws. She was intensely curious about everything, and once the Atares thought

that they had given their *guaard* the slip, Teloa talked freely
to her. Strange scenes and customs laced her speech as she
spoke generally of the Axis Republic and the neutral worlds.
Liel absorbed every word and gesture, clearly fascinated. She
did not pry, however—Teloa wondered if children learned
early not to question off-worlders about their personal past.

Conversation suddenly ceased, as if by mutual agreement. They were content, walking the silent streets of lastday,
ignored by other pedestrians. The festival would end at dawn,
the new year begin. Time enough later for the twins to face
leaving; the *Gerrymander* did not raise until prime.

There was something strange in the brilliant crimson
orange of starset. Tay felt it but could not single it out. Zair
also seemed restless. The air was different, heavier. She heard
frequencies that were not familiar. Teloa stopped walking and
faced the starset. She looked beyond it, above it, waiting for
final, irrevocable proof.

"Tay?" It was Liel, who spoke to the twins and then
hurried back to Teloa.

The off-worlder felt her puzzlement giving way to fear.
Still faint but growing, the pain growing in her head—*Gods,
not again. I cannot, not again!*

"Do you hear it?" Tay's voice was scarcely a whisper.

"Hear what?" Kavan asked as he walked back up the
street.

"They're coming."

"Who is coming?" Kal said, at first sharp with impa-
tience, and then softening as he saw her face. "What do you
sense? Are you an empath?"

"You really don't hear it yet, do you?" She turned to
Liel. "Can't you hear it?"

"There is something..." Liel began uncertainly.

"What, Li? Your hearing has always been good." Kal
suddenly was taut, blazing, cold sober. Just then the air-raid
siren began to wail.

Teloa folded to her knees, the color drained from her
face. "Not again. I can't take it again. So many times...
They came so close, but I got away. Not here, not now—"

"What?" Kavan shook her, dragging her to her feet.

"Lunas. They turned my planet to ash, we had no shields,

no military. They melted the skin from my people. They will
sear the life from this world." She looked up at them, panic
in her face. "They are like living things; they always find
their prey unless destroyed first, they—"

Kavan shook her again, cutting off the growing hysteria
in her voice. "This time it will be different. We have a shield
and can temper the damage. We have to find a shelter; the
radiation cannot touch us there. Come on." Locking an arm
around Tay's waist, Kavan forced her to run. Pain suddenly
filled their heads, the sign of abnormal frequencies.

The impact of the leading bomb half deafened them
and shook the ground beneath their feet, although it landed
on the other side of the river. Zair raised his voice in the
deep-throated bay of his breed. They heard the chain reaction
of explosions as the power lines beneath the street detonated.

Kal glanced back over his shoulder and looked momentarily stricken. "That is the foreign quarter! Shinar is
there—" He started running back.

"Kal, no, you cannot get through, it is—" Kavan's voice
was lost in the groaning sound of the fires, the soft winds of
Amura spiraling to incredible fury.

"What is he—" Liel started to yell.

"He will be back, the fires will stop him. I just hope he
can get back. Come on, I think there is a shelter in the next
block." Kavan indicated that she should help him with Teloa,
and the three joined other Nualans staggering down the street,
Zair leading the way.

There was a shelter, already crowded with children and
several men and women of varying ages. They entered and
rushed down the narrow, winding corridor, which was designed to guard against flying debris.

Still shaking, Tay pulled away, moving to stand alone.
"I'm sorry. I—you don't know, you can't know..." she
whispered, leaning against the wall, her eyes studying the
dim passage beyond where supplies were stored.

"We will know soon enough, will we not?" Kavan replied. At the sound of his name Kavan stepped back to the
mouth of the corridor.

It was Kalith. "I could not get through; Casae Podami
is already blocked off. I am going to try to reach the power

station and cut the lines. Otherwise the whole city will go up," Kal called down.

"Wait! I shall go with you! Two have a better chance!" Kavan raced back up the dark corridor, pushing his way through. He was followed by a man in black—their evening *guaard*.

"No! Don't go! You can't stop it! The lines do not matter, lunas burn from within!" Tay screamed, starting to follow. Liel threw her arms around the woman and hung on, unaware of her disadvantage in height. The two tumbled into a heap at the bottom of the stairs, Zair on top of them both, as another explosion, closer this time, rocked the shelter. Tears streaming down her face, the Caprican made no attempt to get up.

"Tay, we cannot just—" Liel began.

"He's crazy," Teloa whispered. "Lunas throw off their matter as they land. It burns until it is consumed, it takes hours, days! It—"

Her next words were never heard, as a deafening explosion ripped the streets above them, causing the entrance to cave in and debris and bricks to rain down from the ceiling.

"As it was in the beginning, is now and forever, worlds without end . . ." Arrez paused in the litany and found a high-pitched drone interfering with his thoughts. He recognized the air-raid siren. Turning to face the packed house, Arrez imperially tossed his hand in the direction of the main entranceway.

"Open the doors, all of them." He turned to Baskh Atare, who was already crossing the choir area and stepping up into the apse.

"It is starset," Baskh intoned. "The roof of the Mendularion is a perfect target. Quickly, quietly, everyone out. The rows nearest the doors first. There are shelters located at the bottom of the hill. We must reach them." Ignoring Arrez's gestures that he should lead them, Baskh stood firm, a sign of visible stability in the fear of the crowd. The impact of the next bomb set the pillars to swaying, although it was at a considerable distance.

"These pillars have withstood mighty quakes. Do not hesitate, do not panic!" Baskh Atare roared. By now a good third of the people were out, although Arrez saw that the royal family held back, waiting for Baskh.

"Get the children out of here," the priest called, indicating that Tal, Deveah, and Baskh's eldest son should remove their families, the children over ten and old enough to represent their generation at the elderday.

Deveah had just reached the innermost nave door when a bomb lodged in the hill above the temple, collapsing the choir like matchsticks and separating the apse from the nave. The orderly evacuation became a rout. Deveah shoved his son Jared out the door and stepped back into the temple.

The next bomb was a direct hit, dropping through the center of the nave and reaching explosion temperature just below the temple floor, blowing the roof to the sky. Unable to see to the nave through the solid wall of choir stone, Arrez dragged himself off the floor and looked for Drau. He saw her at the altar, attempting to lift the great candle and carry it out the apse exit, which had had its doors blown off the hinges in the force of the last impact. As Arrez tried to reach her he pushed at a pillar. The tiled wall next to him collapsed at the loss of its keystone, and the last thing he remembered was Baskh Atare trying to drag Drau from the altar. Then there was darkness.

———

Braan lay on the ground, trying to clear the sparks from his eyes. Cursing himself soundly into the depths of the Path, he leapt to his feet, preparing to run back to his home for Dylan and Asiai. He looked across the city, flames beginning to burn brighter than the dying starlight. Then he realized what was wrong. He saw no reflection from the Mendularion. Panic rose in his throat, and he tore down the path. *Fool! To think that they would not really abandon us . . .*

He reached the outskirts of town without difficulty and was thankful that he had crossed the river outside the city limits; the bridges still standing were in flames. Racing down a large street, Braan found himself cut off by a fire, several men and women standing before it looking for paths through the inferno. Turning around, he doubled back to another major artery, unaware of his younger brother screaming his name.

———————

Roe awoke with a start, swinging her feet off the bed.

"Moran?" No answer—he must have left her to nap while he changed for dinner. Had Lyte slept, too? He was so tired. . . .

A shudder ran through the building, the plant stand swaying. Roe realized she had felt, not heard, something and had been roused from a sound sleep. A quake? Darkness was falling—she could see nothing from her window. She left the room and went down the corridor to the courtyard. Throwing open a glass door, she looked out into the twilight.

Fire was everywhere, obscured by thick smoke, and she heard screams muffled by the sound of the air-raid siren. The sound connected, and then she was frantically searching the skies. There was a glimmer—another wave coming. She started running back down the hall.

"Moran! Lyte!" She was startled at her own volume and found herself screaming from the pain of the frequencies. Then she was on her stomach, covering her head as the palace buckled and rocked from the impact of a bomb. She heard collapsing stone and tiles and felt herself blacking out. It seemed like only moments later when she could see again, but there was no longer the sound of falling rock.

A voice was speaking softly, urgently, to her; someone was shaking her arm. "Serae, please get up! We must get to a shelter!" It was one of the palace *guaard*, his reserve shattered. His face was white, his neck and shoulders bleeding from superficial wounds. Roe listened—nothing.

"It has stopped," she said aloud.

"But there is no knowing when it will begin again! Please—"

"We must find the injured," she said, interrupting. "Who was here? Three of Baskh's little ones, in the far wing. Moran, Lyte—were my brothers and sister back from the planters?"

"Serae, the temple is destroyed, we must go at once!"

She stared at him, digesting this. Then she stood slowly. "If that is true, Eon, then I may be the Ragäree. If so, I shall

not leave without my man—or his body." She took a deep
breath. "Find help, I will get my bag and extra antidote for
the radiation. You are correct, we must get everyone left into
the shelter. Hurry, I shall meet you at the crossing!"

───────────

Several of the corridors into the watch room were destroyed, but Jaac finally found an open one. Entering the
watch room proper, she found a tight-lipped group of people
still going about their assigned tasks.

"Status report." Immediately a volume of information
was thrown her way. The relief on the faces of her warriors
was plain. Jaac had survived Taos; she would survive this
one. After quickly going over the information she said, "Activate defense system."

"Are we going to let them have it?"

Jaac did not look up as she framed a reply. "We cannot
retaliate without the direct order of the Atare. Have you tried
to reach the *Io* or—"

"No response. Either out of direct range or ignoring us."

"Probably out of range," Henne said bitterly. "They do
not want to listen to the death throes of a planet."

Jaac looked up, mildly surprised. "Who said anything
about Nuala dying?" Henne stared bleakly at her. "It will
take a lot more than a few luna bombs to destroy the radiation
capital of the galaxy. You forget that the shield can detonate
the sensitive luna heads in midair. Order all warriors to the
outskirts of the city, to prepare in case of a troop carrier
landing." She studied the explosion chart, the wide range of
hits, the low density. "Fewhas . . . they might be crazy enough
to land."

"Planet defense activated" came a voice. "The bombs
are beginning to explode in midair. They will stop with the
lunas now and switch to regular forces. We put all legions
on standby before we lost interplanetary communications,
with orders to defend their cities using whatever means possible."

"Then I would imagine that they are ready. Begin preparations to countdown for defense." Every head snapped up.
"It takes a few minutes," Jaac said easily. "The Atare may

have problems getting word to us. We must be ready. This attack is not personal, warriors; the front has moved once again. The Fewhas will try to use plutos bombs and turn us to powder. We may have to retaliate." The warriors quickly bent to their computers.

COMPLINE

Braan took what was left of the temple stairs two at a time, ignoring the voices screaming at him from below. He was conscious of the sound of lunas exploding but felt no impacts. Looking up, he realized that the defense had been activated. The defense shield . . . That could only mean Jaac was still alive.

"We must fight," he said aloud, amazed that he could face the concept so casually. He started into the main entrance, and then saw that there was nothing left of the nave. He backed away quickly, fearful of radiation residue. Instead he cut around the side of the temple and reached the apse door.

"Can anyone hear me?" he called as he entered.

"Braan?" The whisper came from almost at his feet. He jumped and realized that it was Arrez. The priest was buried up to his shoulders in the tiles and plaster but had protected his head. Now he pushed aside rubble and looked up. "I am all right, for the most part. Just the wind knocked out of me." He slapped the tip of a buried pillar at the end of his reach. "This brace saved me, I think. Baskh and Drau were over near the altar."

The Nualan bent and removed one of his scarves, pressing it against a gash in the man's forehead. Glancing around, he was glad to see that several men and women had followed him.

"The high priest says he is all right. Start digging him out. You two come with me. You go find healers and get them up here. And you"—Braan gestured to an especially large man—"you keep everyone else in that shelter. And clear the entrance. We may be coming down in a hurry." Leading the way, Braan climbed over the pillar and dropped down on the other side. He stopped short, shocked at what he found.

When the canopy collapsed, Baskh had saved Drau from the brunt of the flying pieces, but he could not block everything. The woman had taken fragments in the head, and a brief pulse check indicated that she was already dead. Baskh lay next to her, his hands sheltering the eternal fire that, although on its side, still burned. Scarcely a mark was on him, yet he was lying in a pool of blood.

The man's eyelids fluttered. "I thought I heard your voice." It did not sound like Baskh—too soft, his breathing raspy. Braan's eyes traveled the Atare's body quickly, and then he clamped his hands on the leg artery that was swiftly draining the man's life.

"Get a healer and frozen platelet packages!" he yelled, whipping off his other scarf and tightly binding the wound. "The Atare has need!" Baskh gestured weakly with his hands, indicating that they should not waste their time. Braan heard, as if from far away, the words of the death litany. He looked up to find a young priestess kneeling at Baskh's feet, her face white yet serene, oblivious to the smell of death, the smoke, her own broken, bloody arm hanging useless at her side.

"Not y—"

"Let her finish," Baskh said. "I have lost too much blood. Man is not meant to survive such injury. To think I leave my people to this—"

"Had you not maintained the defense shield and the drills, it would have been much worse," Braan interrupted, seizing the man's hands as if he could lend him strength.

"Now you are out of scarves." Baskh attempted to chuckle, reaching for breath. "I always knew that crazy two-scarf fashion would come in handy. I wonder how many lives ...here." Shaking free of his sister's son, the Nualan lifted his head and removed his chain of office, laying it in Braan's hand. "Give this to Tal if he lives. If not, keep it. A mad one shall not lead what remains."

"How do you know I am not mad?" Braan finally answered.

Baskh smiled, almost a grimace in his pain. "Oh, you are. But there are many kinds of madness, and not all are evil. Good luck, my son. Take care of my people. They will need you more than they can know. May Holy Mendulay have mercy on us all." His voice faded off at the end as he slipped away—whether into death or the coma of the dying, Braan did not know. He knelt there a moment, trying to concentrate on the final words of the litany, his mind unable to form coherent thoughts. Slowly he stood, and spoke to the small, stricken gathering.

"There may be survivors here. Let us search the temple." Still clutching the chain of office in his right hand, its deep red stones flashing darkly, Braan continued his wandering.

A woman's voice urgently calling his name forced him back outside and down to the first nave entrance—it was impossible to move through the choir, much less the nave. He found a healer and several others huddled over a body, a few people retreating at the medtech's requests to give the man air.

Braan pushed through the crowd and found Tal lying peacefully on his back. A quick look to the healer produced a negative reply, even as his brother moved an arm.

"His back is broken," the man whispered, fumbling in his bag. "The ribs crushed. All I can do is give him a painkiller." Ignoring him, Braan knelt down and carefully slipped his arms around his brother's shoulders, cradling his head. Tal opened his eyes, the familiar serenity still within the blue one, the depths of the black unreadable. The eldest smiled then, as if reassured by Braan's presence. His eyes strayed to the glint of gold thrown carelessly across his own shoulder. A shadow crossed his face; there was only one reason for Braan to have the chain of office. Tal had loved Baskh as a father. He looked back to Braan's emotionless white face, and slowly, carefully attempted to speak. Braan and the healer bent down to catch the heir's final words.

"Keep it." A smile touched Tal's lips, and it was a moment or two before Braan realized that he had stopped breathing. The healer lowered his hand, the painkiller no longer necessary. Braan gently closed his brother's eyes. Setting the body down, he straightened like an old man, unable to rise to his feet. His right hand hurt, and opening it, he saw he was gripping the chain so tightly that it had drawn blood. He did not feel the healer give him an injection of strong radiation antitoxin.

"We must find Deveah," Braan said, his voice muted among the dead stones.

The healer's eyes widened. "You—you cannot be serious, Seri! We—you—" The man was practically pleading with him, unable to meet Braan's withering stare.

"One way or another it will be settled. The Atare had intended to confine him. We shall need restrainers—"

"There is no need" came a voice from behind him.

Braan tensed at the voice, its pain a weapon against him. He turned, expecting to find a half-strangled child. He found instead one of the twins—squinting in the dim light, Braan guessed. "Kavan?"

"Yes." He moved over and stiffly folded down next to Braan, wordlessly touching Tal's arm. He looked so destroyed, so utterly without hope that Braan was frightened for his spirit.

"Why? Where is he?" The voice was sharper than Braan intended. The healer looked closely at Kavan, pulled out another air hypo, and gave him an injection. Then he stood and indicated that the remaining people should come with him.

"What is left is at the starrise door," Kavan said. Braan flinched. What love there was between them had fled long ago; but he was a brother. Kavan's voice had almost cracked on the final words. Now he saw the chain. Bewildered, he looked around in the growing darkness, awareness dawning. "Where—"

"You are certain?" Braan pressed.

Kavan looked away. "Only one man on Nuala bore the Sheel Split in this generation. Yes?" His voice faded as he lost control, dissolving into silent hysteria. Braan swung the chain violently, scattering the rest of the human gallery like leaves before the wind. There was another line of plutos bombs, closer, in sequence—one landed in the gardens. Braan paid no attention, gathering Kavan into his arms as he had a frightened child many years ago. Kavan did not protest, as in other times, and Braan felt his own fear settling. Finally the young man regained control of himself and pulled away.

"There is much to be done. We are needed," Braan ventured.

"Yes, Atare. What would you have of me?" Kavan answered, composing his face.

It took a few seconds for the form of address to sink in. Braan took a deep breath. "Those here can handle this area. I must go to Jaac. It is fruitless . . . to look for . . . anyone until the bombing stops. Can you make it up the hill and cut off the gas? Perhaps we can kill some of the fires. Try. If not, find me. And get a radiation shot first." Braan managed a faint smile. "I need my third hand healthy." Only then did he notice where the healer had ripped Kavan's sleeve, giving him the injection.

Standing awkwardly, Braan walked out to the top step. An elderly woman sat there, watching him keenly through bright eyes encased in a mass of wrinkles. He stooped to her and started to speak.

"Go on, Atare. They would understand. Of course I shall say the litany—as I know you will. But I shall stay." Rising regally, the woman hobbled inside the small entrance. As Braan started down the steps he heard her ancient, quicksilver voice rising above the commotion of the city.

"Ashes to ashes, dust to dust; as we entered the universe, so we depart—alone. . . ."

FIRSTDAY, 4953   MATINS

One candle burned in the shelter. A tiny candle, ill-made; it sputtered and fought for life between drafts and a pool of oil. Teloa stared at it until almost hypnotized, its flame filling her mind. The bombs came more frequently now, though they seemed less devastating. And they were no longer lunas. The small, cramped shelter was stifling, the odor of fear from the people packed within unmistakable. Time to get out. Teloa stirred. Stretching like a cat, the tall woman stood, shaking herself as if dreaming. At her side Liel glanced up, puzzled— this Teloa was not a shaking child. This woman was quiet, confident, in control.

Teloa met her eyes. "The lunas have stopped. Trying to save money, I suppose. These are plutos or MSMs." Stepping carefully over sprawled limbs, she walked to the back of the shelter, Zair's huge form shadowing her. Liel shivered from the draft as Zair's warm bulk left her side.

"That is a storeroom. Water and food supplies are kept in it," Liel offered.

"What is beyond it?"

"Nothing."

"There must be something," Tay answered. "This draft traveled a long, clean way. It's quite strong." Picking up a piece of hemp lying on the floor, Tay lit it in the candle. Then she started back into the storeroom. "There's a large vent back here," she called.

"How large?" Liel asked, for conversation's sake. The creaking and groaning of rusted metal brought her to her feet, and she stumbled into the storeroom. Teloa looked up from her handiwork. She had snapped an ancient lever—the vent stood open, the entrance taller than Zair.

"Are you coming?" The smile was strong, daring.

Liel stared at her. "You are crazy."

The smile vanished. "No, just stir-crazy. It may take them days to find us, and longer to dig us out. I have survived two wars . . . I shall not be beat by this one," Tay replied, unconsciously falling into the Nualan syntax. Not waiting for an answer, Teloa turned and entered the air vent, Zair right behind her.

Liel looked back into the tiny bomb shelter, crammed with shell-shocked bodies. Only a few of their companions had even bothered to look up during this exchange. Without further hesitation she climbed into the duct.

The path, man-high, changed course often. After what seemed an eternity, a myriad of rest stops and hidden panic, Teloa stopped at a duct that suited her. Throwing her weight on hinges generations older than herself, she managed to open the hatch. They stepped out into cool night air, and silence.

"The bombing has stopped."

"No. It's only begun," Tay answered. She pointed.

They were in the hills above the residential area, Tal's house in plain sight. Liel turned toward the mountains and saw slender ground-to-air missiles slowly, silently, rising from hidden silos.

WATCH ROOM

Jaac sat motionless in the command chair, her eyes never leaving the monitors. One told that the defense shields held but were weakening. Above it another showed the ground-to-air missiles, the first wave GTAs; poised, ready to hurtle the barrier of the radiation belt and sear the missiles before they ever entered the atmosphere. The second wave was a different GTA—one that confused a missile's heading and boomeranged it, sending it back to its origin. She dreaded using them, but things were past the point of return. She waited only for word from her Atare—whoever it was currently. A seal, a note, a presence. Something.

A rush of feet echoed down the corridor outside. The members of the watch looked up, hoping for news. Jaac did not react. Two *guaard* threw open the doors and entered, the palm locks destroyed when the computer system shut down. Behind them came Braan, followed by another pair of *guaard*. Henne stood, extending his hand for the message capsule.

"I came in person." The room froze, absorbing his meaning. Henne took in Braan's form at a glance; saw the chain of office in his hand. Without hesitation the man lowered his head. The others followed suit.

Jaac slowly turned in her command chair and stood. "Our shields weaken. Observations indicate that three ships took off at the beginning of the bombing. They achieved orbit, then we lost them on our monitors. Your orders?"

"Launch the first wave." The words were spoken without tension. Jaac had never doubted Braan's ability to make swift decisions. She did not begin now.

"Launch round one, first wave," Jaac commanded.

"GTA launched." The warrior's reply was a whisper.

"Have you need of my presence?" Braan asked.

Jaac faced him again, not really interested in the ascending missiles. There was no strategy to this, no honor. "The second wave—"

"Use at least half our active first wave. If they do not appear to be slacking off in their attack, fire the first round of the second wave. I do not think we shall need to do anything else." With a brief nod he turned and left the room. Jaac sat down again. There was no more to be said. If the Fewhas persisted, there simply would be no more Fewha battleships; their own bombs would destroy them.

PALACE   FIRSTDAY, 4953   MATINS

It did not take long to rally what servants and *guaard* remained alive in the palace. After several attempts the group finally found a path back to the guest's quarters. Roe had taken the precaution of giving everyone in the party a radiation shot and had left the young children of Baskh outside with a *guaard*. Now they began to dig for Moran and Lyte.

There was no answer to their calls. Roe treated the injured warriors and servants who found their noisy group and waited, swallowing her fear. The *guaard* would allow her to touch nothing—news of the temple's collapse had reached them, and they were terrified that Ronuviel was the last Atare female.

"Serae, we have found a shallow point. The door to a chamber is beyond," a woman called. Roe stepped forward only to be blocked by a *guaard*. "The supports are weak; the living rock could crush us. Stand away, Serae."

The man at the head of the line pushed forward through the soft dirt and crushed stone. They heard an exclamation of surprise, and then a call for aid.

Roe handed an air hypo to the next warrior. "It was a luna that hit this house. Quickly—off-worlders have a greater need of radiation protection than we do." The warrior wormed through the hole and disappeared. People began to widen the crevice, packing the dirt and stone firmly. No one requested they take the serae away—there was hope in that thought.

A stretcher was passed through the opening, and in a little while a warrior came crawling backward through the hole, supporting one end of the litter. Roe was stoic as she realized that it was Lyte, already tossing in a feverish delirium. Activating a monitor, she scanned him. Broken ribs, a punctured lung, radiation poisoning, broken shoulder and arms; mechanically she went to work, injecting the proper antibiotics, immobilizing bones, protecting against shock.

Indicating that the cradle should be placed against the wall, she prepared a second air hypo, an especially potent one. For Moran, if—when—the *guaard* found him. It frightened her; the medication could be worse for her lover than radiation sickness. But it was a necessary risk.

She handed it to a *guaard*. "For the leader—in case it is needed." The warrior nodded and crept back into the darkness of the hole.

A voice spoke from beyond. "Serae, the center is totally collapsed. We shall dig to all door frames—they are the only places he could have survived."

"As you think best," she replied, fighting to keep control of her voice. Roe turned back to Lyte, laying her hands gently on his forehead and shoulder, feeling the healing power well up in her, oblivious to the remaining servants. The group sat in awe of what they could see, aware of a faint light not of stars or of distant torches. All three moons brought their new glory to the sky, yet the light in the shattered corridor slowly engulfed it.

Ronuviel did not know how long it had been since she began the healing trance. She was brought out of it by a gentle touch. "Serae, he lives. Come." Shaking herself awake, Roe stumbled after the man.

They were just lifting Moran through the passage in the debris. He was past delirium, sunken into the spasmodic movements of those poisoned by the planet. Roe activated her monitor, although it was unnecessary, and carefully wiped the blood from the corner of his lips. Setting her features into a mask, she began the work of setting bones and protecting against chill, indicating that someone should carry her bag.

"No one else would be here. Let us meet the others outside and flee this place," Eon ventured.

"To where?" Roe asked between shots, her voice not unkind.

"The hospital complex."

"For supplies, yes," Roe answered. "And then we move on. Amura has become death for us."

Night crawled on to its inevitable conclusion. The group finally found a corridor clear enough to carry the stretchers through the shattered Hall of Mirrors and beyond. The balance of the household awaited them, Baskh's youngest sound asleep under a tree.

A *guaard* efficiently took charge, and soon a wagon crept up to the side doors. It was a panting young woman who stepped down from the driver's niche, a tiny floater seat positioned on the wooden crossbar between the hazelles. "My apologies, it took a long time to find an intact wagon and hazelles calm enough to pull it," she said. "We must hurry before the next—"

Suddenly a rushing wave of sound reached their ears. The children awoke shrieking. Ronuviel turned and looked past the palace to the residential hills and saw flaming streaks of light flash into the sky and vanish. A distant rumble came to them as a slight tremor beneath their feet.

"I do not think we need to hurry," Roe replied softly. "Let us get all injured who cannot walk into the wagon. I am going to the complex for medicine. I shall look for you at Crossroads—we are heading for the Chardonnay caverns. They have withstood millennia of quakes."

"Can they withstand a direct hit?" someone asked.

"Better than the complex," a *guaard* answered for her. "Come, Serae, I shall accompany you." Roe started to speak. She thought better of it and nodded her agreement. Picking up her medical bag, the man slipped into the darkness. The Atare woman paused, looking back to the now still forms of Lyte and Moran. They scarcely seemed to be breathing. But there was nothing to be done until the drug took effect. She rushed after the warrior.

Reaching the bottom of the stairs, they were momentarily blinded by a dazzling burst of light in the heavens, brighter than a dozen moons. The warrior stiffened slightly and hurried on. As they ran, Roe heard snatches of the softly chanted words of the death litany—a canticle of passage for the Fewhas, the self-proclaimed enemies of mankind.

CHAPTER NINE

Tired. So incredibly tired. She felt like she had been walking forever, stumbling through the pre-dawn light. Roe glanced at the warrior beside her. The man had insisted on carrying her medical bags, stuffed to the seams with supplies. They were agonizingly heavy; and finally even he had admitted defeat, setting them in the wagon and carrying instead a small child they had found along the way. No one could manage a jest with the warrior's pride. Too much had happened. They had only another mile. One more mile.

"Serae, you are very pale. Please, into the wagon." Roe shook her head, fearful of crowding those who were lying down.

The young warrior at her left leaned closer, the woman's expression intense. "I have studied medicine well, even though I am not a healer. It is possible that you are with child. It is also possible you are the last Atare . . . and that the off-worlder will not live to sire another. Please do not sacrifice our future for your pride." Roe let the information seep through her exhaustion and felt its truth. Nodding vaguely, she did not protest as they stopped the cart and placed her in front, at the heads of the seriously injured.

Roe considered lying down, but it was not worth the effort. Instead she checked her patients. The medications were beginning to take effect. Carefully, her fingers feather-light, she touched Moran's arm and was relieved to see that a bruise did not immediately form. The injection was arresting the condition. She smiled mirthlessly; first he had to live. If he did, he would suffer no permanent damage. But if they did not check the fevers, the pneumonia that was certain to develop . . .

She prepared herself for the healing trance, unaware that she had already begun to glow. She placed one hand at a temple and the other over his heart, closing her eyes and slowly tuning herself into his body processes. Very slowly— they were in chaos, like an intricate machine run amok. She winced inwardly; it had been a long time since she had worked on such a serious case. Ronuviel forced awareness of her subject away from her self, allowing the healing energy to work. She had to cleanse the body cells, bringing Moran out of the comalike state he had sunk into and up to the delirium Lyte tossed in. Only then could his body attempt to fight the fever that was ravaging it. She could do it; she had mended fractures, aided limb regeneration, reversed external radiation burns. This was merely another problem.

When Roe finally came out of the trance of her own accord, she found that the cart had stopped and the hazelles were gone. So was everyone else—she and Moran were alone. Silence . . . the bombing had ceased. She stirred and looked around. Not entirely alone; three *guaard* sat nearby, awaiting a sign. One noticed her movement and stood. "Are you ready, Serae, for us to take him to the healers' station?" she asked.

Roe looked down. Moran now moved occasionally, as if seeking relief from tight clothing. He was on his way up from deep water. "Yes. Be sure that you set him on soft bedding—and also the other warrior, Lyte. We must be very careful with their external tissue until we are certain that the radiation is checked." She crawled to her feet and, accepting the woman's offer of a hand down, stepped off the wagon.

"It is already done. If you are feeling well enough, there are several elders who wish to speak to you." Roe followed the woman without comment, after seeing the two men gently lift Moran off the cart.

A considerable refugee camp was already in existence. They walked through huge gatherings of people of all ages, more constantly streaming in. Ronuviel managed a smile for them, as always amazed by how happy they were to see her. Soon they arrived at a small tent hastily assembled under tall shade trees. The smell of acid smoke reached her nostrils— she suspected that it was Amura.

Stepping inside, she found the tent crowded. Seven or eight elders were there, standing as she entered. Roe was used to courtesy but not overwhelming homage; strict rules of royalty had been lax in her generation. It was disconcerting. They had prepared a pile of blankets for her to sit on. She remembered the announcement at the Feast of Adel: they believed her pregnant. Why else announce official marriage? Smiling faintly, she sat down, unready for confirmation, suddenly hoping fervently that she was correct.

"Elders," she said, knowing the men and women waited for her to speak.

One man cleared his throat. "Serae, it was with great joy that we received the news of your arrival. So many rumors flying—it is difficult to know what to believe." He paused a moment. "There are a few things we are certain of. . . . The temple is destroyed, and many of those at services also died. Baskh Atare and others of your family have taken the Path." Her smooth, tanned face did not change. The elder went on. "At least one of your brothers survives. An Atare has been acknowledged and gave the order to launch the great defense. I have also heard that Jaacav lives."

"That does not surprise me. She has nine lives, that one," Roe graciously supplied.

Accepting her calm agreement, the woman on her right took up the tale. "We do not know yet what plans have been made or can be made. The troops at the bottom of the hills claim that this is Fewha work and believe that invasion is imminent. But a count was taken in the dark—at least three battleships and two cruisers were destroyed by the GTAs. If so, it will take time for reinforcements to arrive. As you are aware, Fewhas have a reputation for decimating the home population before moving on. Perhaps it would have been safer to play dead, rather than to indicate that the survivors have some fight left in them."

"No 'playing' would have been necessary, elder," Ronuviel replied.

"What else, Serae? We cannot stay here. Shall we return to Amura? The fires must first be brought under control."

"Yes—and more importantly, the danger of disease must be removed. Fortunately it is cold. But we cannot hesitate. Every able-bodied man and woman must return to the city in carefully controlled groups, with special assignments. Even before we seek personal possessions, some must gather wood, others prepare a place for a fire, still others gather materials for the rites. Any recorders that exist must be used to take fingerprints if it is possible, or footprints of infants. This will be very important to the families, to be certain of the fates of their people. We need to establish areas to care for children while their parents help—or for those whose parents have not been found. We must expand the medical area I saw, allow the whole cavern for this."

"We would house you and the other key personnel there also." As Ronuviel started to protest, the woman hurried on. "You are most assuredly the eldest woman of Ila's line left alive. Perhaps the only one. And the only single individual here who can give orders that will be obeyed. I can command my district—if I can find them. So, too, the others. But we are not majority leaders, much less the synod leaders. We cannot command and be followed by all. You must do this, Serae, until the Atare joins us—if he can."

Roe waited. "I would prefer more information before we send groups back. They should seek the Atare and give him my words. Most likely he has instigated the same program."

"Would the words of the high priest suffice?" The gathering turned to the door frame. "Word comes that Arrez approaches and brings his family and others with him. We think he bears the eternal fire," the young man added, nodding his pardon to the small session. His excitement was plain in the way he threw shut the entrance robe. Roe bowed her head, saying a small, swift prayer of thanks that the priest had survived. Now, if only Braan had . . .

She stood slowly. "We must get to the nearest granaries, make sure the food is not contaminated, and build fires to ward off fevers. It may be that come next morning we shall be on our way to Amura—Mt. Amura."

The group stared blankly at her. "Serae?"

"We have jested for years that we could build a city in the caverns of that mountain. Perhaps we shall." She started out the canvas opening. "I have patients to attend to. Please divide up those areas—swiftly—and get to work. If you have difficulties and my name will not serve, I have my signet. Find some wax and seek me." She stepped out into a brilliant starrise and started for the caves.

———

Elana and Arrez found her there when they could finally get away from the crowds. Arrez planted the flame outside the caverns and saw immediately that it would have to be moved to the hill—too many people wanted to light candles from it and pray near it. The elders sought them out, begging Elana to take over the medical area. She was quiet; many of these same individuals had recently sought her downfall. But she did not hesitate. As she disappeared into the caves Arrez inquired about the state of affairs in the encampment.

What he was told both pleased and disquieted him, but his relief over Roe washed out everything else. Telling the elders that the new Atare also wished to begin building funeral pyres as soon as possible, Arrez hurried into the cavern.

He found Elana practically ordering Ronuviel to lie down. A medtech had spread blankets next to Moran, and Roe was in no condition to argue with anyone. Elana had pulled out her diagnostician's box and passed it above Roe's body. She examined the readings with alarm and then looked to Roe again. Suspicion crossed her face. Changing the subject setting, she tried once more. Then she studied the results. "You gave yourself a radiation shot?"

"Yes."

"A strong one? Level two, three?"

"Level two," Roe answered, no longer interested, her

eyes resting on Moran. Arrez looked pained at the sight of the active young man, now so reduced. His firstwife, meanwhile, had asked for a booster hypo and, upon receiving it, gave Roe another injection.

"I was worried—so much medication for it at once—I was not sure."

"I am, and you did well. All of this healing has drained your reserve. You must sleep now and regenerate yourself," Elana said firmly.

Arrez leaned close to her. "Should we tell her now?"

"About Braan—the rest should wait."

"What rest?" came Roe's voice.

Arrez smiled wanly. Her exhaustion had not dimmed her hearing.

"Braan Atare rules, as was meant to be," came a voice. "And he will take things in hand, as should have been done long ago. Do not cross him. His mood is fell now, and shall be for much time to come." They looked up to see Mariah standing at the foot of the makeshift bed, Chaka's youngest asleep in her arms. She turned her gaze on Elana. "I stay with the little ones. Others return to Amura." Elana nodded. Mariah's mystical ability to deal with children could be invaluable.

"Baskh and Rebekah are gone," Arrez went on, not sure what Mariah might say. She had been preoccupied since the bombing, rarely speaking. "Tal, Deveah, Libra, and Persephone are definitely dead—I identified the bodies. Tal's two sons also, and all spouses. Deveah's son lives, although his radiation poisoning is bad and he has broken bones. Braan's two are missing. Kavan is with Braan."

Ronuviel closed her eyes to conceal her relief. Thank Mendulay. Without Braan no one would survive.

"Liel was seen just as the bombing began—they are digging out the entrance to the shelter even now. We know people are in there, we can hear shouts, but nothing intelligible," Elana broke in, not wanting Roe to feel as if she were the only throne-line Atare woman left. "Also, I have seen several members of your mother's family. I shall send for them."

"We shall need the bone fuser, if it was not destroyed,"

Roe said abruptly, the doctor in her taking over. Then she
was vague. "The . . . other planets?" She seemed to be visibly
adding up relatives in her head.

"Nothing since the attack began in earnest," Arrez said
quietly. "Do not be concerned for Deenn or your mother or
the prime minister. They can take care of themselves."

"We monitored their shield activating," Elana added.

"Kal?" she asked finally, fighting sleep. Her serious baby
brother, a child no longer. Lord, she needed his strength.

"Kavan . . . lost him in the crowds. A *guaard* was with
him. We have heard nothing either way."

"He is alive," came Mariah's voice. All turned her way
as she gracefully walked down the aisle to the mouth of the
cave. "Else how could I have dreamt of Kalith Atare?" No
one spoke. Ronuviel felt herself shivering uncontrollably.
There was only one way for Kalith to become Atare. . . .

AMURA   TIERCE

Braan sat quietly beside the body, unaware of the masses
moving around him. This one had been young, the twins'
age; as a matter of record, a friend of theirs. He had been
Braan's assistant, handling correspondence, visitors, art sales,
and all excursions off-world. He was also dead. The name
Carobdus flitted to the surface of Braan's mind. He stoically
punched in the name on his pocket recorder, the instrument
humming efficiently. Then he reached down and removed the
boys' side recorder. Such work would keep someone busy—
Kavan, maybe. He was chopping firewood, trying not to
worry about Kal, telling all who wanted reassurances that he
"would know" if Kalith was dead.

"Do you cheer them or yourself?" Braan murmured aloud.

A warrior approached him. "Atare? We have reached
deep enough to speak to them. There is no hurry, they have
plenty of fresh air, and injuries were minimal."

Braan glanced up abruptly. "And?"

"They say the serae and a tall blonde woman pried the
cover off the air vent and left. A few followed—they were
seeking the source of the current. The fresh air increased later

on; perhaps they knocked out the vent piece at—" Braan had
stood and moved away from Carobdus's body during this
explanation, two men discreetly moving in and removing it;
his movement was a wasted gesture. A huge, long-legged
descendant of Earth's kingly hounds came bounding out of
nowhere, knocking Braan to the street in his delight. Zair
proceeded to clean Braan's face for him, over muffled protests
and strangled sounds.

"Blasted mutt! If you ever want children, will you
g—" Braan's laughing order was cut off by Liel's viselike
grip around his neck. Recognizing her, he pulled her close,
as if trying to protect her from everything around them.
Gasping, choking back sobs, she buried her face in his
shoulder, giving full vent, if only momentarily, to her churning emotions. Her brother said nothing, holding her tightly,
closing his eyes to hide tears. When he opened them, he
found the fresh starlight blocked off. Squinting, he saw the
tall blonde of the gardens and the landing bay—Teloa, was
it? He also sensed immediate, if unvented, hostility from
the gathering. Of course, she was probably one of the few
newcomers left; most were killed by the luna that had struck
the embassy or had departed in the *Gerrymander*, *Griffon*,
or *Hydra*. She was a planter. They needed planters. A smart
one, to find her way through the duct maze. This had to
end, here and now.

Gently shaking Liel, Braan climbed to his feet. To send
them to the mountains or keep them? He decided quickly.
Even with Zair the woman's life was in danger should she
so much as speak a word against the people. "Treason" was
on everyone's lips as it was. Only his family could guarantee
her safety, and he dreaded putting that on Liel.

He turned to Teloa. "Thank you for your care of my
sister." Braan made sure it carried to the group. Then to Liel
he said; "We need assistance. Would you rather... identify
people or go to Roe? She is with child, and I imagine this
has been a severe shock to her system. She will need help,
although she will not admit it. Kavan is at the crossroads.
Take him with you." He paused, digging in the pouch at his
side. He pulled out the chain of office, its stones flashing
brilliantly in the risen star's light. Liel touched it tenderly,

knowing without asking. "Take this to her . . . for safekeeping. And await my return." She gazed up at him, despair and hope flaring briefly in her face. She started to loop it around her neck and then stopped herself.

Dropping the chain down the front of her shirt, she stood, turning to Teloa. "Do you—"

"She will stay with Zair and me," Braan went on smoohtly. "Second Officer, will you please escort the serae to the Chardonnay foothills? Arrez's messenger stated that the Ragäree is there. Pick up Seri Kavan on your way." He waved shyly to Liel in parting and made a brief, funny face for her. She attempted to brighten at his lunacy and followed the *guaard*. Braan then matched Teloa's scrutiny.

"For the time being you will stay with me," Braan said, his voice dropping slightly in volume. "Your life may be in danger from people seeking scapegoats." He took hold of the big dog's collar. "Zair—guard," he said clearly, pointing to Teloa. The hairy deerhound peered up at him, wagged its tail slightly, and walked over next to Tay. "Good dog."

"And what am I to be doing in your company?" she asked.

He abruptly surveyed her. There was no coolness or sarcasm in her voice. "Can you keep records?"

"What kind?"

"All kinds," he answered, extending the recorder to her. "Figures, correspondence, historical—my scripter is dead. For a while you can succeed him and probably later function as a go-between for the city dwellers and the planters." She took the recorder. "That will depend on your talents in both areas and whether you still need protection." Braan held up a package of tape dots. "I want originals of these tonight; we need to get an idea of our losses." Without further comment he began walking down the hill into the city, several *guaard* following.

Teloa stood silent, watching his retreating figure. Zair whined after him and then pawed at her leg. There had been no malice in Braan—she believed he had intended no insult. But too much was upon him, and there was no time to be gentle. Tay threw the recorder strap over her shoulder. One who had been both planter and scripter in her time had no need to fear the demands of Nuala. She started down the hill at a brisk walk, the deerhound bounding ahead.

CHARDONNAY   VESPERS
MOUNTAIN, SOUTH CAVE

Teloa kept her eyes on the rough ground beneath her, aware that she was watching for more than one set of feet. The girl Shinar was exhausted and disoriented and had stumbled more than once. Supporting Shinar's other side was Kalith, who was grim, silent. She knew what he had been doing this long day—helping to find bodies for the fires. It had been hard enough to comb the ruins for survivors. Teloa had not been surprised when the youth became emotional at the sight of Shinar. Nor had his response to Braan amazed her; emotion ran deep in these Atares, for all their cool facades.

She and Zair had found Shinar, half buried in a hallway of the home of Arrez's fourthwife, Chaka. The older woman was dead when they found her—whether from the bombing or her own radiation, the healers still were not certain. Arriving back at the temple, the search group had found Kalith, the last missing Atare; he was burning the bodies of his kin. How long for those scars to heal? Now they approached the mountains—at least they looked like mountains to Teloa. The hills, a *guaard* had said to her. And Ronuviel was there, the people following her without question. Whatever gods there be, you have planned this well. Did so many have to die for your will?

There was a fluttering of blue robes, and Shinar was seized in Elana's urgent grip. The girl began to weep, and though her mother tried to comfort her, neither were fooled. Elana's eldest was dead, Kal had told them—from the bombs. The young Atare slipped away from the two women, and Teloa followed his example. She passed the high priest as she approached the cave; he was oblivious to all save Elana and Shinar.

Ronuviel left the cave and embraced her younger brother.

Kal began to speak urgently; Teloa caught the names Dylan and Asiai. The youth looked concerned. Braan's children...

A crowd pressed up the hill behind them, and Teloa knew Braan had arrived. The excitement, the electricity in the air was tangible. Teloa melted into the gathering within the cave's mouth, the great hound Zair at her heels. Roe pulled Kal to her side and faced Braan. The man appeared composed, but his look was for Ronuviel alone.

They stood mere centimeters apart as the sound of the gathering faded into the breeze. Ronuviel pulled out the chain of office, weighing its trine gold links, achingly touching the rubies studding its length. Then she connected the long circlet and gently slipped it over Braan's head, carefully letting it settle down his chest.

"*Eo Mendulai n Nuala*, for Mendulay and the people," she began, "until our Lord requests your presence on the Last Path. *A-tu yai Atare!*"

"*A-tu yai Atare!*" The crowd roared with one voice the ancient rallying cry. For the first time since the devastation Tay felt there might be a chance.

CHARDONNAY MOUNTAIN   COMPLINE

The activity that night in the camp was subdued. People were too exhausted to notice the warriors arriving with special military equipment, the tireless Jaac giving discreet directions. Low, haunting song rose occasionally, filled with somber thanksgiving to High Mendulay for the salvation of the people. The crying of children had stilled, as well as most weeping. Braan could hear Roe's voice rise and fall as she told a gatuhlpa, a great tale, out of Nuala's past. Now more than ever her place as an oral historian would be important. Who knew what was left in the various computer banks?

For the first time Braan walked into the cave toward the small offshoot that was designated as his. He was having difficulty concentrating, Dylan's face intruding into his thoughts. No amount of comfort would help the boy right now; he blamed himself totally for Asiai's seizure by a fleeing ambassador. Asiai . . . if only the ships made it; if only she were on one. And if so, what then?

As he passed by the makeshift beds he caught sight of Moran and Lyte. Pain was mixed with fury as he looked at them. Had they known, could they have stood by and— He shook his head violently, trying to drive the thought from his mind. That was one thing he could not allow himself to believe—not for a moment. As if aware of his scrutiny, Lyte opened his eyes and met Braan's marbled ones. They stared at each other a long minute. Not sure that Lyte could see him in the darkness, Braan stepped over and knelt down next to him.

A faint smile passed Lyte's lips. Slowly, painfully raising his arm, Lyte grabbed Braan's belt knife and clumsily handed it to him hilt first. "If you . . . believe that, kill . . . now. Else— never—again *men-tsun*." Braan did not answer, not even to match the sardonic smile with one of his own. He reached and took the knife and, delicately taking Lyte's wrist, set the man's arm back down at his side. The warrior took another ragged gasp and closed his eyes. Tucking the knife back in his thong, Braan stood and continued toward the back.

Not a traitor. Lyte was many things, good and perhaps even evil, but not a traitor, not to anyone or anything with honor. Braan rounded the rocky curve and entered the small area that had been prepared for him. A soft bed had been made up on the smooth dirt, and next to it was a basin and a pitcher filled with clear water. Towels were piled on the bed, and a votive candle cast a dim glow over everything.

Braan remembered something; swiftly he retraced his steps and entered the night. He moved around the cave entrance toward the last hill and then stopped. It was ablaze with light. Where the brethren had found so many candles Braan did not know, but they were there, the eternal flame flickering above them. In a daze Braan reached down and picked up a candle from the box at his feet. Lighting it, he set it at the base of the knoll and turned back to the cave.

———

Teloa recognized him as he reentered the hospital and hurried to catch up. He had told her when he had assigned her the task of scripter that he wanted the tapes before she slept, but she had not been able to find him until now.

When Tay reached the niche in the cave well, she rapped softly on her recorder. No answer. Drawing a deep breath, she peered around the rocks. He was there, seated on the blankets, his face pressed to his knees. She could tell that he was shaking; and then she took a half step backward as she realized that he was weeping. Men had not expressed their emotions freely back on Capricorn V. It had not been socially acceptable. And after that first bombing there had been no tears left to weep. She could not bear it—Braan literally had had the future of his race dumped on his shoulders; it was not fair that he was not allowed to share his grief.

She set the recorder at the foot of the blanket and stood, torn and uncertain as to whether any sympathy might be shrugged off angrily, or worse, misunderstood. Finally she reached out and set her hand, feather-light, on his shoulder. They remained that way awhile, and then Teloa glided away to find the one person who might be able to help.

Fortunately Roe was done with her story, and all Tay had to say was "Someone needs you" to get her attention. As the woman reached for her medical bag the Caprican stopped her and then led off in the cave's direction.

Tay stopped just short of the niche's entrance, hesitant to show the way. "He needs someone." Roe gripped her arm in passing and went in. Tay waited and checked carefully. Roe had sat down next to Braan and, without any attempt to get his attention, embraced him. Tay slipped away.

CHAPTER TEN

Tay was rudely awakened by the cold. Shivering, she realized that the star had moved on and Zair had completely taken over the warm spot. She crawled over him and nestled between his paws, flopped over his ribs. He opened one eye slightly, made a soft woofing noise in his throat, and went back to sleep. Chuckling, Teloa stretched luxuriously, aware that it was mid-afternoon and time to get back to work.

Work... Every muscle groaned. She had known hard work on Capricorn V but nothing like this. Back home it had been a matter of economy. Now it was a matter of survival.

They were still digging out parts of the city; Tay was amazed at how the defense shield lessened the effects of the lunas. But it was being done cautiously; off-worlders were restricted to the mountains for fear that the luna radiation would upset their delicate balance with the planet radiation. The work had settled into a routine. Most people had been assigned responsibilities similar to their normal occupations; the others were salvaging important materials and stone from Amura and transporting them to the great mountain, across the Sonoma Valley. The supplies were being carried by hazelle wagon or solar car—the train line would be nonfunctional for some time.

She heard a shout below and looked over the edge. Several men and women were racing triumphantly up the small, curving road the warriors had blasted out. She listened intently in the clear, still air, picking out familiar Nualan words, and gathered that they had finally found what they were looking for in the academy computers. Several university sessions ago, as a final project, a student had examined the feasibility of constructing a city inside a large mountain— Mt. Amura used as the example. Then it was an amusing way to handle a potentially boring assignment. Now they were attempting to do just that and had been seeking the plans since the bombing. The young man's originals had been destroyed, but stored away in the academy computer were the duplicates—and now they had a design with which to begin.

Teloa sat up and surveyed the mountain towering above her, trying to imagine what it would be like to live underground. There were ways to determine the safest place for light and air shafts. . . .

A rustling in the brush disturbed her thoughts. She froze, uncertain. Were there dangerous animals up here? Zair's nose twitched, but he was too comfortable to rouse himself. Surely, if it was venomous . . . Looking closely, she saw two bright eyes peering at her from under the bushes.

"Well, hello there," she cooed in her softest, most persuasive voice. The eyes disappeared. There was more rustling, but Tay could detect no sounds of retreat. "Do you want this warm spot? You may share it, come on. Zair is a sleepy thing, he won't bother you." Bright eyes gleamed at her once again.

Tay dug around in her pockets for the remains of her secondmeal. Slowly pulling them out, she cracked some of the grains together invitingly. "Come here, curious one." The beast slid into view. It was a tiny, furred creature, no longer than her forearm including its long black-and-gray ringed tail. It had a face much like a Terran fox, if a bit flattened, and a short, thick, wooly black coat. Its big scooped ears flicked up, listening to the grains. It sat up on its strong back legs— legs equally suited for speed on the ground or over jagged rocks—and twitched its long black whiskers at her. Tay couldn't help but laugh, and the animal vanished. She waited, the grains on her flat, outstretched hand, and soon, out of the bush almost next to her, a tiny paw slowly reached. Tay carefully pulled her hand back, forcing the creature out. Finally she set her hand on a rock.

There was a long wait. Then, seeing that the woman did not move, the creature crept out, snatched a piece of grain wafer, and scampered back to its bush. It sat beneath the foliage, devouring the piece of wafer and observing her with its soft, dark eyes. Tay cautiously set another piece of wafer on her hand.

"Poor thing, you must be starving," she murmured. Time passed quickly as she set the remains of her meal in her hand and let the animal come get them. Finally it sat right by her hand and ate, now sniffing inquisitively at Zair. Teloa giggled. What kind of creature was this, that it had never seen a dog? It was no longer frightened by the sound of her voice, however, and nonchalantly walked up Zair's side to his head and snuffled his ears. The big animal shook his head and tried to crane his neck around to examine his tormenter. Seeing that the little creature's scent was beginning to excite him, Tay set her arm on Zair's back to calm him.

Too late. Zair jumped up, and the animal leapt for Teloa's sleeve. Running up her arm, it burrowed into her hood. Teloa froze, suddenly afraid that it might bite her.

It had no such intention. Peering around her ear, the creature cheeped once, a *tikki-tikki* noise, as if questioning her, and then proceeded to scold the dog from the safety of Teloa's shoulder. She laughed in delight as the dog thrust his nose down to investigate. Seeing the huge head coming toward it, larger than its whole body, the animal ducked back into her hood. Teloa pulled at the collar, to keep from being strangled by its weight, and carefully stood up.

"Are we friends? Would you like to visit my home and see if you'd care to stay? Let's go take a look." Teloa started down the narrow incline, Zair charging before her. Reaching the road, Teloa heard low, tense voices. She slowed, recognizing one of the voices as Braan's. Carefully looking around into the mountain grotto, she saw him standing there, several angry synod members beside him and one young man before them all. As she approached, the young man turned and left the scene.

The group was speaking Nualan, but she could make out a great deal of it. "This is dangerous, Atare . . . we should follow him . . . I trust no Dielaan dogs."

"And do what? Wipe out their encampment? Do not blame their tribe for the faults of one man and the folly of his immediate family. When the other elders read the information I brought back from Tolis, his plans are ruined. No messenger can change that. But . . . send a tracker. Find out where he goes." Braan sat down on a rock, suddenly looking tired. Seeing Tay, he smiled and nodded to her. "Words from Lars?" he asked, switching to Galactic for her benefit.

"A few. Are you all right? You look pale."

Braan chuckled. "You are worse than Ronuviel."

"Not quite." Roe stepped out of the grotto, moving up behind Braan to knead his back with her strong, delicate hands. "She is learning quickly. Someone must watch you at all times. You push too hard."

"We have to if we are going to be secure come the sno— What in Mendulay's name?" Teloa realized Braan was staring oddly at her, as if she had two heads. She had forgotten that he never glanced casually at anything. What . . . ?

"*Tikki-tikki-tikki!*" came a trill in her ear.

"Oh! Just a friend I found on the ridge." The creature crawled out of her hood and arranged itself on her shoulder, standing on its hind legs and surveying the group. It chirped once at them, as if to dismiss them, and began to groom itself immediately.

Braan laughed. Teloa turned to him with keen interest at this—it was the first genuine laugh she had heard from him since she'd met him. She burst into a lovely smile, pleased that he found the beast as amusing as she did.

"How did you contrive to entrap *that*?"

"I didn't contrive. It came when I offered it some grain."

"More likely decided to come out of curiosity," Roe threw in, gazing at the creature. "An akemmi. I have never seen one during the day, except in a lab. They are engaging little animals, are they not? And very wild. I have never heard of one allowing itself to be handled. Or herself—the color looks like a female."

"Well, it hasn't really allowed itself to be handled," Tay explained. "It's been handling me, much like a climbing post. Maybe it thinks I'm a movable tree!" They all laughed at that as the crowd increased in size.

"Maybe it has not heard that akemmi are afraid of humans," Braan suggested with a wicked grin. "The bombing probably forced it down from the peaks. I have never seen one below the falls. It is a young one." Liel had joined the gathering and now walked up to Tay carefully. The akemmi immediately stopped washing her paw and turned to the woman, hair on end, making horrendous spitting noises.

"Hey!" Tay rapped her on the fanny with an index finger. Surprised, the little female subsided, still warily watching Liel. Tay apologized by rubbing the creature's head with a finger. She began to curl into a ball, a soft humming coming from her throat.

Liel started laughing. "She is protecting you!"

"What will you call this ferocious beast?" Braan asked, standing and moving closer to keep from falling asleep under Roe's healing hands.

"Tikki, what else? That's all she says."

"Truly amazing," an elder murmured as he walked off. "It's obviously never seen a human, so it doesn't know it should be afraid!" The others began to drift away, Liel promising to seek Tay out later.

"Braan." He turned in Roe's direction. "Do not evade the thought. What about Corymb?"

"We will deal with him when he arrives. People are still trickling in; we have no proof that he has known our location the whole time. No reason, no concrete reason to be suspicious." Braan offered the akemmi a finger, which she licked experimentally. "His winning throw is fear. As people become more frightened, they will be more willing to listen to his racist propaganda. We must be sure that there is enough food and shelter for everyone, and that our troops are ready for the Fewhas ... or Axis. Or even pirates. Whoever tries to brave Nuala first."

"Is civil war coming?" Tay asked bluntly, feeling self-conscious. She had never spoken to Braan without his initiating the conversation. As an outsider, it did not seem her place.

"The planters—what do they say?" Braan said instead. He scrutinized her, his gaze piercing. Tay looked away, studying the haze trapped over the valley. And what if the doomsayers were correct and the bombing had changed the climate?

"It will be hard," she finally said, her voice barely carrying to Roe. "There is contamination. The warehouses burned. We have no chemicals and little seed."

"How much seed?"

"Lars is writing it up. I'll bring it to you s—"

He gently took hold of her arm, turning her to face him again. "I want it in layman's terms. The winter plantings?"

"Most of them are in the ground." Teloa looked up at him. "The deep granaries are fine—we shall be fed this winter. And we can plant in the spring. But the harvest will be small, even with optimum conditions. The entire yield here was apparently based on the hybrid seed and chemical infusion. Depending on the rest of the planet's . . . ability to raise food—"

"What you are trying to say is that we shall be often hungry come next winter," Roe broke in. But she looked uneasy as she said it.

"Worse. If we are to maintain the proper nutrition level, there will be no more seed to plant. It will be eaten." There was a tense silence.

Braan was stoic. "So we survive all obstacles to die of the most simple—"

"No." The Atares faced Teloa. "Not necessarily. My planet was unable to use many of the major chemical fertilizers. We used instead a combination of various natural fertilizers, crop rotation—it was harder, but the yield was just as high."

"Could that be done here?" Roe questioned.

"Maybe. If you're asking could I do it, no—there isn't enough time. It took a generation of experimentation to determine just how to adapt to our climate, soil, and weather deviations. And we had Axis food imports until we could support our own people. We would all starve or kill each

other in the fight for dominance over the harvest." Tay felt
very helpless. She had not intended to bring this up; not until
the planters had thought of an alternative plan—any plan.

"Can we help?" Braan replied.

Teloa gave him a searching look. "Lars mentioned something I am curious about. He said, 'If only we had the hands
of the Cied.' He seemed to imply that with its or their talents,
we would be fine. What did he mean?" Was it her imagination
or was Braan momentarily startled?

It was Ronuviel who spoke. "The Ciedärlien. They are
the desert dwellers. Among the people we have had many
branches snap off the parent tree and take root on their own.
Cied was one. Their people turned their back on technology
after the first fall and chose to adapt to Nuala completely.
They are totally self-sufficient, or could be, if they did not
discourage their artisans and deal with us primarily to get
trine gold, which is found in the mountains alone."

"Then they have no respect for you and would just as
soon let you die?"

"She did not say that," Braan interrupted," although you
are not far wrong. The majority of the tribes have a relationship with the Atare house. My ancestors, unlike other
city-state rulers, were not so foolish as to treat them as mere
fanatics." Seeing her confusion, he added, "Nuala has been
a united people for only three thousandyear. Before, we were
a grand division of city-states, with a monarchy or prime
minister and a functional parliament in each."

"Corymb?"

"His family ruled Dielaan. We united under Sheel Atare
Mindbender when famine threatened to devastate us. It was
not a . . . completely peaceful changeover, though the people
favored it and forced it."

"At any rate," Roe continued, "at the coronation of each
Atare and at the marriage of each Ragäree *and* at the birth
of the heirs, the tribes send representatives to pledge mutual
trust and respect between . . . basically the opposing life-styles."

"Are they really opposing? I mean, your people seem
like a people who do things for themselves, you—"

"But major conveniences are taken care of on a larger
scale. A vulnerable scale. A great failing. But then, subcon-

sciously, we may have wanted peace so badly that we were better prepared for paradise than war."

"Then we can expect an emissary within a half year?"

The Atares were silent a moment, astonished. "Yes," Braan began slowly. "I suspect we are being observed. But to deal with our official visitors would only be the beginning. There is little for us to offer them, you see, and the famous Nualan altruism often stops at the desert's edge. There are many tribesmen who would love to step in and take over our gold mines. Others have private ambitions of their own." Someone came up behind them, but Braan was undisturbed, so Tay did not turn. "And there are different . . . levels of Cied. Those of the deep sand mountains are a proud, fierce people, given to warring with their neighbors over the slightest insult. The middle tribes are usually friendly among themselves and others but, in a head-on confrontation, would support the deep people. Then the waste dwellers, the Wasuu, and the Stigati . . ."

"Are marginally human" came Arrez's voice. "Their wants and needs change daily. The danger they could represent, if aroused, is substantial."

Teloa turned and surveyed the high priest. "Could we go to them?"

"Good question. An Atare might. The deep tribes would not accept anyone else. And the Stigati would surely kill any but the Ragäree."

"You're safe. Why?" Teloa asked Ronuviel. Arrez had made the statement in Nualan, but Tay had understood the last line.

"I am the house of Atare," Roe answered simply. "It is my son who shall next rule, not Braan's. And the people would rather take another high family as leaders than any other Atare but the one I carried; for example, Deveah's son and Braan's son would have just as legitimate a claim as my mother's sister's son, and that might bring on a blood feud."

"What about Liel?"

"The eldest of the eldest," Arrez said in Galactic. "Even if Liel had a child first, she is not the eldest daughter and only has a claim if Roe is barren. All royal lines are allowed one generation of solely female issue, you see, before the hierarchy must change. The prophecies say an Atare shall lead us all. May the day come soon." He eyed Braan and spoke in Nualan. "You have called for a tribal council this evening, with the elders as well. I have information for you before then. Concerning Cied, as it were. And Baakche."

Braan studied him. "Tay, do you have your recorder?" he asked in Galactic.

"No, Atare. Shall I get it?"

"Please." The woman hurried off, the akemmi protesting and clinging tightly to her poncho. Zair paused, nosed Braan, and then followed. The Nualan smiled faintly, sadly, at the dog's confusion.

"You keep her close. Why?" Arrez asked, persisting with the Nualan tongue.

"I fear for her. You have seen the dark looks she receives. It has been but fourteenday, Arrez. She is a good scripter and quite mute when others question her about state affairs. The best kind of assistant to have. Also," he went on drolly as she reappeared, "she is the only woman in the city not throwing herself at my feet. It is refreshing."

"She is the only woman not attempting to become pregnant. Fully a third of those who were pregnant have lost the children they carried before the bombing, and Elana fears problems with another third. We revert to the Nualan instinct."

"So pray for Roe," Braan finished, glancing at his sister.

"You think I do not?"

But Braan was smiling at Tay's long leap to the plateau, the akemmi chittering its distress and anger. He was already explaining to Tay that he wanted the following conversation transcribed and a summary prepared for the evening meeting. As Braan led the way, politely gesturing for Arrez to follow, Teloa contained her questions for Ronuviel about the actual power of the Ragäree and quickly brought up the rear.

———

Roe remained alone. She had already heard about Baakche, as she often heard about things before anyone else did, and was not interested in a second recitation. Tonight would come soon enough. She moved on into the mountain, pushing thoughts of starvation out of her mind.

Taking a flight of newly chiseled steps and a natural upper corridor, Roe ducked under a tarp and entered the new medical wing. Her eyes traveled to the back of the cave, and she repressed her alarm. *Stop it, you are acting like a wet nurse*! Moran was sitting up on his bunk, a blanket loosely thrown across his shoulders. He was leaning against an outcrop of rock, eyes closed and face very pale. Roe could tell that he was attempting to control his agonizing breathing. She rushed to support his side, silently cursing the hands that had controlled those bombs.

The bones had fused well, and infection had been kept to a minimum; but these were not the real problems of recovery. The difficulties of dealing with Dielaan poisoning, as the elusive radiation of Nuala was termed, were more subtle. As Braan had hoped, the defense shields had been able to control the luna radiation almost completely. In cases like Moran's and Lyte's, however, the planet had leapt into their weakened defense systems, sweeping past centuries-old protections like a gale wind. And it fed on their body processes, slowing the bone marrow's attempts to replace blood and thereby siphoning the muscles' strength. It was one thing that could not be rushed, this slow cure—bed rest, fluids, slowly increased exercise, and occasional blood transfusions. Because of it all, Moran seemed to need her close to him, physically and emotionally; she gladly obliged.

Moran opened his eyes as she gently brushed his long bangs across his brow. He studied her, his dark blue eyes glazed with pain he could not hide.

"Maybe you should lie down," she began.

"No. I want to go out." Roe started to reply and stopped herself. She stared down the passageway between the ends of the beds. So short—so long. Could she get him down there? And what about back? She took in his form. He wore joqurs and laced skin boots, a thick vatos wool blanket thrown over all. He would be warm enough. Why not? The snow clouds were already forming over the Sonoma range; soon winter would settle in to stay. She sensed chaotic emotion in him—she knew his hatred of caverns.

The walk took forever. Roe felt every step of pain, although Moran said nothing. Finally they reached the broad ledge Elana had chosen as the life shelter walkway. Moran sank down on the bench against the outer wall, exhausted by the movement.

"I am weak," he admitted, a brief smile illuminating his face.

Roe gently traced his cheekbone, appalled by his thinness and enchanted by his beauty. Yes, beauty; he had traveled beyond his usual classic features. It was a bit too close to the pose of an ancient angel for Roe's taste. She outlined the sculptured muscles of his shoulder and arm, glad for him to see that the tone was not completely gone.

"You will be yourself before you know it," she replied, avoiding his direct gaze as she drew the blanket tighter around him.

"You think so?"

"As a doctor, I can tell you the recovery has been swift. Being familiar with your temperament, I can say it will not be nearly fast enough for you."

"Lyte is up and walking alone," he said accusingly.

"You are not Lyte," Roe answered, laying her cheek on his outstretched arm. He looked down on her bowed head and slowly raised his other hand to run his fingers through her hair.

"I don't sleep," he whispered absentmindedly.

"I know."

"Ever since I heard about—those women—I've been worried about you. And it. You're in a dangerous time now—"

"Do not. I am as healthy as—"

"So were they." It was abrupt, unlike him. He stared off over the outer stone wall and down onto the foothills below.

She felt the fear, the need to defuse it. "Nualan women really are different, Moran. We have stone wombs. A radiation blast strong enough to kill me could not touch this child—or children. Stress would. So you have to get well soon; that is my major worry."

"Children? Plural?" His bewilderment was amusing, touching.

"Elana thinks she can hear two heartbeats. We are going to wait a time before we run tests." Moran sighed deep down in his chest, and Roe prayed for the thousandth time to be able to do something, anything, to shake the depression he was sinking into. Often he demanded to sleep at the mouth of the life shelter cave, on the walkway; and he lay awake nights, watching the stars. What did he feel then? Anger? Hopelessness? He had not planned to join them so soon— and in such a way.

An unusual vibration passed through Roe, and realizing what it was, she moved closer to him, seizing his hand and pressing it against her stomach to feel the child's movement. Moran's puzzlement turned to wonder, his deep blue eyes devouring her smiling face as if he could not look at her enough. She lowered her head, her lips brushing the crook of his elbow. Roe could feel his body temperature rise in response to her action and was irritated that months of separation lay between them. She was beginning to show a great deal more than the others as far long as she; by the time he was healed, she would be spending a large portion of the day confined to bed.

"I'm worried about the baby—babies—because, what with the radiation fallout, I've been afraid that I might be ... sterile now." So—at the roots all men feared the same things.

"Highly unlikely. And you are certainly not impotent." Roe grinned wickedly at his mirthless smile. "Do not let it eat away at your mind; that is the danger. It could destroy you." She traced with her lips the muscles of his upper arm and shoulder, pausing at his throat. He bent down and sought her face. She gave into the embrace, pushing thoughts of his condition out of her mind, enjoying something they both had been deprived of too long.

A keen wind knifed through them, and Ronuviel shivered, wrapping her arms around his body.

Moran managed a slight chuckle. "Do you think you can protect me from the elements?" He slowly folded his arms, pulling her close. "Go ahead and try."

"There will be hard frost by morning," she answered. "Snow by the Feast of Souls."

"Another day of rites," Moran mused, "without a temple. Where will they meet?"

"Soon we will be using the great cavern. I just hope we are inside the mountains before the winter strikes. It is not so long, but it is bitter and deep." Roe watched the star creep toward the floating horizon, trying to allow the silva's song to lull her. "Moran," she whispered suddenly, "what is to become of everything?"

Moran did not answer. But he felt her fear, a rare thing in Roe. His arms tightened around her.

CHAPTER ELEVEN

MT. AMURA,   FIFTEENDAY   VESPERS
THE CAVERNS

Smoke, smoke everywhere, rising to the ceiling, and a riot of noise. Teloa carefully picked her way across the cavern floor, avoiding milling adults and racing children. She had lost the dog, Zair, in the crowd. Praise the powers that food was now distributed by tribes—today was calm compared to just after the bombing. Spotting the Atare fire pit, she shifted the cooking pot she clutched in her arms and started in that direction.

A blow behind her knees caused her to stumble, dropping the metal pot with a crash. As Tay turned to see what had happened, a blur of child whisked by, snatching the kettle.

Teloa's arm snaked out, seizing the thief's ankle. "Hold it right there! What do you think you're doing? That pot belongs to my fire group!" she exclaimed indignantly, standing once again. "And that knee trick hurts!" Downcast, the boy did not struggle, and his mother descended upon them, grabbing her son and beginning to apologize.

Suddenly the woman and boy were shoved aside, and a huge form seized Teloa's arm in a bruising grip. Flinching, she pulled back, and the man dealt her a stunning blow to the side of the head. "Bitch! What do you mean, taking food from my son's mouth? You do not belong here; you are off-world, *entiss*, unwanted," the man began to scream, shaking her vigorously as he did so.

Teloa was seeing sparks. She was vaguely aware of the crowd pushing near—some attempting to help her, others trying to aid him. "We will waste no food on murdering Axis warriors, and I shall remove one problem—" and then the scream was of pain as Zair slashed into her attacker.

Two men jumped the hysterical Nualan, and Braan was there, a death grip on the man's wrist, forcing him to release Tay's arm. A healer stepped up with a sedative, assisting the citizens in removing the crazed man. Kalith and Kavan restrained Zair and recaptured the tiny akemmi, depositing it in Tay's hood. Teloa sank to her knees during the spectacle, not fully cognizant of Braan's arm encircling her waist and hauling her up, guiding her to the Atare family fire pit. She was in a dream state, huddled in a crevice, hot saffra being forced down her throat. Among a thousand words and encouragements from Atare relatives both distant and throne-line, Braan's calm, solitary comment stood out. "I asked you to stay with me."

The only other thing Teloa remembered from the meal was watching Braan and his son Dylan. Other family members would seek their ruler's attention, but thirdmeal was clearly Dylan's time. This night there was an edge of excitement to the boy's voice as he related the day's activities, and Teloa heard several whispers indicating the family's pleasure that the boy was snapping out of his depression. She knew he had not forgiven himself for Asiai's disappearance. Tay sank into forgetfulness, her last view of Dylan's shining face.

She awoke with the dying rays of Kee reflecting off her knees. Sitting up, she found Dylan was next to her, hovering near the akemmi. Smiling faintly at him, Tay rearránged herself and offered an arm to the animal. The creature scampered up her sleeve and perched on her shoulder. Dylan pulled out a few nuts and offered one to the beast. Chirping in delight, the creature warily took one from him.

"You are a charmer," Tay murmured, testing the lump behind her ear with her fingers.

"I wish one would stay with me." Dylan sighed. "I have been trying to get her to take that nut since you fell asleep. Do you feel better?"

"Just tired. I will sleep well."

Dylan looked uncomfortable. "The man lost much family—he has been crazed in his grief for days on end. His wife wishes to speak with you tomorrow, when you feel better. She is very embarrassed."

"No permanent harm, I hope. Of course."

The boy nodded, looking pleased with his arrangements. Zair lay beside him; he gave the dog a hug and firmly pushed the beast down when it tried to follow. "Stay with Teloa."

"Tay," she prompted.

He nodded, smiling. "I have to go to bed. I will see you later."

As he started to leave, Tay said, "Dylan, don't worry about Asiai. The ships achieved orbit, and the Nualans off-world will find her and take care of her. Believe it." He just stared sadly at her, and then walked off.

"Poor child, his childhood is over," she said aloud. Shivering at the thought of thirdmeal, she was glad that she had logically traced it out. The man was not angry at her—only at what he believed she represented. It was some consolation, if brief.

The voices in the cavern had grown louder. Almost everyone was gone, hidden from sight beyond the deep recesses of the garedoc, the great cavern, and preparing for sleep. Only the Atare family gathered near, talking quietly among themselves. Arrez was also there, and the surviving synod elders were trickling in. Braan stood alone by the pit, his face and chain of office dazzling in the light, his dark clothes muted against the walls. He did not look quite as grim as he had earlier, she thought; sharing the meal with Dylan had calmed him. Tay had been horribly afraid that the boy would remind him so keenly of Enid and of his missing daughter, Asiai, that he could not tolerate the child's presence. But Braan was making a great effort, and each day seemed easier. She stood, pulling her recorder from under her poncho, and moved to the fire coals. She suspected that Braan merely had given her something to do, but she was thankful for it. It would help her concentrate on the foreign language.

"Brethren, cease thy speech!" It was an older woman who spoke, her poncho design marking her an Atare, not a synod elder. "We have been called for consultation and decision. Let us hear our Atare."

"We have been called" came the answer, almost in unison, confirming Tay's suspicion that the formal words were ceremonial.

Braan stepped back into the fire's glare, fully visible to the whole assembly. Teloa saw that there were more present than she had expected; the house of Atare must have been great to lose so many and yet be so represented. The Atare paused, as if measuring his words.

Then he began to speak. He was not gentle; his tone told Teloa that much. From what she could understand, Braan was saying that they would begin to build within the mountain immediately and would abandon Amura for the duration of the battle emergency. Low speech broke out among the gathering, especially at the words *a siege of generations*.

Ronuviel rose to address the gathering. "The Atare alludes to the last time a maximum offense against the Axis occurred, in the Helix quadrant. It took the Axis sixty-three terrayear to regain its lost colonies. I, for one, do not intend to spend that time living out of a sack, and Amura will be uninhabitable for several years, unless we devise a massive water purification system. We have been tapping the stellar communications scans. We are now deep in Fewha territory." No one chose to comment on this statement.

"Regäree?"

"Speak, friend."

Jaacav rose from her seat on the rocks. Her speech was much swifter than Roe's, and Teloa knew that the tape dots would take a long time to translate. The thrust of the warrior's words concerned their time buffer. The Fewha's spearhead into the outer line had been so great, it might take them as long as twoyear to return to the Nualan System. It was necessary to use that time to guard against invasion by gold pirates or "a zealous Axis force, demanding that we explain our overelaborate defense system."

Teloa found herself sorting out the Nualan words of Jaac's comments; those words hinting around the Axis response. She glanced over at Roe—the Ragäree also looked thoughtful. How was the Nualan defense being interpreted?

"Our main priority is food," Braan continued, regaining leadership of the discussion. "Growing it, storing it, distributing it. We shall not be hungry this winter. That does not mean we can feast, nor does it imply that next year is guaranteed. We must return to the soil and traditional planting methods. Lars sends word that while not impossible, things shall be very difficult for a time."

"A comment." It was Jaac once again.

"Speak."

"For some time the Nualan defense has been attempting to develop a planet-wide shield that could destroy a lesser attack and continue to defuse a luna bomb barrage. As a matter of record, you will find south of Amura numerous growing fields unmarked by bomb craters. These areas were protected by the new test shield, totally forgotten by everyone during the excitement of the devastation. The new shield has its faults—it cannot stop incoming ships, whether they are constructed like Nualan vessels or are general carriers. But it will severely damage even a captured Nualan transport. As always, the radiation will protect us from any other intruders. It has the advantage of being geographically controlled. We can deactivate one beam to allow allies to land, yet continue the protection of the planet as a whole. An active scansearch will be maintained to warn us of the smallest ship's entry into our upper atmosphere. We hope to construct enough power stations to implement this planetwide by the thaw." Teloa felt rather than heard the buzz that answered this; the words were too swift for her to catch. Jaac evidently was finished; she settled herself as if she did not intend to rise again. Braan now spoke, assuring the elders that warriors were monitoring the emotions of their people and that the *guaard* was being replenished by its standby legion.

The last note was directed to an elderly man who had an air of importance. It meant nothing to Tay but apparently answered an earlier question. The elder seemed satisfied in an impersonal way. Tay caught herself picking out *guaard*, all standing near throne-line Atares.

Ronuviel stood up and moved to Braan's side, and the audience immediately gave her their full attention, the undercurrent of whispers concerned with her supposed pregnancy. Their relief and pleasure over her condition was evident.

She is not only Atare, she is Nuala, Tay thought. And they would not want it any other way. She did not fail to notice that Roe did not have to ask for the chair's recognition to speak.

"I am sure many of you can see where these plans are leading, this threefold concern over our defense, our food, and a roof over our heads," Roe started to sum up. "We strive for self-sufficiency, total planet autonomy." Before the crowd could react, she went on. "Before the starships reached for space, all planets were self-sufficient. We can be again. Anything this planet cannot provide us with, we can and shall do without. We do this . . . " She had to raise her voice; many individuals were clearly worried by her inference. "We do this to prepare ourselves for the long siege, to prevent a total collapse of our economy and to give us an excellent bargaining position for reentering the Axis Republican Council. The Axis ignored our mutual treaty obligations and, as well as we can determine, seeks to place the blame on Nuala. Returning to the status quo will be as painful as the next twoyear promises to be."

As the silence dissolved into an undercurrent of words the new head of the synod, Justinian, stood up.

Braan held up his hands, asking for silence. "Our next order of business is more disturbing. I have shown Justinian all of the taped information Ronuviel and I brought back from Tolis, aided by supporting tracts from Amura's transaction computer. He will now relate his conclusions and the voice of his subcommittee."

Justinian stepped forward. Tay studied the elderly man with interest. It was he who had been concerned about the number of the *guaard*, the Atare family's private bodyguard service, as Tay understood it. Justinian and his wife, Url, easily in their eighties, were among the most influential of the synod elders. They were also the most neutral, despite their high placement in the Dielaan house.

The Caprican woman appreciated Braan's shrewdness. Although the majority of the synod supported him without hesitation, there were still enemies: enemies of the house of Atare; personal enemies of Braan's. Anything Braan said to the assembly might be twisted by them. But Justinian was truly independent, as likely to support the throne as to attack it, and was half of the only unbiased pair present. He was the perfect choice to explain about Tolis—and Corymb.

Though his voice was soft, Justinian showed that he was still a masterful speaker and debater. He spoke in detail concerning what the computer had shown and had aides hold up charts explaining how close they had come to absorption by their off-world investors. He indirectly praised Braan's nationalization of the mines and industries and the sending of an interstellar decree to that effect. The old Nualan skillfully reiterated the information about the assassin and then added the scene with the messenger, indicating that Corymb was quite alive and biding his time over his return. Tay let the recorder run; this was too important to risk missing a key concept by abridging as she copied.

Finally Justinian turned and gestured to Arrez, who stood and told the startling news of the presence of Cied in Amura, and of what appeared to be Baakche, the Dragoche himself, in conference with Corymb.

Silence hung in the cavern for a long time after Arrez finished. Even those Corymb supporters who had managed to explain away everything else had trouble with the last charge. The tribes had no use for the cities—this had been the case from before recorded interaction.

The tribes knew of Braan—but not Braan Atare. The difference was important. The Ciedärlien did not acknowledge the rule of Amura, and the point had not been pressed in a millennium. What did they want? Or what did Corymb promise them? And most importantly, how did he intend to deliver?

Braan finally stood up. "I did not request this presentation to set us at each other's throats or to plant doubts in our minds about each other's loyalty. The fact is, there is a hologram awaiting your perusal that was Baskh Atare's last recording. In it he expresses his belief that Corymb was attempting to supplant himself and Tal, setting Deveah on the throne; and that Corymb was aiding off-worlders in what could become a blockade of Nualan economic interests. We cannot make accusations on the basis of this information, but Justinian considered our current situation serious enough to bring this to the synod."

"Atare?" Old Justinian had risen once again.

"Speak."

"The crisis is this: Corymb may return to us a victim of circumstantial evidence; we may even find a blackmailer and slanderer in our ranks. We may also be readmitting a scorpion to our den. Things will be very hard and tense in the next sixhundred fortyeightday. Corymb's experience could be invaluable. He could also seek an opening and wreak havoc among us, destroying monarchy, temple, synod, and masses. A word from him could send sini and 80-20 relationships to fever pitches. My request is this; to those who have supported him in the past, think before backing his words. And those who have never listened, listen; and be not quick to condemn." He looked at Braan expectantly.

"That is all we have prepared," Braan said quietly. "Questions? Comments?" As both Arez and Justinian sat down, several questions were asked, and in them Tay sensed the deep danger they were approaching. The inquiries were specific, current—no one wanted to think too far ahead. And no one wanted to talk about Corymb or off-worlders. Braan dealt with their doubts easily, belaying his exhaustion, and soon the meeting was brought to a dignified end.

Braan turned to Teloa. "May I take the recorder tonight? I would like to go over the complete lecture with no editing or editorializing. It may be that what we think of as useless may in fact be the gold we seek." Tay was not sure she understood any of the cryptic remarks, but the request was clear. And she knew if her record was poor, he'd replace her, so the comment was not aimed specifically at her work. She mutely handed him the recorder.

Braan took it, critically eyeing the amount of tape dots used. "We are long-winded, are we not? A lot of work for you." He glanced up, his expression intense. He moved swiftly, but his touch was sure and gentle, checking the lump above her ear. "How is your head? Are you dizzy, nauseous?" She winced and slowly shook her head. His acceptance of her attitude was uncertain. "If you are sure. Sleep in tomorrow if you have a headache; do not worry about rising duties." Tay started to protest, fearful of others thinking that she'd received preferential treatment. Braan was gone, however, moving into the recesses of the cavern, indicating that the matter was closed.

"Atare!" He stopped and faced her again across a crevice. "Get some rest. If there was no time for a proper coronation, there is no time for a state funeral." He studied her impassively and then disappeared.

"Do not lose any sleep over it. When he drops, I shall just tuck him into bed for a few days." It was Ronuviel.

"And if he keeps staggering on?"

"I will slip him an air hypo when he least expects it," Roe went on reassuringly, forcing a smile.

"I wish I could read people like you all do. I feel . . . handicapped." Tay scarcely realized that she was saying it aloud.

"Relax into it sometime. You might be surprised at how easily you can do it. After all, Lyte and Moran are trained sensitives. And you feel things, Tay—without trying. Good night." Tay nodded at Ronuviel as the woman made her way toward the life shelter. Teloa looked out the portal, saw night deepening, and suddenly felt very tired.

CHAPTER TWELVE

Lyte heard footsteps on the ledge. *It's taken them longer to find me this time*, he thought. *I'm getting better at hiding.* As he had slowly healed, the restlessness took hold of him. He wandered, often sleeping on the life shelter walkway under the pulsing stars. That night he was hiding motionless in a deep, wide niche, accessible only by a ledge leading off the life shelter walkway. Shinar nearly swept by him in her haste to avoid the rising wind.

He was found. She half dragged a heavy quilt around the corner and dumped it next to him. Lyte, arrayed comfortably on his back and studying the stars, pretended to ignore her. Finally: "Can't a man find a little peace around here?"

"Not this way," she replied quickly. "I was sent to be sure your body had not fallen off a cliff and to wrap what was left of it in this." She plopped down beside him. "Are you sleeping here?"

"Have to. Those caves give me the crawlies. Too close, too stuffy. I like to see the night."

"The stars? You cannot see the night."

"I can." There was a pause and he chuckled. Her presence was gentle, lulling, and something began to relax within him that had been tight too long. They shared the moonrise, the trine brethren of Eros, Philios, and Agape rising above the dark, glittering expanse of the Sonoma range. A good healer, this woman-child. No one had to tell Lyte how ill he had been; he still tired suddenly, needing long periods of sleep. But his humor was rising once again, in the face of a strange phenomenon—a growing friendship with Shinar. They rarely played word games anymore. She had sat through too many painful nights with him for that barrier to remain. And the knowledge of that friendship disturbed Lyte. He had never had a woman as a friend; not without other considerations. And Shinar was Kalith of Atare's woman, whether they denied each other or no.

"Did you come to give me a work release?" Lyte asked without looking at her.

"No. I told you why I came."

"Then good night. I'm in a mean mood."

"I have been warned?"

"You have been warned," he continued soberly, shoving the new quilt under his back and shoulders. He was wearing the light, loose pants and long-sleeved shirt of a native, covered carelessly by a wool blanket. Fortunately the rocks slowed the wind. It was amazingly warm in his little shelter, and he had no intention of leaving it for a dark, cramped cave.

"How are the bones?" Shinar started.

Bones? The ones they had fused . . . the ribs and shoulder and—"No pain. I haven't tried any work yet, so I don't know what they can withstand. But if you'd arrange a work release . . ."

"Ha," Shinar answered, leaning over to rap professionally on his ribs for laser misses. "Soon."

As she leaned toward him a tiny shred of wind brought her fragrance to him—an odor of lemon and honey. Brisk, like a slap in the face, with the elusive, naturally feminine scent beneath it all. He reacted without thinking, whipping a strong arm across her back and lightly, teasingly, kissing her. She stiffened, and Lyte sensed her surprise and worry. *Damn, I am not an invalid*! But her response was too swift, not guarded, unexpected. It had never occurred to him to tease a friend, and yet, now he could force thought, and the only coherent one was that she was warmer than he'd expected, softer. Even as thought came he was gathering her in his arms, seeking her lips.

Lyte had always attempted to be a master in every skill he possessed, though he had long ago outgrown his purely mechanical interest in sex. There was no pleasure for him unless the woman was pleased, and so he had learned to please his women. And Shinar was no passive observer, despite her worried detachment. Her natural response was so achingly sweet that by the time Lyte could drag himself to cold-sober awareness, he was on his side and covering her throat with kisses.

He paused, and then icily, cautiously, drew away from her, shaken. "I'm sorry."

"I am not."

"I've never done that before, seriously. I don't know what . . ." He faded off as her words sunk in.

In the growing moonlight he saw her roll over on her right side, touching his shoulder carefully. "Are you nodding off?"

He felt himself ruffle. "No. It's not that again," he replied sharply, using the same emphasis he always did for his recurring exhaustion.

"Then . . . what?"

He stared at her, torn between rage and desire. "I do not molest children," he said stiffly, and flopped on his back.

"Come now, you are not still making that mistake?" she asked softly.

Lyte regarded her without comment. He had seen others' appreciative looks and had been inexplicably irritated by them. They weren't good enough for her. But he wasn't sure he was, either. Damn these Nualans and their crazy lives! But they were happy—only outside interference, such as between Kal and Shinar, caused trouble. "I do not resort to . . . rape . . . to satisfy my needs. I've never had to, and I refuse to believe I'm desperate enough to assault a friend."

"Rape is an act of violence, not of passion. Ask any human who has been attacked. How about mutual comfort instead?" There was a smile in her voice, but it was sad and a bit cynical, as if hiding the tears he had seen so many times in the last few days. He rolled back onto his side, propping up his head with his elbow, but he refused to lift his face to her.

"Look at me," she said seriously.

"No."

"Why?"

"Because I want you so badly, I'm shaking."

Shinar said nothing. She appeared to pause, as if weighing the alternatives, and then she carefully reached over with her free hand and loosened the tie holding his wrap shirt closed, skillfully brushing the stomach muscles. Lyte kept his voice very controlled. "Shinar, I've never allowed myself to get this tight around a woman unless I've been involved with her awhile. My—I can be very—We should wai—"

"I have also been called a demon." She pushed the shirt back, running her fingers through the hairs on his chest.

Lyte moved away from her, shaking out the huge down quilt and spreading it on the ground over his sleeping area. Shinar watched him go through his nightly routine, right down to stripping off the rest of his shirt. Then he dropped back to the blanket and met her gaze, actually more relaxed than before.

"Are you leaving?" he asked.

"Do you want me to?" she countered gently, her eyes not leaving his face.

Don't ask me that. Holy gods, his blood was starting to boil. Tempted by a child—no, not a child. Never make that mistake. Younger than you've fallen for but not a child. But what about Kal? Damn that Atare! Why didn't he tend to his own woman, so she would not—Lyte remembered his conversation with Roe. Was he being used? He studied the young woman's eyes. No. He did not understand what was happening, but he was not being used. Maybe she needed someone as much as he did. Lyte did not answer at first; he merely quietly surveyed the lovely way her soft native shirt and pants clung to her body, and then absently reached over to release the tie holding her top secure. It was hard to remain nonchalant at that sight, but somehow Lyte did. Shinar was impassive, waiting. Lyte felt the expectancy, the question in her mind as well.

Something was crawling around in the back of his mind, and he was ashamed to acknowledge it. "I've never shared love with a woman whom I knew was thinking about someone else," he suddenly blurted out. He kept his tone conversational, but he turned his face away from the light of the rising trine, aware that she could see as well as he.

"I doubt that you ever will," Shinar answered steadily.

Something in Lyte unwound, a wary tenseness he had not recognized. The Nualans were truthful; they did not lie. Is that how Arrez did it? Could he turn his mind on and off among four women? Lyte stopped thinking, stopped worrying, shaking his head ever so slightly. Then he slipped an arm around her ribs and drew her soft flesh to his.

So long . . . not really, but it seemed as if— Gods. He was lost in the moment, the pleasure, wasting no thought on the morrow. Whatever hesitation Shinar had over his physical strength quickly dissolved in his own attempts to increase their pleasure. They were so absorbed in one another that her soft laughter startled him.

She grabbed for her shirt and flicked it across his back. "How did we get out of these?" she gasped, the laughter shuddering through her.

Lyte chuckled and redoubled the flow of kisses and caresses across her full breasts. "Woman, some men are leg men, some neck men. I prefer breasts and had to reach them. Now please, continue whatever you were doing to my back." Still laughing, Shinar complied, her nails once again tracing an intricate pattern down his spine.

And they continued, until the heat was so overpowering that they could only tighten their grip upon one another and seek each other's mouths. Lyte had not expected them to come so close to reaching a peak together—not the first time. Nor had he expected the exhaustion to come afterward in such a rush. His whole body went limp so suddenly, his limbs so heavy, he thought he was blacking out. But no, it passed, and he slowly rolled over on one side to keep from crushing her, his arms reaching out in a warm and protective circle she snuggled into without hesitation.

"Are you all right?" she whispered, and he could feel

her guilt. He stirred slightly, his grip tightening, making no attempt to break their contact.

"I hope you're joking," he answered sleepily. "I may never let you go."

———————

Lyte awoke in a daze, not sure if it was still night or if morning had come. The added warmth so close to him was not startling; the thick, honey hair was. He looked down at the young woman sprawled across his chest and gently raised a hand to smooth her hair. He was having trouble controlling and directing his thoughts, especially about Shinar, and hoped that his restlessness would not wake her.

"What the hell are you doing?" he said aloud, and quickly glanced to see if she was disturbed. What was he going to do about this? He was not a one-woman man—never had been. But there was something special about her, something he couldn't quite place.

She loved Kalith. Yet she had been with him last night, no other. How could you love two people at once? Lyte had never believed it possible. Was it because they both needed someone who cared, and this was just the way it had worked out? Kal had seemed so preoccupied lately.

"Blasted Atare, if I were him, I'd kill me," he muttered. Good luck if you try, fool. You drove her to me . . . keeping her at arm's length, never allowing her to share your hopes and fears. "I'm no good for you, but I'm not sure he is, either." Why did Kal have to take the Atare duties, the traditions, so seriously?

Lyte gently drew away from her, pulling the blanket around her in a comfortable manner. Wait until morning, let it ride, see how she behaves. A stranger or lover? How could hands of healing and loving blend so perfectly; no pity on her part, no gratitude on his. Lords, she was beautiful!

Flopping on his stomach, the man set his head down on his hands, his eyes straying over the stone edge to the last sinking moon. "Mendulay, if you are a g— If you are God, straighten this out to the good of everyone involved, will you? I can't see my way through it." It was his last thought before his eyes closed.

MONTINCOL   SIXTEENDAY   PRIME

   Kee was pale as she rose above the mountain path,
crowded by clouds dark and heavy with the snow yet to come.
Corymb Dielaan rose to his feet and paced slowly before the
mouth of the cave, staring down into the valley separating
Montincol from Mt. Amura. A neutral place, the Dragoche
had requested. The chanting had gone on for hours, the silver
tenor of Baakche Dragoche rising above the rest. Suddenly,
silence. A young Cied, completely veiled in the beige, sand-
threaded robes so common to the desert people, appeared out
of the darkness. They spoke no words; Corymb followed the
Cied back into the meeting area.
   Cloaked warriors of the Ciedärlien stood beside every
seated member. It was impossible to tell by sight which were
male and which female; since a vow of celibacy was a prerequisite to serving as a Cied warrior, it did not matter. Corymb joined the circle, seating himself directly across from
Baakche, the Dragoche. The top portion of their veils, usually
covering their upper faces, were down. None of the chieftains
present dropped their lower scarves, however—that was a
privilege reserved only for intimate family. Genuar's deep-
set brown eyes were among the group. Baakche's heir studied
the Dielaan intently. Baakche was a mad one but would be
the high priest of his people until his death. Genuar, as the
Dragoche tribe war leader, was the actual leader of the Ciedärlien warriors. All the tribes, from high to low, deferred
to the Dragoche tribe. It was purely coincidental—was it?—
that the spiritual heir was also the war leader. The game
began.
   "It has been decided," Baakche intoned, not looking at
the Dielaan. "The brethren have gathered and have discussed
the proposal of Corymb Dielaan. It is agreed that for this
time we shall unite and aid Corymb Dielaan in his lawful
quest to regain the throne of his fathers." Baakche glanced
at Genuar as he spoke. The heir's eyes tightened, but he
remained impassive. There was dispute over the best way to
realize the Cied's ends—many chieftains were absent, refusing to recognize Corymb as the solution but unwilling to
vocally contend with their Dragoche. "In return," Baakche

continued, "we expect a reasonable share of the trine mines, the privilege of living among the cities if we choose, and supplies to aid the tribes destroyed by the alien rain—"

"Your pardon, Dragoche," Genuar interrupted. "There is some misunderstanding, Dielaan, about what it is you require of us. Do you wish us to sabotage their granaries? You have not spoken plainly to us. We would not wish to destroy their seed grain and so put all peoples on short rations."

"No, no—for right now you need only wait." Corymb seemed to consider the simplest way to explain his hopes. Baakche often could not remember much more than that from one day to the next. "The Fewha bombs destroyed most of the chemical and mechanical means the city dwellers used to produce their food. They have enough grain to survive this winter. During it they shall rebuild their cities, and hard work it shall be too. Long hours toward an undefined end. I am trusting that they shall tire of this and want answers."

"You expect rebellion?" Genuar went on. "A thousand years ago the city dwellers might have overthrown a kingdom with less provocation than the attack. It would seem that something has . . . matured? . . . in the character of your people. Their endurance under travail is astonishing."

"Not rebellion. The Atare family is old and rooted. It shall probably be necessary to remove, or detain, the members of the throne line long enough for me to gain a strong foothold among the synod members. It will not take much to convince the masses that we do not need the sinis, and I shall suggest to them that without a surplus of grain, even the 80s may endanger our survival. I shall sow just enough distrust to make them desire a strong leader with direction." Corymb looked distant as he spoke. "The Atares have had three thousand years to lead this planet to ruin. I shall bring our people to a new day."

"Our spies tell us that this Atare is loved. That emotion is stronger than deceit, Dielaan."

"You underestimate my skills as a politician, Genuar. First we watch and see what the Atares shall do. Perhaps they shall even appeal to you for the old knowledge. But *I* am the one who can bring it to Amura. I am the one who shall ultimately rule, I and my line. I am young yet, as Nualans live; I can wait."

Baakche seemed to awaken out of dreams. He touched his forehead and looked at Corymb. "Come, friend, let us break our morning bread." He stood slowly, tightly gripping the arm of Genuar and his chief of security, the assassin. The unknown Cied remained at Baakche's left as they walked out, the position of honor. Genuar excused himself, however, indicating that Corymb was invited and should follow. Corymb made a bow of equality to the seated council and then followed Baakche, looking unsure of how to broach his questions without Genuar's help.

Genuar remained standing until the sound of the passing could no longer be heard. Then he sat down again. "Hot saffra for all," he ordered.

A warrior vanished. The group of men and women sat in silence until several warriors returned with the liquids. Then the young Cied withdrew, leaving the tribal leaders and their advisers. Now the real council began.

"What make you of this, Genuar?" a woman asked, the pattern of the hem of her beige robe marking her a warrior leader of the Tazelle clan.

"I smell treachery. The question is, can it aid us?" Genuar answered, sipping the steaming drink cautiously.

"Then you suspect that he will betray us as the off-worlders betrayed us?" another warrior said.

No one spoke. Finally Genuar stirred. "I think," he started, "that Corymb does not yet know what he will do. He is angry—a great hatred consumes him for the Atares. When Tazelle scouts found him wandering and raving in the Ciedär, revenge was on his mind. Now I think it is in his heart."

"Shall we do as he asks?"

"Wait?" Genuar smiled. "Oh, yes, brethren, we shall wait . . . longer than he thinks. I would send out spies of our own; I do not trust his runners to give us full reports. Riam?" A young Cied stepped back into the chamber. "Tell the brethren what we have discovered about the Atares."

"There have been years of unrest within their walls, but the aliens silenced all dissention. The son who now rules is greatly loved, almost worshiped. The Ragäree is the first Atare-born healer in generations." A murmur broke out at this.

"A born healer," Genuar mused. "Think you the people will back them?"

"As long as logic dictates, and beyond. If this Dielaan removed them, however, caused an 'accident...'" The warrior hesitated.

"Chaos?" came a voice.

"Fear of it," Riam continued. "The younger siblings are honest but untried. I do not think they would have the strength to withstand a concerted attack by the Dielaan. He is old and crafty in the ways of persuasion." Genuar looked as if he were going to speak, but the young woman rushed on. "One other thing. She who is called Ragäree shall become one by spring's full flowering."

"An heir to Nuala..." There was an undercurrent of words whispered in the back, and it was as if a brisk wind had struck Genuar. No matter how often the tribes reiterated their independence, the age-old belief in the eternal power of the Ragäree remained. Perhaps the old prophecies were true. Had the time come to follow the house of Atare?

"What of his policies, this new Atare?" a tribesman said sharply.

Riam's eyes seemed to veil. "No one really knows. It has been five years since he addressed the synod. His wife was dying, his life in ruins. Before that time he was an avid supporter of both 80s and sinis, and as late as the day before the aliens rained upon us, he was dealing with the sinis of Tolis."

"Indirectly, then, a supporter of us." Genuar's vision seemed to drift momentarily. "Not without reason have we always dealt with Atare." He turned again to the Cied. "Did we send greetings to the Ragäree at her temple wedding?"

"It has not yet taken place."

"*Yet*? The Ragarr survives?"

"Yes, but he recovers slowly. The poisonous rain left him open to the planet."

Genuar paused and seemed to consider Riam's words. "A scroll should be left at their eternal flame," he said, think-

ing aloud, "giving greetings and honor to the Ragäree. Such
has it always been. But not this Atare—we shall wait and
see if they come to us, and how they shall bargain." He
scowled fiercely around the room. "I trust you will all keep
your people in order. We must regulate the tribes who refused
to treat with Dielaan . . . or those who pretend not to. Let the
word be spread; the power of Genuar is upon it. All who
bear the name and seal of Atare are under my protection until
I have said differently. And any Cied responsible for the death
of an Atare will answer directly to me."

"So we shall see what use Atare has for us?"

"What use he thinks he has," Genuar corrected. "We
shall see."

MT. AMURA,   TWENTYDAY   VESPERS
NUALA

Lyte watched the star set into embers, the sea turning
gray and chill. The water twinkled fitfully at him in the light
of the firstmoon, a strip of silver on the horizon and then
nothing but twilight. Calmed by the peaceful sight, he moved
to reenter the caverns. As he walked up the path to the mountain's mouth a rolling pebble startled him. Tensing, the commando whirled.

"I am no predator, Lyte."

Kalith. Damn. He did not need this, not now. The knot
began to tighten within him, as predictable as that starset.
"Are you sure?" Lyte returned lightly.

"Why would you fear me? I have no claws, and I am a
terrible infighter."

"You're an Atare," the off-worlder replied bluntly. "And
I have your woman."

"If I could acknowledge her as my woman, you would
not 'have' her," Kal answered.

His voice was so gentle that Lyte relaxed without realizing it. "Why?"

"I do not—"

"Why not acknowledge her?"

"You know our marriage laws for roya—"

"Damn the laws. She's as healthy as I am, and you may be an old man by the time the Axis 'liberates' this planet." Lyte was not sure which angered him most—Kal's reaction or his reasoning.

"Tradition changes slowly, Lyte. And royalty is not like any other job. It is the only position a human is born into— and one of the hardest to escape."

"Then why mope around in a dream, hardly talking to anyone?"

"What would you suggest I do?" The question was so cool, Lyte almost hit him. He started to shout a reply and caught himself. And then coldly began to think. A minute passed . . . two. Lyte still had not thought of anything Kal could do that would not draw criticism from at least one major political or cultural faction. He was a diplomat with no place to serve. "You see? It is not easy. And it affects me keenly, more so than Kavan, because what I decide affects Shinar as well as myself. Soon everyone will know how I feel about her. I cannot disguise it. But it cannot go any further until I determine my own course of action. Does that make sense?" Lyte did not answer. "So I thank you, warrior, for giving her what she needs, the love and security. What I cannot give her, not yet."

"You people have crazy laws," Lyte said flatly.

"Perhaps. But they have worked well for almost five thousandyear. If I toss them away, I must time it and justify it perfectly—or I will fail." The Atare youth's voice dropped noticeably in volume.

"So, married or not, we have one thing in common."

"More than one thing—how do *you* like being utterly useless?" Kal stressed his words skillfully and, without looking back, continued up the path. Lyte stared after him, digesting his hidden meanings.

CHAPTER THIRTEEN

MT. AMURA,   SIXTYDAY   LAUDS
NUALA   (MOONSET)

Braan hesitated at the partition. He knew it was traditional to be as noisy as possible when waking the members of the wedding party, but they had been up late, and Liel slept so soundly. Oh, why not? They could not complain; he was alone and had nothing to pound on. The marriage of Ronuviel and Moran deserved some boisterous celebration.

"Up! Everybody up in there, hurry, hurry, it is a bannsday! You have been chosen; now you are called! Awake!" There was no sound. The *guaard* before the door did not move. Then the temporary partition folded back, and Teloa stood there, eyeing him balefully, completely bundled in a blanket, her hair a wreath of light.

"I hope there is precedent for this," she began, her words dripping ice water.

"He is being nice, Tay" came a sleepy voice from the darkness within. "When Libra got married, I woke up to a twenty-piece band! Go away, Braan, we shall be there."

"We are meeting in the assembly room before we go to the garedoc. Arrez will have candle straws for you. Do not eat anything!" Braan added as a reminder. Teloa, still amazed over the twenty-piece band, closed the partition. Controlling his laughter, Braan slipped back up the passageway toward his room, his *guaard* a shadow at his back.

He was so involved in thoughts about the wedding that he nearly ran into Shinar as she staggered around a corner. The Atare took one look at her face and seized her arm. Looking wildly for the sanitation room, he ripped open the partition and dragged her to a portable commode.

"Get a healer!" Braan yelled at the roommate who had been awakened by Shinar's movement. The women disappeared.

"Atare, I am sorry— you should not," Shinar gasped out between heaves.

"Be quiet and let your stomach settle," he replied, nodding to another bunk mate who had brought a blanket. With the *guaard*'s help the two of them managed to force Shinar flat on her back in the aisle. In a few moments the first roommate returned, Elana behind her. The doctor looked pale for early rising, Braan noticed, but she was not only the final medical authority, she was mother as well. Even with the young adults bunking together by age and sex until proper family units could be constructed, parental rights remained.

The healer checked her daughter's forehead as she pulled out her diagnostician's monitor. Shinar still perspired, her expression wide-eyed but otherwise alert.

"Just my stomach, nothing else," Shinar said, anticipating her mother's questions. Elana played with the dials on her tiny computer, her face betraying nothing. The roommates stood in the doorway, visibly worried.

"Congratulations, you are going to be a mother." The bunk mates responded with gasps of surprise and joy, even as puzzled expressions crossed their faces. "You two—I left the rest of my bag in the life shelter and I need my comp connector to punch in a milk requisition. Go!" The surprised young women took off down the corridor.

"Fortunate that you are billeted so far from other rooms," Braan observed dryly.

"Do you know the father?" Elana went on, lowering her voice despite the absence of Shinar's friends. "If so, he should know before the whole city does." Braan smiled faintly at Elana's consideration, as much as at Shinar's bewilderment.

It clearly had not occurred to the adolescent that she was pregnant. "And how long have you been throwing up in the morning?"

"Not—how far along?"

"Perhaps thirty, fiftyday. Normally we would not say anything yet, but it is bound to get around. Everything does these days."

"Lyte is the father." Shinar sat up slowly. "I am all right, just a little green. It passes quickly. I thought I was just excited about the wedding."

"It should pass in an eightday, if you are like I used to be. I rarely had discomfort after the first sixtyday, until right before the delivery. Atare, I—" Elana turned to Braan.

"I honor the confidence, and there is no problem," Braan said quickly.

Elana frowned slightly. "I hope no problem. . . . I, too, am with child. A full hundredday gone, though it does not show through the robe. And it has been difficult this time, harder. I do not know if the difficulty is the new radiation, stress, my age—" She brushed Shinar's hair out of her face. "We must monitor you carefully. I fear only . . . I fear what the radiation may have done to his genes."

———

It was not a scare tactic, Braan realized as he ducked under the drape and walked down the narrow, winding private aisle to his room. Elana did not tell Shinar about the genetic danger to frighten her— the doctor wished to share all the consequences with a fellow healer. And her daughter took it well, almost abstractly, Braan thought. He doubted that the realization that she was carrying a totally new life had truly hit her. Two more of the people, praise Mendulay! He quickly pulled on the traditional embroidered ivory shirt and black pants. Setting the chain of office around his neck, Braan grabbed his black cape and dashed back up the aisle toward the assembly.

Almost everyone was there; they all had a specific role to play. The bride and groom each had three attendants, and to be asked was a great honor. Braan knew that Jaacav and Liel would be two of Roe's companions and expected Liel to wear the flowers of the future candle, as the youngest woman usually did. But the color of Jaac's blossoms marked her as the past candle. Who—? He scanned the gathering, and his eye fell on Teloa, the orange petals of the present candle entwined in her hair. A feeling of surprise and pleasure washed over him, as well as a slight chastisement for being unobservant. He had come upon Roe and Teloa talking to each other many times—he had been unaware that they had grown so close. Many friendships had both blossomed and withered in the last sixtyday.

Lyte entered the room unobtrusively. Braan studied him as the red firerose buds were arranged down one of the man's shoulders. He looked very uncomfortable.

"You cannot mask before us anymore, can you?" Braan murmured. "The illness has weakened you."

"Atare?" a *guaard* warrior asked.

"Nothing." So Lyte was the past candle. His thoughts were interrupted by Elana, her lovely face beaming, bearing in her hand orange firerose blossoms. He realized that she was speaking to him, explaining that Shinar was to have been flower bearer but still felt unwell. Braan tried to give the scientist his full attention but knew he had failed when she gave his shoulder a gentle, reassuring squeeze in parting.

Interesting to see who was chosen for each candle. He remembered his own wedding . . . not painfully; too much had occurred to think of anything without allowing a proper perspective. Not fireroses. What had been in season during his ceremony? Moran entered the room and also Braan's thoughts. The Atare scrutinized his sister's chosen. Almost grim, too solemn for one so handsome. He had chosen to wear the traditional ivory pants and shirt of the groom. Braan refocused and noticed that Lyte wore a Nualan outfit identical to his own, except that he had on his formal military cape. What to do for Moran, what to do about Lyte? The blond warrior was paying a lot of attention to Teloa . . . Shinar and Lyte. The Atare hid a smile as Teloa laughingly avoided the second officer.

"Atare?" He turned slightly. Jared. In wedding attire, yellow fireroses of the future on his shoulder? He had been in the bed next to Moran's while they were in the life shelter.

What had gone on . . . ? Deveah's Jared. The one good thing Deveah did in his life, helping to bring that boy into existence.

"Jared. You look much better than you did."

"Yes, Atare. Thank you." Jared flushed a bit, both confused and embarrassed. "The high priest asked me to give you this." The boy handed him the stiff, woven, tapered straws he was to use to light his candle.

A murmur at the door captured their attention. Standing, Braan was able to see the entrance of Ronuviel. They had found the family dress— he felt tears momentarily blind him, remembering the older sister who was the last one to wear that gown. A riot of ivory syluan, twinkling in the pre-dawn shadows. He knew he was stepping toward her, as the others did; to touch one with child who was to be wedded was a lucky thing. Moran had been warned and wisely held back. Braan found himself with a handful of hair and ivory lace. Roe suddenly whirled and embraced him.

"Lucky, indeed," she said, chuckling, meeting his glance. She quickly, gently touched the corner of his eye with her thumb, stealing the tear and— holding it to her lips, accepting the gift, be it joy or sorrow— she looked for Moran.

A great deal of pain seemed to fall visibly from the groom's shoulders. Lyte stood nearby, his face fluctuating between confusion and impassiveness. Now the group cleared the way, and Ronuviel walked up to Moran. She moved gracefully, considering her condition; she looked near her time, but of course, that was because it was twins. Roe extended her fist to Moran. Moran understood her gesture and cupped his hand. She hovered above it and set the Stone of the Seri in the center of his palm. Liel laughed out loud as Moran folded his fingers, and the spell was broken, everyone full of cheers, congratulations, and admonishments.

Ah, the stones. Dug out of the ground in their final faceted form except for polishing, they were an old tradition. A Ragäree of ancient times had begun the practice, giving one to her lover off-world so that when he arrived on Nuala without her, none would mistake who he was. They were still called serae stone. Their color was a deep burgundy wine, and they were as hard as diamonds. He had given Enid one.

Normally Roe would have surprised Moran with it before the ceremony, but as always now, there had been no time.

"Atare, will you please?" Arrez indicated that he should take his place in the procession. Braan stepped up next to Teloa, the proper distance behind Lyte, and took the woman's elbow. She flushed crimson under her acquired tan.

"Do not worry, we shall keep you from making mistakes. Arrez explained it all to you, did he not?" Braan whispered, allowing her to take his arm. She nodded quickly. The line began to move.

Lyte and Jaacav led into the garedoc, packed to capacity with Nualans both Amuran and outlander. A carillon announced the hour of prime. Every single person held a candle except the wedding party. The blaze of light within the cavern was still greater than the dawning. Tay released Braan's arm as she went to stand next to Jaac on the opposite side of the altar. Liel was the third of the trio, so different; the sensual, cynical look of Jaac as she eyed Lyte, who was across from her; Tay's hesitant joy; Liel's exuberant glow. Braan wondered if he, Lyte, and the boy contrasted as much.

Moran and Ronuviel were last in, the wandering melody of a gattar covering the soft undercurrent of the gathering's pleasure. It was a good idea, this wedding, Braan thought briefly, not sure that he should have dismissed the idea of a coronation. Then he was lost in the opening words of the ceremony.

"We gather, Brethren, at the dawning of a new day, to witness an occasion as old as mankind and as young as morning. We come together to join in the eternal mystery and gift of our Lord High Mendulay— that joy of two who become one and yet remain two," Arrez began. "I offer to you now Ronuviel and Moran. This woman and this man wish to enrich their separate existence by sharing a life and by bringing new life to our people. I ask you now— be witnesses."

"We are witnesses," the crowd responded.

"You stand before us, man and woman, bringing with you past and present, facing the future yet to come. You each bring three persons, representing your lives and our ancient godhead," Arrez said directly to the pair. "Behold the first of the four great elements: fire. It purifies and purges body

and soul; it lights and warms our being; it represents Mendulay within our hearts. Come." The priest turned and walked
to the eternal flame, which stood to one side of the altar.
Lighting a woven taper, he carried the tiny flame to the great,
dark, bowl-shaped fire basin and ignited the wood within
with a touch. There was a pause as they waited for the fire
to settle into steady flame. Then Ronuviel stretched out a
hand to Moran, and they stood facing one another across the
fire basin. Braan knew it was not purely for decoration that
the sleeves of the wedding gown and shirt were slit, baring
the lower arm when it was bent.

Now the light-bearers' role came into play. Braan studied
the concentration in Lyte's face, wondering if the man was
trying to translate each phrase or if he waited for Jaac's
movement to signal his own. Arrez was pronouncing the ode
to the past life, Roe and Moran repeating it. When they
finished speaking, Lyte and Jaac both moved to the eternal
flame, separately lighting their woven plaits and going to the
altar. Seven candles were set up upon it in an inverted *V* tier.
Silently the two lit the candles at each end.

When they returned to their places, Arrez began the
speech of the present, short and direct, the repeated last words
signaling Braan's movement: "All that I have been, all that
I am, and all that I shall be, Mendulay willing, I shall share
with you." Braan nodded fractionally to Tay, and they stepped
out to light their straws. Liel and Jared followed them a few
moments later, and when Braan finally ceased to study the
firelight reflecting from Tay's hair, he realized that the elemental ceremony was continuing. Arrez was done with the
discussion of air, the mighty wind of the spirit, and had moved
on to soil, the source of all nourishment. Braan watched as
the high priest sprinkled the symbolic dirt over their clasped
hands and into the fire pit, ritually purifying it. Now water
was poured over the couple's hands, steam rising into the
heights of the cavern. Braan knew from experience that their
arms were far enough above the basin to avoid the heat and
boiling steam, but it looked dangerously convincing.

The elemental offerings were through. Arrez had silently, reverently set the most ancient symbols of union and
sacrifice, both essential in a marriage, before the eternal flame.

No words — the wheat and wine needed none. Then, releasing one hand, the couple walked to face the altar. Taking up the prepared woven plaits that were lying on the block, they each set the tip in their three candles, lit by those individuals closest to them. Together they lit the center candle. The company awaited the final words. Moran and Ronuviel turned back to face Arrez and the people. The priest raised his hands in blessing.

"Know that these words are among the most powerful in our language, and that they are spoken in the love of our Holy Mendulay. They bind in this world and all worlds, this life and all lives. It is finished and it is begun. All people are one people; all times timeless; all loves one love; all gods one God. You are One." And when Arrez had spoken the last short sentence, *A-tu Gare*, a deafening roar broke out. Lyte and Tay were both startled, but Roe had spoken to Moran; they raised their clasped hands in a show of triumph as the assembly, as one, extinguished their candles and poured out to greet the dawn.

MT. AMURA   TIERCE

The normal wedding ritual called for a rest day full of feasting, games, and song. Fortunately the weather cooperated and though cold, it was not unpleasant. The elders sat around fire pits with wineglasses in hand, talking about the things that had remained since time immemorial — the children, the neighbors, the harvest, the wedding. Sometimes new topics slipped in, such as the construction of the new city: Nuamura, as they were now saying it. The children chased and hid and teased, and although there was not food in plenty, the cake was the best in anyone's memory. Musicians played a succession of lively tunes, the flat field at the bottom of Mt. Amura's foothills becoming a massive dance floor. And Ronuviel told a new story.

Braan sat as entranced as any of them, listening to the tale unfold in his mind. He could see it now: the blazing ships, the fierce battle, the brilliant deception to get on board a pirate vessel. Roe told it better than Baskh had, and Baskh had been the one to live it. The new Atare occasionally tore himself away from his sister's words to study the faces of his people. They were enchanted, engrossed— some shed a few tears. Time heals wounds and fades memories, Braan thought. Even those who had chafed under Baskh Atare's rule were involved in the story. Of course, it was about something that had happened long ago, before Baskh ruled. The crushing of the pirate gold trade by a clever ruse—

A hand touched his arm. Braan glanced around.

It was Kavan. "I think you had better come."

Caught by this intriguing message, Braan stood and followed him. The young man threaded his way back through the crowd, finally ending up at the hill where Arrez had decreed that the eternal flame would stand, its socket sheltered in a shrine of piled rock. On the altarpiece before it lay a scroll. Braan reached over and picked it up.

A real scroll, made of feathered, scraped tazelle hide. It bore the black-and-gold tassel of the Dragoche clan. Braan slid off the band and slowly unrolled the message.

"Can you understand it?" Kavan asked.

Braan read the epistle twice, to try to glean every possible meaning from the statement. Then he rolled it shut. "It is basically a message of greeting to the Ragäree on her wedding day," Braan said slowly. He started walking back to the crowd. "Wishing her and her child health and long life. They are waiting. And they have some connection with Corymb."

"How so?"

"The Cied place these to be found. True, I had no coronation, but we never came across one acknowledging me as Amura's new ruler. They do not; they wait to see who shall come out on top. I wonder how long they have been dealing with Corymb. . . ." Braan stopped talking and looked at Kavan. "I think we are about to enter into a war of nerves. See if you can slap Kalith out of his solitude. If you think I can help, find me. Use Shinar. The next twohundredday will tell if our house is to survive. Corymb is coming back— soon."

"Another thing; a ship comes. From the north, the sky-watcher says," Kavan added, his face now creased with worry.

Braan gripped his shoulder, not sure if he wished to strengthen his little brother or draw strength from him. "It is long overdue. Have them bring any messages to my quarters. I need some time alone. And . . . if you get around to it, some of the spice cake, when Roe and Moran cut it." Braan managed a faint smile, Kavan returning it.

NONE

It was out of a sound sleep that Braan awoke. Someone was pounding on the metal family seal Kavan had hung next to the private corridor entrance. In the distance he heard the lulling sound of the gathering. Braan sat up, steadying himself against dizziness. He had not realized that he was so tired.

The *Nova* had brought mostly good news. Every 3AV tape showed the Nualans entrenching themselves for winter, storing up food and clothing. Some cities were in better shape than others, and the throne was being asked to negotiate the trade of goods among them. Words came from the border cities— the Cied had suffered during the attack, even with the protection of the shield. There were no bomb shelters in the Ciedär. So far, offers of help from the coast were being refused. The strongest people of the hot city had survived, Gid reported and were rebuilding their homes above ground and below. More news: Tinyan was pregnant, and there was a possibility the child was his. Braan's fingers tightened in his blanket at the thought. Gid would return to Amura, but first there was work to be done in Tolis.

"Great joy and long life, Gid," Braan said aloud, contemplating the responsibility of another child. Asiai . . . He fingered the 3AVs and the Cied scroll, aware that he would have to call a synod meeting the next day.

"Atare! Come quickly!" The voice was urgent. Braan dropped the 3AVs and rushed down the corridor toward the west entrance. It took but a few moments to reach the outside, and when Braan did, he was not really surprised by what he saw.

Standing on the footpath leading into the mountain, surrounded by family, hangers-on, and admirers, was Corymb.

Braan saw that Arrez was also there; he was standing on the outer fringes of the crowd. The priest looked annoyed, an unnatural, impassive expression on his face. Acutely aware of the *guaard* behind him, the Atare drew close enough to hear Dielaan's voice.

"I have heard much of this. I am very concerned about the seed shortage— building within the mountain, you say? I wonder how it will hold up during quakes?"

"There is no seed shortage," Arrez said curtly but pleasantly.

Corymb turned a mild set of black eyes to the high priest. "Oh? Perhaps I was misinformed. I was told our chemicals are gone; that does tend to make many of our farming skills useless. No shortage yet, but that does not mean no problems next fall." The edge of authority in Corymb's voice vanished. He smiled, extending his arms as if to embrace the crowd. "Come, friends— we have returned in time for the wedding feast of our Ragäree. I must pay my respects. I would have come to you sooner, but I did not think I was so important to the people's welfare that it was necessary for me to report in. And my sister's daughter, Odelle, has been ill. Please have her husband take her to the healers immediately, so she may be diagnosed." The note of concern in Corymb's voice appeared to be genuine. And why not? Odelle was the youngest of five children, none of them boys. And the other four had either died in adolescence or were dead from the bombing, Braan seeing no sign of them in the gathering. This frail, black-eyed young woman was just another power pawn. If she did not bear a healthy son and daughter, able to carry on the Dielaan title, it passed to another branch of the family. Only one generation without male issue was allowed. It would be Justinian and Url's branch. Corymb would kill to prevent the title from changing hands; of that Braan was certain. Kill how many? For the second time that day Braan found himself thinking of Corymb and the Cied. Was it coincidence that Corymb missed the temple services on the day the bombs fell?

By now the delighted crowd had noticed Braan, and they parted like grass in the wind, clearing a path for their Atare.

Corymb straightened at the sight of him, his response a nod. "Atare."

"Corymb Dielaan."

"Greetings to you, and eternal peace upon your predecessor."

"Little enough did he find while living," Braan remarked. "We have a council tomorrow, to deal with the news from the north. The computer in the back of the first level holds transcripts of what you have missed, both discussion and vote. I think you will find them interesting." Braan slipped his hands in his pockets, clutching the hard, metallic object he had carried since he had taken it from the Durite's body.

"Thank you for your words, Atare," Corymb answered, nodding and gesturing as Arrez stepped to his side. "I am glad to see that we understand each other's priorities and thoughts. Other than my dear Odelle's condition, my people's situation is foremost in my mind."

Simple words. To repeat them later was to wonder that they once held power. "I understand, Corymb. Most assuredly I understand." With that Braan removed the metal marker from his pocket and pressed it into Corymb's hand, the Durite thong still attached to it. The Dielaan glanced down at the unfinished piece of trine gold, even as Braan turned and walked away. Only Arrez saw the older man's face become momentarily rigid before he slipped on a mask of puzzlement, looking oddly after his Atare.

"Shall we go to the Ragäree, Corymb?" Arrez asked, gesturing with his hand. Smiling demurely, Corymb led the way as if he had trod it all his life.

Braan fought to control himself as he rushed back to finish the 3AVs, wondering cynically how Ronuviel would receive Corymb. In his hurry he almost ran down Teloa, who had been watching the arrival from the obscurity of the cavern's mouth.

"How— how could you even look at that man!" she whispered, staring after Corymb.

"I am sorry, that is twice today I nearly—" Braan stopped when her words registered. He studied the woman, blazing in her fury for the insult given to the throne and to him, and then he laughed. Tay was startled out of her anger and whirled toward him. Braan seized her hand and bowed to press it to his lips.

"Atare?"

"Teloa, did I forget to tell you how beautiful you look and how well you assisted in the wedding? It was a delight to pair with you." He straightened and met her eyes. "I thank you for your concern and request that you continue with those pointed questions. They keep me thinking; with Gid gone, Roe and Arrez alone do that for me, and both are increasingly occupied with other demands. Only you seem to have the nerve to—"

"Atare, I—"

"I insist!" Braan rolled on, ignoring her flaming cheeks. "You see us as an off-worlder, even as you become more Nualan. It is an important duality. And if you fear to jump in, you are welcome to ask permission first! Duty calls me, lady. I must finish those 3AVs, and then I shall send them to you. We shall need a synopsis by tierce tomorrow; things will start early, I am afraid." Not waiting for her response, Braan quickly entered the caverns. He paused inside to let his heart-beat slow, amazed at his response. Troubled dreams, and Teloa had been in them . . . not as a simple scripter. Shaking his head to clear it of such thoughts, Braan returned to his room.

THE GATHERING   COMPLINE

Lyte's head was simply too full of wine. He looked for, and found, a rock more sheltered than most and slid down beside it. That was a mistake; if he didn't end up falling asleep, it would be a miracle. Clutching the mug of hot saffra he'd been carrying, he took a careful sip. Too bad it wasn't coffee; he could use some caffeine.

"There you are!" Lyte was startled but fortunately did not dump the drink all over himself. Shinar—where had she been all day? He had actually taken time out of his wanderings to seek her, something he rarely did. Usually his women sought him. Maybe with Kal. If that man didn't shape up soon, blast him; Shinar needed him. "You look preoccupied. Shall I come back?" the woman went on, hesitating to sit.

"No, no, I was looking for you earlier."

"Uh-huh. Try again."

Lyte looked annoyed. "Stop sounding like Moran. You'd know if I lied, wouldn't you? Yes, I spent a large portion of the day admiring several ladies, and some of them reciprocated. Just for the records, I also like intelligent, beautiful company as an alternative—" He stopped when he saw her smile. *Lords, I'm losing my sense of humor.* It bothered him when he knew he was telling the truth.

"I am sorry. I shall not say it again, not even teasing." She settled down next to him, both careless and confident of their relationship, Lyte slipping an arm around her. Snuggling into their woolen ponchos, thankful for the warmth, they watched the stars begin to pop out.

"Good thing this is what Roe calls south. I'd hate for it to be any colder," Lyte said. "I get frostbite when my liquor's iced."

Shinar hugged him. "Up around Atare city the snow is very deep this time of winter. Tolis also should have snow. I hope they are protected from the weather."

"Are you feeling better?" He looked down at her as she twisted slightly in his arms to see his face.

"What made you say that?"

"I heard you were ill this morning."

It was dark behind the rock; she could not see his face, but his voice was concerned. She relaxed— her friends had respected her right to tell him before any others. "It passes. It is not really illness."

"How can you have a hangover before the party?"

Shinar laughed. "It is because I am pregnant. It will go on for a while."

"You're pregnant?" He sounded puzzled, not surprised. "You should have said something, we could have, well . . . for your comfort—"

"I just found out." Shinar suddenly realized that Lyte had made no connection.

"I didn't think that could be kept a secret from the mother," Lyte was continuing.

"Or the father. It is ours, Lyte. It is barely fiftyday along. I am not even positive I have felt it move yet; it may be my imagination." She paused, remembering that he was off-world, knowing that they handled these things differently. She was not prepared for the reaction.

Lyte literally went rigid, as if he were afraid to move. There was no sound for a moment. "Ours?" A whisper, the question incredulous.

"You understand what this means, do you not?"

"Roe . . . mentioned your customs—"

"But do you remember?" Shinar insisted, turning to face him. "It is, 'Oh, that is great, another little person; be sure to get more rest, drink plenty of fluids, and take your vitamins,' and that is it for now. Do you see? No more, no less." The young woman did not know what else to say. Lyte had not relaxed in the slightest. He was clearly cold sober, though.

Lyte set down his mug, aware that he had begun to shake. Too much wine, way too much wine. *No, you heard correctly, a child. Ours, mine. Lords, what have I done?* He shifted, the firelight silhouetting him, staring out into darkness.

"Of course, that does not mean I can carry it to term. The extra radiation has caused many to lose babies or not conceive at all." She gripped his shoulder. "You do not like children."

"No, it's not—" He lowered his head to hide his confusion. He did not want ties here. What had he done? How could he leave, should he take her, would she go? She loved another man! She also loved him, "differently."

"Lyte, you do not have to marry me. Or support the child financially. Or include it in a will, even! You have given it life. The only other thing you owe it is love and consideration."

"I think the other would be easier." He turned back to her. "Shinar, I am hoping to leave this planet as soon as possible. I don't belong here, and I am not totally convinced Moran belongs here! This is not fair to you, or it, or—"

"How?" she said bluntly.

"What?"

"How do you intend to get off Nuala?"

Lyte paused. "A ship—"

"What ship? Where? Except for the three that had skeleton crews on board, none escaped the bombing. Do you think precious metals will be used to build star transports when we are simply struggling to survive? Be realistic. Only Nualan ships pass the barrier. Even if the *Griffon* and the others made it to free space, to return through enemy lines to Nuala and then return again to the Axis? Even I can tell a better fantasy!"

"Shinar, I—" Lyte's voice had changed subtly.

"All that is required of you is a little emotional support for me and a little affection for the child when it is born. Do not tell me you are incapable of giving it. Unwilling, possibly; afraid, yes. Unable, not likely." She stopped, finished with her speech.

"Shinar, I can only try. . . ."

Something in his voice made her reach up and touch his face. She gasped in amazement to find tears— just tears, no catastrophic upheaval behind them. She pulled him close. "Lyte?"

"It's all right. I'm all right, it's just—" There was no easy way to explain his confusion. He carefully embraced her, suddenly fearful that he might hurt her.

"I will not break, silly."

"I am very . . . surprised," he said, his tone almost sheepish. "I guess I feel . . . old. It's hard to pretend to be a kid when you have one of your own." The last sentence was a whisper.

Shinar held him tightly, trying to comfort him, trying to understand his fear and confusion, which she felt as keenly as the cold. "Come on, it has been a long day. I need sleep!" She released him and pulled him to his feet, grabbing his mug as she did so. "You will feel more confident in the morning. All you *have* to do tonight is keep me warm, and if you cannot manage it, my bed has a nice comforter on it."

Lyte laughed weakly. "I've never spent the night with a woman in my arms without— Well, maybe I'd better learn." He faced her, trying to dredge up a smile. "I get cold sometimes too."

CHAPTER FOURTEEN

NUAMURA   ONEHUNDRED   TIERCE
FIELDS   EIGHTYDAY

Ronuviel heard the carillon chime four bells. Lord, only tierce— what with the heat, she felt as if it were mid-afternoon instead of mid-morning. The bitter cold of the short winter seemed far away. The Amurans had been up since lauds, working feverishly to finish the winter harvest before the monsoons hit. Roe opened her eyes to look toward old Amura and beyond, to the sea. It was dark, threatening. Rain was coming, long, hard rain; and after the rainfall ended, the spring planting would begin.

"Do you mind company?" She looked up. Moran stood next to her, stripped to his joqurs and glistening with sweat. She offered him her water gourd. "Thank you." He took a drink and then settled down under the towering bush for a rest. The eyes studying her were intense. "You have been healing again. You need to conserve your strength. How is Elana?"

"Better. I was able to ease the stress and control the alpha-wave pattern." She flexed her fingers, a faint glow briefly touching the tips.

"Why can you do that?" His voice was neutral, and her reply was a blank look.

Roe shifted her weight. "You have never asked me that before," she answered. "And it is usually the reason off-worlders do or do not talk to me." She studied her hands, wishing that she could use some of the energy to ease her own discomfort; she knew the effort would only tire her more. "We suspect that it is a modification of the sini gene. A mutation of the mutation, if you will. It is the same form of radiating heat, but instead of destroying the body and anything near it, it actually improves health. I do not feel like I really heal anything. It is like using a low-grade electrical charge to speed the recovery of a bone break, for instance." She looked distant. "It can be a burden too. I was always on the outside looking in while I was at Helix University. People envy it, resent it, fear it. Or put great demands upon my time and talents. I cannot work miracles, I cannot keep the dying alive. But people get strange ideas about what can and cannot be done. It does have one blessing attached, though."

"What is that?"

"Never has it been recorded that a family line has had a sini appear once a healer has been born. That is comforting. It would be like a knife in the heart, to lose them after carrying them so long."

"Gid has remained close to his family," Moran objected.

"Gid is an exception. He and his sister were placed together. It made things easier for them to get to Tolis once a year. It has always been awkward, the crossover generation, no matter which way the child travels." Conversation ceased as she spotted Braan and Teloa, walking together in the vine-yard and talking softly. She looked over at her husband, her eyes sparkling.

"You look very pleased," Moran told her, trying to tone down his own smile.

"I admit it. I like Tay; I love her. She is a survivor—she would make a good Atarae."

"Then why doesn't Braan confess that she attracts him and do something about it?"

Roe shrugged. "He thinks he guards his heart. In the meantime Tay steals his soul. She is so beautiful, I believe he keeps his distance so she will not fear she is just one more body. I have a feeling there has been too much of that in her life."

"That's an understatement," Moran agreed.

Roe shot him a sharp glance but said nothing. Teloa's soft laughter floated to their ears. Her laugh was like murmuring water in a shallow creek bed. Only hearing her speak in Caprican was more soothing. The language was swifter and smoother than her humor, but no less delightful. Such a game those two were playing: Tay seeing other men; Braan no longer beating off the flocks of women constantly in attendance.

"Oh!" The whisper escaped before she could control it.

Moran sat up, visibly concerned about her continuing false pains. "Bad?" he asked. She reached over in reply and tightly gripped his hand. "Breathe properly." The spasm passed, and her fingers relaxed. "Another false alarm?"

"I am very tired, belaiss. Can we start back to the caverns? Zair's lady hound is whelping, and Prinz promised me a puppy for each baby. I think everyone knows it is twins, if he does." Moran braced himself behind and to one side of her, helping her to her feet.

Suddenly Teloa was there, her face lined with concern. She reached for Roe's arm. "Are you all right, Roe? You look pale. You've been walking too much, let's get you back to your room."

"I think that is a good idea." Roe gasped. "I do not want these two coming before they are good and ready." She glanced over at her brother, now deep in conversation with his son Dylan. "He shall be a godfather before he knows it."

"He'll be wet before he knows it, the rain's coming. Let's move!" At Moran's command they started across the field toward the foothills. It was usually a ten-minute walk, but Roe knew she would not be able to move at a normal pace. They looked up to see a face briefly appear at the cavern entrance. Roe bent her head to concentrate on walking but was not surprised when Kavan arrived at her side.

"Let me," he said quietly to Teloa, and the tall woman sprinted ahead of them into the cool darkness.

"I do not think . . . this is false labor," Roe got out, doubling over in pain. Kalith was also visible before the cave, his normally expressionless features tense. Together the three of them were able to get her into the cavern and up to her room.

"Good thing some of the family units are completed," Kavan said as they set Roe on her bed. "A little privacy is nice."

"Sure, if you want a room to yourself, get pregnant," Roe replied, gripping the sheets to stop her hands from shaking. "I think I would have reconsidered living on top, if I had known how hard it would be to get up those stairs. I should have demanded that they finish the lifts." Too much pain, too soon. Please, not so soon.

Elana entered the room. "Thank you. Good-bye, Kal and Kavan." She was activating her monitor as she spoke. A few adjustments and she turned to the now present Teloa and Liel, asking them to bring various supplies and two other healers. Then she whirled to Moran. "You are timing?"

"I had nothing to time with, but she's breathing properly," he answered, reaching for the timespot on the built-in shelf.

Shinar breezed into the starlit terrace, radiating confidence. She was not as heavy as some so far along. Roe's grip tightened on Moran's wrist as she gave in to another contraction, oblivious to everything else.

"Liel, I want the Atare *guaard* on this door. And Braan must be found—he should witness the birth of his heir. Good-bye, this is going to take a while," Elana ordered.

"Moran, talk to me," Roe suddenly said.

"No, you talk to me" was the reply. "You said at firstmeal that you had a new story, one about Baskh's predecessor. Tell it!"

"A story? Now?"

"Better than thinking about the pain. There's time until the next contraction. I'll give you plenty of warning," Moran went on. He settled onto one elbow, his head bent close to hers, neither paying any attention to the healers bringing in the standby equipment. Roe took a deep breath and then began to speak, her voice taking on the mysterious and vibrant quality of a master mythmaker.

"Long ago and worlds away, from the second year of

the reign of Curr Atare Moonraker, greatest of the modern
sea monarchs, comes a tale—"

COMPLINE

The small group watched as Agape rose into the dome
of the heavens, taking its place above Eros and Philios. They
were three very slender crescents, their sizes varying depending on how much of Nuala blocked off Kee's light.
Already moonrise. Thunder rolled ominously in the distance.

Gone. The moons. Lyte had only glanced away, and
now blackness. The thunder roared louder. A hand touched
his shoulder, and Lyte looked up to see Teloa.

"The rains come. As long as the planet is good to us,
we have a chance," Tay said quietly. "Are you ready for a
thirtysixday of rain? Liel says sometimes it's like that."

A splatter of rain hit his hand, and then another. He
pulled back from the ledge of the terrace, staring out to greet
the downpour. Steady and hard but not deafening. The thunder still growled, low and menacing. Lyte averted his eyes
as a many-forked tree of lightning leapt across the sky. He
caught himself wondering if it would strike the mountains.

He knew Moran had been a nerous wreck since vespers,
when Elana had determined a possible need for surgery and
had thrown both father and ruler out of the sleeping room.
Shinar had explained why— another off-worlder married to
an Atare serae had panicked recently during a delivery, and
with the possible heirs, Roe's first, no chances would be
taken. It was a matter of state. Lyte knew "matters of state"
could rarely be swept aside; he often forgot that Nuala was
a functional, not a symbolic, monarchy. But next time Moran
would be present. As father of the future Atare or Ragäree,
or both, Lyte knew he would gain power, which he would
enjoy using in just such cases. So long for babies to be born.
And Roe was fragile. Braan said that once, that she continued
on willpower alone.

The rain grew harder. Moran turned slightly to Braan.
"The harvest is complete," Braan said, anticipating his ques-

tion. They both flinched as a great thunderclap shook the room.

"I thought babies were only born during storms in stories," Lyte quipped.

"I was born in a storm," Liel replied. "Elana says her deliveries ran about fifty-fifty. And she prefers storms, or just after. She says it takes her mind off the pain."

"That sounds like Elana," Arrez began warmly. "She . . ." The priest hesitated only a moment, but it was long enough for a thin cry to intervene. The crowd grew silent, listening to the fragile life gain volume in its first protest to the world.

How long until the next? Minutes or hours? It seemed like only seconds later that Shinar came out of the bedroom. Every face except Moran's turned to her as another voice rose to replace the first. It was somehow harsher, more emotional, but clearly a different sound. Moran stood and moved toward the partition. Smiling, Shinar indicated that he should wait a few moments before entering.

"Have I an heir?" Braan asked.

Shinar laughed. "Covered on both accounts. Mendulay has blessed us. Atare and Ragäree to be, and Roe shall be fine, and by the One's will bear others. The womanchild is elder, by almost twenty minutes." Shinar sobered a moment. "One was a breach and caused some anxious moments. But the tearing was mild and surgery not necessary." The small crowd relaxed, conversation bursting from them. Lyte glanced around; Moran had vanished.

⸻

The room was not as dark as the terrace, and Moran blinked quickly in the light. A glow had been activated— a true glow, flickering in the wall's recesses, as mysterious as ever. Roe watched him from beneath veiled lashes. So tired . . . He cautiously sat down on the side of the bed, reaching across to support himself by leaning on the other side.

Roe shifted and completely opened her eyes. "Well? I had almost forgotten what my hipbones felt like. I think the womanchild looks like my mother."

"I hope they both look like you," Moran answered. "Father thought I was a homely baby."

Roe smiled and reached up to run her fingers through his hair. "No chance," she murmured, delicately touching where the starlight had begun to bleach his hair blond.

"Did I ever tell you that you're incredible?"

"Please, not that old line," Roe replied, touching his lips with her long fingers. "It may be painful, but it is instinctive. The body works up to its last breath."

"Let's not talk about last breaths— I've been a basket case" was the answer. He bent over to lightly kiss her shoulder. "Jaac never did come. Did Braan say her mother . . . died?"

"Bearing? Yes. It is a very rare thing. Less than one in, oh, thousands. . . ." She drifted a bit. "I am so excited! What a father you will be!"

"I want to pick one up, but I'm afraid."

"Do not be. They are much more durable than they look. Just remember to support the head," she whispered, closing her eyes for a moment.

"I know— I'm one of eight children, remember? This is different." He brushed her hair out of her face, pulling a long strand to the side of the pillow. "Don't sleep yet, they're hungry."

Her eyes popped back open. "Who says I have to be awake to feed them?" He suddenly looked disconcerted. Moran heard Elana enter the room from the sanitation, and swiftly kissed Roe. Then he leaned over the low-slung cradles. A tiny fist waved furiously above a soft tazelle-hide blanket. Moran carefully pushed aside the flaps of leather and took in his first view of the infant. So little, no bigger than a moment. The hair was very long and dark blond, but the eyes were screwed so tightly shut that he could not look at their baby blue. Not crying but definitely displeased. Roe chuckled at her husband's expression.

"Hello, there. I think you're hungry," Moran managed softly. The second one was no less active but calmer, more testing the new freedom of movement than protesting.

"That big fellow on the left is your son. And this lovely lady your firstborn," Elana said, reaching down to touch a downy hand. "She was quite upset about the arrival, but now I think she likes us. See how her eyes seem to look at you?"

Ronuviel had been noticing just that; and also the deep, original blue irises of birth, with darker marbling that foretold the Atare eyes, though they had not expected that. "She is very aware, very alert for so small a child, and so is he." Reaching in to touch a wisp of her hair, the same toasted honey of his own, Moran scarcely seemed to hear Elana finish. "I think soon they will want to nurse."

Moran scooped up his daughter and turned to Elana. "You were wrong," he said evenly, his face expressionless. "I should have been there." Roe tensed, waiting for what would come next.

Elana shifted the manchild and resolutely faced him. "Yes. You should have. But that does not change the decision. When the house of Atare is involved, I must choose. Miri's husband panicked. I could not take the chance. Though you are a warrior, you are off-world, and it is unlikely that you have witnessed a birth. The pain of a comrade and the pain of your mate are very different things to deal with. I am sorry you had to sacrifice. Next time shall be different. I hope you will come to understand my position." She nodded regally as she handed the now shrieking manchild to Ronuviel, confident that Moran would accept her words. Roe watched him out of the corner of her eye as the baby sought a breast.

It was clear that he did not like them, but he had no choice. Moran looked down at the womanchild. She regarded him with round eyes, seemingly oblivious to her brother's howls.

"It's practically a new world," he whispered to her. "I'm sorry it's such a mess, but I'll do the best I can, and that's all I can ask of you. I wish you weren't born to all of this, but . . . maybe it's better to know your duty beforehand than to have it dumped on you later." He faced the window, careful not to bring her too close. "See out here? Up and beyond? Beyond the Axis, the war, everything. That's truth, God. And I'll show you as much of it as I can. We all will." She gurgled, slapping at his shirt with soft pink fingers. Moran looked up and held her out to the waiting Elana. "I feel ridiculous. She can't understand me."

Elana smiled knowingly and gestured for him to give her to Ronuviel. "Of course she can."

MT. AMURA,   ONEHUNDRED   LAUDS
UPPER POOLS   EIGHTYONEDAY   (MOONSET)

Teloa stood panting, leaning against the sheer rock wall.
Then she was able to examine her surroundings. So this was
the famous northeastern upper pool. At that moment the first
rays of Kee escaped the cloud cover and struck the waterfall.
Tay gasped in amazement as a million rainbows broke out,
casting their glow everywhere. Careful of the deep mud caused
by the heavy rainfall of the night before, she walked into the
stone glade.

Now Teloa could hear the other waterfalls, higher, farther
to one side; they wrapped around this section of the mountains
like ribbons, with similar pools on the western slopes. Roe
had mentioned that there were caves here, too, reaching all
the way to the other side, if one knew the inner paths. This
was Ronuviel's place of atonement, her rock of prayer and
solitude. The Caprican was uncertain as to whether the Nualan
god would speak to her here.

Starting at matins, the garedoc had been filled with the
faithful, coming to be anointed with the healing oils. It was
a simple ceremony, the Feast of Atonement and Anointing;
a blessing and prayers, and then the touching of face, eyes,
ears, lips, heart, and hands with the ointment. This was supposed to be followed by exposure to the elements of Nuala.
For the infirm and less fastidious, this entailed stepping outside for a few moments. For those with deeper faith, or the
weight of many sins upon them, the procedure was usually
to find a high, windy place of rock and earth, within reaching
distance of water, and wait for the touch of Kee's rays. There
was special rejoicing this day over the birth of the twins.

Tay shivered, digging deep into her poncho. The akemmi
stirred, chirping peevishly. High, fluffy dark clouds swept
by overhead, bringing back a touch of winter. She hoped the
heat of yesterday was not a fluke. For a brief moment she
had imagined that she was back on Capricorn V, working the
irrigation trenches. Better not to think too long on that image.
It brought back good times, true; but also sister Meer's scorn,
and brother Tyr's degeneration, his churlishness when he

found her passage on the *Gerrymander*. And where was her little brother Telen?

The clouds to the west, coming from the distant sea, were black. More rain, and more— they needed it so badly. She continued to climb in the gray light of morning, uncertain of where she was going. A scrape of nails against rock told Tay that Zair was finished with whatever curious night scent he was stalking and had caught up with her. Tay found herself in the middle of numerous pools and falls and sat down, enchanted. Like spun gossamer, glittering in the rising star. How wonderful that Kee was rising earlier once again. As she looked off to one side and down the steep drop, she saw several people sitting among the new greenery. Surveying the whole scene, she noticed in front of and slightly above her a familiar profile. Tay stared a minute or two; his back was to her. The man was meditating, and she was shocked to realize that he was naked. Ye gods, the cold! She shuddered at the very thought. This person must feel a need for the total purification of the star's rays. Her thoughts ended as she recognized Braan.

She sat quietly, intrigued, occasionally looking for a hidden *guaard* as Kee swept up into a glorious starrise. When the star had topped a distant mountain pass, Braan moved to his knees and suddenly threw his arms wide, embracing the dawn. Then he whirled and in one fluid motion dove into the dark pool behind and below him. Teloa cut off her gasp and quickly began to climb down.

It took longer to reach the lower pools than she expected. When she reached the edge the lapping rings were quiet. Staring into the water, she considered what horrors lurked beneath the mirrored surface, what sharp-edged rocks . . .

"Looking for someone?" She nearly jumped off the stone shelf. Turning regally, she found that Braan was already dressed in a desert caftan, a towel over his shoulder, his feet bare. He looked more relaxed than she had ever seen him, despite having been up all night. "The water is warm."

She reached down and forced herself not to jerk back. Not cold but certainly not warm. "Only if you've been sitting out for several hours. Does having an heir give you the right to contract pneumonia?"

Braan smiled wickedly. "No chance. Mind over matter. Mendulay spares me for some other end. Have you made your peace with the Almighty? The day of atonement has its superstition attached, but there is something about the purifying, healing oils that is guaranteed to make one feel better."

"And you need to feel better?"

"In a sense." He looked out over the starrise. "I feel clean again. But I shall have to answer for it in the end."

Tay regarded him steadily. "You're not—guilty. You're not blaming yourself for everything that's happened, are you?"

It was Braan's turn to be surprised. "No. I am not so conceited as to think that one man could claim responsibility for all this, though it is the place of the ruler to carry his people's burdens."

"Carry, yes. Absorb, no."

He did not seem to hear her. "I am here because of many things but mostly because I terminated a life, and there is nothing that can make up for that."

"It was self-defense. I think God forgives a truly repentant heart, even of so serious a sin."

"Perhaps." He started down the slope, Tay following. "Thank you for your concern about my body, but I have been diving in that pool since I was a child, and I check for shifting rocks each time I come up here. There is a pole behind the fall, if you want to do it. Always check first. One of my relatives did not, and he broke his neck." Braan glanced over his shoulder. "Why did you climb up here?"

"Because the caves are a closed feeling. I need to breathe occasionally."

He nodded. "I intend to build my quarters up inside here, probably on the western slope. I need the view."

Zair butted Teloa's legs, and it brought her back to reality. So strange to be so close to him, and not a business recorder in sight. She wondered what he was thinking.

Fool! It is a beautiful, crisp morning. Why did you not stay up there and talk? Braan mentally kicked himself.

They descended in silence.

THE CAVERN   ONEHUNDRED   SEXT
                    EIGHTYTWODAY

Such an enclosed feeling, a cavern. Lyte shook his head to clear it of dark thoughts. If he was not careful, he would become as nervous as Moran. Glancing up from the wall he was chipping smooth, he looked over at his friend. The man's discomfort was visible, sweat trickling down his temple. He was tired— two days without sleep— but he was trying to concentrate on his work, giving his all for Nuala. The thought annoyed Lyte each time it occurred to him. Damn planet.

Braan walked by him, his shirt dark with perspiration from digging. The Nualan stopped by Moran, murmuring a word or two. Moran laughed softly and kept digging. Braan moved on.

He is digging like a slave and doesn't even care. The joke between the two men pushed annoyance over into irritation. Lyte attacked the wall with renewed vigor, enjoying the ring of metal against stone. The heavy machinery was destroyed. They had no choice—

Craak!! The sound of the splintering handle was shocking. Lyte stumbled from the shift in weight. A short, violent oath escaped him.

"Are you all right?" Moran asked.

"No, I'm not!" Lyte shouted, throwing the rest of the handle to the ground. Moran just stared at him. "When are we going to do something about leaving this God-forsaken planet?" He no longer cared about the Nualans working nearby.

"How?" Moran queried.

"Don't say that! I'm sick of hearing it! Doesn't anyone else want to get off this rock except me?" Lyte heard his voice rising.

"Wanting to is different from—"

"You could care less! You're not even trying! You don't care if you never get off this planet!"

Moran looked hesitant. "It is now my home, but—"

"Home, dak balls! You're more Nualan than they are!"

"I've got two kids to think about—"

"So do I." The last was a hiss.

Moran's face became unreadable, and Lyte knew that

he was trying to control his explosive temper. "Lyte, I'm sorry we can't—"

"Sorry? You've even decided to jump into politics, old apolitical Moran! You follow that Atare closer than his *guaard*. I never thought I'd see the day when you'd become a boot licker—" Moran's hand shot out, seizing Lyte's shirt in a commando grip. Surprise softened Lyte's shouting. He waited to see if the man would snap and attack him.

The bio-control held. Releasing the shirt, Moran said flatly, "I am not going to leave this planet to starve. Until that problem is solved, I don't want to waste strength even dreaming about ways to get off here. If you have to think about it, keep it to yourself."

"Just watch me."

Moran had already turned and was walking away. Lyte did not attempt to follow him.

CHAPTER FIFTEEN

Ronuviel stirred restlessly in her seat and stifled a yawn. It was not that she disapproved of the formalities. As far as baptisms went, it was remarkably relaxed and informal, without losing any of its dignity. But the last thirtyday had been exhausting, and the temptation to sleep was almost overwhelming. She had been up all night with the babies. Moran had helped her as he could, bringing them to her when she simply could not walk another step; he had changed, held, and talked to them. But he could not feed them, and that was what they needed right now. At least she could feed them together.

The ceremony had reached the important part, the appointing of special guardians. Other than the naming, this was what the crowd wanted most to hear, and the two actions followed on each other's heels. Ronuviel carefully sat up, still more tender than she would admit. Yet Elana had assured her that she was mending properly and swore she would bear again. But not right away— Nualan fertility was delicate and sporadic, and very few women bore children closer than three years apart. Having twins often pushed the time further back. Unfortunately Roe's mother Ila had been an exception to the rule, having borne children as close as a year apart. Roe rather hoped she would take after her grandmother, Chandra, who took twenty-five years to bear her seven children.

Arrez now gestured to Moran to come take the eldest, his daughter. Moran carefully picked up the womanchild, breaking into his gentle smile at the sound of her coos. She tried to reach for his hair, but he quickly settled her into a low carry. Roe knew he was studying her eyes, already showing the blue-and-green marbling. These twins were the first children ever recorded with such irises. The Ragäree smiled faintly. Only she and Moran knew who the guardians were, a prerogative of the parents; and they had talked long over many days to pick just the right child to go with each person. It expressed their hopes for both the child and the adult, each to gain insight from the experience. Moran was to offer the baby to the woman and indicate to the man to follow to the altar; the ancient symbols gave the nurturing to the woman and the protecting to the man, but Roe was grateful that they could work interchangeably. Another onehundred fiftyday or so and Moran could start feeding them solids. And who was fiercer than the female *katt* when protecting her young?

Moran walked out to the huge group facing them, his eyes tracing every individual, looking for the godmother. He finally stopped in front of Jaacav and gave her his entreating, raised-eyebrow look. Jaac appeared to swallow; she had expected this, because of an offhand remark of Roe's. Then she carefully took the bundle, clearly wishing for the protector role. Rarely was the protector a woman or the nurturer a man, though it had been done before. By taking the baby she had agreed to the honor and the responsibility.

Then Moran turned to look several rows back and gestured tentatively with a finger. Roe held her breath. Something had been wrong here for several moons, ever since Moran had become reconciled to remaining on Nuala without reprieve. After an argument with Moran that was loud enough to be heard two rooms away, Lyte had become silent, withdrawn, speaking at length only to Shinar. He still chatted with Roe as if nothing had happened, however. He seemed especially angry with Braan. Because Moran backed him and their friendship grew? She prayed that he would not refuse.

There was a long pause. Elana, sitting before Lyte's aisle, was very uncomfortable, even pale.

The moment passed. Lyte gently moved the woman before him to one side and stepped out. The crowd released its breath. *If only this opens up communication once again,* Roe thought fleetingly. Days ago they had laughed over it, threatening to make Lyte her godfather, both to give him a taste of responsibility for a woman and to keep him from seducing her when she was older. Lyte had passed it off with a smile—then.

Moran had returned for the man-child and, scooping him up, moved to enter the crowd. He had to walk back quite a few tiers, and the gathering parted like blown sand. Finally he reached the object of his search. Teloa blushed in her confusion, the color brushing her shoulders, neck, and face like the touch of a master's paintbrush. Her brilliant smile flashed out, and she joyously gathered up the tiny bundle. The baby immediately reached up and grabbed a long blonde curl. Tay followed Moran back down to the floor of the garedoc, her pleasure in the child evident. Moran was still searching the crowd, and spotting Braan in the corner near the altar indicated that he should come forward.

Now the four were assembled in front of Arrez, and Samara, the sister of Roe's grandmother, came toward them. Three women chose the names for the children: the mother, the eldest female of the Atare house, and one more relative of the mother's choosing. Roe had chosen Liel. Nodding to Arrez, Samara's rich, throaty contralto rolled out.

"Now comes the reason for our gathering, Brethren. Before Most Holy Mendulay and the people we declare these four people to have special bonds to our next chosen ones and announce the naming. They are named by tradition, and as always uniquely. The elder shall be Arien reb Ronuviel Atare. 'Arien' is from the ancients and means 'free-flyer, high soarer, night-rider.' The younger shall be Breeyan reb Ronuviel Atare. The name, from the tiovi, means 'star traveler,' for it is said this one shall travel far before he comes to the throne of his ancestors."

As Samara said the last words Roe glanced quickly to where Mariah had been sitting. That was the first thing the woman said, upon seeing the child: "This one must travel far, 'ere he finds his heart's desire and discovers the burden of the chain." But Mariah was gone, and Elana too. Ronuviel frowned— this, of all things, was something the women would not want to miss. There was more to the ceremony— the baptism with water, the laying-on of hands and anointing with oil— but Roe's mind was on other things, churning, the healer within suddenly terribly worried with a premonition she could not name.

NEW TEMPLE	TWOHUNDRED	LAUDS
HEIGHTS	ELEVENDAY	(MOONSET)

Arrez stood at the entrance to the new temple heights, his grip on his polished wooden beads painful. He stared down the long corridor past the prayer niches to the upper cave opening; the picture window, as it was called. No starrise cut through the murkiness beyond. The last rain from the sea slanted toward the mountains, driving against the rocky overhang. The priest did not hear Ronuviel as she entered the hallway from the direction of the life shelter.

The woman moved slowly— what with the baptism, the twins, and the operation she had just performed, she had found no rest. Her assistant was finishing in post-op; it was her task to talk to Arrez.

Finally the man turned his head, acknowledging her presence. "Well?" he queried, his voice mild. "It is early. Many children have been premature since the bombs fell. But you removed her from her room. What is it?"

Roe hesitated, her face bleak. "She lives."

Arrez seemed to consider her choice of words. "The child?"

The woman shook her head negatively.

"Will there be others?"

"I do not think so."

Arrez looked back out the picture window. Roe glanced toward the opening, wondering what he saw. "Is she awake?" he said at last. "Does she know?"

"Yes. She insisted on knowing everything. I think she

has suspected since the beginning that it was her last. But we could not anticipate..."

"It is all right, Ronuviel" was the gentle reply. "It is Mendulay's will, no matter how we see it. At least he has spared my life's blood. I am blessed." There were tears in his voice. Silently touching his arm, Roe retreated to the life shelter, the man following.

Elana lay in silence, her eyes seeing nothing. Shinar stood near her, a tight, frightened expression on the young woman's face. Arrez sat down on the edge of the bed. "Elana? Belaiss?" The endearment penetrated her fog. She blindly extended her arms for his. They sat that way a long time.

"It was a manchild," Elana whispered.

HARBOR   TWOHUNDRED   TIERCE
                          ELEVENDAY

Braan could not wait until the *Nova*'s gangplank was brought to rest. Grabbing hold of a piece of rigging hanging on the side, he pulled himself up and over the ship's railing with a simple, fluid hand-over-hand action. Leaping over a barrel, he seized Gid in a hard embrace. "You missed the baptism."

"You did not wait."

"Wait? No word, and then you sneak around the point at night with no lanterns. The excuse had better be good."

Gid laughed. "Something unexpected came up, and we had to make an unscheduled stop in Merigwin. I brought you a surprise."

"Not a puppy, I hope." Gid looked blank. "Zair's lady friend whelped almost a dozen, and the owner wants to give me all but the two he promised Roe!"

"Well, I will take one, and you had better get one for the friend I brought you." As he finished, at the opposite end of the moonraker a lovely, dark-haired young woman stepped out of the passenger's cabin, a bundle in her arms.

Braan immediately leaned over toward Gid. "I do not believe you. First you push your mother on me and now—"

"No, no! On the contrary! Not her— him!" The young woman came closer, nodding her fealty, and Braan suddenly recognized the band on her arm, which marked her a member of the practitioner's guild, dealing with mothers and children. Shyly she opened the bundle with one hand. Braan did not move.

The square jaw and dimple in the chin had reached a third generation. And the intense, long-lashed eyes, staring at him, it seemed, were already hinting at the emerald green they would become. Braan extended a finger, which the tiny mite took hold of with an amazingly powerful grip. So small, as small as the twins.

"Atare, may I introduce you to Caran reb Tinyan. He is not much of a talker but has quite a healthy set of lungs, considering that he was sixtyday early. This is Defora, from the Merigwin chapter, who agreed to accompany us as nurse." Gid was watching intently for a reaction. "Needless to point out that my father is not his father. Tinyan originally wished for Arrez and Elana to take him, but Defora's guild said she is expecting her own any moment."

"She had it," Braan managed to say. "It was born dead. Last night." Defora went pale.

Gid winced. "As usual, my timing is superb. We will petition the elders—"

"No." Braan carefully took the manchild from Defora. "Come. Both of you."

NEW TEMPLE   TWOHUNDRED   TIERCE
HEIGHTS   ELEVENDAY

Roe did not know what to say. She had not intended to sit here with Elana and nurse her twins; it seemed cruel. But here was her friend, holding the womanchild, Arien, and actually suggesting that she might function as a wet nurse for other women for a time. Roe was impressed and wondered how much was a brave front.

It was strange and yet relaxing to have Odelle with them. Corymb's sister-daughter was only ninetyday from delivery. Many were delivering prematurely; she was therefore being watched very closely. Odelle was a high-strung woman—no, child— by nature, and this pregnancy only made things worse. It was extremely important to her to have a healthy boy or at least a healthy girl, but eventually a boy as well. She feared that she might not be able to carry more than once or twice, and Corymb was counting on her. Otherwise, he lost his position in the family, unless Dielaan voted to keep him, and would become merely another elder. Of course, there was no basis for her worry. The odds were the same for her as for any other 20. Roe wove her thoughts back into Odelle's speech.

"It was a horrible dream. The infant had two heads, and both sexes and—" Odelle paused, shuddering. "I know, ridiculous, but I cannot rid myself of it. Maybe . . ." Her voice dropped, and she looked quickly to see who was listening. "It is a punishment for the Dielaan's sins."

Shaking her head, Elana said, "Odelle, we cannot promise the child is not sini—the very thing that shields mother and child from each other keeps us from knowing such things. However, I can stake my reputation that it will not be sini-shur."

"You do not understand, Elana. Five generations ago my husband's line had a mock sini— not serious, but the man-child was taken to Tolis. And neither his line nor my branch of Dielaan has yet produced a healer. We are not free!" There was agony in her voice. Roe said nothing. There were no guarantees— all paths were fraught with danger. Elana was a perfect example.

Shinar walked into the room, changing the subject. "The *Nova* is in, and Gid is on it. I heard they are coming this way."

"Felt the baby move yet?" Odelle asked, suddenly looking mischievous.

Shinar made a face. "How would you like your black curls scattered from here to Seedar?" But she also laughed. Shinar had been so excited over the prospect of the baby, she was feeling movement at first with every ache and gas pain. Her peers enjoyed teasing her. Now she turned to her mother, trying to hide her concern. Until an hour ago Shinar had not left Elana since the surgery. She had finally dragged Arrez off for some food.

"Why do you not go bother Kal?" Roe said. Shinar immediately looked as if she were going to object.

"I think that is a good idea, Shinar," Elana said firmly. "He needs pestering, and you look too solemn." Then her voice dropped to a tight whisper. "The best thing for all of us is to get busy with something right away. Please do." Shinar reached over and hugged the woman, and then rushed out. Odelle raised her arms to take Arien, and the scientist gave her up. Elana then held her head high to prevent tears from escaping.

There was a knock at the apartment shield.

"Yes?" Roe asked.

"Ronuviel?" It was Gid's voice.

"I will come out when I am done feeding Bree, just a—"

"We would rather come in if you do not mind. Just Braan and I and a lady friend."

That piqued her curiosity. "Enter." The three walked in, the young woman shy, at the rear, and clearly not Gid's type. Roe turned a puzzled face to them and realized that Braan was carrying not a bundle but a baby.

"I have brought a new playmate for the twins. This is Caran reb Tinyan, and Defora is his travel nurse, from Merigwin."

"A brother! Gid, how nice," Elana said, her voice soft but clear. "Who is the father?"

"I am." Braan paused and then continued hurriedly. "Tinyan and her men originally wanted you and Arrez to take him, if you would, but they did not know you were expecting your own. Are you willing or interested in such a thing?" Elana stared at him. "It is traditional to at least reveal the mother's request. If not, we shall petition the synod. Would you rather dismiss it to the elders or talk with Arrez first or—"

"Braan—" Roe did not know whether to be angry or afraid.

"We must determine if Defora is staying or returning

home, depending on our own chapter's ability to provide for the child. And—" Braan stopped his run-on. Elana said nothing but extended her arms for the squirming man-child. Braan hesitated only a second and then handed her the babe. The child stopped struggling, looking up at the woman with enormous eyes, and then snuggled closer, seeking a reassuring breast and meal.

"I realize that this is a sudden and monumental decision—" Braan started to say, and then saw tears falling on the blanket.

Roe had finished feeding Breeyan and, in one movement, secured her blouse and handed the man-child to a surprised Gid. Moving to Elana, she sat on the bed's edge. "Elana . . . Elana? Do not be upset, they will understand. It is—"

"Get Arrez." Odelle had already slipped away, depositing the sleeping Arien in Braan's arms. Elana did not speak again; only the silent tears gave any sign of her reaction. They waited, and presently an out-of-breath Arrez arrived. He took in the scene with a glance and then pulled up a stool next to the bed. Elana looked up at him, her eyes swimming. "A boon has been asked, a charge laid upon us. This is Caran reb Tinyan, brought to you and me by his half brother, Gid reb Tinyan, and presented by his blood father. Shall we take up his life or shall we pass him to the elders?"

Arrez studied her face and then surveyed the child. "What say you?"

Elana sighed. "I rejoiced at the new chance at life and love we were offered; I cursed Mendulay when it was taken back and cursed myself for the words. For all we know, it is this one who has needed us all along." She touched a dark infant curl, no longer facing Arrez, waiting.

"I have no objections; as you will," Arrez answered.

Roe could see Elana's tears beginning to fall again. "I think you will take them to their cradles," Roe instructed, pushing Braan and Gid out the doorway. "Braan, put her down first. Make sure Gid knows how. I am sure this man-child is hungry . . . and I think things will be all right."

TWOHUNDRED   VESPERS
ELEVENDAY

Braan slipped away from the garedoc gathering early, letting them temper joys and sorrows as they wished. Those who believed in signs from God debated the death of the high priest's child against the arrival of Tinyan's little one and the fact that the heir was the third in a row to have a name beginning with *B*. Of course three was a lucky number, yet purists argued that Tal bore the title a few moments. Braan left it all behind.

The *guaard* had brought word from off-planet contacts; Asiai had been found and relocated with his dead wife's parents. For the time being, she was safe. It was a private joy to be shared only with Dylan. There would be time later to tell Ronuviel and the others.

Roe had stayed with Elana until starset and then finally retreated for the night to her husband's arms. Elana, too, was exhausted; she was in pain and afraid to take medication for fear that it would contaminate her milk. She insisted that she could wait for Roe's healing touch. Braan hoped she was sleeping. He made his way to the new temple heights, to look at Caran reb Tinyan for himself.

The outer opening was merely beads, but no one answered his soft knock on the shield. He peeked in— the partition to the bedroom was closed. Leaving his *guaard* at the door, Braan quietly moved to the cradle. To his amazement the babe was awake and aware of him, calmly sucking on his fist. Braan studied him a moment and then carefully picked him up.

"You have been passed around like a bushel of vegetables, have you not?" Braan whispered softly to him. The smooth baritone voice did not frighten the man-child. Trustingly secure as he lay along Braan's arm, his head fitting perfectly in the man's palm, the infant reached up and out, attempting to seize the glittering chain of office. "You do not really want that— it is a pain in the ass. Believe me, I have been there. I cannot give you two names, but I shall give you what I can, the important things, if you want them. Then you will not need two names— one will be enough. And better than this chain; more. I know."

So absorbed was he with the child that he did not hear the bedroom partition open and close, nor see Teloa pause, a little smile teasing at the corners of her lips as she watched them. The woman slipped off without comment, nodding to Arrez as they passed.

Braan heard the beads move but did not look up. "If you will excuse me, I have to go eat. Your half brother is waiting for me, and right now he needs me more than you do." Braan started to set the baby back down.

"Wait." Arrez stepped forward, a smile lighting his face. He did not tease Braan about his presence there, however. They faced one another, not moving.

"Thank you," Braan said in parting, extending the child to Arrez.

"Thank you," the other replied, embracing the babe with long years of practice. Arrez stood there holding Caran a long time after his Atare had left.

ATARE'S PEAK   TWOHUNDRED   TIERCE
                    TWELVEDAY

Braan settled himself more comfortably, his eyes never leaving the 3AV. For a second he drifted, more interested in the disappearing holographic images than the thoughts they conveyed. Then he admitted defeat, his attention moving to the voices in the private corridor. Dylan and Teloa. She was coming to the mid-morning meeting, and apparently Dylan had been shadowing her. Braan briefly wondered if the child was smitten by the woman or truly was that interested in planting. They did seem to like each other.

"He has been getting more attention lately than I have." He immediately understood what he had said and hoped that Tay had not heard.

"Dad?" Dylan peeked around the side of the stalagmite, not wishing to intrude. Teloa's head followed.

Braan smiled and shut off the AV holographic machine.

"I am feeling neglected," Braan said faintly. "When are you going to come visit me?"

Dylan laughed and ran over to hug him. "We went to the pools yesterday! I cannot see you all the time because it gets—" Dylan stopped, suddenly aware of what he was saying.

"Yes? Boring?"

Dylan made a face. "All they do is talk, talk. Talk to you, talk at you, talk in front of you like you are not there! Until they want you to settle an argument."

Braan laughed. "No one said that being a ruler was fun all the time. So you like planting better? How about classes?"

"Tay makes it interesting!" Dylan looked worried. "I am keeping up my studies, really! I did all the reading up to next templeday!"

"I believe you, I believe you!" Braan met Tay's smile over the boy's head. "I talked to Prinz, and he says in fifteen to twentyday you can go pick a pup from the lady hound's litter. Do you think you can take care of a little puppy?" The boy's eyes grew enormous. "I mean it— I shall confiscate it if you do not feed and brush and love it properly." The boy's head bobbed up and down vigorously. "All right, then it is settled. Go on."

Dylan vanished, a flurry of feet skidding down the dark corridor and an earsplitting whoop at the lifts.

"Such joy! Prinz is going to run out of puppies!"

"I think they are all committed. He did not want to keep any, and it gives him a lot of pleasure to give them away, especially to children."

"And you?"

Braan looked surprised and thoughtful.

"Or you can let Zair stay with you again and I'll take one!"

Braan shook his head. "No, I think your danger is past, but I would like Zair to stay with you a little while longer. I would feel better about it." She smiled graciously at this, and Braan felt fractionally unsettled, as if she were looking right through him. He was even more disturbed by the fact that he was upset. He reached languidly to pull out the 3AV.

"Bad news?" It was an honest question. As scripter, she

would normally be one of the first to know; he had confided in her more than once.

"In a sense. The various com-net startexes we have monitored indicate tremendous pressure building up within the Axis— military secrets exposed, systems up in arms against the republic, attempts to make Nuala take a fall." His voice sank to a whisper. "Tay, I am no longer sure we shall ever be able to reenter the Axis." She said nothing; he looked up, his gaze piercing. "That is not for general hearing."

"I am always discreet, Atare," she answered formally. Irritated by a second of intimacy destroyed, Braan stood and paced to the large thermacontrol window, the first to be placed.

He touched its sill gently. "We have a chance. Several chances. The first we shall discuss today." He was interrupted by pounding on his metal shield. "Enter." Moran, Roe, and Gid appeared, trooping past the two silent *guaard*, another *guaard* in tow. Braan smiled faintly. "I want a real door."

"With a doorkeeper? The *guaard* will not take on anything extra. Some people do not have units yet, and you and Dylan have this to yourself!" Roe answered, amusement in her voice.

"That may change," Braan replied. He gestured to the low chairs. "We have several people to wait for. Sit down. Did you ask Lyte?"

"He said, 'No thank you,'" Roe supplied.

Braan's eyes narrowed. So, he had not imagined it. Lyte was angry and avoiding his friends.

Moran looked momentarily pained. "I'll just lecture it to him later. He has no choice."

By this time the sounds of other participants in the meeting came to their ears. Lars, the head planter, and his major assistant, Brett, were the first through the doorway, followed by Liel and Arrez. Liel was regaining her full spirits, jokes and good humor coming in rapid-fire order. The twins followed, and the gathering was gratified to see that Shinar had been with Kalith. Braan was unable to suppress a smile. He had seen them walking and talking earlier, and for a moment the past year was swept away and they were two young people reveling in the silent intensity of their love. Kal was trying to shake his inhibitions and come to some semblance of peace

with himself, but it was difficult. While Kal took leave of
Shinar, Kavan immediately took a seat, attentive to every
word and movement. He had settled down, Braan reflected.
Still the Atare temper, but he had better control over it. He
took his responsibilities seriously. Jaac slipped in alone.

Finally Justinian and Url entered, the heads of the synod.
The couple brought with them the dignity of royalty, immediately formalizing the meeting. The two settled in on one
couch. After they looked comfortable Arrez offered up a
prayer. Then he looked expectantly at Braan.

Braan's eyes took in the gathering. "I have called you
all here to discuss our immediate course of action, and the
general consequences if we do not move with purpose. Let
no one leave confused." He turned to Lars. "Can you explain
this better than me?"

Lars coughed. He started to stand and then seemed to
think better of it. Leaning back in his chair, he began to
speak. "The winter harvest is stored, and we are preparing
the seed grain for the summer crop, which, if the monsoons
prove to be ended, will be planted this weekend. As everyone
here has heard, several of our sister cities are in desperate
need of food and seed grain. We are the major agricultural
suppliers for this region and everything extending north. It
is a heavy responsibility."

"Was the harvest adequate?" Justinian asked.

"Adequate? Depending on how we look at it, yes. We
produced enough grain to feed ourselves and eleven other
population centers through this fall, and the rest of the seed
grain for this spring. Then there is the fall harvest."

"And?" Arrez supplied.

"We can feed ourselves but not the other cities. Our
farming was artificially controlled to produce that much food.
We no longer have the means, and even with new land under
cultivation we do not have the seed. We will barely have seed
to plant for winter, and it will produce a small crop. To spread
things thinly is to provide an inadequate nutrition level for
everyone."

"Somehow I don't think the people of Merigwin are
going to lie down and starve peacefully. We are left with two
choices; is that what you are suggesting? Find more food or

be prepared for a global war to control what there is." Teloa stared at Moran, amazed that he could announce it so calmly.

"We have numerous tasks. Some will take time, such as rediscovering the farming skills of our ancestors," Braan continued smoothly. "Lars and his fellow planters are convinced that our soil can produce without chemical boosters and pesticides but that involves setting up a complicated crop rotation with tier planting, fertilization, and a natural pesticide system. And, most importantly, getting new seed."

"Smuggled?" Brett asked with enthusiasm. Liel's smothered laughter and Braan's smile immediately dashed his hopes of adventure.

"The rumors in the synod suggest that you intend to deal with the Cied." Justinian let his words hang in the air a moment. "Is this true? Is it wise? We are not sure the Cied have the added resources to help us. Or will be willing to—"

"The resources exist," Gid interrupted. "Braan and I have spent considerable time in the Ciedär, even the interior. And in the midst of that great desert lies an unimaginable oasis, created by the Ciedärlien planters. It is bounty in the midst of endless famine and feeds all the great and middle tribes with extra to barter, which they do on occasion. That land is the one thing their people do not fight over. I have seen it— it exists. And they protect it with their lives. Seed they will sell for the right price. They, too, suffered from the attack, and acquiring material, weapons, metal, and housewares is difficult for them. They are not merchants or artisans— they depend on the coast for these things. Their farming secrets they may be more loath to give up, but it would amuse them to have us in their debt. I am not that proud, Justinian— I know what it is to go hungry."

Lars cleared his throat, capturing their attention. "I agree with the Atare. We must go to the Cied, to the deep sand mountain Dragoche clan, to the Dragoche Baakche himself. We must deal with him one-on-one, with a representative of high standing with the Atare to act as emissary. The Cied call councils of tribal leaders, but they have no permanent, elected parliament— and recognize only one ruler. If we go representing separate tribes or houses, they will see that as a weakness. The fact that we do not have a priest-king is bad enough for our bargaining position, or so records say."

"We do." Arrez did not look away from the window. "Just because he is not anointed a priest does not make him any less a servant of God." Braan winced— the fact that there had been no coronation needed to be rectified as soon as possible.

"What do we have to offer the tribes?" Url asked.

"The usual— and more," Braan answered, satisfied with what was coming out of the discussion. "I have already sent messages causing a temporary cessation of trade with the Cied. As Gid said, they are planters of the highest caliber, but they make nothing— no cloth, no weapons, no lasting abode. They barter for everything, specify their designs for material and weapons, rarely construct their own tents. They are trackers, hunters." The Amurans shivered. The Cied ate meat. Not as much as off-world humans but more than most Nualans.

"They also covet our gold. But can they not make what they have stretch an extra season or two and then take what they want when we are too weak to fight them?"

Braan smiled "No. The Cied were hurt worse than us— their life is a harsh one, and their cities are dependent on the trade caravans. They will not change into craftmasters and city dwellers overnight. And they are Nualans— slavery disgusts them as it would you. They are people concerned with honor and duty to Mendulay above all things; and their own situation not far behind. They will help us. The questions are: How much? At what price? For how long? As friends or as taskmasters? And will they deal with Corymb, with Atare, or still someone else?"

"You mentioned 'more.' What do you have in mind, Braan?" Kavan asked.

"The Cied understanding of weapons is knives and swords, arrow tips to fight animals and one another."

"A debatable difference," Brett threw in. Lars hushed his assistant with a glance.

"I know that several Cied have been off-world in the last tenyear. Baakche's heir is among them. The man Genuar is shrewd and intelligent— he understands the connection between the attack and the probable return of our enemies, I am certain . . . or he can be made to see it. And the Fewhas will make Nuala totally their own, if they return. Even if they want our homes only for an outpost, they will sear the planet to a crisp first. We have the ability to protect the Cied. Tolis builds missiles, and the new shield. However, if we have to threaten to leave them unshielded, we will threaten."

"We may not have to threaten. They remember prophecies from holy books we no longer read," Arrez said cryptically.

"So it is plain that we must go to the Dragoche. I assume you have given thought as to who is to go?" Jaacav broke in smoothly.

"I know who is not going. You are not, my friend. You are the only one experienced enough to supervise the assembly of the shield, and we cannot wait the twentyday for you to finish. *They* must leave immediately. I hope for some aid from the tribes to increase this crop's yield, not just the fall plantings."

Jaac must have expected this, as she did not protest Braan's decision. "You have found someone with my desert skills in condition to travel?" Her gaze at Roe was pointed.

"No. Roe needs a fortyday yet before she will gain her normal strength. We need someone with the equivalent authority to my own, since I doubt that the synod would be pleased with my leaving."

"They would not," Justinian replied just as easily.

"I was thinking that Kalith and Kavan could go." The young men straightened and tried to cover their astonishment. Braan went on quickly. "I feel the synod underestimates their ability to conduct state business, especially together. As a team they are practically unbeatable; and they were also on the last journey to Cied. I trust the experiment is as engraved on their memories as it is on mine. They understand the protocol."

"It would most likely be satisfactory, providing two elders selected by the synod accompanied them."

"May I suggest the two be of personalities not averse to working through the Atares? We need no egos to salve on this trip. And myself—" Lars threw in.

"No. You're too important here. I could just as easily go." Everyone looked at Teloa. "I am Caprican, I was raised on a planet where the daytime temperature averaged forty degrees Celsius. I'll learn the tricks of this desert quickly, and I know what questions to ask."

Braan hesitated, unwilling to admit to himself how much her words frightened him.

"And Brett could go along, to insure that we receive the proper amounts of each type of seed. Tay is not familiar with that part of our work, since our shipments have been cut back to almost nothing," Lars offered. Brett immediately turned to Teloa, looking ridiculously pleased over the idea, totally missing the implications to his future as Lars's assistant. Tay was facing Braan. The Atare let himself go only a moment, his encompassing gaze worried, and then the mask slipped up, his smile barely wavering. He took an intense dislike to the confident young planter Brett, recognized the jealousy, and mentally kicked himself.

"Jaac?" Braan forced out.

"Six warriors with planter skills, one of them *guaard*."

"Six? Is that nec—"

"Yes, Justinian, six," Jaac rushed on. "That is the minimum I shall allow, or I shall insist on the traditional Atare *guaard*. They shall be hard to placate as it is; they have been left in the dark too long."

The idea alarmed both Justinian and Url. "We cannot have too many. It would look as if we were expecting treachery!"

"Agreed," Braan interrupted. "We go to parley, not to fight. But we cannot be foolish. The tribes are never totally united, even behind the Dragoche, and we must not forget it for a second. Any less would not be prudent, any more not only asking for trouble but also a waste of warriors. If a group such as a Stigati tribe intends to attack, you would need a platoon to beat them off. I send these six only to have something between you and a knife in the dark."

"It is settled, then? The synod shall choose the two this afternoon, and the chosen shall leave in the early morning," Url said.

"Agreed." But Braan knew he did not sound entirely pleased with the arrangement.

THE GROTTO   TWOHUNDRED   PRIME
                        THIRTEENDAY

They sat quietly on the rocks, the watchers, as the last packs were secured on the hazelles. Roe looked up at the curving expanse of rock above them, a delicate rose-pink in the reflected light. Teloa had called the yawning opening "the grotto" from almost the very beginning, though it was truly the mouth of the western cavern. The name had stuck. The Atare woman looked over at Teloa, who was off to one side making her farewells to Zair and the akemmi. No wains were going; the long trek over the desert, most of it nothing but mountains and waves of sand, would be too much for their feet. No water could be spared for pets. The big hound whined softly as the Caprican scratched his ears; he knew something was wrong. Tikki scrambled off, vanishing in the brush. Dylan stood nearby, not as overjoyed as expected over gaining Zair's company. He was fond of Tay and worried about her already.

Jaacav was with the half dozen warriors who were to accompany the group. Ronuviel could hear snatches of conversation and instruction. They carried side knives, a few clubs, and Cied swords, and the group leader had a normally forbidden blaster. In the depths of the previous night Jaac had admitted her fears. She did not expect to see them ever again. Roe could not accept it then, and believed it no more by the light of day. Studying the two elders chosen, Roe decided that they were probably an adequate selection. Not distinguished, but honest, fairly objective, and able to keep their mouths shut during the bulk of the negotiations. If only Kal would spring back completely . . . if only Brett would stop annoying Teloa. At least Roe would have found his pronounced attentions vexing. Teloa thought it was terribly amusing. The Caprican woman no longer denied to Roe her attraction to Braan. She merely stated that either the Atare was not mutually interested or not interested at this time. Roe thought her protracted consideration for his shock over Enid's death, the bombing, the loss of Asiai, and the assumption of both kingship and bachelorhood, well. . . . Teloa had been generous with her patience.

Kal had already said his good-byes and stood among the hazelles, his eyes on the distant sea. Shinar had chosen to remain at Roe's side and watched him thoughtfully. The warriors were helping the elders up on their hazelles and seeking their own mounts. Teloa now moved away from Dylan and the dog, starting down the path to the huddled beasts. Braan was standing between Roe's perch and the road and reached out to touch Tay's shoulder in passing. The woman hesitated.

"I have something for you," Roe heard Braan say. "You may need it." The man dipped into a pocket of his poncho and pulled out what Roe recognized as a hunting cat, a deadly knife used to skin tazelles, among other things. It was also known to even up the odds when one was cornered by a *katt*. It was in a case and had a strap attached.

"For me?" Tay was clearly surprised and puzzled.

"Never go far without a good knife and some rope," Braan said briskly, opening the case with the flick of a finger to reveal knife, oil and stone. "Eon can carve the grip to your hand tonight. Do not allow it to rust in the case. Become familiar with it. There are many dangers in the Ciedär." Roe looked up to see Tay quietly studying him, and her expression indicated that she saw beyond the words and the manner. For once Braan did not immediately move away and met the off-worlder's eyes with his own. He closed the case and placed it in her right hand.

"Thank you."

"Be careful."

It was much later that Ronuviel asked Teloa what thought had moved her in those moments, for the woman's final gesture had been unlike the restrained individual they knew. Yet it seemed so normal, so natural, for the scene. Tay had scrutinized him once again, her expression searching, and then had wordlessly reached up and caressed his cheek with her fingertips. Of all Nuala, only Lyte and Braan had patronized the tratores, and only they could know what that motion cost her. But Mercury 7 was in the past, and only a person well trained in the tratore customs would remember long ago and worlds away. No citizens were present to mark boldness in the company of royalty.

The woman turned and hurried toward her hazelle. Mounting with the fluid grace of one familiar with four-legged transportation, she nodded to Eon, the palace *guaard* in charge of the group. A flick of his crop and his beast led off, the others falling in behind. Roe realized that her knuckles were white from gripping her caftan and that she had reached for Braan's sleeve without knowing it. The whole of the distant sea sparkled like silver in the starlight as Kee finally rose above the mountains; the travelers, however, were bathed in shadow as they hugged the rocky terrain, headed for the pass and to the east. Roe trembled in the rising breeze.

PAINTING ROCK, THE CIEDÄR	TWOHUNDRED SIXTEENDAY	PRIME

She sat as still as death, watching the star leap up over the farthest mountains and into the sky. It was the highest point in the region, this jumbled pile of rocks, and her sanctuary against the coming day. Teloa did not even allow herself to stretch; not long ago Brett had come up to join her and had been unable to find her among the boulders. The deception pleased Tay, and she wedged herself tighter into the crevice, reveling in the freedom. She tucked her water flask into her beige robes to protect it from the coming heat.

Three days they had ridden, following a caravan route. The land was blooming in the wake of the recent monsoons, a soft blue-green as far as the eye could see. The hazelles often had to be driven to keep them from eating too much of the fresh grass and foundering. She sighed, thinking about the hazelles. Each animal carried the personal effects and water of its rider, and soon she would have to go down to load her beast. Eon would probably help her, but she didn't want to burden him. The packs were not heavy, just awkward.

Tay shifted, staring off north to the next pile of rocks, a mountain chain in miniature that was slowly wearing away to become more desert. A taller range was beyond them, lost in Nualan mist. The route was easy for those who knew the signs. Eon and Kal had taught them to her, and she amused herself by pacing the trip. This was the easy part, the part that was a day's walk to each water source. But when they passed the painting rock, they reached the open desert, the great sands, which was what Ciedär meant. After that, every oasis and stone formation was found by following the stars—and to fail was to wander endlessly in the ever-changing dunes, until dehydration and starstroke made an end of the story. Then the small, water-seeking crustaceans and the drying winds took care of the rest . . .

The twins were fond of this grotesquely carved place and had chosen it as a wind break. It was called the painting rock because of its major use— as a trysting place for tribes, most of which no longer existed. They met here, at the marker for what was once the edge of the sands, and traded wares, stories, and information, fostering out their children for the season as well. Those few Cied who chose to learn the trade of ceremonial recording then recounted the most important and impressive information on the rock itself, with colors ground from the various delicate berries that appeared just after each monsoon season.

The tribes were gone; even their language was dead and decipherable only by scholars. But the colors in the interior caves were as bright as the day they were crushed into new life, and certainly the rock did not care that the edge of the Ciedär was now three days west of it. Tay had immediately preferred to be on it instead of next to it, the biomorphic cavern entrances reminding her of the sad eyes of some gigantic alien creature. But she had admired the paintings and the rising star long enough.

A sharp cry aroused her. It was harsh, a sound of anger and alarm. Fighting the urge to race back to the camp, Teloa slowly crawled toward the lip of the ledge, at the same time hooking the face veils on her Cied-like robe. She was unarmed except for the knife Braan gave her and unskilled at any other weapons. No matter what the problem was— a small crawly thing dropped down someone's robe or a large predator—

she would be no help and possibly in the way. Trying to calm her overactive imagination, Tay peered over the edge.

Worse than her fears. Large predators— human ones, or marginally human. Teloa at first thought that they were the Cied traders the Amurans had passed the day before, but the robe markings were different. The traders' hems and side seams had been embroidered with an intricate black design— these Cied had a red pattern, bold and abstract, confined to the hem and left side. She stared hard at the pattern, memorizing it before it was obliterated by blood. She realized that the odds were at least six to one and had time to notice that they had captured one of the Atares but killed without hesitation the warrior trying to free him. Then she saw the battle moving her way and crawled back to her hiding place. Damn! Anything for a laser blaster in her hand. But it was not allowed—Eon had the only one.

The sounds of battle ceased. The star rose in the heavens, pulsating its power as the hot spell approached. It was not until vespers, however, when Kee had sunk into the Sonoma Mountains, that Teloa finally stirred. She crept again to the ledge and saw several hazelles moving listlessly. There was no other movement. Standing, Tay looked as far as she could see in every direction. There was no sign of life. She slowly started down the rocks.

The fighting had shed enough blood to attract the krwb, the moisture-seeking creatures of the sand, and they had done their work well. Every single drop of fluid left in the corpses had been drawn out, an orgy of water, enough to last a troop of krwb the rest of their short lives. She could still recognize the victims by their clothes or hair. All six warriors were accounted for, the two elders and the planter Brett. Poor Brett, he had been so pleased to go on this trip and so interested in Teloa since she'd arrived.

"Tikki-tikki-tikki!"

Teloa spun around, the knife in her hand. Several hazelles were grazing nearby, and on top of one of them, perched among the packs, was Tikki. She flicked an ear at Tay and twitched her whiskers. Teloa laughed in hysterical relief. "So you didn't want to be left behind and decided to hide until the trouble was over?" Tay walked to the hazelles and extended an arm, the akemmi running up it to nestle in her hood. "Enough— we belong together."

The hazelles were still hobbled, and after tracking down the food, Tay left them that way. Apparently Eon had been correct when he said that their small group would be of no interest to casual thieves; the packs were untouched and the bodies unsearched. She found five hazelles grazing in the area, three dead and her own trapped in a crevice, afraid to back out. The poor animal must have been in it all day, or the raiders would have taken it: the three missing beasts, along with her own, had been the best of the lot. Eon had mentioned Cied contempt for city-bred animals.

Tay settled in on a ledge, preferring to meet any enemies while on solid rock. Tikki helped to eat the dried seeds and fruits and wanted a tiny sip of water. Akemmi did not seem to need much fluid. As darkness fell, Teloa surveyed her domain and took stock of the situation. Strangely, or perhaps not so strangely, she felt very calm. Her steady family upbringing had prepared her for emergencies in a small farm community. This was merely one more emergency. They had wanted the twins— alive—or several of the attackers would have not allowed themselves to be injured capturing them. Though not experienced, the young men had proven to be fierce fighters when cornered. The warriors had spent most of their time trying to defend the elders and Brett. Eleven of their enemies lay dead to attest to their skills against overwhelming odds. Teloa toyed with taking one of their robes and then discarded the idea. She had no way of knowing which tribes were currently friendly toward each other and which hostile, and she had no intention of falsely allying herself. They came up so suddenly, the guard did not see them until the last moment. How did they know where to seek?

Tay sighed. The implications were not good. Someone had to tell them which of all possible routes would be taken. The question— to turn back or go on? No one would blame her if she went back; a stranger, unfamiliar with the terrain, no weapons or concrete directions. But if she went back, how

long until another group left? If ever? No help would come
for the current plantings, barely in the ground. And could an
army brave the Ciedär? She doubted it. Lack of water would
defeat them, if nothing else.

"Is that all you can offer them, lady— to go back and
starve with them?" Tay asked aloud. She shivered, expecting
an answer from the ghosts of the dead men. She had not
known them, except for Brett, and he was little to her. But
she could mourn strong life ended prematurely. Not knowing
the rituals of the Nualans by heart, she could only say a
Qu'tai prayer for them and light a candle.

There were no candles. So she chose a torch, enough
light for all of them, the Amurans and their enemies. She
went deep into the wind-carved rock to light it, fearing that
curious eyes might come to inspect the glow. And as she sat
inside the cave, the mournful, spectral Cied drawings staring
back at her, Teloa made her decision.

She would go on. Discovering yesterday that she understood the dialect of at least one of the tribes gave her confidence. Her need to listen very closely, and the fact that she
did not expect any words to sound a certain way, improved
her chances for interpreting. She had actually ended up giving
the formal farewells when Kalith realized her talent for language. And a tiny fear was growing within her: What if there
were people who questioned why she had survived and the
others had not? The desert seemed more friendly than her
potential detractors. She would need two hazelles, one to ride
and the next best for packing. The rest she'd cut loose and
hope they'd find their way to a safer place. The food, water,
all the swords—Eon said he would steer by the moons and
two stars.

———————

Teloa never did know (though the mythmakers later recorded it) about her part in the legends of the painting rock.
The newest came from the Pecaio tribe, and they spoke in
low awe and dread of the battle at the monolith, where much

Cied blood was spilled and every enemy slain or taken. Since the Nuala do not believe in ghosts, the only explanation for the eerie glow illuminating every cavern was the presence of angels, sent by Mendulay, to light the paths of the dead.

CHAPTER SIXTEEN

MT. AMURA—   TWOHUNDRED   NONE
UPPER POOLS   THIRTYSIXDAY

They had chosen a stone glade facing the desert. The
pool of water, sheltered from the star's mid-afternoon
heat by the peak above it, was cool and inviting. Roe
dangled her feet in it, enjoying the feel of cold rock and moist
dirt beneath her hands. Braan was stretched out under one of
the mountain evergreens, looking through the crevice to the
plains below. On, on, and still farther, until sight was lost in
an immense waste of sand. She did not doubt that he saw it
as clearly in his sleep as he did now. The *guaard* was hidden,
as always.

There were no more games to play. The search parties
were back, with the report that their group had aroused the
suspicions of the waste dwellers, the paranoid Wasuu. Corymb had openly suggested that the twins were dead and that
the tribes, by their very silence, were refusing to help. Everyone's nerves were on edge, and a pall seemed to have descended upon the mountain. Despite the first blush of turquoise
and gold in the tilled fields, the whispering had begun. Not
enough planted— not enough food. A conspiracy by a small
group to garner controlling interest in the plantings. A Toli
invasion from the north. Other rumors, some even more ri-

diculous. But many people had begun to fear that they were true.

Roe briefly wondered if it was of any use to have accompanied Braan. But he had looked so pleased when she had asked to come, forsaking husband, children, work, and puppies. To what end? She knew that Braan was blaming himself just as surely as she knew that no other way would have been practical. Aircars would have deeply offended the Cied; an army would have been insanity. She sighed. Now someone had to go. But who?

Gid or Jaac. They were the only two with both the authority and the experience to go and return— alive at the very least. Hundreds of tribes to investigate, their invisible territorial lines dividing the Ciedär, their hates as fresh as the new seedlings. How could Braan choose? She twisted a long strand of hair and looked up quickly at the sound of approach from below.

Jaacav stepped into the small clearing, shaking free of evergreen needles. The lump of fur near Braan woofed in greeting and rolled over.

"Such a welcome. At least you could have wagged your tail," the woman said to Zair. Perceiving that he was being spoken to, the dog thumped his tail against Braan's leg. Braan smiled and beckoned for her to join them.

"A good day's work?" he asked.

"The shield is finished." The words seemed heavy, dropping like a stone to the bottom of the pool. Roe wondered at her own reaction and then knew that there was nothing—not even Braan's disapproval— to keep Jaac from going out into the Ciedär.

Braan managed a sigh. "The first test may be all too soon," he murmured.

"I do not intend to be here for it, but I will give you the desert report on its effectiveness." Braan, studying her intently, did not reply. "I am going into the Ciedär to look for survivors from the first expedition. I come to ask your permission to take Moran and Lyte, if they will go."

"But not my permission to leave?"

"I am not only the *watch* officer but the head of the *guaard* as well. You have failed to honor our rights on several occasions, and in this case especially I have let you have your way."

"And?"

"This shall redeem for all. I believe they are still alive and that a Stigati or Wasuu tribe is holding them, awaiting outside orders. Whether the Dragoche's, Corymb's, or another's orders is not important. I also think that they will not be alive much longer and that we must act quickly. We have perhaps thirtyday to check every Stigati and Wasuu tribe in the 200 Kilon—no more. I cannot believe Genuar is condoning this action. He is probably unaware of it now, but he has his spies. If the perpetrators think the Dragoche's heir is onto their scheme, whatever it is, they will dump the survivors immediately. It calls for action—no more conversation."

"Agreed." Braan's voice sounded very grave. "I do not want this, but I cannot deny it. Why Moran and Lyte?"

"I want fresh eyes and hearts to help the search, and no conflicts over what paths to take within the spiral. They are trained in ways like ours and have improved these last long days with hazelles and lack of weapons. Lyte no longer leaps for a blaster that is not there. Besides, they need to feel as if there is something they can do. I regret taking him from you, Roe, but I believe it is right."

Her heart twisting suddenly at the loss of both of them, Roe whispered, "Yes. Do you think Lyte will come?"

"No. But I intend to ask. He will want to, even if he refuses."

"Gid?" Braan asked.

"No. You need him here, Atare." It all appeared settled in her mind.

"Tomorrow?"

"I think tonight," Jaac replied. "With the proper witnesses, of course."

"Of course," Roe echoed. "Of course." To be going...

| NUAMURA, | TWOHUNDRED | VESPERS |
| MT. AMURA | THIRTYSIXDAY | |

Lyte waited, sitting at a crossways, watching through a

hole in the wall the glittering star fall toward the sea. He felt the tightness in his face, cursed it, but could do nothing to stop it. Moran would be coming soon. And what was he going to say to him?

Jaac had been straightforward. Pure clandestine work, in and out, not a soul aware— he and Moran were the only ones she wished to have accompany her into the Ciedär. Spy out the situation, find and free any living travelers and silently return. Nine shriveled bodies had been found, only the Atares and Teloa unaccounted for. Briefly he wondered which was harder on Braan, his missing brothers or the Caprican woman. A chance to be moving once again, a chance to do what he and Moran were best at.

Why do I hesitate? He had asked himself the same question for an hour, ever since he had turned Jaacav down. *Whom do I punish?* That pulled him up short. Was it spite? Was his anger at this planet superseding everything else? This damn planet. Holding him, trapping him. It already had Moran. He had ceased to think of leaving, was actually supporting Braan's decision as the Nualan tossed out law after law. Damn these crazy Nualans!

Moran charged around the corner and stopped abruptly. Lyte did not give him time to assess the situation. "Packed?" he asked conversationally, knowing that his tratore face would not fool Moran.

"Yes. You?"

"I'm not going."

"Why?"

"Because I'm not."

Moran sat down next to him on the stone ledge. "That doesn't make the slightest bit of sense. A chance to do what we're trained for and love to do, and the possibility of recovering Kal alive so you can resolve your problem with Shinar."

"There's no problem with Shinar. She's near her time. I think she'd like me around."

"But you don't intend for it to be permanent; nor does she. She wants Kal, and I think he still feels the same. Have you changed your mind?" There was a pause. "You've never let a difference of opinion keep you away from the action

before. Not trouble with coworkers, not trouble with superiors. Why should this be different? Lyte, in the names of
the gods, what are you going to do?"

"I don't know." He heard the edge to his voice and the
bleakness behind the words. Moran did not answer. Lyte
suddenly wondered if Roe had figured out what was bothering
him and had spoken to Moran. *Wish she'd tell me* . . . The
Axis Republic was dead or dying— he was a warrior without
a war to fight. Except against this planet. On whose side?
He was not sure about Braan, or anyone else, except possibly
Shinar. And Corymb. He knew where Corymb stood. At least
he knew where he, himself, did not.

"I'll miss you," Moran said finally. Lyte waited for the
famous Moran temper to blow, but the man was quiet, his
expression sad. Reaching out, Moran gently took hold of his
friend's shoulder a moment. Then he stood and walked toward
his apartment to take leave of his wife.

Lyte sat there until long after dusk.

UPPER	TWOHUNDRED	VESPERS
CAVERNS, MT.	THIRTYSIXDAY	
AMURA		

Ronuviel leaned against the ledge of the enclosed porch,
her eyes idly scanning the horizon. The child she held close
did not move; he slept soundly, oblivious to all that had passed
above him in the previous hour.

They were gone. Just the two of them; Lyte had refused
to the end. But she had questioned Moran at length when he
had appeared, for every word, every thought. And she began
to understand what was troubling Lyte. She also saw that it
was something none of them could help him with— he had
to resolve it on his own. A soft sigh escaped her, and Bree
stirred slightly in response. She clasped the infant closer, as
if trying to draw comfort from him. Then, deciding that she
was being selfish, she gently set him back in his cradle. Roe
carefully pulled the light blankets over both babies, her eyes
caressing them. She could see Moran there— mostly in Arien
but in Bree also. She knew that someday she wanted more

children but hoped that Mendulay arranged it in the future. Exhaustion crept up on her, scattering her thoughts. She wanted Moran to be the father. She wanted him for herself. Please, Lord, sweet Mendulay...

She sat at her desk, trailing her fingers along the dark, polished wood, surveying the communiqués, the history 3AVs, the theology texts. For the last fifteenday she had done nothing but sleep, be with the babies, and study. She remembered Moran's amusement when she admitted she needed to hire a homekeeper, and her relief when Liel volunteered to take on the work. Ronuviel had grown accustomed to the privacy of the apartment and was not ready to return to the huge entourage of palace days. Sometimes she could even forget who she was and what she represented.

What lay before her was everything the Amuran archives possessed on the Ciedärlien. She had analyzed it and tried to find answers. Her major finding was the simple fact that she needed more information. That could be easily accomplished; surface communication had been reestablished, and it was once again simple to send a message across the continent. Reaching for a message capsule, she punched out brief requests to the prime ministers of Atare city, Merigwin, Tolis, and Seedar, along with several minor coastal towns. They all had something in common; they traded with the Cied. She asked them the same question. Did they have any recorded information on the tribes? If so, would they send a copy of each notation, no matter how obscure, to the Ragäree by private communiqué? She sealed it with her name seal, now combined with the stars of the Bréthren, the traditional addition marking the Ragäree's sign. Moving to the entranceway, she softly asked one of the two warriors at the door to take the capsule to the communications station, wait while they were all sent, and then destroy the capsule. Roe stressed the need to make sure no one else gained knowledge of its contents. The capsule vanished into a pocket, and with a brief nod the warrior disappeared.

Roe returned to the window, knowing that the *guaard* would take care of everything. It did not matter if spies in the various cities discovered her inquiries. By the time the

information reached Corymb, Roe hoped to have formulated
some concrete answers for his and the synod's questions.

Darkness was falling when a knock came at the bronze
shield.

"Enter."

The dark-haired young woman swept in, setting a tray
on the desk with a flourish. Liel dropped into the rocker with
an exaggerated sigh, pushing her hair out of her face and
looking momentarily younger than her sixteen standard. "The
lifts had lines a kilometer long, so I took the stairs! I was
worried when you did not come to dinner."

"I forgot. The babies were hungry, and with Moran leaving . . . You should not have bothered."

"You must eat," Liel replied sternly. "You do not need
to lose any more weight, just tone up what you have left!
Time to start running up and down the stairs." She uncovered
a dish. "Cheese and noodles, fresh fruit, whole-grain bread,
and—"

"Do you think they are alive?" Roe interrupted.

Liel was silent. "I am naive enough to believe that somehow we would know if they were gone. Have you felt any
sendings from the hereafter?"

Roe smiled. "No."

"Then eat your dinner. No more talk about morbid things.
I have had enough of that. Lyte is in the hall. I think I shall
go tempt him with one of these loaves. Oh, several groups
requested a story tonight, if you are not too tired. Something
hopeful, please, they are still scrubbing the tearstains off the
rocks from the last one you told." Liel flew out the door.

"But a mythmaker is not supposed to tell stories people
want to hear," Roe said aloud. "A mythmaker is a seeker of
legends . . . an interpreter of the truths that rise from the sub-
conscious. My historical tales are merely pastry cream." She
picked up a piece of fruit and nibbled on it, wondering how
the year really had gone for Liel. Her sixteenth birthday had
ended with the destruction of her city. A tale was buried in
there somewhere.

Roe ate quickly of what she wanted, a mood growing

on her. Finishing the passion fruit, a fine ending to a comforting meal, Roe slipped on her sling carry.

As if by magic Liel appeared, no doubt summoned by the *guaard*. "Will you speak tonight?"

"Yes. Put Arien in the sling and bring Bree." They gathered up the blankets, body liners, and other paraphernalia required for baby travel, and then walked into the corridor. One warrior led them, one appeared from the darkness to watch the room, and the third followed as they walked toward the lifts. Passing the crossways, Roe found Lyte was still sitting by the hole in the cave wall, his hands playing with the bread loaf.

"Coming?" Roe asked. "I am going to tell a gatuhlpa." Lyte did not turn his head. "I would like you to come."

That got through to him. "In a little while." Roe nodded for the warriors to continue.

In the garedoc a large crowd had already formed. Shinar came forward over the rocks as swiftly as her advanced state of pregnancy would allow, scooping up Arien from Roe's basket.

"Odelle wants to hold her," Shinar explained. Liel was settling in with Bree, the liner bags piled at her feet. Ronuviel pried herself loose from her thoughts about her children, her sister, and the fragile Odelle, whose pale face glowed at the prospect of holding Arien. The Atare woman walked slowly toward the great fire in the cavern's center. All the family fires had burned down to nothing, the only light source in the garedoc the central pit. Several people threw more wood on the pyre, and Roe stood next to it, letting the warmth creep into her bones. Even with the approach of summer it was always so cool in there.

She took a small sachet from her pocket and threw it into the fire's center. Green, blue, and purple flames spouted among the red and gold. Slowly the garedoc grew silent, so quiet that the absence of sound was almost tangible. Roe lifted her head and hummed a few soft, tentative notes. Then a melody went up— mournful, almost poignant— and at the sound of it even the faxmur birds in the trees outside the cavern ceased to sing. The woman continued. Her tune was lonely and yet dignified, as if no other song could hold court in its presence. None of the people seated around the fire had ever heard it before, and those who could still separate heart from mind knew that it would not be heard again. Finally an end was reached. The notes faded into silence.

"Hear, oh my people, the words of the Ancients. Twenty thousand times has Sol traced his ecliptic migration since mankind first recorded life. Cities, nations, rose and fell, rise and fall. Peoples reach for the pinnacle and collapse into dust. Great works are begun, laws set down, civilization finds its heights— all is forgotten. All ash, death in the winds. Once mankind was a free people, a seeking people, doomed to mortality, doomed to curiosity, never seeing Truth. Now they are in bondage of their own making; and they do not dare to raise their eyes to the stars."

Roe was walking, circling the fire, her arms raised in entreaty. There were faces out there, faces she knew, but the trance cared not, refused to acknowledge them. She was absorbed, ready to perform, to interpret.

"Among the peoples, among the seed of Earth, of Terra, we alone have survived. We alone flourish. Others forget and are forgotten, while we seek the secrets left to be found. For five thousandyear we have been the Brethren. We are the Brethren. We are Nuala."

She could feel Braan's presence as she warmed to her work, feel the power within her, in her words; the recognition of it in her people. The story continued, of a mechanical probe that certified Nuala as a paradise for colonization; of the brave peoples who chose to test their skills against new elements. The *Atare*, the *Dielaan*, and the *Seedar*, three transport ships; well seasoned for their voyage. Perhaps newer or older vessels would not have made it. Disaster, almost total disaster, wreckage everywhere, deaths by the hundreds, by the thousands.

"The hard rains fell on the burnt-out transport ships, spreading disease and deformity. And the people lifted up their voices for help, but no help came. And the lingering generations passed." Her own throat tightened here, as did the others, but she left the thought, moving on to the next sequence. Perhaps the most tragic words in their history.

Turned around. Their past, their future, held on a string

and turned around by one family, one man. Habbukk, the first Atare, though he would not have called himself that. The shield laws—no, she had bypassed them, but they could be woven in, later, at the first crisis.

More wood on the fire, and it burned low again. The whole history . . . not at once, too much; a thousand lifetimes must be told, and still it is not everything. So she left it at the birth of Habbukk's sister's son; born normal, born fertile. Born to lead the people toward a new beginning. Out of death, madness, despair . . .

"We move toward new life!" Her voice rang in exultation, and she was standing on the ceremonial rock, arms outstretched to embrace the willing crowd, though she had no memory of climbing there. As if a spell had been broken, the people withdrew, shaking themselves awake. The light of the three moons pierced the darkness of the chamber, natural and man-made shafts bringing the bittersweet joy of the planet to their feet scant nights before the trine.

A question was asked concerning the story, the history of it. She answered as if in a dream. Another question, the reply coming from Liel as she brought Arien to Roe. Cuddling the child, exhausted, ready to feed them and sleep, Roe faced her people, their faces visibly marked from the spiritual and emotional intensity of the telling. "Is there anything else, Brethren?" she asked the group.

"Yes" came a penetrating whisper she recognized as Lyte's. She turned toward the stairs, the source of the voice. "The rest of the story."

Ronuviel bowed her acknowledgment.

CHAPTER
SEVENTEEN

Lyte had not been at the Ascension Day celebration long when he realized that someone was missing. A pregnant woman walking by focused his thoughts, and he immediately went to find Shinar. He made a thorough search of the grounds; it took nearly an hour and brought no results. Finally he saw one of her roommates preparing to enter the dance floor and caught her arm. "Where's Shinar?"

The young woman looked startled. "You did not know? She went into labor early this morning. Still is. I checked about a half hour ago. I am surprised that you—"

"Where is she?" Lyte's grip tightened on her arm, his face betraying nothing.

"In the life shelter, since she is still in the dorm. . . ."

Lyte was already gone.

———

Moments later he reached the entrance to the life shelter, one of the few sets of solid doors existing in the mountain.

Pulling on it, he found it locked. He began to pound. This brought swift results.

The door cracked a few millimeters, and a man's harried face appeared. "What do you want? Is there an emergency?"

"Yes. I've been told my child is being born here, and I demand to be present."

"Who told you such a thing?"

"That's not important. She told me she wanted my support during this, and I'm here to give it."

The man looked tired and impatient. "That is impossible. She has no chosen, no husband, and that is always a requir—"

"Then it is true; you want only my genes. I am allowed to make a genetic contribution but not an emotional one, is that it?" Lyte interrupted, hiding none of the mocking anger in his voice, letting his expressive Nualan pour out.

From within the shelter Lyte heard Elana's voice say, "Let him in." The healer sullenly gave way, swinging the door toward the warrior. Lyte quickly slipped inside. Moving through the ward to the birthing room, he was surprised at what he found. Shinar was just dropping down on her side after rocking on her hands and knees to ease the contractions. She looked tired and strained but not in pain.

A smile brightened her face, and she held out a hand to him. "I wanted you to come, but I thought it would be worse for you than it was for me," she said softly.

Lyte sat down on a stool next to the bed and took her hand, gently caressing her cheek. "Hey, healer— you didn't tell me."

"So now you know."

"Soon we'll all know."

ATARE'S PEAK   TWOHUNDRED   COMPLINE
                      FORTYSIXDAY

Closing the thick beads behind himself, Braan gave an inaudible sigh of relief. Here he could shut out everyone and everything, even the *guaard*. A flicker of irritation passed through him. For several days not one but two *guaard* had been constantly in attendance, and he noticed even more around Ronuviel and the young ones. And they were obvious, in a manner he could not remember. When questioned, they would merely reply, "We have reason to believe that you may be in danger."

He could not stay angry long. The warrior clan had shadowed him since birth, even off-world. Braan could not remember ever being without them, except for the trek through the wadeyo forest. They had to be operating on instinct or on an unsubstantiated tip, or they would explain the circumstances to him. Feeling persecuted, Braan removed his overtunic and went into the bathing room to test the water.

The festival of Ascension Day had always been one of his favorites, but it was an exhausting time. It symbolized the day of soul-rising, demonstrated by brightly painted handmade kites that were released to the four winds. Dylan had run him ragged while creating their kite, and the afternoon dancing and general celebration had worn Braan out. The women were constantly in attendance as always, and for the first time since Teloa had left, Braan had found himself truly interested in a woman. She had looked a bit like Jaacav.

That woman. . . . she had been coy, secretive, female in the most mysterious sense. He had met her at a wine stall. She was not from Nuamura but from the outlands of the valley, probably the daughter of a grape grower. She wore a holiday skirt and blouse bordered with the emblem of the Tarn clan, a schism group of Atare. In the end he decided that she knew who he was, though she treated him like any other attentive male. Bold, that one, aware of her charms and how to use them. Braan spent the early hours of evening with her; they shared thirdmeal and some dancing.

At the night's full darkness, final carillon, Braan parted from her. Not that he was not tempted. Just not tempted enough. She was different from Teloa, very different, but Tay kept creeeping into his thoughts. He had always been gifted with a rich fantasy life by day and the real thing at night. He had no desire to confuse the two.

"Atare . . ."

He froze, placing the voice, and confused as to why it should be here. She was at the outer door, the lovely of the

festival, edging around the warrior. The young *guaard* had
not let her through the main beads, however, and was keeping
his body between her and Braan. Where was the other? Of
course, he had sent the man to reassure Ronuviel over the
increased number of *guaard*.

"Let her through," Braan said. As he spoke, his eyes
turned from her to the *guaard*. Suddenly the young warrior
gestured, that unmistakable movement that meant only one
thing. Braan reacted instinctively, dropping to the floor, then
reaching for his cat knife. In the hall?

What happened next was a blur, and a knife went by,
millimeters above his shoulder, slicing the shirt fabric. The
warrior was facing Braan, crouched in the door frame, his
right blade still in his hand, the other empty. The woman was
heaped between them. The young man carefully flipped her
over with his foot; the crimson flood across her back was
great. Touching a cord at her neck, the blond pulled out a
gold-and-black tassel— the colors of the Dragoche tribe.
Then the man spun again to the corridor, his knife held at
vital's height as a voice said, "Baakche's assassin."

Braan stared as a desert-robed individual stepped into
view, holding empty hands away from his hips. The Cied
continued in a flat, controlled Nualan dialect. "I am impressed. I thought I would come too late, that she would fool
you. Was she too eager or did not find favor with you?"

"Neither." Braan found his voice and slowly rose. "I
lost my heart before she came, and I am at my soul a one-
woman man." The *guaard* moved toward the Cied and, flick-
ing aside part of the Cied's outer robe, removed a wicked-
looking cat.

"You knew?" Braan asked the *guaard* in a conversational
voice, indicating the woman.

"I knew she was not Tarn clan. Mendulay smiled upon
you, Atare. I am Tarn-bred and raised, and I know every
women tenyear each side of my age. The question was, why
the deception?"

Braan studied the blond's handsome, smooth face, unreadable as his gaze pierced the Cied man. "You are—"

"Noah, Atare."

"What tribe is this man?"

"Deep sand-mountain Dragoche."

Braan stepped forward. "You are full of interesting information, Noah. Stay with me." The young man flinched, his reserve shaken. Those three words were ceremonial. Most Atares had their own *guaard*, who never left them except when ordered; obedience was one of the first laws of the elite warriors. Braan had been alone since his off-world companion had died defending him. But he was not one to turn down an omen.

"We must speak, Braan Atare. I have kept silent and watched a mad one and a liar bandy words too long." The Cied removed his upper veil.

"Welcome, Genuar reb Ibsn Dragoche. Noah, send for hot saffra. Have you eaten, Seri?"

"It is not necessary. We have little time. The Ciedär loses its water as we speak, and I would deal with this before I return to my tribe," Genuar replied. Noah moved to a com and ordered the tray. A flick of the wrist and his cat vanished. Walking to the assassin's body, he removed his other knife and wiped the blade across a clean section of shirt.

"Noah, do not let the Ragäree hear of this yet, and increase the *guaard* on her and Liel." Braan offered the Cied a seat on the plush rug near the window. The man gracefully folded to the floor in acceptance. The second *guaard* returned and did not raise an eyebrow to discover a body to be removed. By the time he had left with the assassin, Braan and Genuar were past superficial talk and deep into the reason for the Cied's arrival.

Genuar handed Braan the scroll of congratulations, to be given to Ronuviel and Moran. "It was twins?"

"Yes. One of each, healthy and bearing Atare eyes. The Ragäree thinks they already show the healer traits." Genuar started visibly at the information. "I am grateful for their births, especially since the disappearance of my brothers while en route to your encampment."

Genuar's eyes narrowed slightly. "I had heard these rumors, but those who engineered the feat are keeping their own counsel. I warned my Brethren of the danger of touching Atare blood. When I find the fools, my hand shall fall heavily."

"Could they be alive?"

The Cied appeared surprised. "I believe so. To kill one of royal blood is a heavy sin. Baakche, in his sanity, would not have done such a thing. They will only be in danger when it is known that I am actively searching for them. There are many ways to end life without using knife or hands. A lone man in the Ciedär with no water. . . . And no proof of the deed. I shall move swiftly."

"Several of the *guaard* are in the desert, seeking them."

"My people shall not hinder them and shall help if they can."

"You know why we sought you?" Braan went on, getting to the heart of the discussion.

"I suspected. For years you have found faster, easier ways to grow food. An admirable goal and result. But you pushed too far, too fast. And the planet turned on you. You need seed and our methods of growing. What do you offer in return?"

"That depends on what the Cied want."

Genuar paused a long time. "What I want and what others want may differ. Until I am the Dragoche, I am merely first of many clan leaders. But Baakche's health is fading. He will not live the year; by High Festival he will be gone."

"We may not have that much time."

"It must be peaceful. If we go warring, the laughter of the off-worlders shall be our only spoil of battle, as they take our gold and leave us to die. We lost many people during the rain of alien bombs. Some tribes have scarce a dozen people left. They need to be completely restocked. Tents, clothing, weapons, herbs grown from the special buds. Some will want trine gold."

"And you?"

The man met Braan's eyes. "I want protection. So they cannot touch us again. Is this possible? I know of the overlapping shield that kept the death bombs from us, the ones that kill the ground. You have given us this defense for many years and never asked payment for the vigil. I know there is nothing in the Ciedär worth protecting, yet you did."

"There are Nualans in the Ciedär. That is enough."

"Can we keep the bombs away?" Genuar insisted. "Not just the death bombs. All bombs."

"Yes." Braan let the word settle. "There is a new shield, recently activated."

"Is invasion possible?"

"Not unless they have found the Dielaan cure or can bring enough water for an army. The new shield has openings to land friendly vessels. Unauthoritzed ones will be severely damaged passing through it. Unless they can build ships as we do, we are safe."

Genuar mulled over the words as Noah set a tray of saffra and kriska next to them. He reached for a mug and held it protectively, lost in thought.

"If the twins are dead," Braan ventured carefully, "this will be difficult. A synod member sows seeds of mistrust among the people. They want Cied skills but shall not forget the deaths of the royal brothers and their ten companions."

"Ten?" Genuar raised an eyebrow. "The traders who met them counted twelve total, but only nine bodies were spotted."

"We hope the planter Teloa, a tall woman, is with the twins." Braan replied neutrally.

"The translator. I shall inquire. Which synod member speaks against us, Atare?" The Cied's eyes widened ever so slightly in protesting innocence.

"You might be surprised."

"If it is Corymb, I am not." Genuar took a sip of his saffra. "He plays both sides and wins the hour. But I think he has already lost. Dissent brews among the tribes. When word spread of the assassin leaving for the coast, Corymb's support was severely eroded. He seems to think us barbarians, but the damnation reserved for king killers . . . They have their own section of hell. It is true we often resort to thin lines when removing enemies. We never kill outright."

"Then you think we have a chance to gain Cied support?"

"A chance." Genuar's eyes flicked to Noah. "Your people are well trained, considering that they grew up soft, in peace. I say the same for their Atare. I warn you now. I must convince the tribes to gather, to listen to me and to you. You must make them believe that you are worthy of the ancient title you bear and the responsibility you hold in your hands. I have long suspected you would be. Prove it."

Braan studied the Cied. "Must I show how long it has been since I fought with cats for my life? How many necks must I break to show this?" His voice was cool.

"You cannot pretend to be nought than what you are. Some Atares are diplomats, some warriors, some saints. The current situation may require all three. I feel and see some of each in you. Whether the priests and chieftains think it is enough?" Genuar shrugged. "Trust High Mendulay."

"You leave immediately?"

"Yes. I will travel this night and tomorrow before I rest. You can still travel by day for a time. Follow me. The grasses die. Soon even hazelles cannot brave the sands safely. Remember— by attempting to have you killed, Corymb destroyed his edge. You can tip the balance." Genuar nodded gracefully and stood. "Fare you well, Atare, until our next meeting." Parting the beads and receiving his knife from Noah, the Cied vanished into the darkness of the corridor. Braan was not concerned about him slipping away safely.

The Atare sat alone for some time and then called the *guaard* at the door. Noah entered the main room. "I go to the Ragäree. Leave someone on the room and accompany me."

LIFE SHELTER   TWOHUNDRED   MATINS
                      FORTYSEVENDAY

Lyte sat near the outer doors, staring at the stars but not really seeing them. Around him the many healers moved silently, blending into the faint light of the glows. The only thing he was truly conscious of was the sound of his son having his first meal. Shinar's remarks punctuated the baby's, fluctuating between delight and difficulty mastering the nursing.

Standing, the man moved over next to the bed. Shinar was lying on one side, a folded comforter under the child to make it easier for him to reach the breast. She seemed shrunken again, tiny, the long, thick hair like a cascade of light around them both. She glanced up at him with a sleepy expression on her face, tryng to relax but looking uncomfortable.

"I thought breast feeding was a normal, natural thing," Lyte said.

"It is. A lot of 'normal, natural things' are not the easiest in the human condition— at first. Remember your first time with a woman? It is one thing to watch someone feeding and another to do it yourself."

"He's not going to go hungry, is he?"

Shinar laughed. "He is not even getting regular milk yet. This special fluid is higher in protein and helps stabilize his immune system, among other things."

"Did I ever tell you I delivered a baby once?"

"No! When?"

"In a war zone. A civ went into labor, and the unit medtech was dead. Fortunately it was her fifth or something like that. She told me what to do and I did it. A healthy girl."

"No wonder you took it so well. It was your second."

"You were fine," Lyte whispered in reply, touching a tiny hand. "At least it— he— wasn't too premature." He was unaware of Shinar's intense scrutiny, his mind spinning. His son. His gift to the planet. What could it give him in return? Did he want anything from it? Shinar— but she was a loan, not forever. For some reason he kept thinking of Corymb. The man did not like him, of that Lyte was certain. Not because of Moran, or being off-world, or even the Axis. Corymb hated anyone with grit, anyone who could outmaneuver him in thinking. If this baby boy, this man-child, grew up with even a fraction of Lyte's own attitude toward hypocrisy and high authority . . . For a season Lyte had dug and pounded beneath the mountain, often working side by side with Braan Atare. Their forced partnership had led to a grudging admiration on Lyte's part, and he had been careful to make sure that Braan had no justifiable criticism of him. All this time Lyte had sworn to himself that he did not belong here, had no desire to be here; but where else would he belong? Not CSSI. He could not stomach returning to the Axis, even if that was possible. For all he knew, he was outlawed. "What is his name?" he asked suddenly.

Shinar looked surprised. "I would not name him without asking you. Look, he is staring at you, he is a watcher. I wonder how much he sees. This may be your only chance, Lyte. If you find a high-house woman—"

"I know, strict naming rules. We have thirtyday until baptism at the earliest. There's no rush."

"What is *watcher* in your tongue?" Puzzled, Lyte repeated her Axis word. "No, no, your native tongue. Every planet has its own."

"Not Secundus CSSI."

"You jest."

"It is believed that Axis roots are in the CSSI system; old Terran, you know. The first colonies. My grandmother was Caprican. A maverick, although it was grampa who bucked the system by marrying her. I take after her, I guess."

"Do you speak Caprican? What is *watcher* in that tongue?"

Lyte thought a long time. Shinar did not speak as the minutes passed. "I think it's *ried*."

"Ried. A good name for an observant baby, do you not think so?" she asked, trying it out on her tongue.

"Ried reb Shinar. Too simple?"

"If it were three or four syllables, we would end up shortening it, like the Ragäree's name. It is the *R* that bothers you. I do not think it is common on Nuala for names, because of the word *reb*, 'child of.' Shall we think on it?"

"I like Ried. I shall think on you both often."

Shinar was silent, not pointing out the Nualan syntax in the Axis tongue. Then she asked, "When are you leaving?"

The man glanced up. He had just reached that conclusion for himself. "I may not. I'll go to Braan and find out what needs to be done."

She reached out in response and touched his cheek. "I am glad."

If Lyte heard the catch in the Nualan words, he did not acknowledge it. Good-byes were too hard as it was. "Good luck, Ried. With your mother's flair, my hedonism, and Kal's discipline, you're going to be something. Don't ask me what." Reaching out and touching the now sleeping baby's hand once more, Lyte kissed Shinar's fingertips in parting and stood to leave.

RAGÄREE'S   TWOHUNDRED   MATINS
PEAK   FORTYSEVENDAY

The silence on the mountain was almost unnnatural. Ronuviel sat watching the planets spiral above her, fingering the sharp blade of her knife, thinking on Braan's words. Her brother sat across from her, watching for reaction. But she did not allow any.

"Where do you want us to go?" she finally asked.

"There is a meditation peak that has been prepared for Arrez. It is above my quarters, almost to the tree line. Go there. Take the children, take Liel— tell Arrez and Gid where you go, no others. Have you chosen *guaard*?"

"No. I do not think Liel has, either."

"Noah and Jaac's second in command will take care of it for you. At least six— I would prefer more. Under no conditions see any representatives of the house of Dielaan. And see Odelle only when the *guaard* is present." Roe eyed him, thinking his precautions excessive. "What if the next assassin is a child? I would rather you see only those you know personally. And please order those Cied supplies from the other cities at once. I want them here in a fifteenday."

"You go to the deep mountains?"

"Yes. I will take a *guaard* with me, or perhaps Lyte. I will ask him."

Ronuviel looked mildly surprised. "You trust him?"

"In so many words. He will feel obligated, whether he personally cares for my welfare or not."

"He is a better man than even Moran thinks."

"I agree." Braan faced her. "You have studied the writings, all we know of Cied. I need you, but..."

"Elana does not think it wise. I shall know when I am strong enough. I may even follow you." Braan chuckled. Roe raised an eyebrow, smiling slightly. She sighed. Staying up this late increased her exhaustion. Standing, she went to the window. "There is something missing; what you tell me of Genuar's words and actions confirms it. The twins, *my* twins, are important, and so is their relationship to you and the throne. That seems simple enough, but the Cied are people

of signs, of superstition, even. We may win the battle on the
basis of that and at least feed our people."

"And lose the war?"

She regarded him steadily. "Possibly. But is it not a
chance we have to take? If we believe, they will. And they
cannot go to war claiming deceit if we treat with them in
good faith."

Braan looked puzzled. Glancing outside, he stood. "Night
lengthens. You can explain that later if we are spared.
I—"

Roe moved over to him quickly, holding him close in a
long embrace. "Come back safely. Bring my man back to
me. And . . . I hope they find Teloa." The expression on his
face did not change, but Roe felt him tense in surprise.

"Look to yourself. And guard my heir and throne."

TWOHUNDRED   LAUDS (MOONSET)
FORTYSEVENDAY

The corridors were very dark, the glows set on their
lowest level. Braan had forgotten how dark a cave was, especially far from the outlets. The small pack slung over his
shoulder seemed incredibly light, the chain around his neck
insufferably heavy. Noah moved with feline grace beside him,
the *guaard*'s tread as noiseless as his own. Another level up
and over and they would be at Lyte's quarters.

"Late for a stroll, isn't it?" Noah already had his knife
out. The silvery man moved toward them. "What brings you
to this part of the mountain? No sense in going up. I'm here."

"Looking for you, Second Officer," Braan replied easily.

"Just Lyte. What a coincidence. I was looking for you."

"Why?"

"The Atare is gracious, but his words are first," Lyte
said ceremonially.

Braan smiled. Even when Lyte seemed to concede an
edge, he did not. "I go to Ciedär to confront the Dragoche
and to bring back as many of our people as live."

"Oh? And how do I fit?"

"The only substitute for a *guaard* is a commando. They

will not let me out of here without one or the other. Care to come?"

"Why?"

Braan did not pretend to misunderstand. "It is your battle too. Moran and Jaac wanted you there. I do. Come with us Lyte. Find your place on this world."

"There's an assassin looking for you," Lyte said conversationally. "Leaving Nuamura is probably the best thing."

"Why?" Noah said abruptly. Braan flicked a glance at him. It was rare that a *guaard* would break into an Atare conversation.

"Because I have a vested interest in keeping you alive," Lyte said. "I'll need a robe and a water gourd."

"And a blaster. The grass withers and desert returns. The great predators stalk the Ciedär nights. Meeting a *katt* with only a sword or a knife is not pretty. Go. We will wait on the stairs."

"How do we leave without being seen? The synod won't be thrilled about this."

"The south exit."

Lyte shook his head. "I personally know the Dielaan who watches it— casually, of course— after dark. Perhaps I'll go pay him a visit before I go off on one of my nightly jaunts. While you slip past."

"Agreed," Braan replied, making a mental note to have a private exit built. Lyte slipped away. Braan turned to Noah and removed his chain of office. He held it out to the young man. "I go now. Keep this against the return of myself or my brothers . . . or my sister's son if all else fails, though I do not see him reaching maturity if we do. And guard Dylan. He is your charge if Corymb Dielaan takes power. He is safe until then, as he is no threat to Dielaan's plans, only a mark for revenge." Braan started to remove the new seal ring, his own crest now bordered with a chain of office, the mark of an Atare. He hesitated.

"Any could use it, Atare, if it was taken, and you not alive to defend it," Noah said gently. "I shall keep it safe until you return if you intend to go through with this."

"I do."

"Then Holy Mendulay be with you," Noah finished, and,

spying Lyte bounding down the stairs, added in a voice loud enough to be overheard, "And if you do not guard him well, off-worlder, then I shall personally cut your throat. I do not advise you to appear again without him."

CHAPTER EIGHTEEN

The hazelles loped along in their constant, almost staggering, gait, their hooves causing the sands to bark like a cavern of yelping puppies. The strange scuffing noise was almost soothing to Lyte, who had ceased to look ahead toward the mountains. Another set of mountains...

"Far enough" came Braan's voice out of the darkness. Lyte straightened on his saddle blanket and stretched as his beast halted next to the leader. He could barely make out Braan's beige robe in the faint light of the rising firstmoon; the embroidery appeared black.

"Do we travel by night yet? I thought you wanted to go on," Lyte said.

"I do. But something is wrong."

Lyte's hand went to his blaster, safely tucked back under his robe for the first time since landfall nearly two hundred sixty days before. "Direction?" he whispered casually.

"Not *katt*. Weather."

Lyte hauled impatiently on the reins of the pack animal, stopping its attempts to wander off. "I thought the rain was over. Long over."

"It is. But pressure changes can bring windstorms. I am

not exaggerating when I say that one summer's wind can grind a stone column into sand."

The warrior did not like the sound of that at all. "Where do we go?"

"These boulders. That is why I stopped. I hope there is an opening large enough to take the hazelles through. Without them I doubt that we would survive." Braan jumped off his hazelle and reached into a pack. Lyte heard the sound of something striking against rock. "Cover your eyes and hold those animals! I am going to check for *katts*."

For once the off-worlder was glad of his authority-response training when a flare erupted before his eyes. Braan quickly found a cave opening to his liking and tossed the cylinder inside. Leaping back, the Atare drew his blaster and reached to calm his hazelle. There was an explosion of high-pitched sound from within the dark hole, and hundreds of tiny winged creatures fled to the black skies.

"What?"

"Vaaze. Harmless but they have a habit of passing their droppings when artificial light strikes them. If you need to seek shelter without time to use flares, be prepared for a damp head!" Snorting his disgust, Lyte slid off the beast and began to drag it inside.

It was not long before they had a small fire burning and water boiling. Lyte once again secretly marveled at the tiny pressed disks, which, when burned, gave off considerable and long-lasting heat in a multitude of colors. Braan dropped some sealed pouches into the water to heat and then reached for the plates.

"No, you've had to do everything. I'll do it," Lyte said, holding up a warning hand. "Sit."

Braan sat down. "Did it ever occur to you that I get tired of other people doing everything?"

"So we'll take turns. Eat." He settled against one wall, looking out at the stars. "That low one, what planet is that?" He had watched it for several nights. It had come to herald ride's end.

"I believe it is Niamh." Braan burrowed down next to a hazelle, pouring himself some saffra.

"Niamh? I thought Niamh was the morning star."

"In winter. In summer it is the evening. It will set soon; the season is early yet."

They sat in almost companionable silence, watching the planet set. Lyte let his thoughts drift, following them down a path leading back to his illness and a question that had bothered him. "Braan," he began, "something I've wondered about . . . Corymb has hated you for how long? And has even tried to kill you. But you were the third son; whatever his warped mind wants—the trine mines, the throne, power, a new hierarchy—logically you are out of the running. Why kill you?"

Braan did not turn his head. "If something happened to Tal, I was next in line. Deveah would have been ruled unfit by the *guaard*. That is the one thing Corymb could not and cannot get around—the *guaard*. The synod might have taken Deveah with a strong prime minister, because of the twins' youth and Deenn's wild ways. But not the *guaard*."

Lyte felt uneasy. "So Deveah was a front all along? Then what was he—Braan, did Corymb know that *both* Tal and Deveah would die? Was he hoping that Jaacav and the *guaard* would fail if the Axis pulled out and a coup—" Lyte sat up. "Do you realize—How long has he dealt with the Cied?"

"Let it go, Lyte." Braan's voice was easy. "If it is true, only Corymb, Baakche, and his assassin know the truth of it. The assassin is dead, Baakche a mad one, and Corymb certainly will not tell us. The *guaard* watches."

The commando considered the implications of the Nualan's words, and a vision of power flickered at his mind's edge. A form of democracy? But what if a corrupt Atare and *guaard* . . . "Do you check out the genes of off-worlders who marry Atares?" Lyte said abruptly. He was ashamed of his rudeness, but it was another question that had gnawed at him during the dark nights.

"After staying among us so long you still fear without thinking—for Moran and for yourself?" Soft, but still a question. "Do you think Shinar would allow anyone to touch, to change the child she carries? And you have the nerve to ask me that. Do you think a council appointed to look for 'healthy stock' would have allowed me to marry Enid?"

Lyte was silent. Wrapped up in his concern for Moran and his own paranoia, he had completely forgotten about Enid. "My apologies. I did not live with it, and it slipped from me. Did you check out Moran?" he persisted.

Braan smiled. "No. Where would we check? Our file person knew Moran and said that there was nothing to investigate. He was as he appeared. Moran told Roe about his parents, siblings, and temper before he knew who she was. It was enough. The biases of observers are not for us. Each person stands on their own merits here."

"You sure a commando is enough for a *guaard*?" Lyte asked a mug of saffra later. "That guy with you didn't sound as if he were joking. His last words, I mean."

"He was not. Loyalty—total loyalty to the Atare and Ragäree—is the first criterion of a *guaard*. He would die without hesitation for me. He does not think you would. Therefore, in his eyes you are an unsatisfactory guardian. Let us drag this fire farther in." Braan grabbed the edge of the fireproof tarp and hauled it deeper into the cave. One hazelle flopped down with its spine to the curved opening, another crowding to stand in the back. Braan tended the fire so that it was burning brightly again. Lyte, uneasy, moved away from the cave opening and around the boulders to the fire.

"Anyway, the kid didn't look happy that I was going and he wasn't."

"You are not much older than that 'kid.' He was irritated because although I had just asked him to remain with me, obedience to the Atare is very important to a *guaard*. Dylan needs him now. With me he would have been unnecessary— or dead."

"I don't—"

"All Atares have a special *guaard*; first, one chosen for them as a child, then one they choose in their adolescent years. Mine died while I was off-world, and since I was not the heir and times were peaceful, no one pressured me to find another. As Atare, I must have several companions to protect the office. Negligent of me to wait so long. I took Noah the night we left."

"Why?"

"His finesse at saving my life, among other reasons." Braan had told Lyte briefly about the assassin and Genuar's visit on their first night of riding. He had a right to know the danger. "I thought you knew about the *guaard*."

"I have thought about it; why it still exists when the Axis requires its members to hold no standing armies except Axis Forces."

Braan poured another mug of saffra. "The standing Axis law applies to whatever body governs the planet or system. The *guaard* is what the name implies—the Atare family's private guard. They are accountable only to the ruling Atare and his eldest sister and take any orders from them."

"Convenient."

"As Moran has said, I wonder how many other planets have similar bodies of warriors."

"So that evades the standing-armies law. How many *guaard* are there at any one time?" Braan did not answer at first. He smoothed his new facial growth and massaged a knot in his shoulder while staring into the fire. It occurred to Lyte that even now the Nualan did not trust him. Then the man spoke, and Lyte was ashamed.

"To be a *guaard*, and to be under the ruling house, is special. There are only, by tradition, five hundred active *guaard* and one thousand standbys. The thousand are on leave, raising families or pursuing alternative careers. Some serve—served—in the Axis Forces. But there are only two ways to leave the *guaard*, save death: if the current-generation Atare or Ragäree ask one to, for positive or negative reasons, and by one's own request. It is a lifelong trust that can be short in times of trouble. There are thousands more who have had much of the training and then go off-world to serve the Axis, for the glory of Nuala. When they return here, they are auxilary, continuing *guaard* training and on the list for consideration, should a position open up. And every Nualan, from childhood on, is trained in elkita. It is part of the religion—also for health."

"Thousands of *guaard*, or potential *guaard*. What do you use them for?"

The Atare smiled faintly. "The last three thousand years—for ceremony. And general family security. Before that, to unite Nuala."

For a time Lyte considered the place of royalty and listened to the swiftly rising wind. Suddenly his ears popped.

Braan reached out to soothe the prone hazelle, which was beginning to look wild-eyed. "It comes. Soon. That is the warning."

"Elkita. That was how you subdued the Durite?"

Braan nodded. "The priests and priestesses teach it. It is very fancy gymnastics and mind over matter. They train openly, but you have avoided the temple areas, and therefore the kita, the training ground."

"What are the oaths?" Braan looked up, surprised. "I heard two children talking about becoming *guaard* and 'sharing the oaths.'" Lyte had to raise his voice; the wind had increased. He was receiving a lot of information and decided to take advantage of it.

"They are simple. The *guaard* swears to obey the orders and follow the eldest male and female of the Atare throne generation, as long as those two do not violate the ancient laws of Nuala. In return, all Atare heirs, no matter how distant from the throne, are always trained in desert commando fighting, elkita, and self-defense. They should be able to succeed as commander-in-chief at any reasonable age."

"Such as?"

"Sixteen or so. Also, the Ragäree and Atare must always put the raising, training, and nurturing of the heirs foremost in their minds, above all other pursuits, and be willing to swear before Mendulay that they have done so." The last was shouted. Then Braan shook his head and gestured negatively in the direction of the cave opening. It was plain that there would be no more conversation. Lyte clapped his hands over his ears, thankful that he was not beyond the boulders, much less outside. Braan was already curled up next to the now banked fire.

"Sleep?" Lyte joked. "Through this?"

It went doubly unheard through the wind. Braan was asleep.

THE CIEDÄR   TWOHUNDRED   TIERCE
                    FIFTYTWODAY

They were kilometers from the boulders by starrise. Lyte had awoken only once in the night, when the wind stopped. It had been so sudden. Lyte suspected that another pressure change had actually disturbed him. Remember to watch for pressure changes. . . .

"Is there anyone far from here who weighs on your mind?" Braan asked as they rode.

Lyte shrugged. "A little curly-haired Vergean hustler, and occasionally my mother; without her protection I wouldn't have lived to my majority."

"Parents can be helpful."

"Parent. Singular. My old man would try to kill me with his bare hands, and my mother would use her threat of leaving with the family name, fortune, and reputation as a way to stop him. So I owe her more than the average child. I did the best thing I could for her. When the old man disowned me, I cleared out completely." Lyte's tone did not encourage further comment.

"I can see why Moran became everything for you" was the reply. Braan glanced at him as he said this and suddenly pulled up his hazelle, seizing the reins of Lyte's mount.

"What the—"

Braan reached back to the pack animal and lifted off the largest water gourd. "Why is this not under your robe?" The words had an edge of incredulity and irritation to them, a tone Lyte remembered from a day of discipline, when Braan had both appointed new judges and passed down sentences for crimes. The Nualan had removed his lower veil. "There is no way to fully explain the danger! If a storm arose, we could be separated from each other and the animals in seconds! *Always* carry water on your person, under your robe and against your body. Do not drink out of it while we have the others. It is only for emergencies."

Braan pressed against his own robes, outlining the other large gourd, strapped to his ribs. "And for Mendulay's sake never open one during a storm!" He held it out by its strap to Lyte.

Neither commented on the obvious: that Lyte had watched Braan do this every day of their trip since they passed out of the Sonoma Mountains. The warrior had not thought Braan was hoarding water; he realized that he had not thought about it at all. Lyte masked his own personal irritation, as he saw that Braan was more furious with himself for not explaining it thoroughly than with his companion. Nodding, he took the gourd.

"Now," Braan added.

Lyte parted the robe, lifted his caftan, and carefully wrapped the gourd's strap around his body above his joqurs waistband. "Anything else?" Lyte asked.

"You have spoken to the *guaard* about diablos, sand spouts?"

"Yes."

"If I think of anything, I will mention it." Veiling again, even the upper veil, Braan pushed the hazelle into its trotting gait. Following suit, Lyte fell into line behind the man. He caught himself wishing that he could reassure the Atare. Lyte had heard about the sandstorms, but the season for them was not now, and they were more frequent farther south. The *guaard* had not thought it important enough to expound on. Last night was bothering Braan. A freak storm . . .

Your mortality shows, my friend, Lyte thought without rancor. *Too much is on your mind, and your hopes wither with every step we take.* Lyte was not ready to offer words of comfort aloud, though he did not know why—why he wanted to, why he could not. They rode in silence until well past sext.

In the distance, looking deceptively close, were mountains. A range rose high before them, its baked face a smoldering menace. The tips of the peaks beyond were half hidden in haze. There was no visible vegetation. In the crevices, Braan had said, usually only in light for an hour. Water could be drained from them; they could be eaten. Emuvv was one; tropc was another.

Secondmeal had been sparse, eaten without shade, mainly to rest the hazelles. They had sat in a circle of the animals, the dry, tumbling remains of monsoon grasses whirling by them. Braan had lifted a small rock, revealing a flurry of small crustaceans digging into the sands. Krwb, the major scavengers of the deep desert. The scene had given Lyte involuntary shivers.

"Why did you come?" The question startled Lyte, snapping him out of daydreams. An answer burst from him. "Because I belong here."

"Agreed. Why now?" Lyte pulled alongside to look at the man. "I mean, with Shinar's time so soon . . . I intended to ask you to come, anyway, but . . ." Braan trailed off when he realized that Lyte was chuckling.

"My error. Shinar had the child the night we left. A healthy boy, and she appears fine. We're going to call him Ried."

"Sounds good. I have never named any of mine. It must be nice. A name is important. So, your responsibility to stay ended, you decided to follow Moran?" Braan rolled on.

"You know better, Atare. Let us not play games. You need help, and I'm vain enough to think that I'm just the warrior to give it to you. If Corymb seizes power, I am one person he won't want around. The kid? Shinar being Arrez's daughter might protect them, but then again, maybe not. I've got a stake in your liegeship, and I intend to keep my eye on you at all times," Lyte replied, flickering the reins at a cloud of tiny insects swarming around the hazelle's head.

"We will let that stand as the whole reason. Noah would be pleased."

Lyte did not comment. Everything in his head was very confused "Could you have gone alone by sea safely, if your goal was there?" he asked instead.

"Certainly. I was well trained by my childhood *guaard*."

I'll say. Lyte's next question was forgotten. His ears suddenly popped. Braan reined up and scanned the horizon.

Sand, sand forever, and the last peaks of this mountain range, stretching away north.

"Veil. Let us go." Braan slapped his hazelle into a run, dragging the pack animal behind him; Lyte followed, fighting both his mask and his beast. A quick glance to his right showed dark clouds coming from the southeast, dimming the mid-afternoon light.

"Can we beat it?" Lyte yelled.

"We can try. Remember what the *guaard* told you!" was the answer, Braan's anger evident in his voice. Pushing the beasts hard, too hard in this heat? The warrior stole another glance over his shoulder and was appalled to see how fast the storm was moving. The mountains were so close, they had to reach the mountains, to endure the storm without the mountains . . . The hazelles needed no urging; they sensed that something was wrong. The mountains were perhaps a league northwest—

Darkness. It descended so abruptly, the animals slowed to a walk without signals. Lyte reached forward, his hand closing on the pack hazelle's tail just as visibility vanished. Where was the sand?

It struck. Lyte shriveled into his caftan, unable to absorb the fact that he could feel the stinging grains through two layers of cloth. There was nothing but wind; Braan could have been screaming into his ear without effect. Sliding off his beast, careful to retain his grip on the second hazelle, Lyte wrapped one arm around his mount's neck and waited. In a few moments the pack animal started moving. Hoping desperately that he was following Braan and not a loose creature, Lyte pushed his rider beast forward.

The *guaard* spoke the truth. The blowing sand was not as bad closer to the ground. The off-worlder felt nothing on his feet except wind gusts. He had not thought about the darkness— of course, it would be dark. Rocks, small ones, but large enough for both he and the hazelle to trip over. Lyte's grip on the pack animal loosened. Only for a moment; long enough. Lyte forced his beast to keep moving, trying to catch up. Then he stopped.

Braan would not be able to find him, even if he noticed that his partner was missing. Lyte could no longer see the hazelle he was holding, and the temperature had dropped, rivaling the previous night's cold.

He decided. Forcing the hazelle to lie down, he banked himself against it, pushing at the sand to pile it to either side. The animal had already curled up as best it could, burying its face in Lyte's robes, its horns across his legs. The man made sure that the special veil filter was in place over his nose and mouth, dug himself down as deep as he could, and waited.

CHAPTER NINETEEN

It was past nightfall when the storm finally blew itself out. Braan stuck his head out of the opening cautiously. Nothing. A faint evening breeze had begun, but no sand, no gale-force winds. In front of his crevice lay the half-buried carcass of the pack hazelle, already drained of its fluids by krwb. He had lost his rider beast entering the mountains: It had stepped in a rock fault and broken its leg. Sand, the deadliest enemy of hazelles, had killed the pack bearer. Their lungs could not veil to protect them from the blowing, burning grains.

Braan sat a moment, his head bowed, trying to face the loss of Lyte. Even the elements conspired against them. If he had made it to the mountains . . . It was not until the hazelle broke its leg that Braan realized he had lost him. In the storm season groups always traveled roped together. If he was ever in the desert with an off-worlder again, he would use ropes, no matter what the time of year.

An agonizing scream rent the darkness, chilling the man to the bone. *Katt*—an adult male, a hungry one. On the scent of prey he was confident of— Here? The main diet of *katt* was tazelle and brush rodent, timid fare but swift. Lyte. Braan jumped up, pulling out his blaster and setting it on high beam. Mastering the rush of adrenaline, he swiftly crept in the direction of the cry, up into the mountains.

———

The third new moon had just popped up when Braan reached the *katt*'s plateau. He almost jumped back off the ledge when the beast roared again, until he saw the caves. An echo made the animal seem closer. Moving as noiselessly as possible to the entrance, Braan pulled out one of the two flares he had brought up and lit it. He heaved it as far into the cave as he could and stepped back to hide in the scrub brush. Nothing. No vaaze, no *katt*. Whispering a quick prayer Braan stepped into the cave.

Not a cave, a cavern. A maze of openings stared him in the face, the ceiling rising to incalculable heights. Cied paintings trickled down the walls, mournful eyes staring at him. He heard another scream from the left, and it occurred to him that the male might have lost the scent. Then there was a rush of footsteps; someone was running toward him. He ducked in the first opening, the tip of his blaster peeking around the corner. A Cied robe flashed by him, fluttering wildly and Braan leaned against the stalagmite nearest the entrance, steadying his weapon. A flash of black and gold came tearing out of the darkness, and he fired. The animal collapsed onto the stones lining the cavern floor. There was a pause, and Braan stepped out quickly, checking the beast. The blaster had ripped its chest open. A female...

Trembling, Braan slowly backed away from the body. Not a young one, a full adult, and her mate had acted as a ruse. He looked wildly for the other person. Cied? The robed figure had been too slight for a man. A small rock slide started within the cave. Braan whirled and ran to the entrance where the Cied was huddled, gasping for air. Grabbing a wrist, he pulled the human along and toward the left cave slot. At the same time he lit the other flare. The individual began to fight him, swinging a drawn cat knife.

"We cannot outrun it. We must find an opening too small for it to pass through!" Braan hissed softly, forcing some of the Cied dialect. "It will circle to the other side!" The other

immediately complied. Light from the flare revealed a fairly
smooth, wide path, and they began to run. They had until
the *katt* found their trail; then they had nothing. Twists and
turns and false trails, always taking the narrower lead. The
wall paintings accompanied them; some were of *katt* hunts.
In one picture the *katt* was hunting the man. Braan, himself,
was becoming winded when he found what he sought. An
opening, a bit high but human-sized, too small for *katt*. He
tossed the blaster into the opening; until it recharged, it was
useless. Jamming the flare into a hole, Braan grabbed the
Cied and pushed her—it was female—up the wall. The
woman must have been on the run for a long time. She was
exhausted and having trouble finding footholds. There was
no time to be chivalrous. When she slipped and fell for the
second time, Braan pushed her aside and was up the wall in
a bound. Two steps and he was pulling himself inside. Turning, he reached down for the bundled woman. She had found
the first foothold.

Braan heard sliding pebbles. Using his last strength, he
dragged her to his level and flipped her over his knees into
the hole. Fumbling to drag her completely inside and feeling
for his cat knife, he saw a pair of gleaming golden eyes. The
katt crouched and sprang; high, arcing, hurtling at them with
the weight of five men. Braan brought the knife down.

The *katt* screamed in pain and fell to the path, clawing
hysterically at the rocks. The blade had punctured the top of
the skull, just as it was designed to do. Ignoring his now
tattered sleeve, Braan sagged against the lip of the hole,
stretching his legs and undoing his veils, using them to wipe
the sweat from his brow and neck. Dear sweet Mendulay . . .
The woman was still draped over one of his legs, shaking
but silent, the dignity of her people wrapped around her more
securely than cloth. She sat up slowly, curling her knees close
to her body and wrapping her arms around herself, weaving
in her dream as if to pass out from exhaustion. Braan grabbed
her to steady her movements, and then pulled her closer when
he realized that her body was icy to the touch. She did not
protest—she was that tired.

He listened to the *katt*'s dying whimpers as its brain
stopped functioning and then noticed that the woman's veils

were loose and bent to see the age of his fellow survivor.
She glanced up; gray eyes met green and brown ones. Amazement crept over her smooth, thin face, and Braan wondered
if he looked as shocked as he felt. He had prayed to find her
but had expected her to be with a tribe.

"Thank you" came a whisper; tight, high-pitched, like
water reeds in brisk wind. How well she controlled fear.

It was too much for him. He cautiously touched her face,
as if afraid that she would vanish. Then he let her head drop
to his arm and bent to kiss her; gently, thoroughly, as he had
wanted to do for so long. Reaching to hang on to his other
arm, she did not try to stop him. They clung to one another
a while, and then Braan straightened.

"Are you alone?"

"Except for my hazelle." Teloa must have read more in
his face. "Your companions?"

"Lyte is . . . gone. We were separated in the sandstorm.
And the three animals are lost or dead." He eyed her search-
ingly. "You have heard, seen nothing?"

"Tikki. No humans." She gripped his arm in sympathy.
"He is a commando. He'll make it."

Braan did not answer. He flicked on the safety of his
recharged blaster. "Come. Before the flares die." He helped
her down from the ledge, and they slowly made their way
back up the path. Braan was thankful for his memory, which
had saved him in mazes before. He pinpointed the *katt* in his
mind. Krwb did not venture into a cave, and he wanted the
skin if there was time.

"The blaster." Teloa stopped him before they reached
the front of the cavern. He looked surprised. "There is another
katt, smaller."

The pit of his stomach grew cold and knotted. For an
adolescent to prowl the same range as an adult pair, it had
to be desperate.

They soon learned how desperate. They went down several plateau levels to where Tay had hidden her hazelle and
supplies in a narrow cave. Crawling through the tiny opening
facing south, they were greeted by Tikki, who immediately
burrowed into Tay's hood. The hazelle was behind the fire,
its body caked with dried foam. It turned a wild eye on them.

The cave smelled of blood. Puzzled, Tay went to the beast while Braan built up the fire. Then Tay gasped and pointed to the other exit where she had brought in the hazelle.

Braan stared, astounded. She had gathered and kept all the Cied swords from painting rock, and planted them, blade-up, in the dirt, the shorter blades extending from the sides of the cave opening. The young male *katt,* determined to reach the hazelle, had slashed its face and neck trying to squeeze between the weapons. Finally it had attempted to jump over them and had impaled itself.

The Atare went outside and pulled the carcass off the swords from the front. Then he asked if she was going to boil water.

"I have none."

"None?"

"I use these plants." She held up a stalk of tropc. "Not the freshest but palatable."

"I have water with my things. Wait here."

———————

The packs were untouched. Any small, furred scavengers would wait several days to make their meals, until the hazelle was so sweet with death, a *katt* would not touch it. The krwb had left little for their fellow predators to find. Braan stripped off the equipment and returned to Teloa's level.

The woman had dug out what rations she had left, including some roots from mountain plants. She had also removed her tattered outer robe, piling it like a pillow next to the fire. As Braan entered, Teloa straightened abruptly, and he knew she was nearly asleep. His own exhaustion weighed on him.

"How long did you hide from those *katt*?" Braan asked, surveying the pitiful pile of food. No wonder she looked thin. She had improvised well, though, her planter's knowledge helping her find the tubers and stalks most likely to provide nourishment.

"The pressure changed while I looked for food, so I sought a cave. I thought rain was coming. Unfortunately it was the same cavern the *katt* were in. I avoided them several days, through two storms—I've been here four days," she

added, anticipating the next question. "I'm afraid I finally
got lost. I was looking for the Dragoche camp."

"You did well. Across this range is sand and, in the
distance, the mountains we seek. It would take us six or eight
days riding from the far side of this mountain. I will explain
how to hide from sandstorms. I do not intend to lose you as
I lost Lyte." He poured one canteen into a pan. "Saffra?"

"Please," she answered, and then caught her breath. "But
we need—"

"There is a free well near here. We will stop there tomorrow, before we cross this range, and clean our faces."

"The sand works very well," Tay offered.

Braan smiled. "That is how the Cied bathe, and how we
must too. But nothing feels like cool water on the face or
down the throat." He sacked the yellow tubers and dropped
them in the boiling water. "Fish them out when they start to
burst their skins. I have something I need to do. I may be
awhile." Checking to be sure that his blaster was recharged
and secure, Braan slipped out into the chill night.

He sat outside on a rock for several minutes, controlling
his breathing, watching the stars above. He deserved highest
laurels for that casual performance. He had forgotten how
beautiful she was. How to begin? He had no idea, but he had
to keep his physical attraction to her under control or he would
fail. The only way to do it right now was to cool down and
work himself into sleep. Tightly gripping the flares he had
palmed, Braan adjusted his eyes to the sinking moons and
started up the mountainside.

TWOHUNDRED   MATINS
FIFTYTHREEDAY

The adult *katt* were as he had left them, stiff as a board
and dyeing the stones crimson. Braan quickly stripped off
his clothes and began to cut away the first pelt. The skin of
a *katt* was worth its weight in diamonds off-world; the skin
of one killed with a knife thrust was beyond price. And that
pelt would be his major gift to Baakche Dragoche. The
others . . .

It took less time to skin the female. He folded them the way his *guaard* had taught him and walked back down the rocky slope. After cutting up the adolescent *katt*, Braan moved away from the carcass and scrubbed himself clean with the fine sand in the bowl of the glen. Then he sat awhile, watching the last moon set and the night grow old. Peace washed over him, the presence of Mendulay settling like a mantle. It was not until the cold reached his bones that he remembered he had eaten nothing. Regretfully detaching himself from the meditative mood, Braan reached for his joqurs and caftan.

━━━━━━━━

Tay was asleep next to the fire, her caftan and one blanket wrapped warmly around her, the other coverlet folded and set next to his pack. She had found several other bits of food in the bags and had arranged the brightly colored seeds and dried fruit on the second blanket's edge. In a tightly sealed sack balanced precariously above the pan were his tuber and beans. The water was now saffra.

"Warm without being overcooked. Nicely done, my lady." Braan sat across the fire from her and began his meal, wishing briefly for fresh bread. He was grateful that her hunger had overcome whatever desire she would have had to allow royalty to eat first.

One hazelle to carry their food and water. Six days riding. But both of them on one beast? Both of them walking with a pack animal . . . Maybe twelve or fourteenday, if they were lucky. And maybe a dead hazelle at the end of the trip; even hazelles needed some water. He would regret that, but otherwise it could be their own deaths. He looked long at the beast. It was sinewy, as if it had thrived on the trip. Tay must have fed it every plant from the last range to this one. There would be boulders in the desert, crevices to shield from the light and heat of the day, though they were not on any proper map. Some had free wells, unclaimed by any tribe, for the use of all.

He quietly searched the packs, and his heart leapt to see a long string of gourds. She had kept them with no hope of finding water; or she had kept faith.

Braan closed the satchels and banked the fire for the night.

RAGÄREE'S   TWOHUNDRED   VESPERS
PEAK   FIFTYTHREEDAY

Liel was studying the ancient parchment so intently that she was unaware of Ronuviel's entrance. Roe smiled faintly, her amusement fading as she saw what her little sister was reading. Trouble—the girl could draw parallels as easily as she and Arrez had.

"Broadening your horizons?" Roe heard herself say.

"Working on an ulcer," Liel replied without turning.

Ronuviel forced a chuckle. "Coming with me?"

Liel spun around. "You are crazy! You are really going to go east! You could get killed, and the babies too! Ever since the night Braan and Lyte left, things have been crazy. The councils have not met, nor the synod; Arrez issues orders and Gid carries them out. People are becoming worried and suspicious. Not one member of the male throne line left in Nuamura, and now *you* are planning to leave!" A moment's pause, then, "Why are you asking me to go?" Liel forced out. "Are you so confident of success that you will take our whole family into the Ciedär? I would think you would be ordering me to stay here!"

Ronuviel sat down on the edge of the desk, facing her little sister. Not so little; a woman, thinking with adult concern. "Liel," she started gently. "Do you disbelieve the prophecy just because you may be a part of it?" Liel did not answer. "I am not crazy, dreaming about my children becoming great leaders and taking Nuala into a new age. I am practical. And I am willing to do anything moral to bring about the safety of our people. Have you looked in the fields? Healthy plants, yes, but small, and likely to bear small yield. We will not last another year without assistance. There will be no off-world help. We know that; we merely laugh and jest as night closes in around our fragile fortress. The Cied can aid us, but we must convince them that the house of Atare is their lifeline, just as they are our future. Dielaan will not waste energy shielding the Ciedär, no matter what his promises; and if the Fewhas land, Ciedärlien will die. No race of semi-barbarians would dare leave a nomadic people ripe for rebellion within striking distance of their installations.

"We must show them their danger, show them that Braan is worthy of their confidence, and show them that the house of Atare continues. Genuar can convince them of the danger. I believe in Braan's ability to prove to them his worthiness. And I think the prophecy of Naitun can be applied to me: 'In a year of flame and thunder, from the womb of a healer life shall be born, bearing sight no one has seen before. And ye shall bow down to the one before them,' and so on!"

"I know the prophecy," Liel finally interrupted.

"Do you understand it?"

"I know what you want to make of it. In a year of great upheaval 'them'—the twins—are born with Atare eyes never before recorded, and the one to lead is that ruler born before them, Braan. You think you can get away with this?"

A knock came at the bronze shield. "Enter." Arrez walked into the room. He studied their faces, his own unsmiling, and then his glance fell upon the open manuscript.

"Are you going?" he asked conversationally.

Liel stared at him in amazement. "You as well?" she breathed.

"It rips my heart. But it is the only guarantee of success. I believe in Mendulay's providence."

The young woman leapt up. "Then I am also going! Someone in the party must have common sense! I will be ready in ten minutes." She flew out the doorway before either of them could answer her.

"You are resolved on this?" Arrez said a moment later.

"For me. I do not know if I am right to take her. But who else can I ask to take the risk? This is Atare business, in the end. I do not think I can handle the children in the desert alone, and can you see a *guaard* tending one of them?"

Arrez reached out and gently touched her cheek. "Be cautious. Let them recognize you for what you are. Do not force your hand. I pray for a safe journey and a swift return. There is no way to determine what will happen."

"Have faith, my priest."

"I should be saying that to you."

THE CIEDÄR   TWO HUNDRED   PRIME
                    FIFTYSIXDAY

When Lyte opened his eyes, he could see the rising star of morning swiftly topping the horizon. It was so large, he could almost reach out and seize it. A blur detached itself from the shadows in his vision and came to him. He felt his head and shoulders being lifted and water being poured down his throat, streaming down his pale beard. It was as if his body belonged to another person. Lyte no longer seemed to exist.

"Don't breathe it, you're not a fish." Moran. How did Moran come into the dream? A day or so ago Moran had appeared, shaking his head in irritation and telling him he was a stupid, selfish fool for waiting so long to come into the Ciedär. And then to lose the Atare! And to share his water with the hazelle even though starstroke had set in. Starstroke? Lyte had wondered, even as he had drained his gourd, much thirstier than a commando ever had right or reason to be. He had staggered on, looking for shade, for water, until his head swam so badly that he could no longer stand.

"Bra-an . . ."

"You were alone, except for your beast." Another voice. Jaacav. A dream? Not a dream. Lyte slowly opened his eyes again, focusing on the shadowy lumps. A vatos wool blanket was spread over him. There was no fire that he could see.

"What are you—what were you doing out here? What happened to Braan?"

"Where . . . find me."

"In the sand, west of here. The hazelle stayed with you, and we spotted movement. Where is my Atare?" Jaac asked, her voice sharp.

"Sandstorm." Lyte tried to sit up, his head clearing. He felt weak, almost as weak as when he had radiation poisoning.

"From the beginning. Take your time. We're not leaving until you can ride out of here," Moran said. The warrior helped his friend sit upright, leaning him against a stone.

Lyte explained it all, from the arrival of the assassin to the last thing he remembered, collapsing at the feet of his hazelle. Jaac sat still a long time after his story ended, watching Kee rise higher in the sky. Then she stirred, rearranging her robes and reaching for a tool to kindle the banked fire.

"He lives," she said definitely.

"Mendulay spares him for some other end?"

She turned fiercely at this, but there was no trace of mockery in Lyte's voice. "This thing with Genuar is dangerous. If you left on Ascension Day, then word must be spreading through the campsites. And their captors will attempt to remove all traces of the deed."

"Have you narrowed down the possible places they could be?"

"Pecaio tribe, Stigati," Moran answered curtly. "Or so all signs indicate. We have been in fifty tribal areas in the last twentyday, all in the 200 Kilon. We have had no time for details."

"That is no longer important." The men turned to her. "If Genuar is actively seeking those who flout his orders, then the rebels will attempt to rid themselves of the twins without leaving evidence. But that is not as simple and obvious as it sounds. Even in the wastes, land is strictly divided, and borders are not crossed without incident. To dump them with no water and have the deed unwitnessed would be nearly impossible. There is only one place to take them."

"Which is?"

"Bloodsand. We are at least a full day and night's journey from it. We should leave at dusk. That means arriving at vespers the following day, but—"

"I can travel." Moran choked back a laugh at Lyte's statement.

"A day's rest, then we ride hard," Jaac threw back at him. "If not too worn out, they could survive a day in the heat without permanent injury; it is not yet summer. We must be there by stardown tomorrow." As the fire blazed up, she poured a gourd of water into a pan.

Lyte turned his attention to the bleak rocks heaped behind him. "Dismal place."

"Quite the opposite. This is the rock of Evermind," Jaac

answered. "There is a stream that always flows from the inner dell. Legend says it sprang from the stone at the unvoiced command of the prophet Naitun—from the mind of Naitun, hence the name. We will fill our gourds before we leave."

"What is Bloodsand?" Lyte glanced to Moran, who was facing toward the sea. Not talkative today, on edge. He probably missed Roe. Or was alarmed by finding his friend half dead in a deep desert.

Jaacav grimaced. "A place of final punishment. The Cied are long sundered from us and have their own laws and judgments. One of the nastiest is to stake a human out until he dies of dehydration. Bloodsand is used by all the tribes for this purpose. They do not kill the accused. Kee does."

"Convenient scapegoat."

"Deadly. Between the winds and the krwb, little is left by morning."

"Jaac, what are the Cied? Renegade Toli? Outcasts?" Lyte began hesitantly, hoarsely. He still felt dry and a bit light-headed.

Jaac chuckled maliciously. "We are the outcasts. Almost four millennia ago many Nualans decided that we were all being punished for using technology to change our planet. Given the proper time, Mendulay would heal both us and Nuala. That was what the followers of Lien believed. So they went off into the Ciedär, following their prophet. He did not agree with the way of life that was being conducted on a large scale and felt that if the rest of the people could not see his point, then let them choose damnation. So the Ciedärlien live forever apart."

"Were they right?" Moran asked in a low voice.

"Their prophets have a high accuracy rate. Naitun, the fellow who created this spring, was one of them. They live harshly yet, from many viewpoints, quite well. They do not have more 20s, though. That was their goal."

"I would think a combination of their simplicity and coastal ingenuity would be best," Lyte proposed.

"Agreed. Convince the Cied. Saffra? We must seek shade in the rocks until vespers." And that ended conversation, until shortly before they left for Bloodsand.

The last star was fading from the sky when Braan spotted the Stone Ring. Finally, a place with shade to spend the next twelve hours. Without turning he spoke to Teloa. "The Stone Ring. We shall spend the heat of the day here and continue at vespers." Tay did not answer, so Braan assumed that she had nodded. He had taken great pains to point out their destination to her; the great slash in the Dragoche Mountains. If something happened to him, she could reach other humans. But she did not comment on day-to-day landmarks.

On other subjects she was quite talkative, even outspoken. The fortyday in the Ciedär had been lonely. The akemmi could not answer her, even if it listened. She was full of questions about every imaginable topic, from new births and deaths to interstellar eavesdropping. In the course of the three days and four nights they had been company for one another, they had exhausted the matter of Nuamura, at least to Braan's taste. He had too much on his mind and no way to begin speaking.

Teloa had been shocked and disturbed over the assassin's attack; quiet when he explained Genuar's visit and the subsequent trip east. Was it the office she was concerned about? What kind of thought was that, Atare? Again, for the hundredth time, his body responded to his straying thoughts, and he was grateful that his caftan hid the evidence. Damn, he would have to keep the fire between them at all times.

One hazelle. She had lost the other earlier; it had not been strong enough to survive the desert. Braan now led the remaining beast inside the standing circle of stones. They were tall, at least four meters, and some had lintels across them. In the center was a round, flat stone, the symbol for fresh water carved into its face. Teloa looked pleased. "Shall we check?"

"If you wish. Even if it is dry, we have enough." Untying the hazelle's rope from around his waist, he hobbled the animal, staked it on a long line within reach of some stubby brush, and pulled the pack off its back. Tay undid the rope that connected her to the beast and immediately dug through the pack for fire crystals. While she built the fire, Braan began to prepare their food. Tay set out eating utensils and then pushed the rock over a little bit and lowered a weight and tube. She drew some water back up and examined it in the growing light. Clear of debris . . . She dropped in a tablet; the color would determine if they could drink it. Pale yellow. Not a single problem. Pouring the tube into a cooking pot, she settled down to wait. The last few days had shown her that Braan preferred to do the cooking. And he did know more ways to prepare the Ciedär rations.

Tikki finally stuck her head out of the hood, complaining peevishly until Tay offered her a snip of dried fruit. The akemmi took it graciously and scurried to the packs, where she proceeded to burrow, and then nibbled the delicacy. When Teloa lifted up the saddlebags to be sure that the creature was under them and not tearing through them, her hand touched fur. She carefully removed the topmost *katt* skin, which was properly rolled.

"What are you going to do with these?"

Braan glanced up. "They may have several uses. The young male's is yours; you set the trap for him. One I will probably offer to Baakche as a gift; only trine gold would be more impressive, and I have that as well. The other I will make a cape or robe out of . . . maybe a wedding gift."

Teloa had already wrapped the big forepaws around her, looping them in front. "How do I look?"

"Like a child playing dress-up, using a rug for a stole."

Her brilliant smile flashed out, and she took several graceful dance steps. "What shall I do with mine? It's too little for a poncho and too pretty to walk on! I'd hate to hang it over a hole in the wall."

Braan tried to hide his laughter and failed. "How do you and Moran do it? I have never met anyone before who could simplify Nualan and have it sound correct. Usually that mix sounds like strangled Axis. I think you two have invented a new tongue." He studied her a second, stroking his beard, trying to remain objective. "A skirt," he said at last. "Or if you are nice to me, maybe I will give you my skin."

She danced off again in excitement. "Up to my chin in fur! I love it! I never thought I'd live somewhere cool enough to wear them!" She dropped down next to the fire and slowly, correctly, rerolled the skin. "It grows quiet. A strange place, this desert. The nights are lively and full of sound, the days dead and silent."

"Very quiet. This is the most 'alone' I have ever been. Starting with that sandstorm when I lost Lyte. This is the first time I have ever felt totally free."

"Ever? I am here."

"Ever. Even with you. This is the first time a *guaard* or commando has not been with me. I am always a twosome, at the minimum."

"Always? I mean . . . there must be times . . ."

"No. Always. Every waking and sleeping moment."

"No privacy?"

"I ignore them and they ignore me. The mountain is refreshing to live in. They stay outside in the corridor or, at the worst, in the meeting room. In the palace and my home they were in the sanitation, in my sleeping room—one gets used to them, like a glow or a chair."

Teloa seemed genuinely surprised. "Everywhere. Just one? Or more than that? Do they follow your whole family wherever they go?"

Braan smiled. "Not just my family. My immediate circle. At various times Gid has been guarded, or Prime Minister Lennard, even Arrez."

Tay looked thoughtful. "The day I was attacked, were the men who saved me *guard*?"

"One. The other was a citizen. Yes, a *guaard* was watching you. But thirdmeal was the time for a change of *guaard*, and as fate would have it, that was when your problems began. I had ordered them to shadow you, and they did."

"Can't even scratch in private," she replied coarsely, barely concealing her irritation.

"Oh, they do not watch you every second. They know normal sounds and abnormal ones. They listen, smell; they do not have to see us all the time. Do not misunderstand me. I am grateful for their vigil. But sometimes . . ."

Teloa reached for the tongs and began fishing for the dinner pouches. Braan pushed the plates in front of her and settled back to open a sack of nuts. Finally, without looking at him, Tay spoke. "That's hard to understand. I'm used to being alone. Even when I left home and was working. I knew what they meant by the saying 'being alone in a crowd.' In a way it was nice. The Ciedär, the endless desert, and no one out here except Tikki and Telen and me."

"Telen?"

Tay blushed. "My little brother's name. The hazelle has the same wise, gentle look, and yet he is very patient with me. Like Telen. For someone so mechanically oriented, my brother was very concerned about people."

"Where is he now?"

"I don't know. At the displacement camp I gave him everything I had left, my last cubiz, and told him to find a guild that would take him. I was already a planter. As the war stretches on and on, fewer planets take in skilled refugees; they'd rather train their own workers." She passed him a plate of the tasty red tubers and black beans and accepted a handful of nuts in return.

There was a long stretch of silence but not an uncomfortable one. The fire burned low; Braan finally banked it. They moved their packs as far away from it as possible. Wincing at the pain the movement cost him, Braan slowly lowered himself down behind a cool rock.

"Are you all right, Atare?"

He shot her a glance. "It is nothing. Some people get ulcers; my tension goes to my muscles, especially my back and neck."

"Muscle tension can become serious. I am a trained masseuse. May I assist?"

He answered honestly. "I am not sure that would be a good idea."

"Why?"

Braan hesitated. Then, "I have learned to control my emotions in your presence, lady. I doubt I could keep such reserve under your touch."

Teloa looked puzzled. "There are two basic types of massage, Atare: therapeutic-sensual and erotic. One relaxes, the other arouses. To the one giving the massage, and the receiver, it is easy to differentiate technique. My people had need of such a skill. I offer it to you." She held up her head with dignity as she spoke, but the flush in her cheeks was not starlight.

"I would rather have plain speech. It would ease the tension," he replied. "I apologize for delaying so long. But I had to be sure that I was not merely lured by your physical charms, which are considerable. I value our friendship too much to make that mistake now. I have learned to appreciate all the other special qualities you have; I have missed your wit, your compassion, even your barbed questions." He knew what he wanted to say, but the words were wrong now. So he did not say "I love you."

"Do you understand?" He was startled to realize that Teloa was shaking. He started to reach out to steady her and stopped himself.

She did not notice. "Do you know what it is like, Atare, to want something badly and yet to fear it just as strongly?" It was a tight, barely controlled whisper.

"The name is Braan."

"This cannot be." She hid her face in her hands to hide her tears.

"Teloa, this is not an absolute monarchy. If you cannot stand to look at me, tell me to go away! You will not lose your head!" Braan was terribly puzzled. Someone else? Had she made a crazy vow while praying to be saved? "My lady, I am simply asking to pay court to you upon return to Nua-mura. I believe we shall survive this."

"No! No, I am wrong for you. I hoped it could be different, but I've thought—" She folded over to muffle her sobs. Braan knew the comfort of a touch, even an unfavored one. He stiffly moved before her and set his hands on her shoulders. In a little while the woman began to gain control. Soon she became aware of him; her whole body went rigid.

Braan pulled back, slipping his hands into his robe pockets but not moving away. "Please. Explain. What do you want me to say? If it is truth, I will say it."

"I thought your people were bolder," she said, straightening and looking him in the eye.

"They are," he replied without a pause. "If I was merely interested in your body, I would have made it plain. I feel I was quite straightforward concerning your work, which improved daily. Were you almost anyone else, I would have begun with the words *I love you*." Tay's face became even whiter. "But I feared you would react just as you have. Why are those words so frightening?"

"Because. Do you know what I did before I came here?"

"You were a planter somewhere—"

"Between home and Nuala."

"No."

Teloa looked away. "I was a hustler."

"So?"

Tay faced him, her face a tratore mask. "Are you mad? I thought you knew."

"I knew you worked on a sumptuary planet. There are countless professions practiced there."

"I was a hustler! How long do you think your kingship would last if you associated with a hustler? Admitted you loved one?"

Braan swallowed quickly to stifle a laugh. "With the exception of Nuala, almost every royal house in the known universe keeps male and female courtesans within its walls—"

"Not a courtesan! Not someone trained to be a walking pleasure palace, pampered and protected! A hustler! Alone, a mark for every sadist, psycho, and molester in the galaxy! To be beaten and treated as a doll with no emotions and no response! Where not reacting is what keeps you alive!" Her voice edged on hysteria. She fought to control it. "No guild would take a trained planter; they wanted raw talent to mold to their own rules. And I was crazy enough to think that nothing was worse than death."

"My great uncle married a hustler. I almost did, too, but she vanished one night, just before I asked her. She left for much the same reasons, I suppose, though she never said them aloud. A severe inferiority complex—"

"You don't understand!" The tears came again, in frustration.

"I do not." The reply was gentle.

"You need the acceptance and neutrality of the non-aligned planets. If they found out you were consorting with a hustler—"

"Who would connect the planter Teloa with the hustler of another name?" There was silence. "You did use another name, did you not? Tay, I love you. How do you feel about me?"

"There is something else." She clutched the material at her side. "There is a scar along my rib cage. It is from the one time I forgot myself." As she spoke, her voice diminished to barely a whisper. "To be a hustler is a delicate thing. To be successful one must perform on command—to be passive or active as the patron dictates. He looked so much like my long-dead Caprican love I forgot myself. One does not forget one's place when a patron desires a passive partner. Were it not for the affection a cantinamaster held for me, I would be long dead. I learn very well. I have not made the same mistake since. Can you imagine a body so well trained that it goes rigid when a child touches its arm?"

"I have never lifted a hand in violence to a woman in my life. I swear by my Lord Mendulay."

Teloa looked up at his soft answer and could not meet the pain—her pain—in his face. "You need a lover, my lord, not a hustler. I have relaxed a bit these many long days. But enough to pretend that I am a real person? Even if I could overcome this affliction I prolonged my life with, I would be flinching every step of the way. It has been so long. Unless I am passive, or have a passive partner, I am lost."

"Teloa. You say you learn well. You can unlearn just as easily! Lord, we are not talking about gymnastics! Sex is not a spectator sport, but it is not all games, either! Are you trying to tell me that kiss back in the cave was nothing?"

"I am trying to spare you great pain," she replied, her words slow and spaced to keep control of them. "You cannot imagine the pain my fears and memories will cost you."

"They can only bind us closer." He suddenly pulled her into his embrace. She was startled but not exhausted, as she had been the time before. And she did freeze. Braan did not break off their kiss until he felt the slightest relaxation, the touch of her fingers to his shoulder. He faced her as he arranged his robes to guard against the heat. "There was response. You are not lost to us yet. I am willing to take the chance. If you are."

"I love you. But I cannot love you."
She was right. That hurt most of all.

They posted no guard, for no *katt* prowled so far from the mountains, and they could not defend against human attack. Braan tossed at the threshold of sleep, forced to lie on his stomach, stirring sand and gravel in his pain. He had the strangest dream; he heard a voice in it.

"You are keeping me awake. Do you know you are kicking rocks? Trust me, I know what I'm doing." The pressure on his spine and ribs was firm but not hard. And sleep spun away.

When he awoke at vespers, the ache in his back was gone.

BLOODSAND   TWOHUNDRED   VESPERS
                     FIFTYSEVENDAY

Kee was dropping in the western sky, but the night wind had not yet come. Lyte was silent, twisting a broken piece of whip, watching the fire burn low. Moran seethed beside him, his anger barely under control. It was he who had broken the hazelle whip. They had found the young Atares at Bloodsand and dispatched their Cied guards, as Jaac had predicted. The twins were alive . . . just barely. Dehydrated, and Kavan bleeding internally from a beating administered after an escape attempt. Moran was furious—with the Cied, with Corymb, with how long it had taken to find the Atares. Now Kalith watched the fire as well—grim, silent, almost menacing in his scraggly beard, but no longer detached from them. There was calculated thought in his movements.

No longer afraid . . . of anyone or anything including appearances, public opinion, or the future. And when a man fears nothing, he becomes dangerous, Lyte thought, studying the young Atare. Nearby, Kavan slept, oblivious to pain and the rising wind.

"May I intrude?" Jaac stood before them, a ghost in the moonlight.

"Of course," Lyte said graciously.

"We must speak of tomorrow." The woman dropped to the sand. "The Atares must be returned to Nuamura. My original plan, if we found them strong and healthy, was to continue on to the clan mountains. There I hoped to accomplish what the first party set out to do. But Kavan needs immediate medical attention, more aid than I can give him. However much I wish to go present our case to the Dragoche, even to help my Atare, I have in my hands the lives of the heirs."

"Must we all go?" Lyte asked. "I was thinking of trying to find Braan."

"I was going to send you two back with the twins. But we are deeper in the Ciedär than I thought. It is easier to explain how to find the Dragoche tribe than how to retrace our path home. Therefore I must return to Nuamura. Moran must come with me. He is the Ragarr, and his safety is as imperative as Kalith and Kavan's. Also, I need help with them. To the life shelter, Kavan's injuries are simple to attend to, but if we are too late in returning, he could die of blood loss within. That leaves you to journey on, Lyte. You must take three gourds, for there is no water between this camp and mountains, unless you stumble onto a spring." She stood and pointed east. "Do you see, by the light of the three, the deep slash in the distant range? It grows more obvious as you journey closer, and a free well lies just inside it to the left. That is the mouth to the Dragoche tribe's domain. You must choose your entry—announced, by the slash; or stealthy, through the valleys running south. Braan may need your assistance. The range grows immense as you see more of it. Do not be dismayed. Keep your eyes on the slash!"

"Roe is not in Nuamura."

Jaac turned to Moran at this, her eyes narrowing slightly. "What did you say?"

"I don't think she's there. I know that sounds crazy, but I have the strangest feeling that she's ahead of me."

Lyte was suddenly very worried about Moran, but Jaac only studied them both, her gaze unflinching. "Strange are the bonds between sworn lovers, and they are strong. But whatever madness has come upon Ronuviel, I remind you of

your children and ask you to return with me. I think we must
be up at lauds and journey until high sext. Then we rest until
vespers and travel the night through dawning. Summer approaches, and we do not have the countenance of the Cied
to travel in this heat."

"I think I'll leave at the same time. Let's all get some
rest," Lyte suggested, bothered by Moran's tratore face. Not
like him . . .

THE CIEDÄR   TWOHUNDRED   LAUDS
                    FIFTYEIGHTDAY   (MOONSET)

Jaac was up with the false dawn, tending a low fire and
checking the water gourds. Some were already missing. She
had heard Lyte in the night, gone with the stars. She had
walked past the sleeping twins and counted bodies; there had
been only one by the small boulder. He had been eager to
leave then. The missing hazelle was the one with a white
ankle. It was the strongest of the group, one of the Cied's
beasts, so adapted to desert life that it was more tazelle than
hazelle. A good choice.

She was preparing a solid firstmeal and packing the rest
of their supplies when she heard someone stirring behind her.
"Let us finish packing the gourds. I want to leave as soon as
we have eaten," she said.

"Fine by me."

Jaac froze at the voice. Standing slowly, she turned to
face Lyte, who briefly returned her glance and went to pick
up a mug. Then she sprang away to the boulder. Using a
smaller rock as a step, she quickly reached the top. In the
faint light of the coming dawn there were few shadows across
the sand. Their group approached the deep desert, and little
was found here except sand and rock. Jaac could barely make
out hoofprints leading away east. He was long gone.

"Sear the Path!" exploded from her lips. "Fool! Idiot!"
She leapt back down.

"What?"

"Moran has gone."

Lyte's face passed swiftly from incredulity to fear to fury. "I'll kill him." He ran to the hazelles.

"No! Stop! You cannot, especially without water."

"Then get me some gourds fast. I want to catch him before starrise—"

"No. He is kilometers from here. You cannot hope to find a commando when he does not wish to be found! He took a Cied hazelle, a beige one. You could pass them and never know it!" She snatched the reins from him, fearless in the face of the frightened, plunging animal. "Calm yourself and the beast! I cannot get Kavan back alone. Kal can barely support himself. Our path is sundered from his, Lyte. I need your help."

The man was silent, but the hazelle settled into a light prance. Dismounting, Lyte stepped out of the pack line to face the dawn. When he finally spoke, his voice was thick with harnessed anger. "I would have gone with both of them, but it's beyond me." He switched to Nualan. "Let us head for Nuamura."

"We shall make straight the path of their return."

CHAPTER TWENTY

Braan adjusted the fire once more and settled against the hazelle. The beast tossed its head impatiently at the confinement of the cave. Cursed sandstorm! This one sounded like a diablo: narrow, treacherous, and scraping the rocks above them to sand.

The woman was sitting over in a crevice, her eyes on what could be seen of the opening. The evening was already cool, but she had not bothered to put on her outer robe. Braan found himself following the intricate knotting of her tattered caftan, which gave the material more shape and caused it to pull in closer to her body. He had seen the Cied wear such involved garments, but where? She must have thought it up independently. It had not occurred to him that her inner outfit might be as ragged as her outer. He had given her his extra embroidered outer robe, but he had only one inside wrap. Three pairs of joqurs; could she wear—?

For almost a fourday they had continued on, not talking except at meals, avoiding the obvious topic. Now that the subject had been brought up, no matter how confusingly, Braan felt strangely at ease. Much of his tension had left him, and he was no longer disturbed by Tay's physical closeness. His mind strayed often to his sojourn among the tratores, and the lifestyles of the hustlers. So many things he had never understood. One memory disturbed him. The youth had been one of the preeminent hustlers of Mercury 7. His eyes—they had had no life, no spark in them. . . .

"Is this entire world desert? Except by the sea, where the mountain tropics prevail?"

Braan showed no surprise, though it was her first question in days. "No. There are mountains, prairies, swamps, deserts, tundra, glaciers, tidewater—everything you can imagine is probably found here."

"I would like to see it someday, if we live."

"I am planning on it. I would enjoy showing you the magic of Nuala."

She did not look at him. "Have we lost much time?"

"More than I care for; tonight and tomorrow. We need a full night for this step of our journey."

"Couldn't we leave when the storm quits and walk until dawn?"

"It is a full twelve hours to the next shade. We should not be out by day at all. Even the Cied avoid the daylight during summer, and the hot time comes early this year."

"At least we can talk. I know a diablo is more dangerous, but it's quieter!"

Braan smiled. "We are deep in these rocks. They would muffle the sound of a normal sandstorm." He reached to remove his thigh-high boots and set his feet near the fire to warm his toes. He glanced clandestinely at Teloa and saw that she was distracted, staring off into space. There was something familiar about the way she was sitting. Not the hair; she had twisted it up into a loose figure eight. His insides congealed as he realized that it was an ancient hustler pose, an invitation to disrobing. She did it instinctively. What were her thoughts? Confused? Had her body retreated into the known and accepted? "All we need is a bottle of wine," he heard himself saying.

She reacted by turning her head slightly, a flush on her cheek. "Wine? On a life-or-death expedition?"

"It does not feel that way right this moment. I am tired of Ciedär rations already. You must be sick of them. The owner of the Minotaur restaurant has opened up again, within the mountain. We can go there for an excellent meal when we get b—"

"No!" He was startled at her abruptness. "There's no use in— We shouldn't pretend it can be something it can't."

"Shall we start at the opposite end? I will seduce you first and romance you later." At those words she did look over at him. Braan's smile was so wicked, she laughed, and it was her own laugh, not forced. "Better yet, you may seduce me. I am yours." He folded over dramatically in a heap next to the hazelle.

Tay muffled her giggles, shaking her head in disbelief. Then a sad expression crept across her face.

"Thank you. But I could not accept what our relationship would do to—"

"Have you ever thought that each individual is responsible for his own life?" She stared at him. Braan propped himself up on one elbow. "Tay, is it wrong to be happy?"

She stared at him a moment longer and then looked into the fire. "Perhaps things, perhaps people, are different here. Maybe I am the one who does not understand. You are really willing to take this chance?"

"The whole chance. We cannot give up if things are difficult at first. I have learned that happiness is fleeting. I will grab it anyplace I can find it and hang on tenaciously."

"Very well." There was pause in her voice, a neutrality. Braan started grinning again. "You sound as if I just sentenced you to life imprisonment. Come on over to my side of the fire anytime you want to talk about it. Or do anything else." He flopped down on his back.

A while later there was the rustle of material, and she came and knelt down next to him. She reached up to pull out the comb holding up her hair.

"Wait. Why are you doing that?" Tay looked puzzled. She clearly had not thought about it. "You only do things like that when you want to."

She managed a ghostly smile and touched her wrap collar. "And clothing?" she asked.

"Same thing. Do not remove it until you want to . . . or

it gets in the way." He sat up then and turned sideways, facing her.

She studied him for a long time. Finally she leaned over and brushed his cheek with her lips. Braan did not move. He held himself so tightly in check, he was afraid to breathe. She started toward him again and stopped herself short. Casting her eyes down in embarrassment, she spoke, and there was a tinge of wonder in her voice. "The last time I impulsively kissed a man on the cheek, he beat me."

Controlling the sick rage that rose up in him, Braan understood that they had a long way to go. No matter how successful the surface recovery, some things never healed. "I think we might do better if I seduced you," he said gently, slipping his arms around her and drawing her close. An orgasmic ripple passed through her, and then she tensed, her face scarlet beneath her tan, not looking at him. Braan was stunned and pained, first by the realization that she had so successfully masked her physical attraction to him, and then by the fact that she had lost her control so abruptly. He had not even brushed her back, the safest erogenous zone he could think of. This time the pain was more personal. *Sweet Lord, she thought I was going to hit her*! Carefully—the wrong words . . .

"Has it been that long?" he said very gently. Her answer was falling tears, bright against the fire before they vanished into folds of material. He cradled her closely, privately thinking every violent and obscene thought he could manage, all directed at the tratore worlds. A few well-placed luna bombs and—no, too many there did not know the evil they perpetuated. Was ignorance a permissible shield?

He did not know how long it had been since his thoughts started wandering away from him, but a peep from the akemmi brought him back to the moment. Something was different. Teloa had relaxed a bit, one hand resting lightly on his arm. He bent over and kissed the top of her head. She did not flinch—good—or she did not feel it. He had his own theory on how to draw her out of her trained passive state.

"Tell me, belaiss, have you ever been kissed on every square centimeter of your body?" He could not keep the smile out of his voice. She looked up at him, half puzzled, half amused. "Or has no one ever bothered?"

"Can't say that I have." Pink touched her cheeks and throat again. A modest hustler—Lord, the galaxy may collapse into a black hole.

"Do you wish to say good night and place the fire between us? If you . . . object, I shall be able to tell, you know."

"Just remember, it's not you. It's . . . memories." She faltered, meeting his gaze.

"I shall try to remember."

THE CIEDÄR	TWOHUNDRED FIFTYNINEDAY	NONE

It was very warm in the small cave when Teloa awoke. And quiet; the storm was over, the animals dozing. The subtle scent of the hazelle reached her nose. She lay still, orienting herself. Then she stretched for Braan's gold timespot, lying on top of the pack. Almost vespers: time to build up the fire and start packing. But it was so pleasant not to move. Of course, the strangeness . . . She became fully conscious and knew that Braan was lying beside her; indeed, had an arm draped loosely over her ribs. Ah, the ribs; the problems that scar had caused. Her heart ached for his unvented fury at the perpetrator of the deed, a man dead so long that only his bleached bones would be found. That had helped her emotional flood start, when she immediately tried to reassure him that there was no longer pain, physical pain. How foreign to wake next to a man. Never in her life, not even at home, had she done that. Always slipping off by herself or being left in the dark alone.

I must not become a parasite, she thought suddenly, fiercely. *Expect nothing, hope for nothing.* She reached out to touch his back, her fingers as light as blown seed. *My love, do you know the fire you dare to play with?* They had tried to talk, as night wove into day, but Teloa discovered that the pain was still too fresh, even after all this time, and spent most of their conversation sobbing. Braan had asked no more questions. He merely accepted each strange revelation as it came out. And when this trek was through, then what? She sighed. Back to sneaking down corridors, probably. She no longer cared. She knew she would have no rivals, at least until he took a wife. She could not say it aloud, but with this man it was enough to be loved.

"Do not stop." Surprised, she glanced over and discovered that she was massaging his neck. One green and brown eye studied her. "I had a dream about such a massage."

"Oh?"

"The day we discussed it. When I woke up, I felt better." Teloa started laughing silently. "So it was not my imagination? I thought not, but I saw fit not to bring it up. Now I can say thank you."

"You are welcome."

"I am not done saying thank you."

Her smile was heartfelt, and she was able to force herself to relax before he embraced her, so he never knew what that kiss cost.

NUAMURA—   TWOHUNDRED   PRIME
THE GROTTO   SIXTYTWODAY

For the first time in his life Lyte saw a *guaard* on duty register surprise. The dark, narrow-faced man gestured, and the woman across from him nodded and vanished.

"Send for the healers, bring a stretcher!" Jaac called.

"You are victorious?"

"We have accomplished what we set out to do," she answered, leading Kavan's hazelle forward. Kal dropped the reins of his beast and rushed to help the *guaard*, who was untying Kavan from the cloth saddle. "We need a legion of *guaard* to unpack and watch over these items. It is imperative. And I need six *guaard* on each Atare." Her voice lowered. "Two outside the cubicle, the others within," she murmured to one as she gestured to Kavan.

Suddenly *guaard* were everywhere, swarming over the animals, easing Kavan down on a stretcher, inquiring about everyone's health. Lyte remembered that some *guaard* were also healers. One of them, a young man, stepped up to Ka and knelt. Slipping a hand into his own shirt, the *guaard* produced the Nualan chain of office. Kal started to shake his head negatively.

"It was his wish, Atare, that you should hold it until he returns." Kal did not move at first. Then he reached out and held the chain in his right hand.

"The conferral must be witnessed. Send for the high priest and the Ragäree, and for the heads of the synod," Jaac said, glancing at the scene. Kal did not seem aware of what was happening. He was studying the chain. In his other hand the youth still clutched a leather thong. Strung on it was five ounces of trine gold. Riding back to the mountains, the group had come upon a decimated Stigati smuggling operation. After killing the young *katt* that had destroyed the camp, Jaacav had insisted that they search the packs. They found weapons, luxuries—and five ounces of trine, the ransom of kings. The embargo had been violated.

Not a ransom, Lyte thought with a grim smile, remembering Kal's face when he found a Cied whose robe was not shredded. The embroidered emblem was bold, abstract, and blood-red. Recognizing it from his days of captivity, Kal had carefully folded and kept it, along with the gold, saying only, "We have found the blood payment for the deaths of two Atares. They should have demanded more."

Jaac had spoken differently. "Mendulay guided us to them. There shall be a reckoning."

"The Ragäree is not here," the *guaard* continued, and then spotted Lyte. The warrior stopped speaking and stood. "I told you not to return without him." Almost conversational.

It was the last thing Lyte expected, and a lesser commando would have been left gasping his life out on the rocks. As it was, he barely was able to turn the blade, so lightning-fast was the *guaard*. What? He was fresh and young and wanted blood. Lyte was exhausted and confused.

The *guaard* backed off, looking for another opening, while Lyte palmed the cat knife he had lifted from the other's belt. Everyone has gone crazy, was all he could think. Circle, feint, circle again, watch the eyes, the neck muscles, the chest—Jaac was giving orders, the other *guaard* falling back. What was she saying? The smell of blood was intoxicating.

"Noah! Explain!" *Noah*. Where had he heard . . . Then Lyte remembered. This *guaard* belonged to Braan. *He's going to kill me*.

"Noah! He is mine!" It was soft, chilling, and carried across the silence. Someone was behind Lyte. Whatever he saw made Noah drop the knife into the dust. Lyte remained crouched, suspecting a trap, using a quick-glance technique. Common sense said to jump him now. "Lyte! Enough!" He recognized the voice. Kal. Turning, he saw that the young man was close to him, hand stretched toward the off-worlder. Lyte offered him the blade, but Kal took his other hand, holding it so he could see where the knife had ripped his palm when he turned it away. "This should be attended to." Kal faced the silent troop of *guaard*. "Given either following a healthy Atare or returning to guarantee the life of an heir, Lyte chose. Does anyone deny the choice?" Silence prevailed. Glancing at Noah, Kal said, "My elder lives. The other commando is at his back. It is enough?"

Noah nodded, his handsome face impassive. Lyte offered him his knife back, expecting him to walk away. To his veiled surprise the man graciously accepted it and then bent to gather up the other weapon.

"Nothing personal," Kal murmured drolly. Then he gestured toward the *guaard* removing his brother. "Make certain Elana operates," he said to Jaacav, "and take *guaard* to Shinar. I must prepare for the council, but tell her of my plans . . . to see if our hearts are still one. I would speak to Justinian— I have an ultimatum for him." Glancing to Lyte, he asked, "Are you coming to the anointing? To do this thing I must become Atare." And then the young man swept into the cavern.

GAREDOC   TWOHUNDRED   SEXT
                   SIXTYTWODAY

Lyte watched the monstrous cavern fill, silenced by the sheer number of elders who had seats in the synod. Too many people with power for Lyte's taste. Would they understand the point that Kal was trying to make? The morning had been hectic. Lyte had not been privy to the meeting in Kal's chamber, although he had heard the raised voices. Instead he met with a healer to have his hand laser-sealed. His presence as a witness was requested for the anointing, however. It was swift, the battlefield version, naming the youth Kalith Atare, the onehundred sixtyeighth of his line. And Kal now walked with a confidence far outweighing the chain of office he wore. Even Justinian did not hesitate to address him as sovereign. Lyte wondered what Kal had forced upon the man—what Justinian was willing to do to insure a royal line. Only after the ceremony was through did Jaac depart to tell Shinar the news and leave *guaard* with her. Did Jaac fear for Kal?

"Brethren, cease thy speech!" It was Url, the wife of Justinian, calling the synod to order. Lyte, seated in the visitor's gallery, moved until he could see the permanent dais. Kalith had arrived, scrubbed, shaved, and dressed in a deep burgundy-red caftan. He was a vivid sight, easily seen even by those in the uppermost tiers. "We have been called for consultation and decision. Let us hear our Atare."

"We have been called" came the unanimous response.

Kal stood and walked to the edge of the dais. "There is no time for soft words of diplomacy. Our fate is balanced on a pinnacle, between the warriors of the *guaard* and *watch* and the favor of the Ciedärlien. We have one of these. Braan Atare has gone to the Ciedär at the invitation of Genuar, heir of Baakche Dragoche, to gain the other. Our existence rides with his success or failure. I have agreed to take up the chain—with conditions. Justinian shall conduct this discussion." The Atare sat once again.

The old politician stood and moved to the portable podium. He paused, as if considering his words. Lyte's tension-sensitive training was running riot—Justinian seemed to feel as if the roof were about to blow off the cavern.

Finally the Nualan began. "Brethren, we have been gifted by Mendulay—the house of Atare has returned to us. And they bring high hopes and faith in their siblings. Therefore Kalith Atare has specified two conditions to his rule. The first is that it shall be interim, as the ancient codes demand, and that he shall step down upon the return of Braan Atare. The second condition is that in the near future, upon the woman's acceptance, Kalith Atare shall take to wife Shinar reb Elana." There was a moment of absolute silence. And then almost every man and woman present began to speak.

Justinian banged on the podium. "Brethren, please! Am I not entitled to the courtesy of being heard? As you all shall be, after I finish presenting this case. I shall try to show you why I, representing the synod, agreed to these conditions." He took a sip of water, purposely slowing his movements, as the shouts from the floor died down to an undercurrent. "Elders of Nuala. The law that you are screaming about at the top of your lung capacities is well known to me. I have pondered it many years but have never considered doing anything about it, because no Atare has protested loudly enough. Now one has, and now I think I can make you see the sense of this; see things we have all been blind to for centuries.

"The law of the royal line was made thousands of years ago, both to help the genetic mixing and to keep any one royal family from becoming too greedy and conquering a planet for a son, a city not being enough. I see no reason why the safety measure of the joint power of Atare and Ragäree should not continue, especially since the responsibilities include a solar system; it balances as easily and cleanly as the throne and synod. But the law of marriages—that law was made when genetically we were only marginally human. Now the 20s have a better genetic rating than any other human group! I exempt no race from that statement. And we have discovered that since the bombing, the vast majority of the survivors are 20s. This is a planetwide phenomenon!

"Fellow elders, I wish to remind you that the last time the Axis lost a front, it took them sixty-three years to regain the captured systems. Sixty-three terrayear, friends! And in that case, like most cases, no interplanetary Axis shipping was possible for the duration of the occupation. Now, do we deny Braan Atare, the three single throne-line Atares, and their house the privilege of a legal line? Do we doom our royal family to extinction? Kalith Atare brings to us a jewel of the new generation, the daughter of our high priest Arrez and Elana, the most skilled scientist and surgeon among us. She is a lovely, educated woman of a line as clean as Atare itself, and a proven 20. Do we dare insult our people and all they have sacrificed for these last five thousandyear by saying a woman any human should be proud to marry is not suitable for our ruler? Do we say Nualans are inferior? Will always be inferior? We might as well!

"And I remind you, only Atare is still bound by this law. Only Atare of all the royal houses does not intermarry among the other royal lines and the masses, does not take two spouses if a relationship with an 80 is desired. How long, Nuala? How long must we wait to call ourselves human?" Applause from many fronts greeted the end of his speech, and Lyte leaned back in amazement, shaking his head as the leader of the synod seated himself on the dais. Crisp, concise, to the point, and with just enough melodrama. Justinian was a master speaker, that was certain. One would think he had been planning this for years. He had hinted at as much—had Kal and Shinar always been his star examples? No matter. Immediately several dozen elders leapt to their feet to demand recognition from the chair. Lyte settled down for a long, drawn-out argument.

THE CIEDÄR   TWOHUNDRED   VESPERS
                SIXTYTWODAY

Wavering heat, rising from the scorched sand until Ronuviel was convinced that there were two stars, mirroring one another, broiling the group between them. She lay on the tarps without moving, drenched with sweat, afraid that evening would never come. The babies were quiet as they nursed; so calm this trip, as if they were also lulled by the shimmering desert.

The tent suddenly flapped, announcing a visitor.

"Who is it?" Roe asked. She was usually not modest about feeding the twins, but when she nursed both of them at once, she felt too much like a tazelle to handle strangers, even among *guaard*.

"Liel."

"Enter."

The woman slipped in like a whisper. "Can I help you pack?"

Roe did not miss the note of concern in her voice. *Too tired, I am too fragile.* "Yes, please. The blue satchel—that is the last of it."

"The camp is almost closed up," Liel said after a pause. "We leave soon."

"How far?"

"Six or sevenday."

"Too long." Liel glanced up at this, slowing her packing. "From now on we must be ready to ride at vespers and travel until nearly tierce. I feel time is running out."

"But—"

"We must, Liel. Or the rest makes no difference. The Cied travel day and night."

"When they have truces, yes—they stop and exchange for fresh hazelles. We cannot do that. But if we go to tierce, we might cut a day . . . a day and a half, perhaps." She laid the last garment on top and pulled the sides of the bag together.

"It will have to be enough. Tell the first officer."

Liel yanked the satchel shut and dragged it out the tent entrance, ill-concealing her anger and fright.

DRAGOCHE   TWOHUNDRED   VESPERS
MOUNTAINS   SIXTYSIXDAY

Teloa was aware of light first. It had been such a long night; they had walked until well past starrise, but they were finally in the Dragoche Mountains. She opened her eyes. Starset. The cave's mouth was wide and low, facing west. She slowly sat up and stretched. If only she could wake up instantly, like Braan did. They had slept the morning away, and then hobbled the hazelle so it could graze. Tikki had left to search for seeds.

"You are inhumanly beautiful by starset." Teloa did not turn, forcing herself not to blush. Failure. It whipped from her stomach to the extremities like an elaborate body painting.

"Another fantasy realized. I have wanted to see the total blush."

She slowly maneuvered around to face him, one fist defiantly on her hip. "I think you lie awake nights—days—thinking up phrases to make me do that."

"You are right. But I never use any of those." Braan allowed himself a stretch, and Teloa watched the muscles ripple. He did not give the impression of being a big man—Moran and Lyte were half a head taller—but he was so compact, yet fluid, even graceful. Nothing extra; no fat, no fleshiness. She could count his ribs, yet he was not skinny. Even the whorls of light brown hair were more artistic than—

"Were you always self-conscious about your body?" he asked, his mischievous grin creeping out.

"Not at home, although total nudity was not common there. The fields were nightmarishly hot, and garments were sparse."

"It is also uncommon here. But no one is surprised by it, unless the person wears no jewelry. Then they look out of place."

"When I worked the tratores, I was dressed. People who wanted sex did not care how you looked in private. A light was never ignited, to my memory. I started to feel obscene when I was unclothed. They wanted glamorous showpieces. I wore designer gowns in the tratore itself, and the illusion boudoir items when I was playing statue."

"Statue?"

Teloa smiled and unwound her long legs, moving closer to his tangle of blankets. He knew the heart and soul of the tratores but had not played the game. And the hustlers he had met clearly did not waste any time educating him concerning the crueler aspects of hustling. "The wealthier and more powerful patrons were, the more likely they were to want beautiful hustlers of all sexes lounging around their private apartments in various stages of undress. For visitors to look at, envy, but never handle. They, themselves, rarely touched us. I had a regular, a gem merchant, who never spoke, never acknowledged my presence; but he had me sit with him through a whole day of semiprivate meetings with professional buyers. I stayed on a couch behind and to one side of him, wearing nothing but his jewelry. I was his favorite—his assistant told me I was the only one who could wear any stone, any metal. And he paid me in cut, unset gems. But he never spoke to me."

Braan would not look at her. "Did you hate them?" he asked at last.

She did not answer. Her thoughts drifted back to the starset, now splashed across the sky like crushed blossoms. Their last starset. What if the Cied— A gentle touch along her jawline brought her mind to clarity. She looked over at him, lying on his side, waiting for her reaction. She had learned that it was his way of calling her back when depressing thoughts threatened to overwhelm her. She raised her left hand and caressed his growing beard, letting her fingers trail across his lips. Then she bent over and softly kissed each eyelid.

Braan struggled for control. It was the first move toward him she had made in eightday that did not reek of conscious thought and worry. For the first time, it seemed, old bruises did not throb for her, bones did not ache in response. Mendulay, to act upon this . . . But that was not how he wanted the Cied to find them. Despite his notoriety, Braan was fiercely protective of his lovers—especially this one. His reputation was one thing he hoped did not precede him into the Dragoche camp. He was content with merely looking at her. Sweet Mendulay. He did not allow the silence, her thoughts, to deepen.

"We will have company soon," he said, sitting up. "We must get the hazelle closer to the cave and be ready to welcome them."

"I'll miss the privacy. Cied everywhere; and if we get back, I'll never see you without a *guaard* present." She pulled away and stood, reaching for her inner robe, refusing any nonverbal consolation.

Braan took up his joqurs and looked for his caftan. "The *guaard* will not interfere with us," he replied, amused by the thought.

"For they have eyes, even when they have orders to ignore things." She sighed and instantly felt contrite for burdening him. "I thought I was done forever with sneaking down corridors."

"The *guaard* see nothing, even on the few times they must be stationed in the private quarters. They do not ever discuss things among themselves, unless they think an Atare is in danger. What sneaking?"

"Oh, you have a private entrance?" She turned to face him as she said this, winding long, smooth ropes of hair around her head, crisscrossing the circles to make them appear woven. Braan stopped halfway into his caftan and took his time pulling it down, trying to fathom what she meant. Then he understood.

A hasty smile crossed his face, but he cut off a laugh before it passed his lips. Suddenly the answer was balanced in time, amusing or devastating. He answered simply, not betraying his caution. "Teloa . . . I am not looking for a mistress," he began, slipping into Axis. "We do not even have a Nualan word for such a thing. I want a wife. I need an Atarae—a legal partner to bear my legal heirs. Personally I search for a bondmate. I want that woman to be you." He had looked her in the eye while he said it but could not tell what she registered.

She stood there with her hands to her head, arrested in mid-gesture as she freed the few shorter hairs to lie around her face. "You have lost your mind," she finally whispered. "Do you wish to call into question the authority of your kingship? I am . . . touched, but you cannot—"

"My grandmother's brother did, and no one pulled him off the throne."

"Braan! You're mad!"

He caught her up in an embrace. "No! I am quite sane! You are not thinking! A courtesan, yes, then we might have problems, criticism. Too many of them in the past have schemed their way into power here. But a hustler! A vivid reminder of everything they detest about the Axis and its war; a war we fought hating it, our enemies and our allies." Braan spoke swiftly, his words tumbling over each other. "Tay, we need not announce it, but should it become public knowledge, we merely say, 'It is true. She was a victim of Axis insensitivity, doomed to the prison of a resettlement camp or the fate of a hustler.' You would be the object of ready, honest, heartfelt sympathy and fiercely shielded!"

Teloa stared at him, wide-eyed. "But—"

"My lady, even if you were the lowliest of planters, which you will never be because Lars wants you as his personal assistant, some people could—and may—discover your secret and try to make you feel badly about it. It was an evil of war, and you the victim. It is paid for; let it go. Have you not suffered for it long enough?" She could not answer and merely reached up, touching his arms carefully. "Think on it. You must have no doubts. At least about me."

"I will boil some water if you will get the beast," she whispered. She would not call it Telen in his presence. He whirled and, grabbing his outer robe, threw it on loosely and ducked out the cave entrance. Tay reached for the small boiling pot and filled it, her hands shaking. Then she reached for her outer robe, caressing the dragon of the Atare line.

"They are here." She spun around, startled by his voice. "We might as well use the dry rations." He threw some saffra into the water.

"The beast?"

"They have it."

"If we had stayed awake . . . guarded?" She asked hesitantly.

He shook his head. "We want them to find us. These are the Dragoche Mountains; only the Dragoche prowl here. Eat as much as you can," he instructed, handing her a twisted food stick. "It is a good six hours to their encampment."

"You have been there?" she asked after a time.

"When my mother's brother negotiated a treaty with them. It is no makeshift city but a permanent tent site. You will find it interesting." He pointed to her knife. "Keep that hidden. And within reach. We do not want them to think you are a warrior but also do not want them to think you are khatta."

"Khatta?"

"A young man or woman who does not have the talent to become a warrior, a hunter, or a scholar. The choices are to flee to the coast, die, or fall into a servant class of sorts— chattel, khatta. I do not think that is the original meaning of the word, but it suffices. We must be sure that they know you are of the scholar class. Be as proud as you can honestly manage, my beauty. Attitude and truth is everything. Do you remember what I told you of their customs?"

"I think so."

"Good. Do not be intimidated by them. You are my liaison. It is not proper for me to press for the rights of the royalty class. You have a good memory. Use it—demand our rights. It improves our standing as word spreads."

Tay kept her face impassive, determined not to show her fear. *He will tell me if I press too hard....*

"Remember how you flared at Corymb? Keep that in mind." He watched her quietly, his eyes sparkling in the flickering light of the fire. Amused? Excited about the coming challenge?

Why do I have a knot in my chest? She did not ask the question aloud. Mechanically chewing the food stick, she felt the numbness creep to her stomach. At the same time an excitement grew, a tension in her arms and thighs. Such a game they were about to play . . .

———————————

Tay was grateful that she was between bites when the silhouette rose up in the entranceway. Somehow she managed not to flinch but glanced to Braan. He dipped up a cup of saffra and turned to the robed figure. "Break your fast with us?"

The warrior nodded thanks but did not take the cup. "We are nearly finished." He faced Tay again. She swallowed, unable to believe that he left his back exposed. But he was right: If there was treachery, they were already lost.

She stuffed what was left of the dry saffra into her bag and then was startled when a dark streak flashed by the fire pit and into her outer robe. The Cied stepped into the light, his drawn blade glittering. Braan held up a hand to stop the warrior as Tikki ran up Teloa's arm. The Cied's dark eyes flickered in amazement. He sheathed his sword and then left the cave.

"Are we in trouble?" she whispered.

"No, you just increased your stature by having a wild

animal that looks to you. Come. Put on your robe." He began
to extinguish the fire.

———————

The moons crept to hang suspended in the center of the
sky, and still they walked on. Another two or three hours; in
a valley, he had said. The light was bright enough to see an
occasional pattern on a robe. She was certain that she saw at
least two different ones, possibly three. What ... ?

"Braan, the robe patterns ..."

"I know. We are heading toward the camp. Do not worry."
It was swift and low.

Do not worry.

Her feet felt leaden when they finally topped the last
crest. Teloa sat down in the middle of the trail, caring little
for their reactions. Climbing mountains was different from
walking in sand. She looked out over the valley and forgot
about her feet. Light. Thousands of twinkling lights, like a
hill of temple candles or the ceremony of Lastday. Camp
fires, lanterns, torches—from this distance nothing but tiny
points of light. Braan extended a hand to her. She stood, and
they started down the narrow, winding path.

The road eventually broadened and became smooth once
more. They were on the floor of the valley. Huge, irregular
tents loomed up on either side of them, pallid heaps under
the near-trine. Cied, in flowing robes, went about their business along the side routes, but Teloa did not miss the occasional sidelong glances. Braan had thrown back his hood,
something he had asked her not to do. She risked a turn of
her head; he walked like a ruler should walk, brisk and yet
unruffled, with a proud carriage.

He could not be mistaken for anything else. She saw a
difference in the robes now, reflecting strangely in the torchlight. The hem and side-seam combination was on every Cied
accompanying them, even if it was not the black-and-gold
Dragoche emblem. A few of their guides had embroidery on
the backs of their robes, as well. Leading the way was an
older Cied—his robe's black-and-gold markings were from
the right hip to the left corner hem in a widening arc across
the front. She could not tell if it was the same design. A few

smaller figures—women—stood in tent doorframes. Their black-and-gold pattern was also a curving slash, but it was an inverted arc from the left shoulder down between the breasts to the belt. Several shrouded forms had more than one area embroidered.

Finally the greatest tent was reached. The older man indicated that Braan should follow him. A warrior stepped next to Tay, and inwardly she froze. Braan remained impassive.

"I am the Atare's eyes and ears," Tay heard herself say. The warrior disappeared again, and she was following Braan under the canopy. He had not exaggerated—he would truly do nothing to press for rights, not even to request the mandatory scripter. She had spent the last six hours reciting the information he had given her. She hoped it was enough.

They were seated on soft pillows across from an elderly man wearing a white outer robe with the Dragoche warrior border, the lower skirt design, and trim on his long cuffs and hood. The younger man to his right possessed intent, dark eyes; the trim on his sand-colored robe was identical, except for the plain hood rim. It suddenly occurred to Teloa that these designs were very important. She looked casually at Braan as she surveyed the group, politely dropping her upper veil. His robe was also richly embroidered, as was the one she was wearing—his extra. Various shades of violet, and royal purple—the true, deep pink—in a fierce, convoluted dragon, metallic threads highlighting the design. Kell swirls bordered the cuffs and hood. Lords, she wore the mark of the royal line.

Braan had removed both veils with his hood, the ultimate in compliment and trust, Tay assumed. She did not expect them to reciprocate. Not yet. Figures in solid beige robes appeared, bearing trays of saffra, dried fruits, and various cheeses and breads. Teloa riveted one young man with her stare when he attempted to serve a clansmember after the Dragoche but before Braan. He quickly repaired his error.

"Welcome, Braan Atare. When Genuar told me you came alone to our borders, I could not believe my ears. And that you would bring one of your house! You bring honor upon our heads." Baakche had a strong tenor with just a touch of silver in his voice. A mad one, Braan had said, and dying. The old warrior was their high priest and spiritual conscience, able to command every leader present with the wave of a hand.

"The Serae Teloa is one of our finest planters and was a representative of the first expedition, when my brothers were lost," Braan supplied graciously. "I found her in the Ciedär, and she accompanies me on the same mission." Teloa wondered about those words as Baakche quickly named the tribes present, four deep around the circle. Somewhere in this camp were the traders her group had met, and they would know that her original robe had been unmarked. Why did that bother her?

The discussion began in earnest, and Teloa settled back to listen very carefully. She segmented the bread as he had told her to, conscious that those present were expecting her to behave like royalty. Watching eyes and listening to inflection would be her greatest help here. Later Braan would have questions.

It was the Ciedärlien's turn to ask questions. Genuar had briefed them on many things, that was apparent. Teloa sensed a subtlety behind the words. Some of the inquiries were deceptively simple, such as asking about the health of his family, of the high priest, of their people in general. Questions about industry, trade, mining, defense. When they reached defense, the voices took on a new edge. A planetwide shield? Why include the Ciedär? Though not enemies, the Cied and the cities were not allies.

"But that must change," Braan answered gently. "If we read the signs correctly, a time is fast approaching that shall demand all our resources and cunning. We—"

"Why Cied? Why should we not let this enemy destroy you and go on as we have always lived? Did not the prophets foretell this day?" The woman's voice was hard, broken; Tay had the feeling that her tribe had suffered greatly under the attack and blamed the cities for provoking it.

"This enemy is not my enemy, chieftain," Braan replied, his voice perfectly controlled. "It is senseless, without direction, and burned through our system on its way to its goal, the heart of the Axis. Only our retaliation kept it from searing this planet to a crisp. They shall return, Brethren. May Mendulay strike me dead if I do not speak what I believe. Certainly they want the cities, the mines, the industry, the most pleasant places to live. But, warrior, do you seriously think the Fewhas, the Malvevenians, even the Axis will allow a warrior nation to remain within striking distance? The Cied might die later, but surely they would die." There was no response as Braan reached for some yellow cheese. "And when they finally leave, Nuala a barren rock, devoid of gold or minerals; shall you learn a trade, Brethren? Shall you take to the seas, the mines, to weaving?"

"You come to bargain?" said a voice in the back. Stigati at this meeting. Interesting . . . Not the Wasuu, the outbounders, the hard-core waste dwellers, but Stigati, those who had some semblance of a tribe.

"In so many words."

"Speak plainly."

Braan paused, settling his thoughts, though his face betrayed nothing. How to phrase this politely yet firmly? Teloa wondered. "Generations ago," Braan began, "the Atare came to the Dragoche with a proposition. Neither of them trusted the Axis—or the Wasuu, who were raiding and destroying both Cied and city alike. So the Atare proposed a mutual defense pact. The technology of the city and the cunning of the Cied—together. The Atare had ordered the construction of a defense shield. It would not be a solid shield and could be detected when activated, but it would prevent our total destruction. The Cied, in turn, would keep the Wasuu under control, stop the raiding and the deaths. A bargain was struck. The shield was extended to the Ciedär, and the Dragoche ordered the Wasuu contained.

"Years passed. Most of the Wasuu became Stigati, and the vigil was relaxed. The city of Seedar can attest to fewer warriors walking the boundaries. It still has tumbled walls and abandoned homes to show for the desertion. Yet when the Fewhas attacked, the shield held, and we are alive because of it. Fewer but alive."

"This is known to us, Atare. The Cied destroyed the Wasuu tribes, and the contract was fulfilled. It was later we discovered that the cities expected a perpetual vigil. Yet your protection of us continued."

"The *Atare*'s protection continued. The word of Curr Atare, and Baskh Atare after him, is what saved the Cied. Just as I now bring my word to you."

"Your word is better than any other's word?" someone asked bluntly.

Braan looked him directly in the eyes. "The *guaard* is mine. The *guaard* control the shield. Therefore the shield is mine. Do not make the mistake of thinking that the *guaard* passes with the kingship. It does not. And the synod is in an uproar over the disappearance of Kalith and Kavan of Atare. If the *guaard* limits the shield to the walls of old Amura, the synod will not—and cannot—prevent it."

Sneaking a glance at Genuar, Teloa felt he looked pleased. Perhaps he, himself, had not phrased things in quite the same way, but an effect clearly had been made on the group.

"You come with a new offering, Braan Atare?" Baakche said.

Braan did not miss the formal use of his name. "I do. Before, desert and coast united for their mutual defense. Now we must unite for our mutual survival. A new shield exists. It can still detonate the lunas in the air; it can also destroy the power of the lesser warheads. Debris will fall into our atmosphere, but the rain of death ends. Enemy ships would be severely damaged passing through it, while friends could be shown safe passage."

"What use is this to us?" a chieftain interrupted. Teloa sent him a withering glance.

"You need the protection of our shield. We need the instruction of your planting. I propose a trade. Teach us to make this planet fruitful without chemicals, without forced yield, and we shall protect the planet itself." Tay counted the minutes as they ticked by.

"And if we do not believe this? How can you exclude us? I think we are protected whether we agree or not." Teloa tried to see the speaker.

"If we can open the shield anywhere for a ship to land, we can deactivate it to leave an area unprotected. Accept it." Now Tay could see the speaker, a man bearing a recent scar in a half-moon over his left eyebrow. He was visibly nervous and looked unfriendly. She studied him a moment as another pause mantled the gathering.

"And if this offer is refused?" Baakche's voice was almost tender.

"Then you condemn the cities to warfare over food and to deterioration. And yourselves to eventual death at the hands of the invaders—possibly even from the Axis. As long as we live, they cannot gain the controls. You cannot operate them, even if you take them away from us. If we starve, the secret dies with us."

"Perhaps the bargaining with the synod would be easier."

"Unlikely. The Ragäree would rule until my heir was of age, and after losing three brothers to the desert, she would not feel kindly toward the Cied. I am your hope."

A soft buzzing rose as various chieftains began to talk among themselves. Teloa sipped her saffra, trying not to gag at its strength, and considered the words. These people respected strength, honor, and truth. Braan clearly had the honor of his ancestors and his own name; and they were Nualan, they could sense truth. Strength? She felt the air within him. What would they make of it? Baakche and Genuar were not joining in the whispering, and they were clearly in charge.

"Dawn approaches, Atare. Our scholars wish to show you what you have come so far to see, and then to the day's rest." Baakche signaled, and three Cied entered the tent, one of them the man who had escorted Braan inside. "Elder, take them . . . take them . . ." Baakche faltered, visibly weak in the growing light.

"It is done, O Dragoche." The planter turned and bowed to Braan. "Atare, my fellow scholars and I would show you the results of our labors." Braan stood and gave the nod of equality to Baakche, who looked distant. Then he reached to steady Teloa, the woman gracefully standing and, at his slight urging, falling into place beside the scholar as they all walked out of the tent. Only after the tent flap settled into place did conversation burst forth within.

———————

The light of day was welling into the valley as they
walked through the village toward the fields. Teloa casually
refastened her upper veil, not certain if it was proper for a
stranger to walk around without it on. Braan left his hood
down. Smoke floated before them as they reached a path
slanting downward. Cooking fires—for their last meal before
retiring? Cied reversed the normal schedules in the summer.
They passed a group of children playing, their romp part
dance, part throwing and catching. The small robed figures
stopped and boldly stared as the quintet went by, until the
head planter hissed a warning to them, scattering them to
their own tents. Then Teloa saw the fields, and she forgot
about everyone and everything else.

Turquoise and gold as far as she could see, and taller
than the tallest human. She stepped into the forest of poles
and grain without asking leave, dropping her veils and reaching with the skilled, gentle fingers of one who knows growing
things. None of the planters tried to stop her; they looked
knowingly at one another, as if she had passed some sort of
test. Gesturing to Braan to follow, two of them started down
an aisle.

Fragile turquoise plants, already hip-high, and golden
gourds vining up around them, keeping pace in their mutual
race for the sky. Directly next to each row was a trench box
filled with floating seedlings. Short, leafy plants needing
shade grew beneath them, and the grain swept away toward
the hollow of the valley. Tay stooped to examine the irrigation
system. It was completely enclosed, and a trickle of water
from a modified tropc tube ran to each individual plant. She
saw no yellowed vegetables, no insects devouring the crop.
Standing, she stared off at the fields, where morning had not
yet come, and saw fruit trees in the draw.

"The retchii grow swiftly and are harvested first," a
planter said slowly, carefully, to Teloa. Touching the waist-
high trench boxes, she added, "The gourds then drop into the
shallow liquid." Tay nodded.

The man and woman accompanying Braan were more
verbose but did not go into any specific information. All too

soon for Teloa, the tour was over. As the young woman brought Tay back to the main path, she said, "I hope we shall be able to show you more."

"I also. We burned all ties with the Axis. Now we turn to fellow Nualans," Teloa answered cautiously, refastening her veils. The shrouded Cied nodded thoughtfully, as if dissecting her words.

Climbing easily to the village level, the head planter escorted them to an unoccupied tent. Something of the *guaard* in Tay took over, and she threw back the flaps, examining every corner of the structure. It was clean, cool, and dry, with soft pillows the depth the size of mattresses completely covering the floor. A tray of hot saffra and delicate cakes sat in one corner, a pitcher and basin of water in the other. Their packs were in the center of the tent.

Satisfied, Teloa indicated that Braan could enter. The young planter behind her ventured a low question. "There are other tents. You will stay here?"

Teloa nodded. The planter bowed and turned to follow the other two scholars. Tay remained, appearing regal and actually shocked by the royal treatment. Her gaze traveled to the largest tent, the meeting place, and her eyes widened. Frozen, she waited as the warriors entered Baakche's tent, and then the spell was broken. Tay spun around and followed Braan inside, drawing the flaps. Two Dragoche warriors stepped up to stand at the door.

Braan had already removed his outer robe and had poured half a mug of saffra. "Care to wash your face in real water?" Teloa merely knelt down, an exaggerated sigh escaping her lips. Laughing softly, he leaned over and gave her a quick hug. "You were magnificent! Strong without being arrogant. If I was not madly in love with you, I would make you chief of protocol!" A rap at the tent frame disturbed him. He frowned slightly, the first real expression she had seen on his face in hours. "We have our own sanitation behind that curtain; we should not be disturbed for anything until vespers." He whipped back the flap. A servant knelt there with a tray on the ground before him and another in his arms. Controlling a smile, Braan gestured, and the man stepped in, setting the food by the

saffra tray and returning for the pitcher, basin, and towels
Bowing pardon, the khatta vanished.

Pulling the canvas down, Braan faced Tay. "It appear
that your position has been defined. They were confused unti
now. I did not think we looked enough alike to be mistaker
for relatives." Teloa shook her head incredulously at the game
going on in his head and then removed her veils and oute
robe. She untied her hair, letting it fall heavily to her thighs
So good to be free of restrictive clothing . . .

Braan had vanished. He reappeared again and went t
the first basin, pulling off his caftan and bathing face, hands
and neck. The water sounded good to Teloa, so she als
retreated to the sanitation. To remove the dust of the day . .
The light of the rising star cast strange, muted brights an
shadows through the sides of the structure, but Tay did no
notice. She had seen something before Baakche's tent tha
disturbed her, and she was not sure if she should tell Braan
If she was correct; if it was important.

———

"Observations?"

"We are not home yet" was her answer.

"No, we are not."

"I wish you had had time to teach me the tribes' symbol
and the pecking order."

He shrugged, pulling off his boots and then his joqurs
"Other things were more important. Have you figured out th
inner tribal markings?"

"The embroidery?" She paused to pull off one boot
waving her foot to cool it. "The hem and lower side-sean
combination is the mark of a warrior. Only royalty has mark
ings on cuffs and hood."

"Cuffs for royalty; priesthood is marked by the cow
design. The scholar is the lower skirt crescent, and the ar
over the heart is a makermother. Hunters have the crescen
on the right shoulder blade, trackers the arc on the left. Mor
than one can be possessed, which increases status."

"Except the makermother." Braan looked oddly at her
"Baakche does not have that one." Braan laughed and stretche
out to let the fine perspiration dry on his body.

"No, he cannot have that one. His predecessor was a woman, and she had all the markings. Very impressive, like the high priest's ritual robes." While he spoke, Braan eyed her critically. She was disturbed. Why? "Did you like the oasis? Impressive, is it not?"

"Very. They can save us, Braan—if they want to." She impatiently removed her caftan and then stretched, catlike, her blond mane a glittering curtain around her. She was too much woman to hide behind that hair; nature did not allow it. He pushed that thought away. They were both very tired— he felt it in himself and could see the exhaustion and tension in her. She had called him Braan and was outwardly unself-conscious about it. Praise Mendulay. What was going on in her mind? He could almost see the brain activity.

He reached for a blanket, so lightweight that it felt like silk. So they chose to treat him like an Atare, at least until they decided what to do with him. "The saffra has a hot rock under it; it will stay warm. We should rest while we can. I hope we do not have to leave hastily." He meant it lightly, as a joke, but Teloa moved abruptly in reply, as if she had made up her mind about something. She folded down de-murely next to him, her hand on his knee.

"Were you bluffing, back in that council? About with-holding the shield?"

"No. Suppose you tell me what is really bothering— Tay?" He forced himself not to move suddenly as his body told him that her hand was wandering, tracing a delicate design on his inner thigh. "Beauty, what are you doing?"

"Doing?" she repeated innocently. "Merely relaxing my mind, Atare. It has been a stressful day."

"Indeed. And is becoming more so. I warn you, my control is very good in dark caves with nervous off-worlders, but in bright tents with bold women— Teloa!" He half sat up. A game—what kind of game? A role playing? The smile was mischievous and knowing, almost confident, a joke on them both. Like he felt she had been long ago, before other forces shaped her life. Yet he felt tension and a thin edge of fear. Why forcing herself into the role? He had based their physical relationship on slowly cracking her trained passivity and encouraging her pleasure. If she persisted, he would not be able to do that.

"Do you think Tikki will like staying with the hazelles? I was not sure about leaving her there."

I hope you do not think words will take my mind off what you are doing. Do not insult yourself. Her hands were so warm and still soft, even after many days in the Ciedär.

"If she becomes bored, she will find us. I trust her ability to sneak past Cied, if she could fool Eon and the other warriors." She was shockingly bold; he could count on one hand the women who could look you in the eye and—of course, he was passive. It made the role easier. But why? Should he play it through? Did he have a choice? "Lady, my control is slipping."

"Oh?" The next caress was strategic, the response immediate. He grabbed for her; she swept out of his way, a teasing chuckle all that was within reach. "Atare, are you trying to tell me something?"

Braan checked his movement with effort but not his racing blood. "My name is Braan," he replied softly.

"I know." She glided sinuously over the satin pillows toward him, and this time Braan did not miss. The struggle was brief and spirited, but joyful, anticipated. Even as he tried to pin her, half his mind slowing his efforts while the other half was an incoherent frenzy of color, she touched his upper thigh invitingly, winningly, in control of the moment. She whispered his name and something else, in Caprican, and then they were linked, a diffusion of feeling, the elusive tension gone. Braan no longer attempted to control himself, lost against the smooth, warm hardness of her body, razor-keen from desert paths and winds. He tangled his arms in her hair and sought her neck while she gently held his sides, steadying, coaxing. She had such a teasing tongue. . . .

Tired. So tired. He had lost a moment, a total blackout, as he always did when his nerves were worn. He had not known he was so tight . . . Warm and soft, cradled in her arms and curls, one hard leg a lock to keep him close. He pulled totally away, to allow her to move freely if she cared to, listening to the twin sounds of her heartbeat in his ear and soft gasps of air, slowing. The tension in the air had returned.

She was shaking. Suddenly fearful, he lifted his head to meet her eyes. Tay reached for his neck, her arms encircling his shoulders, all boldness gone, seeking comfort. Braan gathered her into his embrace and rolled over on his back, holding her so close that he could not distinguish her heartbeat from his own. He was not mistaken. She was crying.

"Belaiss, what is wrong?" He barely heard the words himself, dreading the answer, not wanting to break the silence.

"I . . . am . . . so afraid. He will kill you, I know it. I will stab him if he tries to touch me, I will not—not again . . ."

"Teloa, who? What?" No point in saying that they were under Genuar's protection. Something had terrified her, and he had totally missed it. He reached for the sheet, to add warmth to her now icy form. He tucked the silky folds around them, hoping his presence would help steady her. *Thank the Lord, it is not me she fears.*

"I wanted—just once—for things to be as they should, in case . . . you—" He touched her lips to hush her, understanding now and not wanting her to think more on it. "I just . . . block out the mind. The heart knows. . . ."

"What did you say? I do not know that language."

"What—oh, Caprican."

"I thought so." He eyed her.

"It means 'I love you.'" She pulled him close again, hiding her face against his shoulder.

"Tell me."

When she was calm, she finally began in a low voice, "The Stigati who spoke in the council; the man who doubted you could turn off sections of the shield? I saw him, Braan. Outside Baakche's tent, with the other chieftains, I think. His robes . . . The mark was the same one as the warriors who attacked us, I am positive of that. I thought I saw it when we walked out earlier, but I ignored it. Now I have seen the entire design clearly. You cannot miss the angle of that slash, the way it tapers to a point. He took your brothers, his people."

"The warrior with the half-circle scar around the brow? It is recent, still purple?"

"Yes! And the way he—he scrutinized me, he knows I know, from what you said here, about my being with the first group. A terrible look . . . and then he did not see me anymore. He was staring at this tent. He hates you."

"That last knife fight addled his brains."

"It is not funny." She clutched him tightly.

"I know. Sleep. We can do nothing about it now. I cannot speak to Genuar alone until this is over." But Braan lay awake, thinking, long after Teloa's breathing slowed, knowing what he had felt in the air and not sure how he would deal with it.

CHAPTER TWENTY-ONE

Lyte forced himself to stay awake by sitting on the edge of a rock outcropping. Sheer survival did wonders for his cognizance. Four days they had argued, every tribal and political rivalry of the past five thousand years rising to the surface of the discussion, obscuring the main issues. One group was upset about the broadening multiple marriages to include the royal family. Should this be allowed only when one spouse is an 80, or with more than one 20 as well? What if an heir to the Atare name died and his next eldest brother had a different mother; was monetary pecking order determined by which marriage came first or the children's date of birth? What if the Ragâree wanted to marry a sini? Were humanoids and aliens next?

Lyte laughed without sound. They were so flustered, they no longer made sense! But one thing was clear to him: They would not oppose the marriage. An elder of Seedar made that plain when he stood and said, "This is getting into the hypothetical, and I assume that means there is no objection to the current reality?"

An elder stood to address the synod leader. "Justinian, I have a more pertinent question. Do we still need a royal house at all? Could we not develop another judicial branch of government? The Axis has always frowned on all forms of planet royalty," the Dielaan elder said, stubbornly avoiding Corymb's riveting stare.

"The Axis frowns on a great number of the things we do, elder," Justinian replied. "I am not certain the Axis will allow any of our government to remain standing."

Corymb did not like that suggestion. Why? Lyte considered the man's reaction. Of course. If he cannot have the throne for himself, a descendant of his might.

"Justinian, what do you mean about the Axis not allowing our government to remain standing? Are you withholding information?"

"Idiots!" Everyone looked to see who had spoken. It was Kavan, lying upon a cot near the dais, refusing the comfort of the life shelter. He had demanded to be present for the debate. Now he shook in his rage; a *guaard* extended a hand to keep him lying prone, but the acoustics carried his voice. "Can you not see what is coming? What Braan Atare is doing? The reason we are alive is because of the old shield and the missile sites, the very things the Axis decreed we were not to have! Not only can we survive alone when Braan returns with the secrets of the Cied; we must! We are not reentering the Axis Republic, even if there is a republic to rejoin. Rebellion sparks on hundreds of planets. Intelligent beings can see through this so-called 'investigation' of Nuala. Our ambassador is being held—" Kavan finally stopped, unable to contain his fury, reduced to silence. He fell back, exhausted. An undercurrent of speech was heard, barely audible.

Kal stood and walked to the center of the dais. He closed his eyes a moment, as if collecting his thoughts. Then: "Brethren, my brother speaks much truth. The shield and GTAs are expressly forbidden items, even with our gold mines to protect. The *guaard* and their fellow Axis-trained warriors we keep only by virtue of their Atare origins. If the Axis returns, or we 'return' to them, do you think they will allow us to keep our defense missiles? Our planet shield? Especially the new shield, when it damages non-Nualan ships? They will want to establish a large military 'peacekeeping' force here. After all, we probably will be the Fewha line once again. They will keep the peace; by making sure our defense shield is no longer operative, by detonating our missiles in their tubes. They will police our people, our trade, our mines, the *guaard,* and the spaceport, where Axis ships built from our planet's patents shall land. Then, elders of the synod, when we are expendable again, we truly shall end as a people."

"You are talking treason!"

Kal's intense green eye bored into Corymb. "Would you like to open that topic for discussion?" He gestured to the crowd. "Have you not questioned the people you represent? What has the Axis given us, except a larger inferiority complex than the one we already had? Occasionally an off-worlder came to love our people and chose Nuala. So we gained our perverted system of royal marriage! Name one good thing the Axis has given us! Only one! Do not tell me of trade or industry. I will tell you of the enormous profits they made every year off our planet. *One thing!*"

It was so silent in the garedoc, Lyte could hear a pebble moving under someone's foot. Kal began to speak again, gently and with love, of what he had seen in his short life on this planet. The good and the bad, the beauty and ugliness—of the Ciedär and the people living in it. Of their pride, ignorance, and confusion; of bringing them slowly into modern technology and understanding, even if they preferred to choose older life-styles. Kal spoke of a united Nuala, a free and self-determining people once again. He spoke only briefly of their captivity—he preferred to leave tale telling for when Braan Atare returned. But it had been hard and had revealed a traitor in their midst; else how could the Cied have known which trail to follow of the dozens leading out of Nuamura? And then there were the weapons and other goods found in the destroyed smuggler camp. It was not a small-time trader, dodging the embargo, but someone with the power to include five ounces of trine gold in the bargain. This last caused a great deal of speech among the elders. Five ounces! Even on Nuala that was not an amount to be tossed about lightly. Kal held up the thong of gold and then nodded to Justinian.

"Forgive me, Brethren, but I am drained of strength. These petty arguments weary me; the end result cannot be changed. Make your decision. The life or death of Atare— and Nuala—is in your hands. I leave you to your choice." With that the young man turned on his heel and left the dais. Lyte rose from his seat to catch up with him. Too many things to deal with . . .

DRAGOCHE   TWOHUNDRED   VESPERS
CAMP   SIXTYSEVENDAY

He had dozed fitfully, unsure of what was bothering him. Waking, he remembered—he felt death in the camp. His death? Braan sat up carefully, trying to avoid waking Teloa. She had seen the danger, read it for what it was. Reaching for fresh joqurs, he considered all the possibilities. Ruler of a people concerned with life, he drew death wherever he went. Had his luck run out? Two attempts on his life within the year. Did the third time count for all? Would Genuar allow it? Could he stop it?

The Ciedärlien dealt with honor above all things. So far he had not suffered his name or rule to be challenged. But the desert was no place for mercy, no place for rest. That was seen as weakness, and advantage would be sought in it. How would this Cied do the deed? To come straight out and kill an Atare, no, he would not bring such a sin upon himself or his people. Cied chieftains took up their peoples' sins, but the people answered for known evil done by their rulers. Unless he was a mad one . . .

Shaking out his caftan, Braan remembered his own mocking words, words others had used before him: "Mendulay spares him for some other end." Was this the end? Would his death act as a catalyst, crystallizing Nuala's future, sending it down the only path left to it? What did he leave? Confusion, an infant Atare, enemies on every front, and five blood children, perhaps more—he was busy last winter. Was it enough? Suddenly he felt old, used up.

"Braan?" He glanced over and saw how intently she studied him, no trace of sleepiness about her.

She knows. He had not wanted to distress her with his fear. But only a fool would not be afraid. A Cied warrior was a perfect fighting machine, programmed to kill. He had only cut off a life force once in his life, the dying Durite. Now he knew why Nualans made such poor Axis warriors; the blood lust, the urge to attack had been bred out of them. They had to reacquire it, and only the most diligent, such as Jaac and his brother Deenn, succeeded. This Cied most likely had engineered the deaths of the twins.

Teloa crawled over and laid her head on his thigh. "There is great danger, isn't there?"

"To you? I do not think so. To me—quite likely. We shall know soon." He reached down to touch her face gently, meeting her upturned eyes. "Remember, I love you. Now and the woman you will become. Beauty may grow or fade, but the true mark is character, and you have it. Never let anyone convince you otherwise. Let us eat; they will come soon."

━━━━━━━

Up, hidden in the darkening hills from Kee's fading rays and Cied eyes, Moran observed the camp. He had seen the city hazelle among the pale desert breed and found the tame akemmi that came to his call. Braan Atare—and Teloa? Possibly. Fate had taken stranger turns in the past; they had used the same path into the desert. His own beast now grazed with the herd and with luck would not be discovered before starrise. Hopefully no one looked at tribal brands too closely, especially with so many different Cied present. But present for how long? And where were the leaders, which tent? It was important. He wanted to be as close as possible to Braan, should trouble start; and slipping into the camp unseen was a different thing from spying out the tumultuous valley. The warrior began to move down the hill, the akemmi clicking softly in his ear.

━━━━━━━

An escort came at twilight, before the day was totally withered. This time Braan hated walking to the council tent, for it was dark enough outside to wash away all color of the

living. He felt as if surrounded by walking corpses, all shrouded
in dirty white. They were unclean, their thoughts, their feelings. Much of Cied life was honorable, free, good. But beneath, it stank of blood and death. The entrance loomed up
before them. He signaled for Teloa to stand directly behind
him. If she was his wife, they could enter together, but there
were certain traditions the Cied did not allow tampering with,
and the law of rank was one of them. He briefly wondered
about Baakche. So far he had been remarkably lucid. If their
luck held . . .

It did not. Braan could see that the old man was in a
dream before they were seated. Genuar was conducting the
meeting. The chieftains had reassembled, four semicircles
around the inside of the tent. Braan felt Tay stiffen and followed her gaze. The last row . . . one Stigati chief was gone.

"Atare"—Braan returned his thoughts to Genuar—"the
council has long discussed the proposition you have brought
to us. We are aware of the great sacrifice your people have
made, destroying their trade and defense ties with the Axis.
We are not blind; we know there is likely no return from your
stance. We know you want the skills we have developed over
the centuries. But we ask, what of next year? Your winter
planting was lean; the spring will not be that much better,
even with our help."

Braan casually adjusted his robes. "Why, Seri, as the
cities need grain and produce, the desert needs cloth, weapons, and refined metal. Our factories would love an excuse
to begin production once more. I am sure a separate, short-
term treaty can be arranged by council and syn—"

"Enough of the lies!" Braan stopped in mid-sentence,
keeping his composure. Out of the corner of his eye, he saw
that a warrior had entered the great tent and was standing at
the door.

"What means this?" Genuar snarled, gesturing for the
Cied to be removed.

"I challenge!" The man's voice was rasping, vicious. At
those words the guards fell away from him. He had bought
the right to speak. Braan glanced at Tay; beneath her veils
she was wide-eyed. Turning to face the warrior, Braan saw
that he was completely unveiled, his black beard matted with

dust, the new scar vivid purple. The Stigati, of course. But his robe was hanging in shreds on him, the front panel of the outer robe slashed away. No pattern, no tribe.

Scourged and thrown out for violating . . . the twins are alive, was Braan's first thought. Why challenge? He had lost all face by disobeying Genuar's words. Unless he believed death in combat was more honorable than freedom and banishment. Unless . . . Braan looked over at Genuar and Baakche. The younger man was shocked and angry over the insult, his eyes flashing a warning. Baakche was staring at his hands, a smile playing about his eyes. So, with one hand he tells his heir that this test is not necessary, and with the other he concocts combat.

"What challenge? You know not this man!" Genuar was openly scornful, part of Cied justice, the treatment for an avowed rule breaker. How—?

"I know this woman. Long my people spied their train, and only two wore the Atare mark, not three! If you lie for this, dragon, what other tales do you spin?" The gathering stiffened as one at the insult. There was no greater offense than to call a Nualan a liar.

"I did not lie. Her robe was destroyed by Ciedär winds. I gave her my second."

"And implied that she was of the royal house!"

Braan reconsidered the previous conversation. "Not implied. I called her serae, for so every intended bride is named. In but a little while it is my intention to make her Atarae. That business was not the council's concern."

The warrior's face pulled into a sneer. "As with the shield, there is no proof. So I claim her as truth-price, to found my new line." With one swift movement he reached for and jerked Tay to her feet. The response was sudden. Genuar leapt up, but it was a wasted motion. The Stigati froze, and as his grip loosened, everyone could see why. Teloa had worked her cat knife free during his little speech and, at his movement, had pressed the tip of the blade into his groin. The look in her eyes told him that she did not bluff. But he could not back away—Braan's cat was in the hollow of his knee, against tendon and muscle. One move and he would be crippled for life.

"Challenge accepted." Nicely done, Baakche. You cast him out for attempting to shed royal blood, and then give him another chance at it, all the while hiding your own guilt behind the robes of your position. Planned or coincidental? No matter—if he won, it proved his worthiness to the Cied and guaranteed their council support, at least for a season. If he lost, the Cied would say it was meant to be. But he could not let an Atare be called liar. Anything else he could ignore but not that. Such leechings would be repeated, gathering force and conviction, until no claims, no disavowal, could stop them. And the house would fall. Empires had tumbled on less.

"I have not the stomach for the darker side of kingship." Was that what Roe had said? Can you kill a man in cold blood, Atare? That is what it is, license to kill. What does it prove if you do?

Two warriors came forward and indicated that the Stigati chieftain should follow them. Only then did Braan's knife disappear. "Teloa. Stay with the scholars, please." It was mildly spoken, belying his thoughts. If fate was kind, he would at least take this Cied down the Path with him, and Teloa could return to Nuamura to do what little might help. He followed the trio outside, a brief prayer to Mendulay illuminating his thoughts. He knew his skills and training. Now he had to live up to it. As a body, the council stood, waiting for Baakche and Genuar to lead them. Teloa stayed with the three planters, aware that they would also go out to . . . what?

———

Darkness had settled over the valley. The fire in the tribe's common, the center ground of the camp, was burning brightly, fed by scrub brush and hazelle dung. Braan wondered about the acid tinge to the smoke's smell, from nix dung—he had seen no nix in the herd. They were precious animals, shy breeders; the finest worth their weight in yellow gold. He forced his thoughts back to the wide circle. The chieftains were gathered around the fringe, some standing, some seated in tent entrances. He saw the scholars scurrying to an unoccupied spot and hoped Tay was with them. He could tell they approved of her. Good.

Would this be free or tied combat? He did not relish the idea of fighting with their left wrists tightly secured together. Braan looked over at his opponent, who stood beyond the fire pit, swaying with emotion or exhaustion—Braan could not tell which. Would he not even name himself? The Atare sat down by the fire and waited, his eyes on Genuar.

The chieftain was distracted, a young warrior racing into the circle to command his attention. The newcomer spoke swiftly, in tones too low to overhear. Genuar raised his head and stared oddly at Braan. Then he said something to the youth in reply. The warrior vanished out the circle exit leading to the valley. Braan did not like the feel of that at all, but now was not the time to ask.

Genuar walked over to Braan, who stood. "I am sorry. I tried to avoid this. He is weak, but his fury makes him dangerous." The Cied pulled out a gleaming cat knife. "This blade has served me well. I give it to you, as a token of my good faith, that it may speed your hand. Finish this quickly or you will walk the Path this night."

"See to my woman."

Genuar's eyes seemed to smile. "I pray that will not be necessary." He turned to face the now massed group. "The man Robis has challenged Braan Atare, who has accepted. The combat shall be free—and to the death." The Stigati stepped up to the fire pit, across from Braan, flames and Genuar between them. *They did not even leave you your mother's name.*

"It begins." Genuar moved out of the way, to sit beside the muttering Baakche.

This is ridiculous, Braan thought. But very real. The Stigati crouched low, starting to creep around the circle. Braan stood his ground, balancing carefully on the balls of his feet, letting his body relax into the elkita. He knew his training, the sound skills of a warrior; but not commando-honed, not *guaard.* Elkita was something else. Defense, more than movement; he was an expert. Only that fact and endurance could save him. But the survival strength of the Cied might be more than even a rested Atare could handle. The warrior was there, almost next to him, and suddenly lunged with the speed of a striking milee, pinning his fighting arm. Just as quickly the Cied was flying through the air, landing on his back at the common's edge. Braan flipped himself to his feet, remaining low, the knife now held with the thumb-and-full-finger grip of one who understands weapons. As he suspected, the teaching of elkita had waned in the Ciedär. If a chieftain did not know it, very few would. Interesting. He hoped Teloa remembered what she saw, in case he could not.

The Cied approached again, this time more cautiously, respect in his eyes. Also confusion and anger. He had not wanted this duel, Braan suspected. He was a scapegoat. No time to consider it. Circling . . . a feint, and then another lunge. Braan was ready for him. Shifting the knife to his left hand, Braan grabbed for nerve and artery with his right. At the same time he caught the Cied's right arm between his left knee and fist with a crunch no one missed. He was trying for the nerve; whether he found it or not, the warrior dropped his knife. The Cied grabbed for his throat; knocking them both to the ground. Seeing his intent, Braan frantically applied pressure on the man's windpipe, trying to render him unconscious. The Stigati was becoming glassy-eyed, but his hand moved relentlessly toward the discarded knife. No choice— Braan whipped his left arm down, still clutching Genuar's cat. Too late, the Cied released Braan's throat, reaching for his arm. Braan slid the knife to his side and then thrust up and out, under the rib cage and toward the heart. Abruptly the Cied's struggles ceased, his eyes widening slightly; they no longer saw his adversary. Braan quickly heaved the warrior over and leapt for the other knife. It was unnecessary. The Stigati was dead.

Dazed, Braan did not notice that two Cied had stood and were walking toward the fire. He did hear an animal's chittering, and saw a dark streak zip by him. Turning, he realized that Teloa and the scholars were at his back and that the creature was Tikki, creeping into Tay's hood, ignoring the exclamations of the surprised tribal leaders.

Looking back to the fire, Braan found that a warrior was blocking the light. The warrior held a drawn cat knife in each hand and was facing down the other Cied. The crowd was deathly silent, as if shocked by his appearance in their midst. Only the keening of the rising wind could be heard.

One of the two standing Cied dropped his upper veil. "Even those who would kill kings deserve rites and a light ceremony," the khatta said.

"Do they?" a familiar voice responded. Startled by his presence, Braan froze within and then reached to close the dead Stigati's eyes. Braan moved over to the circle's edge, sitting before Teloa. "Then take him." Moran backed up until he was between Braan and the body. The khatta came forward and dragged the Cied out of the fire circle. Braan relaxed, was aware of blood between his fingers, tensed again; then Teloa's hands were skillfully rubbing the taut muscles running down his spine, forcing away the exhaustion he felt to his bones. So grateful that it was not his blood . . . Composure, everything rode on composure.

"My apologies for taking so long, Atare. I had storms and guards to avoid. I thought to find my woman here," came a voice out of a fog.

"I am glad to see you, though my questions are multitudinous. But we two are alone. She, of all the first expedition; I lost Lyte in the basin. Unless Genuar will tell me good news of the twins," Braan replied slowly.

"Much we have to say to one another, Atare. Justice has been met. You have avenged the insult to your kin. They were alive when taken from Bloodsand. Not by my people, though as they arrived, they saw it done," Genuar offered.

"We took them—Jaac, Lyte, and I. They were alive when I left them." Moran spoke to Braan, not to Genuar, and did not relax his stance.

"They sent you?"

"I came. Lyte would have, but I felt Roe's presence and decided to travel east."

"Then you can explain the caravan in the valley?" No one answered Genuar, but he appeared satisfied by their puzzled glances. "If you will have your warrior take his place, Atare, we were discussing a treaty, were we not? Short-term and affecting trade? And we would offer gifts to your house. Saffra for everyone."

As Genuar finished speaking, two Cied warriors appeared before him, addressing their leader. Then they turned and indicated that an entrance should be made in the circle. The glow of torches rose above the tent path, and soon two Dragoche warriors walked into the ring, planting their firebrands at either side of the opening. They were followed, to Tay's amazement, by several warriors in solid beige robes, with a curiously entwined dragon over their hearts. Eon's uniform . . . The four men arranged themselves in a defense posture around the commons while Teloa looked back to the entrance. Eight large *guaard* slowly processed, carrying an enclosed litter. It was small and made of sprung wood and plastic, covered with light material drifting in the breeze. It also bore the Atare dragon on its sides. Braan inhaled audibly, and Tay glanced over, worried. He was very pale—injured— and he had said nothing?

"Nix. They brought a litter on a nix." He was clearly stunned by the development and looked even worse when the tall, lively hazelle pranced in behind the carrier, a slight figure on its back.

"What?" Tay whispered to him.

"We are lost. What is she doing? Our house dies." She gripped his arm, afraid. He was dropping his mask. Why? "The only reason I agreed to follow Genuar was Breeyan. I knew I left an heir behind me. Silly, I suppose. If I die, if the Cied refuse, there will be no Nuala and no need for an Atare. But if she brought them . . ."

"Jaacav took the twins back to Nuamura."

"That is Liel, Tay, on that hazelle. And only Roe's health and the tiny ones would demand a litter. We trace our line through our Ragärees! Do you not see? If Baakche refuses to acknowledge her, Kal will be the last Atare ruler!" The woman went as pale as Braan, the full gamble laid before her. The Cied did not bow to the coast—they never did. The future hung on a mad one.

The *guaard* carefully set the carrier down, six more of their brethren coming in behind them. One young woman stepped up to open the curtains, while another *guaard* held the hazelle's tossing head. Liel slipped down and walked gracefully to the litter. Tay detected the slightest tremor of her hand. *She is as terrified as I am.*

A bundle was extended through the parted curtains, and Liel gathered it close. Then Ronuviel stepped out, the other babe held tightly. She wore no hood or veils, and immediately a soft hum began. The chieftains knew who she had to be but were as puzzled as Braan. On her part, Roe surveyed them swiftly, imperially, her gaze resting on Baakche and Genuar. Her magnificent, intimate smile lit up her face, and she slowly walked toward them. Tay glanced at Moran—he was gone, mingling with the *guaard,* finding an access point to Roe. She . . . she was glowing

Tay sat back on her heels, astonished. But she only did that when she was healing someone! Surely she would not try to cure Baakche's madness? Yet Teloa had never questioned her about it; for all she knew, it was an emotional reaction Roe normally held in check. It raised her body temperature—that Tay did know. Lords, the baby. Which one? Framed by the coals of the fire and the trine moons, especially since Roe shielded her charge from torchlight. The bundle also glowed—but lighter, more silvery than Roe's golden aureole. The Ragäree gestured for Liel to bring the other infant forward, but the young woman had reached her limit; she stood frozen. Moran stepped to her side and scooped up the baby, smiling at whatever reaction the tiny one shared with him. How strange to feel a smile through a veil. Liel did not move back, unwilling to give up the small victory with her fears, but she did not follow Moran to Roe's side.

Now Teloa was aware of figures standing behind her—many figures. The clan had gathered to find out who the visitors were. She heard one child ask who the pretty lady was. "A healer" was the reply. "*The* healer," whispered another.

Baakche did not react, not even when Roe reached for her other child and the wrap of blankets in Moran's arms began to glow with the same gold of its mother. Not from Ronuviel—separate, self-generated. Tay was enchanted and could sense that the crowd was as well. The gathering was as disarmed as their chieftains were confused. Genuar was on his feet, his veils down, revealing a dark, well-trimmed beard and mustache. He was looking at Braan warily, wonderingly. His nonchalance was as shattered as Braan's.

The Atare woman knelt by Baakche, waiting, so close that they could touch without effort. Genuar, in the meantime, was examining Moran's bundle, appearing visibly shaken. Baakche raised his head and met Roe's eyes. He was not aware of the baby's reach until the child seized his robe in an urgent grip. Then he looked at the glowing pair. He sighed quietly, tapping the tiny hand with one finger. A *guaard* brought a low seat and had Roe sit upon it. Baakche looked up at the fragile woman holding her son and then stood slowly.

"My people," he whispered in a silvery voice, revealing the extent of his physical illness in his trembling upraised arms, "I have sinned greatly these many days, in my fear and the need of us all. Instead of punishing you for my crimes and striking me dead, Mendulay has most richly blessed us. For many years, in many forms, the prophecies of Naitun have puzzled me. Now dream takes flesh and walks our mother planet. I praise the Holy One that I have lived to see this!" Baakche faced Ronuviel again and, in a move startling almost everyone, knelt before her. "Thank you for bringing me peace. I am forgiven." His last words visibly shocked her as his actions had not, but Roe kept her composure. Though her gentle touch was for Baakche, her eyes were on Genuar. He was struggling with something within.

Teloa was conscious of the whispers of the crowd growing louder; of excitement, tension. The grip Braan had on her hand was bone-crushing. He was watching several chieftains. They looked bewildered, torn between prophecy staring them in the face and their desire to retain autonomous control over their clans. They turned to Genuar for help. The gathering was ready to follow Baakche's lead, Tay had no doubt, but they looked to Genuar for their daily law and order. Only Baakche ignored them—he had made his peace.

Braan did not dare move, but he had to. He stood silently waiting. This man desired protection for his people, yet feared absorption by the cities. Braan could prevent the latter, at least during his own lifetime; he intended to educate his heir along the same vein.

Did Genuar believe that?

The Cied was composed once more, and his piercing gaze was only for Braan. One word either way and a riot would break out. On his decision their lives depended. *He came to warn me, yet he did not stop the fight. He wanted help from an equal. Will he accept a sovereign, even in name only?* Pride or the safety of the Ciedär and its people . . . Genuar walked around the fire and stopped within a meter of Braan.

Teloa thought she would scream. Say something! Yes, no, talk, anything!

He did not. He made the slight formal bow of the *guaard* to royalty, accompanied by a barely raised eyebrow. Braan replied with the upswept arm of greeting and honor. Pandemonium broke out. The chieftains were nearly trampled by the crowd in its effort to see the infant twins. The *guaard* locked into a barricade, keeping them from pressing too close but allowing them to look. Braan could see Liel being lifted up into the litter to protect her from the crush, and then arms encircled him from the back.

"It's all right? Is it?" It was Tay.

He swung an arm around her and in reply pulled her close for a second. Then he turned to Genuar, who stood as firm as a rock among the swirling waves of people. "Why?" Braan could not stop his quizzical smile. "Why take the chance?"

"Because," Genuar started, a laugh brightening his dark face, "I am curious." At their puzzled looks he went on. "The story begins, Braan Atare, and I want to see what you do next. It must be impressive to top this!"

CHAPTER TWENTY-TWO

The healers made Odelle as comfortable as possible. gave her a tranquilizer, and then left her in peace. There was nothing else to be done. Shinar told her she was going to the common ward, beyond the beads, and would be back in a moment. Did she want a priestess? No? Soon, then She would return.

Odelle did not pay attention; the painkillers and relaxan were soothing her harassed and convoluted mind. Now to sleep. It was over. A healthy child but a mock sini . . . Wha had Elana said? "Her jaw is like Tinyan's. She will be a strong leader, Odelle. Know it." Sweet Mendulay, what next" The drugs lulled her. Her husband had taken it stoically, with words of concern and comfort. "The next you will nurse yourself." Yes, Corymb would be so angry.

"Bitch!" It was a hiss, an intake of breath. Odelle's eye shot open. She recoiled more from the tone than the word "Do you understand? Do you know what you have done?"

She stared blankly at him. He was so furious, he wa

vhite, his lips compressed, his teeth clenched. "It is life. Mendulay has de—"

"Mendulay be damned!" Odelle blanched at the blasphemy. "You destroyed it! The greatest action of your life nd you have shattered everything!" Corymb raged on, heedess of discretion. In the great ward Shinar caught one look hrough the beads at his face and ran for the outermost door nd her *guaard*. "All my plans, ruined, and—"

"We do not stand on one child. Elana said so. The tribe vill vote to keep you, I am sure, and there are ways to increase he chance of a boy, though they usually do not try them ntil—"

"Foolish twit of a child! To rule Nuala the line must be lean! How can you bear the next to reign if you bear sinis? 'ou chose that insipid idiot—we will find you a better! We ave been clean for generations; it is his fault! A distant Dielaan relative would be better. I will check the genealogy. Do you realize that I must remove the Atare myself? I cannot ive him time to entrench himself." This was no longer to er. He was pacing, muttering.

"Our line has no healers—" Her voice shook.

"Do not speak to me of healers! The planet is balanced t the point of civil war, and you speak of healers! I have lans for the healers. They are too close to sinis—"

"You are the one who divides us. If Justinian and High 'riest Arrez did not keep the peace—"

The look on his face stopped her in mid-gasp. "I shall ile the order immediately. If anyone asks, the family synod greed on removing his house status. Keep him at your peril, ut he shall not father any more Dielaans!"

"It was a temple marriage—"

"What is done can be undone! If you fight this—" He tepped toward her, his face set. "You remember the last time ou crossed my wishes, do you not?" The last was so soft, o gentle, she barely heard it. They faced one another, Odelle rrified and shocked out of her trance, Corymb blazing in is determination, the pulse at his throat visibly throbbing.

"Seri Corymb, the serae is tired. No visitors except her usband are permitted, and that includes all family." The *uaard's* mild speech did not disguise his warrior's posture.

Corymb locked eyes with him and then whirled and stamped out of the ward.

Shinar immediately rushed from behind the *guaard* to Odelle. "That . . . horrible man!" She burst out. "Whatever he said, Odelle, do not pay any attention to him, he is—he is a mad one!"

"He is . . ." Odelle whispered, her eyes darting to Shinar like a frightened bird's.

Puzzled, Shinar continued hurriedly. "I have brought 3AVs, Odelle, about the Serae Lyn of Seedar, who bore a mock sini as her firstborn son and a healer next, the healer Arunn. And of— Odelle, will you listen? The delivery was normal, the baby is fine! And the odds are in the millions— *billions*—against non-sini parents having more than one sini child. You and your husband will have children you can raise in your own home."

"Who in Tolis will raise the heir of Dielaan?" Odelle's voice still shook, her lips now thin with mockery.

"You are the friend of the Ragäree, who is the best-loved of the house of Atare and the personal friend of the ministers. I have already asked Kalith to speak via 3AV to them, to insure privacy. They will make sure she is received as the daughter of Odelle, not the heir of Dielaan. Feel better?" Shinar's words were as soothing as she could make them. What else could be said? Her son was with her—Odelle's daughter would be sent north with the next ship. "I grieve with you, friend," she whispered, tears filling her eyes. "But Mendulay has a plan, and we are not consulted. Have faith."

"She is my firstborn," Odelle replied brokenly. "The line rightfully goes through her. The old tyrant will dominate her life, too, unless she has no brother, and it ends. . . ." Her mind seemed to drift, and Shinar reached for her, gripping her chin, turning her head.

"Odelle?"

Odelle moved quickly, for all the drugs were affecting her, seizing Shinar's hand. "Do something for me. Remember, her name is Valleri. Will you remember? Valleri."

Shinar stroked back her dark curls. "You can tell your eldest when she comes, Odelle. They usually take the mother's preference."

"Please, it is my wish. Upon the child's life I wish it!"

Her oath visibly startled Shinar. "It is from the Nualan, is it not? The word *freedom*." Odelle had turned away. "A good idea. A name charms its owner, protects her. If you like, I will go tell your eldest now. I can leave the shelter; you are the only one here." The girl nodded. "Do you want me to hook up the viewer?"

"No! No, I want rest ... peace."

"Of course." Shinar tucked the light blanket around her. "Sleep." She started for the private exit.

"Shinar?"

"Yes, Odelle?"

"Thank you. For all things." The young healer smiled, feeling an ease to the tension in the room. Odelle smiled back. Shinar left the room.

Odelle carefully raised herself, swinging her legs over the bed's edge. She sat there, oblivious to pain, looking through the dividing beads into the common ward. A surgical table stood near the sealer drawers, where Shinar had left it, unlocked. The steel and laser scalpel tips were in labeled containers; Shinar had been putting them away.

She stood and stepped toward the shimmering wooden curtain.

MT. AMURA   TWOHUNDRED   PRIME
                         EIGHTYTWODAY

Over the swirling sands to the east, a pale salmon dawn was brightening. It was steady light, without any specific source. The priest pulled his white wool poncho tighter around his body.

Since lauds he had been sitting there, looking out on the scrub slopes and barren rock of the Sonoma Mountain's Cie-är face. The *guaard* had come to him in the deadness of the dark, saying the words he had waited too many days to hear: "Travelers from the desert—they will be here by dawn." Arrez rose from his bed, seized his robe and poncho, and followed her. The questions that needed answering had no answers yet.

Word had spread like a thunderhead, just as swift an
devastating. Arrez had spoken briefly to Kalith, and the *guaar*
now watched the pass behind them, Jaacav and her second
below at road's end. At the grotto the crowd gathered, hopin
for any word that could be interpreted as favorable. Besid
him stood a pale Kavan, his family's emissary. In the grott
two hours distant, Kalith fretted, Arrez knew, waiting to hea
whether friends or enemies approached—praying to be abl
to give up the chain of office.

Kee burst over the broken peaks in the distance, an
Kavan turned his head to avoid the glare. He could see Arre
sitting below him, eyes squinting, poncho wavering in th
thin breeze, looking like a giant bird of prey. Kavan's gaz
traveled back to the foothills below, and in the dazzling ligh
he could see the leaders, barely a kilometer distant, a hug
pack train behind them. As the star rose higher, the illusio
of black figures against white sand vanished, and he bega
to pick out tribal patterns.

"Eleven, twelve . . . Do you think every tribe sent a
ambassador?"

"Possibly."

"Then he made it? She made it?"

"Possibly."

Kavan sat down behind the priest, his irritation apparent
"What do you mean?" He scowled. "Surely if they intende
to fight us—

"The banner they carry is white—a truce flag. The
may come to parley or to challenge. And since they carry th
mark of passage, even if they throw your brother's body dow
before us, we cannot retaliate. Be patient."

After another period of silence Kavan exclaimed, "Th
nix! Roe's nix is returning." Arrez did not answer, refusin
to hope, wanting only an end to waiting and prayer. H
watched several of Jaac's subordinates ride out to the leadin
group, to be met by a messenger in Cied robes. The ap
proaching convoy did not slow its pace. Then the *guaar*
bolted back to where Jaacav was, motionless on her blac
hazelle. The ensuing conversation was brief and widely heard
for a warrior started up the hill on foot toward them.

"My seri! He comes, the Atare comes! Ragäree, Ragarr

and heirs are with him, as is the Serae Liel. And he found
the planter! The Dragoche himself approaches!"

"Will they help us?" Kavan interrupted.

"They bring planters and seed from all the tribes!"

━━━━━━━

Now he could relax. Arrez stood slowly and turned to
leave. "Thank you. Come, Kavan. It is not proper that we
should be sitting like oads on a stone when Atare and Dragoche come to call. Did you tell them we are in mourning?"

"I do not think they did."

"It should be done—see that your commander hears my
words." Arrez topped the rise and stepped onto the road.
"They must come up by pairs; it will take them until tierce.
We have some time to ourselves."

━━━━━━━

When the travelers finally reached the grotto, escorted
by several dozen warriors, a multitude greeted them. The
crowd filled the half circle before the arch, packed the bowl
of the garedoc, overflowed down the western road, and hung
from the cliffs, all to catch a glimpse of the Cied. Arrez and
Kavan had agreed while riding back that they would announce
that the house of Atare had returned intact and that the planter
Teloa was found. Of their guests, only general mention would
be made—"Cied are with them." Arrez wanted no disgruntled
Amurans trying for Genuar's—or Braan's—life.

The spectacle waiting at the city's entrance was as colorful as the one riding through the pass. Arrez had donned
the summer robes of state, white syluan with embroidered
green on stole, cuffs and hem. The twins were both brilliant
in syluan joqurs and long-sleeved tunics, Kal's emerald with
a yellow cape, Kavan's deep violet with white, embroidery
rich on both outfits. The representatives of the houses, synod,
and guilds were no less splendid in their finery. Only the
black arm bands marred the occasion.

Lyte looked out of the corner of his eye at Shinar. She
was very pale, dark smudges hollowing her eyes, but otherwise she was bearing up well. It was she who had found
Odelle's still warm body, blood splashed over bed and floor.

The girl had been ignorant of technique but thorough, to the shock and horror of the city. Suicide was considered a dignified end for the terminally ill but not for one with so much life ahead. Family pressure and shame was the suspected reason, though the Dielaan council issued an epistle stating that Odelle had had mental problems for some time. Shinar's answer to that had been brief, bitter, and unrepeatable.

Corymb, himself, stood among them, but not the same Corymb. He was shrunken, closed, almost unaware of the gathering near him. For the first time Lyte saw him using a cane, though he had been told that the man had walked with a sight limp for decades. His presence made the twins visibly nervous. What if he had a pact with these Cied to harm Braan? Noah stood beside Kavan, seal in hand, ready to step to his ruler's side the moment he reined up. Shinar pointedly ignored the Dielaan; Lyte was sure that only her new visibility kept her from spitting at him when he passed.

Braan Atare and Teloa were the first up the rise, followed by Ronuviel's huge, shaggy nix. *Guaard* came forward to take their hazelles, Braan helping the woman off the animal. The nix stood silent, its wedge-shaped head turned to survey the gathering, its polished, curved horns glittering in the growing light. Ronuviel's *guaard* took the children from her and pulled down a small ladder to aid her descent from the litter on the nix's back. The beast was herded through the scattering crowd to make room for Liel and Moran, who were next in line. Warriors of the *watch* kept a chain of bodies between the new arrivals and the Nuamurans, and few objected to this precaution.

Beside Lyte, Kalith stirred. The young man walked toward his older brother, a *guaard* on either side of him. He had removed the chain of office and held it in his hands. The *guaard* Noah knelt first, presenting Braan's seal to him, which he immediately slipped on his finger. Then Kal dropped to one knee and offered him the chain.

"In a hurry to get rid of it, are you?" Lyte heard Braan say. Kal answered softly, and his elder laughed. Braan took the chain from him and put it on over the desert robe, looking as regal through dust as any monarch could. He nodded across the bowl to Arrez, then raked the group of house leaders behind Kal with his glance. Baakche and Genuar had walked through the departing hazelles to Braan. They placed themselves carefully, to be able to greet all the leaders and be part of Braan's words to the gathering, yet to avoid offending any who had questions about their presence. Stepping to Teloa, Kal managed a broad smile, which she gently, shyly returned. The High Atare now faced the delegations of elders, led by Corymb and his Seedar counterpart.

What happened next was swift and unexpected. Braan caught one good look at Corymb's face and saw that something was terribly wrong. Odelle's death? Then he saw the knife flash. A blow from the side knocked Braan to the ground, and Moran continued right through the small group, his foot slashing out to catch Corymb in the knee. Noah had seized the Dielaan's right wrist even as he buckled. But the man had carried two blades, hoping to be doubly lucky, and Genuar was not fast enough to cut off Baakche's action. The old man leapt between Corymb and Braan, desert reflexes responding one more time, and he took the short, delicate stitto blade in the chest as Corymb was dragged flailing to the ground.

The Cied leapt around their leaders, expertly pinning Corymb to the rocks. One whipped out a cat knife, but Genuar spoke swiftly in Ciedärlien Nualan, and the warrior froze. The Dragoche clan leader was not looking at his fallen ruler or the would-be assassin but at the warriors and a healer, on the fringe of the crowd working their way to the exit where the hazelles had walked on through. The warriors carried a sealed container between them, its lid glass with a two-way breath hatch. And Genuar knew what a sini box looked like.

"Hold!" The Cied walked quickly to their side.

The healer paled—he nodded to Braan, who was now standing again and with a nervous glance to the desert monarch, said, "Pardon, Atare, but the *Emon* is leaving with the tide, and we were not to place her on board until the last moment. We ride to the harbor." Braan was watching Genuar, who was scowling darkly, his deep eyes riveting Ronuviel to the mountain as if doubting her existence.

"Whose child is this little one?" the chieftain demanded.

The healer looked for help, saw none forthcoming, and

whispered, "This is Valleri reb'Odelle, the last heir of Corymb, bound for Tolis." A soft, rising wind carried his words
to the now silent crowd. There was little else, not even the
cry of birds. Baakche's breathing was labored and heart-
rending above the whisper of the stunted mountain trees.
Genuar nodded, turned, and went back to Baakche. Ronuviel
was with the old man and shook her head fractionally at the
new Dragoche.

"He . . . is necessary. My time is past," Baakche said to
the tall chieftain, a whistle in his throat. "So it was written."
The warrior's grip tightened on Genuar's shoulder as his
breathing became light, shallower; and then the tortured lungs
ceased.

"Release him," Genuar told his warriors. "Mendulay has
punished him enough. Death would be too merciful for his
deeds." He looked at Baakche and, to no one in particular,
added, "He was my father."

All eyes were on Ronuviel, who had moved to Corymb,
her glowing fingertips spanning his forehead. "Something has
snapped," she murmured, her eyes closed. "He is a broken
man." She released him, and several *guaard* helped her up
from her kneeling position. "Come," she requested of those
around her. "We have many candles to light."

———

Genuar's marshals attended to his followers, and a tent
site was established at the western foot of Mt. Amura. A
prodigious amount of food was prepared and taken to both
returning *guaard* and guests. Genuar chose to eat with his
people and to wait with them until Braan took care of immediate Nuamuran problems. What to do with Genuar and
his chieftains had been the first problem—Braan was then
free to take Roe, Liel, Moran, Teloa, and Jaacav to the assembly where Kalith, Kavan, and Arrez tried to explain all
the dealing, double-crossing, and general turmoil that had
occurred in his absence. Ronuviel had told him little during
the ride back. They had been careful not to give the Cied
reason to suspect treachery.

Gid came in during the end of the discussion and added
his thoughts on the situation. When the man finished, Braan

sat with the air of a shock victim. He closed his eyes and leaned back against the wall.

"I was angry and prideful, Braan. Things may be difficult because of my behavior," Kalith said tightly, afraid of his brother's reaction.

Braan opened his eyes. "No, I do not see that as a problem. I only wonder how much further to push events. They have had a lot to digest in the last twentyday. I suppose it will depend on how well they accept the news that I concur with you. Let us leave off storytelling until we have dealt with the synod. The worst problem you have left me is the need for an immediate coronation." He smiled at his younger brother.

"They are getting restless," Arrez remarked. He was standing at the opening to the garedoc.

Braan loosened his outer robe, smoothed his desert beard, and flicked the dust off his worn boots. "Let us reward their patience." He stood. Noah started down the assembly steps, and Braan followed, another *guaard* directly behind him.

"You can go rest if you prefer," Roe whispered to Teloa.

"When you need it more than I? I think not," Tay replied, and stared, mystified, at the Ragäree, who laughed in delight at the woman's totally Nualan speech. Roe encircled Teloa's arm with her own, and they walked together to the floor of the garedoc.

"Brethren, cease thy speech!" Justinian's voice rang out above the conversation. "Out of our blackest dreams, hope fulfilled—our Atare has returned, and he has triumphed!"

Braan stepped up next to the man and waited for the roar of approval to subside. "I hope you all feel that way when I have finished speaking. To say we have 'triumphed' is perhaps premature. We have a long road ahead and, most likely, a hungry winter. We shall not starve, barring catastrophe; that is truly a great victory. Even now Jaacav shows the Dragoche the material preparations we have made to reimburse the Ciedärlien for their extra grain. I have offered shield protection in exchange for their knowledge. Planters and seed have come to us, as well as the secrets of their fertilizer. I intend this to be the beginning of a long and fruitful relationship for both Cied and the coast." He paused.

"The matter of my brothers' capture and the deaths of the elders Tig and Piral, along with their escort, has been settled. The Dragoche and tribal council were unaware of treachery in their midst, and Cied justice has been dealt out. That aspect of this sordid mess is over. There is another part— what to do with Corymb Dielaan. What shall we do with him, Brethren?" Braan had begun to pace the length of the platform, Justinian melting away into the background. "In the past many of you have been dissatisfied with the evidence against him—dealing with monopolies, selling out his planet, even blackmail and murder. Though you were loath to trust a dead Durite, you saw his latest attempt, made with his own hand. Whether it was against my royal person or directed toward Baakche, the result is unchangeable. Baakche, the Dragoche, is dead. The Cied are appeased—they feel Mendulay has punished the Dielaan sufficiently. The code of this planet is justice tempered with mercy. Has he been punished enough? His line has ended; his career and community standing are destroyed. As one who has willfully terminated a life he must be barred from any position of authority or responsibility for the rest of his days. Do we entrust him to his family? I feel I must have assistance with this; as his intended victim not once but three times, the temptation to be too harsh—or too lenient—is great." Braan sat on the throne after his pronouncement, his eyes taking in the assembly.

Ronuviel watched him and knew his fear; of being too gentle and fighting the tendency with a heavy hand.

One elder was recognized by Justinian and slowly stood. She cleared her throat and looked to Braan. "I think, Atare, that it is necessary to be sure that Corymb Dielaan can never pursue his personal vendetta against the house of Atare ever again."

"Suggestions?"

"Can we not place a special guard upon him, to watch his every move and be certain that he spends his time in research and composition, no threat to our people?"

Another individual demanded recognition. "An important question must be answered. Is he sane?"

Justinian turned to the foot of the podium and indicated that Elana should step up. The woman faced the synod. "All physical tests have been conducted. I would prefer to allow more time for observation, but at this moment I can say that hate and uncontrollable rage provoked Corymb into this murder. He is aware of what he has done and is unrepentant." This brought forth a murmur from the crowd.

Braan smiled briefly. "Shall we then return him to his ancestral home and bar him from all tribal and governmental activities? Being what he is, we must expect him to attempt to infiltrate the synod. Is it better to have him in Nuamura where we can watch him? Send him to Dielaan and monitor all visitors and correspondence? Imprison him?"

The discussion continued, but an end was finally reached. The *guaard* brought Corymb Dielaan in. Braan said nothing at first, studying the man. Corymb glared back, much of his vigor restored.

"Corymb Dielaan. Due to my personal involvement in this case, I have asked the synod of Nuala to declare your fate. It shall be this: You are stripped of all authority and responsibility within the Nualan synod, and the tribe and house of Dielaan. Your staff and all fringe assistants will be removed, though the new Dielaan will arrange a scripter, if you desire one. Your name shall not be stricken from the Dielaan line or the synod records. That is the mercy of the elected elders. As penalty for the death of the Dragoche Baakche and other nefarious deeds, the following is added: You shall never attempt to leave the planet Nuala, or even the city Dielaan, without the express permission of the ruling Atare. You shall remain permanently in the upper east wing of the Dielaan palace. And, most importantly, any attempt to communicate with or influence a person of authority in temple, synod, or ruling house shall be considered treason and dealt with as such. The same applies to your heir, Valleri. Her mother's last wish was that she be removed from your sphere. To the best of our ability it shall be done. Your skills as writer and historian are unrivaled—it is hoped you shall atone for past deeds by using these researching and recording talents for the betterment of our people. That is all."

"Atare?" Justinian nodded to him.

"One more thing. I would appreciate the synod attending to the matter of my brother's marriage as soon as possible.

I realize it is merely formality but there is clearly no longer need to have the law within our code." He broke off then and scanned the crowd for emphasis, his gaze piercing. "Our own planters shall meet with the Cied late this afternoon. I intend to have definite news for you by morning; about potential crop yields, future projections—a new day dawns, Brethren. Please forgive me, but it has been a long thirty-sixday." Standing, Braan nodded to the gathering and walked up the assembly steps, Noah in tow. Other dignitaries to see ... Justinian raised an eyebrow and turned back to conduct the meeting.

TIERCE

The ride up the lift was smooth and silent, the faint glow causing a luminescence to appear in her skin. Tay examined her hands, the glowing whiteness of them. She suspected where her personal things were—she was not certain she wanted to go looking for them. Tikki occupied herself by climbing Tay's hair and swatting her paw at the glow in the back wall. Teloa quailed inwardly as she opened the bronze doors to the transport; there was only one apartment on this floor, and she would die of embarrassment if the *guaard* questioned her reasons for being on the level.

Standing within the lift a few moments, Tay swallowed her fear and then walked resolutely to the dark-beaded door. The *guaard* was oblivious to her. She summoned her voice. "Has he returned from synod?" she asked in her best Nualan.

"No, Serae. He had dignitaries needing attention," one woman replied tonelessly. Nodding her thanks, Teloa pushed aside the beads and walked in. No one attempted to stop her.

Inside, letting the beads settle, Tay calmed herself and surveyed the room. The akemmi leapt down and vanished under a chair. How his quarters had changed—how everything had grown since the hole at Chardonnay Mountain. She went to the tempra-controlled window and looked out over the Sonoma Valley. The cool, new green of the grapevines flickered before her eyes, now visible, now unseen. Soon dotted with grapes...

She stood on a plush rug made of some natural fiber—her fingers touched it. A wool? Tay removed her dusty boots and shook the rug for caution's sake. Then she took in the immediate room. A new woven mural on the wall—Braan's seal. The *katt* pelts were lying on the couch. She reached to touch one. Peering into the smaller sleeping room and sanitation, she recognized Dylan's heavy boots. Ah, Dylan. He had clung to her in the assembly, moving Tay to tears. He promised he had taken good care of Zair, and his own p— She jumped as something cold touched her. The big dog bumped her hip with his nose. She bent over and hugged him.

"I did not hear you come in!" she whispered. He wagged his tail and thrust his face against hers. "Or have you been here all along?" Straightening, she walked to the larger sanitation. It had two entrances, one from the inner hall and the other from the main sleeping room. There were two large stone basins, pools compared to tubs off-world; a carved rock grille rose between them, from floor to ceiling, polished to a glossy black. Shallow stairs curved from one basin to the other. Several mirrors and a dressing table, face basins, and a portable commode . . . She went into the sleeping room.

Larger than she expected. *He does not intend his woman to live separately, as some cultures do, she thought.* Two immense wardrobes, hidden by heavy curtains of deep blood-red velvet. There was another window to the outside, newly inserted, and a light shaft above. The bed would have been monstrous in any other room. *Large enough to think you are alone or know that you are not . . .*

Attendants? They had had them in the palace, she was sure. Now? She could tell Braan's wardrobe—a boot peeked out from under one corner, casually sprawling against its mate. She opened the other curtains. Her missing sandals and clothing . . . And something else. She pulled out the long red garment. Syluan, translucent syluan . . . The syluan lace, as fine as a babe's hair, was black. Sleeveless, no back, a low front . . . A red robe of opaque syluan was with it. Who? Elana. Tay sat down on the bed's edge, holding the gown. So she knew, knew long ago, to have had this made. How many knew . . . ?

My tratore face is gone. A shriek from Tikki drew her
to her feet. Now the animal was scolding. Tay rushed into
the sanitation. Then she began laughing. The creature had
apparently climbed to the dresser and taken Tay's rake, which
had been left in the logical place. The akemmi was making
off with the prize when Zair burst in and wanted to play.
Tikki's reaction was to defend her new toy fiercely. Zair
looked very confused. Tay reached to the floor and picked
up her rake. "That is *mine*."

Zair in turn clamped his mouth around the little creature
and gingerly carried her down the hall into the main room,
where he set her on the center rug. Spitting, hissing, making
outlandish faces, Tikki batted him on the nose and ran to hide
under a table. Laughing again, unfettered, as she had not
laughed in days, Teloa dug in the dresser for a dry cloth and
tested the constantly swirling water.

She sanded her hair and body twice, unable to get enough
of the hot water. Drying off, she raked out her hair to help
it dry. Then she found a softly scented lotion and rubbed it
into her dry skin. A glance in the mirror startled her. Too
thin. Too much muscle. And her hair was now so long, past
her waist! She had not noticed. Shaking her head, she turned
away. Too slender for a hustler, but she did not have to worry
about that anymore. Tay put on the red gown but hung up
the matching robe in favor of the vatos wool poncho. She
felt cold inside the cave after so long in the Ciedär. Her timing
was perfect; she heard the beads rippling in the outer room
as she finished drying her hair.

Lifting one strand of beads to the side, Tay saw that he
was alone. Braan moved to the window slowly, finally relaxing his stance. Every moment indicated exhaustion. He
leaned against the windowsill, the picture of dejection. As
she considered whether or not to enter the main room, she
heard him whisper, "What price, Holy One?"

Parting the beads, the woman chose. Now she could see
Zair lying at his master's feet, Tikki curled up in a tight ball
under the beast's chin. Braan opened his eyes and saw her;
a smile lit his gaze, but it did not reach his lips. Discarding
her usual caution, Tay walked over the slipped her arms

around him. He embraced her, gently stroking her hair; his arms had no strength.

"You need a hot whirlpool and a massage. Shall I offer?"

Now Braan smiled. "It would not help. The pain is within, lady, and I know no cure. I have seen my soul, and it is black." She did not interrupt him. "Do you understand the price I paid for this fragile truce, beauty? So fragile we must wait until vespers for the planters to meet, to make sure their words are rested and unlikely to flare?"

When the silence became strained, she knew he expected an answer. "I know how many lives you saved by sealing this agreement."

"I bought it in blood, Teloa. The blood of a Cied warrior. I did not have to kill him—the rules were Cied law, not Nualan law, not my moral code. But I allowed it to happen, by my very passiveness. And a life has been taken."

"Better for you to have died?" she asked, her voice sharp.

"Perhaps. Who knows? It might have been a test of will—to see who would prevail. If I had refused, they might have merely tossed him out and—"

"You speak like Moran. 'What if.' I will tell you 'what if.'" She pulled away, angry in her fear for his mood. "There is evil in this universe, Braan Atare. Evil sentience, evil laws, senseless violence. A single warrior cannot do a thing about it, so Moran needs his abundant trust in the basic goodness of mankind. But you know better, for you are more than merely a man. If good beings fail the vigil, evil ones shall triumph. Simple words but full of meaning. You cannot change the universe, but you may change Nuala. Instead of an infant heir and an unprepared ruler to make sense of starvation and civil war, you have a chance to lead your people to something better. A chance—a gift from Mendulay."

"Tell me, woman. Why should I be so certain that I am the only one who can do this?"

"Say not *only*—say *best*," Tay answered. "How do you know? The entire reason for that man's existence may have been to die at your hand! A catalyst to push you ever forward to a bright future for your people."

"How do I not know that I should have—"

"Or a warning," she went on, overriding him. "Of the

dark—the rottenness so close to us, Braan, where one slip can send us into the pit. Life is so good, Atare, yet so evil—a balance. You must strike a blow for the good and leave judgment for later."

"Does God or man judge man?"

"Neither, and both. Let history judge," she said, whispering finally, reaching for him once again.

"I cannot forget. I could block it then, but I cannot forget."

The intensity, the pain in his voice, frightened her. "You should not. And you would not have won those chieftains unless you had showed them you meant business. One man for the future. So it will be, until the Cied themselves change. With your help maybe he will be the last."

"Maybe." He sighed softly and, releasing one arm, walked her down the passageway to the sanitation. He reached over to test the water and was half out of his over-robe before he knew it. He stood stiffly straight. "You are good at that."

"Practice." She did not blush or flinch or even smile.

Braan faced her. "Will you stay . . . here?"

"Yes."

"Will you marry me?"

"I don't know. I think so. I need time to consider, and to orient myself to Nuamura once again."

"How can you do one and not the other?" he started, but she stopped him with a touch.

"I have to." He looked irritated, hurt. Tay hurried on. "No law or authority can bind, belaiss. Not as securely as the human heart . . ."

Trembling, she dropped his robe as he sought her embrace.

MT. AMURA   TWOHUNDRED   TIERCE
                   EIGHTYTWODAY

Moran had looked for Lyte several times since they arrived back in Nuamura. Finally he found the warrior, sitting alone on the boulders outside the grotto. Lyte heard someone coming and stood, facing into the darkness of the cavern. Moran walked up and paused before him, studying his friend.

A smile crept over Lyte's face. "Is this all the greeting I get for sparing your demented hide?" Moran laughed aloud and hugged him tightly. Shoulder-to-shoulder, they moved back to the rocks. "I'm serious. If you hadn't left so early, I would have followed you and beat your ass to mush."

Moran snorted. "You might have lost a few teeth."

"True," Lyte agreed amiably. "Jaac prevented our finding out. But if you ever—*ever* take off again without inviting me first—"

"Never."

"—the reason had better be good," Lyte finished.

"What are you doing out here?" Moran asked.

"Enjoying the view."

"Try again."

"Seriously. This is a...beautiful planet, Moran. Turquoise and white and black, three moons, a long hot summer coming..."

"What's with you?" Moran stared at him. "You look... happy."

"I am."

"Why?"

"Because...I've been thinking a lot about a gatuhlpa Ronuviel told right after you left." Lyte stared back out at the valley. "These people have roots, Moran. They belong here, in this strange world. Just as surely as my parents belong in CSSI. And they've offered it to me—freely. No strings attached. You can ignore it, you know. But I don't want to. What is in the outer galaxy that I can't find here? We've got everything."

"Even brewing civil war," Moran said dryly.

"No—interlopers, maybe, who will keep us busy; but the Nualans put peace higher on the scale than profit. Maybe it's the trine gold." He turned to Moran, a startled expression crossing his face. "I never thought of that! Every Nualan has enough trine to buy a planet—it's not worth as much here, did you know that? Maybe it isn't as important when it's always there! And I'd like to watch Ried and the others grow

up. And your kids—you're a lousy authoritarian, so this
should be fun."

"Kids are different."

"We'll see. But my first priority is . . ."

"Yes?"

"To climb this mountain." He looked up, up, craning
his neck to see the rising Sonoma range, the peak of Mt.
Amura lost in rolling clouds. "We've barely touched it."

"Tomorrow?"

"Today."

"I'm beat . . . and this partnership is a two-way path."

"Tomorrow." Lyte extended his hand for the oath grip.

NONE

Moran found Ronuviel right inside the grotto. Only her
guaard was present, standing next to her. Moran did not
recognize the warrior—undoubtedly the regulars were already resting. Roe was sitting on the ground, leaning against
the cavern walls; she appeared to be asleep.

Moran squatted down beside her. "You should lie down.
Come."

She held up her hand, a languid gesture. "Not yet. Listen." He sat down. The arguments of the synod filtered out
to them.

"What are you waiting for?"

"The official decision on Kal and Shinar."

"It will pass, won't it?"

Roe smiled and reached for his cheek. "How you murder
our language, you and Teloa. Just speak Axis when you are
not sure. It will pass. I hope they will strike all laws concerning it. Humans should not pass judgment on individuals
when it comes to their private lives."

"Aahmn. But you do look thoughtful."

"I am. I am thinking about what kind of future we are
creating for our children. About what Kal told them, about
the things Braan and I discussed. Do you realize the challenge, Moran? The possibilities? In our lifetimes we may be
able to improve the situation of not only Nuala but other

planets as well. For millennia we have been a sanctuary. We must spread it, love; spread the word that justice shall prevail. I hope for peace among Fewhas, Axis, Malvevenians, and Nualans."

"We are not Axis?"

"No. It was a mistake—well, not a mistake—to go back. But it has outlived its usefulness. Self-sufficiency is the key. Harmony with the universe. We must throw out the old, racist prohibitions, must impress upon people the need for system rule and mutual survival by helping friends, not dominating them."

"Shall we be the new masters of the galaxy?" Moran asked.

She opened one eye, thinking he was mocking her, but his expression was serious and tinged with his love. "I pray not. I hope we are willing to help the oppressed no matter where they be. If asked, we shall aid them. When any group exploits another, it threatens the balance, Moran. I believe, as you do, in the ultimate triumph of right. But there will be so many mountains to climb."

He reached for her hand. "We will show our children the balance. What they do with it is up to them. We cannot anticipate their universe. We must prepare them for all possibilities." Roe nodded wearily, and he saw the narrow line within her—the optimism and the fear.

A shadow fell upon them, between the glow and the *guaard*. Glancing up, they saw the ghost that was Arrez. "Seri?" Moran said, using the title of respect for the man.

"I have left inside many confused elders, Ronuviel, fearful and belligerent," the priest started carefully, and Roe sensed relief in him. "They are hesitant about the future, yet no longer distrusting of their Atare, it seems. He may lead us to destruction, but they are willing to follow. Many laws fell this morning, under a simple catch-all statement that will undoubtedly cause many arguments in the next few years. 'We are Human.' And Url has pronounced the declaration of our freedom to be the wedding of Kalith reb Ila Atare and Shinar reb Elana—whenever they blessed well please!"

Roe leapt to her feet, half strangling the older man in her delight. "Come, we must tell Kal. He is waiting!"

NUALA, MT.   TWOHUNDRED   NONE
AMURA   EIGHTYTWODAY

"Kal! Kalith!" Ronuviel rushed past the *guaard* in front of his door, nearly tripping over the step up. "It is done, it is done!"

"What is done?" he asked steadily, looking away from the window to meet her eyes.

She seized his hands. "Where is Shinar?"

He knew then. He opened his hand a moment to reveal the hard object within, and then swiftly left the room, racing for the departing lift, his *guaard* running to keep up.

Roe turned to Moran and hugged him tightly, refusing to let go. "Did you see his face?" she started, laughing.

"The most incredible mixture of joy, relief, and arrogant assurance I have ever seen," Moran agreed.

"Come! I must see her reaction!"

The lift was hours too slow. Kal flew down the corridor to the life shelter, nearly knocking over a medtech at the bronze door and not apologizing for it. Fortunately the door, itself, was open. She was in the main room with her fellow students, watching a ward healer prescribe medication. Kal's sudden arrival stopped all conversation and turned every head. Embarrassed but undeterred, he abruptly extended his fist to her. She stared at him, not understanding, and then, at his repeated gesture, offered him her palm. Kalith slowly, forcefully unfolded his fingers, pressing the serae stone into her outstretched hand and covering it with his own.

"For better or worse, serae, we have won."

She folded into his arms, her answer in the fierceness of her grip.